# Adobe
# Illustrator CS5
## one-on-one™

Also from Deke Press

*Adobe Photoshop CS5 One-on-One*

# Adobe
# Illustrator CS5

## one-on-one.

DEKE McCLELLAND

deke™
PRESS
O'REILLY®

BEIJING • CAMBRIDGE • FARNHAM • KÖLN • SEBASTOPOL • TAIPEI • TOKYO

# Adobe Illustrator CS5 One-on-One

by Deke McClelland

This title is published by Deke Press in association with O'Reilly Media, Inc., 1005 Gravenstein Highway North, Sebastopol, CA 95472.

O'Reilly Media books may be purchased for educational, business, or sales promotional use. Online editions are also available for most titles (*safari.oreilly.com*). For more information, contact O'Reilly's corporate/institutional sales department: 800-998-9938 or *corporate@oreilly.com*.

| | | | |
|---|---|---|---|
| **Managing Editor:** | Carol Person | **Mastermindus Designus:** | David Futato |
| **Associate Editor:** | Susan Pink, Techright<br>Linda Laflamme | **Video Producer:** | Max Smith |
| | | **Live-Action Video:** | Taymar Pixley<br>Andrew Brown<br>Lucas Deming |
| **Organizeuse:** | Toby Malina | | |
| **Indexer:** | Julie Hawks | **Video Editors:** | Kim Bubar, Bryce Poole,<br>Andy Ta, Roon Tamuli |
| **Technical Editor:** | Ron Bilodeau | | |
| **Manufacturing Manager:** | Sue Willing | **Software Development:** | Charles Greer |
| **Editrix Emerita:** | Colleen Wheeler | **O'Reilly Online Wranglers:** | Kirk Walter<br>Adam Witwer |
| **Editrix Depraesentiarum:** | Mary Treseler | | |

## Print History:

October 2010:    First edition.

Special thanks to Michael Ninness, Lynda Weinman, Bruce Heavin, David Rogelberg, Sherry Rogelberg, Stacey Barone, Kevin O'Connor, Mordy Golding, Betsy Waliszewski, Sara Peyton, and Tim O'Reilly, as well as Patrick Lor, Garth Johnson, Chad Bridwell, Megan Ironside, Danny Martin, John Nack, Bryan O'Neil Hughes, Zorana Gee, and the gangs at Fotolia, iStockphoto, and Adobe Systems. Extra special thanks to our relentlessly supportive families, without whom this series and this book would not be possible.

This book was typeset using Adobe InDesign and the Adobe Futura, Adobe Rotis, and Linotype Birka typefaces.

ISBN: 978-0-596-80801-3        [C]        RepKover™ This book uses RepKover,™ a durable and flexible lay-flat binding.

*To Dan Brodnitz
and
Colleen Wheeler
who fought to keep
this Illustrator's
dream alive.*

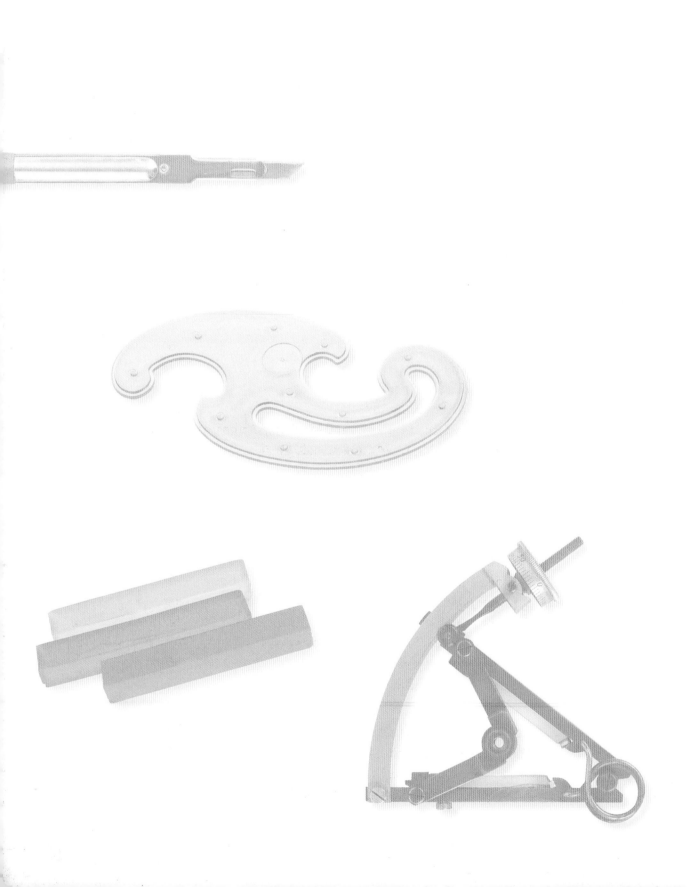

# CONTENTS

# PREFACE

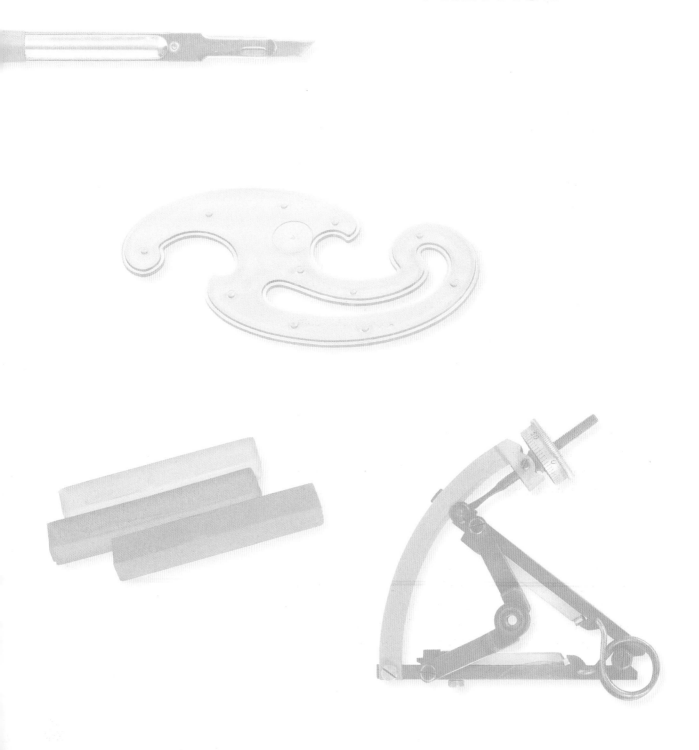

# HOW ONE-ON-ONE WORKS

Welcome to *Adobe Illustrator CS5 One-on-One*, another in a series of highly visual, full-color titles that combine step-by-step lessons with more than six hours of video instruction. As the name *One-on-One* implies, I walk you through Illustrator just as if I were teaching you in a classroom or corporate consulting environment. Except that instead of getting lost in a crowd of students, you receive my individualized attention. It's just you and me.

I created *One-on-One* with three audiences in mind. If you're an independent graphic artist, designer, or Web content creator—professional or amateur—you'll appreciate the real-world authenticity of the tutorials and your immediate ability to apply what you learn in your own work. If you're a student working in a classroom or vocational setting, you'll enjoy the personalized attention, structured exercises, and end-of-lesson quizzes. If you're an instructor in a college or vocational setting, you'll find the topic-driven lessons helpful in building curricula and creating homework assignments. *Adobe Illustrator CS5 One-on-One* is designed to supply beginners with all the guidance they need to get started in Illustrator, while giving more advanced users the depth of knowledge that will fortify their expertise. And I've seen to it that each lesson contains a few techniques that even experienced Illustrator users don't know.

## Read, Watch, Do

*Adobe Illustrator CS5 One-on-One* is your chance to master Adobe Illustrator under the direction of a professional trainer with more than 20 years of computer design and graphics experience. Read the book, watch the videos, do the exercises. Proceed at your own pace and experiment as you see fit. It's the best way to learn.

Figure 1.

*Adobe Illustrator CS5 One-on-One* contains twelve lessons, each made up of three to six step-by-step exercises. Every lesson in the book includes a corresponding video lesson (see Figure 1), in which I introduce the key concepts you'll need to know to complete the exercises and see features that are best explained in action. Best of all, every exercise is project-based, culminating in an actual finished document worthy of your labors (like the examples in Figure 2). The exercises include insights and context throughout, so you'll know not only what to do but—just as important—why you're doing it. My sincere hope is that you'll find the experience entertaining, informative, and empowering.

All the videos and sample files required to perform the exercises are available for download at *oreilly. com/go/deke-IllustratorCS5*. If you already have an oreilly.com account and are logged in, you can click straight through to a site where you can play the videos, download them to your computer if you like, and get the sample files. (If you don't have an oreilly.com login, you'll be invited to create one, and then be sent properly on your way.) Together, the book, sample files, and videos form a single, comprehensive training experience.

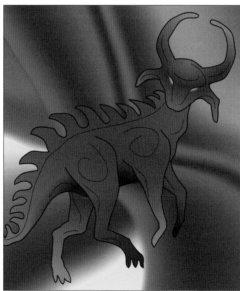

Figure 2.

Previous installments of *One-on-One* provided the video and practice files on a DVD bound in the back of the book. I've made the decision to deliver video and practice files online instead. It's a more flexible, less wasteful approach that gives you the same great *One-on-One* instructional experience. Plus, I'm not limited with regard to sample file selection or video length—and I have a place to post updates, bonus material, and anything else I might want to share with you.

## One-on-One Requirements

The main prerequisite to using *Adobe Illustrator CS5 One-on-One* is having Illustrator CS5 installed on your system. You may have purchased Illustrator CS5 as a stand-alone product or as part of Adobe's Creative Suite 5. You *can* work through many of the exercises using an earlier version of Illustrator, but some steps will not work as written. All exercises have been fully tested with Adobe Illustrator CS5 but not with older versions.

*Adobe Illustrator CS5 One-on-One* is cross-platform, meaning that it works equally well whether you're using Illustrator installed on a Microsoft Windows-based PC or an Apple Macintosh.

Any computer that meets the minimum requirements for Illustrator CS5 also meets the requirements for using *Adobe Illustrator CS5 One-on-One*. Specifically, if you own a PC, you need Windows XP with Service Pack 3, Windows Vista (Home Premium or better) with Service Pack 1, or Windows 7. If you own a Mac, you need Mac OS X version 10.5.7 or higher.

Regardless of platform, your computer must meet the following minimum requirements:

- 1GB of RAM
- 2GB of available hard disk space
- 16-bit color graphics card
- Color monitor with 1024-by-768-pixel resolution
- Broadband Internet connection for sample files and videos
- QuickTime Player software (if it is not already installed and you want to watch downloaded versions of the videos offline; available at *www.apple.com/quicktime*)

# One-on-One Installation and Setup

*Adobe Illustrator CS5 One-on-One* is designed to function as an integrated training environment. So before embarking on the lessons, I'm going to request that you install a handful of files onto your hard drive:

- Lesson files used in the exercises (Around 200MB in all)

- *One-on-One* Creative Suite color settings (*Best workflow CS5.csf*)

- Custom collection of keyboard shortcuts called *dekeKeys*

- The twelve lesson videos (if you want to view them offline; playing them online doesn't require any downloading)

- QuickTime Player software (if it is not already installed and you want to watch downloaded versions of the videos offline)

---

As you'll see, these files are all available at *www.oreilly.com/go/deke-IllustratorCS5*, with the exception of QuickTime Player, which you can download from *www.apple.com/quicktime*.

---

I'll also have you change a few preference settings. These changes are optional—you can follow along with the exercises in this book regardless of your preferences. Even so, I advocate these settings for two reasons: First, they make for less confusion by ensuring that you and I are on the same page, as it were. Second, some of Illustrator's default preferences are just plain wrong. So, welcome to your first one-on-one style exercise:

1. *Go to* **www.oreilly.com/go/Deke-IllustratorCS5.** This is the companion site for the book, where you can get all the supplemental materials you'll need. It's also where I'll be posting technical updates (in the event that Adobe makes significant changes to Illustrator), bonus content, and other things I find relevant. If you already have an oreilly.com account, you'll be asked to log in to the site straight away. If you need to create an account (it's free), you'll be taken through that process and returned to the companion page when you're done.

2. *Examine the table of contents.* At the companion site, you'll notice that each lesson has an entry in the table of contents. That's where you'll find each lesson's complement of sample files, archived in a separate *.zip* file for easier downloading. Once you get those files on your hard drive, you can right-click the *.zip* file and choose **Extract All** to create an unzipped folder for each particular lesson.

Stash the files somewhere convenient and memorable, so that when I direct you to open one during an exercise, it won't be hard to find. I suggest you make a *Lesson Files-AIcs5 1on1* folder on your desktop into which you drag those separate folders for each lesson. If you follow this suggestion, the instructions I've supplied at the beginning of each exercise will lead you right where you need to go.

3. ***Decide whether you want to watch the videos at the site or offline.*** At the outset of each book-based lesson, I'll ask you to play the companion video lesson. These video lessons introduce key concepts that make more sense when first seen in action. On the companion site, click the **Watch** button next to the video you want, and it will play in a spiffy online player (see Figure 3), which doesn't require that you download the movies or acquire a separate piece of software for playing them. I think it's a fairly nice experience, actually.

But if you have an unreliable Internet connection or you'd just rather have the freedom of keeping the videos where you can always get to them, click the **Download** button next to each lesson to save them to your hard drive (and remember you'll need QuickTime to watch them if you choose that route).

PEARL OF WISDOM

The video lessons were crafted by the talented folks at lynda.com. These high-quality videos are not excerpts from other training materials but created expressly to complement the lessons in this book.

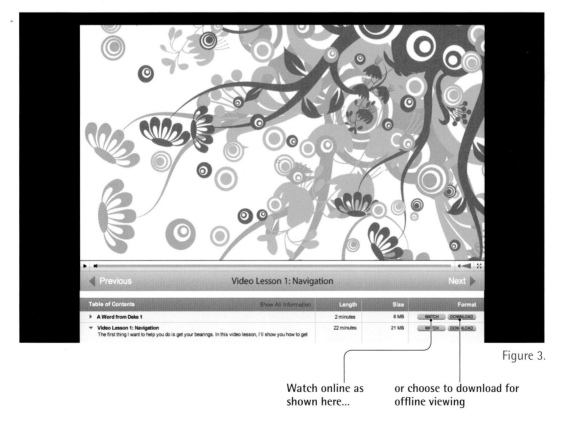

Figure 3.

Watch online as shown here...

or choose to download for offline viewing

I recommend Apple's QuickTime Player software because it's free and offers great playback functions.

4. *Download the dekeKeys and color settings files.* While you're online, notice that I've also provided two files to streamline and improve your Illustrator experience. One contains my custom keyboard shortcuts, and the other, my preferred color settings. So download *Best workflow CS5.csf* and *dekeKeys-Illustrator-CS5.zip*, put them somewhere you'll remember, and I'll show you how to install them in the next steps.

5. *Move the color settings to the appropriate folder.* Move the *Best workflow CS5.csf* file to one of two locations on your hard drive, depending on your platform and operating system. (Note that, in the following, user indicates your computer login name.)

   • Under Windows 7 and Vista, the location is
     *C:\Users\user\AppData\Roaming\Adobe\Color\Settings*

   • Under Windows XP, it's
     *C:\Documents and Settings\user\Application Data\Adobe\Color\Settings*

   • On the Mac, choose **Go→Home** and copy the color settings to the folder
     *Library/Application Support/Adobe/Color/Settings*

If you can't find the *AppData* or *Application Data* folder on the PC, it's because Windows is making the system folders invisible. Choose **Tools→Folder Options**, click the **View** tab, and turn on **Show Hidden Files and Folders** in the scrolling list. Also turn off the **Hide Extensions for Known File Types** and **Hide Protected Operating System Files** check boxes. Then click the **OK** button.

6. *Move the dekeKeys file to the appropriate folder.* I'm also going to suggest you install my custom keyboard shortcuts for working in Illustrator. I've created these shortcuts because there are some handy features inside Illustrator that you'll use often enough to warrant the availability of convenient keystrokes. You don't need to install my shortcuts to make the exercises work, but doing so will make your Illustrator life more efficient.

Return to the desktop level of your computer (or wherever you stashed *dekeKeys-Illustrator-CS5.zip*) and unzip the file. Then move *dekeKeys Illustrator cs5.kys* to the appropriate location depending on your operating system:

- Under Windows 7 and Vista, the location is
  *C:\Users\user\AppData\Roaming\Adobe\Adobe Illustrator CS5 Settings\en_US*

- Under Windows XP, it's
  *C:\Documents and Settings\user\Application Data\Adobe\ Adobe Illustrator CS5 Settings\en_US*

- On the Mac, choose **Go→Home** and copy the color settings to the folder
  *Library/Preferences/Adobe Illustrator CS5 Settings/en_US*

7. *Start Illustrator.* If Illustrator CS5 is already running on your computer, skip to Step 8. If not, start the program:

   - On the PC, go to the **Start** menu (🌐 under Windows Vista) and choose **Adobe Illustrator CS5**. (The program may be located in the Programs or All Programs submenu, possibly inside an Adobe submenu.)

   - On the Mac, choose **Go→Applications** in the Finder. Then open the *Adobe Illustrator CS5* folder and double-click the Adobe Illustrator CS5 application icon.

8. *Change the color settings to Best Workflow.* Now that you've installed the color settings, you have to activate them inside Illustrator. Choose **Edit→Color Settings** or press the keyboard shortcut, Ctrl+Shift+K (⌘-Shift-K on the Mac). In the **Color Settings** dialog box, click the **Settings** pop-up menu and choose **Best Workflow CS5** (see Figure 4). Then click the **OK** button. Now the colors in your images will match (or very nearly match) those shown in the pages of this book.

   I created Best Workflow CS5 settings to work for the entire Creative Suite. There is one setting particular to Illustrator that you'll want to tweak in order to keep yourself from going crazy responding to warning dialog boxes. In the Color Management Policies section of the dialog box, click the **CMYK** pop-up menu and choose **Preserve Embedded Profiles**. This ensures each of the sample documents I provided will open without displaying an annoying, in this case irrelevant, warning. Then click the **OK** button. Now the colors in your images will match (or very nearly match) those shown in the pages of this book.

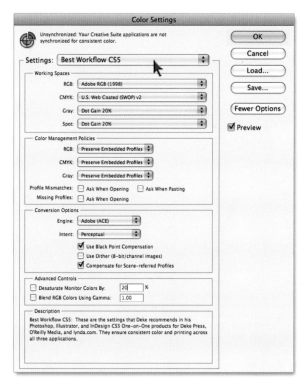

Figure 4.

9. **Switch to the dekeKeys keyboard shortcuts.** To load dekeKeys, choose **Edit→Keyboard Shortcuts**. In the **Keyboard Shortcuts** dialog box, choose **dekeKeys Illustrator CS5** from the **Set** menu, as in Figure 5, and click **OK**. To confirm that you now indeed do have my custom shortcuts working, open the File menu and check to see that there is now, indeed a shortcut next to the Place command of Ctrl+Shift+Alt+D (⌘-Shift-Opt-D), as you can see in Figure 6.

---

If you don't have a file open, the Place command will be dimmed, but you should still be able to see the keyboard shortcut listed.

---

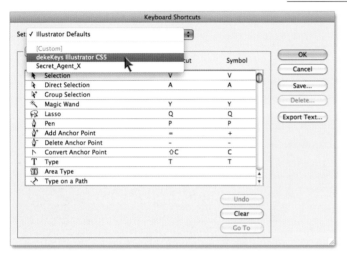

Figure 5.

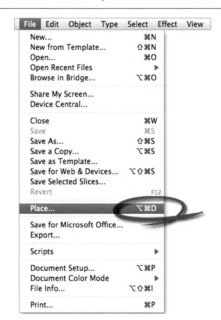

Figure 6.

10. **Adjust a few preference settings.** To minimize confusion and maximize Illustrator's performance, I'd like you to modify a few preference settings. Choose **Edit→Preferences→General** (that's **Illustrator→Preferences→General** on the Mac) or press Ctrl+K (⌘-K). You'll start with the General panel of the manifold Preferences dialog box. I've highlighted the settings I want you to change in Figure 7 and the next four figures. Red means turn the option off, green means turn it on or change the default value. Yellow indicates optional consideration.

The first setting I want you to change is already selected for you. So change the **Keyboard Increment** to 0.2 by simply typing that value into the already selected field, as in Figure 7. This will allow you finer control when you move items with the arrow keys, which we'll be doing often in this book.

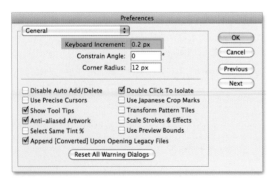

Figure 7.

11. *Switch to the Selection & Anchor Display settings.* Click the pop-up menu to the right of the word **General** and choose the next set of preferences. The key setting change I want you to make here is to turn on the **Object Selection by Path Only** check box. If you're new to Illustrator, this may mean nothing to you yet and you'll have to take my word for it. If you have some experience with the application, then know that this means you must click on the outline along the edge of an object in order to select it, rather than just clicking inside it. So the result is that turning this feature on, as I've done in Figure 8, gives you much finer control inside complex illustrations.

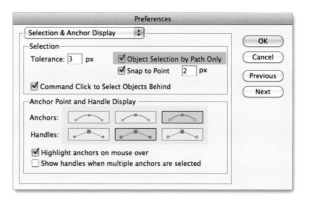

Figure 8.

You may want to also change the size and shape of your anchor point and handle display to something suiting your eyesight needs. I notice that the older I get, the larger I like them to be.

12. *Move to the Units panel.* Next, choose **Units** from the pop-up menu at the top of the Preferences dialog box. Your **General**, **Stroke**, and **Type** units should be set to **Points**, as in Figure 9. A *point* is $\frac{1}{72}$ of an inch (or $\frac{1}{12}$ of a pica for those familiar with that term).

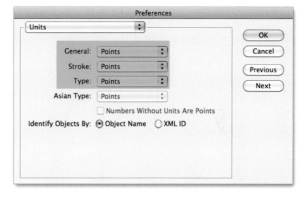

International users may find or want some other measurement in the units setting, which is fine and won't keep you from completing the exercises. Just be aware that I'll be working in points.

Figure 9.

13. *Navigate to the Appearance of Black panel.* Press the **Next** button inside the Preferences dialog box eight times (to take a whirlwind tour of some of the Preference options I'm *not* going to have you change) so that you arrive at the **Appearance of Black** panel, as shown in Figure 10. In the world of CMYK graphics (like those you'll be creating in this book) black areas are treated in two ways. There's 100 percent black which is made up of only black ink, or *rich black* that has some cyan, yellow, and magenta mixed in giving it a richer appearance. It seems to me that you should know which one is which inside your artwork, so change the **On Screen** setting to **Display All Blacks Accurately**.

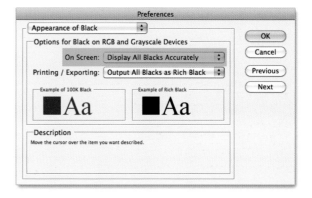

Figure 10.

14. *Quit Illustrator.* You've come full circle. On the PC, choose **File→Exit**; on the Mac, choose **Illustrator→Quit Illustrator**. Quitting Illustrator not only closes the program but also saves the changes you made to the color settings, keyboard shortcuts, and preference settings.

Congratulations, you and I are now in sync. Just one more thing: If you use a Macintosh computer, please read the next section. If you use a PC, feel free to skip it and move along to the following one, "Structure and Organization."

## Reassigning the Mac OS X Shortcuts

Adobe intends for the function keys to display or hide common panels. Meanwhile, pressing ⌘ and Option with the spacebar should access the zoom tool. But in recent versions of OS X, these keys will tile or hide windows according to Apple's Exposé or will invoke search functions via Apple's Spotlight. To rectify these conflicts, do the following steps:

1. *Open your OS X System Preferences.* From the  menu, choose **System Preferences.** Click the **Keyboard & Mouse** icon, and then click the **Keyboard Shortcuts** button.

2. *Reset the Dashboard & Dock settings.* In the left panel, click **Dashboard & Dock.** In the right panel, click the **F12** shortcut to highlight it, as shown in Figure 11. Then press Control-F12 (which appears as ^F12 in the window).

Figure 11.

3. *Switch to the next group of shortcuts.* Click **Expose & Spaces**, replace **F9** with Control-F9, **F10** with Control-F10, and **F11** with Control-F11.

4. *Reset the ⌘-spacebar functionality.* Spotlight, Mac's questionably useful search feature, has taken over the ⌘-spacebar and ⌘-Option-spacebar shortcuts. In Illustrator, these shortcuts let you zoom in and out of your images with immensely convenient efficiency. Reclaim this handy feature by choosing **Spotlight** in the left panel. Next, click **⌘Space** and replace it with **⌘-Control-F1**, and click **⌥-⌘-Space** and replace it with the shortcut ⌘-Control-Option-F1 (which shows up in reverse order as ^⌥⌘F1).

5. *Close System Preferences.* Finally, click the ⊗ in the top-left corner of the window to close the system preferences.

From now on, the panel and zoom tool shortcuts will work according to Adobe's intentions, as well as the directions provided in this book.

## Structure and Organization

Each of the lessons in the book conforms to a consistent structure, designed to impart skills and understanding through a regimen of practice and dialog. As you build your projects, I explain why you're performing the steps and why Illustrator works the way it does.

Each lesson begins with a broad topic overview. Turn to the first page of each lesson, and you'll find a section called "About This Lesson," which lists the skills you'll learn and provides you with a short description of what you'll find in the video-based component of the lesson.

---

As you read in "One-on-One Installation and Setup," on page xiv, the videos can be streamed or downloaded from the book's companion Web site, found at *www.oreilly.com/go/deke-IllustratorCS5.*

---

These video lessons are an integral part of my plan for helping you really get your bearings in Illustrator. Ranging from 15 to 45 minutes apiece, these high-quality videos introduce key concepts, focusing on those features and techniques that make more sense if you first see them in action.

---

Theoretically, you can watch the video lessons in any order you like. However, each video makes the most sense and provides the most benefit when watched at the outset of the corresponding book-based lesson.

---

Edited and produced by the trailblazing online training company lynda.com, the video lessons were made specifically to work with the exercises in this book, not excerpted from versions of my full-length video training. A great deal of care—both in form and in content—has gone into making the video lessons.

---

One final note: Unlike the exercises in the book, most of the video lessons do not generally include sample files (although on a few occasions they do). The idea is that you work along with me in the book; you sit back and relax during the videos.

---

Next come the step-by-step exercises, in which I walk you through some of Illustrator's most powerful and essential graphic illustration functions. A globe icon (like the one on the right) appears whenever I ask you to open a file from the *Lesson Files-AIcs5 1on1* folder that you created on your computer's hard drive.

To make my directions crystal clear, command and option names appear in bold type (as in, "choose the **Open** command"). The first appearance of a figure reference is in colored type. More than 900 full-color, generously sized screen shots and illustrations diagram key steps in your journey, so you're never left scratching your head, puzzling over what to do next. And when I refer you to another step or section, I tell you the exact page number to go to. (Shouldn't every book?)

To make doubly sure there are as few points of confusion as possible, I pepper my descriptions with the very icons you see on screen, critical icons like ◉, *fx*, ⅋, and ✋. So for example, when I direct you to add a layer to your document, I don't tell you to click the Create a New Layer icon at the bottom of the Layers panel. (The only time you see the words *Create a New Layer* is when you hover your cursor over the icon, which is hard to do if you don't know where to hover your cursor in the first place.) Instead, I tell you to click the ▣ icon, because ▣ is what it is. It has meant hand-drawing nearly 400 icons to date, but for you, it was worth it.

**PEARL OF WISDOM**

Along the way, you'll encounter the occasional "Pearl of Wisdom," which provides insights into how Illustrator and the larger world of computer graphics work. Although this information is not essential to performing a given step or completing an exercise, it may help you understand how a function works or provide you with valuable context.

---

More detailed background discussions appear in independent sidebars, which consist of one or two complete pages so they don't interrupt the flow of working through your exercise. These sidebars might go into deeper detail about the basic features of the interface or the basics of color inside Illustrator. Sometimes they shed light on the mysteries of sophisticated techniques like creating text on a path, tracing a full color photograph, or turning your artwork into pixels inside Adobe Photoshop

A colored paragraph of text with a rule above and below it calls attention to a special tip or technique that will help you make Illustrator work faster and more smoothly.

Some projects are quite ambitious. My enthusiasm for a topic may even take us a bit beyond the stated goal. In such cases, I cordon off the final portion of the exercise and label it "Extra Credit."

### EXTRA ★ CREDIT

If you're feeling oversaturated and utterly exhausted, the star icon is your oasis. It's my way of saying that you deserve a break. You can even drop out and skip to the next exercise. On the other hand, if you're the type who believes quitters never prosper (which they don't, incidentally), by all means carry on; you'll be rewarded with a completed project and a wealth of additional tips and insights.

I end each lesson with a "What Did You Learn?" section featuring a multiple-choice quiz. Your job is to choose the best description for each of twelve key concepts outlined in the lesson. Answers are printed upside-down at the bottom of the page.

### FURTHER INVESTIGATION

A "Further Investigation" marker includes information about further reading or video training. For example, let me use this one to refer you to the lynda.com Online Training Library, which contains tens of thousands of movies, more than a thousand of them by me. And all available to you, by subscription, every minute of every waking day. Just to be absolutely certain you don't feel baited into making yet another purchase, I've arranged a time-limited back door for you. Go to *www.lynda.com/deke* and sign up for the 7-Day Free Trial Account. This gives you access to the entire Online Training Library. But remember, your seven days start counting down the moment you sign up, so time it wisely. Then again, if you find the service so valuable you elect to subscribe, we're happy to have you. You'll be happy, too.

## The Scope of This Book

No one book can teach you everything there is to know about Illustrator. Here's a quick list of the topics discussed in each lesson and its accompanying video, as well as a visual preview (in Figure 12) of what you'll encounter in the videos that accompany each lesson.

- Lesson 1: Opening, creating, and organizing your artwork; establishing artboards, guides, and layers, setting up your workspace, and navigating inside Illustrator.

- Lesson 2: Drawing lines, arcs, and basic and complex shapes; choosing, mixing, and applying color to your art; adjusting fill, stroke, and object order.

- Lesson 3: Drawing with the pen tool, creating fluid Bézier curves, anchor points, combining paths.

- Lesson 4: Working with text, placing type on a path, advanced text formatting, ligatures, glyphs, and other special characters.

- Lesson 5: Moving, cloning, and scaling elements; offsetting paths; selecting, transforming, and aligning objects.

- Lesson 6: Using Pathfinder operations, employing the Crop, Exclude, and Intersect functions to create complex shapes using Shape Builder.

Video Lesson 1: Navigation

Video Lesson 2: The Basic Shape Tools

Video Lesson 3: The Pen Tool

Video Lesson 7: Gradients

Video Lesson 8: Blend Modes

Video Lesson 9: Freehand Painting

- Lesson 7: Working with gradients, designing custom gradients, blending between paths, editing and masking blends, using clipping masks, gradient meshes.

- Lesson 8: Opacity and knockout groups, working with opacity masks, applying blend modes, cropping entire layers.

- Lesson 9: Dynamic brushstrokes, symbols, and instances; art brushes; replicating symbols; using the symbolism tools; free-hand painting.

- Lesson 10: Dynamic effects, applying and editing graphic styles, exploiting the transform effect, creating 3D text and graphics.

- Lesson 11: Using Live Trace to turn raster images into paths, filling in shapes with Live Paint, changing all the colors in an illustration into different colors automatically, drawing with the Perspective Grid tool.

- Lesson 12: Prepping your file for commercial printing, using local printers, optimizing your artwork for posting on the Web, rasterizing in Photoshop.

Figure 12.

Video Lesson 4: Working with Type

Video Lesson 5: Selecting & Aligning

Video Lesson 6: Shape Builder & Pathfinder

Video Lesson 10: Dynamic Effects

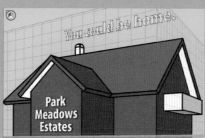
Video Lesson 11: Perspective Grid Tool

Video Lesson 12: Commercial Printing

Now that you have everything set up so that you and I are in sync, I invite you to turn to Lesson 1, "Starting a Document." I hope you'll agree with me that *Adobe Illustrator CS5 One-on-One*'s combination of step-by-step lessons and video introductions provides the best learning experience of any Illustrator training resource on the market.

LESSON

# 1

# STARTING A DOCUMENT

**I'VE BEEN COVERING** Adobe applications for years, and I'm intimately familiar with most of them. So I really shouldn't play favorites. But if I were to pick the one closest to my heart— purely my personal pet, clearheaded reasoning be damned—it would be Illustrator. Compared with such powerhouse applications as Flash, After Effects, or InDesign, Illustrator may seem like an odd choice. I mean, hello, have I forgotten *Photoshop*? Don't get me wrong, I think all those programs are wonderful. And I must admit, I spend more time in Photoshop than any other application. But I'd still go with Illustrator.

I'm not saying Illustrator is the best thing Adobe's ever released. Honestly, it's impossible to compare one Adobe product to another; they all serve different purposes. Nor is Illustrator the most entertaining application in the Creative Suite. While there are times I quite enjoy using Illustrator, I can't deny that drawing an intricate path with the pen tool can be grunt work of the most menial order. And between you and me, Illustrator is not the most elegantly designed piece of software. After twenty years of haphazard updates— some really great, some not—the program is about as organized as a mad tea party.

Figure 1-1.

I find Illustrator so particularly captivating for three reasons. I don't expect you to identify with the first one: Illustrator was the subject of one of my earliest books (an illustration from which appears in Figure 1-1), and you never forget the mind-numbing pain of your initial efforts, even if you hatched them, as I did, two decades ago. Second, and this one benefits you, Illustrator is a much deeper program than most people imagine, deeper even than Photoshop in terms of the number of things it can accomplish, the variety of ways you can approach a project, and its sheer quantity of features.

# ABOUT THIS LESSON

## Project Files

Before beginning the exercises, make sure you've downloaded the lesson files from *www.oreilly.com/go/Deke-IllustratorCS5*, as directed in Step 2 on page xiv of the Preface. This should result in a folder called *Lesson Files-Alcs5 1on1* on your desktop. We'll be working with the files inside the *Lesson 01* subfolder.

Before you can take advantage of Illustrator's first-rate drawing functions, you must know how to open a file, set up a new document, adjust columns and guides, and save your work to disk. In this lesson, you'll learn how to:

## Video Lesson 1: Navigation

In this first video lesson, I'll give you a sense of how to get around inside of Illustrator. I'll show you how to zoom in to a particular area of your artwork, zoom out to see more at a time, pan around to see details, and move between and organize your artboards.

To learn your way around your artwork, visit *www.oreilly. com/go/deke-IllustratorCS5*. Click the **Watch** button to view the lesson online or click the **Download** button to save it to your computer. During the video, you'll learn these shortcuts:

Video Lesson 1: Navigation

| Operation | Windows shortcut | Macintosh shortcut |
|---|---|---|
| Zoom in or out | Ctrl+⊞ (plus), Ctrl+⊟ (minus) | ⌘-⊞ (plus), ⌘-⊟ (minus) |
| Zoom in with the magnifying glass | Ctrl+spacebar-click or drag | ⌘-spacebar-click or drag |
| Zoom out with the magnifying glass | Ctrl+Alt+spacebar-click | ⌘-Option-spacebar-click |
| Zoom to 100 percent or fit page | Ctrl+⊡ (one) | ⌘-⊡ (one) |
| Fit artboard in window | Ctrl+⊙ (zero) | ⌘-⊙ (zero) |
| Fit entire artwork in window | Ctrl+Alt+⊙ (zero) | ⌘-Option-⊙ (zero) |
| Switch between open documents | Ctrl-Tab | ⌘-~ (tilde) |
| Move to next artboard | Shift+Page Down | Shift+Page Down |
| Move to previous artboard | Shift+Page Up | Shift+Page Up |

And third, once you get a feeling for how Illustrator works—as well as how it doesn't—something about it is positively addictive. The program has been compared to a Swiss Army knife due to its versatility and functionality. But it's more like a collection of tools held up to a looking-glass with something more wonderful reflected back. The strangeness of Illustrator and the promise of still more just beyond the next doorway is a large part of the program's attraction.

Embracing the twisted logic that permeates the program requires a determined psychological commitment. When you come to the bottle labeled "Drink me," you would do well to drink it (it is not marked "Poison" after all), every last drop. When you do, when you chase every last word of this book as it leads you down the rabbit-hole into the very deep well and beyond, your view of sense and nonsense may well shift a few degrees. It's not that you'll suddenly decide that Illustrator is reasonable and the other applications are un. That would be madness! It's just that regular logic—actual, quantifiable, incontrovertible, commonsense logic—seems awfully mundane compared with the Mad Hatter logic of Illustrator. Lewis Carroll's dormouse never actually said "Feed your head" (or anything of the sort!), but nothing can prevent Illustrator from doing just that. And once you get a headful of this vast Jabberwocky of a program, it's hard to return to a normal program without feeling a tiny sense of loss. As Alice herself said, "Somehow it seems to fill my head with ideas—only I don't exactly know what they are."

## What Is Illustrator?

Illustrator is at its heart a drawing program. This means it excels at the creation of graphic art that involves smooth lines, bold colors, and crisp text. The simplest real-world analogy is a coloring book. As you may recall from the dim, dopey days of childhood, life in a coloring book is simple, an impossible cardboard-cutout world distilled to its most primitive components, as in Figure 1-2. Each detail is plotted out with straight lines and curves, all of which intersect to describe an array of codependent shapes. As a young coloring-book artist, it was your job to fill those careless shapes with colors, usually continuous hues applied with crayon or marker but sometimes a more varied—that is to say, messy—blend from one color to another. This blend of predefined lines and colored spaces made up the finished illustration.

But a coloring book is hardly the only real-world analogy. Any traditional pen-and-ink graphic, schematic pencil drawing, stylized type treatment, or high-contrast painting falls to Illustrator's digi-

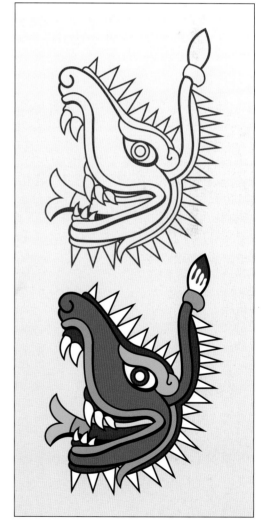

Figure 1-2.

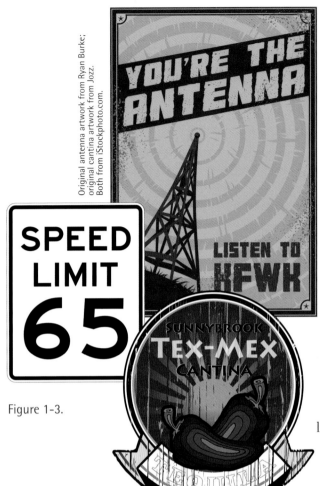

Original antenna artwork from Ryan Burke; original cantina artwork from Jozz. Both from iStockphoto.com.

Figure 1-3.

tal domain. And lest you think such artwork is rare or refined, think again. We all see Illustrator artwork on a daily basis. Just about every corporate logo in use today has passed through Illustrator. Nearly every bag, carton, or container you see at the grocery store comes to you from Illustrator. Buying a new toy, computer, or piece of sporting equipment? That box was most likely designed in Illustrator. Movie posters, glossy magazine ads, schoolbook illustrations, architectural renderings, stamps, decals, DVD and CD cases, billboards, transit signs, retail signage, bumper stickers, credit cards, gift certificates, crap you get from McDonald's, fragments of screaming paper and colorful plastic buried in landfills the world over—in short, virtually every ounce of still, single-page graphic commerce and public-service labeling is to some extent a by-product of Illustrator (see Figure 1-3). For better or for worse, Illustrator artwork surrounds you.

## Illustration versus Image

Illustrator's main purpose is to create line art. Each line, shape, and character of text is independent of its neighbors. These independent elements are known as *objects*. Illustrator describes each object using a basic coordinate-based mathematical equation. (Fortunately, Illustrator doesn't assail you with this math; it calculates the equations in the background.) Because these equations describe the course and contours of the object, they are sometimes called *vectors*. Hence, Illustrator is said to be an *object-oriented* or *vector-based* drawing application. Illustrator prints the lines, shapes, and text by sending the vectors to a printer and letting (or helping) the printer sort out the details.

Compare this approach to that employed by the more popular Photoshop, which brokers in tiny colored pixels. Each pixel is a perfect square, arranged adjacent to its neighbors like squares on a checkerboard. The purpose of most of Photoshop's vast collection of functions is to adjust the colors of these pixels.

That's great for digital photographs and continuous-tone artwork, in which one color gradually transitions into another. But it also means that Photoshop imagery is resolution-dependent. An image contains a finite number of pixels. Print the image too large, and the jagged transitions between one block of pixels and the next becomes all too apparent, even to people who have no idea what a pixel is. (The fact that most moderately educated people *do* know what pixels are and can identify low-resolution imagery at a glance makes matters that much worse.)

In contrast, vector-based graphics—even poorly rendered ones—are output at the maximum resolution of a printer. The result is uniformly smooth artwork with clearly defined edges and sharp, exacting corners. And because each line or shape is a separate object, you can pick it up and move or modify it at a moment's notice, whether you bothered to place it on an independent layer (as is necessary in Photoshop) or not.

A document created in Illustrator is called a *drawing* or an *illustration*. You can also call it a *graphic* or a *design*, depending on its content. A file from Photoshop is a *photograph* or a *bitmapped image*. For purposes of this book, the term *image* will always mean a piece of artwork that comprises pixels. I'm much more lax about my vector nomenclature. Illustrator is mostly about vectors, but it lets you import and integrate images into your vector artwork as well. So any word that's synonymous with *graphic art* will and does suffice in this book.

## Opening an Illustration

Opening a drawing in Illustrator is pretty much like opening a document in any application, Adobe or otherwise. It all begins with the Open command. In this exercise, I'll show the basic method of opening a file. In the next, we'll see a different (and arguably better) way.

1. *Bring up the Open a File dialog box.* Choose **File→Open** from the menu bar. Or you can press Ctrl+O (⌘-O on the Mac). You get the **Open a File** dialog box. Figure 1-4 shows the dialog box as it appears on the Mac under OS X Snow Leopard (10.6), where it is simply called the **Open** dialog box.

2. *Navigate to the Lesson 01 folder.* Assuming you installed the lesson files on your desktop, here's how to get to the *Lesson 01* folder:

   • Click the desktop icon located along the left side of the dialog box to display the files and folders on your computer's desktop. (If you don't see a desktop icon on the Mac, press ⌘-D.)

Figure 1-4.

# Illustrator's Interface and Document Windows

With Illustrator CS5, just like the other Creative Suite apps, much of the interface is hidden when you first run the program—but you can unleash a whole host of panels and interface options. The following list, in alphabetical order, describes the more essential elements:

- **Application bar:** Introduced in CS4, the application bar (combined with the menu bar under Windows) includes buttons and menus to make accessing the Bridge and workspaces quick and painless.

- **Artboard:** The defined margins of a piece of artwork make up what is known as the *artboard*. A single document may be simply one artboard or may contain many artboards—and the artboards can even be different sizes.

- **Artboard controls:** The controls you see in the bottom-left corner of the document window let you switch between artboards, either sequentially or by entering a specific artboard number.

- **Cluster bar:** I call a set of stacked panels represented by side-by-side tabs (such as Layers, Appearance, and Graphic Styles below) a *cluster*. The dark gray area to the right of

the tabs is the cluster bar. Drag the bar to move a cluster. Click the double arrow in the bar to collapse a cluster.

- **Community help search:** This quick-search box will launch your default browser and return search results of Adobe's online help, developer notes, and tutorials.

New in CS5 is the concept of CS Live, an online collaborative environment that allows for document review, browser compatibility testing, and more. To learn more, select Explore CS Live Services from the drop-down menu.

- **Control panel:** The horizontal panel along the top of the screen provides access to Illustrator's most commonly used options. The panel is context sensitive, changing to accommodate the selected object or active tool.

- **Cursor:** The cursor tracks mouse movements and changes to reflect the active tool or operation. Keep an eye on it and you'll have a better sense of what you're doing.

- **Docking pane:** A docking pane contains many panel clusters, stacked one atop the other. Drag a cluster bar and drop it onto a docking pane to add panels to the pane. Drop a panel next to a pane to begin a new pane.

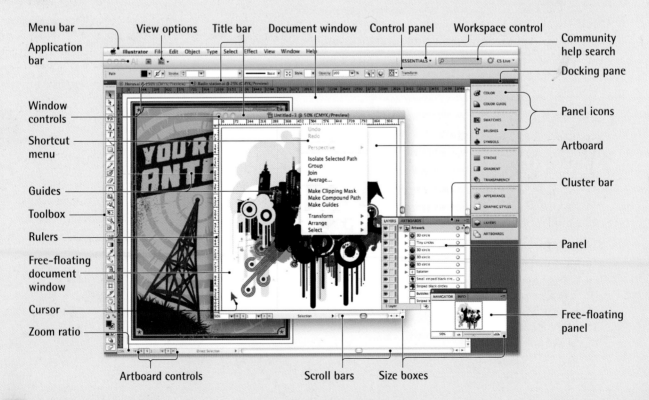

- **Document window:** By default, each open document appears as a tab in the main document window. You can view a document in a separate, free-floating window by dragging its tab away from the top of the window.

- **Guides:** The colored lines in the document window are nonprinting "magnetic" guides, meaning that objects or points snap into place when dragged close to them.

- **Menu bar:** Click a title to display a list of commands. A command followed by three dots (such as Export...) displays a *dialog box*; others work right away.

- **Panel:** A panel is a window of options that remain visible as you work. To switch between panels, click a named tab. Move a panel by dragging its tab. Drop a panel outside a docking pane to make it free-floating. Click the tiny ▾≡ in the top-right corner to bring up the panel menu.

- **Panel icons:** When you collapse a docking pane, Illustrator shows its panels as icons. Click an icon to temporarily display or hide the panel. Drag the left edge of the pane to hide or show panel names next to the icons.

- **Rulers:** Press Ctrl+R (or ⌘-R) to frame the document window with two rulers, one above and one to the left. Tick marks track your movements. In the U.S., the default unit of measure is *points*, where a point is $\frac{1}{72}$ inch.

To change the unit for a single ruler, right-click (Control-click on the Mac) the ruler and select a different setting. To cycle both rulers from one unit to the next, press Ctrl+Shift+Alt+U (or ⌘-Shift-Option-U).

- **Scroll bars:** Located opposite the rulers, the scroll bars let you pan the document horizontally or vertically.

- **Shortcut menu:** Also called a *context menu*, you can display this menu of options by clicking the right mouse button. (On the Mac, press the Control key and click.) Like the control panel, the shortcut menu is context sensitive.

- **Size box:** Drag the bottom-right corner of a window or scalable panel to make it bigger or smaller.

When you resize a panel using the size box, Illustrator scales neighboring panels to accommodate. Some panels, however, cannot be resized or can be resized only to a limited extent.

- **Title bar:** The title of the last-saved version of a file appears at the top of the document window, or in the document title tab. An asterisk indicates that the file has unsaved changes. Click the title bar to make a document active so you can edit its contents.

To switch between open windows—including tabs—from the keyboard, press Ctrl+`\`` (⌘-`\``). On a U.S. keyboard, the `\`` key is located in the upper-left corner of the keyboard next to the `1` key.

- **Toolbox:** Click an icon in the toolbox to select a tool; then use the tool in the document window. A small black triangle at the bottom-right of an icon means multiple tools share a single *slot*; click and hold the icon to display a flyout menu of alternate tools. Or press Alt (or Option) and click a slot to cycle between tools.

Press the Tab key to hide the toolbox and all panels. Press Tab again to bring them back. To hide or show all panels except the toolbox and control panel, press Shift+Tab.

- **View options:** Use this pop-up menu in the application bar to auto-arrange document windows.

- **Window controls:** The title bar contains three controls that let you hide (min), size (max), and close a document window. As illustrated below, the Mac controls are on the left; the Windows controls are on the right.

Apple Macintosh OS X            Microsoft Windows 7

- **Workspace control:** Use this pop-up menu to switch quickly between workspaces. (See "Creating Custom Workspaces" on page 28 later in this lesson.)

- **Zoom ratio:** The percentage value on the left side of the application bar lists the magnification of the document on screen. Raise the value to zoom in; lower the value to zoom out.

- Locate and double-click the *Lesson Files-AIcs5 1on1* folder.
- Lastly, double-click the *Lesson 01* folder.

3. *Select a file.* Click the file called *Radio station.ai* to select it. This is the first of the documents pictured in Figure 1-3, promoting a fictional radio station and based on a poster illustration by Fotolia illustrator Absent Anna.

---

If you're using a Windows-based PC and you don't see the document you want, you probably need to change the setting in the Files of Type pop-up menu at the bottom of the dialog box. Although this menu is useful for narrowing the choices in a folder full of files—you can view just one of many file types (PDFs, or Encapsulated PostScript documents, for example)—these options may prevent you from seeing the piece of artwork that you want. For day-to-day work, the default setting of All Readable Files is your best bet.

---

4. *Open the artwork.* Click the **Open** button or press the Enter or Return key to open the document in Illustrator. If the document appears on screen, all is well. However, if you established your own color settings—something other than what I asked you to do in the Preface (see Step 8, page xvii)—Illustrator may greet you with a **Profile or Policy Mismatch** message; just click **OK** or **Continue** to make it go away.

I'll be asking you to open and modify many files during the course of this book. Explore these files if you want, seeing how the different shapes are put together to create the overall effect. When you arrive at the successful conclusion of an exercise, as you have now, you may do with the document as you will—inspect it, modify it, or ignore it altogether. (Sometimes I will ask you to save the file.) To tidy up and move on, click ✖ in the title bar (⊗ on the Mac). Or you can choose **File→Close**.

## Organizing Your Artwork

In the previous exercise, we saw the simple way to open a file, but there is a better way—using the standalone Adobe Bridge. The Bridge is no mere image opener, however; it's a complete *digital asset manager.* In the Bridge, you can review images and illustrations, rotate them, delete them, move them to different folders, organize them into collections, and flag them for later use. You can even preview artwork at full size, filter which documents you see and which you don't, and group related assets into stacks. If you have just a few dozen files lying around your hard drive, this may seem like overkill. But if you have a few hundred, a thousand, or a hundred thousand, the Bridge is an absolute necessity.

To get a sense of what the Bridge can do, try the following. (These steps assume that the Bridge is set to the Essentials workspace, as it is by default.)

1. *Open the Bridge.* Click ▶Br in the application bar. Or press the shortcut, Ctrl+Alt+O (or ⌘-Option-O).

2. *Navigate to the* **Small thumbs** *folder.* The Bridge window is, by default, divided into five main panels: two panels on the left, the large *content browser* panel in the middle, and two more panels on the right, each labeled black in Figure 1-5. (Violet labels show ancillary options.)

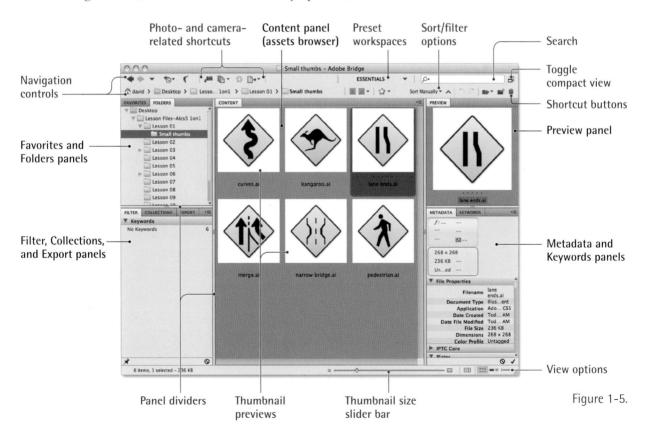

Figure 1-5.

The top-left section contains tabs that let you switch between the Favorites and Folders panels. The Favorites panel gives you instant access to commonly used folders, as well as a few places that Adobe thinks you'll find useful. The Folders panel lets you navigate to a specific folder on your hard disk or other media that contains the file or files you want to open. With that in mind, here's what I want you to do:

- Click the **Folders** tab in the top-left corner of the window to switch to the *folder tree*, thus termed because it branches into folders and subfolders.

- Scroll to the top of the list until you find the blue desktop icon. (This assumes you installed the lesson files on the desktop, per my instructions in Step 2 on page xiv of the Preface.)

- See the gray "twirly" triangle (▶) in front of the word *Desktop*? Click it to expand (or twirl open) the desktop and reveal the folders on your computer's desktop.

- Locate the folder called *Lesson Files-AIcs5 1on1* (the folders on your desktop should appear in alphabetical order) and click its ▶ to expand it.

- Click the ▶ in front of the *Lesson 01* folder.

- Finally you'll find a folder called *Small thumbs*. Click that folder to fill the content browser with a collection of six tiny *thumbnails*, as in Figure 1-5.

3. ***Enlarge the thumbnails.*** By default, the thumbnails in the content browser are tiny. That's great for assessing the broad contents of a folder but less than optimal when gauging the artworks' appearance. To increase the size of the thumbnails, drag the slider triangle in the bottom-right corner of the window, labeled as the thumbnail size slider bar in Figure 1-5.

---

Alternatively, you can zoom thumbnails from the keyboard. After selecting a thumbnail, press Ctrl+⊞ (or ⌘-⊞) to make the thumbnails larger; press Ctrl+⊟ (⌘-⊟) to make them smaller. The maximum thumbnail size is 1024 pixels in either direction, though many times your Illustrator documents will appear smaller—most likely including all the files in this lesson folder—regardless of the zoom level you set. See the sidebar "Bridge Preview and Document Size" on page 21 for more information as to why.

---

4. *Move the Preview panel.* When working with large thumbnails, the Preview panel serves little purpose. So let's tuck it away. Grab the **Preview** panel by its tab and drag it all the way to the left side of the window until a bright blue outline appears around the Folder panel. Release the mouse button to drop the panel into the top-left section of the Bridge.

5. *Rearrange more panels.* Choose **Window→Collections Panel** to hide that panel, and repeat for the Export panel by choosing **Window→Export Panel**. Drag the **Metadata** panel from the top-right corner of the window to the bottom-left, as demonstrated in Figure 1-6. And drag the **Keywords** panel as well. This empties the right panel.

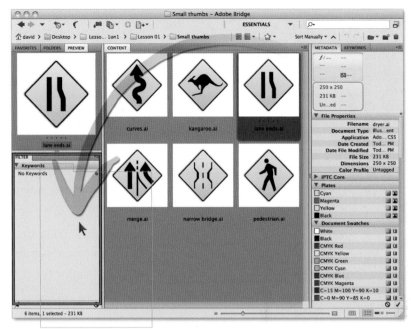

Figure 1-6.

6. *Hide the empty panel.* Double-click the vertical divider that runs along the right edge of the content browser to hide the now-empty right panel. Then click the **Preview** and **Metadata** tabs to bring these important panels to the front, as in Figure 1-7.

7. *Save this workspace.* In nearly all the Creative Suite apps, a *workspace* stores the basic configuration of the interface—which panels are visible, how panels are arranged, and (in the case of the Bridge) even the size of the thumbnails in the content browser. (I'll discuss how to save custom workspaces for Illustrator in the exercise "Creating Custom Workspaces" on page 28.) To save your current Bridge workspace, click the ▼ on the far right

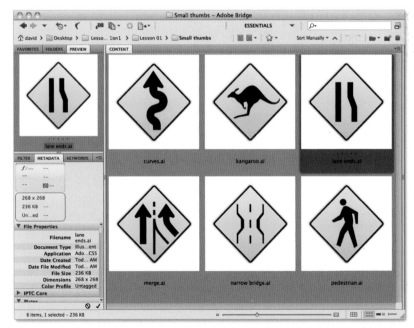

Figure 1-7.

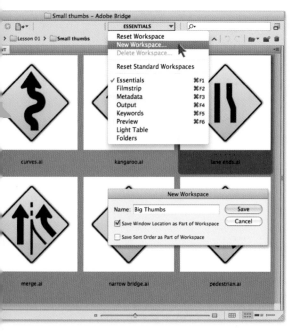

Figure 1-8.

of the application bar (it appears immediately to the right of the word *Essentials* in Figure 1-8) and choose the **New Workspace** command. Then do the following:

- Name this setting "Big Thumbs."

- If you like the size and placement of the Bridge window, leave the **Save Window Location as Part of Workspace** check box turned on.

- To maintain some flexibility, turn off the second check box, **Save Sort Order as Part of Workspace**, so that you can preserve custom sort orders even after switching workspaces.

- Click the **Save** button. The saved setting appears in the Workspace pop-up menu, above Essentials, and is automatically assigned the keyboard shortcut Ctrl+F1 (⌘-F1 on the Mac).

8. ***Increase the size of the content browser.*** One of the downsides of larger thumbnails is that you can see fewer of them at a time. The solution? Increase the amount of screen real estate devoted to the content browser:

- Maximize the Bridge window so it fills the entire screen by clicking the ▢ on the far right of the Windows title bar or the ⊕ on the far left of the Macintosh title bar.

- To gain still more room, press the Tab key to turn over the entire Bridge to the content browser. And by all means, feel free to drag the bottom-right slider triangle again so that the thumbnails adequately fill their new space.

---

At this overblown size, you might feel a bit intimidated by the sheer magnitude of the Bridge. Luckily, the program includes a *compact mode* that lets you toggle between the full view and a pocket-size view. To toggle the compact mode, click ⬚ in the top-right corner of the window or press Ctrl+Enter (⌘-Return on the Mac). The compact Bridge stays in front of other applications. This means you can preview the contents of a folder while editing artwork in Illustrator. Or drag a thumbnail into Microsoft Outlook or Apple's Mail program to create an email attachment. To exit the compact mode, click ▢.

---

**FURTHER INVESTIGATION**

The Bridge offers lots of ways to rate, label, and filter your assets, add keywords, edit metadata, and otherwise intelligently manage your files. (These tools are particularly popular with photographers.) For a more in-depth look at the Bridge, check out my book *Adobe Photoshop CS5 One-on-One*. Or start your complimentary 7-Day Free Trial Account at *www.lynda.com/deke* (as introduced on page xxiii of the Preface), and navigate to my introductory Photoshop series *Photoshop CS5 One-on-One: Fundamentals*, Chapter 3.

9. ***Restore the Bridge to a more manageable size.*** While all this real estate is good for previewing your thumbnails, it's not the most helpful for navigating your folders. Restore the other panels by pressing the Tab key again, and if you're so inclined, return the Bridge to its windowed mode by clicking the ⬚ on the far right of the Windows title bar or the ⊕ on the far left of the Macintosh title bar.

10. ***Add a folder to the Favorites panel.*** One of the most helpful bits of navigation the Bridge provides is the ability to add your folders to the Favorites panel. Let's add this ability now since you'll be accessing the lesson files regularly throughout the book:

- In the folder tree under the Folders panel, navigate to the desktop, which should be at the top of the list; click to select it. In the content browser, you should see the folder *Lesson Files-AIcs5 1on1* (along with whatever you have on your desktop).

- Switch from the Folders tab to the **Favorites** tab in the top- left panel.

- Finally, drag the thumbnail for the *Lesson Files-AIcs5 1on1* folder from the content browser to the Favorites panel.

Now you have a shortcut to the lesson files directly from your Favorites panel. Those are the basics of the Bridge; close it or send it to the background as you see fit, and return to Illustrator.

## Setting Up a New Document

Just about every program lets you create new files—if they didn't, they would soon be extinct. But Illustrator lets you specify a slew of settings when you create a document, giving your artwork a solid frame in which to sit, ready to take on the world.

The goal of this exercise is to create a new document. For the sake of example, we'll create a document with a single square artboard, suitable for use as a CD cover. (In the exercise after this one, we'll learn how to add additional artboards, even after the file is created.)

1. ***Choose the New command.*** Choose **File→New** or press Ctrl+N (⌘-N on the Mac). Illustrator displays the **New Document** dialog box, as in Figure 1-9.

2. ***Give your document a name.*** Ever helpful, Illustrator highlights the first option, **Name**, so you can hit the ground running. Change the name to something like "CD Cover."

3. ***Choose a profile.*** Illustrator comes with a set of seven basic document profiles, each geared toward a different end product.

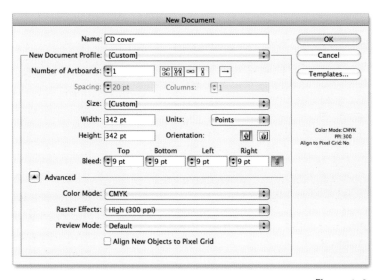

Figure 1-9.

While you don't have to choose a document profile—all the values are editable regardless of what profile you start with—doing so helps get the basic settings in order. In this case, our final artwork will be printed, so select **Print** from the **New Document Profile** menu if it isn't already.

4. ***Review the artboard options.*** For the moment, we'll focus on just one artboard in this document, but it's good to know all your options. The artboard settings will be dimmed, since the number of artboards is set to 1, but we can still review them:

   - The first set of icons indicates whether the artboards should be arranged in rows (⊞), columns (⊞), a single row (▯▯), or a single column (▯). The separate button at the end (→) toggles the ordering between left-to-right and right-to-left (or top-to-bottom versus bottom-to-top), the latter being common in Hebrew, Arabic, and a few Asian alphabets.

   - The next setting is Spacing, which determines the amount of room between each artboard. (Generally speaking, this should be at least double the bleed on the document, to prevent the artwork from overlapping.)

   - The final setting, Rows (or Columns, depending on the ordering you're using), sets the number of rows (or columns) for the artboards. The value automatically changes to try and keep the artboards as close to a square arrangement as possible, but you can override this value.

Note that you can create only equal-size artboards from the New Document dialog box. To make the artboards different sizes, you must edit the artboards, which I explain in the next exercise.

5. ***Change the size to a custom size.*** By default, the Print document profile sets up a single artboard at standard letter size, or 8½ by 11 inches. Other paper sizes are listed, but don't be fooled into thinking these are the only options available to you. Illustrator allows you to make documents at any custom size.

The standard card used for the front cover of a CD is 4¾ inches square. However, you may notice that Illustrator's default units are points, not inches. (An inch is 72 points.) You could change your units to inches here in the dialog box, but I recommend you don't—points are the industry-standard unit of measurement for Illustrator artwork. And why change the units when Illustrator will convert them on-the-fly for you?

Here's how to have Illustrator convert units. Press the Tab key one or more times to advance to the **Width** value. Then type 4.75 inches (4.75in or 4.75" for short). Press Tab to advance to the Height value. The moment you do, Illustrator converts your inches to points, making the Width value 342pt, or 342 points. Next, repeat for the **Height** value.

---

Just for fun, Figure 1-10 shows many other ways to enter alternative measurements, including picas and millimeters. Note that you can spell out units or use abbreviations. You can also perform small bits of math, but you are limited to a single operand.

---

Finally, the Orientation options switch the artboard between portrait (⊞) and landscape (⊞) mode, although they make no difference in this document because it's square.

| | | |
|---|---|---|
| 4.75 inches | 28 pica 6 | 4in+54pt |
| 4.75inches | 28pica6 | 4in+p54 |
| 4.75 inch | 28p 6 | 5in-1.5p |
| 4.75inch | 28p6 | 5in-1p6 |
| 4.75 in | 342 points | 5in-18pt |
| 4.75in | 342 point | 120.65 millimeters |
| 4.75" | 342pt | 120.65mm |
| 4"+.75" | picas 342 | 12.065 centimeters |
| 5"-0.25" | pica 342 | 12.065cm |
| 19/4" | pica342 | 12cm+0.65mm |
| 19*0.25" | p342 | 12065/100mm |
| 28.5 picas | 4in+4.5p | |
| 28.5 pica | 4in+4p6 | |
| 28.5pica | | |
| 28.5p | | |

*40 different ways to say "4³⁄₄ inches" in Illustrator*

Figure 1-10.

6. ***Establish the Bleed settings.*** We need to establish settings for the *bleed*—the artwork that runs off the edge of the page to make sure no gaps appear when the art is printed and trimmed. (For art destined for the Web or mobile devices, a bleed is not only unnecessary but can cause issues when it's time to output the art.) I explain bleeds in more detail in Lesson 12, because they're essential for printed art, but for now, know that a bleed of ¹⁄₈ inch, or 9 points, is sufficient for a typical print job. Make sure the link icon (🔗) is active—that is, dark gray as opposed to light gray. The link icon locks all four values, so that any value entered is set for all sides. Change any of the values to "9 pt" and press Tab; all the other values update automatically.

7. ***Review the Advanced settings.*** Lastly, we'll review the Advanced settings. (You may need to click ▾ to see them.) The three main settings are Color Mode (CMYK for print, RGB for screen), Raster Effects (determines the resolution for rendering certain effects when output), and Preview Mode. These three are fine as is, because we started from the Print document profile.

PEARL OF WISDOM

New in CS5 is the Align New Objects to Pixel Grid option. In previous versions of Illustrator, output for the Web was a hit-or-miss operation; sometimes objects would straddle a row or column of multiple pixels, causing the edges to look lighter or fuzzy. This option remedies that problem. Since this illustration is destined for print, leave the box unchecked; for Web or mobile device artwork, imake sure this option is turned on, ensuring crisp output to the screen.

PEARL OF WISDOM

Bear in mind that most values you enter in the New Document dialog box can be modified later. You can add or delete artboards, change artboard dimensions, rearrange the order and placement of artboards, and even change the color output settings. If you have only a vague idea of how you want to set up your new document, don't fret. Just rough in some numbers and consider the result a work in progress.

Figure 1-11.

I always leave Preview Mode set to Default, which provides the most flexibility. It's easy enough to change to the other preview modes from the View menu. For more information on the preview modes, see "Video Lesson 1: Navigation" from the videos.

8. *Click the OK button.* Or you can press the Enter or Return key to accept your settings and create a blank document inside a new document window. Your document should look like the one in Figure 1-11, with a perfectly square artboard and a red bleed boundary.

Now that you have created a pristine new document—complete with a custom-sized artboard, bleed boundaries, and output settings—you'll learn a few ways to change it in the next exercise, as well as how to add a second artboard with a different size.

## Changing the Document Setup and Modifying Artboards

Creating new documents is fine—but invariably specifications get updated, you (or your client) change your mind about the artwork's size, or any of a host of other issues arise. Rather than recreating your meticulous efforts, you need your documents to change with the times—and now I'll show you how to do just that, through a series of hypothetical (but sadly, all too common) scenarios. Instead of being contained in one dialog box, however, these options are scattered in several places across Illustrator's user interface. We'll walk through them one by one.

1. *Create a new file.* If you have the file open from the previous exercise, great; you can simply continue to use that file. If you closed the file, not to worry—when you create a new document, Illustrator remembers the settings you last used. Choose **File→New** or press Ctrl+N (⌘-N on the Mac) and then press **OK** to accept the new document. (If you closed the file *and* created another document between the last exercise and this one, there's not much that can be done, so I've stashed a catch-up document called *CD cover.ai* in the *Lesson 01* folder. Open that file to continue.)

In creating the new file back in Step 8 of the preceding exercise, you updated the default settings that Illustrator automatically remembers. But there's a shorter shortcut: to bypass the New Document dialog box entirely and use your most recent default values, eschew File→New and press Ctrl+Alt+N (⌘-Option-N) instead.

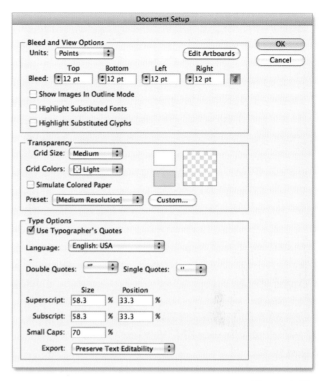

Figure 1-12.

2. *Bring up the Document Setup dialog box.* The first dialog box to examine is Document Setup. You can get to it by choosing **File→Document Setup** from the menu, pressing Ctrl+Alt+P (⌘-Option-P), or pressing the **Document Setup** button in the control panel. The dialog box is shown in Figure 1-12.

Whoa! You might be wondering what you've stumbled into, because this looks nothing like the dialog box from the previous exercise. (Through the looking glass, indeed.) With the advent of multiple artboards in CS4, Illustrator moved much of the New Document dialog box into different places. The only commonality immediately visible in this dialog box are the bleed settings. We'll start there.

The other Document Setup options—Transparency and Type Options—will be discussed in their respective lessons (Lesson 4 for type and Lesson 8 for transparency).

3. *Adjust the bleed settings.* Suppose that you've received an urgent missive from your printer informing you that they now require a 1-pica (or 12-point) bleed on all artwork. Easy enough to fix. Making sure 🔒 is still turned on, change one of the bleed values to 12 points by either highlighting the value and typing "12 pt," or pressing the up arrow next to the value three times. Notice that all the values update in sync. One problem down!

You won't see the update to the bleed boundary in the document window while the dialog box is open, but rest assured, the change will occur momentarily.

4. *Switch to artboard-editing mode.* As is often the case with changes, there's rarely just one. Also in the printer's letter is an update to the CD card template; the new jewel cases require a nonstandard card size of 4.675 inches square. Yet there's no document size to be found in this dialog box. What to do?

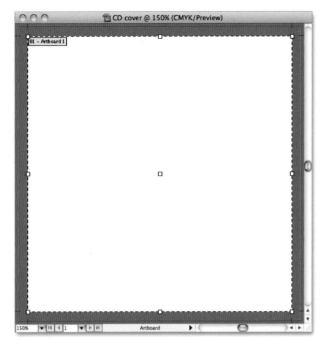

Figure 1-13.

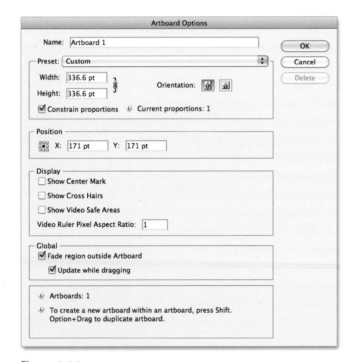

Figure 1-14.

Lurking in the upper-right corner of the dialog box is the **Edit Artboards** button. Whether your document has one artboard or twenty, the artboard-editing mode is the only way to edit an artboards's size and position. (Some options are available via the Artboard panel.) Click the button to switch to this mode.

Several things happen at once: First, your document window turns gray, except for the area bounded by the artboard itself. Second, the bleed boundary updates to the new setting you specified in the preceding step. Last, *crop marks*—black lines outside the print area—appear, indicating the edges of your artboard. You can see these changes in Figure 1-13.

Note that you can also access the artboard-editing mode at any time by selecting the Artboard tool from the toolbox (□) or by pressing Shift+O.

5. *Modify the size of the artboard.* Now that you're in edit mode, you can edit the artboard's dimensions in a number of ways. You could simply drag a corner, holding the Shift key to constrain the proportions and preserve the perfect square—but that would require knowing off the top of your head how many points are in 4.675 inches. You could also use the W and H values in the control panel, entering the value 4.675in and letting Illustrator handle the conversion. That would be more precise, certainly, but another way affords you even more control. And Illustrator thrives on precision and control.

With that in mind, I'd like you to click ⊞ in the control panel; it's the last icon before the origin point grid and the X and Y values. (In this too small icon, Adobe is quixotically trying to represent a dialog box with a miniscule 18×18 pixel square.) The Artboard Options dialog box, shown in Figure 1-14, opens. This dialog box also provides access to all the other options in the control panel, with the exception of options to add or delete an artboard.

For now, we just want to change the size of the artboard to the new specifications. Click the **Constrain Proportions** box, type "4.675in" in either the Width or Height value field, and then press the Tab key. The other value updates automatically, and you'll

If you're familiar with the thumbnail previews in the Bridge when working with Photoshop images, you know that bitmap image thumbnails scale beautifully, even to large sizes. So why do some of the pieces of artwork made in Illustrator insist on staying eye-strainingly tiny?

The answer is fairly straightforward: The thumbnail is limited by the original document size. This is true for bitmap images as well, but nearly all professional photographs—not to mention snapshots taken with your average digital camera or even a decent cell phone—are at least 1200 pixels in at least one dimension. This size puts these images well above the 1024-pixel threshhold the Bridge uses to draw its thumbnails.

The preview of vector art, however, is based on the size of the document, or in the case of Illustrator files, the artboard. The problem arises if you have an illustration on a small artboard (as is often the case with an icon or a company logo)—the thumbnail refuses to budge over a certain size no matter what.

---

There is another reason for small thumbnails. Illustrator limits the size to which you can scale a thumbnail of an extremely complicated file, say one with many anchor points, regardless of artboard size. (*Urban chaos.ait* in the *Lesson 01* folder is an example of this.)

---

I can hear you saying now, "But vector art is infinitely scalable! Isn't that the whole point?" Indeed it is. And why Adobe has chosen not to allow vector art thumbnails to scale beyond their document size is a mystery to me. Thankfully, there is a workaround. Stick with me and I'll walk you through it.

---

Some of the steps I'm about to use, such as scaling artwork and saving your file, are discussed in this lesson or in later lessons. For now, follow along, knowing that the details will be fleshed out in future exercises.

---

- If it's not already open, open the Bridge by clicking the ▶Br icon or by pressing Ctrl+Alt+O (⌘-Option-O on the Mac).

- Using the folder tree, navigate to the *Lesson 01* folder inside the *Lesson Files-AIcs5 1on1* folder. Twirl open the *Lesson 01* folder to reveal the folder called *Small thumbs*. Click that folder to select it.

- You should now see previews of six traffic icons in the main content panel of the Bridge. (These icons come

from Fotolia artist Alexander Kurilchik.) Scale up the size of the thumbnails; at some point, you'll notice that the spacing around the thumbnails, but not the thumbnails themselves, becomes larger. Houston, we have a problem.

- For brevity, we'll make the fix to just one of the files, rather than to all. (You could create an *action*, much like those in Photoshop, to automate the process.) Double-click the thumbnail for *curves.ai* to open it in Illustrator.

- Now that you're in Illustrator, you need to do two things: resize the artboard and scale the artwork. You learned how to adjust the artboards in the current exercise, so start there: Click the Artboards tool (⼞) or press Shift+O to switch to artboard-editing mode. In the control panel, adjust the W and H values (for width and height, respectively) to 500 pt each to double the size of the artboard. Press the Esc key twice to exit back to the document.

- The artboard is resized, but what about the art itself? We'll need to scale it similarly as well. Press Ctrl+A (⌘-A on the Mac) to select all the art. In the control panel, make sure your anchor point is set to the center square (like ▦), and adjust the W and H values to 450 pt each.

---

You can achieve the same effect using simple math in the value boxes. Type *2 (that's an asterisk followed by the number two) after both values to double them.

---

- Finally, save your file to a new document by choosing **File→Save As** or pressing Ctrl+Shift+S (⌘-Shift-S). Give the file a name like "curves_big.ai."

Now, if you return to the Bridge, you should see your newly created file, with its thumbnail now scalable to twice the size of the original file. It's a convoluted way to fix the problem of small thumbnails, but unfortunately it's the only way to get around this issue until Adobe ponies up.

---

It's best to keep this limitation in mind when creating new artwork and make sure to use a size large enough to have a decent preview. With these traffic icons, the preview was legible enough at the smaller size, but more detailed files at similar sizes would be a complete mess. Also, a word of warning: If you use this scaling technique on existing artwork that has already been placed in an external program such as InDesign, you will need to readjust the scaling factor in that program.

---

see your new artboard size previewed in the document window, complete with a newly resized bleed boundary. Click **OK** to accept the new artboard size.

6. *Create a new artboard.* Imagine that while wrangling the CD cover, your boss requests that you make a back for the CD as well, known in the biz as a *tray card* (because it sits under the tray that holds the CD). Thankfully, she gives you the dimensions, rather than just having you guess—the tray card should be 4⅝ inches tall by 5²⁹/₃₂ inches wide. (At this point, it's appropriate to bless Adobe for building conversion into Illustrator—but don't give too much thanks yet, as there's a caveat we'll see in the next step.)

You should still be in artboard-editing mode; if not, select the ⟂ tool or press Shift+O. Again, you have many options open to you: You could try to draw the artboard freehand, though once again you would run into the unit conversion issue. (Also, since you checked the Constrain Proportions box in the Advanced Options dialog box, the artboard tool will currently let you draw only constrained proportions—in this case, squares.) You could also Alt-click (or Option-click) the existing artboard to duplicate it, and drag it to a new location.

Here, your best option is to simply use ⊡ in the control panel to create a new artboard, and edit it from there. Click ⊡, and your cursor is loaded with an artboard that matches the original. Place the new artboard somewhere to the right of the existing one, as shown in Figure 1-15; we'll tweak its final position when we've finished the editing. To see the canvas well enough to place the second artboard, you may need to zoom out by pressing Ctrl+⊟ (⌘-⊟ on the Mac).

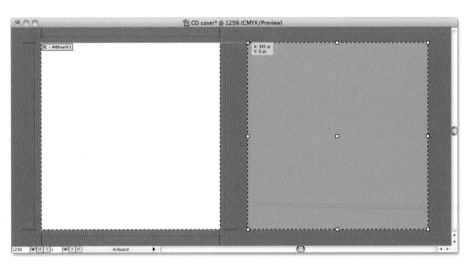

Figure 1-15.

7. *Edit the new artboard's size.* Again, bring up the **Artboard Options** dialog box by clicking ▦ in the control panel. Start by changing the Width value—but now

comes the caveat. If you enter 5 29/32in, you will be greeted you with an "Invalid numeric value" alert. Illustrator can't deal with whole numbers and fractions together in a numeric field. (Illustrator doesn't even consider them fractions, but rather numbers separated by a division sign.) 5+29/32in also won't work because Illustrator limits you to one operand per field.

Here's the workaround: First, make sure the Constrain Proportion box is not checked. Then, enter the fraction value "29/32in" in the **Width** field, tab to the next field (prompting Illustrator to convert the value to 65.25pt), Shift+Tab back to the **Width** field, and then append "+5in" to the value, so that the box reads "65.25 pt +5in". When you tab to the Height value, Illustrator dutifully does the math, for a final width of 425.25 points. For the **Height** value, enter "4.675in" (the equivalent of 4⅝ inches), and then click OK to accept the artboard's new size.

8. *Reposition the second artboard.* You should still be in artboard-editing mode. Click and hold somewhere in the second artboard; you can now drag it to any position in the document. Drag the artboard to the right, leaving enough room so that the crop marks don't overlap (or barely overlap) into the bleed of the first artboard. Finally, align the vertical centers of the artboard. Illustrator will snap it into place and draw a green smart guide connecting the centers of the artboards when you are in the proper position, as seen in Figure 1-16. (I introduce guides and smart guides in the next exercise.) When the artboard is in position, release the mouse button.

And there you have it! Multiple artboards, each built at a custom size. After all this hard work, you might want to save your document; press Ctrl+Shift+S (⌘-Shift-S on the Mac) to bring up the **Save As** dialog box. Give it a name like "CD artboards.ai," and click **Save** to preserve your work. (If you see a second dialog, click **OK** to save the file using the default settings.)

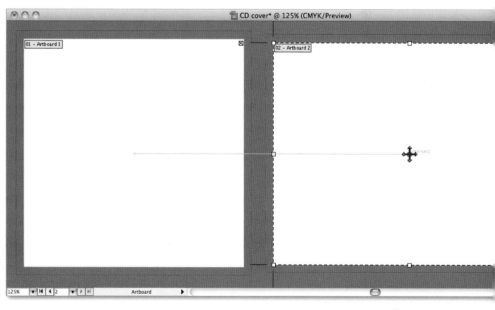

Figure 1-16.

Figure 1-17.

Figure 1-18.

## Introducing Guides, Smart Guides, and Layers

Knowing how to set up a document and customize your artboards means that your artwork will have a good foundation. But even the best of illustrators can use some assistance keeping his or her ducks in a row. Layers and guides give you the tools to do just that. *Guides* provide a nonprinting framework to keep your art aligned. *Smart guides*, which were overhauled for CS4, are guides that Illustrator creates on-the-fly to help you align to objects in your illustration. *Layers* allow you to organize your objects into distinct groups and manipulate those groups as a whole.

In this exercise, I'll introduce you to each of these tools in turn. I'll also show you how to create custom guides, isolate your guides on their own layer, and more.

1. *Open a sample file.* Press Ctrl+O (⌘-O) to bring up the Open a File (or Open) dialog box. Navigate to the *Lesson 01* folder inside the Le*sson Files-AIcs5 1on1* folder. Select the file *Horus. ai*, and click the OK button.

2. *Examine the guides.* When you first open the document, it will look like the one in Figure 1-17—a black-and-white line drawing of the eye of Horus. Conspicuously absent, however, are any sign of guides. The document does indeed contain guides, but they are currently hidden. Display the guides by pressing Ctrl+⌑ (⌘-⌑ on the Mac) or by selecting **View→Guides→Show Guides**. You should now see three cyan-colored squares, as in Figure 1-18.

If you're new to Illustrator but familiar with guides in other programs like Photoshop or InDesign, you may be wondering how these squares can be guides. Aren't guides limited to horizontal or vertical rules? In most programs, yes, but Illustrator allows you to take any path, of any shape, and convert it to a guide—something we'll be doing later in this very exercise.

3. *Make sure your rulers are visible.* No, I'm not suggesting you go looking for the president, or prime minister, or even the queen herself. I want you to make sure your *document rulers* are visible. If they aren't, you can show them by pressing Ctrl+R (⌘-R) or choosing **View→Show Rulers**. Your rulers must be visible to create a horizontal or vertical guide, which is our very next step.

4. *Create a new guide.* You can create new guides simply by dragging down from the horizontal ruler or to the right from the vertical ruler. First, make sure the black arrow tool is selected, either by clicking the ▸ tool in the toolbox or by pressing the V key, and then drag down from the horizontal ruler. Release the mouse button when the guide is anywhere in the artboard.

5. *Delete the guide.* Let's assume the guide you just created isn't exactly where you want it (which is almost certainly the case, since I didn't provide any direction as to where to place it). Sadly, if you try to move or select the new guide, you probably can't. Why, you may be asking, can't you move a guide you created 30 seconds ago?

   Most likely, your guides are locked—meaning they can't be moved, edited, or deleted. To unlock them, select **View→Guides→Unlock Guides** or press Ctrl+Alt+⎀ (⌘-Option-⎀ on the Mac). Now you should be able to select your guide by clicking it (the guide turns a dark blue); delete it by pressing the Backspace or Delete key.

6. *Place a guide using smart guides.* When placing the guide this time, you'll get positioning assistance from smart guides. First, make sure smart guides are turned on by confirming that a check mark appears next to the **View→Smart Guides** option. (They should be on by default.) Again, drag down from the horizontal ruler, but this time move the cursor over the bottom of the vertical line under the eye, as in Figure 1-19. You should see a smart guide with the label *anchor* and a smart measurement, letting you know that the guide has snapped to that anchor point. When your screen looks like Figure 1-19, release the mouse button.

Figure 1-19.

Figure 1-20.

7. *Repeat for a second guide.* Repeat the process for a second guide, this time snapping the guide to the anchor point at the top of the vertical line, as shown in Figure 1-20.

8. *Create a custom-shape guide.* The last guide we're going to create is a custom rectangle guide to accompany the three that already exist in our document and complete a grid of four squares. To draw this guide, we'll use the standard rectangle tool to create the shape, and then convert the shape to a guide.

Switch to the rectangle tool by clicking the □ tool in the toolbox or by pressing the M key. Draw a rectangle from the upper-right corner to the lower-left, as shown in Figure 1-21. (You should see the word *anchor*, which is a smart guide label, at each corner while you are drawing.) Once the cursor snaps into place, release the mouse.

Illustrator draws a rectangle with the current fill and stroke settings—your results may vary from mine. In my case, I get a thick black stroke and no fill. Regardless of the visual results you get, the next step is the same: Convert the shape to a guide. To do so, choose **View→Guides→Make Guides** or press Ctrl+5 (⌘-5 on the Mac). The results are shown in Figure 1-22.

Figure 1-21.

Figure 1-22.

9. *Bring up the Layers panel.* The last task in this exercise is to create a new layer to house all our guides. To that end, bring up the Layers panel by pressing the F7 key or choosing **Window→Layers** from the menu. You'll notice that the document has just one layer at the moment, Horus, which holds all the artwork and guides.

10. *Create a new layer.* The guides need a new home. Alt-click (or Option-click) ⬚ to create a new layer and bring up the **Layer Options** dialog box simultaneously. Name the layer "Guides," and change the color to something of your choosing. (I like orange against the blue of the other layer.) The dialog box should look like that in Figure 1-23; when it does, click **OK**.

Figure 1-23.

11. *Select and move all the guides.* Using the black arrow tool, click one of the guides to select it (if the rectangle guide isn't still selected), and then Shift-click the rest of the guides one by one to add them to the selection. (It's easiest to click the guides well away from any of the artwork.) You should select six guides in total. In the **Layers** panel, you'll notice a small blue square to the right of the layer name, **Horus**, shown in Figure 1-24. Click and drag that square up to the **Guides** layer. You've successfully moved all your guides to their own layer!

Figure 1-24.

PEARL OF WISDOM

The small square in the Layers panel allows you to drag the currently selected object or objects, regardless of what they are, to any other layer (assuming the target layer is not locked). Also, clicking the square (or the area where the square would be, if no objects are selected) selects all the objects on that layer.

12. *Lock the Guides layer and toggle its visibility.* The guides are on their own layer, but what practical purpose does that serve? One advantage of placing objects on their own layer is that they can be locked or hidden independently of the other layers. To lock the Guides layer, click the second (empty) column, just to the right of the 👁. A 🔒 appears, which indicates that the layer is no longer editable, as shown in Figure 1-25. (To unlock the layer, simply click 🔒.) To hide the layer, click 👁, and to "wake up" the layer, click the empty space in the 👁 column.

Figure 1-25.

In the case of guides, there is a bonus—isolating the guides on their own layer saves you the hassle of going through the rather long View menu every time you want to toggle the guides on and off. You can simply access this functionality via the Layers panel.

Starting back with CS4, you can snap objects to guides using smart guides, even if the guides are hidden or locked at the layer level; this wasn't the case for previous versions of Illustrator.

If you'd like to save your work, press Ctrl+Shift+S (or ⌘-Shift-S on the Mac) to bring up the **Save As** dialog box. Name your file "Horus with guides.ai," and click **Save**. Otherwise, discard the file, and move along with me to the next exercise, which also deals with organization—this time, of your workspace.

## Creating Custom Workspaces

Like most Adobe software, Illustrator's interface can be described as panel intensive. Lurking under the Window menu are 34 panels (not counting the toolbox and control panel, and certainly not including the vast number of libraries, which are also housed in panels), though mercifully the various workspaces narrow them down. A *workspace* is a predefined collection and placement of panels. Illustrator CS5 has nine (that's right, *nine*) default workspaces, each geared toward different uses. Some are designed to mimic applications you may be familiar with, such as Freehand, Photoshop, or InDesign. In each workspace, a panel can either stand on its own or be nested with other panels inside a *docking pane*. Illustrator's Essentials workspace places just eleven panels (in five clusters) on the right side of the screen in a single docking pane. As you can see in Figure 1-26, they appear simply as icons. Clicking any icon temporarily expands the corresponding panel until you click to send it back in line.

So with all these workspaces for different uses (and different users), why make a custom one? Chances are none of the default workspaces will have all the functionality needed for the most important user—you.

By way of example, this exercise shows you how to set up and save a custom workspace well-suited for the work you'll be doing in Illustrator as you go through this book. You'll also learn how to switch between a custom workspace and the defaults.

Figure 1-26.

ESSENTIALS ▾

Automation
✓ Essentials
Like FreeHand
Like InDesign
Like Photoshop
Painting
Printing and Proofing
Typography
Web

Save Workspace...
Manage Workspaces...

Figure 1-27.

1. *Start with the Essentials workspace.* Assuming you haven't done any panel redecorating that you care to keep, choose **Window→Workspace→ Essentials.** Better yet, select Essentials from the workspace control pop-up menu, as in Figure 1-27. Either method switches to the Essentials workspace.

2. *Open a sample document.* To ensure that we're on the same page, open the *Retro blisco.ai* file, from iStockphoto artist Bulent Ince, located in the *Lesson 01* folder. The art-work appears in Figure 1-28.

Figure 1-28.

3. *Zoom in on the leaf tips.* Zoom in on the area around middle dancer's head and shoulders. Press the Z key to access the zoom tool, and click to zoom in to 400 percent. (It took me four clicks, but your experience may vary.)

4. *Detach the document from the docking pane.* For the most part, I like using tabbed documents so that I can switch easily between them, without all the window clutter. In this case, however, I want the interface to stand on its own as much as possible. Click the tab in the top bar, drag it anywhere in the applica-tion window, and release. Then click the size box in the lower-right corner of the document window and drag it so that only a small amount of the artwork is visible, as shown in Figure 1-29.

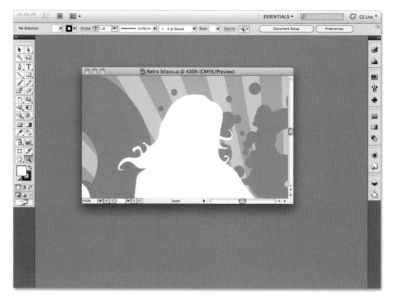

Figure 1-29.

If, after you detach the window, your size box isn't visible, no worries. You can resize a document window from any visible side. Just drag the top of the window down, and then grab the title bar to move the window back into view.

Figure 1-30.

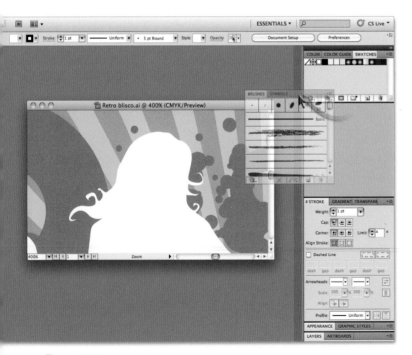

Figure 1-31.

5. *Expand the docking pane to reveal the panels.* The default view gives you an icon for each of the default panels. To start, you have five clusters of light gray panels nestled inside a larger dark gray *docking pane*, which is anchored to the right edge of your screen. Click the double arrow (◄◄) or anywhere along the top of the docking pane to expand the pane and see the full contents of the front panel from each cluster, with tabs for the other panels visible behind them.

6. *Move the Swatches panel.* Especially at this resolution, screen real estate is a hot commodity. Condense the color-related panels into one pane by clicking the title of the **Swatches** panel and dragging it up to the right of Color Guide, as shown in Figure 1-30. When you see the blue box, release the mouse button.

7. *Create a new docking pane for Brushes and Symbols.* While clicking and holding somewhere in the *cluster bar* (the gray area to the right of the panel tabs), drag the **Brushes** and **Symbols** cluster to the left, until the vertical blue bar appears as in Figure 1-31. This creates a new docking pane to the left of the original; click the double arrow (►►) to collapse the panels back to their icons.

8. *Move the Appearance and Graphic Styles panels.* The Layers panel is a screen hog, so give it some more room. Repeat the move you did in Step 6 for the Appearance and Graphic Styles panels, moving **Appearance** into the pane with Layers and Artboards, and **Graphic**

**Styles** just below Symbols, as shown in Figure 1-32. Drag the **Appearance** tab between Layers and Artboards to adjust the order.

9. *Open the Transform panel cluster.* One essential missing from the Essentials workspace is a cluster of three panels: Transform, Align, and Pathfinder. Choose **Window→Transform** to open this panel cluster.

10. *Dock the Transform panel cluster in the narrow docking pane.* Again while clicking and holding somewhere in the cluster bar, drag the **Transform** panel cluster over to the narrow docking bar below the icon until you see a blue line appear. (If instead you see a blue box, move further below the graphic styles icon into the gray bar underneath.) Release the mouse button, and the panels will now be grouped at the bottom of the docking pane.

11. *Add a cluster of text-editing panels.* Another essential set of panels missing from this workspace, assuming you plan to set any copy in Illustrator, are the text-editing panels. Choose **Window→Type→Character** to bring up a cluster of text-related panels (Character, Paragraph, and OpenType). Drag this panel cluster to the bottom of the docking pane, below the Transform panel cluster.

12. *Repeat for two more panel clusters.* Repeat the last step for the Navigator and Info panel cluster, and then again for the Document Info and Attributes cluster. Choose **Window→Navigator** to open the first cluster, and drag it into place beneath the text-editing cluster. Then Choose **Window→Document Info** to open the second. This time, release the mouse button inside the Navigator cluster, when you see the blue box instead of the blue line; this combines the four panels into a single cluster.

13. *Extract the Navigator panel to its own cluster.* The Navigator panel doesn't quite fit with the others in its group; move it to its own group by dragging the ✳ icon down until you see the blue bar below the original cluster. Your final results are shown in Figure 1-33 on the following page.

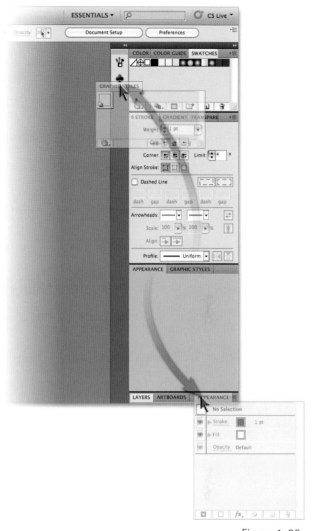

Figure 1-32.

Figure 1-33.

14. ***Rearrange the other panels as you see fit.*** You now have a collection of panels on screen that are more useful than the default arrangement. Still, you may want to make some adjustments to better exploit your screen real estate. Here are a few techniques you can use:

- Expand or reduce the width of a docking pane by dragging the left edge of the pane. You can also use the left edge to hide or show the panel names when the panels are collapsed to icons.

- Click ✦ in the panel tab to cycle between different expansion settings. Or double-click the panel's tab. (The latter technique gives you extra options when the panel is free floating.)

- Resize the height of a panel by hovering over the dark bar separating the clusters until your cursor becomes a double-headed arrow, as in ✤. Then drag the bar up or down to resize the panel's height.

- Collapse a panel to only tabs by clicking the cluster bar above the panel title. Click again to restore the panel.

- To bring back a hidden panel, choose its name from the Window menu. All panels are listed in alphabetical order, although the Type-related panels are squirreled away inside a submenu.

- Collapse the docking pane to icons by clicking ►► in the upper-right corner (or on the top of the docking pane). Restore it with another click.

- Note that you can not drag a docking pane, but you can create one—on the other side of the screen, for example— by dragging a panel to a new location and waiting for a blue vertical bar to appear. You can make multiple docking panes side-by-side as well. Note that adjacent docking panes "stick" together; dragging one will drag all adjacent panes. To detach a docking pane, you must instead detach all its cluster panes.

15. *Save your custom workspace.* Now that you have your panels arranged just the way you want them, save which panels are visible as well as their position and scale by choosing **Window→Workspace→Save Workspace** or selecting Save Workspace from the workspace control pop-up menu. Name the workspace "One-on-One Workspace" (see Figure 1-34) and then click the **OK** button.

16. *Restore one of the default workspaces.* Having saved your custom workspace, you can now switch between it and any other workspace, including any of Illustrator's defaults. Choose **Window→Workspace→Essential**. All the panels return to their layout from back in Step 1.

17. *Bring back the One-on-One workspace.* Now comes the real test. Choose **Window→Workspace→One-on-One Workspace** and, presto, your saved workspace reappears.

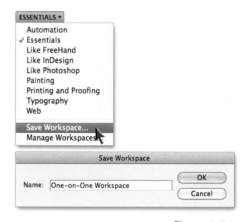

Figure 1-34.

---

To delete a saved workspace, choose Window→Workspace→Manage Workspaces. Then choose the name of the workspace you want to delete from the Manage Workspaces dialog box and click the trash icon.

---

Although the New Workspace command might seem to give you complete control over the interface, it actually has no bearing on the document window itself. Try this: Resize the document window, and zoom out from the page so it looks approximately the way it did in Figure 1-28 on page 29. (You zoom out by Alt-clicking or Option-clicking with the zoom tool.) Then switch back and forth between the Essentials workspace and One-on-One workspace configurations. Throughout, the window remains unaffected. In Illustrator and other Adobe CS5 applications, the workspace is all about panels; settings applied to the document window, such as zoom level and position, are stored with the document file itself.

PEARL OF WISDOM

Note that unlike either the Bridge or InDesign, Illustrator does not remember the last state of a workspace—meaning that switching to a new workspace will switch to the default state of that workspace, rather than the last arrangement. To keep your custom workspace settings, you need to explicitly save your workspace.

# Saving Your Artwork

Illustrator is packed with so many tools, panels, and commands that it can be a bit dizzying at first. But there's one absolutely critical command in the program, the Save command. Without File→Save, you couldn't preserve your hard-earned art. In this exercise, you'll learn how to use the Save command in Illustrator as well as your different options for saving a file.

1. *Open a document.* **Choose File→Open** or press Ctrl+O (⌘-O on the Mac). Open the file *Urban chaos.ait* in the *Lesson 01* folder inside *Lesson Files-AIcs5 1on1*.  This piece of artwork comes to us from Fotolia illustrator Rama Rajan and is pictured in Figure 1-35. Imagine that you just created this file; now you're ready to save it for posterity.

## PEARL OF WISDOM

Because this file was last saved as a template (hence the *.ait* extension), Illustrator opens an untitled copy of the file. This prevents you from accidentally saving over the original. More importantly where this exercise is concerned, it exactly simulates the experience you would have if you were to create a new document—so far as Illustrator is concerned, the document has never been saved. Unfortunately, Illustrator also considers a newly made document, or a freshly opened copy from a template, as *unmodified*—and therefore does not make the File→Save command available to you until you've made some sort of modification; we'll do that next.

2. *Make the smallest of modifications.* Since Illustrator in its apparent helpfulness won't let us save the file without some modification, we'll need to trick it into thinking we've made a change. Bring up the **Layers** panel by pressing F7, click the 👁 to hide the **Artwork** layer, and then click the empty space where the eyeball was to "wake up" the layer. That small change is enough for Illustrator to flag the art as modified.

Figure 1-35.

3. ***Choose the Save command.*** Press Ctrl+S (⌘-S) or choose **File→Save**. If the document had been saved before, Illustrator would update the file on disk. But because it hasn't, the **Save As** dialog box appears, as in Figure 1-37.

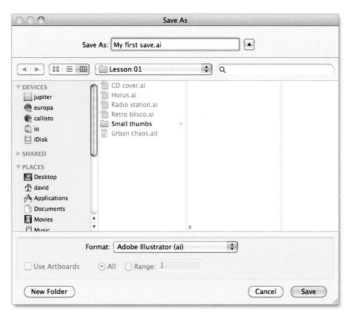

Figure 1-36.

4. ***Choose the desired format.*** Leave the **Save as Type** option (called **Format** on the Mac) set to **Adobe Illustrator (ai)**. This saves the artwork as an everyday native file that opens as a titled document. But what are these other options, you may wonder?

- Illustrator EPS (eps) saves the file in a format called Encapsulated PostScript. For years, this format was the cross-platform, cross-application standard—but it's falling out of favor now that Adobe is dominating the design world with the Creative Suite. This format is most useful for backward compatibility with legacy versions of programs, most notably QuarkXPress.

- Adobe Illustrator Template (ait) saves the file as a template file, causing future openings of the file to open a copy rather than the original. The only way to change a template file is to open a copy, make the modifications, and then resave the file as a template over the original.

- Adobe PDF (pdf) outputs the file to Adobe's ubiquitous Portable Document Format. This file is viewable by anyone with Mac OS X and any Windows user who has Adobe Reader installed.

- FXG (fxg) is a new format, short for Flash XML Graphics. It's designed specifically as an interchange format between Illustrator, Flash, and Flex (Adobe's Internet application development framework).

- SVG Compressed (svgx) and SVG (svg) are standards for Web-based vector graphics and are supported by nearly every Web browser except Internet Explorer. (SVG is short for Scalable Vector Graphics.)

5. *Specify a name and location.* I recommend that you save the file inside the same *Lesson 01* folder that contains the *Urban chaos.ait* document, but feel free to save it elsewhere if you'd like.

---

You can name the file as you please, with one proviso: Leave the extension unchanged for the file format you're choosing (in this case, *.ai*). It's difficult to override this extension on the PC, but it's easy on the Mac. *Don't do it!* Files without extensions or, even worse, the wrong extensions, won't successfully transport across platforms (via email or servers), they go unrecognized by Windows, and they might not work properly under future versions of the Mac OS.

---

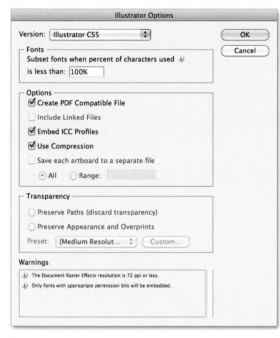

Figure 1-37.

6. *Save the file.* Click the Save button or press Enter or Return to save the file to disk. Or not! A second dialog box pops up, shown in Figure 1-36; Illustrator has a few more questions for you.

- First, select the **Version**. Unless you have a specific reason to save to a previous version, it's best to stick with CS5. Multiple artboards are supported only in CS4 and later, and some features are CS5-specific; saving to an older version might cause information to be lost.

- In the second area, **Options**, turn on all available check boxes. Create PDF Compatible File ensures maximum compatibility with other Creative Suite applications. Embed ICC Profiles stores the color profile information with the file. Finally, Use Compression helps reduce the size of the saved file.

- The third area, Transparency, is currently dimmed—the document contains no transparency. We'll cover the Transparency options in Lesson 8.

From this point on, you can update the file to reflect any changes you make by choosing File→Save. To again invoke the Save As dialog box—whether to save a different version of the document, save it in a different format, or store it in a different location—choose File→Save As or press Ctrl+Shift+S (⌘-Shift-S on the Mac).

# WHAT DID YOU LEARN?

Match the key concept in the numbered list below with the letter
of the phrase that best describes it. Answers appear upside-down
at the bottom of the page.

## Key Concepts

1. Vector-based
2. Pixel-based
3. Artboard
4. Files of type
5. Adobe Bridge
6. Workspace
7. Bleed
8. Guide
9. Smart guide
10. Layer
11. .ai format
12. .eps format

## Descriptions

A. The native file format for Illustrator, usable across the Creative Suite.

B. A setting that allows you to filter the list of files in the Open (or Open a File) dialog box by selecting Illustrator, PDF, EPS, or a number of other formats.

C. The boundaries of a piece of artwork as defined by Illustrator.

D. The Creative Suite's stand-alone digital asset manager.

E. Artwork that is made from discrete shapes and can therefore be scaled to any size without loss of quality.

F. A collection of objects that can be hidden, locked, selected, or otherwise manipulated as a group.

G. A collection of settings that define the layout and visibility of panels and other user-interface elements.

H. A nonprinting line or shape that forces other objects or paths to snap to it, allowing for precise alignment

I. Artwork created from individual blocks of color; it cannot be enlarged without a loss of quality.

J. A legacy file format, once the industry standard for vector artwork.

K. An area outside the final trimmed artwork used in print to prevent gaps from appearing around the final printed piece.

L. A nonprinting element created by Illustrator on-the-fly, aligning to existing objects and paths in the document.

## Answers

1E, 2I, 3C, 4B, 5D, 6G, 7K, 8H, 9L, 10F, 11A, 12J

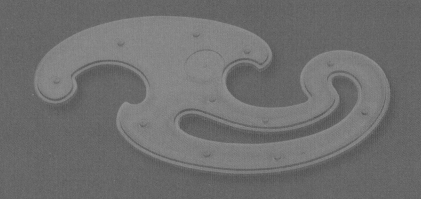

# LESSON
# 2

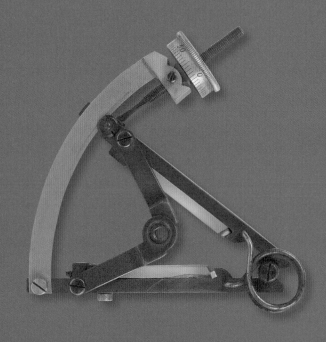

# LINES, SHAPES, AND COLOR

**THE FUNDAMENTALS** of any illustration are lines, shapes, and colors. These are the elements that define your artwork—whatever it may be—and it's their interaction that creates the final composition. Even the most complex art starts with these basic elements, as shown in Figure 2-1.

Not surprisingly, Illustrator gives you a host of ways to create and manipulate these basic elements. Illustrator has five dedicated tools for creating lines (or in the case of two tools, groups of lines) and six for shapes. But things don't end there. Once you've drawn these building blocks, Illustrator gives you tools to split apart the lines and shapes and stitch them back together. You can layer simple lines and shapes on top of one another to create more complex art, even applying discrete strokes and fills to each element. Like Dr. Frankenstein, you can combine all these pieces into one singular creation, with Illustrator as your faithful Igor. (It's my job to help make sure *your* creation won't be chased by an angry mob with torches.)

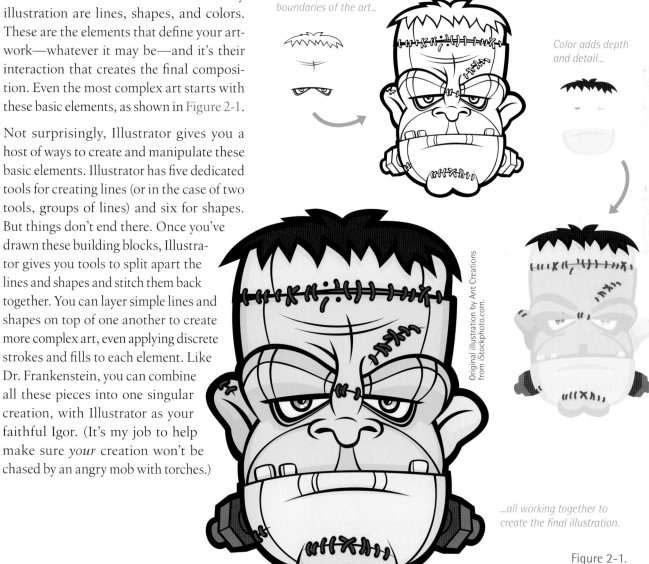

*Lines and shapes create the boundaries of the art...*

*Color adds depth and detail...*

Original illustration by Ant Creations from iStockphoto.com.

*...all working together to create the final illustration.*

Figure 2-1.

# ABOUT THIS LESSON

## Project Files

Before beginning the exercises, make sure you've downloaded the lesson files from *www.oreilly.com/go/Deke-IllustratorCS5*, as directed in Step 2 on page xiv of the Preface. This should result in a folder called *Lesson Files-Alcs5 1on1* on your desktop. We'll be working with the files inside the *Lesson 02* subfolder.

It's time to take advantage of Illustrator's basic drawing functions, including the various incarnations of the line and shape tools. In this lesson, you'll learn how to:

## Video Lesson 2: The Basic Shape Tools

In this video lesson, I'll introduce you Illustrator's fundamental drawing tools, the geometric line and shape tools that allow you to create path outlines. You'll also see how to apply fills and strokes to the paths you create. Starting with this basic introduction, we'll build on these drawing skills throughout this book.

To start with the basics, visit *www.oreilly.com/go/deke-IllustratorCS5*. Click the **Watch** button to view the lesson online or click the **Download** button to save it to your computer. During the video, you'll learn these shortcuts:

| Operation | Windows shortcut | Macintosh shortcut |
|---|---|---|
| Constrain the rectangle tool to a square | Shift-drag | Shift-drag |
| Draw a shape from the center outward | Alt-drag | Option-drag |
| Draw a square from the center outward | Ctrl+Alt+drag | ⌘-Option-drag |
| Undo the last action | Ctrl+Z | ⌘-Z |
| Toggle between fill and stroke | Press the X key | Press the X key |
| Set stroke to "None" | Press the ⧄ key (forward slash) | Press the ⧄ key (forward slash) |
| Select All | Ctrl+A | ⌘-A |
| Deselect All | Ctrl+Shift+A | ⌘-Shift-A |
| Add or subtract sides to a shape | Press the ↑ or ↓ keys | Press the ↑ or ↓ keys |

## Endpoints and Closed Paths

Where to begin? Let's start simply and build our way up. First, we'll look at lines, which Illustrator calls *open paths* because they have *endpoints*—points at the end of the lines, points that stop. (The upper half of Figure 2-2 shows one of an open path's endpoints.) They're out there, on the market. They're single points. Maybe they find another point, maybe they don't. They're not quite ready to settle down.

Then we'll move on to shapes. Illustrator calls these *closed paths* because they don't have endpoints. These shapes aren't closed in the sense of "shut down," it's just that they aren't accepting new points. The points are married, really. Except that they're binogamous—every point is joined to two other points, so the shape continues forever and ever, as shown in the lower half of Figure 2-2.

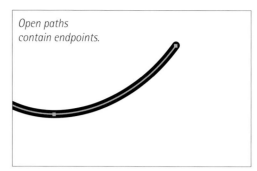

*Open paths contain endpoints.*

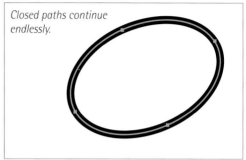

*Closed paths continue endlessly.*

Figure 2-2.

## Drawing Lines, Arcs, and Spirals

In these first two exercises, we're going to be working with a file you first saw in the preceding lesson—the eye of Horus. This time, however, you'll get to actually *illustrate* in Illustrator, not simply set up guides. The first exercise will focus on drawing paths using the various tools available from the line segment tool (\) flyout menu. Time to start drawing!

1. *Open an illustration.* Choose **File→**  **Open**. Navigate to the *Lesson 02* folder inside the *Lesson Files-AIcs5 1on1* folder, which should be on your desktop. Open the file named *Horus is go.ai*. You should see the same familiar eye, but this time in a light gray, as shown in Figure 2-3.

2. *Examine the document's layers.* Bring up the **Layers** panel by pressing F7. This document is split into three layers—one to house the tracing template (Horus), one to hold the guides (Guides), and finally the layer where you'll be drawing (Draw Here). The first two layers are locked and should stay locked. Click the first column to the left of the **Draw Here** layer to turn on the 👁 and make the layer visible. (You'll

Figure 2-3.

Figure 2-4.

Figure 2-5.

see that I've already drawn the eyebrow and the outline of the eye for you, as in Figure 2-4.)

3. *Detach the group of line tools from the toolbox.* You're going to be using a number of these tools, all grouped under the \ tool in the toolbox. Rather than having to click and hold, waiting each time you want to switch tools, you can detach the group and make a standalone minitoolbox. Click and hold the \ tool until the flyout menu appears, and then move over the tear-off bar shown in Figure 2-5 before your release the mouse. Presto! You now have a minitoolbox you can position anywhere in your workspace.

You can repeat this tear-off as many times as you want. If you have a large monitor, for instance, you might want to create multiple copies of this minitoolbox and position them around the screen so that you always have one nearby.

4. *Draw the center vertical line.* The \ tool should already be selected; if not, press the ⌐ key to select it. (The tool itself looks like a backslash, which is why the ⌐ key is the keyboard shortcut.) Starting at the top of the center vertical line, click and hold the mouse, dragging down toward the bottom of the line. Hold the Shift key while dragging to constrain the line to regular angles (45 degrees, 90 degrees, etc.—only multiples of 45 degrees). When you've reached the bottom of the line (a smart guide should appear with the label *anchor*, as in Figure 2-6 on the facing page), release the mouse.

5. *Fix the line's attributes.* You have your first line, but it might be hard to see at the moment—its attributes don't match the other lines in the drawing. Fortunately, you can lift the properties of other objects and apply them to the selected object using the eyedropper tool. Here's how:

- Switch to the ✐ tool by clicking it in the toolbox or by pressing the I key.

- Move your cursor over one of the existing heavy paths; when the green smart guide path appears under your cursor, click to lift that path's attributes and apply them to your newly drawn line, as in Figure 2-7.

6. *Draw the large arc.* Next you'll draw the large arc on the right leading to the spiral. Switch to the ⌒ tool in the minitoolbox, and click and hold at the upper-left end of the arc. If your arc is bending the wrong way, press the F key to flip it (while keeping the mouse button down). Keep dragging until your cursor snaps to the smart guide anchor point, as in Figure 2-8.

7. *Draw the spiral.* Drawing the spiral is a little trickier. Select the ◎ tool from the toolbox, and start dragging from the center of the spiral down toward the end of the arc. Your spiral will probably look completely wrong at first, but quite a few keyboard tricks are available to help you. (All these shortcuts can be used only while the mouse button is still pressed; once you release the mouse button, the spiral cannot be changed using these shortcuts.)

   - Press the R key to reverse the direction of the spiral.

   - Press the ↑ and ↓ keys to add or subtract *winds* (quarter-circle arcs) from the spiral.

   - Hold the Shift key to constrain the spiral to regular angles, as described in Step 4.

   - Hold the spacebar to move, rather than resize, the spiral.

   - Hold the Ctrl (or ⌘) key to change the *decay rate* of the spiral (that is, how loosely or tightly the spiral is wound).

   - Hold the Alt (or Option) key to change the length and size of the spiral while adding winds.

Unless you've changed the default settings of the spiral tool, you'll most likely need to reverse the spiral with the R key and press the ↓ key four times to get to the correct number of winds. Then you have the rather finicky matter of adjusting the decay with the Ctrl (or ⌘) key, and using the spacebar frequently to reposition the spiral after each adjustment. Don't worry if you can't get the spiral to line up precisely

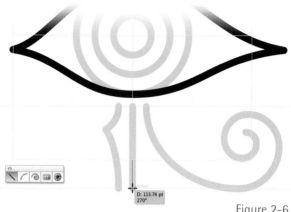

Figure 2-6.

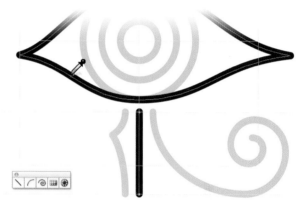

Figure 2-7.

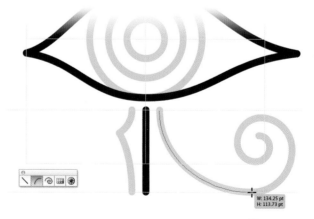

Figure 2-8.

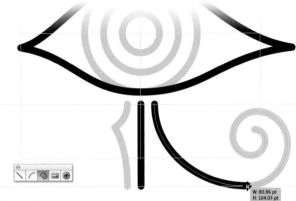

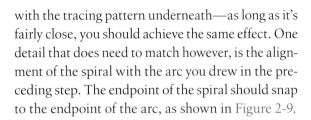

Figure 2-9.

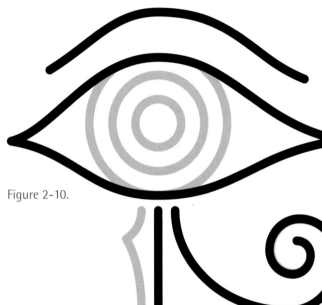

Figure 2-10.

with the tracing pattern underneath—as long as it's fairly close, you should achieve the same effect. One detail that does need to match however, is the alignment of the spiral with the arc you drew in the preceding step. The endpoint of the spiral should snap to the endpoint of the arc, as shown in Figure 2-9.

Now that you have an introduction to the basic line-drawing tools, it's time to move to the next exercise. Your results so far should look like the illustration shown in Figure 2-10. Choose **File→Save** to save your work. Give it a name like "Horus in progress.ai," and save it to the *Lesson 02* folder. We'll be revisiting this file in the next exercise.

## Splitting, Joining, and Aligning

So far we've seen a few of the basic line tools. But if you look at the Horus drawing just to the left, you'll see some elements that can't be drawn or perfected with the tools you've learned thus far. Sure, the line on the bottom left is made up of arcs, but they're not the nice, symmetrical arcs the ⌒ tool lets you draw. Likewise, the arc and spiral on the right may look like a single continuous line, but they're two discrete paths, and should they end up misaligned, you may see a break in your final art. I'll show you how to tackle these issues in this exercise.

1. *Open an illustration.* If you have your file open from the previous exercise, just continue along with that file. Otherwise, open the file *Horus slice & join.ai*, located in the *Lesson 02* folder.

2. *Draw the first arc.* The line just to the left of the vertical line is made up of two arcs; they need to

be drawn one by one. Select the ⌒ tool, and draw the lower arc, starting from the bottom and dragging up and to the left. It's important to start the arc precisely where the template arc starts; a smart guide should snap the cursor into place with the label *anchor* when you start drawing. To give the arc the proper shape, you'll need to draw past the end of the tracing template, as shown in Figure 2-11.

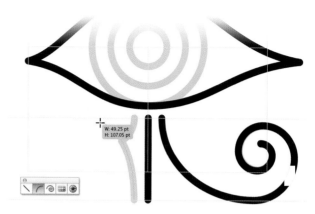

Figure 2-11.

---

You may encounter the same issue that you did in Step 5 of the preceding exercise—namely that your new line doesn't share the attributes of the rest of the artwork. If so, switch to the ✐ tool (or press the I key) and pick up the attributes from one of the other paths. Be sure to switch back to the ⌒ tool when you've finished.

---

3. *Draw the second arc.* Still with the ⌒ tool selected, draw the upper arc from the top, dragging down and to the left. Again, make sure your starting point snaps to the anchor on the tracing layer beneath. You'll need to draw past the end of the template with this arc as well, as seen in Figure 2-12.

4. *Switch to outline mode.* Now it's time to cut the arcs you just drew into two pieces each. We want to cut the arcs precisely where they intersect, but with the wide stroke on the paths, it's impossible to determine exactly where that point is. That's where Illustrator's outline view comes in handy. Outline view displays the basic paths and points, without any stroke or fill attributes visible. Choose **View→Outline** from the menu or press Ctrl+Y (⌘-Y on the Mac) to switch to outline mode.

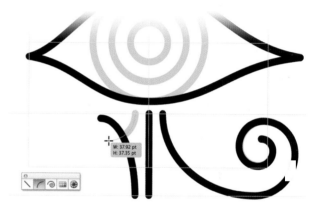

Figure 2-12.

Suddenly your lovely artwork has become sparse. Every line and shape is now drawn as its most basic path, including all the guides. The arcs you want to edit are jumbled with the arcs from the tracing layer, making it difficult to see where to cut them. This won't do at all, so press Ctrl+Y (⌘-Y) again to switch back to preview mode.

---

Ctrl+Y (⌘-Y) toggles between outline and preview modes. Also, when in outline mode, the View menu displays the option for preview mode in place of outline mode.

---

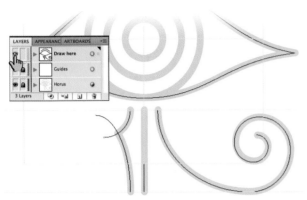

Figure 2-13.

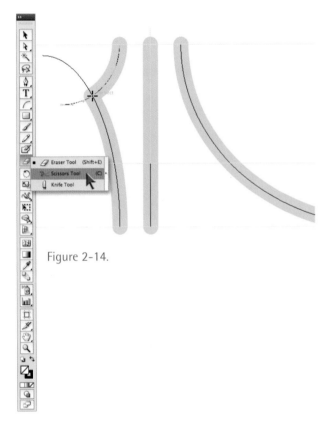

Figure 2-14.

Figure 2-15.

It would be ideal if only the active layer would be in outline mode, while the tracing template and guides stayed in the more helpful preview mode. Thankfully, Illustrator gives you a way to do just that. Bring up the **Layers** panel by pressing F7 (if it isn't visible already), and Ctrl-click (⌘-click on the Mac) the 👁 icon next to the **Draw Here** layer. This switches this layer, and this layer only, to outline mode, indicated by the layer visibility icon (◎). Your art should know look like Figure 2-13.

5. *Slice the first arc with the scissors tool.* Now that you can see where to make the cut, it's time to split the arcs. Select the ✂ tool by pressing the C key (C for s*c*issors), or by choosing it from the flyout menu under the ⟋ icon. With the tool selected, click the arc at the intersection point with the second arc, as in Figure 2-14. The arc will split into two halves.

6. *Delete the extra piece of the arc.* Switch to the ▶ tool by selecting it from the toolbox or by pressing the V key. Then click the left half of the arc and press the Delete key to get rid of it.

7. *Slice the second arc.* Switch back to the ✂ tool by pressing the C key, and click the intersection of the two arcs again (the same location you clicked in Step 5). Instead of slicing the second arc in half, Illustrator greets you with the rather grumpy dialog box shown in Figure 2-15. What's going on here?

Some of you may already know where the problem lies: When you hover over the intersection point, Illustrator's smart guides highlight the arc that's already been cut. Illustrator considers the highlighted path to be active, and in this case, where you've clicked is the endpoint of a path; Illustrator can't use the scissors tool on the endpoint.

The problem stems from the fact that the already-sliced arc is on top of the other arc. Every path in Illustrator has a position in a front-to-back stack of objects. Each path is either below or above each of the other paths in the document. Where two paths overlap, Illustrator selects the path on top by default.

The solution: Bring the arc to be sliced to the front of the stack. Do this by selecting the arc with the ⬚ tool, right-clicking (or Control-clicking on the Mac), and choosing **Arrange→Bring to Front**. (Conversely, you can use the keyboard shortcut Ctrl+Shift+⬚ or ⌘-Shift-⬚.)

If you want to temporarily use the black arrow tool without actually changing tools, you can do so by holding down the Ctrl key (the ⌘ key on the Mac), and clicking the object you want to select.

Switch back to the scissors tool and click at the intersection to slice the second arc. Finally, repeat Step 6 to delete the extra section of the arc. The results of this hard work can be seen in Figure 2-16.

8. *Change the layer view back to preview mode.* Ctrl-click (⌘-click) the 👁 icon next to the **Draw Here** layer to return that layer to preview mode.

9. *Join the arc to the spiral.* We've split paths apart; now it's time to join some together. To join paths, you must select the endpoints to be joined, and those points only. The black arrow tool won't help you here, as it selects the entire path and all its points. You need the white arrow (what Adobe calls the direct selection) tool.

Start by switching to the ⬚ tool by selecting it from the toolbox or pressing the A key. On the right side of the illustration, drag a marquee around the two points you want to join, as shown in Figure 2-17. (When you drag a marquee, it selects the points—or in the case of the black arrow tool, objects—that it encompasses or intersects.) Once you have the points selected, press Ctrl+Alt+Shift-J (⌘-Option-Shift-J).

Illustrator now presents you with the dialog box pictured in Figure 2-18. By joining the points, you are combining the two separate points into one, and Illustrator needs to know the type of point you want. Selecting Corner produces a sharp corner, while selecting Smooth produces a point with gentle curves on either side. In this case, we clearly want **Smooth**. Select it, and then click **OK**. (You may see your arc or spiral adjust slightly when the points are joined; if so, there's no need to worry.)

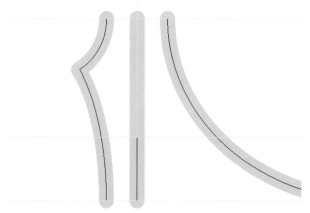

Figure 2-16.

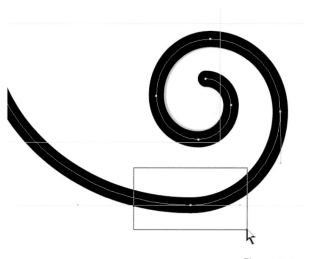

Figure 2-17.

Figure 2-18.

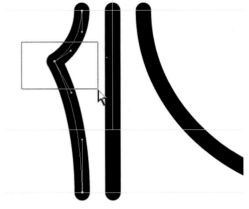

Figure 2-19.

If you are lucky enough—which, when talking about distances this small, is very lucky—to get the Join dialog box, it's because Illustrator's smart guides helped to align your points precisely. If that's the case, choose Corner and click OK, and then just sit back and read along through the next two steps. You won the alignment lottery.

New in Illustrator CS5, if you simply press Ctrl+J (⌘-J) or choose Path→Join from the Object menu, Illustrator automatically joins the two points as a corner join, without prompting. Use the keyboard-mashing shortcut described previously to get the option dialog every time. (Well, nearly every time; see my caveat in the next few steps.)

10. *Join the two arc segments.* On the left side of the illustration are the two arc segments you spliced in the previous steps. Again, using the white arrow tool, drag a marquee around the points you want to join, as in Figure 2-19, and press Ctrl+Alt+Shift-J (⌘-Option-Shift-J). This time, Illustrator doesn't present you with the dialog. What gives?

Even with the most precise of clicks, and even aided by the smart guides, these two endpoints are most likely not aligned perfectly with one another. When two points aren't exactly co-incident (i.e., directly aligned on top of one another) and you combine them with a standard join (Ctrl+J/⌘-J), Illustrator simply connects them with a straight line segment. (As you'll see in Step 12, this isn't how Illustrator handles a join performed with Ctrl+Alt+Shift-J/⌘-Option-Shift-J.)

How precise do you need to be? In my case, my points were separated by $^2/_{1000}$ of a point in one direction, and $^5/_{1000}$ of a point in the other. That's just under two microns of space between the two points—or $^1/_4$ the size of your average red blood cell. We're literally talking microscopic here. (To give you some context, the dot in this lowercase "i" is 300 microns across.) Illustrator, bless its heart, is just that sensitive.

11. *Undo the join and reselect the points.* Press Ctrl+Z (⌘-Z) to undo the join from the last step. With the white arrow tool, draw the marquee again to reselect the two points.

12. *Align and join the two points.* Now it's time to align the points, then join them to create a single corner point. You have a few options, all of which take you to the same destination:

    • You can align the points using the align options in the control panel, highlighted in Figure 2-20. You can align the points using the ⊟ and ⊪ buttons, which align the vertical center and horizontal center, respectively. Once the points are aligned, press Ctrl+J (⌘-J) to join them.

Figure 2-20.

- Choose **Path→Average** from the **Object** menu, or press Ctrl+Alt+J (⌘-Option-J). This brings up the dialog box shown in Figure 2-21. Select **Both**, and click **OK**. Finally, press Ctrl+J (⌘-J) to join the points.

- The fastest (and my favorite) method to align and join points is the now familiar key-masher. Press Ctrl+Shift+Alt+J (⌘-Shift-Option-J on the Mac). If the two points aren't coincident, this combines the Average and Join commands into one simple step, with no dialog boxes to respond to.

However you choose to get there, you now have one single path consisting of the two arc segments. Only one element is left before your Horus eye is complete!

13. *Draw the concentric rings of the eye.* The last element you need to draw is the group of concentric rings that make up the iris and pupil of the eye. While you could use the shape tool and draw each circle individually, there's a faster way—using the polar grid tool. Select the ⊕ tool from the minitoolbox, and start dragging from the intersection of the guides in the center of the eye.

Much like when drawing the spiral, the outline you're drawing looks quite different from the desired results. And like the spiral, a number of keyboard shortcuts can help:

- Hold the Shift key to constrain the ellipses to perfect circles.

- Press the ↑ and ↓ keys to add or subtract concentric circles. In this case, you want a total of three circles.

- Press the → and ← keys to add or subtract *radials* (the lines running from the center to the outer circle). For the eye, reduce the radials to zero by pressing the ← key repeatedly.

- Hold the Alt (or Option) key to draw the shape outward from the center, rather than from corner to corner.

It's easiest to adjust the circles and radials with the arrow keys first, and then hold Shift and Alt (or Shift and Option) to fix the shape and position of the outlines. (Remember, all these keyboard shortcuts work only while the mouse button is still pressed.) Once your outline looks like that in Figure 2-22, release the mouse.

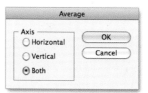

Figure 2-21.

I can't explain why Adobe changed the default behavior of the Join command in CS5. Sure, it may save you some time if the bulk of your joins are corner joins, but now you get no warning if your points are noncoincident, and I prefer having control over how points are joined. Therefore, I recommend using the full key-mashing shortcut for nearly all joins.

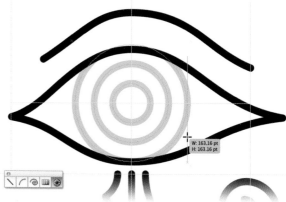

Figure 2-22.

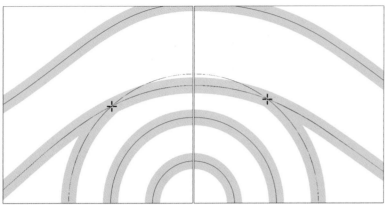

Figure 2-23.

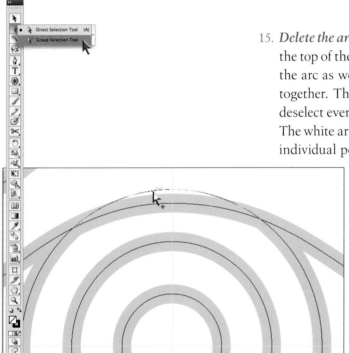

Figure 2-24.

14. *Slice the extraneous arc from the outer circle.* That made the creation of the concentric circles easy, but unfortunately the outermost circle is extending beyond the frame of the eye. Once again, it's time for the scissors tool to do its magic:

    • Bring up the **Layers** panel by pressing F7, and view the **Draw Here** layer in outline mode by Ctrl-clicking (⌘-clicking on the Mac) its 👁 icon.

    • Switch to the ✂ tool, and click the points where the outer circle intersects the eye path, as shown in Figure 2-23. (It helps to zoom in to get the precise cut.)

15. *Delete the arc slice.* Switch to the ▶ tool and select the arc across the top of the circle. Unfortunately, the black arrow tool selects the arc as well as all the circles—these elements are grouped together. This won't work; press Ctrl+Shift+A (⌘-Shift-A) to deselect everything, or choose **Deselect** from the **Select** menu. The white arrow tool doesn't fare much better, as it selects only individual points or segments. Fortunately, there's a third selection tool, under the ▷ tool flyout menu, called the group selection tool, shown in Figure 2-24. Select the ▷ tool, and click anywhere on the arc across the top of the eye. Press the Delete key to get rid of it. Be sure to click only once on the arc; clicking a second time will select the entire group.

---

If you don't want to switch tools via the flyout menu, or you just want to save some time, you can temporarily access the group selection tool by holding down the Alt (or Option) key while the white arrow tool is active.

---

16. *Return the art layer to preview mode.* Ctrl-click (⌘-click) the 👁 to return the **Draw Here** layer to preview mode. Turn off the other layers by clicking their 👁 icons.

You now have your completed Eye of Horus, shown in Figure 2-25 on the facing page. This artwork was built using only the basic line tools, and yet with just a little manipulation, you've used those tools to create more complex and sophisticated shapes. Save or discard the file as you see fit.

# Drawing Primitive Shapes

So far we've been working primarily with open paths, that is, paths that have endpoints. In this exercise, we'll be working with closed paths—simple shapes known as *primitives*. A primitive is a basic shape, such as a rectangle, a circle, an ellipse, a triangle, a polygon, or a star. These primitives, along with the basic line shapes, are the elements that make up every drawing produced in Illustrator.

For the rest of this lesson, we'll be working on one file that will continue from exercise to exercise. But this isn't just any old piece of art. It's a stylized *tonalpohualli*, an ancient 260-day Mesoamerican calendar used primarily by the Aztecs. In the first exercise, you'll create a tracing template and draw many of the basic shapes that make up the illustration.

1. *Open the tonalpohualli.* Navigate to the *Lesson 02* folder inside the *Lesson Files-AIcs5 1on1* folder. Open the file named, appropriately enough, *Tonalpohualli. ai*. You'll be greeted with a round piece of artwork, replete with primitive shapes like rectangles, circles, ellipses, and stars.

Figure 2-25.

2. *Examine the Layers panel.* Bring up the **Layers** panel (if it's not already visible) by pressing the F7 key. You'll see that this document has a total of five layers. One issue I have with the Layers panel as it stands is that the thumbnails are so small as to be nearly useless. That's something you can easily rectify. Click the ▾≡ button in the upper-right corner of the panel, and choose **Panel Options** from the panel menu. This brings up the dialog box as seen in Figure 2-26. You could change the thumbnail option to Large, but why when you can create your own custom size? Select **Other** in the dialog box, and enter a value between 60 and 100, depending on your available screen real estate. (I went with 70.) Now your thumbnails are large enough for you to see the details on each layer.

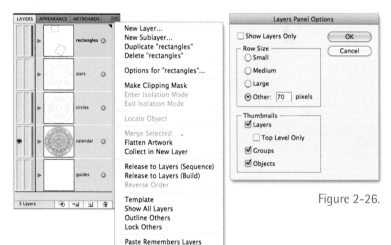

Figure 2-26.

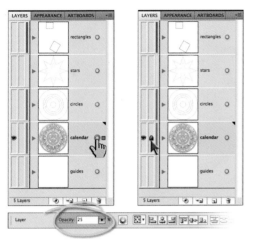

Figure 2-27.

3. *Make a tracing template from the Calendar layer.* Now it's time to turn the existing artwork into a tracing template to follow. You can accomplish this in a few simple steps:

- In the Layers panel, click the ○ icon (affectionately known as "the meatball," shown in the left side of Figure 2-27) to the right of the **Calendar** layer name. This selects the layer and all the artwork on it.

- In the control panel, set the **Opacity** to 25 percent.

- Finally, back in the **Layers** panel, click the square to the right of the 👁 to lock the Calendar layer (indicated by the 🔒 icon, shown in the right side of Figure 2-27). Note that locking the layer also deselects all the artwork on that layer.

4. *Repeat for the Circles layer.* You'll notice that I've placed some other tracing templates in this document: three additional layers that provide templates for the primitive shapes you'll be drawing. For now, focus on the Circles layer:

- Make the **Circles** layer visible by clicking the leftmost square, waking up the 👁 icon.

- "Meatball" the layer (by clicking the ○ icon). This time, set the **Opacity** to 50 percent via the control panel.

- Lastly, lock the layer.

5. *Turn on and lock the Guides layer.* Using the same methods, make the **Guides** layer visible, then lock it to prevent the guides from being moved.

6. *Create a new layer.* One layer that is conspicuously missing from this document is a layer for drawing your artwork. Create a new layer by clicking the 🔲 icon at the bottom of the Layers panel. Double-click the new layer (by default named Layer 6) to bring up the **Layer Options** dialog box, as seen in Figure 2-28. Name the layer "My drawing" and change the layer's default color. I chose orange, because it stands out well from the other layer colors, but feel free to pick whatever color you'd like.

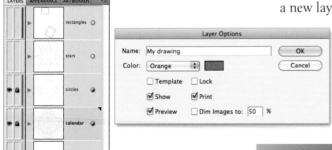

Figure 2-28.

PEARL OF WISDOM

A shortcut when creating new layers will save you a lot of time in the long run. Rather than creating a layer by clicking the 🔲 icon, then double-clicking the layer to edit its options, you can Alt-click (or Option-click) the 🔲 icon. This creates a new layer and brings you directly to the Layer Options dialog box without the need for a second step.

7. *Drag the My Drawing layer to the top of the stack.* There's one last layer change before we're ready to start drawing—the **My Drawing** layer needs to be on top of all the other layers. Drag the title area of the layer to the top of the stack in the Layers panel. When the cursor is above the Rectangles layer, release the mouse button.

8. *Tear off the Shapes tool panel.* As you saw in Step 3 on page 42, the tools in Illustrator that have flyout menus also have tear-off options, allowing you to pull the group of tools into a minitoolbox. Click and hold the ▢ icon, and release the mouse button over the tear-off bar, as seen in Figure 2-29.

9. *Draw the innermost circle.* Select the ⬯ tool from the **Shapes** tool panel, or press the L key. Starting from the intersection of the two blue guides in the center of the artwork, drag while holding the Shift and Alt keys (or the Shift and Option keys on the Mac). As we've seen in previous exercises, the Shift key constrains the shape (in this case, to a perfect circle), and the Alt or Option key draws the shape from the center out. Once your circle snaps into place like in Figure 2-30, release the mouse button and then the keys.

Figure 2-29.

This drawing scenario is one case where Illustrator's smart guides may be more of a bane than a blessing. As you draw your circle, Illustrator tries to snap it to every object on the page, even those on locked layers—all the rectangles, the various star segments, each of the circles that make up the god's face in the center of the art—and it can be pretty maddening when you're trying to align the shape precisely to the circles template. The alignment is easiest when you drag the circle out along one of the blue guides, particularly toward the top; a smart guide will appear with the label *anchor*, as shown in Figure 2-30, letting you know that you're aligned to one of the anchor points of the circle on the tracing template underneath. If you're still not having any luck, temporarily hide the Calendar layer, which greatly reduces the number of possible "smart" alignments. As a last resort, if you're ready to throw your hands up and be done with it, you can turn off smart guides completely by choosing View→Smart Guides or pressing Ctrl+U (⌘-U on the Mac).

Figure 2-30.

10. *Adjust the fill and stroke of the new circle.* Most likely, your new shape picked up the attributes from the Circles layer, meaning you have a circle with a 2-point red stroke. Change the at-

tributes to the default by pressing the D key or by clicking the small ⬚ icon in the lower part of the toolbox. (The large icon shows the current stroke and fill colors.)

As is true for nearly all drawn objects, the default is a 1-point black stroke with a white fill. Although closer to the original art, it's still not quite right. The fill and stroke attributes are shown in the control panel in Figure 2-31. For the fill, click the ▾ arrow and select **None**, indicated by the ⊘ icon. Bump up the stroke weight to 2 pt by selecting it from the pop-up menu.

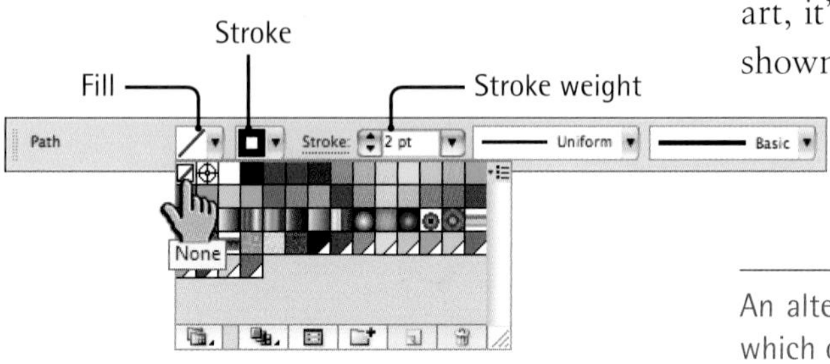

Figure 2-31.

An alternative method for changing the fill (or stroke, depending on which object is active) to None is to press the ⧄ key. Why the ⧄ key? Because the icon for None (⊘) also looks like the / character. You can confirm whether the fill or stroke is active by looking at the Color panel (bring it up by pressing F6)—the shape on the top is active.

11. *Draw the second circle.* With the ⬭ tool, start at the halfway point of the upper-left quadrant of the circle guide, and drag diagonally down and to the right, as in Figure 2-32. Hold the Shift key to constrain the shape to a perfect circle. Unfortunately, by default Illustrator draws your shape from corner to corner; what you really want is to draw the shape from arc to arc. While keeping the Shift key down, add the Ctrl key (or Command key on the Mac) to change the way Illustrator draws the shape. If you need to, hold the spacebar to move the shape into position. (You may need to temporarily turn off the Calendar layer or your smart guides, given the number of objects on the layer.) Don't worry if the circle isn't perfectly aligned; we'll address that later in this exercise. When you're happy with the size and position of the new circle, release the mouse button. Illustrator has used the settings from the previous shape, so your stroke and fill are correct as is.

W: 189 pt
H: 189 pt

Figure 2-32.

12. *Add the third circle mathematically.* There's yet another way to draw ellipses. What this method lacks in visual clues, it more than makes up for in precision. With the ⬭ tool selected, click in the very center of the illustration at the intersection of the two blue guides. Illustrator presents you with the **Ellipse** dialog

box, as seen in Figure 2-33. As it happens, I know this circle is supposed to be 238 points in diameter, so I'd like you to enter "238 pt" in the **Width** field of the dialog box. Rather than tabbing to the next field and reentering the same value, however, you can use a clever trick built in to Illustrator to make perfect circles (and squares). Click the word **Height**, and Illustrator copies the value from the Width field for you. Finally, click **OK**.

Figure 2-33.

Whoops! What went wrong? When placing shapes mathematically—just as when you draw them— Illustrator by default starts from the top-left corner; you need to add the Alt (Option) key to draw the shape from the center out. Press Ctrl+Z (⌘-Z on the Mac) to undo this circle. Now Alt-click (or Option-click) at the intersection of the guides, and click **OK** in the dialog box (which remembered your values from the last circle). Illustrator now dutifully draws the circle from the center, positioned perfectly.

13. *Draw the remaining two circles.* You've mastered the various ways to draw circles, so now it's your choice: Draw the remaining two circles however you see fit, using any of the methods shown so far. The size of each circle is more important than the position; the diameters of the two circles should be around 290 and 420 points, respectively. Your results should look like Figure 2-34.

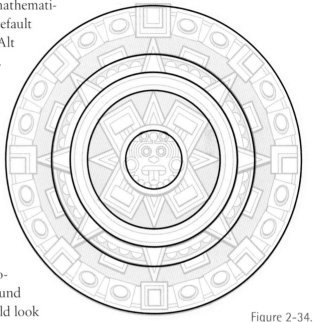

Figure 2-34.

14. *Deliberately misalign the circles.* After all that work, why would I ask you to vandalize your own illustration? Sadly, it's the only way to demonstrate the power and simplicity of Illustrator's align functions. While the drawn circles were close, not all of them were perfectly aligned; we're simply magnifying the misalignment. Using the ➤ tool, grab the circles and drag them willy-nilly around the artboard. Just be sure to leave the smallest of the circles in place, as it will be the anchor for the alignment steps to come. Sufficiently trashed, your artwork should now resemble something similar to Figure 2-35. Quite the mess, to be sure, but everything will be put right in the next few steps.

15. *Select all the circles.* To align the circles, you first need to select them. You can't simply meatball the layer (by clicking the ○), as that would select not only

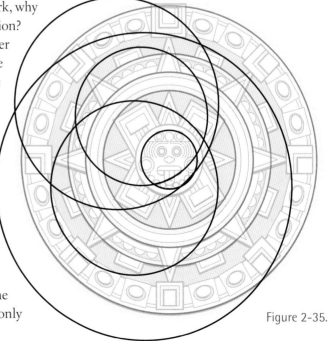

Figure 2-35.

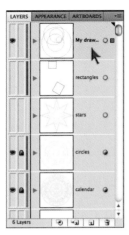

Figure 2-36.

Figure 2-37.

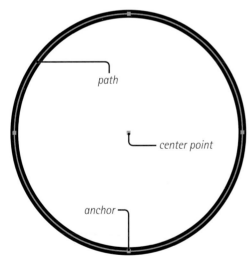

Figure 2-38.

the objects, but the layer as well. You could click one circle, and then Shift-click the rest of them, but why take that much time? The quickest way: Alt-click (or Option-click) the layer title area (anywhere inside the orange area in Figure 2-36, other than the meatball—your highlight color may be different). This selects all the objects on the layer, but not the layer itself.

16. *Align the circles.* Now that you have the circles selected, examine the control panel. You'll see a group of align icons, circled in Figure 2-37. The two you want for this step are horizontal align centers (☐) and vertical align centers (☐).

Click the ☐ icon and then the ☐ icon. All the circles are now concentric but unfortunately in the wrong place; press Ctrl+Z twice (⌘-Z on the Mac) to undo the alignment.

We need to make sure that all our circles align to the smallest one, the only one in its proper position. To that end, Illustrator lets you specify a *key object*, that is to say, an object against which all others will be aligned. Still with the ➤ tool, click once (and only once) on the smallest center circle. Illustrator highlights it with a thick orange stroke (or your color choice, if you picked something different in Step 6 on page 52), indicating it is now the key object. Again, click the ☐ icon and then the ☐ icon. Presto! All your circles are now aligned to the center of the art and to each other.

17. *Hide the Circles layer.* You're finished with the circles, so you no longer need the tracing template. Bring up the **Layers** panel, and click the ● to hide the Circles layer.

18. *Set up the stars tracing template.* Now we'll move on to drawing more complex shapes, but to do so, we need to prepare the stars tracing template. Make the **Stars** layer visible by clicking the leftmost square next to the layer name in the Layers panel, waking up the ●. Next, meatball the layer (by clicking the ○ icon) and set the **Opacity** to 35 percent using the control panel. Finally, lock the layer, and click the **My Drawing** layer to make it active.

19. ***Draw the first star.*** Select the ☆ tool from the **Shapes** panel. Unlike the other shapes, stars and polygons are always drawn from the center out, and are always regularly sized (i.e., contained by a square bounding box).

---

In this and the next few steps, all the functions work for both the polygon and star tools, with the exception of the Alt/Option and Ctrl/⌘ modifier keys; those keys are specific to the star tool. The star tool is really nothing more than a specialized polygon tool—the stars are simply polygons with the midpoint of each side inset.

---

Since all stars are drawn from the center, position the cursor at the intersection of the guides at the center of the illustration. Drag toward one of the points of the outermost star. Your star will likely be five-pointed—great for drawing a traditional schoolroom star or the star most commonly seen on world flags—but for the *tonalpohualli*, you need an eight-pointed star. Many of the same keyboard shortcuts you used with the spiral will work here as well:

- Press the ↑ and ↓ keys to add or subtract points from the star (or sides, in the case of polygons).

- Hold the Shift key to constrain the star so it has one point facing exactly toward the top. (For polygons, the Shift key constrains the bottom edge to be perfectly horizontal.)

- Hold the spacebar to move, rather than resize, the shape.

- Hold the Ctrl (or ⌘) key to drag the radius of the outer points of the star, while leaving the inner points in place. (See the upper half of Figure 2-39.)

- Hold the Alt (or Option) key to constrain the sides of the star to regular angles (the same angles found in the polygon with the same number of sides), as seen in the lower half of Figure 2-39.

In this case, you'll need to press the ↑ key three times to achieve an eight-pointed star. Hold down the Shift key to constrain the angle. Size the star to align the inner points. Once you have the inner points aligned, add the Ctrl key (or Command key on the Mac) to adjust the distance of the outer points. When your star looks like that shown in Figure 2-40, release the mouse button.

Your star may have picked up the attributes of the stars tracing layer (in this case, a green stroke); if so, press the I key

*The Ctrl (or ⌘) key adjusts the outer points of a star, while leaving the inner points fixed.*

*The Alt (or Option) key adjusts sides of the star to regular angles.*

Figure 2-39.

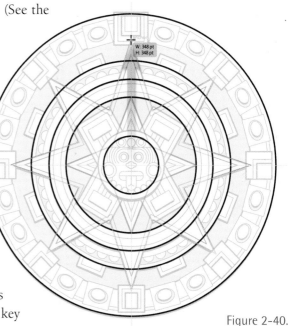

Figure 2-40.

to switch to the eyedropper tool and lift the attributes from one of the circles. Switch back to the ☆ tool when you're finished.

20. *Draw the second star.* Now it's time to draw the second star, using the same method as the previous step. Some of you who are familiar with Illustrator or other drawing programs may be asking, "But Deke, why don't we just copy and scale the existing star?" Sure, you could do that. But scaling wouldn't allow you to keep the distance between the sides of the two stars equal—things would be just a smidge off.

It's just as easy, and more precise, to draw a new star from scratch. Start dragging from the center, and size the star to line up your inner points. Then, with the Ctrl (or ⌘) key down, move your outer points into position. Constrain the angle with the Shift key, and release the mouse button. Finally, change the stroke **Weight** in the control panel to 1 point, to better match the original artwork. The results are shown in Figure 2-41.

21. *Draw the third and final star.* The last and smallest star in our calendar illustration is a four-pointed star. Drag from the center to start drawing your star, and then press the ↓ key four times to reduce the number of points to four. Align your inner points first (they should be just inside the smallest circle), then align your outer points while holding Ctrl (or ⌘). Constrain the star's angle and release the mouse. Switch the stroke back to 2 points to match the original art.

22. *Turn off the stars tracing template.* That's it for the stars! Bring up the **Layers** panel, and click the 👁 icon to hide the **Stars** layer.

23. *Draw your first rectangle.* It's now time to draw the rectangles. Not exactly the most exciting of shapes, but one of the most common. It's up to you whether you want to use the rectangles tracing template or not; if so, follow the same instructions as Step 18 on page 56 to lock this layer and make it a tracing template. Otherwise, it's easy enough to follow along on the calendar tracing template itself.

Select the ▨ tool from the **Shapes** panel, or press the M key. All the same keys apply to the rectangle tool as the ellipse tool—Shift constrains it to a perfect square, Alt or Option draws from the center out—but we just need a simple rectangle drawn from corner to corner, as shown in Figure 2-42. No modifier keys needed. Once your rectangle is aligned, release the mouse button.

Figure 2-41.

Figure 2-42.

W: 49.33 pt
H: 45.27 pt

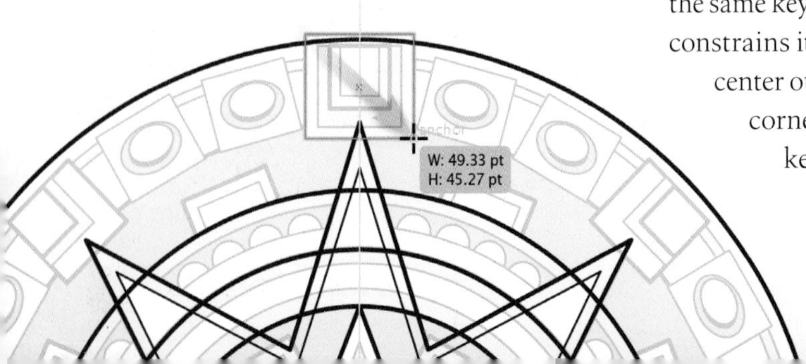

You've seen nearly all the line and shape tools in action at this point, and if you find yourself dreading drawing another rectangle, you can skip ahead to the next exercise, "Combining Simple Shapes into Complex Ones" on page 62. But by far the coolest drawing trick in this lesson is coming up, mixed in with a few other tidbits you haven't yet seen. So stick with me; I promise it will be worth it.

24. *Examine the decorative group near the god's face.* Look at the group of rectangles highlighted in Figure 2-43. This group is composed of standard rectangles, but they're drawn at an angle. All five rectangles are drawn at the same angle, in fact, which is something we can use to our advantage. Sure, you could draw one of the rectangles, rotate it, resize it to match the template—and then repeat the whole process for the other four!

However, a simpler way is to take advantage of one of Illustrator's earliest features—present since version 1.0, over two decades ago—and one of its most over-looked: the amazing *constraint axes*. The constraint axes determine the angle at which shapes, text, lines—heck, Illustrator's entire world—are based. Rotate the constraint axes, and *everything* you draw will be rotated to the same degree.

25. *Rotate the constraint axes.* So, you may be wondering, just how do you rotate these near-omnipotent constraint axes? Easily enough: Press Ctrl+K (⌘-K on the Mac) to bring up Illustrator's **Preferences** dialog box, as shown in Figure 2-44. Tab to the second value, **Constrain Angle**, and enter the value 60. Click **OK**. You won't see any visible change, but just wait for the next step.

26. *Draw your first rotated rectangle.* Start at the corner at the top of the largest rectangle, and drag down to draw your rectangle. As if by magic, the rectangle is drawn at the perfect rotation, seen in Figure 2-45.

27. *Draw the next two largest rectangles.* Repeat the process for the next two largest rectangles. (We'll deal with the two smallest in the next two steps.)

Figure 2-43.

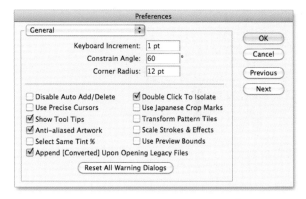

Figure 2-44.

Figure 2-45.

Figure 2-46.

Figure 2-47.

Figure 2-48.

28. *Draw one rectangle and duplicate it.* Using the tried-and-true method you've by now mastered, draw one of the smallest rectangles. Switch to the ▸ tool by pressing the V key, and drag the rectangle toward the other position, as in Figure 2-46. While dragging, hold the Alt (or Option) key to duplicate the rectangle (the cursor will change to look like ▸). Add the Shift key to constrain the direction of your drag. Note that even dragging is constrained to the specified angle. Once the duplicated rectangle is in position, release the mouse button.

29. *Clean up the stroke weights.* You've now created all the elements of the decorative ornament, but the stroke weights don't match the original artwork very well. Select the three rectangles shown in Figure 2-47 by clicking one and Shift-clicking the remaining two, and change the **Stroke** in the control panel to 1 point.

30. *Reset your constraint axes.* Now that we're finished creating our tilted decoration, it's time to reset the constraint axes. Doing this is critical—otherwise, all subsequent elements you draw will still be constrained to the specified 60-degree angle. Press Ctrl+K (⌘-K) to bring up Illustrator's **Preferences** dialog box, reset the **Constrain Angle** value to 0, and click **OK**.

31. *Further refine the ornament.* The ornament is looking pretty good, but we need to make a few tweaks in preparation for flipping and cloning the art to the other three positions around the god's face:

   • Select all five rectangles, either by clicking and Shift-clicking or by drawing a marquee as shown in Figure 2-48. (The marquee merely has to intersect any part of the shape.)

   • Fill all the rectangles with white by choosing white from the fill arrow (▾) in the control panel.

   • Group the five rectangles by pressing Ctrl+G (⌘-G) or choosing **Object→Group** from the main menu.

   • One last step. The two smallest rectangles are overlapping another piece of the art, when it's clear from the tracing template that they should be behind that piece. First, make sure nothing is selected by pressing Ctrl+Shift+A (⌘-Shift-A). Switch to the  tool, and Alt-click (Option-click) the larger of the rectangles to select the shape without selecting the group, as shown in Figure 2-49. Then press Ctrl+Shift+🔲 (⌘-Shift-🔲 on the Mac) to bring the shape to the front of the group.

Figure 2-49.

32. *Flip the ornament.* Now to duplicate the ornament to the other positions around the central face. First, select the grouped ornament with the ⬈ tool. To flip the selection, we'll use Illustrator's reflect tool (⬕). You can access the reflect tool by clicking and holding the ↻ tool in the toolbox or by pressing the O key.

Once you have the tool selected, Alt-click (or Option-click) at the intersection of the guides at the center of the artwork. This sets the reflection axis and opens the **Reflect** dialog box, shown in Figure 2-50. The *reflection axis* is simply an invisible line that the artwork will flip (or reflect) across—you can think of it as a mirror that the artwork will reflect across. Make sure the **Preview** check box and **Vertical** are selected. Do *not* click OK; instead, click **Copy**, which duplicates the ornament.

Figure 2-50.

33. *Select both ornaments and flip them again.* Once again switch to the ⬈ tool, and Shift-click the original ornament to add it to the selection. Change back to the ⬕ tool, and Alt-click (or Option-click) at the guide intersection again. This time in the Reflect dialog box, select **Horizontal** and click **Copy**.

Figure 2-51.

You've navigated the fundamentals of drawing and manipulating Illustrator's primitive shapes, and picked up a few more advanced techniques along the way. After all that work, the results of which can be seen in Figure 2-51, perhaps a break is in order. Grab a coffee, stretch a little. And for heaven's sake, save your work. I'll be here, ready to lead you into the next exercise, where we'll revisit this file and learn to combine primitive shapes into more complex ones.

Figure 2-52.

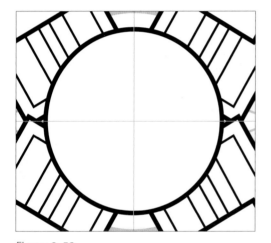

Figure 2-53.

Figure 2-54.

## Combining Simple Shapes into Complex Ones

Primitive shapes are fine and all—you'd be hard-pressed to draw any illustrations without them—but where Illustrator really shines is in the combination of these primitives to create more complex objects. This is the bread and butter of the work in Illustrator, and knowing the best ways to create these complex shapes will prove indispensable. What follows is your first taste of these methods; we'll explore them further in later lessons.

In this exercise, I'll demonstrate the variety of ways Illustrator provides to cut shapes apart and join them back together. We'll be working with our *tonalpohualli* again, this time filling in some of the facial details.

1. *Open the tonalpohualli.* If you have your file from the preceding exercise still open, great. If not, open the file you saved or open the file *Topo face time.ai* in the *Lesson 02* folder.

2. *Zoom in on the face.* Since we're going to be working exclusively with details in the god's face in this exercise, zoom in tight on the center of the illustration, as in Figure 2-52. (I found around 800 percent to be a good amount, but your value will vary depending on the room available on your screen.)

3. *Select the inner circle and bring it forward.* With the ⬉ tool, click the circle surrounding the face. Press Ctrl+Shift+⬚ (or ⌘-Shift-⬚) to bring the circle to the front. Fill the shape with white by clicking the ⬚ in the control panel, and selecting white from the pop-up palette. You should now see something like Figure 2-53.

4. *Set the My Drawing layer to outline mode.* The white circle is a nice clean canvas to work on, but it's unfortunately obscuring the tracing template. Let the Calendar layer show through by setting the **My Drawing** layer to outline mode. Bring up the **Layers** panel, and Ctrl-click (⌘-click on the Mac) the 👁 next to the My Drawing layer. The results are shown in Figure 2-54.

5. *Draw the primitive shapes that make up the nose.* If you examine the nose, you'll see that it's comprised of three overlapping circles. Switch to the ⬭ tool, and draw each in turn:

   • Start with the center circle, dragging from the intersection of the guides, using the Shift and Alt (or Option) keys to constrain the shape and draw out from the center.

- Next, draw the left circle. Start from the intersection of the first circle and the blue guide, and again use the Shift and Alt (Option) keys.

- Finally, switch to the ▸ tool, and drag the left circle horizontally across to the other side. Hold the Alt (or Option) key to duplicate the circle. Once it snaps into place, release the mouse button.

Press Ctrl+Shift+A (⌘-Shift-A) to deselect everything. Your three circles should now match those in Figure 2-55.

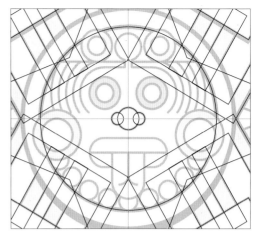

Figure 2-55.

6. *Return the My Drawing layer to preview mode.* Back in the Layers panel, Ctrl-click (or ⌘-click) the 👁 to return the **My Drawing** layer to preview mode. The two nostrils are overlapping the center circle, with their strokes cutting in, shown in Figure 2-56. Combining the shapes will address the problem.

7. *Select and combine the circles.* Using the black arrow tool, click one of the circles, and then Shift-click the other two to select all three circles. Bring up the **Pathfinder** panel by choosing **Window→Pathfinder**.

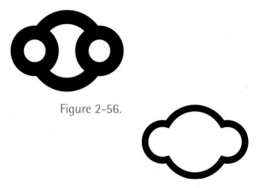

Figure 2-56.

---

The Pathfinder panel has many options, each performing various mathematical transformations on the selected paths. Pathfinder operations are one of Illustrator's most powerful tools for manipulating shapes. So powerful, in fact, that an entire lesson (Lesson 6) is devoted to them. Consider this the Pathfinder appetizer.

---

Figure 2-57.

From the Pathfinder panel, click the ⧉ icon (the first choice in the top row). This adds the shapes together, giving them a single stroke around the outside of the newly formed nose. Adjust the stroke **Width** down to 1 point, and you should see the perfect schnozz for our calendar (see Figure 2-57).

8. *Examine the lozenge-shaped mouth.* Next on the agenda is recreating the mouth. Return the **My Drawing** layer to outline mode to allow you to see the tracing layer underneath. Looking at the original artwork, you might be thinking that you could combine two circles and a rectangle to get the basic shape. That would work, but another way uses just one shape—splitting a circle and splicing it back together

9. *Draw a circle at one end of the mouth.* The first step in creating the mouth is to draw the circle. Select the ellipse tool, and drag diagonally from the upper left to lower right, using the Shift key to constrain the shape, as in Figure 2-58.

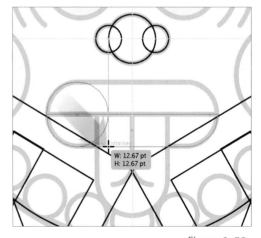

Figure 2-58.

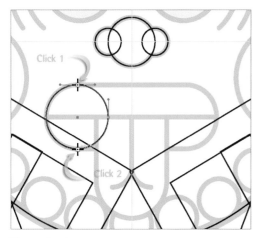

Figure 2-59.

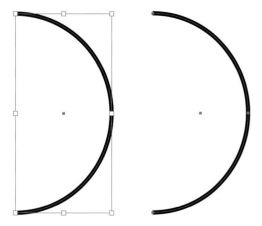

Figure 2-60.

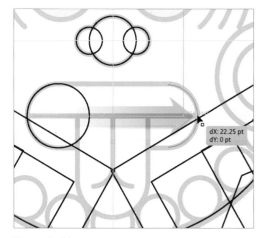

Figure 2-61.

10. *Split the circle in half.* Access the scissors tool by clicking the ✂ icon in the toolbox or by pressing the C key. Click the top and bottom points of the circle, as in Figure 2-59, to split the circle exactly in half.

---

You may be wondering why I'm not using the knife tool (🔪), also available under the ✄ icon, to slice the circle. While I love Illustrator, I avoid the knife tool at all costs—it is Illustrator's most poorly designed tool. It lacks any and all precision, drawing a freehand line that slices any and all shapes it crosses. You can constrain the line to be perfectly straight with the Alt (or Option) key, but even then, the tool doesn't snap to any points or paths, making it so haphazard as to be functionally useless. Stick with the scissors.

---

11. *Ditch Illustrator's bounding boxes.* With the black arrow tool, select the right side of the circle. See the frame with the eight white boxes around the edges, like in the left half of Figure 2-60? This is the *bounding box*, and the white squares are the *handles*. Illustrator creates this bounding box by default around all paths. It provides convenient access to scaling by dragging one of the handles; or, if you move just beyond the handle, you can rotate the path. Unfortunately, the handles often get in the way of some of Illustrator's other functions—including the one we need next, which is dragging the arc by its rightmost point. Tell Illustrator "thanks, but no thanks" for the bounding boxes by choosing **View→Hide Bounding Box** or by pressing Ctrl+Shift+B (⌘-Shift-B on the Mac). Don't worry about the scale and rotate options; you can still access those from the tools in the toolbox. Your arc should now look like the right half of Figure 2-60.

12. *Drag the right side of the circle into position.* Now that the pesky bounding box is out of the way, drag the rightmost anchor point in the right half of the circle into position, illustrated in Figure 2-61. Once the path snaps into place, release the mouse button.

13. *Join the bottom points of the arc.* Switch to the white arrow tool (either choosing ▷ from the toolbox or pressing the A key). Click the bottom point of the left-hand arc, as shown in Figure 2-62 on the facing page. Notice that when you hover over the point, Illustrator highlights the point with a white-filled box—this micro-feature is fantastic for helping you find points in your paths, regardless of their complexity. Next, Shift-click the bottom point of the right-hand arc. Finally, join the points by choosing **Object→Path→Join** or by pressing Ctrl+J (⌘-J). The

Join command automatically connects the two points with a straight segment.

14. ***Join the top points to close the shape.*** You could repeat the process for the top two points, but since there are only two endpoints left on this path, Illustrator can join them automatically. Press the Ctrl (or ⌘) key to temporarily switch to the black arrow tool, and click anywhere on the path to select the whole shape. Press Ctrl+J (⌘-J), and Illustrator automatically closes the path.

---

The Join command will work only on single shapes that have two open endpoints, and only if the entire shape is selected. If you attempt to use this command on multiple shapes, or on a shape that is only partially selected, Illustrator will complain and refuse to cooperate.

---

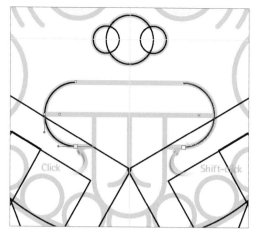

Figure 2-62.

15. ***Draw the seam across the lips.*** To finish the lips, draw the line across the center. Select the \ tool by pressing the ⌐ key, and drag from the left side of the lips to the right side while holding the Shift key, seen in Figure 2-63.

16. ***View your work.*** Ctrl-click (or ⌘-click) the ◎ for the **My Drawing** layer to see the fruits of your labor. The face is progressing nicely, with two of the primary features complete.

EXTRA ★ CREDIT

These last few steps will illustrate another way to split and rejoin shapes using Illustrator's context-sensitive control panel; we'll trash and recreate the lip lozenge in the process. If you're satisfied with the scissors tool and Join command, feel free to skip to the next exercise, "Coloring Your Artwork" on page 66. But you can stick around for just a handful of steps more, right?

---

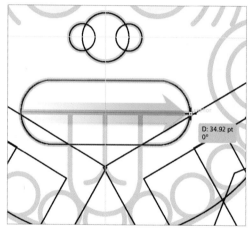

Figure 2-63.

17. ***Delete the lozenge shape.*** For the sake of illustration, I'm going to ask you to redraw the outer edge of the lips. Select the lozenge with the black arrow tool and press the Delete key.

18. ***Redraw your starting circle.*** Change the My Drawing layer back to outline mode so you can see the tracing template underneath. Next, draw the starting circle the same way you did in Step 9 on page 63.

19. ***Split your circle.*** With the white arrow tool, click the top point of the circle and Shift-click the bottom point, as shown in Figure 2-64. Up in Illustrator's control panel, you'll see three buttons next to the label **Anchors**. Click the ⌐ button to split the shape at the selected points.

20. ***Drag the right half of the circle to the other side.*** Repeat Step 12 to position the right half of the circle.

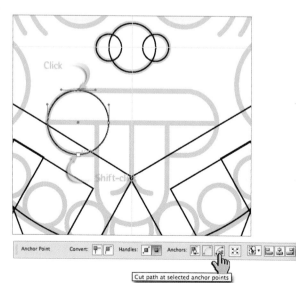

Figure 2-64.

21. *Join the bottom two points.* Select the two bottom points with the white arrow tool, just as you did in Step 13 on page 64. Rather than choosing the Join command, however, we'll select another of the buttons from the control panel—in this case, the second of the Anchor buttons (⌢), which connects the selected endpoints.

22. *Join the top points.* Join the top points using the same method you used in Step 14 on the previous page.

23. *Send the lozenge backward.* Ctrl-click or ⌘-click the 👁 icon for the My Drawing layer. As you can see, the lozenge is now blocking the seam of the lips; to reveal the seam, choose **Arrange→Send Backward** from the **Object** menu, or press Ctrl+[ (or ⌘-[) to send the lozenge back one step.

And there you have it! The final art is seen in Figure 2-65. This exercise has only scratched the surface of breaking apart and restitching shapes, but you're off to a great start. You may not be quite at mad-scientist level yet, but later lessons will help you master the madness that is Illustrator.

## Coloring Your Artwork

Shapes are an indispensable piece of any artwork. They define your overall composition, like the outlines in a coloring book. But just like in a coloring book, the outlines are empty, hollow, waiting to be filled with vibrant color. Color adds life and character to an otherwise nondescript illustration. More color is not always better, however. Color should be used judiciously, as it communicates just as much as the other elements of your drawing. An explosion of vivid colors may be perfect for a child's birthday invitation but would quickly make a business card look garish.

Illustrator lets you apply color in several ways: via predefined *swatches*, a group of colors saved with the illustration itself; through the color mixers, or *sliders*, available in the Color panel; and lastly through the Color Guide panel, which uses mathematical formulas (based on color theory) to create swatches on-the-fly based on your starting color.

In this exercise, we'll continue with our *tonalpohualli*, coloring the shapes to resurrect our ancient Aztec calendar. Before you begin, you may want to check out the sidebar "Color in Illustrator: A Whirl-

Figure 2-65.

wind Tour" on page 68which provides background on color theory, Illustrator's various color modes, using color sliders, and working with the built-in swatch libraries that ship with Illustrator.

1. *Open a new version of the calendar.* Navigate to the *Lesson 02* folder inside the *Lesson Files-AIcs4 1on1* folder. Inside you'll find a file named *Topo shapes. ai.* When you open the file, you'll notice that I've added a few more shapes (mostly the rectangles around the outer edge of the calendar) to give you a more robust calendar for coloring.

2. *Select the circle that encompasses the innermost star.* Start your adventure into color by selecting the circle that surrounds the innermost (i.e., the four-pointed) star using the black arrow tool, as shown in Figure 2-66.

3. *Set the fill color.* Access the color sliders by bringing up the **Color** panel. Choose **Window→Color** or press the F6 key. (Alternately, you can access the color sliders by Shift-clicking ▾ (the fill arrow) in the control panel.)

   However you choose to get there, you should see CMYK sliders. Currently, the stroke is the active attribute (indicated by the stroke icon being on top of the fill icon, like so: ▣); the stroke currently has the *focus.* Click the fill icon to make it active, or simply press the X key to swap the focus from stroke to fill. (Pressing Shift-X swaps the colors without changing focus.)

   Once the fill is active, enter the values shown in Figure 2-67. Click in the cyan value (**C**) to enter 0, then press Tab to advance to the magenta value (**M**) and enter 10. Press Tab again, and enter 25 for the yellow value (**Y**), and repeat for the black value (**K**). With each press of the Tab key, Illustrator updates the fill color. Your circle should now be filled with the soft clay color seen in the fill box.

4. *Create a new swatch.* I like the terra-cotta color so much that I want to create a swatch for it. Like nearly everything in

Figure 2-66.

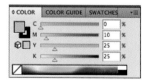

Figure 2-67.

# Color in Illustrator: A Whirlwind Tour

Working with color in Illustrator can be a bit daunting at first. You can choose different color spaces and choose colors in multiple places. More than 70 color libraries are built in—and that's not including the industry-standard color books, such as Pantone, Trumatch, HKS, and Toyo.

Scratching your head already? Let's start at the foundation and work our way up.

A *color space* is simply the way the colors in a document are defined. The two most common color spaces are RGB (red/green/blue), used primarily for graphics intended for the screen, be it computer, television, or even film; and CMYK (cyan/magenta/yellow/black, where black is the key color), used exclusively for print output, on everything from home inkjets to commercial presses. RGB is an *additive* color space, meaning the more color you add, the brighter the color becomes, while CMYK is *subtractive*—adding more color makes the result darker, as shown below.

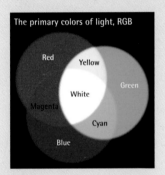
The primary colors of light, RGB

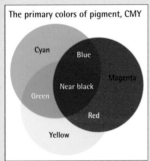
The primary colors of pigment, CMY

Illustrator requires that each document you create be assigned one of these two color spaces; it's best to pick the one that matches your ultimate output destination. (You can change the color space by choosing File→Document Color Mode and then the color space you'd like to use.) Because each color space is able to produce only a certain range of colors (known as a *color gamut*), choosing the correct color space ensures that your colors will output as you expect. (For more on output, see Lesson 12, Printing and Export.)

After you've established your color space, it's time to choose your colors. Illustrator provides two ways to specify color: swatches and color sliders; let's examine the color sliders first. You can find the color sliders in the Color panel (which

you can bring to the front by pressing the F6 key), or you can bring them up by Shift-clicking the color pop-up arrow (▾) in the control panel. The figure below shows the CMYK and RGB color sliders in the Color panel, identifying the key components.

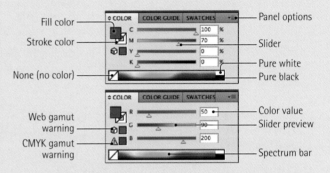

The CMYK sliders are based on a scale of 0–100 percent, which specifies the percent of ink coverage. Conversely, the RGB values use *luminance*, which is a scale of 0–255. Because CMYK is subtractive, reducing all the values to 0 produces white; doing the same in the additive RGB space produces pure black.

You can adjust the color by dragging the slider or by entering a new value in the color value field. As you drag a slider, the color previews of the other sliders are updated to show you the colors you could achieve by moving those sliders.

At the bottom of the panel are the none, white, and black options, as well as the spectrum bar. Clicking any of the options, or anywhere in the spectrum bar, will immediately assign that color to the selected element (either fill or stroke, depending on what has focus). The spectrum bar attempts to display all possible colors at once, with solid hues moving along the central horizontal axis, adding white as you approach the top and black as you near the bottom.

Click the panel options button to pop up a menu that allows you to change the color space of the sliders. In addition to RGB and CMYK, there are a few other choices:

- *Grayscale* (a black slider only).

- *HSB* (short for hue/saturation/brightness). HSB specifies the hue as a value between 0 and 360 degrees (with 0 being red, 120 being green, and 240 being blue, and the other hues gradually transitioning between them), and the saturation and brightness as a percentage from 0–100. While brightness is self-explanatory, saturation indicates the relative strength of the color, with 0 being gray and 100 being a vivid hue, fully saturated.

- *Web Safe RGB* is the RGB space confined to "Web safe" colors. These values are entered in the hexidecimal values common to Web applications, such as Fireworks or Dreamweaver.

Last are the gamut warnings. The Web gamut warning alerts you that the specified color is not in the default Web color space. Even if you're creating an illustration for the Web, it's most likely safe to ignore because nearly all modern computers and browsers are no longer limited by this color space. (It was created in the early days of the Internet.) For maximum compatibility, you can click the small swatch next to the warning, which shifts the color to the closest Web-safe version.

Similarly, the CMYK gamut warning cautions you that the RGB (or other non-CMYK color space) color you specified cannot be reproduced accurately in print. If your final destination is print output, you would be wise to heed the warning. Clicking the small swatch takes you to the closest CMYK equivalent. (Due to the limitations of the inks used for printing, CMYK cannot produce as wide a color range as RGB.)

Dialing colors with the color sliders is all fine and dandy, but what if you have many colors you need to apply over and over again to objects in your illustration? Or perhaps you need a spot color, perfectly matching your client's corporate color scheme. Maybe you're not even sure what color you want, and would like to see a selection presented to you.

That's where Illustrator's swatches step in to the rescue. Illustrator has two basic homes for swatches: swatches stored directly in the document and swatches housed in libraries. (Swatches from libraries can easily be added to your local document swatches, making them easier to apply and ensuring that they are saved with the document.)

To see what swatches are stored in the document, bring up the Swatches panel by pressing F5. Assuming you have a document open, you'll see an assortment of tiny squares, each one a discrete color that can be applied to any stroke or fill simply by clicking it (with the appropriate object selected).

Swatches aren't limited to just colors. You can also apply (and even create) gradient and pattern swatches, as well as sort swatches into groups. You'll learn more about gradients in Lesson 7, Blends, Masks, and Gradient Mesh, and more about patterns later in this lesson.

The figure below shows the layout of (and the tools available from) the Swatches panel.

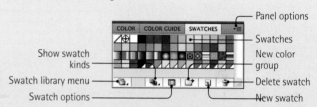

The swatch library menu provides access to Illustrator's built-in swatch libraries, as well as the industry-standard color libraries (stored in the group Color Books). Selecting any of these libraries will open the library in its own panel; multiple libraries will open as tabs in the same panel. This panel can be moved, docked, and hidden just like any other panel; however, if you'd like to add it permanently to your workspace, select Persistent from the library's panel options menu. To add a swatch from a library to your local document swatches, select the swatch in the library, and from the panel options menu, choose Add to Swatches.

The ▦ icon allows you to filter the kinds of swatches displayed, while ▤ brings up a dialog box, allowing you to edit the swatch's values. The ▤ icon also brings up the same dialog box but creates a swatch from scratch.

Lastly, the ▭ icon allows you to create a group of swatches in the panel. To add swatches to a group, simply drag the swatch to the folder icon at the start of the row. Each group is kept on its own row in the Swatches panel, allowing you to organize your colors into tidy blocks.

Whew! It may be a lot of information to absorb at once, this whirlwind tour of color. But don't worry, you'll be seeing this all in action soon enough, and nothing commits knowledge to memory better than making good use of it—which you'll do throughout the remainder of this book.

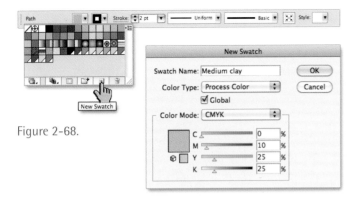

Figure 2-68.

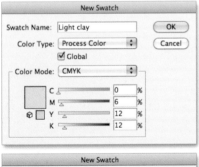

Figure 2-69.

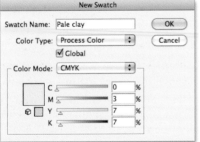

Figure 2-70.

Illustrator, there are several ways to accomplish this task. You could select Create New Swatch from the Color panel options, or you could bring up your Swatches panel and click the ⬜ icon. But the fastest way—and my favorite—is to use the control panel, because it's always on-screen. Click the fill ⬛, shown in Figure 2-68, and then click the ⬜ icon at the bottom of the panel. In the **New Swatch** dialog box, Illustrator names the color with the CMYK values by default, but I recommend you use a more meaningful name; in this case, I picked "Medium clay."

Of the other options in the dialog box, leave **Color Type** set to **Process Color**. This ensures that the color will print properly when sent to a commercial printer; generally you will want to use Spot Color only when using a color from one of the specialized swatch libraries (such as Pantone solid coated, for example). Make sure the **Global** check box is turned on, as this instructs Illustrator to link all the objects using this swatch with the swatch itself. If you later edit the color values of the swatch, the items tagged with it will update automatically. Click **OK** to close the dialog box. Your new swatch is added to the end of the grid.

5. *Clean up your swatches.* Before I ask you to dig in to more coloring, you need to create a few more swatches. Right now, though, the swatches are a bit of a mess—there are a host of colors that would never be appropriate for our ancient Meso-american calendar. Make sure no artwork is selected by pressing Ctrl+Shift+A (or ⌘-Shift-A), and then click the fill ⬛ in the control panel. Click the Global Malt swatch, which is just to the left of your Medium Clay swatch, and then Shift-click the Magenta swatch to select all the swatches in between, as in Figure 2-69. Finally, click the trash icon to delete the swatches. Illustrator pops up a warning, asking you to confirm the deletion; click **Yes** to dismiss the dialog box.

6. *Create two more swatches.* With the extraneous swatches gone, your panel should contain just five boxes. Click the Medium Clay swatch to select it, and then click the ⬜ icon. Enter the values **C**:0, **M**:6, **Y**:12, **K**:12 in the upper half of Figure 2-70, name the color "Light clay," and click **OK**. Click the ⬜ icon again, and enter the values from the lower half of Figure 2-70 (**C**:0, **M**:3, **Y**:7, **K**:7). Give the swatch the name "Pale clay," and click **OK**.

7. *Change your strokes from plain black to rich black.* If you select one of the objects in your calendar and examine the stroke color, you'll see that it has the CMYK values C:0, M:0, Y:0, K:100. "So what," you're probably thinking, "black is black, right?"

In the RGB color space, that's true. But not so when working with CMYK. Black in this case is just one ink out of the four. Much of the black printed artwork you see is printed using *rich black*—a black that is composed of all four inks. Rich blacks tend to print darker and look, well, richer than their one-ink counterparts. Also, using a rich black helps prevent *trapping* issues—printing errors that show white gaps between two colors that share no inks in common. (See Figure 2-71 for an example.)

Plain black

Rich black

Figure 2-71.

To switch all your strokes to rich black, do the following:

- Select the black swatch in the **Swatches** panel as a starting point, and click the ⬑ icon. Change the values to **C**:50, **M**:50, **Y**:50, **K**:100, and name the color "Rich black." Be sure the **Global** check box is turned on. Click **OK** to save your swatch.

- Select any of your objects with the black arrow tool. From the control panel, click the ⬙ next to the ⃰ icon (the last item on the control panel, called the Select Similar Options menu). From the pop-up menu, choose **Stroke Color**, as shown in Figure 2-72. Illustrator automatically selects all the objects whose stroke color matches the original selection.

- In the **Color** panel, make the stroke attribute active by clicking its icon. Back in the **Swatches** panel, click the rich black swatch to apply it to all selected strokes.

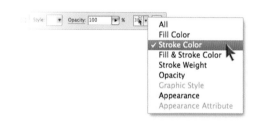

Figure 2-72.

Now to confirm that all your strokes have switched to the rich black. Press Ctrl+Shift+A (or ⌘-Shift-A) to deselect all objects, then double-click the rich black swatch to bring up the **Swatch Options** dialog box. Turn on the **Preview** check box, and adjust the CMYK values to something in the neighborhood of **C**:0, **M**:100, **Y**:50, **K**:0. *Do not click the OK button.* All your strokes should now change to a bright pink—all except, strangely, the nose. Make a mental note, and click the **Cancel** button.

8. *Fix the nose.* Select the nose with the black arrow tool, and (making sure the stroke attribute is active) click the rich black swatch to fix the color.

A few notes about rich blacks: If you didn't adjust your Appearance of Black preferences in the Preface as I instructed, you should do so now. Choose **Preferences→Appearance of Black** from the **Edit** menu (or the **Illustrator** menu on the Mac). Change the **On Screen** setting to **Display All Blacks Accurately**, and click **OK**. This will allow you to differentiate between plain black and rich black on your monitor.

Also, when specifying a rich black, keep the total of the four inks below 300 percent. Most paper used in commercial printing can't absorb any more ink beyond that point, leading to smudging at best and paper tearing at worst.

Figure 2-73.

Figure 2-74.

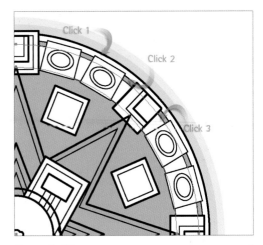

Figure 2-75.

9. ***Open a new version of the artwork.*** At this point, you can save your artwork or discard it. I'd like you to open a new version of the calendar called *Richer artwork.ai*, located in the *Lesson 02* folder, which includes the rich black strokes and yet more shapes for your coloring attention. (If you'd like, you can also open *Our goal.ai*, which shows the results you're working toward.)

10. ***Make sure your Swatches panel is easily accessible.*** In the next few steps, you're going to be using the Swatches panel almost exclusively. If you've already got yours docked (which you should, if you followed along with "Creating Custom Workspaces" in Lesson 1) great. If not, bring the panel to the forefront by choosing **Window→Swatches** from the menu; drag the **Swatches** panel to your docking panel, positioning it in a location convenient for you.

11. ***Change the fill and stroke of two circles.*** Select the outermost circle. Make sure the fill is active, and click the lightest of the swatches, Pale Clay. Select the next circle in, and click the Light Clay swatch to change the fill. Now select both circles (either by drawing a marquee, as in Figure 2-73, or clicking and Shift-clicking), press the X key to make the stroke active, and set it to none by clicking the ⊠ icon (or pressing the ⬚ key). The results are shown in Figure 2-74.

12. ***Change the fill of the next three circles.*** Press the X key again to return focus to the fill attribute. Click the third circle in, and fill it with white. Next, click the fourth circle, and fill it with the Medium Clay swatch. Finally, click the fifth circle in. You'll notice Illustrator highlights the fifth and sixth circles; this shape is a compound path, something we'll learn more about in later lessons. For now, just fill the shape with white, as shown in Figure 2-75.

13. ***Select the circles and send them backward.*** The fills look great—but unfortunately they're now blocking some of the artwork in the center of the piece. Select all five circles by clicking the outermost one and Shift-clicking the rest. Send all the shapes to the back layer of the illustration by pressing Ctrl+Shift+⬚ (⌘-Shift-⬚ on the Mac).

14. ***Fill more elements by dragging swatches.*** You're not limited to changing the fill of selected objects. You can change the fill (and stroke) of any path in your illustration by dragging swatches onto that path. Here's how:

- Deselect all objects by pressing Ctrl+Shift+A (or ⌘-Shift-A).

- Drag the Pale Clay swatch to the outermost circle in the second grouping, as shown in Figure 2-76.

- Drag the Medium Clay swatch to the second circle in, then the white swatch to the third circle. Drag the Pale Clay swatch to the fourth circle (the thickly stroked one), white to the fifth, and finally Light Clay to the innermost one. (See Figure 2-76 for guidance.)

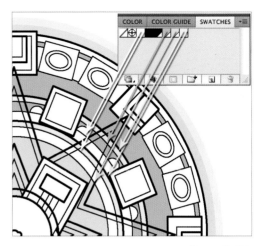

Figure 2-76.

---

It's important when you're dragging the swatches that you release the mouse over the outline, rather than inside the shape, due to the Object Selection by Path Only preference I had you set back in the Preface. You may think that dragging the swatch over the outline would change the stroke, but instead it changes the active attribute of the object. If you'd like to change the inactive attribute (in this case, the stroke) while dragging a swatch, hold the Shift key as you drag.

---

15. *Recover the lost circle.* You may have noticed that the first circle you filled, way back in Step 3 on page 67, has gotten lost under all the other shapes. (To confirm this, Ctrl-click or ⌘ click the 👁 icon of the Paths layer to switch to outline mode; Ctrl-click again to change back to preview mode.) With the black arrow tool, slowly move the mouse over where you think the shape might be, as in Figure 2-77. When you move over the shape, your cursor will change from ▸ to ▸., and the path will be highlighted in orange (or whatever you set your layer color to oh-so-many steps ago). Click to select the circle. Rather than bringing the shape to the front of the stack, which would cover up most of the central art, I want you to move the circle up the stack incrementally. Press Ctrl+🄻 (⌘-🄻 on the Mac) to bring the shape forward. Keep repeating this until the circle becomes visible—in my case, seven times in total. The final results are shown in Figure 2-78.

Figure 2-77.

While we're not quite finished, that's it for this exercise. Save your progress so far, with a filename like "Halfway there.ai" or something similar, in the *Lesson 02* folder. We'll revisit it in the next exercise, where we learn more advanced ways of applying fills and strokes and more powerful methods of moving objects up or down the stack.

Figure 2-78.

## Filling, Stroking, and Stacking

In the previous exercise, we focused primarily on how to color objects, with a few instances of moving objects forward or back. In this exercise, I'll show you how to move shapes directly in front of or behind the selected object, as well as how to manipulate entire groups, even when those groups may be nested inside other groups.

We'll wrap up by restoring the face in the center of the artwork. This is our last exercise with the *tonalpohualli* (and the last exercise of the lesson), and by the end you'll have a complete (and complex) high-quality illustration.

1. ***Open the calendar art.*** If you have your file from the last exercise open, you can keep working with that; if not, open the file *Topo halfway.ai*, found in the *Lesson 02* folder.

2. ***Fill the two outermost stars.*** Using whatever method you'd like, fill the outermost star with Light Clay, and the star just inside it with white, as in Figure 2-79.

3. ***Move the stars to their proper place in the stack.*** If you temporarily turned off the Paths layer (by clicking its 👁), you'll see that the stars are supposed to be behind the thickly stroked circle about halfway out from the center. You have to move them, but how?

---

So much of Illustrator is a building process, rather than a traditional pen-and-ink process. The stacking order is a crucial part of building a successful illustration, and while the stacking order may seem inscrutable at times, the next few tricks will prove indispensable.

---

Make the **Paths** layer visible again, and select both stars with the black arrow tool. Rather than pressing Ctrl+⌷ (or ⌘ -⌷) countless times, trying to get the stars into position, do the following to get them just where they need to go:

- Press Ctrl+X (⌘-X) to cut the stars. This moves them to the clipboard.

- Select the heavy circle with the black arrow tool, as shown in Figure 2-80.

- From the **Edit** menu, choose **Paste in Back**, or press the keyboard shortcut, Ctrl+B (⌘-B). (The keyboard shortcuts for Paste in Front and Paste in Back are *extremely* useful, and I highly recommend you commit them to memory.)

Figure 2-79.

Figure 2-80.

Your illustration should now look like Figure 2-81. (I clicked the background to deselect the stars to make them more visible.) With the Paste in Back and Paste in Front commands, Illustrator leaves the horizontal and vertical position of the elements unchanged, and changes only the stacking order.

4. *Repeat for the ring of squares.* See the ring of large white squares, evenly spaced between the star points? Those squares should be behind the dark outer ring they overlap so that only the edges are showing. Click one square—and they all get selected! I created these squares as a group, so they could be manipulated as one object. Press Ctrl+X (⌘-X) to cut the squares, and select the outer heavy ring. Finally, press Ctrl+B (⌘-B) to position the squares in back, as shown in Figure 2-82.

5. *Fill some more shapes.* It's time to fill in some of the shapes at the center of our artwork. Using the black arrow tool, click the outermost four-pointed star, and then Shift-click the innermost star. Fill both shapes with white by clicking the white swatch in the **Swatches** panel. Click the middle four-pointed star to select it, and fill it with the Light Clay color, as pictured in Figure 2-83.

6. *Fill and move the circle just outside the god's face.* There's one circle left to fill—the one just outside the face. Click it with the black arrow tool, and fill it with the Medium Clay color swatch. Immediately, it obscures the rest of the face; it's sitting at the top of the stack. Press Ctrl+X (⌘-X) to cut it, and then click any of the rotated rectangles. (They'll be selected as a group.) Finally, press Ctrl+F (⌘-F) to place the circle just in front of the rectangles, as in Figure 2-84.

Figure 2-81.

Figure 2-82.

Figure 2-83.

Figure 2-84.

Figure 2-85.

Figure 2-86.

7. *Fill groups inside groups.* You're nearly there—only the outer ring shapes and the rotated rectangles still need fills applied. However, if you try to select one of these shapes, you select the entire group. You need to select into the group, as introduced in Step 15 on page 50, using the group selection tool. Easier yet, use the standard white arrow tool and simply Alt-click (or Option-click). Here's what to do:

- Switch to the ▷ tool by pressing the A key.

- Alt-click (or Option-click) *twice* on the rectangle shown in Figure 2-85. (The first click selects the single shape; the second selects the subgroup inside the group. A third click would select the entire group.) Fill the selected shapes with Pale Clay.

- Alt-click (or Option-click) twice on the thin rectangle shown in Figure 2-86. Fill these shapes with the Light Clay swatch.

- Now for the outer rectangles. Alt-click (Option-click) twice on the shape shown in Figure 2-87. (Note that this selects all the objects in this subgroup around the entire ring; the figure is zoomed to show which rectangle to click.) Fill these shapes with Light Clay.

8. *Fill and clone the ellipses.* Now turn your attention to the ellipses ringing the outer band. On the original artwork, these shapes had a three-dimensional effect; you'll create this by cloning the artwork. There are a few substeps involved, outlined in the enlightening bullet points below:

- Alt-click (or Option-click) twice the outer ellipses, shown in Figure 2-88. Fill the shapes with the Light Clay color.

Figure 2-87.

Figure 2-88.

- Next, Alt-click (or Option-click) twice on the inner ellipses, and fill them with your Rich Black swatch.

- Duplicate the ellipses by pressing Shift+Alt+↑ (on the Mac, Shift-Option-↑). The ↑ key would nudge the art 0.2 points, but adding Shift multiplies your nudge distance by ten. Finally, adding the Alt (or Option) key clones the selection as you move it. Your current art should look like Figure 2-89.

---

If your art doesn't look like the figure, it's possible you neglected to change your Keyboard Increment preference, as I suggested in the Preface. In that case, press Ctrl+K (⌘-K) to bring up Illustrator's preferences, and change the **Keyboard Increment** value to 0.2 pt. Click **OK** to dismiss the **Preferences** dialog box.

---

Figure 2-89.

- Finally, fill the cloned ellipses with white. The final effect is shown in Figure 2-90.

9. *Copy the face from the tracing layer.* One element is still missing from our Aztec calendar, and that's the face of the ancient god in the center of the calendar. Here's how to get the face from the tracing template directly into your artwork:

- Bring up your **Layers** panel by pressing the F7 key, and hide the **Paths** layer by clicking the 👁 icon next to it.

- Unlock the **Calendar** layer by clicking the 🔒 icon. Click the layer title to make it active.

- With the black arrow tool, click anywhere on the face *except* the nose or mouth. The face elements are grouped, and will be selected all at once. Your selection should look like Figure 2-91.

Figure 2-90.

- Press Ctrl+C (⌘-C) to copy the paths, or choose **Copy** from the **Edit** menu.

- Back in the **Layers** panel, hide the **Calendar** layer, show the **Paths** layer, and make the Paths layer active by clicking the layer title.

- Still using the black arrow tool, select the innermost circle.

- Press Ctrl+F (⌘-F) to paste the face in front of the circle, as seen in Figure 2-92 on the following page.

You've not only changed the stacking order with this operation but also copied artwork from one layer to another (something that can't be accomplished with the Send to Front and Send to Back commands). Even better, Illustrator has restored the face

Figure 2-91.

Figure 2-92.

details to full opacity—the transparency was an attribute of the layer, and not of the paths themselves. By moving the art to the Paths layer, the paths become fully opaque.

You may notice a few issues with the details in Figure 2-92. The mouth is in front of the tongue—something that never happens in real life—and the stroke on the nose and mouth is too heavy. Sharp-eyed readers may spot the third issue—the black strokes of the newly pasted face are plain black, rather than rich black. We'll fix these last few issues in the remaining steps.

10. *Nudge the mouth back.* Using the black arrow tool, click the lozenge shape, and Shift-click the seam of the lips. With both paths selected, press Ctrl+⬚ (⌘-⬚ on the Mac) to send the shapes behind the tongue.

11. *Change the stroke width of the nose and mouth.* The mouth should still be selected; Shift-click the nose to add it. Now to change the stroke width—but sadly, Illustrator isn't providing that as an option in the control panel. No matter, you can get to the stroke weight by bringing up the Stroke panel. Press Ctrl+F10 (⌘-F10) or choose **Stroke** from the **Window** menu. In the **Stroke** panel, change the **Weight** to 1 point.

12. *Make the face elements rich black.* Click any face element (except the nose or mouth) to select them all. Make sure your stroke attribute is active, and apply the Rich Black swatch. Figure 2-93 shows the before and after.

Figure 2-93.

These last few steps are finicky and deal with tiny details in the artwork. But that's what Illustrator's all about, right? Besides, it's the only place in this lesson you'll learn about the stroke options beyond simple weight as well as Illustrator's isolation mode, which is critical for working in artwork with an overabundance of shapes. Finally, I wrap up with a special treat—a very cool pattern fill based on, of all things, a nose. How could you pass that up?

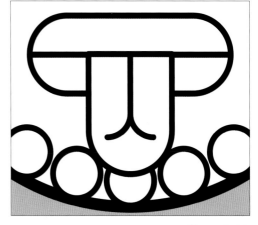

Figure 2-94.

13. *Examine the tongue.* Your artwork looks pretty sharp, but if you look closely at the shapes that make up the tongue (enlarged in Figure 2-94), you'll see some alignment issues at the top, along the seam of the lips. (Try a zoom level of 1600 percent to get the necessary level of detail.)

14. *Delete the top line of the tongue.* Select the ▷ tool from the toolbox, or press the A key. Click the top line of the tongue— but *not* on one of the corner points—to select that line segment, and press the Delete key.

15. *Bring the lip seam to the front.* That's better, but now the fill of the tongue is hiding part of the seam of the lips. Switch to the black arrow tool and click (or alternately, just Alt-click or Option-click with the current white arrow tool) the seam to select it. Press Ctrl+⬚ (⌘-⬚ on the Mac) to bring the seam over the tongue, as shown in Figure 2-95.

16. *Bring up the Stroke panel.* If it's not still visible, bring up the **Stroke** panel by pressing Ctrl+F10 (⌘-F10). The panel has a number of options, all labeled in Figure 2-96. You're familiar with weight, but what do these other options mean, exactly?

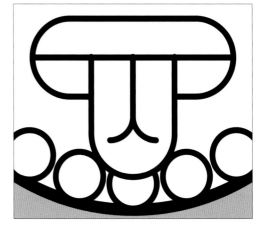

Figure 2-95.

- There are three types of stroke caps: *butt cap, round cap,* and *projecting cap.* These caps determine how a path's endpoints appear.

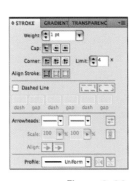

Figure 2-96.

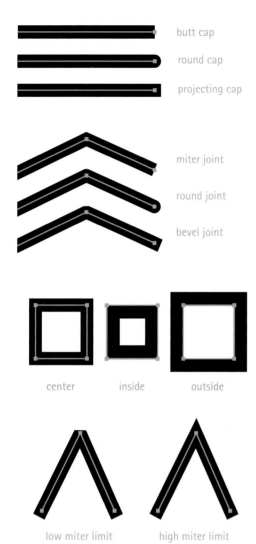

butt cap

round cap

projecting cap

miter joint

round joint

bevel joint

center  inside  outside

low miter limit  high miter limit

Figure 2-97.

Figure 2-98.

- Likewise, there are three types of joins: *miter join*, *round join*, and *bevel join*. These affect the appearance of a path's corner points.

- The *miter limit* specifies how sharp the corners of acute angles can become. It's used in conjunction with the miter join option.

- The Align Stroke options determine the position of the stroke relative to the path. You can center the stroke on the path or have the stroke align entirely inside or outside the path.

- The dashed line options allow you make the stroke a dashed line—and even specify the length of the dashes and the gaps between them independently.

- New in CS5, the arrowhead options allow you to add arrowheads to your strokes, specifying a host of parameters. (In CS4, the arrowheads were created as effects.)

- Also new in CS5 is the stroke profile, which allows you to vary the width of the stroke.

Figure 2-97 demonstrates some of the stroke options, with the underlying paths in orange.

17. *Change the cap on the outside of the tongue.* Now back to our regularly scheduled artwork. See the little round bits sticking up over the seam of the lip? Those are round caps on the tongue strokes, and they just won't do. Select the outside U-shaped part of the tongue by Alt-clicking (Option-clicking) with the white arrow tool. (It's still part of a group, so you can't select it with the black arrow tool.) Switch the cap type to a butt cap. (No snickers, please.) That takes care of two of the problem spots.

18. *Change the cap on the tongue cleft strokes.* The cleft of the tongue is made up of two strokes (one forks left, the other right). Select them both by Alt-clicking the first and Shift+Alt-clicking the second. (That's Option-click and Shift-Option-click for you Mac users.) Switch the cap style to butt cap. That fixes the issue along the lip seam but unfortunately also changes the ends of the cleft, as seen in Figure 2-98. This method won't work; press Ctrl+Z (⌘-Z) to undo.

19. *Select the problem points and nudge them down.* The only solution we have is to nudge the problem points down because Illustrator won't allow us to specify two different cap styles on the same path. Select the problem points by marqueeing with

the white arrow tool in a small square around the top of the tongue cleft.

Whoa! Instead of selecting just those points, you've selected a slew of paths, as indicated by the mess of orange now on your screen. You could try to select the points by simply clicking them, but given all the objects that overlap, it would be a futile effort. Here, we need to take advantage of Illustrator's *isolation mode.*

First, make sure nothing is selected by pressing Ctrl+Shift+A (or ⌘-Shift-A). Switch to the black arrow tool and double-click the tongue cleft. Illustrator now enters isolation mode, dimming all the art except the face elements you double-clicked. You can now work with the isolated artwork without the worry of selecting other objects. (Indeed, you can't select any of the dimmed artwork, no matter what.)

Switch back to the white arrow tool, marquee around the problem points, and nudge them down by pressing the ↓ key. Exit isolation mode by clicking the ⇦ in the upper-left corner of the window (you may need to click it twice) or by pressing the Esc key. The tongue is now perfected, as shown in Figure 2-99.

20. *Create a pattern swatch.* Now for the promised treat. Bring up your **Swatches** panel. With the black arrow tool, select the nose shape, and drag it into the Swatches panel. Illustrator creates a new pattern swatch, based on the shape of the nose.

Deselect the nose, and then double-click the swatch. Give it a name like "Nose" and click **OK**.

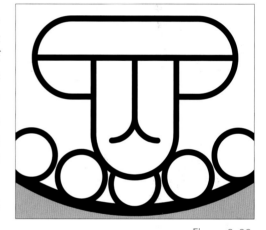

Figure 2-99.

---

It's important to deselect the nose before you double-click the swatch to edit it; otherwise, you'll apply the Nose swatch to the nose itself! The results aren't pretty. If you accidentally do this, just press Ctrl+Z (⌘-Z) to undo.

---

21. *Examine the Appearance settings for one of the circles.* If you're still zoomed in on the face, zoom out so you can see all your artwork. Select the outermost circle filled with Medium Clay (the second circle in with a black stroke). Bring up the **Appearance** panel by choosing **Window→Appearance** or by pressing Shift+F6.

You'll see values for the stroke, fill, and opacity of the selected shape. Working with Illustrator, you'll spend a lot of time in the Appearance panel; this is the Appearance panel teaser.

22. **Duplicate the Fill value.** Click the **Fill** entry to select it. Press the ⬓ icon at the bottom of the Appearance panel to duplicate the fill. It may seem strange to have two fills assigned to the same object. Just one more example of the madness that is Illustrator. We'll take advantage of this double-fill in the next step.

23. **Apply the Nose swatch to the first of the fills.** You should see ⬇ next to the fill swatch in the first Fill entry. (If not, click the entry to make sure it's active.) From the pop-up menu, choose the **Nose** swatch. Presto! Your artwork updates with a tiled pattern (from a swatch you created)—and it doesn't even look like noses at all.

It's time to put the *tonalpohualli* to rest. You've worked hard to create the simply stunning piece of art shown in Figure 2-100—and all through the use of primitives. Stacking, slicing, stitching together—you've run the gamut of manipulating these shapes, and it will serve you well in the lessons to come.

Figure 2-100.

# WHAT DID YOU LEARN?

Match the key concept in the numbered list below with the letter of the phrase that best describes it. Answers appear upside-down at the bottom of the page.

## Key Concepts

1. Open path
2. Closed path
3. Join
4. Average
5. Anchor point
6. Center point
7. Constraint axes
8. Bounding box
9. Handle
10. RGB
11. CMYK
12. Swatch

## Descriptions

A. A color mode used primarily for print.

B. A function that makes two points coincident without combining them.

C. A rectangular frame drawn around a path.

D. A point that is not drawn in the path but acts as a snapping point for the middle of the shape.

E. A continuous path with no endpoints.

F. A point on a bounding box that provide access to scale and rotate functions.

G. A function that combines two points if they are coincident; otherwise, it connects the two points with a straight segment.

H. The corner point, endpoint, or curve point location on a path.

I. A path with two endpoints.

J. A color mode used primarily for the screen.

K. A predefined color, pattern, or gradient.

L. A setting that determines the angle of all artwork drawn in Illustrator.

## Answers

1I, 2E, 3G, 4B, 5H, 6D, 7L, 8C, 9F, 10J, 11A, 12K

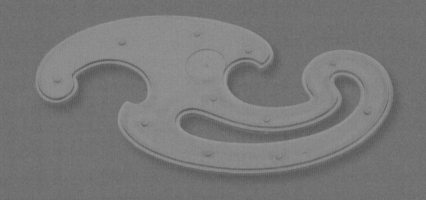

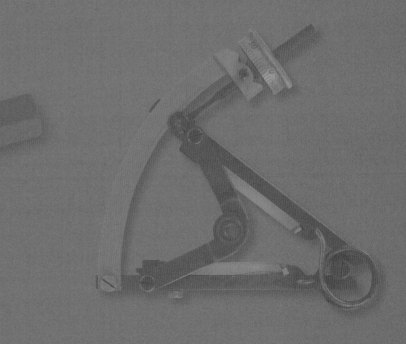

# USING THE PEN TOOL

**WHILE LINES AND SHAPES** are the building blocks of any illustration, the line and shape tools we saw in the last lesson aren't by any means the only way to create them. The pen tool (✒) is Illustrator's most powerful drawing tool and perhaps the most difficult to master. It allows you to draw open and closed paths of any shape you can imagine; you aren't limited to simple, regular shapes. You can also manipulate and edit paths with infinite variety, from the most basic to the very complex (see Figure 3-1). Even the letters you are reading now began as paths drawn by a pen tool, crafted and shaped by the skilled hands of a type designer.

The pen tool may seem a bit daunting at first, and it does take some practice to use skillfully. Throughout this lesson I will guide you through the basics of bending the pen tool to your will, but it is a two-way street. If you're willing to have patience, the pen tool in turn will give you control. One very sound piece of advice: Don't be afraid to experiment. (Heck, that's what Undo is for.) Play around drawing different shapes, using different techniques. See how moving points this way or that changes the shape. While I cover the "how's" of using the pen tool, mastering it requires a mix of experience and experimentation.

Shapes drawn with the pen tool can be fairly simple...

...or maddeningly complex.

Hibiscus by pringletta; floral border by Julio E. Chandia. Both from iStockPhoto.com.

Figure 3-1.

MIDDLESEX FLORIST

# ABOUT THIS LESSON

## Project Files

Before beginning the exercises, make sure you've downloaded the lesson files from *www.oreilly.com/go/Deke-IllustratorCS5*, as directed in Step 2 on page xiv of the Preface. This should result in a folder called *Lesson Files-Alcs5 1on1* on your desktop. We'll be working with the files inside the *Lesson 03* subfolder.

It's time to take advantage of Illustrator's basic drawing functions, including the ubiquitous pen tool—a tool that is simple to learn, yet requires patience and practice to master. In this lesson, you'll learn how to:

## Video Lesson 3: The Pen Tool

With the powerful pen tool, you can create any freeform shape you want. Although indisputably useful and flexible, this tool also has a reputation for being hard to understand, let alone master. In this video, I'll show you the basics of working with the pen tool, so that with a little practice you can draw any path outline you need.

To see the pen tool at work, visit *www.oreilly.com/go/deke-IllustratorCS5*. Click the **Watch** button to view the lesson online or the **Download** button to save it to your computer. During the video, you'll learn these shortcuts:

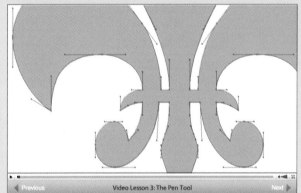

| Operation | Windows shortcut | Macintosh shortcut |
| --- | --- | --- |
| Select the pen tool | Press the P key | Press the P key |
| Expand (or "twirl open") a layer | Click the ▶ before the layer name | Click the ▶ before the layer name |
| Select the black or white arrow | Press the V or A key | Press the V or A key |
| Target (or "meatball") an object | Click the ◎ in the Layers panel | Click the ◎ in the Layers panel |
| Hide all panels or just those on the right | Press the Tab key or Shift+Tab | Press the Tab key or Shift-Tab |
| Toggle between the view modes | Ctrl+Y | ⌘-Y |
| Cut or redirect a control handle | Alt-click or -drag the point | Option-click or -drag the point |
| Nudge a selected object | Press ↑, ↓, ←, or → | Press ↑, ↓, ←, or → |
| Clone a path outline | Ctrl+C, Ctrl+F | ⌘-C, ⌘-F |
| Join two open paths to form a closed one | Ctrl+J | ⌘-J |

# What Makes the
# Straight Line Bend

Shapes and lines consist of anchor points and paths, as you learned in the last lesson. You can think of the shape like a subway system: Anchor points are the stations, and paths are the tracks. You can move a point, but the path still has to travel through it, so the path follows the point, wherever you move it. Anchor points are just that—they anchor the path in specific locations.

You can also think of anchor points as a dot-to-dot puzzle. Each anchor point is a dot, and you connect those dots with what Illustrator refers to as a *segment*, so-called because it is just one piece of the whole path.

Unlike dot-to-dot puzzles, however, segments in Illustrator don't have to be straight; they're free to curve. But how does Illustrator know which way to curve the segment? And by how much?

That's where Illustrator relies on another kind of point. Not an anchor point, mind you, because this point is not part of the path, but a point that I refer to as a *control handle* (or just *handle* for short). Control handles have a more indirect, almost gravitational, effect on the shape of a path. Pull the control handle one way, the path bends toward it; push it the other way, and the path is repelled, as in Figure 3-2. (The original path is shown in light gray for comparison.) These control handles are what make Illustrator; they've been there since the very beginning, one of Adobe's first patents. And the pen tool is the only way to have complete control of these handles as you draw. (Control handles are first covered in the exercise "Drawing Fluid Bézier Curves" on page 96.)

In this lesson, we'll start out using the pen tool to draw straight-sided polygons, eschewing the control handles until later on in the lesson. With a little perseverance, by the end of this lesson you'll have created a full-fledged piece of vector art, using only a handful of paths.

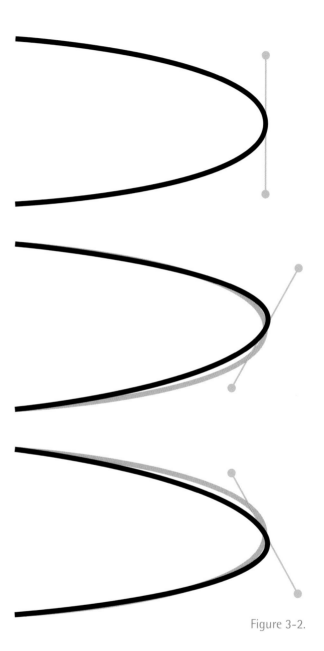

Figure 3-2.

## Establishing a Bitmapped Tracing Template

In the previous lesson, I demonstrated how to draw artwork using a tracing template based on Illustrator paths. A much more common way to work is to take a digital image—whether a photograph or a scan of traditionally drawn pen-and-paper art—and use that image as a tracing template to recreate the art in Illustrator.

Throughout this lesson we'll be recreating artwork based on a pictograph I saw at Agawa Rock in Ontario, along the shore of Lake Superior. The pictograph is of a *mishipizheu*, or underwater panther, painted by the native Ojibwe people.

1. *Examine the evolution of the artwork.* Open the Bridge by choosing **File→Browse in Bridge** or pressing Ctrl+Alt+O (⌘-Option-O on the Mac). Conversely, you can click the ▸Br icon in the application bar. From the Favorites panel in the upper left, navigate to the *Lesson 03* folder inside the *Lesson Files-AIcs5 1on1* folder, as seen in Figure 3-3. (This assumes you followed the instructions in Step 10 on page 15 in Lesson 1.) Inside the *Original* subfolder, you should see three bitmap images: *Mishipizheu.jpg*, *Mishi sketch.jpg*, and *Mishi painting.jpg*.

   The first file, *Mishipizheu.jpg*, is the original photograph I took at Agawa Rock, while *Mishi sketch.jpg* is a rough digital sketch I created in Photoshop. Finally, *Mishi painting.jpg* is a digital photograph I took of an acrylic underpainting I made, inspired by the original photo. (I subsequently ruined the painting, but that's another story.) We'll use this final image for our tracing template.

2. *Open the Illustrator file.* After navigating back up to the main *Lesson 03* folder, double-click the file *Mishi drawing.ai* to open it in Illustrator. You should see a document with

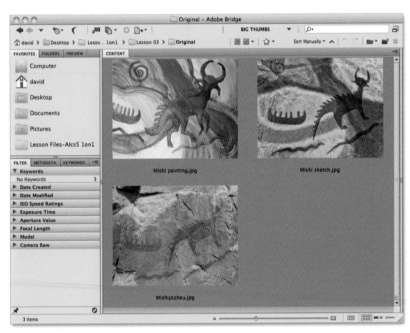

Figure 3-3.

two layers, as shown in Figure 3-4. (If you
don't see the **Layers** panel, press the F7 key
to bring it to the front.)

3. *Delete the existing template layer.* While it's
great that you have the template layer already
in this file, we need to delete it to recreate the
tracing template. Delete the layer by dragging
it to the trash can icon at the bottom of the
panel, or by selecting the layer and choosing
**Delete "Template"** from the ▾≡ menu. If you
see a warning dialog, click **Yes** to dismiss it;
you're sure you want to delete the layer.

4. *Import the tracing template into the
file.* Choose the **File→Place** command;
the resulting **Place** dialog box is shown in
Figure 3-5. There are a couple of options in
this dialog box that you should note:

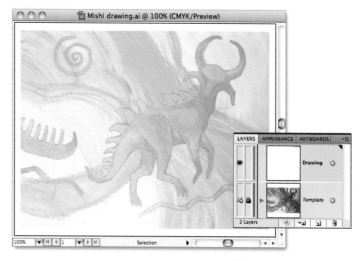

Figure 3-4.

- The **Link** check box determines whether Illustrator *links* to the selected file or *embeds* a copy of
  the file inside the Illustrator document. If you're
  concerned you might lose your original file, you
  can embed it so a copy is saved with your illustration—but I generally don't recommend this
  option. Doing so increases the document size
  significantly and makes it more difficult to edit
  the embedded artwork. This option should be
  turned on by default.

- The Template check box instructs Illustrator
  to automatically perform a bevy of steps when
  placing the file. Choose *Mishi painting.jpg* from
  the *Originals* folder, make sure the **Template**
  box is selected, and then click the **Place** button.

Figure 3-5.

Because you selected the Template check box, Illustrator automatically created a new layer behind all the other layers, placed
the image on this layer, locked the layer, and dimmed the artwork. Unfortunately, the artwork may or may not be aligned
to the artboard; we'll fix that in the next few steps.

5. *Unlock the template layer and select the artwork.* In the **Layers** panel, click the 🔒 icon to unlock the **Template** layer. Then,
   using the black arrow tool, click somewhere along the edge of
   the artwork to select it.

Figure 3-6.

Figure 3-7.

6. *Align the artwork.* From the control panel, shown in Figure 3-6, make sure the align to artboard icon (⊞) is selected. A series of icons will now appear on the right; click the ≞ icon and then the ⬚ icon to align the artwork to the artboard by horizontal and vertical centers respectively.

7. *Lock the layer and change its options.* Click the empty box to the left of the **Template** layer name to relock the layer. Double-click the layer name to bring up the **Layer Options** dialog box shown in Figure 3-7, and rename the layer "Template."

You'll see a few other options in the dialog box. The Template check box was set automatically by Illustrator, and as we'll see later, it ensures that the layer will be visible in both preview and outline modes. The **Dim Images** setting specifies the percentage bitmapped images should be dimmed to. (It has no effect on vector-based shapes.) Change this value to 35% and click **OK**.

That's it! You now have a tracing template, ready to use to create your illustrated mishipizheu—which you'll start in the very next exercise. Save your file as "Mishi tracing.ai" or something similar before moving on.

## Making Free-Form Polygons and Spline Curves

Now that you've seen how to create a tracing template, it's time to put it to good use. In this exercise, you'll use the pen tool to trace the strange-looking canoe (or is it a giant comb?) at the far left of the image. The pen tool launched Illustrator more than 20 years ago and is arguably still the most powerful and essential tool in Illustrator today. Although using the pen tool requires patience, it affords you the most control over your artwork—you create each path one point at a time. You'll start by drawing the simplest shapes the pen tool offers: free-form polygons.

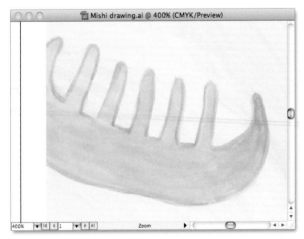

Figure 3-8.

1. *Open your tracing template.* If you have the file open from the last exercise, great; if not, open the file you saved at the end of the last exercise or the *Mishi drawing.ai* file in the *Lesson 03* folder.

2. *Zoom in on the canoe.* Select the ⚲ tool from the toolbar (or press the Z key). Click a few times on the canoe to zoom in closely on that part of the artwork, as shown in Figure 3-8. Make sure the Drawing layer is active before proceeding.

3. *Select and examine the pen tool.* Select the pen tool by clicking the ✍ tool in the toolbox or pressing the P key. You'll notice that the pen tool appears as ✍ₓ when it's over the artwork. What does that little *x* mean? It's Illustrator's way of letting you know that the next click you make will create a new path. (You'll see the *x* vanish in the next step.)

4. *Place your first six points.* With the pen tool, click on each of the five points shown in Figure 3-9 to start tracing the canoe. The first click creates a single point, and when you move the cursor away, the *x* is gone, and the pen tool now appears as ✍. Each subsequent click creates a new point and connects that point to the previous one, creating a path. After you've drawn your six points, your path should look like Figure 3-10.

5. *Switch to outline mode.* Houston, we have a problem. While your path is roughly following the outline of the canoe, the white fill of the path now covers the tracing template to such an extent that the template is no longer usable. This is easy enough to fix—what I want you to do is switch to outline mode by pressing Ctrl+Y (⌘-Y on the Mac). The path switches to outline mode, but as I discussed in Step 7 on page 90, the tracing template remains visible, as seen in Figure 3-11.

6. *Add a slew of other points.* Keep clicking counter-clockwise around the outline of the canoe, using the dots shown in Figure 3-12 on the next page as reference. When you get to the final point and are ready to click again on the starting point, notice that your cursor changes to ✍ₒ. The little circle indicates that you are about to close the path. Click to close the path.

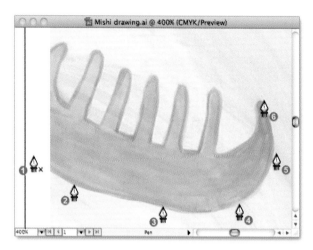

Figure 3-9.

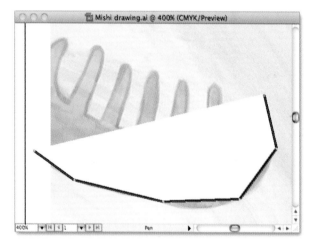

Figure 3-10.

---

PEARL OF ⬤ WISDOM

If you manage to deselect the path, don't panic. Keep an eye on your pen cursor; ✍ₓ means you'll start a new path, which you don't want. However, if you move the cursor over the last point on the path, your cursor will change to look like ✍. Clicking with this cursor reselects the path and allows you to pick up where you left off. Another possible pitfall: You place a point where you don't want one. You can always press Ctrl+Z (⌘-Z) to undo the point—but there's a little trick you can use, as long as the mouse button is still pressed. With the mouse button still down, press and hold the spacebar. You can now drag the current point; when it's in the desired position, release the mouse button first, then the spacebar.

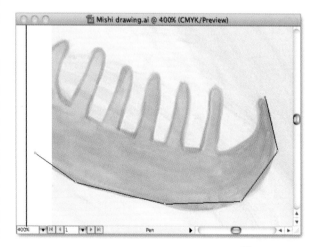

Figure 3-11.

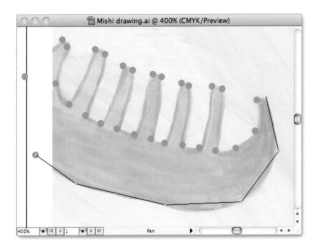

Figure 3-12.

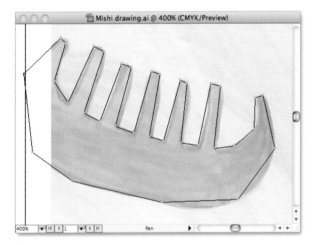

Figure 3-13.

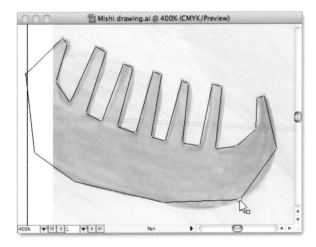

Figure 3-14.

7. *Adjust the canoe using the white arrow tool.* Now you have a complete path, as shown in Figure 3-13, but if you're a perfectionist like me, you may not like how some of the segments aren't terribly close to the original outline. To change a segment, you can adjust individual points with the white arrow tool. (Adobe refers to the white arrow tool as the direct selection tool.) Select it by clicking the ⬚ tool in the toolbar or pressing the A key.

Why the white arrow tool and not the black arrow tool? The white arrow tool allows you to select individual points, while the black arrow tool always selects the entire path.

Armed with the white arrow, click anywhere away from the path to make sure it's deselected—or alternatively press Ctrl+Shift+A (⌘-Shift-A on the Mac). When you hover your cursor over a point, your cursor will change to ⬚, and you'll see a white highlight square showing you the point, as in Figure 3-14. Click to select the point, and drag the point to the desired position. Use your discretion as to what points need to be adjusted, and don't worry about making things perfect. (I tweaked some of the points around the oarsmen.) We'll see a few more tricks in the next step.

PEARL OF WISDOM

You've probably seen the flurry of green smart guides as you've been drawing this path. If the automatic snapping behavior of the smart guides is getting in your way (as it was mine), you can temporarily turn off the guides by pressing Ctrl+U (⌘-U).

8. *Make more tweaks with the pen and white arrow tools.* Your canoe should be looking better, but there may still be room for improvement. Select the pen tool (by pressing the P key) to look at some of the other options you can use to edit paths.

If you click and hold the pen tool to show the flyout menu, you'll see a few other options, shown in **Figure 3-15** on the facing page: add anchor point tool, delete anchor point tool, and convert anchor point tool. These tools are certainly useful, but there's almost never a need to select them from the flyout menu because they are available directly from within the pen tool itself—something we'll see in the rest of this step and in the sidebar "The Three Kinds of Anchor Points" on page 98.)

- As you move your cursor over an existing segment, the pen tool changes to ♦+, indicating that you will add an anchor point if you click.

- If you move your cursor over an existing point, the pen tool changes to ♦-. This indicates that clicking the point will delete it, and Illustrator will reconnect the two adjacent points on the path.

- Pressing the Ctrl key (the ⌘ key on the Mac) temporarily switches to the last arrow tool you used, which in this case is the white arrow tool. The white arrow tool, just as in the previous step, will let you move individual points in the path, including ones you've just created.

Now that you know what these tools do, use them to further refine your canoe outline. I added a point to each side of the canoe to make the outside a little rounder, and moved a few other points around. Be careful when creating a new point: Click and release the mouse button to create the new point, then press the Ctrl (⌘) key, and finally drag the point to the desired location. If you click and drag without releasing the mouse button, you'll create a smooth point, which we haven't yet discussed. (They're first discussed in the next exercise, "Drawing Fluid Bézier Curves") If you accidentally create a smooth point, press Ctrl+Z or ⌘-Z to undo. You should end up with something similar to Figure 3-16.

9. *Round off the canoe with the Round Corners command.* The outline of the canoe is now quite close to the tracing template, but it is still too angular. We'll solve this problem by applying a *live effect.* (While live effects aren't described in full until Lesson 10, consider this a teaser.) From the **Effect** menu, choose **Stylize→Round Corners** to open the **Round Corners** dialog box, as pictured in Figure 3-17. The Radius (for me, at least) defaults to 10 pt. Select the **Preview** box so you can see the effect that Round Corners will have on the artwork.

Disappointingly, nothing seems to happen. That is because Round Corners, being a live effect, does not change the shape of the path in Illustrator—rather, it changes how the stroke is drawn, and the stroke can be seen only in preview mode. For the time being, leave

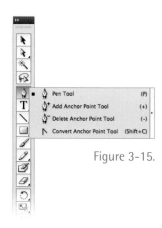

Figure 3-15.

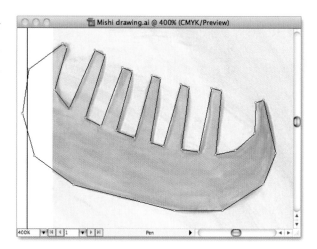

Figure 3-16.

Figure 3-17.

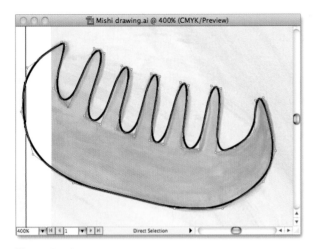

Figure 3-18.

Figure 3-19.

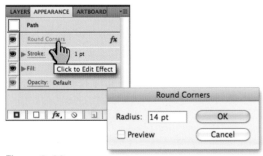

Figure 3-20.

the default Radius as is and click **OK**, having faith that something has, in fact, changed.

10. *Switch to preview mode, and change the canoe's fill.* Press Ctrl+Y (⌘-Y on the Mac) to switch back to preview mode. You should now see your rounded canoe, stroked with black, filled with white. Here's what I want you to do:

- Make sure the fill is active (the icon at the bottom of the toolbox should look like ▣). If the fill is not active, press X.

- Set the fill to None by clicking the ☑ icon or pressing the ⟨ key.

You should now be able to see through your rounded canoe, as in Figure 3-18.

11. *Edit the round corners effect.* The rounded corners help, but the effect isn't perfect. Once again, choose **Stylize→Round Corners** from the **Effect** menu. Illustrator pops up the rather obtuse warning shown in Figure 3-19. What gives?

Illustrator is warning you that you are about to apply a second helping of the round corners effect, which we definitely don't want—we want to edit the original effect. Click **Cancel** to dismiss the warning.

To edit the original effect, bring up the **Appearance** panel, shown in Figure 3-20, by pressing Shift+F6 or choosing **Appearance** from the **Window** menu. Click the underlined **Round Corners** to bring up the **Round Corners** dialog box. (Astute readers may notice that the dialog box from Figure 3-19 says to double-click the name of the effect; the dialog box is incorrect because only a single click is necessary.) Change the **Radius** value to 14 pt, and click **OK**.

Why did I choose such a high radius value when it completely rounded the stylized oarsmen in the canoe? The high radius value works best for the outside of the canoe, and I have a trick to square off the oarsmen to better match the original sketch, which you'll see in the next step.

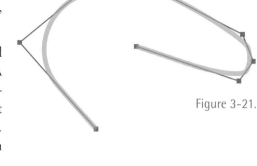

Figure 3-21.

12. *Add points to fix the oarsmen.* To square off the oarsmen, we'll take advantage of the way Illustrator handles spline curves. A *spline curve,* as shown with its base path in Figure 3-21, follows the path and runs along the segments between points, but curves away from the points themselves to smooth the corners. (This differs from how Illustrator handles Bézier curves, which we discuss in the next lesson.)

Illustrator uses spline curves to calculate how to draw the round corners effect, a fact you can exploit to your advantage here. If you look closely at the right side of Figure 3-21, you'll see that the curves are much less rounded, due to the fact that there isn't enough room between the points for Illustrator to achieve a smooth curve.

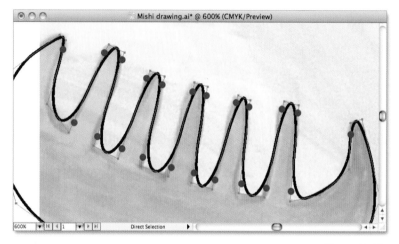

Figure 3-22.

Now to put the spline curves into practice. Press the P key to switch to the pen tool (if it isn't still active), and add points to the path as shown in Figure 3-22, being careful to click near *but not on* the existing points. (It helps to zoom in; if you click an existing point and accidentally delete it, press Ctrl+Z or ⌘-Z) to undo. There are close to two dozen points to add, but adding them should go quickly. As you add each point, you'll see the curves become more angular but still keep a smooth edge. Your final result should look like Figure 3-23.

That's it for this exercise. Be sure to save your work. We'll pick up this file again in the next exercise, where you'll draw your first honest-to-goodness curved path as we start tracing the mishipizheu.

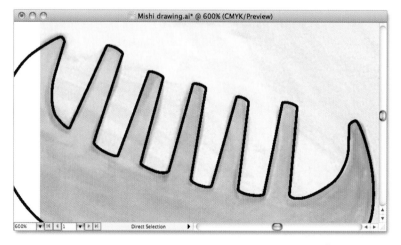

Figure 3-23.

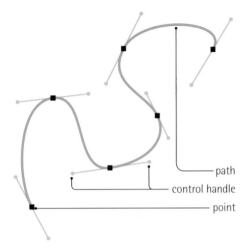

path
control handle
point

Figure 3-24.

# Drawing Fluid Bézier Curves

So far we've seen how to draw corner points with the pen tool, and even soften those corner points using spline curves via Illustrator's round corners effect. But the true power of the pen tool, and of curves, can be realized only by using Bézier curves and the two new types of points it introduces: the smooth point and the cusp point. (For a full explanation of the different types of points, see the sidebar "The Three Kinds of Anchor Points" on page 98.)

*Bézier curves* are calculated differently than spline curves. Rather than connecting to the center of each segment and curving to avoid the corner points as spline curves do, Bézier curves run through each point, and the control handles determine how the path bends, as illustrated in Figure 3-24. (The path is shown in light blue, the points in dark blue, and the control handles in green.) With a Bézier curve, the path always bends toward the control handle, almost gravitationally. Also unlike spline curves, Bézier curves affect the path itself, rather than simply how the path is rendered.

In this exercise, we'll trace the head of the fearsome underwater panther, the fabled mishipizheu, taking full advantage of the Bézier curves that the pen tool makes available.

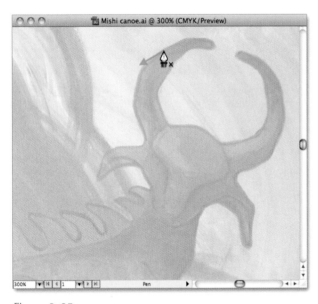

Figure 3-25.

1. *Open the artwork.* If you have your file from the preceding exercise, open it now. Otherwise, you can open an in-progress document called *Mishi canoe.ai*, found in the *Lesson 03* subfolder inside the *Lesson Files-AIcs5 1on1* folder. You should see the now-familiar tracing template as well as a completed canoe.

2. *Add your first point.* First, confirm that your fill is set to None. Zoom in close to the mishipizheu's head, as shown in Figure 3-25. Press the P key to make the pen tool active. Instead of clicking to add a point (which would add a corner point), I want you to drag from the pen pointer to the end of the arrow seen in Figure 3-25, releasing the mouse button when you roughly reach the spot marked by the arrowhead. This creates a smooth point, complete with control handles.

The farther you drag from the start, the longer the control handle. A longer control handle exerts more "pull" on the path, pulling it farther from a straight segment. While you won't see any difference on this first point, as you add more points to your path the effect will become clear.

3. *Add four additional points.* Drag four additional points as shown in Figure 3-26. Click and hold at each start point, drag to the arrowhead, and then release the mouse button. You should get a nice, smooth path tracing the left edge of the mishipizheu's face.

---

As you create each point, note how the control handles always remain opposed to one another—that is, wherever you drag the control handle under your cursor, the other control handle is 180 degrees from it. This behavior what defines a smooth point.

---

4. *Adjust the path as necessary.* Switch to the white arrow tool by pressing the A key. Using the white arrow tool, you can move the anchor points, just as you did in the previous exercise—but you can also adjust the control handles. Move the control handles around to see how they affect the path. Pushing the control handle toward the path makes the curve shallower; pulling the handle away makes the curve more pronounced. Try to line up the path as best as possible with the tracing template.

You're not limited to just moving points and control handles. You can move entire path segments; click the center of a path segment and drag it left or right to adjust the control handles at either end simultaneously, increasing or decreasing the curve. Your final result should look something like Figure 3-27.

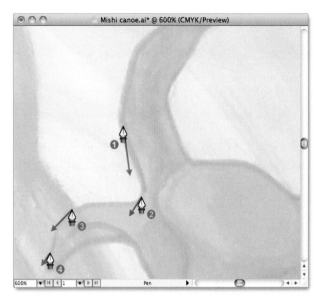

Figure 3-26.

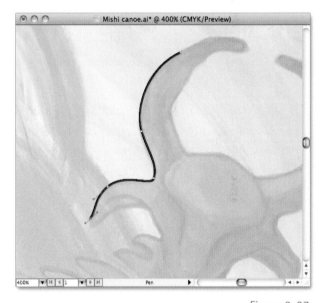

Figure 3-27.

**PEARL OF WISDOM**

Working with Bézier curves can be daunting at first, but there are some guidelines to making sure your curves look smooth and consistent. One rule: When working with Bézier curves, each segment should have a control handle at both ends or at neither end. Mixing smooth points with corner points can create some odd flattening of the path's curves, so is best avoided. (For sharp corners, use cusp points, which are explained in the next step.) Another helpful guideline: The control handles should each be approximately $1/3$ the length of the segment—so the segment would be roughly $1/3$ initial control handle, $1/3$ open, $1/3$ final control handle, as in **Figure 3-28**. If you want to adjust a control handle so that it's significantly longer, shorten the other control handle to maintain about $1/3$ of the open segment.

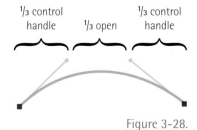

$1/3$ control handle   $1/3$ open   $1/3$ control handle

Figure 3-28.

5. *Add the first cusp point to continue the path.* Once you're satisfied with the start of your path, you're

# The Three Kinds of Anchor Points

Three kinds of anchor points are available in Illustrator: corner points, smooth points, and cusp points, shown in the figure on the right. The dimmed versions on the right side of the figure show how each type of point is drawn; let's examine these points in more detail.

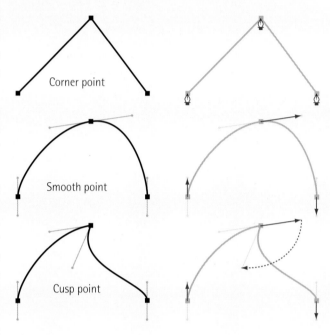

Corner point

Smooth point

Cusp point

The *corner point* is the simplest of the points in Illustrator. It has no control handles and is drawn by simply clicking where you would like the points to be with the pen tool. Corner points are by default used in all regular and irregular polygons.

The *smooth point* is the basic point used in Bézier curves. Smooth points are drawn by clicking at the point's desired location, and dragging out the control handle, as indicated by the purple arrows in the figure. The control handles for smooth points are always directly opposed; that is to say, there is always 180 degrees between them. Smooth points are used automatically in all circles, ellipses, and spirals.

Lastly, the *cusp point* is the most complex point in Illustrator. Basically, you can think of it as a hybrid of a corner point and a smooth point. While it has two control handles, like a smooth point, those handles are joined at an angle, like a corner point. Being the most complex of points, it's also the most difficult to draw. You start by drawing the same way you would draw a smooth point, but once you have the trailing control handle in place (the one opposite your mouse cursor), press and hold the Alt key (the Option key on the Mac), and move the second control handle into place (indicated by the dotted purple arrow in the figure above). Only custom shapes you draw take advantage of cusp points; none of the standard Illustrator shapes include them.

Knowing how to draw these points is all well and good, but what if you've already drawn a point and now realize it's the wrong kind? You have several options for converting points from one type to another:

- *Convert the point using the buttons in the control panel.* When you have an anchor point selected, the context-sensitive control panel will show the following options:

The first option converts the selected point to a corner point; the second, to a smooth point. While it's quick and easy, it offers nothing in the way of control and is my least preferred method for converting points.

- *Use the convert anchor point tool.* You can access the convert anchor point tool (Ν) from the flyout menu under the pen tool. With this tool, click a point to convert it to a corner point. Drag from a point to convert the point to a smooth point. Drag from a point and then Alt-drag (or Option-drag) to convert the point to a cusp point.

- *Access the convert anchor point tool on-the-fly.* If you want to be a true power user, don't bother switching tools back and forth; you can access the convert anchor point tool at any point while using the pen tool. Press and hold the Alt (or Option) key and your cursor will change to Ν, indicating that the convert anchor point tool is active. You can click or drag from a point, just as you can with the standard version of the tool. However, to create a cusp point (since the Alt/Option key is already held down), drag your first control handle as you usually would, release the mouse button, and then, still with the Alt (Option) key pressed, drag the second control handle into place.

ready to continue the path around the floppy ear and on to the neck and scales along the spine. Reactivating the path and drawing the cusp point can be a little tricky, so here's what you should do step-by-step:

- Switch to the pen tool by pressing the P key.

- Move your mouse over the bottom point on the path until your cursor changes to ♦.

- Drag and drop as indicated by the blue arrow in Figure 3-29 to make the path active again. (The reason for the drag is to preserve the point as a smooth point; simply clicking the point to reactivate the path would convert the point to a corner point.)

- Click at the point indicated by the start of the green arrow in Figure 3-29 to add an anchor point. Drag and drop to the end to pull out the first control handle. Then, while keeping the mouse button down, press the Alt (or Option) key, and drag along the second arrow to the end. Release the mouse button.

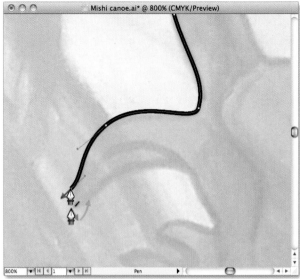

Figure 3-29.

You'll notice that with the Alt (Option) key held down, the second control handle now pivots independently of the first. The Alt (Option) key is essential for both drawing cusp points and converting smooth points to cusp points (as I'll demonstrate in the next step). Congratulations on your first cusp point—but there are more.

6. *Add more points using the methods learned so far.* Using the markers in Figure 3-30 as a guide, add more smooth and cusp points to the path to trace along the neck and over the first four scales on the mishipizheu's back. The darker arrows indicate the primary drag; the lighter arrows of the same color indicate the Alt-drag (or Option-drag). Follow the tracing template as best you can, but don't worry too much if you're off here and there; you'll be adjusting the path next.

7. *Make the control handles visible for multiple points.* If your path looks anything like mine, it's passable, but there's

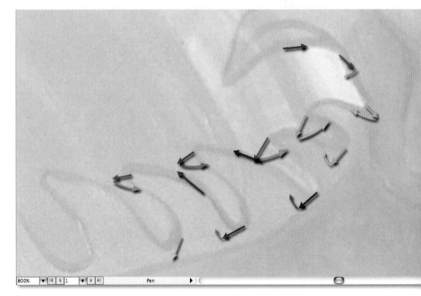

Figure 3-30.

Some shortcuts are worth remembering when working with the pen tool. Remember the spacebar trick to move points back on page 91? It works with smooth and cusp points as well, but with these points you want to release the spacebar before you release the mouse. (Releasing the spacebar first allows you to continue adjusting the control handles after you've moved the point.) If you accidentally draw a smooth point where you had intended to draw a cusp point, no problem. While holding the Alt (or Option) key, drag from the point. You'll draw the second control handle out as you drag, converting the smooth point to a cusp point on-the-fly.

Figure 3-31.

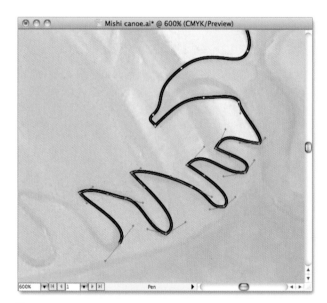

Figure 3-32.

room for improvement, especially along the spiky scales down the creature's spine. Unfortunately, adjusting control handles for each individual point can get tedious—trying to find the point to click it, adjusting its control handles, then searching for the next point to edit.

Thankfully, there's an easier way. Since CS3, Illustrator has allowed you to edit the control handles of multiple points, but the feature is well-hidden. Here's what you need to do:

• Switch to the white arrow tool, and select a single point anywhere along the path.

• In the control bar, look for the handle icons pictured in Figure 3-31. Select the ⌖ icon, which shows handles for multiple selected anchor points.

• Marquee around the points of the spikes, as shown in Figure 3-32. You should now see the control handles for all selected points.

> You can also change the default for this setting by choosing **Preferences→Selection & Anchor Display** from the **Edit** menu (the **Illustrator** menu on the Mac) and making sure the Show Handles when Multiple Anchors are Selected box is selected.

8. *Adjust the control handles to refine the path.* Now that you can see all the control handles, adjust them to refine the path. You can move them individually without deselecting any points. Your path will invariably look a little different from mine; experiment with moving the control handles to get the path as close to the tracing template as possible. The adjusted path should look similar to Figure 3-33 on the next page.

That's it for this exercise. By all means, if you want to continue tracing the mishipizheu, don't let me stop you. It's excellent practice for getting comfortable using the pen tool. (You can take a peek at *Mishi paths.ai* in the *Lesson 03* folder if you want to see what my finished paths look like.) Save or discard your work as you see fit.

## Cutting, Separating, and Closing Paths

You've seen how to draw and edit paths, but we have a few operations left to cover—namely, how to cut a single path into separate paths and how to close a path. As with the other exercises in this lesson, the best tools at your disposal are the white arrow tool and the pen tool.

For the last exercise, I've provided a file with the complete path outlines of the mishipizheu. You'll split an existing path, learn how to draw multiple paths without leaving the pen tool, and close open paths. Finally, we'll wrap up the exercise by coloring our various paths to match the underlying painting.

1. *Open the artwork.* If you were dili-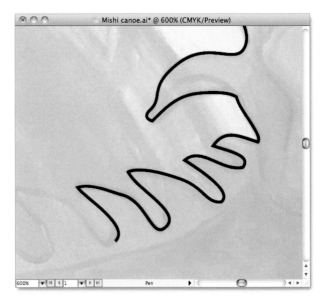
   gent and drew all the paths after the end of the last exercise, congratulations—and by all means use your file. Otherwise, open *Mishi paths.ai* located in the *Lesson 03* folder. You'll notice that this file contains a total of five paths for the water panther—one closed path that traces the outline of the body and scaly spine, and four open paths (one for the backbone, and three for the remaining legs), as shown in Figure 3-34.

Figure 3-33.

2. *Split the path that composes the backbone and muzzle.* The path that makes up the backbone also traces along the bottom edge of the creature's muzzle. I think the art would be much improved if these were two separate paths, and thankfully Illustrator gives us a way to do just that:

   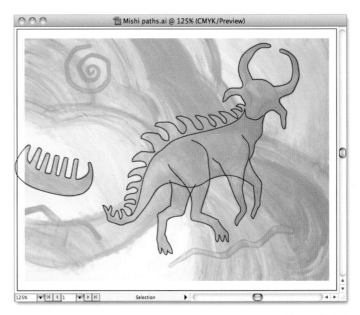

   Figure 3-34.

   • From the toolbox, select the scissors tool, or press the C key.

   • Position the crosshair cursor over the path approximately at the point shown in Figure 3-35 on the next page.

   • Click to split the path. You now have two distinct paths, even though they may be hard to see, as their endpoints overlap.

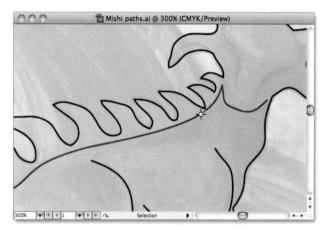

Figure 3-35.

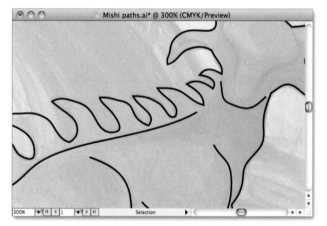

Figure 3-36.

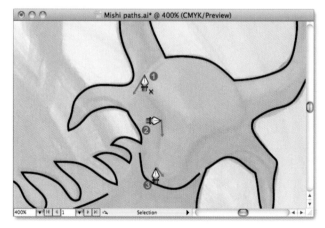

Figure 3-37.

3. *Open the space between the two paths.* If you're lucky, as I was, the point that was selected when you split the path was the endpoint of the muzzle portion. If that's the case, simply press the Backspace key (or Delete on the Mac) to get rid of that point and separate the muzzle from the backbone. If the lower part of the path is selected, however, you'll have to follow a few more steps to achieve the desired result:

- Switch to the white arrow tool by pressing the A key.

- Marquee around the points you just split.

- Shift-click the lower portion of the path to deselect it.

- Press the Backspace (or Delete) key.

You should end up with two separate paths like those in Figure 3-36.

4. *Draw the left contour of the face.* Switch to the pen tool, and draw the left side of the creature's face, using the arrows in Figure 3-37 as a guide.

5. *Draw the right side of the face.* The guide points you should use to draw the right side of the panther's face are shown in Figure 3-38 on the facing page. However, if you just start clicking, you'll continue the path you made in the last step, as indicated by the plain ♦ cursor—obviously not what you want. You need to deselect the current path first, and you can do so in two ways:

- Press Ctrl+Shift+A (⌘-Shift-A on the Mac) to deselect all. (You can also choose Deselect All from the Select menu.)

- Hold the Ctrl key (the ⌘ key) to temporarily access the white arrow tool and click anywhere off the path.

Now the pen cursor should once again indicate that it's ready to start a new path by appearing with the small *x*: ⬦ₓ. Draw the three points to create the right edge of the face.

6. *Close the rear leg path.* The leg closest to the tail is meant to appear behind the creature's body in the final artwork. I'd like to close this path with an arching segment to make sure that no gap is visible between the body and the leg. To close the path, do the following:

   - Deselect the currently active path.

   - Move the mouse over the top-left point in the shape, until the pen tool looks like ⬦.

   - Alt-drag (or Option-drag) from that point to the end of the first arrow in Figure 3-39. (I've dimmed the path to make the arrows easier to see.)

   - Move the pen tool over the top-right point; the cursor should indicate that you are about to close the path (⬦ₒ).

   - Alt-drag (Option-drag) from that point to the end of the second arrow.

---

Wondering why I had you Alt-drag from both points? Doing so created the arching shape. Simply clicking the two points would have connected them with a straight segment, which is not ideal. Even worse, if you had dragged with no key held, it would have converted the points to smooth points and completely changed the outline of the leg. By Alt-dragging (or Option-dragging), the original path was preserved, and these two points were joined by a cusp segment.

---

7. *Color the main body shape.* Assuming you're satisfied with your shapes, put the pen tool away and get ready to color the finished outlines. A color from the original painting would work best, and the eyedropper tool is the perfect tool to use. Here's how:

   - Switch to the black arrow tool by pressing the V key, and select the outermost path (the main body shape) by clicking it.

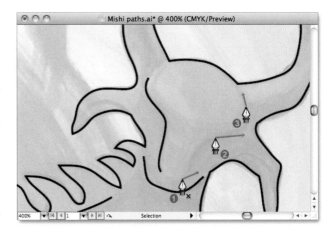

Figure 3-38.

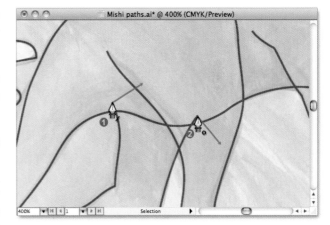

Figure 3-39.

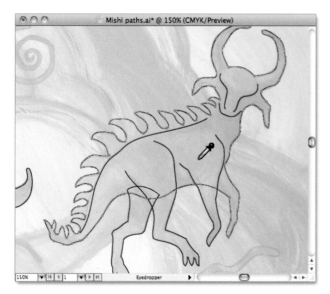

Figure 3-40.

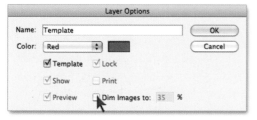

Figure 3-41.

Figure 3-42.

- Now, switch to the eyedropper tool (✐) by pressing the I key. Click somewhere in the reddish background, near the spot marked in Figure 3-40. That fills the shape with the color of the underlying pixel in the tracing template, but it also unfortunately gets rid of the stroke (as there is no stroke associated with the bitmap image). Press Ctrl+Z (⌘-Z) to undo.

---

If you're having trouble seeing the stroke, press Ctrl+H (⌘-H) to hide the selection. Press Ctrl+H (⌘-H) again to make the selection visible.

---

- This time, Shift-click with the eyedropper tool. This fills the active attribute with the eyedropped color. (The active attribute should be the fill; if your stroke changes color, press Ctrl+Z/⌘-Z to undo, press the X key to make the fill active, and click with the eyedropper again.) There is still an issue, however, as the eyedropper is picking up a sickly pink color, rather than the rich red of the original art. The reason? The eyedropper is grabbing the dimmed color, rather than the undimmed original. Again, press Ctrl+Z (⌘-Z) to undo.

- Bring up the **Layers** panel by pressing F7, and double-click the name of the **Template** layer. In the **Layers Options** dialog box shown in Figure 3-41, deselect the **Dim Images to** check box, and click **OK**. The artwork should now appear in full, vibrant color.

- Shift-click with the eyedropper one last time. Your shape should look like Figure 3-42.

8. *Color the other paths of the mishipizheu.* Now that the main body is filled with the appropriate color, you can start coloring it's time to color the legs. With the black arrow tool, marquee around the bottoms of the legs to select them, as shown in Figure 3-43. Then, back with the eyedropper tool, click somewhere along the stroke of the main body. *Voilà!* All the shapes are now consistently colored.

9. *Rearrange the stacking of the paths.* The color may be good, but unfortunately the legs are all wrong. The main body path is covering the legs that should appear in front. Select the main body with the black arrow tool, and press Ctrl+Shift+[ (⌘-Shift-[) to send that path to the back of the stack.

   While that fixes most of the legs (and reveals the muzzle and backbone paths), the far left leg is still problematic. Click that path with the black arrow tool, and again press Ctrl+Shift+[ (⌘-Shift-[). Your mishipizheu is now complete, and appears in Figure 3-44.

10. *Color the canoe.* One last shape to color. Select the canoe with the black arrow tool. Switch to the eyedropper tool, and Shift-click near the point indicated in Figure 3-45 to lift a rich green fill.

11. *Restore the dimming of the artwork.* Back in the **Layers** panel, double-click the name of the **Template** layer. In the **Layers Options** dialog box, check the **Dim Artwork to** box and click **OK**.

Figure 3-43.

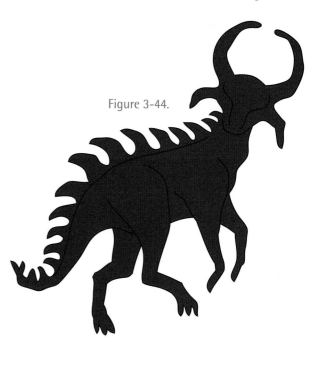

Figure 3-44.

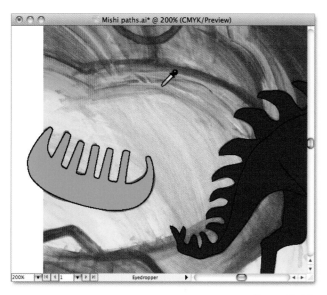

Figure 3-45.

And there you have it! As seen in Figure 3-46, you now have a vector-based pictograph, based on a bitmapped tracing template—artwork created entirely with the sometimes obtuse, occasionally frustrating, but ultimately limitless pen tool.

Figure 3-46.

# WHAT DID YOU LEARN?

Match the key concept in the numbered list below with the letter of the phrase that best describes it. Answers appear upside-down at the bottom of the page.

## Key Concepts

1. Pen tool
2. Control handle
3. Link option
4. Template option
5. White arrow tool
6. Black arrow tool
7. Spline curve
8. Bézier curve
9. Corner point
10. Smooth point
11. Cusp point
12. Eyedropper tool

## Descriptions

A. Also called the selection tool, this tool selects and manipulates entire paths.

B. The most powerful, flexible, and complex of Illustrator's drawing tools.

C. A point with two opposing control handles and no distinct angle in the path.

D. A point that is not part of the path but rather affects how the path curves.

E. An import option that specifies whether or not to embed a copy of the file in the Illustrator document.

F. A type of curve that follows the segments and curves away from the points. It does not affect the underlying path.

G. Also called the direct selection tool, this tool allows the selection and manipulation of individual points and control handles.

H. A point with two control handles positioned independently, usually with a distinct angle in the path.

I. An import option that causes the imported artwork to be placed on its own locked layer with any bitmapped artwork automatically dimmed.

J. A point with no control handles and a distinct angle in the path.

K. A tool that allows you to lift colors or other attributes from an object in the document.

L. A type of curve applied directly to the path. The path moves through all the points, and the segments bend based on the control handles.

## Answers

1B, 2D, 3E, 4I, 5G, 6A, 7F, 8L, 9J, 10C, 11H, 12K

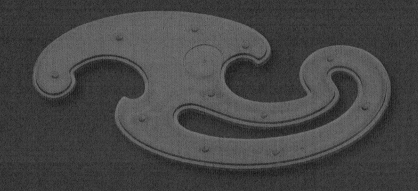

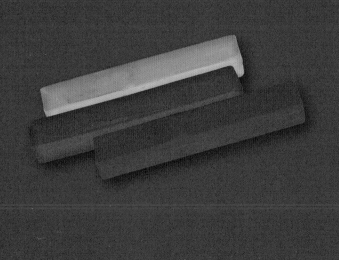

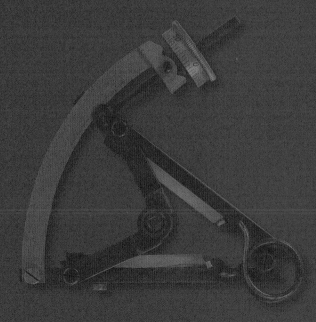

# LESSON

# 4

# CREATING AND FORMATTING TEXT

**THE ART OF TYPE** is a very nuanced thing. If you've seen one typeface, you've seen them all, right? Why not just enter the text, print it, and be done with it. After all, your artwork is what really shines in Illustrator—so why should you worry about the text formatting?

Even given my predilection for typeface geekery, I have to admit that the differences between one typeface and another are at times incredibly subtle. Consider Figure 4-1, borrowed from *Adobe InDesign CS4 One-on-One*. There are seven uppercase O's from seven different sans serif fonts. (To learn more about serif and sans serif typefaces, see the sidebar "The Look of Type" on page 114.) A type nerd like me could wax poetic, explaining how remarkably diverse these letters are, hailing from three distinct sans serif traditions. But to the untrained (or less fanatical) eye, the letters are just a bunch of ovals. Some look like rings; others look more like donuts. But in the end, they're all still ovals. The overwhelming majority of your readers can't tell a Grotesque O from a Humanist O, and furthermore they probably don't care. It makes you wonder why Max Miedinger put so much care into creating his ubiquitous typeface Haas-Grotesk (renamed Helvetica in 1960)—and why in the world I know that he did.

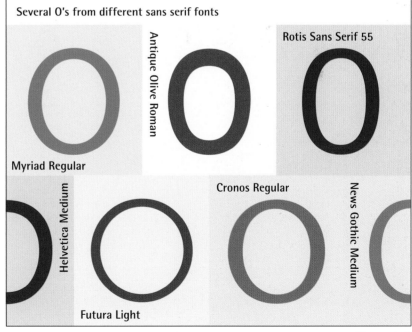

Figure 4-1.

# ABOUT THIS LESSON

## Project Files

Before beginning the exercises, make sure you've downloaded the lesson files from *www.oreilly.com/go/Deke-IllustratorCS5*, as directed in Step 2 on page xiv of the Preface. This should result in a folder called *Lesson Files-Alcs5 1on1* on your desktop. We'll be working with the files inside the *Lesson 04* subfolder.

It's time to put Illustrator's type tools to work, including the point type, area type, and type on a path tools. In this lesson, you'll learn how to:

- Place and edit text . . . . . . . . . . . . . . . . page 112
- Change the formatting and appearance of type . . . page 117
- Edit blocks of type (known as area type) . . . . . . page 122
- Place type on a path . . . . . . . . . . . . . . . page 127
- Work with advanced formatting, ligatures, glyphs, and other special characters . . . . . . . . page 129

## Video Lesson 4: Working with Type

Illustrator does an excellent job of letting you create text-based elements inside your artwork. In this video lesson, I'll demonstrate three different ways you can create type inside Illustrator: affixed to a single point inside your illustration, filling the area inside a path outline, or flowing along the contours of a path.

To see how to place type into your illustrations, visit *www.oreilly.com/go/deke-IllustratorCS5*. Click the **Watch** button to view the lesson online or click the **Download** button to save it to your computer. During the video, you'll learn these shortcuts:

| Operation | Windows shortcut | Macintosh shortcut |
|---|---|---|
| Select the type tool | Press the T key | Press the T key |
| Create a new document | Ctrl+N | ⌘-N |
| Advance from one field to another | Press the Tab key | Press the Tab key |
| Select the rectangle or ellipse tool | Press the M or L key | Press the M or L key |
| Align anything to the artboard | Choose ⬛ in the control panel | Choose ⬛ in the control panel |
| Display the Move dialog box | Double-click the black arrow tool | Double-click the black arrow tool |
| Create and name a layer | Alt-click ⬚ in the Layers panel | Option-click ⬚ in the Layers panel |
| Accept your text edits | Press Esc or Ctrl+Enter | Press Esc or ⌘-Return |
| Show or hide the bounding box | Ctrl+Shift+B | ⌘-Shift-B |
| Align type to the outline of a closed path | Alt-click with type tool | Option-click with type tool |

I'm here to tell you Miedinger and the others did what they did because the appearance of type can determine whether or not it gets read. Single letters may be endlessly entertaining to us type nerds, but fonts and other type characteristics take on real meaning when applied to larger passages of text. By way of example, Figure 4-2 shows each of the typefaces from Figure 4-1 applied to a full sentence. (Believe it or not, the size specifications are consistent throughout.) Suddenly it becomes evident just how much a typeface—in addition to color and other factors—affects our perception of what we read. Each face infuses a piece of Illustrator art with its own particular weight, texture, and style, which in turn affect the appeal and mood of the finished piece. Much as I love graphics, text is the reason most printed documents (including this one) exist. And that makes the humble font a vital contributor to your final artwork, worthy of your attention.

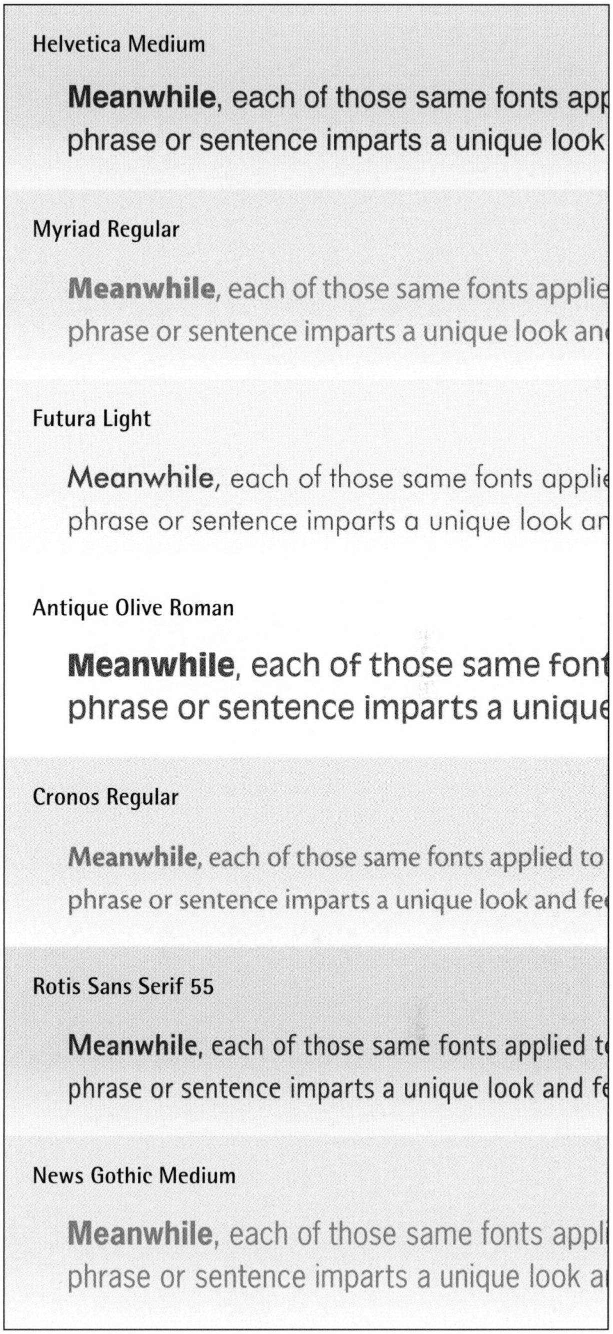

## The Mechanics of Type

Illustrator has three basic methods of handling lines of text: point type, area type, and type on a path. *Point type* is the most basic; it creates lines of type anchored to a single point, and moving that point moves the type with it. *Area type* allows you to create a bounding box (which can be any shape you'd like, though rectangular is the most common) and flow the text automatically inside the frame, much like in a traditional page layout program, such as InDesign or QuarkXPress. Lastly, *type on a path* allows you to place type along any existing path, regardless of its shape; you can bend type around spirals, sharp corners, or gentle arcs.

In addition to the way Illustrator handles the placement of type, characters and paragraphs can have other formatting attributes—such as typeface, size, leading, and alignment—also known as *styles*. Not only does Illustrator allow you to set these on a case-by-case basis, but (beginning with CS3) you can create and save specific character and paragraph styles to apply over and over to your heart's content.

**Helvetica Medium**

**Meanwhile**, each of those same fonts app phrase or sentence imparts a unique look

**Myriad Regular**

**Meanwhile**, each of those same fonts applie phrase or sentence imparts a unique look an

**Futura Light**

**Meanwhile**, each of those same fonts applie phrase or sentence imparts a unique look ar

**Antique Olive Roman**

**Meanwhile**, each of those same font phrase or sentence imparts a unique

**Cronos Regular**

**Meanwhile**, each of those same fonts applied to phrase or sentence imparts a unique look and fe

**Rotis Sans Serif 55**

**Meanwhile**, each of those same fonts applied t phrase or sentence imparts a unique look and fe

**News Gothic Medium**

**Meanwhile**, each of those same fonts appl phrase or sentence imparts a unique look a

Figure 4-2.

## Placing, Entering, and Editing Text

In the first exercise, we'll start with the basics: getting text into Illustrator and editing it for content once it's in your artwork. As we move through the lesson, I'll demonstrate progressively more sophisticated ways to manipulate type, but we've got to start somewhere.

Figure 4-3.

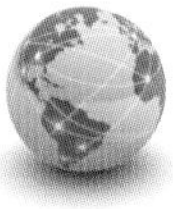

1. *Open a piece of artwork.* Navigate to the *Lesson 04* subfolder inside the *Lesson Files-AIcs5 1on1* folder. Inside you'll find an Illustrator file called *Early poetry.ai*. This poem is so named not because it was one of my first forays into metered verse; I wrote it when my eldest son was very young and had a penchant for removing his socks. You should see artwork like that shown in Figure 4-3.

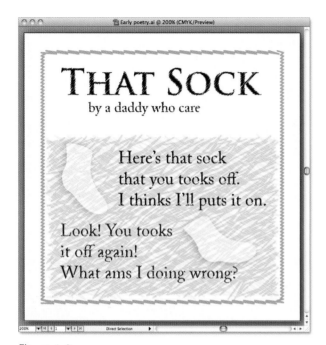

2. *Hide the Type layer.* Bring up the **Layers** panel by pressing F7 (or choosing **Windows→Layers**). This document has two layers, Type and Card. In the next few exercises, you'll be recreating the Type layer, so click the 👁 icon to hide the layer.

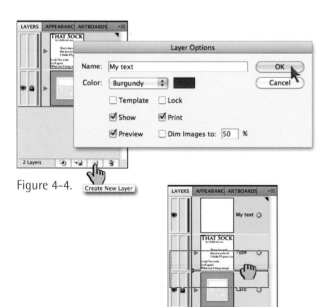

**PEARL OF WISDOM**

If you examine the Card layer (you can twirl it open by clicking the ▶ arrow), you'll notice only three objects in the layer—two socks and a rectangle labeled *scribbles*. All the strokes and fills you see on the Card layer are created by live effects, which I cover in Lesson 10, but you can check them out by selecting the scribbles object and viewing the effects in the Appearance panel. You don't need to concern yourself with these effects, but if you're interested to see how the effects are done, they're there to explore.

Figure 4-4.

Figure 4-5.

3. *Create a new layer for your type.* From within the Layers panel, Alt-click (Option-click) the ◻ icon to create a new layer, as seen in Figure 4-4. Pressing the Alt (or Option) key creates a new layer and simultaneously opens the **Layer Options** dialog box. Name the new layer "My text," change the **Color** to something unique (I chose burgundy), leave the other options unchanged, and click **OK**.

4. *Move the new layer below the old layer.* Move the newly created layer by dragging it down between the Type and Card layers, as in Figure 4-5. Release the mouse button to complete the move.

5. *Import some text to the new layer.* Choose **File→Place** to open the **Place** dialog box, as shown in Figure 4-6. Navigate to the *Lesson 04* subfolder inside the *Lesson Files-AIcs5 1on1* folder. Inside is a Microsoft Word document labeled *That sock.doc*. Select the file, and click the **Place** button. Illustrator now presents you with a **Microsoft Word Options** dialog box, seen in Figure 4-7.

Figure 4-6.

---

Note that Illustrator is capable of importing plain text documents (ending with .txt) or rich text format documents (ending in .rtf) in addition to Word documents.

---

6. *Dismiss the Word options dialog box.* The table of contents, footnotes, and index are fantastic features when working on a long document (such as this book), they tend to be overkill for Illustrator. While the multiple artboards introduced in CS4 certainly allow you to simulate a multipage layout in a document, Illustrator is poorly suited to manage documents of any significant length—the very kind of documents that require these features.

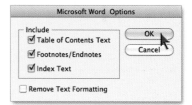

Figure 4-7.

The only option that will likely be useful to you is Remove Text Formatting, which strips the placed text of all the formatting applied inside Word. In this instance, you'll be reformatting the text regardless, so don't bother to check the box. Click **OK** to dismiss the dialog box.

7. *Turn on the bounding box.* Your text should now be in your illustration, as shown in Figure 4-8. If your text looks anything like mine, the frame is oddly sized and positioned. In nearly every layout or design program, you could simply grab one of the corners to resize the text box. But at the moment, Illustrator is treating the corners of the box as standard corner points, just as though you had drawn the shape with the rectangle tool. (The standard corner points are indicated by the small filled squares at the corners.)

To resize the text box, we need to make the bounding box visible. Choose **View →Show Bounding Box**, or press Ctrl+Shift+B (⌘-Shift-B on the Mac). The corners should now turn into open squares, revealing handles to manipulate the text box.

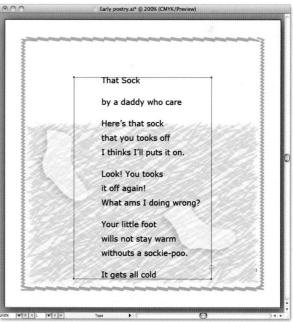

Figure 4-8.

Subtle crafts demand meticulous tools, and typography has more meticulous tools than you can shake a finely carved stick at. Let's begin at the beginning, with fonts—specifically, the two fonts that ushered in electronic artwork, Times and Helvetica, both pictured below. In Times, the lines of each character change gradually in thickness and terminate in tapering—or *bracketed*—wedges called *serifs*. Created in 1931 by Stanley Morison for *The Times* of London, the font was designed as a revival of the 18th-century Transitional serif faces. Meanwhile, the "naked" sans serif Helvetica drew its inspiration from the turn of the 20th century. With its uniform strokes and disdain for ornamentation, Helvetica came to dominate typesetting and remains one of the top-ten selling fonts to this day. It even inspired its own revival, Robin Nicholas's 1982 Arial, now an online standard.

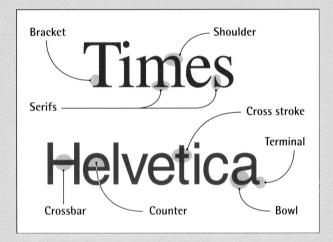

The number of fonts available to digital creative staff has grown exponentially over the last 20 years. In addition to a few thousand serif and sans serif faces, you can choose from slab serif, monospaced, blackletter, script, display, symbol—the list goes on and on. Fortunately, even the wackiest of these fonts subscribes to a few basic formatting conventions.

For example, regardless of font, type is measured in points, from roughly the top of the highest letter to the bottom of the lowest. But that doesn't mean that 12-point text set using one typeface matches the size of another—in fact, far from it. To show why, the illustration at the top of the opposite page

shows three lines of 52-point type. Only the font changes, from Franklin Gothic on top to Künstler Script and finally the Adobe face Garamond Premiere. The first line appears the largest thanks to its relatively tall lowercase letters. Like most script faces, Künstler offers short lowercase letters and thus appears the smallest.

When gauging type size, bear in mind the following:

- Each row of characters rests on a common *baseline*. The parts of characters that drop below the baseline—as in *g, j, p, q,* and *y*—are called *descenders*.

- The line formed by the tops of most lowercase letters—*a, c, e,* and others—is the *x-height*. Those characters that fit entirely between the baseline and x-height are called *medials*. Large medials usually translate to a larger looking font and remain legible at very small sizes.

- The portions of lowercase letters that rise above the x-height—*b, d,* and the rest—are called *ascenders*. Two letters, *i* and *t*, do not typically rise to full height and are considered medials.

- The unlabeled white lines in the upper-right illustration indicate the *cap heights*, which mark the top boundary of the capital letters. When working with a standard text face such as Garamond (as well as Times, Helvetica, and their ilk), the cap height falls slightly below the ascenders. Franklin Gothic (and many other sans-serif faces) makes caps and ascenders the same height; Künstler Script raises the cap height well above the ascenders.

In the old days of metal typesetting, *point size* was calculated by measuring the piece of lead that held the letter. This meant the size was slightly larger than the largest character of type. Typesetters added room between lines of type by inserting additional blank strips of lead. Now that everything's digital, the lead is gone but not forgotten. Designers still call line spacing *leading* (pronounced "ledding"). And while modern type houses can size their characters any way they want, the actual height of the characters is typically smaller than the prescribed size. For example, in the upper-right illustration, each colored bar is exactly 52 points tall; the characters fit inside the bars with a point or two to spare.

In addition to height, you can measure type by its width and weight. The difference is that you don't typically scale these attributes numerically. Rather, you select from predefined styles, such as those pictured for the fonts Benton Sans and Antique Olive to the right. Because few fonts include width variations, Illustrator lets you stretch or squish the letters manually. But doing so can make the text look ridiculous. As indicated by the brown text in the right-hand figure, scaling the width of a letter changes the proportions of its strokes as well as its proximity to other letters. If you decide to stretch, I recommend going no narrower than 80 percent and no wider than 125 percent.

Most font families include at least one italic or oblique style. These slanted variations are used to stress foreign or unfamiliar phrases, as well as titles of books and other publications. Although Illustrator also offers underlines, they aren't commonly used. (You may notice that underlines do not appear in this book, for example.) These days, the underline is relegated to marking hyperlinks, such as those on the Web, and that's about it. So in virtually all cases, if you're tempted to underline, use italics instead. If an italic style is not available, Illustrator (unlike InDesign or Photoshop) has no built-in method of slanting type, but applying a Shear transformation of about 12 degrees will have a similar effect; you can read more about the Shear transform in the next lesson.

| Benton Sans, Width | Benton Sans, Weight |
|---|---|
| Compressed Condensed Regular 150% Stretch | Thin Light Regular **Bold** **Black** |

| Antique Olive, Width | Antique Olive, Weight |
|---|---|
| **Condensed** Regular **Compact** 50% Squeeze | Light Regular **Bold** **Black** |

Figure 4-9.

Figure 4-10.

8. *Resize the bounding box.* Now that the handles are visible, resize the bounding box to fit in the lower area of the artwork (the peach scribble area). Don't worry about getting the box precisely aligned; we'll refine the positioning in a later step. If you want to move the text, it's easiest to grab it by a baseline and drag it into position. Once your text box looks similar to that in Figure 4-9, you're ready for the next step.

---

See the little red ⊞ icon at the lower right of your text box? This icon indicates *overset text*—that is, text that is in the flow of the bounding box but cannot be displayed due to a lack of space. For now, it's safe to ignore; I'll show you how to flow text from one text box to another in a later exercise in this lesson.

---

9. *Move the title and byline.* The title and byline need to be moved to the top of the artboard. Switch to the type tool by clicking the **T** icon in the toolbox (or by pressing the T key).

   - Select the first line of type (*That Sock*) by triple-clicking somewhere in the line. (Don't triple-click too quickly, as it may confuse Illustrator; rather, pause for about a half-second between clicks.)

   - Then press Shift+↓ to select the next line of type, the byline *by a daddy who care.* (I've taken some grand liberties with verb tense in this poem.)

   - Finally, press Ctrl+X (⌘-X) to cut the text and move it to the clipboard.

10. *Paste the type.* Make sure that nothing is selected by choosing **Select→Deselect** (or pressing Ctrl+Shift+A/⌘-Shift-A). With the type tool still active, click somewhere toward the upper-left of the artboard; you'll see a blinking insertion point cursor. Paste the title and byline by pressing Ctrl+V (⌘-V). Illustrator creates the text as point type, with the two lines floating free, as shown in Figure 4-10. (However, you can't see the baseline or the anchor point while the type tool is active; see the Pearl of Wisdom on the next page to learn a quick way to exit the type tool.) You should notice the extra carriage return, indicated by the blinking cursor on the third line by itself; get rid of it by pressing the Backspace key (Delete key on the Mac).

If you're like me, you tend to rely heavily on keyboard shortcuts to switch tools and access commands. But keyboard shortcuts won't work when editing text, right? There's one that will, and it will allow you access to all others. When editing text, press Ctrl+Enter (⌘-Return on the Mac). This exits the type tool and returns you to the black arrow tool; all keyboard shortcuts now function normally. And you don't even need to switch back to the type tool to resume editing—simply double-click anywhere in the text, and you'll return to the type tool automatically.

That's it for this exercise. You now know the basics of how to place and edit text. In the next exercise, I'll explain how to work with point type, as well as cover basic text formatting. Save your work because we'll be picking up where we left off.

## Applying Formatting and Effects

Getting text into your artwork is the obvious first step, but without being able to format the text, your illustration is unfinished. In this exercise, I'll show you how to apply character and paragraph attributes to your type, and even preview live effects (fully explored in Lesson 10).

1. *Open the poem document.* If you saved your file from the preceding exercise, open it now. Otherwise, open the catch-up document *Placed text.ai* in the *Lesson 04* folder.

2. *Select the title and byline type.* With the black arrow tool, click the baseline of either the title or the byline. (Press the V key to make the black arrow tool active if it isn't already.) You should see a burgundy rectangle around the lines and a tiny point off to the left, as shown in Figure 4-11. This point is the anchor point for the type.

For mysterious reasons known only to Adobe, Illustrator can be flaky about displaying the anchor point. If you don't see it at first, try minimizing and restoring the document window.

You may be asking, "But why is the point so far from the type? What gives, Deke?" Well, observant reader, the text that was pulled over from the original Word document was formatted with an indent,

Figure 4-11.

Figure 4-12.

which Illustrator happily preserved. Not to worry; in the next few steps we'll fix the formatting of the title and byline, and our strange floating anchor point will be just a memory.

When working with point type, it's best to hide the bounding box to prevent accidental scaling of the type. Hide the bounding box by choosing **View→Hide Bounding Box** or pressing Ctrl+Shift+B (⌘-Shift-B on the Mac).

3. *Remove the indent from the title.* Double-click anywhere in the first line of type to make the type tool active. In the control panel, shown in Figure 4-13, click the word **Paragraph** to bring up the **Paragraph** panel, and change the first-line indent value from 36 pt to 0 pt and press Enter to accept the changes. Finally, press Ctrl+Enter (⌘-Return) to return to the black arrow tool. (Note that you *can't* use the number pad Enter for this step.) The first line should now be flush left, aligned with the anchor point.

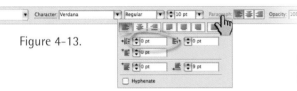

Figure 4-13.

4. *Update the size of your font preview.* It's time to change the font used for the title, but first, you should make the job easier by changing your type preferences. Press Ctrl+K (⌘-K) to bring up the **Preferences** dialog box, and switch to the **Type** option in the main pop-up menu, as shown in Figure 4-14. Change the **Font Preview** option to **Large** and click **OK**. Depending on the number of fonts installed on your system, it may take a minute or two to update.

You won't see any change right away. Rather, updating this preference determines the size of the font preview displayed when you choose Font from the Type menu.

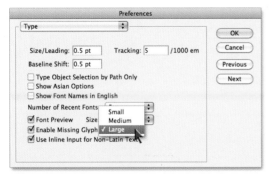

Figure 4-14.

5. *Change the typeface of the title and byline.* From the **Type** menu, choose **Font→Adobe Caslon Pro→Regular**. This updates all type selected with the black arrow tool to Adobe Caslon Pro.

---

Type attributes can be edited when text is selected either with the arrow tool or with the type tool. With the arrow tool, changes are applied to all the type; whereas with the type tool, changes are made only to the selected characters or paragraphs.

---

6. *Change the point size of the title.* Double-click anywhere on the line reading *That Sock* to switch to the type tool, and then triple-click that same line to select the entire line. You can change the point size of the type in a number of ways, all shown in Figure 4-15: You can enter a value directly in the control panel, you can use the ⬍ arrows to the left of the point size, or you can select a preset type size from the ▼ menu to the right of the point size. Choose 36 pt from the pop-up menu to start.

There is, however, a better way—a keyboard shortcut that will save you a lot of time if you commit it to memory. (For all the shortcuts available while working with type, see the sidebar "Formatting Shortcuts" on page 120.)

- With the type selected, press Ctrl+Shift+⬚ (⌘-Shift-⬚ on the Mac) to increase the point size; conversely, press Ctrl+Shift+⬚ (⌘-Shift-⬚) to decrease the point size. By default, these shortcuts will increase and decrease the size by two points, but I recommend more fine-tune control.

- Bring up the **Type Preferences** dialog box by choosing **Edit→Preferences→Type** (or the **Illustrator** menu on the Mac), pictured in the sidebar figure on the next page. Change the **Size/Leading** value to 0.5, the **Tracking** value to 5, and the **Baseline Shift** value to 0.5 as shown. Click **OK** to confirm your changes. Your keyboard shortcuts will now change the point size in half-point increments. Adjust your point size to exactly 44 pt using the keyboard shortcuts.

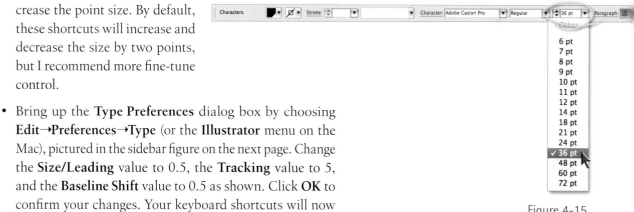

Figure 4-15.

# Formatting Shortcuts

When it comes to text formatting, Illustrator is shortcut crazy. And for good reason—shortcuts let you experiment with various text settings while keeping your eyes on the results. Quite simply, by committing a few keyboard shortcuts to memory, you can dramatically increase how fast you work with type. Assuming you have a rough feel for the location of keys on the keyboard, you can adjust formatting settings almost as fast as you can think of them.

I should note that I'm not asking you to do anything I wouldn't ask of myself. This is not a comprehensive list that I've assembled by pouring through help files; these are the shortcuts I use routinely, lodged in the nether regions of my brain. Sure I had to displace some information—my phone number, my kids' birthdays, what my mom looks like—but it was worth it.

Before trying out these shortcuts yourself, I recommend that you confirm the keyboard increments in the Preferences dialog box. Choose **Edit→Preferences→Type** (**InDesign→Preferences→Type** on the Mac). Then make your way to the type increment options, circled in the figure. I recommend setting **Size/Leading** to 0.5 point and **Kerning** to $^5/_{1000}$ em. I also suggest that you

change **Baseline Shift** to 0.5 point, as shown below. Then click the **OK** button to confirm.

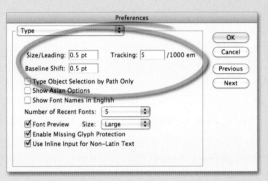

Whatever values you decide to use, bear in mind that you can change them anytime you like. Because these increments are variables, I refer to them in the following table by their initials—*SI* for the Size/Leading increment, *BI* for the Baseline Shift increment, and *KI* for the Kerning increment. In all cases, text has to be selected for the keyboard shortcuts to work.

| Operation | Windows shortcut | Macintosh shortcut |
|---|---|---|
| Increase type size by SI | Ctrl+Shift+⦗.⦘ (period) | ⌘-Shift-⦗.⦘ (period) |
| Increase type size by 5× SI | Ctrl+Shift+Alt+⦗.⦘ (period) | ⌘-Shift-Option-⦗.⦘ (period) |
| Decrease type size by SI | Ctrl+Shift+⦗,⦘ (comma) | ⌘-Shift-⦗,⦘ (comma) |
| Decrease type size by 5× SI | Ctrl+Shift+Alt+⦗,⦘ (comma) | ⌘-Shift-Option-⦗,⦘ (comma) |
| Increase leading by SI | Alt+↓ | Option-↓ |
| Increase leading by 5× SI | Ctrl+Alt+↓ | ⌘-Option-↓ |
| Decrease leading by SI | Alt+↑ | Option-↑ |
| Decrease leading by 5× SI | Ctrl+Alt+↑ | ⌘-Option-↑ |
| Increase baseline shift by BI | Shift+Alt+↑ | Shift-Option-↑ |
| Increase baseline shift by 5× BI | Ctrl+Shift+Alt+↑ | ⌘-Shift-Option-↑ |
| Decrease baseline shift by BI | Shift+Alt+↓ | Shift-Option-↓ |
| Decrease baseline shift by 5× BI | Ctrl+Shift+Alt+↓ | ⌘-Shift-Option-↓ |
| Increase kerning/tracking by KI | Alt+→ | Option-→ |
| Increase kerning/tracking by 5× KI | Ctrl+Alt+→ | ⌘-Option-→ |
| Decrease kerning/tracking by KI | Alt+← | Option-← |
| Decrease kerning/tracking by 5× KI | Ctrl+Alt+← | ⌘-Option-← |
| Restore kerning to Metrics and tracking to 0 | Ctrl+Alt+Q | ⌘-Option-Q |
| Toggle automatic hyphenation | Ctrl+Shift+Alt+H | ⌘-Shift-Option-H |
| Left-align paragraph | Ctrl+Shift+L | ⌘-Shift-L |
| Right-align paragraph | Ctrl+Shift+R | ⌘-Shift-R |
| Center-align paragraph | Ctrl+Shift+C | ⌘-Shift-C |
| Justify all lines except last one | Ctrl+Shift+J | ⌘-Shift-J |
| Justify that last line, too | Ctrl+Shift+F | ⌘-Shift-F |

What if you want to change the font size in larger increments without resetting your preferences? You can by adding the Alt (or Option) key to your shortcut. In other words, Ctrl+Shift+Alt+⌐ (⌘-Shift-Option-⌐) on the Mac) will now increase the point size by 2.5 points, or five times the value set in your preferences.

7. *Change the typeface again.* Now that the title is an appropriate size, I'm not sure I like the look of it. I want to change it to Trajan Pro, a font that ships with Illustrator and the Creative Suite. You could choose it from the Character pop-up menu in the control panel, or even from the Type menu. Instead, I'll show you a quicker way. Double-click the name of the current font (Adobe Caslon Pro) in the control panel, and begin typing the name of the font you want—in this case, Trajan Pro. On my system, I only have to type *T-R* before Trajan Pro is selected. Press Enter (or Return) to accept the new typeface and update your text, as in Figure 4-16.

Figure 4-16.

8. *Move the title.* The title looks good, except for its position. Rather than switching back to the black arrow tool, you can access it on-the-fly by holding down the Ctrl key (the ⌘ key on the Mac). Drag the headline to a better position like that in Figure 4-17, then release the mouse button and finally the Ctrl (⌘) key.

Figure 4-17.

9. *Adjust the size of the byline.* The original typeface is fine for the byline, but it's far too small when compared to the size of the title. Select the byline by triple-clicking anywhere in the line *by a daddy who care* and increase the point size to 18 pt using any method you've learned thus far. (I find the keyboard to be the quickest way, but it's your choice.)

10. *Change the byline's leading.* Leading, as you learned in the sidebar "The Look of Type" on page 114, is the space between lines of type. In this step, we'll adjust the leading of the byline to create appropriate space between it and the title.

Choose **View→Type→Character** or press Ctrl+T (⌘-T on the Mac) to bring up the **Character** panel. If your panel appears short, click the ▾≡ icon in the upper-right corner of the panel and choose **Show Options**. Your panel should look like that in Figure 4-18.

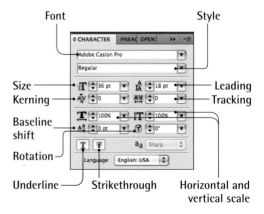

Figure 4-18.

You can adjust the leading value directly from the Character panel (or from the Character panel pop-up menu by clicking the word **Character** in the control panel), but there's also a keyboard shortcut that allows you to adjust it without changing tools and see your changes as you go. Press Alt+↓ or Alt+↑ (Option-↓ or Option-↑) to adjust the leading up or down by 0.5 points (assuming you changed your preferences as directed in the sidebar). Adding the Ctrl (or ⌘) key increases the change to five times the normal value. After each keypress, the value updates in the Character panel; once you've reached a leading of 15 pt, you should have the spacing shown in Figure 4-19.

11. *Change the byline tracking.* I'd like the byline to fill out more of the space under the title, but I don't want to change the point size. What I want is to increase the space between the charac-ters; this attribute is known as *tracking*. You can adjust the tracking directly from the Character panel, but there is (you guessed it) a shortcut. Press Alt+← and Alt+→ (Op-tion-← and Option-→) to adjust the tracking out or in by $5/1000$ of an em space. A tracking value of 0 uses standard spacing. Negative numbers reduce the space between letters, or *tighten* the tracking, while positive num-bers increase the space, or *loosen* the track-ing. Keep loosening the tracking until the byline takes up roughly the space under the six center capitals in the title (around a value of 130 or so), like that in Figure 4-20.

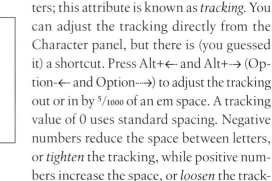

Figure 4-19.

That's it for now. Save your work, because we'll be returning to this poem once again in the next exercise. I'll demonstrate how to work with area type, and flow text from one text frame to the next.

Figure 4-20.

## Editing Area Type

Now that you've learned the basics of formatting text, it's time to turn your attention to working with area type. Area type behaves much more like type in traditional layout programs: Text automatically wraps inside its text block, and text can flow from one block to the next. The best use of area type is for longer passages of text—say, body copy for an advertisement or the legalese present on nearly every piece of printed material. In this exercise, you'll use area type to work with the first two stanzas of our poem.

1. *Open the poem in progress.* If you have your file from the end of the preceding exercise, open it now. Otherwise, open the document *Area type.ai* inside the *Lesson 04* folder.

2. *Make the bounding box visible.* Armed with the black arrow tool, click anywhere on a line of type in the body of the poem to select the text box. Make the bounding box visible by pressing Ctrl+Shift+B (⌘-Shift-B on the Mac) or choosing **View→Show Bounding Box**. The eight white-filled square handles should now be visible.

3. *Resize the text block.* Still using the black arrow tool, resize and move the text block into the approximate position shown in Figure 4-21. Don't worry about the red ⊞ icon warning you of overset text; we'll fix that in a later step.

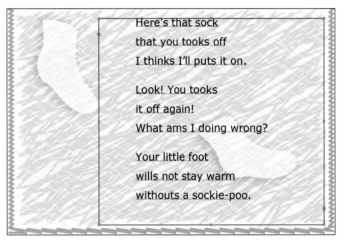

Figure 4-21.

4. *Lift the text attributes with the eyedropper tool.* Remember the eyedropper tool introduced back on page 42 in Lesson 2? In addition to fill and stroke attributes, the eyedropper tool can lift text formatting attributes. Switch to the 🖋 tool in the toolbox (or press the I key). Move the cursor over the byline to pick up its formatting. Note that when you pass the cursor over the text, it switches to 🖋. Click when you see that icon to lift the text formatting, as shown in Figure 4-22.

5. *Remove the indent.* Unfortunately, the indent on the type is still hanging on from the original Word document. (You removed it from the title back in Step 3 on page 118, but not from the byline.) Click the word **Paragraph** in the control panel to bring up the paragraph options, shown in Figure 4-23, and change the left indent from 36 points to 0 points.

6. *Edit the point size, leading, and tracking.* Now that you've removed the indent, it's time to clean up the character-level formatting. Start

Figure 4-22.

Figure 4-23.

Figure 4-24.

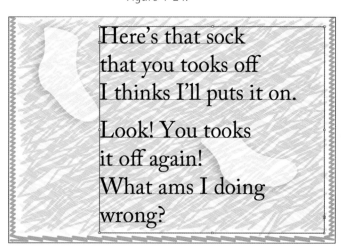

Figure 4-25.

Left side bearing    Right side bearing

← Character width →

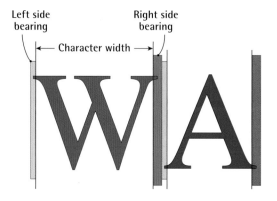

Automatic (metrics) pair kerning

Figure 4-26.

by clicking the word **Character** in the control panel to bring up the character formatting options, shown in Figure 4-24. Change the point size to 22, the leading to Auto, and the tracking to 0. Your results should look like those in Figure 4-25.

---

When you change the leading value to Auto, Illustrator updates the value to (26.4). The parentheses indicate that the value is automatically generated; it's based on a default auto-leading setting of 120 percent. This default percentage cannot be changed globally; it can be changed only on a per-paragraph or per-text block basis using the Justification option in the Paragraph panel menu. (It can be changed globally on a per-document level by choosing the Justification option with no text selected; however, this default only affects text created after the change is applied.)

---

7. *Change the kerning of the body text.* I'd like to change one last character attribute, called kerning. *Kerning* is similar to tracking in that it affects the space between characters, but unlike tracking, the space is determined for adjacent pairs of letterforms. For example, Figure 4-26 shows a classic combo, *WA*, with and without kerning. *WA* is so well known that nearly all fonts contain instructions to automatically kern this pair of letters; *WA* is referred to as a *kerning pair.*

The kerning on the poem stanzas is currently set to zero, as seen in Figure 4-24 (and your Character panel, should that window still be open on your screen; if not, click the word **Character** in the control panel to bring it up again). Change the value to **Auto**. You should see a subtle improvement, as shown in Figure 4-27 on the facing page.

PEARL OF 🔵 WISDOM

With the different kerning options available, you may be wondering what the best choice is. Auto will, by default, use the font's built-in metrics if they are available. Optical allows Illustrator to examine the letterform shapes and use its best guess as to appropriate kerning. Metrics forces Illustrator to use the font's built-in metrics.

So which is best? In general, Auto or Metrics are best for most professionally produced fonts because their kerning tables are meticulously set to space the characters correctly. On the other end, freeware fonts often have poor or no kerning data and benefit greatly from Optical kerning. Optical kerning really shines, however, when kerning two different type sizes—or even typefaces.

8. *Update the title and byline kerning.* Now that you know the importance of kerning, it's time to apply it to the title and byline. (Turning on kerning is helpful with all type but especially important when working with large point sizes.) With the black arrow tool, click either the title or the byline. Bring up the **Character** panel, and switch the kerning value to **Auto**.

9. *Adjust the height of the text block.* Back to the poem's stanzas. Select the text block with the black arrow tool. Grab the handle at the bottom center of the block, and drag it up to hide all but the first stanza, as pictured in Figure 4-28.

10. *Flow the overset text into a new text block.* Finally you'll see one of the great advantages of area type: flowing text from one block to another. Click the ⊞ icon to load the overset text to the Place cursor (🖼). With the Place cursor loaded, drag from the top-left corner to the bottom right, defining the area where you want the new text block, using Figure 4-29 as a guide. Release the mouse, and your new text block will appear. A dark red line connects the two, indicating the text is linked from one box to the next.

11. *Move the text blocks as necessary.* The placement of the two stanzas could use some polishing. Still using the black arrow tool, move the text blocks into the desired location, as shown in Figure 4-30 on the following page. (You can also nudge selected frames with the arrow keys on the keyboard.) Depending on how wide you drew your text block in the last step, you may need to widen it to get the word *wrong?* to appear.

12. *Apply a live effect to the type.* These last steps are really a preview of live effects, which I cover fully in Lesson 10. They'll add the finishing touches to our document. I've already created

# Here's that sock that you tooks off I thinks I'll puts it on.

Metrics kerning      No kerning

Figure 4-27.

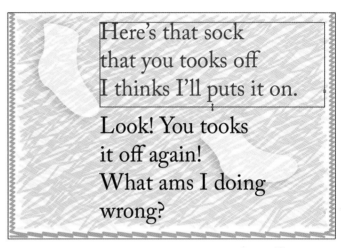

Figure 4-28.

Figure 4-29.

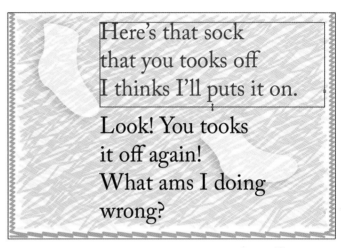

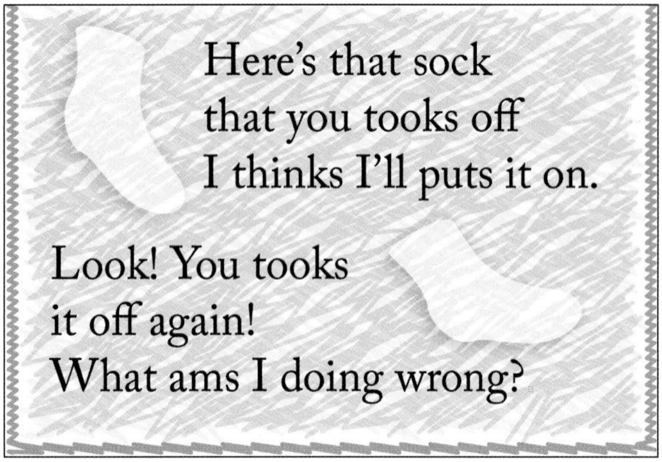

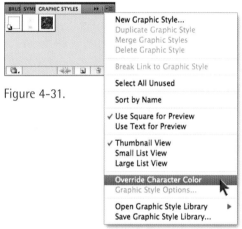

Here's that sock
that you tooks off
I thinks I'll puts it on.

Look! You tooks
it off again!
What ams I doing wrong?

Figure 4-30.

Figure 4-31.

New Graphic Style...
Duplicate Graphic Style
Merge Graphic Styles
Delete Graphic Style

Break Link to Graphic Style

Select All Unused

Sort by Name

✓ Use Square for Preview
Use Text for Preview

✓ Thumbnail View
Small List View
Large List View

Override Character Color
Graphic Style Options...

Open Graphic Style Library          ▶
Save Graphic Style Library...

Figure 4-32.

THAT SOCK

by a daddy who care

Here's that sock
that you tooks off
I thinks I'll puts it on.

a style called Graphite and saved it with this project. This is the style you'll apply. You have a number of little changes to make:

- Select all the elements in the **My Text** layer by pressing Ctrl+A (⌘-A on the Mac). (Don't worry about this command selecting elements on other layers, because they're either locked or hidden.)

- Bring up the **Graphics Styles** panel, shown in Figure 4-31, by clicking the ▢ icon or pressing Shift+F5. Before you apply the style, however, you need to change a default preference. From the ▾≡ pop-up menu in the upper corner of the panel, deselect **Override Character Color**.

- Click the final style (the gray square) to apply the graphic style to the selected text. *Voilà!* All the text is now drawn in the style of colored pencil, and yet remains fully editable.

13. *Change the title color.* One final touch: The title could use a little color, and given the change we made in Step 12, it's now possible:

- Switch to the type tool, and triple-click *That Sock*.

- Press F6 to bring up the **Color** panel, and make sure **Fill** is active. Click the ☒ icon to switch from the black slider to the CMYK sliders. Click in the CMYK spectrum to choose a color. (I went with a rich blue.) Deselect everything by pressing Ctrl+Shift+A (⌘-Shift-A on the Mac) to see your final results.

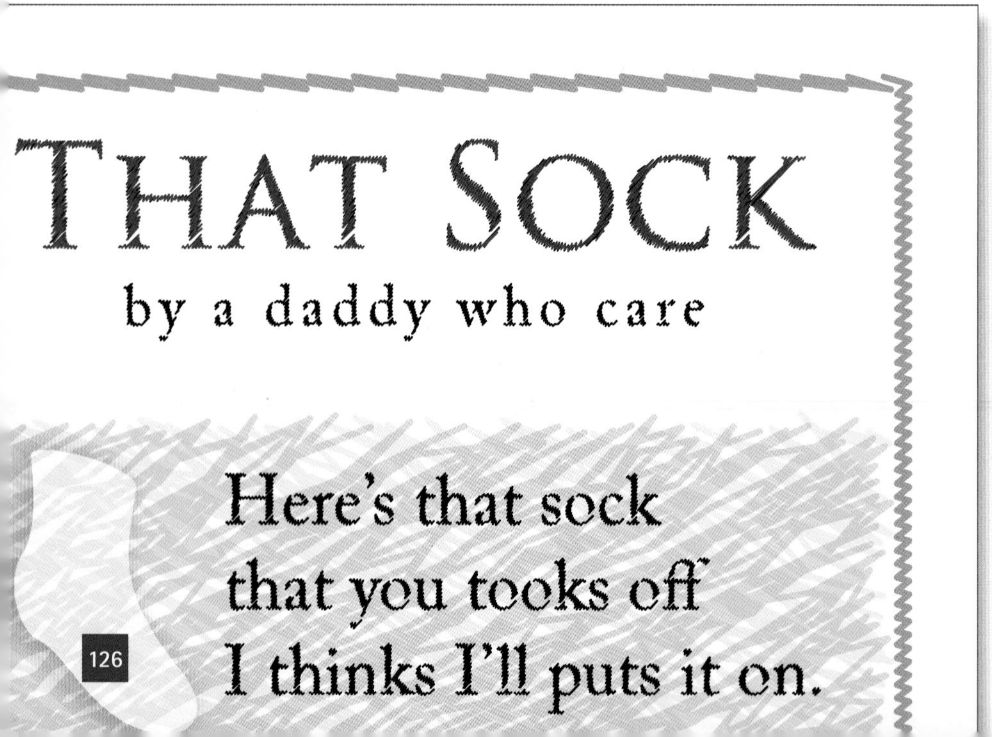

And there is your finished poem, as seen in Figure 4-32. You've learned how to work with point and area type, link text blocks, and even preview some live effects. Save or discard your work as you see fit; in the last exercise you'll move on to a new file with the full version of the poem. But next up, we have a brief diversion with a completely separate project.

## Placing Type on a Path

While point and area text are probably the most common ways to handle text in Illustrator, there's a third kind: text on a path. Text on a path allows you to wrap a line of text around any shape you can create in Illustrator. To help demonstrate type on a path, I've created a document that features a guest appearance by Professor Shenbop, an entirely fictitious (and sadly dead) frog that rose to fame in the *Adobe InDesign One-on-One* books. (Check out *InDesign CS4 One-on-One* for more of Shenbop's story.)

Figure 4-33.

1. *Open the Shenbop artwork.* Inside the *Lesson 04* folder you'll find a file called *Shenbop.ai*, seen in Figure 4-33. This document was rebuilt in Illustrator, based on Shenbop's first appearance in the InDesign book. (The document has three layers, two of which are locked, because you won't need to edit them for this exercise.) Note the type placed outside the artboard; this is the type you'll be adding to the circular paths.

2. *Cut the first line of text.* With the black arrow tool, click the line *Professor Shenbop's* to select it. Press Ctrl+X (⌘-X) to cut the text and move it to the clipboard.

3. *Paste the text on the upper path.* Switch to the type tool, and move the cursor over the red circular path, just above the three o'clock position. (The red circle is actually two separate paths. I already split the path horizontally for you using the scissors tool, using the method you saw in "Splitting, Joining, and Aligning" in Lesson 2.) Your cursor should change to look like ⌁, as shown in Figure 4-34. Click to convert the path to allow type, and press Ctrl+V (⌘-V) to paste the text.

Figure 4-34.

When you click on a path with the type tool, Illustrator automatically removes the stroke from the path, rendering the path itself invisible. Paths with type can have only stroke or fill attributes on the type, not on the paths.

4. *Adjust the indents and the flip.* Switch back to the black arrow tool. You'll see blue guides appear perpendicular to the path itself, which is also shown in blue—all pictured in Figure 4-35. As you mouse over these guides, your cursor will change to look like ▸▎, ▸▎, or ▸▎. The first two arrows allow you to adjust the left and right margins of the type on the path; drag these guides to the far ends of the

Figure 4-35.

Figure 4-36.

Figure 4-37.

Figure 4-38.

Figure 4-39.

path (the nine o'clock and three o'clock positions). The last icon, ↖, appears over the guide in the center of the path; drag it upward to flip the type to the other side of the path. Your final results should look like Figure 4-36.

5. *Cut the second line of text.* Select the second line of text with the black arrow tool and press Ctrl+X (⌘-X) to cut the text to the clipboard.

6. *Paste the second line on the lower path.* Repeat Step 3 for the second line of type, this time clicking with the type tool just below the nine o'clock position. Figure 4-37 shows the results.

7. *Change the Type on a Path options.* The second line of text presents a problem. The text is partially hidden under the Shenbop artwork, but if you flip the text to the other side of the path, it will be upside-down. Fortunately, Illustrator provides an easy solution. Choose **Type→Type on a Path→Type on a Path Options**. This brings up the dialog box shown in Figure 4-38. Turn on the **Preview** check box, select **Ascender** from the **Align to Path** pop-up menu, and click **OK**. The well-aligned type is shown in Figure 4-39. (Don't worry about the overlap of the gold ring; we'll address that in the next step.)

PEARL OF ⬤ WISDOM

Other options are available to you in the Type on a Path Options dialog box. First, the Effects option: I don't recommend changing it. The default setting of Rainbow may sound flighty or impractical, but it's the most useful and conservative of the choices. Figure 4-40 on the facing page illustrates all the possible Effects options. The remaining option, Spacing, acts much like tracking seen earlier in this lesson; the Auto setting usually produces the best results.

8. *Adjust the indents.* There's one last step before we can put this frog to rest. You may have been curious as to why there was so much extra space between *Music* and *Quiz*; but the answer should be clearer now—that space provides clearance for the text to wrap around Shenbop's pull-string ring. All that's left to do is to grab the right margin guide with the black arrow tool, and gradually pull it to the left until the text gap falls across the ring.

Professor Shenbop is now ready to greet his students with his apparently terrifying music quiz; the final art is shown in Figure 4-41. Note that these techniques work for any path, not only simple arcs—you could just as easily wrap text around spirals or polygons. Now that you've completed your break with the academic frog, it's time to return to the land of sock poetry for the final exercise in this lesson. Save or discard your file as you like.

Figure 4-40.

Figure 4-41.

## Advanced Formatting, OpenType Fonts, and Special Characters

In this last exercise, I'll show you some advanced type formatting, including area type options and the Adobe line composers, Open-

Type features, and a myriad of special characters and how to access them. This time, you'll be working on a full version of the "That Sock" poem and focusing exclusively on advanced type features.

1. *Open the full poem artwork.* Open the file *Full poem.ai* located inside the *Lesson 04* folder. The document should look like that pictured in Figure 4-42.

2. *Examine the document layers.* Bring up the **Layers** panel by pressing F7. This document has three layers: Background, Final Text, and Raw Text. Final Text shows what the text should look like at the end of this exercise; hide the **Final Text** layer by clicking the 👁 icon next to the layer name. Next, turn on the **Raw Text** layer; we'll be working with this text.

3. *Select the text frame.* Using the black arrow tool, select the main text frame by clicking a line of type. Note that the text block is the same size as the artboard; the edges of the bounding box have been snapped to the artboard. This ensures that the text is aligned, but leaves no margin around the text—something we can remedy in the next step.

4. *Update the area type options.* Choose **Type→Area Type Options** to bring up the **Area Type Options** dialog box, shown in Figure 4-43. This dialog box allows you to specify the size of the text block, as well as the number of rows and columns—but for now we'll focus on the **Offset** options.

    - First, make sure the **Preview** box is checked. Next, change the **Inset Spacing** value to 30 pt. This brings all the margins—top, left, right, and bottom—in by 30 points.

    - Next, change the **First Baseline** pop-up value to **x Height**, allowing the first line to float up slightly outside the margin and vertically align the rest of the text.

    With each change, you'll see your document update. After you've made the changes, click **OK** to accept them. Your text should now look like that in Figure 4-44 on the facing page.

5. *Justify all the lines of the type.* That small change has made a big difference, but the alignment of the type is still all wrong. Bring up the **Paragraph** panel either from the control panel or by pressing Ctrl+Alt+T (⌘-Option-T), and select the last of the alignment icons, as shown in

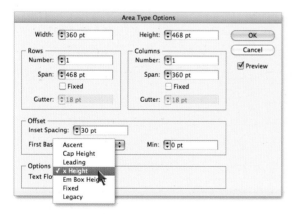

Figure 4-42.

Figure 4-43.

Figure 4-45. This forces all the lines to be fully justified across the text block.

---

The first three icons are the standard alignments: left, center, and right. The second group of three justify all lines but the last, which is either aligned left, center, or right. Only the final icon forces *all* lines to be justified.

---

6. ***Select the body of the poem.*** Examine the body of the poem in Figure 4-46. See how now that the lines are justified, the spacing has become very uneven? As evidence, compare the fourth line with the sixth, or the last. (I've removed the background so the type is clearer.) We'll fix that in the next step, but first we need to select just the poem body. Switch to the type tool, and triple-click in the poem body to select the entire paragraph.

7. ***Switch to the every-line composer.*** Still in the Paragraph panel, choose **Adobe Every-line Composer** from the ▾≡ menu. This causes Illustrator to calculate the line wraps based on all lines in the paragraph at once, rather than determining each line break individually. Basing line wraps on all lines nearly always produces better results, as evidenced by Figure 4-47.

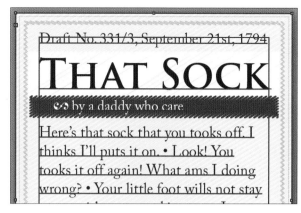

Draft No. 331/3, September 21st, 1794
THAT SOCK
by a daddy who care
Here's that sock that you tooks off. I
thinks I'll puts it on. • Look! You
tooks it off again! What ams I doing
wrong? • Your little foot wills not stay

Figure 4-44.

PARAGRAPH
0 pt
Justify all lines
0 pt
Hyphenate

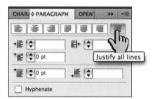

Figure 4-45.

Here's that sock that you tooks off. I
thinks I'll puts it on. • Look! You tooks
it off again! What ams I doing wrong?
• Your little foot wills not stay warm
withouts a sockie-poo. • It gets all cold
and freezes off. Your feets won't adds to
two. • One foot don't matters when you
crawl or roll or flop or flump. • But
when you starts a-walkin', you'll hates
you gots a stump. • So please, Dear,
leaves your sockie on and keeps your
footsie hot. • Then Daddy wills rest
easy that you'll grows a safely tot.

Figure 4-46.

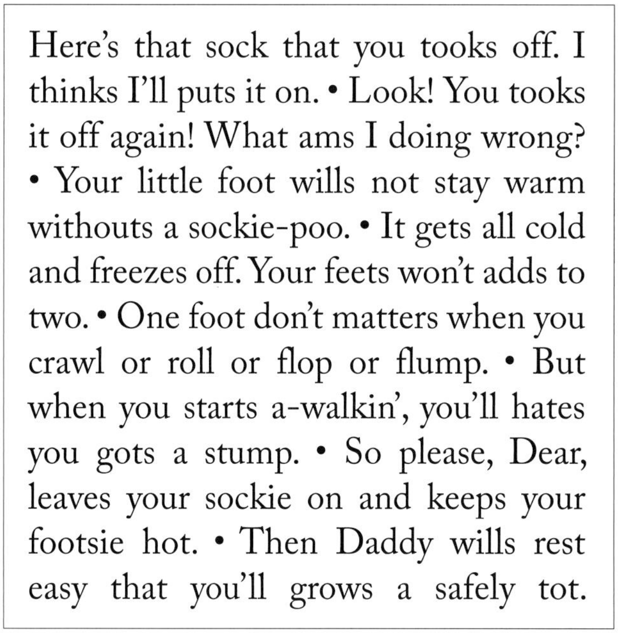

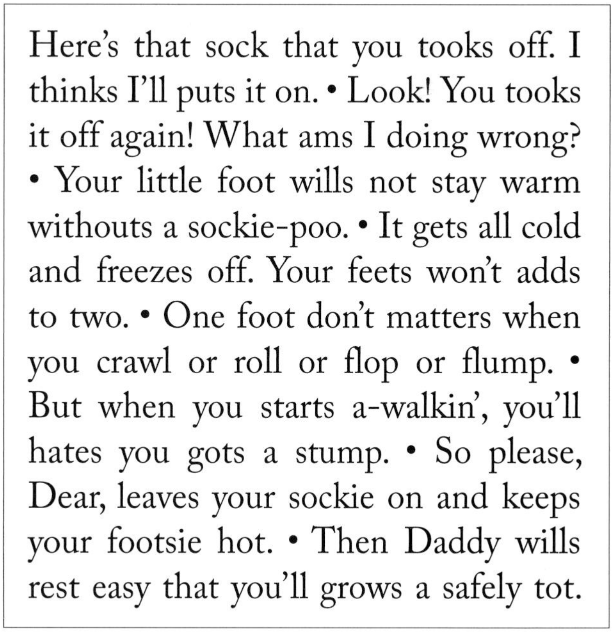

Here's that sock that you tooks off. I
thinks I'll puts it on. • Look! You tooks
it off again! What ams I doing wrong?
• Your little foot wills not stay warm
withouts a sockie-poo. • It gets all cold
and freezes off. Your feets won't adds
to two. • One foot don't matters when
you crawl or roll or flop or flump. •
But when you starts a-walkin', you'll
hates you gots a stump. • So please,
Dear, leaves your sockie on and keeps
your footsie hot. • Then Daddy wills
rest easy that you'll grows a safely tot.

Figure 4-47.

**PEARL OF WISDOM**

Steps 8 through 14 specifically deal with OpenType font features. But what exactly is OpenType? It is a font standard developed by Microsoft and Adobe that has many advantages over the old Type 1 or TrueType formats, including cross-platform support (no need for separate Windows and Mac versions!), extended character sets, and automatic substitution of many typesetting characters and variants. Adobe converted their entire type library to OpenType in 2002, and nearly every major type foundry now offers most, if not all, their typefaces in OpenType format. All the fonts shipped with the Creative Suite are OpenType fonts, though only those labeled Pro have the full range of OpenType features.

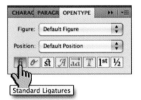

Figure 4-48.

Here's that sock that you tooks off. I thinks I'll puts it on. • Look! You tooks it off again! What ams I doing wrong? • Your little foot wills not ſtay warm withouts a sockie-poo. • It gets all cold and freezes off. Your feets won't adds to two. • One foot don't matters when you crawl or roll or flop or flump. • But when you ſtarts a-walkin', you'll hates you gots a ſtump. • So please, Dear, leaves your sockie on and keeps your footsie hot. • Then Daddy wills reſt easy that you'll grows a safely tot.

Figure 4-49.

8. ***Turn on standard ligatures.*** The most helpful of OpenType features for everyday use is automatic standard ligatures. *Ligatures* are single letterforms that are used to represent multiple letters—for example, the *fi* in *fine*. (The same word without ligatures: *fine*.) Different fonts supply different ligatures, but with OpenType fonts you needn't concern yourself because Illustrator places them automatically.

   Press Ctrl+Alt+Shift+T (⌘-Option-Shift-T) to bring up the **OpenType** panel, shown in Figure 4-48. Click the **fi** icon to turn on standard ligatures. You'll notice the *ff* and *fl* pairs all update to use ligatures.

9. ***Turn on discretionary ligatures.*** Discretionary ligatures are significantly less common and generally relegated to antique documents (or documents mimicking antiques), but they can also be used for decorative purposes. Their name is apt—they are to be used at your discretion. Turn them on for this document by clicking the ſt icon. Figure 4-49 shows the result of the text with both standard and discretionary ligatures. (In the case of Adobe Caslon Pro, the only discretionary ligatures that appeared were the *st* pairs.)

10. ***Create a fraction in the first line.*** Notice the fraction *331/3* in the line across the top of the document? Properly typeset, it should appear as $33^{1}/_{3}$. OpenType makes creating the fraction straightforward; simply select the characters 1/3 with the type tool, and click the ½ icon. Illustrator automatically builds the fraction.

    Note that if you select all the number, Illustrator will build the fraction $^{331}/_{3}$, so it's important to select only the part you want to become a fraction.

11. ***Create an ordinal in the date.*** Just to the right of the fraction is an ordinal. *Ordinals* are used after numbers, such as $12^{th}$ or $23^{rd}$, or even $2^{e}$ in French. Building proper ordinals is as simple as building fractions; select the ordinal text (in this case, *st*) and click the $1^{st}$ icon.

12. ***Set all the numbers to proportional oldstyle.*** Another feature of OpenType fonts involving numerals is oldstyle versus lining figures. *Oldstyle* figures, much like discretionary ligatures, have an antique feel, and many descend below the baseline. *Lining*

figures are the standard numerals you're accustomed to seeing; they're called lining because they all line up along the baseline. To further complicate matters, each style of figure also has tabular versus proportional variants. With *tabular* figures, each digit is the same width, so the numbers line up nicely when presented in a table. *Proportional* figures, on the other hand, vary in width. Figure 4-50 shows the difference between the styles.

| Lining | Oldstyle | |
|---|---|---|
| 4,571 | 4,571 | Tabular |
| 4,571 | 4,571 | Proportional |

Figure 4-50.

In this case, since the date is in the 18th century, oldstyle figures seem completely appropriate. Triple-click the first line, and back in the OpenType panel, choose **Proportional Oldstyle** from the **Figure** pop-up menu. The cumulative results of the past few steps can be seen in Figure 4-51.

Draft No. 33⅓, September 21st, 1794

Figure 4-51.

13. ***Change the initial caps to italic swashes.*** The first line has been dressed up quite a bit, but there's yet another decorative function of OpenType left to be seen. *Swashes* are alternate versions of characters, usually with some kind of flourish or embellishment. Using the type tool, select the capital *D* at the start of the first line. Unfortunately, if you attempt to apply a swash by clicking the *A* icon, you're greeted with a ⊘ cursor—swashes aren't available. What gives?

 As is the case with many (but not all) fonts, swashes exist only in the italic style of Caslon Pro. In the control panel, change the **Style** from Regular to **Italic**, and then click the *A* icon. Presto, your first swash! Repeat this for the *N* and *S*; when you're finished you should see a line like Figure 4-52.

*Draft No.* 33⅓, *September* 21st, 1794

Figure 4-52.

14. ***Apply small caps to the byline.*** There's one last OpenType function to take a look at, and that's small caps. *Small caps* are capital letters reduced in height, usually to the font's x-height or slightly taller. Unlike the other OpenType functions, however, small caps can't be accessed in the OpenType panel.

 Select the entire byline *by a daddy who care* by triple-clicking the line of text. Next, bring up the **Character** panel, and from the ▾≡ menu select **Small Caps**. Illustrator dutifully changes the type, as shown in Figure 4-53.

Why isn't this function in the OpenType panel? Small caps can be applied to any typeface; if an OpenType small cap is not available, Illustrator will do its best by reducing the size of the font's full capitals.

BY A DADDY WHO CARE

Figure 4-53.

15. ***Add an ornamental glyph via the Glyphs panel.*** I've saved what I consider the best for last. The Glyphs panel (seen in

The options for ordinals, fractions, and small caps are more than just conveniences in OpenType fonts; they're superior design. Rather than simply making the characters smaller, as was the case with Type 1 or TrueType fonts, OpenType fonts have special letterforms—created by the typeface designer—that are smaller in stature, but match the weight of the full-size typeface. Figure 4-54 illustrates the difference.

Fake fraction
33¹/₃

Fake ordinal
21ˢᵗ

OpenType fraction
33⅓

OpenType ordinal
21ˢᵗ

Fake small caps
BY A DADDY WHO CARE

OpenType small caps
BY A DADDY WHO CARE

Figure 4-54.

Figure 4-55.

Figure 4-56.

Figure 4-55) is one of the most useful type tools in all of Illustrator because it gives you access to every character a font has to offer. (You can bring up the **Glyphs** panel by choosing **Type→Glyphs**.) The ⬙ and ⬘ icons decrease and increase the size of the character previews; the pop-up menus at the bottom allow you to choose the font and style to view. A small ▸ icon in the lower-right corner indicates that alternates are available for that character. Simply double-click a glyph to insert it (assuming the text tool is active).

I want to insert a second ornament in the byline to match the first. With the type tool, click at the end of the byline to set the insertion point. (Be sure to include the trailing space.) The ornament is from Adobe Garamond Pro Italic; change the font at the bottom of the Glyphs panel to **Adobe Garamond Pro** and the **Style** to **Italic**. Scroll all the way to the bottom to find the glyph highlighted in Figure 4-55, and double-click to insert it.

And with that, you've wrapped up your *tour de force* of text formatting in Illustrator; Figure 4-56 shows the fruits of your labor. You've made it through quite a bit of information in just a few exercises, but my hope is that this lesson leaves you well-prepared to delve into the meticulous yet rewarding craft that is typesetting.

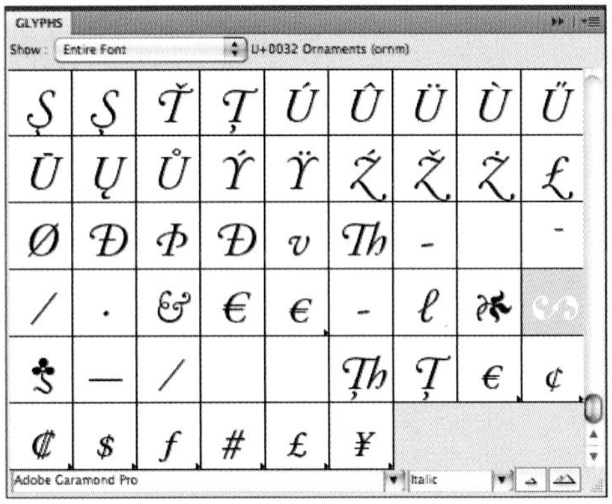

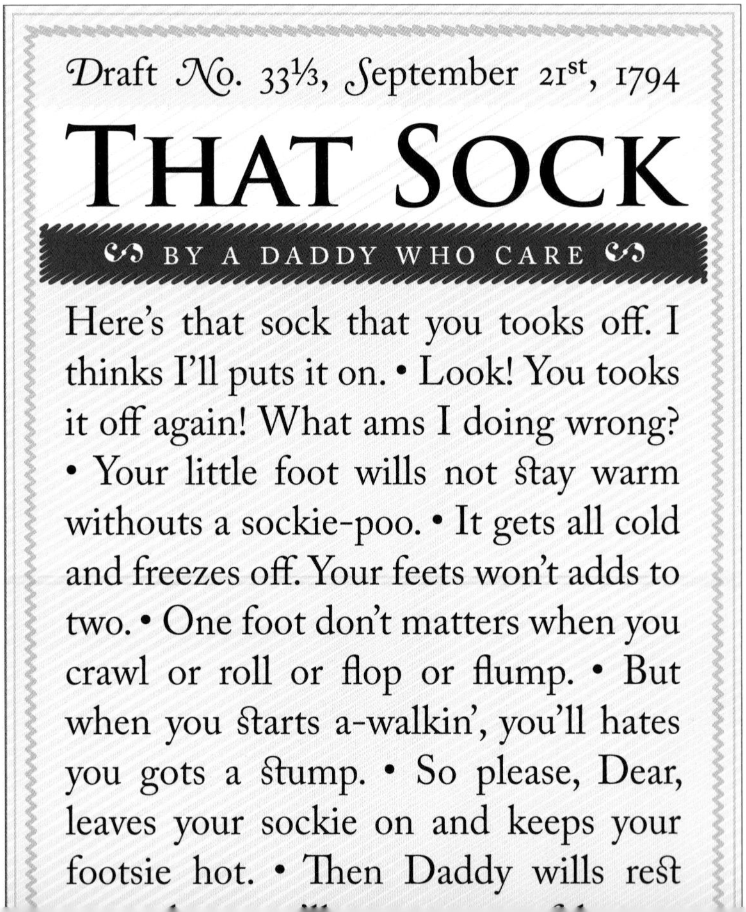

Draft № 33⅓, September 21ˢᵗ, 1794

## THAT SOCK

❧ BY A DADDY WHO CARE ❧

Here's that sock that you tooks off. I thinks I'll puts it on. • Look! You tooks it off again! What ams I doing wrong? • Your little foot wills not ſtay warm withouts a sockie-poo. • It gets all cold and freezes off. Your feets won't adds to two. • One foot don't matters when you crawl or roll or flop or flump. • But when you ſtarts a-walkin', you'll hates you gots a ſtump. • So please, Dear, leaves your sockie on and keeps your footsie hot. • Then Daddy wills reſt

# WHAT DID YOU LEARN?

Match the key concept in the numbered list below with the letter of the phrase that best describes it. Answers appear upside-down at the bottom of the page.

## Key Concepts

1. Point type
2. Area type
3. Type on a path
4. Baseline
5. x-height
6. Ascender
7. Leading
8. Tracking
9. Kerning
10. Ligature
11. Ordinal
12. Swash

## Descriptions

A. A special letterform that replaces two or three characters, with *fl* being a classic example.

B. A line of type anchored to the outline of an Illustrator shape.

C. The height of the majority of lowercase letters, such as *a*, *m*, or *s*.

D. The space between lines of type.

E. A line or lines of type that have a single anchor point; you must do line breaks by hand.

F. A special character used to replace a standard character, usually for decorative purposes.

G. The height of tall lowercase letters, including *d*, *h*, and *l* (but generally not *t*).

H. An imaginary line on which all characters of type rest.

I. The space between characters in a line of type.

J. A line or lines of type that fit within a text block; the text wraps automatically and can flow from one block to another.

K. A special formatting applied to letters that follow numerals, such as *14^th*.

L. The space between individual pairs of characters.

## Answers

1E, 2J, 3B, 4H, 5C, 6G, 7D, 8I, 9L, 10A, 11K, 12F

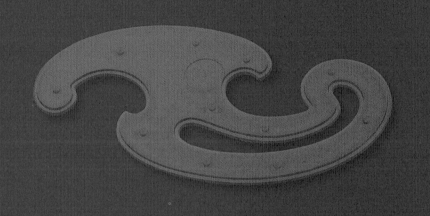

# TRANSFORM AND RESHAPE

**IN REAL LIFE**, a transformation is a complete change, an overhaul that forever improves something. In Illustrator, a transformation is very nearly the opposite—much less grand, much more common, definitely not an overhaul. A *transformation* is any operation that changes a path without compromising its original structure. After transforming a path, its points and segments remain basically in the same position relative to each other.

An example is scaling. If you enlarge a five-pointed star, it's still a five-pointed star—it's just bigger. Rotation is also a transformation. So are reflecting and slanting (what Illustrator calls *shearing*). These are the main four transformations, as shown in Figure 5-1, but you could argue that there are others as well. Offsetting a path moves all the points outward or inward. The reshape tool rearranges points, but the stretched shape remains recognizable. Even the simple act of moving a path is a transformation.

While transformations are hardly transformative, they are undeniably powerful. They permit you to size paths to match. You can repurpose paths and build ambitious illustrations. And with a few seconds' work, you can transform and duplicate paths to create symmetrical shape sequences that would take minutes (or even hours) to render with traditional tools.

## The Fine Art of Reshaping

The reshape tool isn't the only way to reshape a path. (In fact, it may be my least preferred way—although the results are often interesting, they're only sometimes helpful and seldom predictable.) Instead, the pen tool offers such extreme control that it's possible to position every anchor point and control handle exactly where you want them so you never need touch them again. These are the kinds of manipulations that I refer to as *reshaping*. While it's pos-

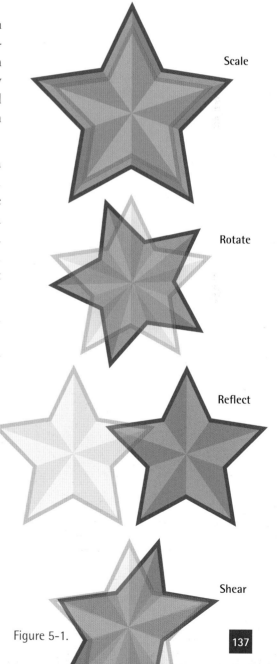

Scale

Rotate

Reflect

Shear

Figure 5-1.

# ABOUT THIS LESSON

## Project Files

Before beginning the exercises, make sure you've downloaded the lesson files from *www.oreilly.com/go/Deke-IllustratorCS5*, as directed in Step 2 on page xiv of the Preface. This should result in a folder called *Lesson Files-Alcs5 1on1* on your desktop. We'll be working with the files inside the *Lesson 05* subfolder.

Transformations are simple operations, but they can produce powerful results when used wisely. In this lesson, you'll learn how to:

## Video Lesson 5: Selecting and Aligning

Selecting an object or set of objects allows you to edit, alter, group, or move items inside your artwork. In this video, I'll show you how to select objects with Illustrator's two selection arrow tools, the black and white arrows. And then I'll show you how to align objects precisely and efficiently with Illustrator's Align options.

To see selections live, visit *www.oreilly.com/go/deke-IllustratorCS5*. Click the **Watch** button to view the lesson online or click the **Download** button to save it to your computer. During the video, you'll learn these shortcuts:

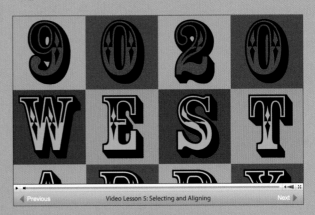

Video Lesson 5: Selecting and Aligning

| Operation | Windows shortcut | Macintosh shortcut |
| --- | --- | --- |
| Select the black arrow tool | Press the V key | Press the V key |
| Display the Preferences dialog box | Ctrl+K | ⌘-K |
| Select the next object below | Ctrl+Alt+[ (left bracket) | ⌘-Option-[ (left bracket) |
| Select through one object to another | Ctrl-click with the black arrow | ⌘-click with the black arrow |
| Turn on or off smart guides | Ctrl+U | ⌘-U |
| Select entire objects inside groups | Alt-click with the white arrow | Option-click with the white arrow |
| Ungroup everything | Ctrl+Shift+G | ⌘-Shift-G |
| Display the Appearance panel | Shift+F6 | Shift-F6 |
| Select the lasso or magic wand tool | Press the Q or W key | Press the Q or W key |
| Display the Align dialog box | Shift+F7 | Shift-F7 |

sible you won't need to edit your artwork, that's usually not the case. The addition of a new path often forces you to reassess another path. You may decide to construct a complex path in pieces and then join them. And some reshapings that you can do after drawing a path are simply easier (and more fun) when applied with tools other than the pen.

Which is why Illustrator lets you select and enhance your artwork. As I demonstrate in the Video Lesson 5: "Selecting and Aligning" you can select through one shape to another below it in the layers stack, select a range of points with the lasso tool, select related objects with the magic wand, select all segments in a path independently of their anchor points, and save selections for later use. Once you've selected precisely those parts of those paths you want, you can enhance them by adding center points, copy colors independently of their fill and stroke attributes, transform paths from independent origin points, scale and filter individual segments, and merge a single stroke across multiple paths.

Illustrator's white arrow tool gives you a surgical level of control over the nipping, tucking, trimming, and ultimate reconstruction of any path in your illustration. It's indisputably one of the most basic and powerful editing tools. But the best illustrations ultimately use a combination of the white arrow tool and the transformation functions; you turn to whichever tool provides the best control and the most efficient means to the desired end.

Start here...

...follow these steps...

...and end up here.

## Moving and Cloning Path Elements

In the first two exercises, I'll walk you through creating a fanciful (and utterly fictitious) ancient Pueblo stop sign, a stylized hand symbol that I invented to warn the cliff-dwelling Native Americans of dangerous intersections. You'll start with two simple shapes, a line and a spiral, shown in the upper half of Figure 5-2. Then through a series of pictured transformations, you'll create the final art shown in the lower half of the figure. (You'll also add a few effects to polish the final shape, as you'll see at the end of the second exercise.) These exercises entail no drawing: simply a series of manipulations to create the final artwork. And with that, let's get started.

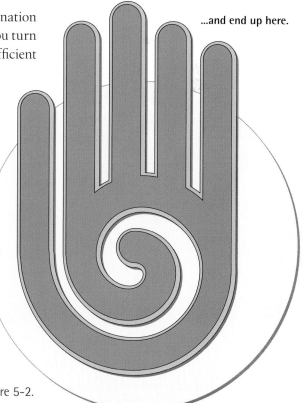

Figure 5-2.

Figure 5-3.

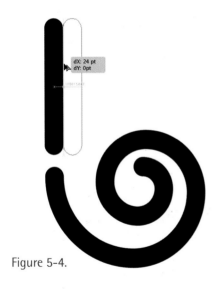

Figure 5-4.

1. *Open the Pueblo stop sign art.* Navigate to the *Lesson 05* folder inside the *Lesson Files-AIcs5 1on1* folder, and open the *Pueblo stop.ai* file.

2. *Make sure the Shapes layer is active.* Examine the **Layers** panel, and notice the file's two layers: One contains the fundamental shapes you'll be working with, and the other, a finished art layer I've provided for reference. Turn off the **Finished Art** layer by clicking the 👁 next to it, and click the first empty column by the **Shapes** layer to make it visible. Finally, click the name of the Shapes layer to make sure it's active. Your Layers panel should look like that shown in Figure 5-3.

3. *Outline the stroke of the thumb.* With the black arrow tool, select the line that will compose the thumb of the stop-sign hand. Right now, the line is a simple line segment, with rounded caps and a 24-point stroke. Although it's easiest to draw the thumb this way, it's much easier to manipulate it as a filled shape—that is to say, a closed path. With the path selected, choose **Object→ Path→Outline Stroke**. (If the bounding box is visible when you select the line segment, hide it by pressing Ctrl+Shift+B or ⌘-Shift-B on the Mac.) Illustrator replaces the original stroked path with a new closed shape that matches perfectly.

4. *Duplicate the thumb.* I want to duplicate the thumb to use it as the other four fingers, but I also want the fingers to be exactly one finger-width apart. You can achieve this by duplicating the thumb for use as a "spacer" finger. Click anywhere on the left edge of the new shape, and drag it to the right until it snaps to the right edge of the first shape, as shown in Figure 5-4. (Press the Shift key to constrain your drag to purely horizontal.) Before releasing the mouse button, press the Alt (or Option) key; your cursor will change from ▸ to ▸, indicating that you are now cloning the shape, rather than simply moving it. Once you see the duplicate cursor, release the mouse button.

---

If your shapes aren't snappy—that is to say, they aren't snapping into place when you bring the edges close together—confirm that your smart guides are turned on by choosing smart guides in the View menu.

---

5. *Change the color of the spacer thumb.* Now that you have your first spacer, you need to change the color to allow this spacer and its fellow spacers to be easily deleted once they've served their purpose. Shift-click the Color swatch in the control panel, shown in Figure 5-5. Adjust the **K** slider down to 0, and the **M** and **Y** sliders up to 100, making the spacer finger a rich red.

6. *Select and duplicate the thumb pair.* Marquee around the top of the two thumbs to select both, and then repeat the method used in Step 4 to duplicate both shapes, as shown in Figure 5-6.

7. *Repeat the transformation three times.* In this step, you'll see one of the very handy shortcuts that transformations offer. Choose **Object→Transform→Transform Again** to automatically create a third finger/spacer pair, appropriately positioned. Did you notice the Ctrl+D (⌘-D on the Mac) keyboard shortcut on the menu? Press it twice to round out the hand with a total of five digits and five spacers, as shown in Figure 5-7.

8. *Select and delete the spacers.* Using the black arrow tool (which should still be the active tool), select one of the spacer shapes. At the far right of the control panel, click the ⬝ icon next to the 🔲 icon (select similar options), and choose **Fill Color** from the pop-up menu. Since all the spacers now have the same fill (and a fill different from all the other art), only the spacers will be selected. Press the Backspace (or Delete) key to get rid of them.

9. *Select the four fingers and move them up.* Now it's time to move the fingers so that they look more like fingers on a hand and less like Popsicle sticks on a spiral. Marquee around the four fingers to select them, as shown in Figure 5-8. You could nudge the fingers up using the ↑ key, or even Shift+↑, but that could take a long time, depending on your keyboard increment. Instead I'd like you to move them by the numbers. Press Enter (Return on the Mac) to bring up the **Move** dialog box. Positive values move the selection down or to the right; negative values move the selection up or to the left. (You can also specify a distance and an angle, but for our purposes, we'll stick with vertical movement only.) Make sure the **Preview** check box is turned on, enter a **Horizontal** value of 0 pt and a **Vertical** value of −50 pt, and press the Tab key. (You should see the preview update as soon as you press Tab.) Click **OK** to dismiss the dialog box.

10. *Move the index, middle, and ring fingers.* Repeat Step 9, this time marquee just the three central figure shapes.

Figure 5-5.

Figure 5-6.

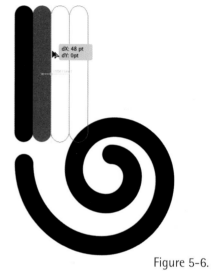

Figure 5-7.

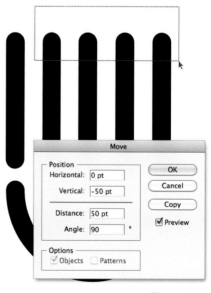

Figure 5-8.

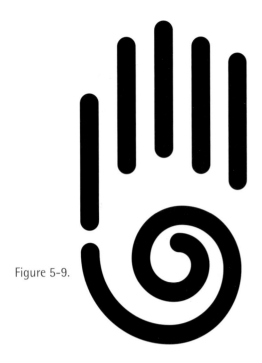

Figure 5-9.

Figure 5-10.

Figure 5-11.

Press the Enter (Return) key. In the Move dialog box, move these three fingers up 20 points by entering a Vertical value of −20 pt, and click **OK** to accept the transformation.

---

You may have noticed that the Move dialog box remembered your value of −50 pt from the last step. All the transformation dialog boxes remember the last values you supplied, which makes repeating transformations easy. But there's an even easier way to repeat the transformation, as you'll see in the next step.

---

11. *Repeat the transformation for the middle finger.* Select the middle finger, and repeat the transformation to move it up 20 points, either by choosing **Object→Transform→Transform Again** or by pressing Ctrl+D (⌘-D). Your arranged figures should look like those in Figure 5-9.

12. *Make the Finished Art layer a template.* The rather clumsy spiral needs some work, but to know how to transform it, you need the guidelines provided by the original. Here's how to transform the layer into a template:

   • Turn on the **Finished Art** layer by clicking the empty box in the far left column.

   • Select all the elements on the Finished Art layer by meatballing it (clicking the ⊙ icon to the right of the layer name).

   • In the control panel, change the **Opacity** value to 50%.

   • Lock the layer by clicking the second column just to the right of the 👁 icon.

   • Finally, drag the layer to the bottom of the stack, and click the **Shapes** layer name to once again make it the active layer.

13. *Move the spiral into position.* Now that you have your template layer in place, you can go about fixing the spiral—but first, you have to position it properly. With the black arrow tool, drag the spiral up into position so that the lower-left arc is more or less centered on the template, as in Figure 5-10. (Again, you can hold the Shift key to constrain your movement to purely vertical.)

14. *Use the reshape tool to adjust the spiral.* At this point, you could adjust the points and control handles of the spiral by using white arrow tool, but there's another way—using the reshape tool. Click and hold the scale tool to reveal the flyout menu, as shown in Figure 5-11, and select the final tool, the reshape tool. Move the endpoint at the spiral's center into position; note that as you drag the point, the other points move relative to the

drag, except for the spiral's other endpoint, which stays firmly anchored in place. Then, start moving the various midpoints into position. Both endpoints will stay locked in their positions, but all the intervening points shuffle around rather elastically. (The effect is not unlike a taffy pull, frankly.) As you move the points, you'll notice that points you've already positioned will move out of place, so you'll need to keep revisiting them as the shape gets closer and closer to perfect. Once you have something that approximates Figure 5-12, you're ready to move to the next step. (It took me about a dozen drags of various points to get the spiral into a shape that more or less matched the template.)

Figure 5-12.

---

**PEARL OF ⬤ WISDOM**

Unlike nearly every other tool in Illustrator, precision is the reshape tool's enemy and ease-of-use its friend. You can't completely control the shape because each move has consequences on other points, not just the one you drag. However, the reshape tool maintains the overall curves, making sure everything stays smooth, even as you manipulate multiple points on the path. With the pen tool, you'd need to adjust each point and control handle manually, which could quickly get complicated and persnickety.

---

15. ***Convert the spiral to a filled shape.*** Before you can join the spiral to the fingers, the spiral needs to be a filled shape, rather than a stroked path. Switch back to the black arrow tool and select the spiral, then choose **Object→Path→Outline Stroke**.

    As soon as you do, note the rather alarming number of points that make up the shape; drawing this shape by hand with the pen tool clearly would have been unnecessarily difficult.

---

**EXTRA ⭐ CREDIT**

Speaking of persnickety, this last group of steps could certainly qualify. But they're the only place where you'll learn how to manipulate discrete portions of a path and how to select and deselect just one of several overlapping paths—not to mention the place where I introduce the Pathfinder panel. So stick around, if you're so inclined. Otherwise, meet me at the next exercise, "Offsetting Paths to Simulate Depth" on page 146.

---

16. ***Zoom in and change the Shapes layer to outline mode.*** It's time for some detail work, so you need to make sure your view is as clear as possible. Zoom in on the area where the thumb overlaps the spiral—something in the 600% to 800% range works best, depending on your screen size. Bring up the **Layers** panel (if it's not still visible), and Ctrl-click (⌘-click) the 👁 icon next to the **Shapes** layer to switch that layer to outline mode. Your art should now look similar to that in Figure 5-13.

17. *Align the spiral to the thumb.* Chances are good that your art, like that in Figure 5-13, doesn't quite line up. With the black arrow tool, select the spiral, and drag it until it snaps into alignment with the thumb (most likely, just a fraction of a point).

---

Unlike earlier versions of Illustrator, CS5 uses smart guides, so you don't necessarily have to grab the path by an anchor point; the path will snap into place without a point to act as an anchor.

---

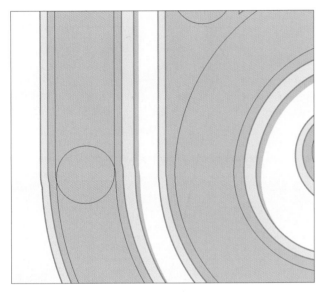

Figure 5-13.

18. *Extend the index finger to intersect the spiral.* Switch to the white arrow tool by pressing the A key, and marquee around the bottom curve of the index finger to select just those points, as shown in Figure 5-14. Drag those points until they align with the bottom of the thumb, adding the Shift key to constrain the movement to vertical.

19. *Nudge the curve of the spiral into alignment.* Once again, the spiral is out of alignment; this time with the index finger. You need to select some of the points on the spiral to move them; marquee the area shown in Figure 5-15 to select the necessary points.

Unfortunately, that also selected some of the points of the finger, which you don't want to move. Shift+Alt-click (or Shift-Option-click) the index finger once to add the entire shape to the selection, and Shift+Alt-click (Shift-Option-click) again to deselect the entire

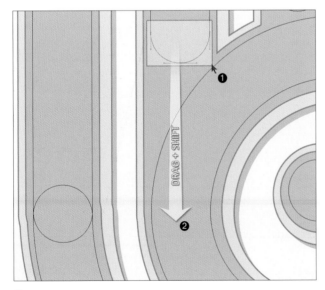

Figure 5-14.

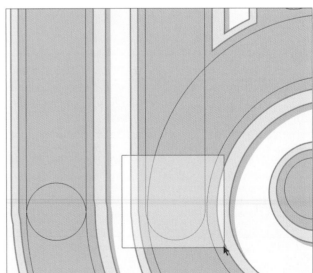

Figure 5-15.

finger. Now nudge the points with the arrow keys so that they align with the finger, as in Figure 5-16. (I did four nudges to the left; your nudges may vary.)

20. ***Repeat the extension for the middle finger.*** Repeat the procedure from Step 18 with the points at the bottom of the middle finger.

21. ***Extend the ring finger down.*** Marquee around the bottom of the ring finger to select the points along the bottom curve, as shown in Figure 5-17. Unfortunately, this also selects an arc of the spiral; press and hold the Shift key and draw a second marquee that intersects just the arc segment to deselect it. Move the bottom of the finger down, again adding Shift to constrain the move.

22. ***Extend the pinky.*** Drawing a marquee around the bottom of the pinky also selects part of the spiral; while holding down the Shift key, marquee again over the arc to deselect that segment. Drag the bottom edge down to overlap the spiral, as shown in Figure 5-18.

23. ***Align the spiral to the pinky.*** Marquee around the area shown in Figure 5-19 on the next page. As with the index finger, this selects a few points you don't want. Shift+Alt-click (Shift-Option-click) the pinky *twice* to select, and then deselect the entire

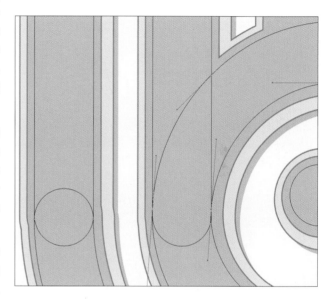

Figure 5-16.

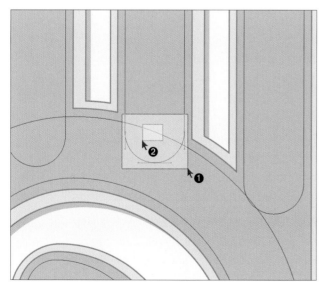

Figure 5-17.

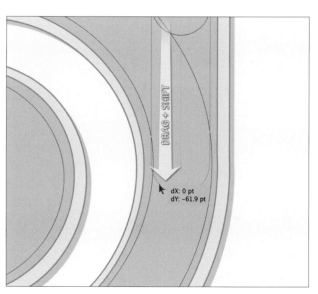

Figure 5-18.

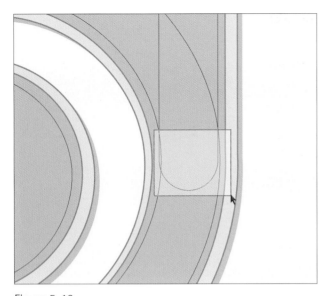

Figure 5-19.

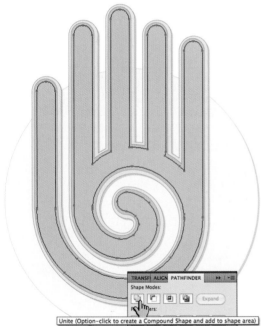

Figure 5-20.

path. Then, using the arrow keys, nudge the spiral into alignment.

24. *Zoom out and select all the shapes.* Now that everything's aligned properly and your shapes are overlapping, zoom back out so you can see the full artwork. Select all the shapes by pressing Ctrl+A (⌘-A).

25. *Join the shapes with the Pathfinder panel.* Bring up the **Pathfinder** panel by pressing Ctrl+Shift+F9 (⌘-Shift-F9) or choosing **Window→Pathfinder**. Click the 🔲 icon to join (or unite) the shapes into a single filled path, as shown in Figure 5-20.

---

After you click 🔲, you should see one single outline with no points left inside the shape. If your shapes look unchanged, however, not to worry—Illustrator joined them into a *compound path*, that is, a path made up of multiple shapes, rather than a new single path. Simply click the Expand icon in the Pathfinder panel to complete the step. I discuss the Pathfinder panel fully in the next lesson.

---

The hand is now complete, and you accomplished all those steps without using a single drawing tool. Save your work because in the next exercise you'll be returning to it to put the finishing touches on your stop sign.

## Offsetting Paths to Simulate Depth

In the last exercise, you used various transformations to create the basic shapes of the stop sign. But Illustrator has still more transformations in store. In this exercise, I'll walk you through a transformation creating the illusion of depth, and you'll put the final touches on your artwork with graphics styles, swatches, and transparency.

1. *Open the work in progress.* If you still have the art from the last exercise open, skip ahead; otherwise, open your saved file, or navigate to the *Lesson 05* folder inside the *Lesson Files-AIcs5 1on1* folder and open the file *Joined shapes.ai*.

2. *Offset the path to thicken the fingers.* Comparing the hand on the Shapes layer to the Finished Art layer, it's clear that the fingers could use a little more weight. While you could simu-

late the effect with a stroke, why not just transform the path itself? Here's how:

- With the black arrow tool, select the hand on the **Shapes** layer.

- Choose **Object→Path→Offset Path**.

- In the **Offset Path** dialog box, shown in Figure 5-21, change the **Offset** to 3 pt, and make sure the **Preview** box is checked so that you can see the offset. (The other options are fine left at their defaults.)

- Click **OK** to accept the transformation.

Note that Illustrator clones the path before applying the transformation; you now have two hand paths, one inside the other.

Figure 5-21.

3. *Offset the path again to create the bevel.* Select the inner hand path with the black arrow tool, and again choose **Object→ Path→Offset Path**. This time, set the **Offset** to 7 pt, and click **OK**.

4. *Delete the original path.* The original skinny path has served its purpose. Select it for the last time, and delete it by pressing the Backspace or Delete key.

5. *Draw the circle for the background.* Only one element is missing at this point—the large circle that serves as the background of the stop sign.

- Switch to the ellipse tool by pressing the L key or choosing it from the flyout menu of the ▩ tool.

- Drag diagonally down from the upper-left part of the arc, shown in Figure 5-22, toward the lower right. After (and only after) you start the drag, add the Ctrl and Shift keys (⌘ and Shift on the Mac) to draw from arc to arc and constrain the shape to a perfect circle. If your circle still isn't in quite the right position, hold down the spacebar to temporarily drag the circle to a new spot, and release it to continue drawing.

- Once you're satisfied with the circle, release the mouse button, and *then* release any keys you pressed.

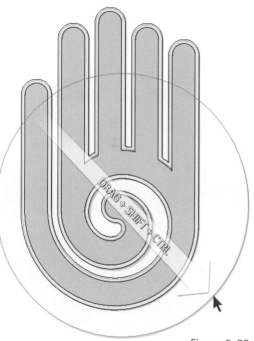

Figure 5-22.

6. *Turn off the Finished Art layer.* You don't really need to see the template any more at this point. Bring up the **Layers** panel, and click the 👁 icon next to the **Finished Art** layer to hide it.

7. *Switch back to preview mode.* Now that all the shapes are in place, it's time to fill in the details. Switch the **Shapes** layer

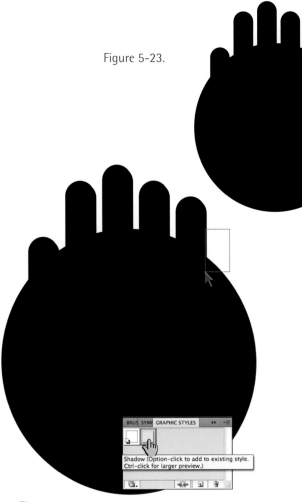

Figure 5-23.

Figure 5-24.

back to preview mode by Ctrl-clicking (or ⌘-clicking) the 👁 icon. As you can see in Figure 5-23, right now the artwork is just a big blob of black, but you'll address that in the next step.

8. *Apply a graphics style to the oval and the outer hand.* With the black arrow tool, marquee the circle and outer hand to select them, as in Figure 5-24. Press Shift+F5 to bring up the **Graphic Styles** panel, and apply the **Shadow** style by clicking the small yellow square. I made this style in advance for this exercise; I go into detail about graphic styles in Lesson 10.

9. *Fix the stacking order of the circle.* If you click off the shapes to deselect them, you'll see that the circle is in front of the hand. That just won't do. Select the circle with the black arrow tool, and choose **Object→Arrange→Send to Back** from the menu (or press the keyboard shortcut, Ctrl+Shift+[ or ⌘-Shift-[ ).

10. *Fix the stacking order of the outer hand.* We've fixed the circle, but the outer hand is still on top of the inner hand. Select the outer hand, and send it back one level by pressing Ctrl+[ (⌘-[ ). The result of the last two steps can be seen in Figure 5-25.

11. *Use the eyedropper tool.* The inner hand is now visible, but it still has its solid black fill. Switch to the 🖊 tool by pressing the I key, and click somewhere on the outer path to lift its stroke and fill attributes. Then press the Alt (or Option) key—your cursor will change to look like 🖊—and click the inner hand path to apply the attributes.

---

Note that the eyedropper tool picks up stroke, fill, transparency, and other attributes, but by default does not pick up or apply live effects, such as the drop shadow appearance. (Live effects are covered fully in Lesson 10.) You can change the default attributes picked up by the eyedropper tool by double-clicking the 🖊 icon in the toolbox.

---

12. *Apply a swatch to both hands.* All the stroke attributes now match the template, but the fill color for the hands is wrong. Select both hands with the black arrow tool, and confirm that the fill attribute is active. (You should see the yellow fill on top of the 🔲 icon at the bottom

Figure 5-25.

of the toolbox; if the fill isn't active, press the X key to make it active.) Choose **Window→Swatches** to bring up the **Swatches** panel. Finally, click the brown swatch to apply it to both hands; your results should look like Figure 5-26.

13. *Apply transparency to lighten the shapes.* The stop sign is in pretty good shape, but I'd like to lighten the beveled hand and the background. Rather than messing around with swatches to try to create a new tint of my color, you can accomplish the task much more easily with transparency. Here's what to do: Marquee to select the circle and outer hand, and from the control panel, change the **Opacity** value from 100 to 50.

Unfortunately, as you can see from Figure 5-27, that didn't have quite the intended effect. Certainly, the shapes are lighter, but the beveled hand is now translucent, and you can see the circle through it. We need a different approach. Press Ctrl+Z (⌘-Z) to undo the opacity, and leave the two objects selected.

14. *Create a group and apply transparency.* What we need is transparency as a group. Group the two objects by choosing **Object→Group** (or press Ctrl+G or ⌘-G). Now change the **Opacity** value back to 50. The hand in Figure 5-28 is opaque relative to the circle, but both are translucent against the background.

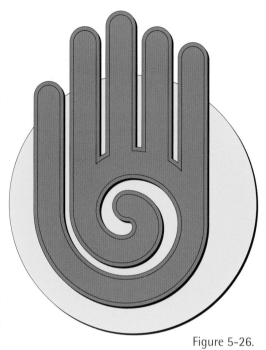

Figure 5-26.

Figure 5-27.

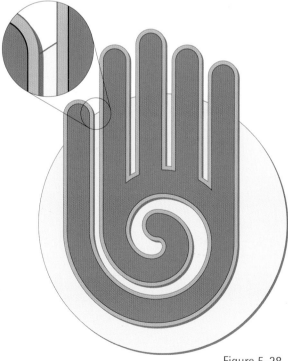

Figure 5-28.

15. *Copy the beveled hand out of its group.* We're nearly there. While I like the look of the paler brown hand, I wish the stroke were still 100% black. Unfortunately, since I asked you to change the opacity of the group, the opacity of that stroke alone can't be restored because—as you'll see in this step—the opacity of the stroke is still set to 100. Here's the trick for copying an element out of a group:

    • Switch to the white arrow tool by pressing the A key.

    • Alt-click (or Option-click) the outer hand path to select the entire path.

    • Press Ctrl+C (⌘-C) to copy the path.

    • Deselect the path by clicking anywhere off the artwork, and then paste the new hand at the front of the stack with Ctrl+F (⌘-F).

    ---

    It's crucial that you deselect the path before pasting. With nothing selected, Illustrator pastes to the front of the entire layer. However, if a piece of artwork is selected, Illustrator pastes it in front of that piece (in this case, just in front of the group).

    ---

    Once you paste the path, you'll see that its opacity is 100%—demonstrating that while the group itself is translucent, the individual pieces retain their original opacity.

16. *Change the fill of the hand to none.* Last step—you've restored the dark stroke, but the fill is now obscuring the inner hand underneath. Remove the fill by pressing the Ⓘ key.

And there you have it! Starting with a simple black line and spiral, you've recreated the fictional stop sign, first shown all the way back in Figure 5-2 on page 139, using a myriad of transformation tools. Along the way, you've learned a few other tricks dealing with groups. In the next two exercises, we'll keep with our Native American art theme and return to the *tonalpohualli* you first saw in Lesson 2.

## Working with the Scale Tool

It's time to revisit the *tonalpohualli* from Lesson 2. In this exercise, you'll be working exclusively with the scale tool—not only scaling artwork from its center point, but also scaling around a specified transformation origin. The *transformation origin* is the point around which all of Illustrator's transformation tools are calculated. While the transformation origin defaults to the center of the selected object (or objects), you can position it wherever you'd like—flexibility you'll take advantage of over the next two exercises.

1. **Open the new tonalpohualli artwork.** Navigate to the *Lesson 05* folder inside the *Lesson Files-AIcs5 1on1* folder, and open the file *Tonalpo-new-alli.ai*. You'll see the familiar smiling face, but this time, the calendar is decked out in flashy Vegas colors, as shown in Figure 5-29.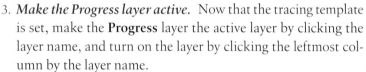

2. **Create a black-and-white tracing template.** While the new colors might be great for the final art, they'll likely distract you as you work through the next steps. Open the **Layers** panel, and select everything on the **Calendar** layer by meatballing the layer (clicking the ○ icon). Make the selected art grayscale by choosing **Edit→Edit Colors→Convert to Grayscale**. In the control panel, set the **Opacity** value to 35. Finally, lock the layer by clicking the second column in the Layers panel, shown in Figure 5-30.

---

Note that the Convert to Grayscale function is not an effect but a permanent change—once you convert objects to grayscale using this method, the color information is gone forever (short of an undo).

---

Figure 5-29.

3. **Make the Progress layer active.** Now that the tracing template is set, make the **Progress** layer the active layer by clicking the layer name, and turn on the layer by clicking the leftmost column by the layer name.

4. **Clone and scale a circle.** The *tonalpohualli* may not look like it needs more circles—it has plenty already—but to match the template, you need precisely three more. With the black arrow tool, start by selecting the innermost circle that isn't part of the god's face (the light brown one). Here's how to scale and clone the circle:

   - Switch to the scale tool by pressing the S key.

   - Start dragging from one of the corners. You'll have much more control with the scale tool if you start your drag on a diagonal, rather than directly horizontal or vertical. As you drag toward the center, the circle will be reduced; dragging outward enlarges the shape.

Figure 5-30.

# Scale, Rotate, Reflect, Shear, and Move

Illustrator provides four core transformation tools—scale, rotate, reflect, and shear—plus the black arrow tool, which allows for basic movement. These tools all share some common functionality.

For instance, with each of the four core tools, you click once to set the origin point, and then drag to begin the transformation. While dragging to complete the transformation, Shift constrains the transformation (in the case of rotate, reflect, and shear, to 45-degree angles; in the case of scale, to purely horizontal, to purely vertical, or to a uniform aspect ratio). The Alt (or Option) key instructs Illustrator to clone the object, creating a second object with the transformation applied while preserving the original. These modifier keys function for the black arrow tool as well, with Shift constraining the move to 45-degree angles.

Double-clicking any of the tools brings up the appropriate transformation dialog box—pictured in the figures below— setting the origin point at the default (the center of the selected object or objects). Alt-clicking (Option-clicking on the Mac) sets the origin to the point clicked and brings up the same dialog box. (Double-clicking also works for the black arrow tool, but Alt-clicking does not.)

Some of the options are consistent across all the transformation tools. For instance, the Objects and Patterns options select whether the transformation affects the paths themselves, the pattern fill, or both. (Yes, it's possible to transform the pattern fill without changing the outline of the base shape, but see the Tip on page 161 for a caveat about the Patterns option.)

Other options, however, are specific to each transformation. The Scale dialog box allows uniform (proportional) scaling, nonuniform scaling, and the scaling of strokes and effects. (The last option is most useful when you like the proportion of a shape's stroke, drop shadow, and so on; selecting this option causes Illustrator to scale the stroke weight or effect size proportionally to the object's new dimensions.)

Rotate's Angle option is straightforward, indicating the degree the object will rotate *counterclockwise* around the transformation origin. Likewise, the Reflect Angle option specifies the angle of the "mirror" Illustrator will use to calculate the transformation; Illustrator reflects all the points of the object across this axis.

The Shear options are perhaps the least intuitive. The Angle option determines the angle at which Illustrator will slant the path, moving the points above the axis in one direction. The Axis option determines the points that will remain fixed during the transformation; the object shears on either side of this axis.

Limited transformations are available from the Transform panel. Full numerical transformations are available for scale (both proportional and nonproportional), shear, rotate, and move. (Shear transforms, however, are limited to the horizontal axis.) Reflect transformations from the Transform panel

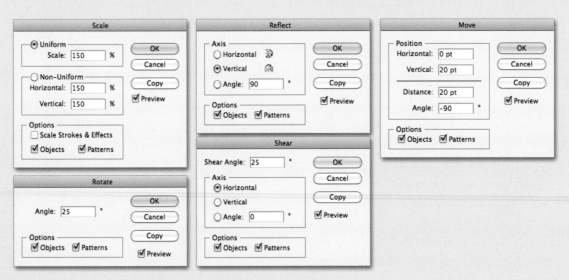

are limited to flipping either along the horizontal or vertical axis. Finally, the Transform panel is accessible also as a pop-up panel from the control panel by clicking any of the blue highlighted labels (X, Y, H, or W).

The easiest way to see how the transformation tools work, though, is to see them in action. A variety of transforma-tions are shown below; each star shows the settings used to achieve the results. Experimenting on your own is the best way to explore the options available. And remember when working with all the transformation dialog boxes, turning on the Preview option will help eliminate a lot of the guesswork involved in achieving the desired effect.

Original

Scale: 75% uniform,
no stroke scaling

Scale: 50% uniform,
pattern only

Scale: 50% H, 100% V,
stroke and object scaling

Rotate:
-12°, object only

Rotate: 27°,
pattern only

Reflect: Horizontal,
object only

Reflect: 45°,
object and pattern

Reflect: Vertical,
pattern only

Shear: 30° shear,
horizontal axis, object only

Shear: 27° shear,
vertical axis, pattern only

Shear: 20° shear,
45° axis, object and pattern

W: 88.31%
H: 88.31%

Select this circle

Figure 5-31.

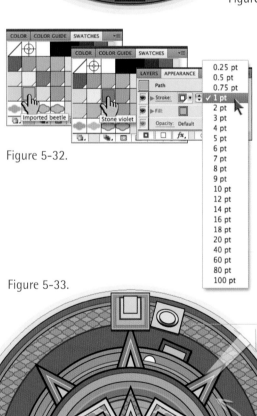

Figure 5-32.

Figure 5-33.

COLOR COLOR GUIDE SWATCHES

COLOR COLOR GUIDE SWATCHES

LAYERS APPEARANCE

Path

Stroke:
Fill:

Opacity: Default

Imported beetle

Stone violet

0.25 pt
0.5 pt
0.75 pt
✓ 1 pt
2 pt
3 pt
4 pt
5 pt
6 pt
7 pt
8 pt
9 pt
10 pt
12 pt
14 pt
16 pt
18 pt
20 pt
40 pt
60 pt
80 pt
100 pt

intersect

W: 156.05%
H: 156.05%

Select this circle

- Add the Shift key to constrain the shape to a perfect circle; add the Alt (or Option) key to create a clone of the shape. Drag in toward the center to reduce the size of the circle. When your circle looks like that indicated by the blue guide in Figure 5-31 (about 88%), release the mouse button and then the keys.

5. *Assign a new stroke and fill.* Bring up the **Swatches** panel (if it's not already visible), shown in Figure 5-32, by choosing it from the **Window** menu. Make sure the fill is active, and apply the Imported Beetle swatch. Press the X key to switch to the stroke, and apply the Stone Violet swatch. Finally, press Shift+F6 to switch to the **Appearance** panel, and reduce the stroke width to 1 pt.

---

As a shortcut, you can change the fill, stroke, and weight in the control panel; they are the first three attributes shown. Alternately, you can make all the changes in the Appearance panel itself.

---

6. *Clone and enlarge another circle.* Two circles are still missing from the outside of the calendar; if you look closely, you can see the vague gray shapes showing through from the tracing template. Ctrl-click (⌘-click) the light brown circle indicated in Figure 5-33 to select it. Clicking again, drag away from the center to enlarge the circle. (I chose this circle because it has no live effects applied to it and will require the fewest attribute changes in the next step.) Add the Shift and Alt (Option) keys to constrain the shape and create a copy; when the circle is the size shown by the blue guide in Figure 5-33, release the mouse button.

**PEARL OF WISDOM**

Pressing the Ctrl key (or the ⌘ key on the Mac) gives you temporary access to the last arrow tool you used. This is a great shortcut for selecting objects without having to switch tools back and forth and definitely one worth committing to memory.

---

Sadly, Illustrator by default places a cloned object directly in front of the original object—which, in this case, means the clone is covering almost half the artwork. We'll fix that in the next step.

7. ***Change the stack order, stroke, and fill.*** Press Ctrl+Shift+[
(⌘-Shift-[) to send the circle to the back of the stack. Assuming the stroke attribute is still active, press the ☐ key to set it to none. Lastly, change the fill to the Medium Clay swatch in the **Swatches** panel, as shown in Figure 5-34.

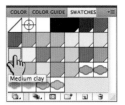

Figure 5-34.

8. ***Create a third circle.*** Your new circle should still be selected, meaning you're ready for more scaling and cloning. Drag just a short distance from the point indicated in Figure 5-35, add the Shift and Alt (Option) keys, and release when the circle is in position, as shown in the figure.

9. ***Change the stack order and fill.*** Again, press Ctrl+Shift+[ (⌘-Shift-[) to send the new circle to the back. In the Swatches panel, set the fill to Light Clay, as in Figure 5-36.

10. ***Select the green square.*** Moving on from the circles, it's time to complete the square ornament on the left side of the circle. If you turn off the **Progress** layer temporarily, you'll see that the square ornament is comprised of three squares, as shown in Figure 5-37; you'll use the same scale and clone techniques used for the circles to complete this ornament. Select the square by Ctrl-clicking it (⌘-clicking on the Mac).

11. ***Move the transformation origin.*** Before you can scale the shape, you need to move the transformation origin. It's specified on screen by a light blue ✛ icon and appears in the center of the object by default. Click the lower-left corner to move the origin, as shown in Figure 5-38.

Figure 5-35.

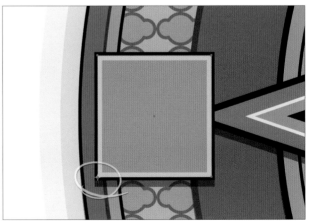

Figure 5-36.

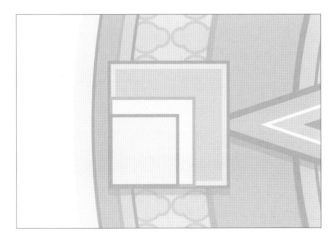

Figure 5-37.

Figure 5-38.

Working with the Scale Tool    155

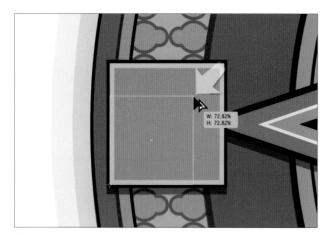

Figure 5-39.

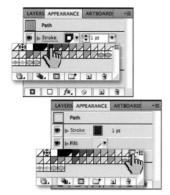

Figure 5-40.

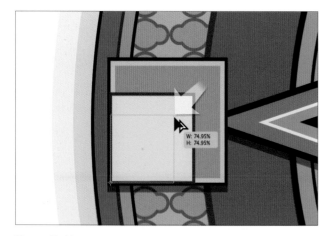

Figure 5-41.

12. ***Clone and scale down the square.*** Starting from the upper-right corner, drag down toward the lower left. Add the Shift and Alt (Option) keys to constrain and clone the shape. Once the clone is positioned like that in Figure 5-39, release the mouse button.

13. ***Assign new attributes via the Appearance panel.*** The new square needs only one stroke, but the current shape has two. Here's what to do:

    • Bring up the **Appearance** panel and delete one of the stroke attributes by selecting it and dragging it to the trash icon in the lower-right corner of the panel.

    • Do the same for the drop shadow effect.

    • Change the remaining stroke to the Darkness swatch (a dark brown color) and a weight of 1 pt, and change the fill to Aztec Gold, as shown in Figure 5-40.

14. ***Clone the square again.*** Scale down the square again, using the Shift and Alt (Option) keys to constrain and clone the shape, as in Figure 5-41. (In the figure, I changed the smart guide from yellow to green to make it more visible.)

15. ***Assign a new stroke and fill.*** This time, set the stroke to Rich Black and the fill to Plains Grass, as shown in Figure 5-42.

16. ***Group the squares.*** Switch to the black arrow tool, and Shift-click the other two squares to se-

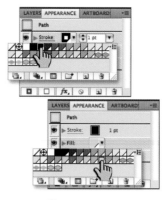

Figure 5-42.

lect all three. Group the squares into a single ornament by pressing Ctrl+G (⌘-G) or by choosing **Object→Group**.

That's it for the *tonalpohualli* for now. You've seen the start of what you can do armed with only the scale tool. Save your work, grab a snack, maybe get up and stretch—or dive right in to the next exercise, where the real magic of power transformations and series duplication shines.

# Rotate, Reflect, and Series Duplication

The ancient Aztec calendar still has some wisdom to impart—namely, the use of the transformation tools to quickly recreate the repeating ornaments around the circles of the calendar, also referred to as *series duplication*. The current art contains just one of each of these elements. In the Lesson 2 files, I had pre-created the bulk of these ornaments; here, you'll learn the secrets of how I made them.

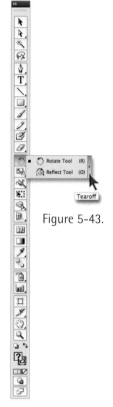

Figure 5-43.

1. ***Open the art in progress.*** If you have your artwork from the last exercise, by all means, use it. Otherwise, make your way to the *Lesson 05* subfolder inside the *Lesson Files-AIcs5 1on1* folder, and open the file called *Ready to rotate.ai.* You'll see just a smattering of ornaments; by the end of the exercise, you'll have recreated the full set.

2. ***Tear off the rotate and reflect tools.*** In this exercise, you'll be switching between the rotate and reflect tools, which share a spot in the toolbox. But there's a better way to access them. Click and hold the ↻ tool, and when you move over the tear-off bar, as shown in Figure 5-43, release the mouse button. This creates a floating minitoolbox that you can position anywhere on the screen.

3. ***Turn on the Guides layer.*** Click the far left column next to the **Guides** layer to turn it on. You should now see two guides, bisecting the horizontal and vertical centers of the art.

4. ***Select the ornament and set the origin.*** With the black arrow tool, select the ornament you grouped in Step 16 of the last exercise. Press the R key to switch to the rotate tool, and click at the intersection of the two guides to set the transformation origin, as shown in Figure 5-44. (In the figure, I've changed the origin point to orange to make it easier to see; by default, the ✛ icon will appear in the same color as your guides.)

Figure 5-44.

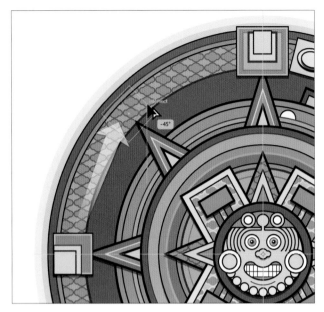

Figure 5-45.

**PEARL OF WISDOM**

It may seem counterintuitive, but for rotation purposes, positive values rotate the object counterclockwise and negative values rotate clockwise. I'll spare you the gory details, but it stems from the polar coordinate system (that forgotten lesson from high school geometry), which is the same system Illustrator uses to calculate rotations.

5. ***Rotate and clone the square ornament.*** Drag the ornament clockwise around the calendar, as shown in Figure 5-45. Add the Shift key to constrain the rotation to 45-degree angles. Finally, add the Alt (or Option) key to clone the shape, and then release the mouse button.

6. ***Clone the ornament again.*** The cloned ornament should still be selected; repeat the preceding step, this time dragging counterclockwise. Your smart measurement should read 90° when you release the mouse button, as in Figure 5-46.

7. ***Reflect the three square ornaments.*** Now that you have one half of the ornaments complete, it's time to clone them to the other side:

   - Switch to the black arrow tool, and add the first two square ornaments to the selection by Shift-clicking them; all three ornaments should be selected.
   - Switch to the reflect tool by pressing the O key, and click somewhere along the upper part of the vertical guide.
   - Next, Alt-click (or Option-click) somewhere along the lower part of the vertical guide, as in Figure 5-47.

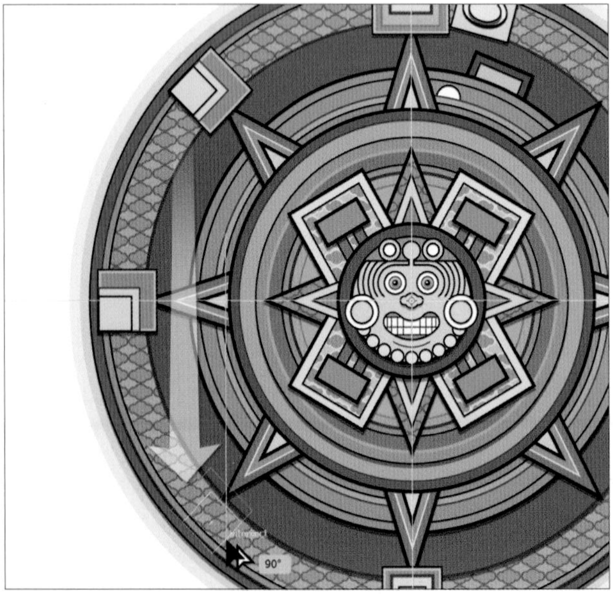

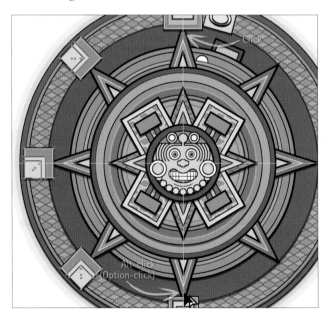

Figure 5-46.

Figure 5-47.

Illustrator treats the two transformation origins as points on a mirror, reflecting the artwork across the axis you defined. (The Alt/Option key, as is true with all the transformation functions, instructs Illustrator to clone the shapes.)

8. **Clone the elliptical ornament.** Switch back to the rotate tool by pressing the R key, and Ctrl-click (⌘-click on the Mac) the elliptical ornament group in the upper-right quadrant of the circle. Click to set the transformation origin at the intersection of the guides, and then drag slightly clockwise to move the ornament. When your smart measurement reads –15° (as in Figure 5-48), press the Alt (or Option) key to clone it, and then release the mouse button.

Figure 5-48.

---

If you don't get a measurement of precisely –15°, don't sweat it. Chances are good that Illustrator's smart guides keep snapping you to some object or another; there's certainly plenty on the page to snap to. You'll be fine as long as you're close. Just as a reminder, if the smart guides are getting in your way, you can turn them off at any point by deselecting smart guides in the View menu. Just be warned: Turning off your smart guides also turns off your smart measurements, so you won't be able to see the angle measurement on-the-fly.

---

9. **Group the two ornaments with the blue square.** Again, press the Ctrl key (or ⌘ key) to temporarily access the black arrow tool. Add the Shift key (which, if you'll recall, adds to the selection) and click the original elliptical ornament and the blue square, as in Figure 5-49. Press Ctrl+G (⌘-G) to group them.

Figure 5-49.

10. **Rotate and clone the group.** If all is well, the group is still selected and the rotate tool is still active. Once again, click at the intersection of the guides to set the origin point, and drag the group clockwise, as shown in Figure 5-50, holding down the Shift and Alt (or Option) keys to constrain and clone the group.

11. **Repeat the transformation.** That's one quarter of the circle; fortunately, the rest is much simpler. Remember the **Transform Again** command, which I first showed you way back in Step 7 on page 141, in the first exercise of this lesson? Use it again here by pressing Ctrl+D (⌘-D on the Mac). You'll need to

Figure 5-50.

Figure 5-51.

Figure 5-52.

press that keyboard shortcut a total of six times to complete the circle. Your first series is duplicated!

12. ***Rotate and clone the egg.*** There's another way to rotate objects—by the numbers, rather than by hand. Ctrl-click (⌘-click) the small circle just below the original elliptical ornament to select it, as shown in Figure 5-51. Instead of clicking at the intersection of the guides to set the origin point, however, Alt-click (or Option-click) at that intersection. This sets the origin and brings up the **Rotate** dialog box. For this little decorative egg, I want an Angle value of –7.75. Change the value and click the **Copy** button to clone the egg.

13. ***Repeat the transformation twice.*** Press Ctrl+D (⌘-D) twice to repeat the cloning and complete the row.

14. ***Group the row of eggs.*** Ctrl+Shift-click (or ⌘-Shift-click) the first three eggs to add them to the selection, and press Ctrl+G (⌘-G) to group them.

15. ***Clone, rotate, and repeat.*** Again, Alt-click (or Option-click) at the intersection of the guides to bring up the **Rotate** dialog box. Enter an **Angle** value of –45, and click the **Copy** button. Press Ctrl+D (or ⌘-D) six times to repeat the transformation all the way around the *tonalpohualli*. Your results should look like Figure 5-52.

16. ***Select the patterned circle and star.*** In the last few steps of the exercise, you'll be working with the patterned ob-

jects in our calendar: the outer circle, the outer four-pointed star, and the rectangular decorations just around the god's face. Start by switching to the black arrow tool and clicking the outer patterned circle to select it. Then Shift-click the star to add it to the selection, as in Figure 5-53.

17. *Rotate the objects and patterns.* Double-click the rotate tool to bring up the Rotate dialog box. Change the **Angle** value to 90, make sure the **Preview** check box is selected, and press the Tab key.

    What gives? Nothing really happened. To rotate the pattern fill along with the shape, you have to make sure that both the **Objects** and **Patterns** check boxes are selected. (Only the Objects box is selected by default.) Once you select the Patterns check box, shown in Figure 5-54, you should see the pattern rotate. Click **OK** to accept the transformation.

Figure 5-53.

18. *Select the grouped rectangles.* One other group in the artwork has a pattern fill—the rectangles framing the god's face. Switch to the black arrow tool and select the rectangles by clicking them.

19. *Rotate the objects and patterns.* Double-click the rotate tool to bring up the Rotate dialog box. By default, Illustrator remembers your last settings. In this case, that's not exactly what you want—the shapes are now awkwardly rotated, as shown in Figure 5-55 on the next page—but unfortunately it's the best you can do for now. Click **OK** to accept the transformation, and resign yourself to fixing things in the next (and final) step.

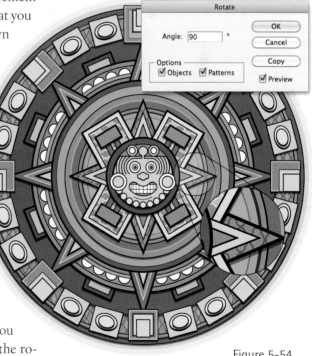

Why not rotate just the patterns? Illustrator gives you that option—in the dialog box in this step, you could have deselected the Objects check box while leaving the Patterns box selected. Sadly (or perhaps buggily), this doesn't always work. With objects that have multiple fill attributes, Illustrator applies pattern-only rotation to just the *active* fill attribute, which in this case is the solid color fill and not the nose-based pattern.

20. *Reverse the rotation of only the objects.* Well, even if the last step didn't give you the results you wanted, you can fix the shapes easily enough. Again, double-click the rotate tool. This time, deselect the **Patterns** check box, and click

Figure 5-54.

Figure 5-55.

**OK**. This rotates the rectangles back into position, while leaving the pattern vertical. The final artwork is pictured in Figure 5-56.

And that, dear reader, is the end of our adventures with the *tonalpohualli*. With just a few simple shapes as your base, you've managed to create an elaborately ornamented illustration—without once using any drawing tool.

Figure 5-56.

## Transforming with Respect to Independent Origins

Allow me to introduce Uzz, cloying corporate mascot extraordinaire. Based on another found petroglyph (seen in Figure 5-57), Uzz will plead with, guilt, or cajole his audience into brand loyalty—or at least that's the hope. Over the course of the next exercise, you'll recreate Uzz's trademark cyclops eye-head using some of the techniques demonstrated earlier in the lesson as well as some new transformations. You'll also learn about saving selections and how to use saved selections to speed up future work.

1. *Open the Uzz artwork and examine the layers.* Navigate to the *Lesson 05* subfolder, inside the *Lesson Files-AIcs5 1on1* folder. Open the file called *Wuv Uzz.ai*, where you'll find our corporate mascot (sans eyelashes), waiting for the final touches before being set loose on the public.

   Bring up the **Layers** panel if it isn't open already. The *Wuv Uzz.ai* file has five layers, three of which are locked and can be safely ignored for the time being. In this exercise, you'll be focusing primarily on the Circle Eye layer.

2. *Hide the Primitives layer.* For now, the Primitives layer is going to be distracting to the work needed on the Circle Eye layer. Click the 👁 icon next to the **Primitives** layer to hide it.

3. *Turn on the Circle Eye layer.* Click the leftmost column of the **Circle Eye** layer to make it visible. You should see a perfect circle, adorned with a single eyelash.

4. *Switch the Circle Eye layer to outline mode.* Ctrl-click (or ⌘-click) the 👁 icon by the Circle Eye layer to switch it to outline mode, as in Figure 5-58.

5. *Rotate and clone the eyelash.* With the black arrow tool, select the eyelash by clicking it. Switch to the rotate tool by pressing the R key, and Alt-click (or Option-click) the center of the circle to bring up the **Rotate** dialog box, as shown in Figure 5-60 on the next page. Enter an **Angle** value of 15.5, and click **Copy** to clone the eyelash.

6. *Repeat the transformation five times.* Press Ctrl+D (⌘-D) five times to copy the eyelash around the left side of the circle.

7. *Select the left eyelashes and save the selection.* Switch to the black arrow tool, and marquee around the group of eye-

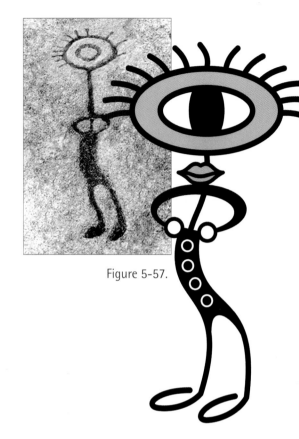

Figure 5-57.

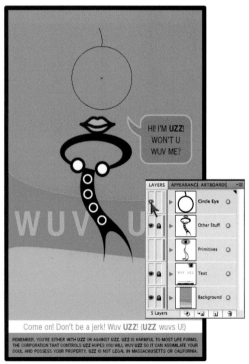

Figure 5-58.

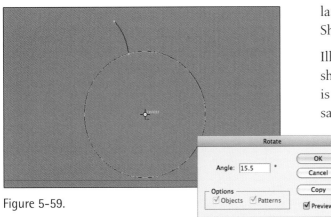

Figure 5-59.

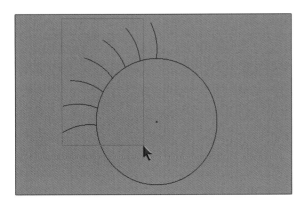

Figure 5-60.

lashes (not including the original), as in Figure 5-59. Shift-click the circle to deselect it.

Illustrator allows you to save selections, much as Photoshop does, but Illustrator's method of saving selections is quite different in its implementation. Rather than saving the selection as a channel, Illustrator remembers the specific objects that are part of a saved selection, even if the objects are later moved or transformed. As shown in Figure 5-61, choose **Select→Save Selection**. In the **Save Selection** dialog box, enter "Left Eyelashes" as the name and click **OK**. This group is now available under the **Select** menu at any time.

8. *Reflect the eyelash group.* Now it's time to put lashes on the other side of the eye. Switch to the reflect tool by pressing the O key. Click at the top-center point of the circle, and Alt-click (or Option-click) at the bottom center point, as in Figure 5-62, to reflect and clone the eyelashes to the other side.

9. *Save another selection.* Again choose **Select→Save Selection**, and save the new group as "Right Eyelashes."

10. *Clean up your existing saved selections.* If you choose Right Eyelashes from the Select menu, things work as expected. However, if you choose Left Eyelashes, both groups are selected. What gives?

Illustrator remembers what objects were part of a selection when it was saved, even if transformations are applied after the save—and cloning is included in these transformations. To fix the problem, repeat the first part

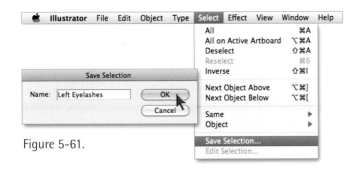

Figure 5-61.

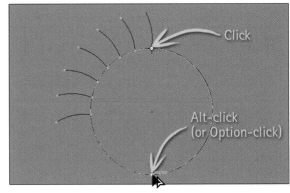

Figure 5-62.

of Step 7 to select just the left eyelashes. Save the selection as "Left Eyelashes."

Now, unfortunately, you have two selections saved with the same label. Choose **Select→Edit Selection** to bring up the **Edit Selection** dialog box pictured in Figure 5-63. Click the first Left Eyelashes entry, and change the name to "All Eyelashes." Click **OK** to accept your changes.

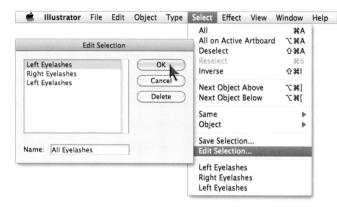

Figure 5-63.

PEARL OF ● WISDOM

If you're anything like me, seeing the selections in their current order—All Eyelashes, Right Eyelashes, Left Eyelashes—makes you just a little crazy. You might think that Illustrator would let you reorder the saved selections in the **Edit Selection** dialog box. Unfortunately, you'd be wrong. The saved selections *always* appear in the order in which they were saved. Short of resaving them and deleting the old ones, there's no way to reorder them.

11. *Adjust the layers in the Layers panel.* To properly scale the eye, you need to see both the new work and the original. Switch the **Circle Eye** layer back to preview mode by Ctrl-clicking (or ⌘-clicking) the 👁 icon. Turn on the **Primitives** layer by clicking the leftmost column by the layer name, and lock it by clicking in the second empty box, as shown in Figure 5-64.

12. *Scale all elements on the Circle Eye layer.* Select all the elements in the Circle Eye layer by meatballing the layer. Switch to the scale tool by pressing the S key, and drag as shown in Figure 5-65, pressing the Shift key to constrain the scaling to just the horizontal axis. Once the eye matches that on the Primitives layer, release the mouse button.

13. *Delete the extraneous circle.* Now that the eyelashes are scaled, you no longer need the circle that they were based on. Switch to the black arrow tool, and click anywhere off the artwork to deselect all the objects. Finally, click the circle and press the Backspace or Delete key to get rid of the circle.

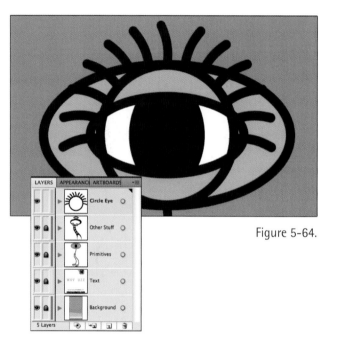

Figure 5-64.

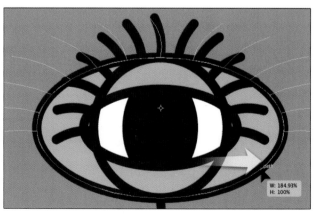

Figure 5-65.

Figure 5-66.

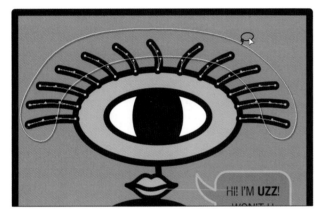

Figure 5-67.

Figure 5-68.

14. *Scale the eyelashes down.* All the eyelashes are now in position, but the scale transformation has left them looking the worse for wear. Those farthest to the sides are now nearly twice as long, and that just won't do.

In the **Select** menu, choose **All Eyelashes**, and switch back to the scale tool by pressing the S key. Drag from the outside back toward the center, as in Figure 5-66, once again pressing the Shift key.

Unfortunately, the results are even less acceptable—Uzz now has eyelashes sprouting directly from its eyeball. We need a different method. Press Ctrl+Z (⌘-Z) to undo this last step.

15. *Select the outer points of the lashes with the lasso tool.* Switch to the lasso tool (⌀) by pressing the Q key. (Q because the lasso itself looks somewhat like a Q.) Draw a shape around the eyelashes' outside points, as shown in Figure 5-67.

16. *Scale the eyelashes again.* Switch back to the scale tool, and once again drag from the outside toward the center while pressing the Shift key, as in Figure 5-68. While these results are better—the eyelashes still start from the edge of the eye—the control handles are now behaving badly, causing all sorts of crimps and strange corners in the outermost lashes. Again, press Ctrl+Z (⌘-Z) to undo.

17. *Select all the lashes and use the Transform Each command.* So what's a corporate mascot to do? Fortunately, there's yet another method—the Transform Each command. First, select all the lashes by choosing **All Eyelashes** from the **Select** menu. Then, choose **Object→Transform→Transform Each**. You'll see the **Transform Each** dialog box shown in Figure 5-69 on the facing page.

First, make sure the **Preview** option is selected. (By default, it's off in almost every dialog box. Why Illustrator insists on this, I have no idea.) Change the **Horizontal** value to 70, and press Tab to see the results. So far, this looks the best—Illustrator is now transforming each object on its own independent origin point—but some of the eyelashes have started to float away. That's where the Origin option (indicated by the ⠿ icon) comes into play. Click the center box on the left edge, to make the matrix look like ⠿. This fixes the right lashes but makes the left ones worse. Likewise, the ⠿ option fixes the left lashes but wrecks the right side. Clearly, this is a two-step process. Click **Cancel** to exit the dialog box.

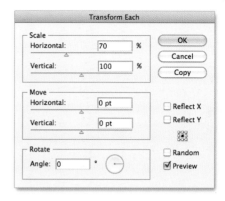

Figure 5-69.

18. *Select the left lashes, and transform them.* Choose **Left Eyelashes** from the **Select** menu, and then press Ctrl+Shift+Alt+D (⌘-Shift-Option-D) to bring up the **Transform Each** dialog box. Enter a value of 70 for the **Horizontal** scale, and set the matrix to ⠿. Click **OK** to accept the transformation.

19. *Repeat the process for the right lashes.* Repeat the process for the other side, choosing **Right Eyelashes** from the **Select** menu. Again, set the **Horizontal** scale to 70, but set the matrix to look like ⠿. Click **OK**.

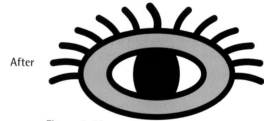

Before

20. *Move the Circle Eye layer down.* The eyelashes are just about perfect, but if you look closely, you may see a few little points where the lashes extend slightly into the eyeball. To fix this, go to the **Layers** panel and drag the **Circle Eye** layer below the **Primitives** layer. Figure 5-70 shows the before and after.

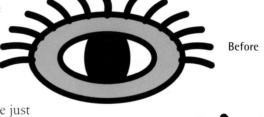

After

Figure 5-70.

21. *Unlock all the layers.* Since you'll need to fix all the black elements, that means fixing the elements on all layers. Click all four 🔒 icons in the **Layers** panel to unlock all the layers.

Figure 5-71.

Figure 5-72.

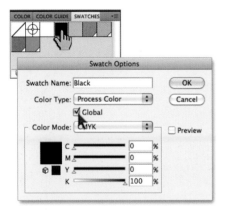

Figure 5-73.

22. ***Select all paths with a plain black stroke.*** Switch to the magic wand tool by selecting it from the toolbox (or pressing the Y key). Before you can use the tool to select objects, however, you need to make some adjustments. Choose **Window→Magic Wand** to bring up the Magic Wand panel as shown in Figure 5-71. Alternatively, you can double-click the magic wand tool in the toolbox.

---

If your window doesn't match that shown in the figure, make sure to choose Show Stroke Options and Show Transparency Options from the panel (▼≣) menu.

---

In the panel, deselect **Fill Color** and select the **Stroke Color** option. Now click any one of the eyelashes. Note that all the black paths are now selected—but so are the shapes that make up the speech bubble, which clearly do not have a black stroke. Sadly, the magic wand tool in Illustrator can get confused by compound shapes—while the compound shape itself has a non-black stroke, the individual elements that make up the shape *do* have black strokes, and Illustrator is trying to do its best with the information it's given. Switch to the black arrow tool, and while pressing the Shift key, marquee as shown in Figure 5-72 to remove the extraneous shapes from the selection. (Be careful not to accidentally marquee the text.)

23. ***Assign the black swatch and make it global.*** Bring up the **Swatches** panel, and make sure the **Stroke** attribute is active. Double-click the black swatch to bring up the **Swatches** dialog box, shown in Figure 5-73. Select the **Global** option to convert the swatch to a global color. Click **OK** to close the dialog box.

**PEARL OF WISDOM**

Global colors are indicated with a small white triangle in the lower-right corner of the swatch. Changes made to a global swatch affect all objects in a document that use that swatch. Nonglobal swatches, however, cannot be automatically updated—changes made to a nonglobal swatch affect only the objects created after the change.

24. ***Select all paths with a plain black fill.*** Switch back to the **Magic Wand** panel. Deselect the **Stroke Color** option, and select the **Fill Color** option. Finally with the Magic Wand tool selected, click the outside edge of the pupil, as in Figure 5-74 on the facing page, to select all the objects with a black fill.

25. ***Assign the global black swatch.*** Press the X key to make the **Fill** attribute active. In the **Swatches** panel, click the global black swatch to apply it to all the selected fills.

26. *Select the blocks of black text and assign the global swatch.* With the black arrow tool, click the line of text *Hi! I'm Uzz!* to select that text group. Next, Shift-click the legalese at the bottom of the illustration to add that text block to the selection. Finally, click the global black swatch in the **Swatches** panel to apply the swatch to all the selected text. Press Ctrl+Shift+A (⌘-Shift-A) to make sure nothing remains selected.

27. *Edit the black swatch to make it a rich black.* Now that the black elements have been assigned the global swatch, all that's left to do is edit the swatch to make it a rich black. Double-click the swatch, and change the **C**, **M**, and **Y** values each to 50. Click **OK** to accept the changes. On screen, you should see the black go from a dull gray to a rich, true black. Figure 5-75 illustrates the difference between the plain black and rich black in print.

Figure 5-74.

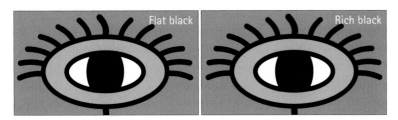

Figure 5-75.

Uzz is now ready to make his public debut, and you're now armed with a number of new tools to deal with selections and transformations. Save or discard your work as you see fit; you'll be starting with new artwork in the next exercise.

## Scaling Partially Selected Paths

In this final exercise, you'll use the scale and rotate tools to transform three simple circles into an elaborate lace pattern, as in Figure 5-76. While the results may seem like an impossibility, Illustrator's scale function, when applied to path segments rather than whole paths, can create some lovely Spirograph-style effects.

1. *Open the lace-pattern art.* Navigate to the *Lesson 05* subfolder inside the *Lesson Files-AIcs5 1on1* folder. Open the file called *Lacemaking.ai*.

   This document has four layers. The Final Lace layer shows the final artwork; this will be used as your guide as you recreate the other bits of art. The Just

Figure 5-76.

Figure 5-77.

Figure 5-78.

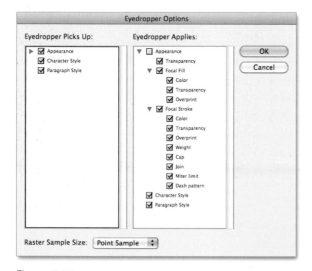

Figure 5-79.

Circles layer houses the circles you'll use later in the exercise; you can ignore it for now. The One Shy layer contains many of the background elements.

2. *Turn on the One Shy layer.* You'll begin the exercise with the One Shy layer—so-named because it's shy one rounded square from the final art. Turn off the **Final Lace** layer by clicking its 👁 icon, just to make sure it stays out of the way. Turn on the **One Shy** layer by clicking the leftmost column by its name in the **Layers** panel, and make that layer active by clicking the layer name.

3. *Draw the final rounded square.* Select the rounded rectangle tool by choosing it from the rectangle tool flyout menu, as shown in Figure 5-77. Draw from the upper-left to lower-right corner—with smart guides enabled, you should snap directly to the anchor points at the corners—and while holding the mouse button down, press the ↑ arrow key to increase the roundness of the rectangle's corners. (Depending on whether you had a previous value for the rounded corners, you may need to hold the ↑ key down for a little while; if you go too far, press the ↓ key a few times to nudge the outline back.) Once your outline looks like that in Figure 5-78, release the mouse button.

4. *Pick up the live effects from one of the other squares.* The square is the right shape, but it has all the wrong appearance attributes. If you examine the other rounded rectangles, you'll see a lighter edge along the top and a shadow along the bottom. This effect is achieved by using two separate drop shadows—both of which are live effects. By default, the eyedropper tool doesn't pick up live effects, but that can be changed easily:

   • Double-click the eyedropper tool in the toolbox.

   • In the **Eyedropper Options** dialog box, shown in Figure 5-79, select the **Appearance** check box in the **Eyedropper Picks Up** column. Click **OK**.

- Now that the eyedropper tool is active, click one of the other rounded rectangles, taking care not to click the translucent star shape, as in Figure 5-80.

Illustrator lifts the color and fill, as well as all the live effects.

5. *Fix the stacking order.* The new rounded square is obscuring much of the rest of the art. Switch to the black arrow tool, and click a visible portion of the star; this selects a total of three shapes (the star, a circle, and a square), as shown in Figure 5-81. Press Ctrl+Shift+⌈ (⌘-Shift-⌈) to bring the group to the front, revealing the salmon-colored circle and the star in its entirety.

6. *Select the outermost square.* If you take a quick peek back at the Final Lace layer, you'll notice a white-square-and-circle combination frame around the lace. The square that you need to start building this frame, however, is now unfortunately hidden under the group that you just brought to the front. If you are lucky, you could Shift-click through the stack to select it—but if you are unlucky, you will end up isolating a group of artwork you don't want. (Should that happen, press the Esc key to exit isolation mode.)

Another method is similarly finicky, but it won't accidentally send you somewhere you don't want to go. First, make sure the square/circle/star group is still selected. Next, right-click (or Control-click on the Mac) somewhere in the upper-left corner of the square, as shown in Figure 5-82 on the following page, and choose **Select→Next Object Below**. This should select the square; if not, rinse and repeat—you should be able to select it after a few attempts.

7. *Copy the square to the front.* Choose **Edit→Copy**. Click off the artwork to deselect the square, and then choose **Edit→Paste in Front** to paste the square at the top of the stack. (You must deselect the artwork before pasting; otherwise, Illustrator simply pastes it in front of the currently selected object.)

Figure 5-80.

Figure 5-81.

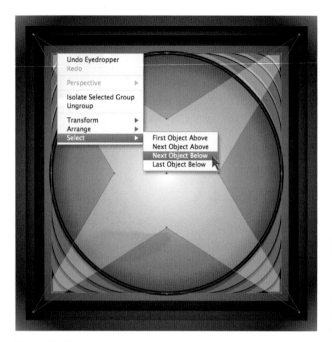

Figure 5-82.

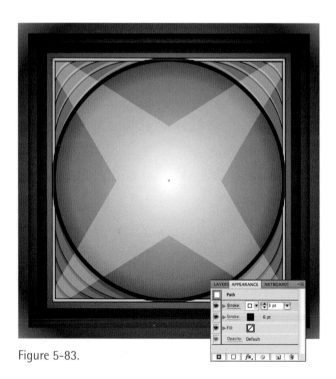

Figure 5-83.

8. *Remove the fill from the square.* Confirm that the fill is active (if it's not, make it so by pressing the X key), and then press the ⃞ key to remove the fill.

9. *Select the circle.* The second part of the frame is the circle shape, but as you saw in Step 5, that shape is currently part of a group—you'll need to use some selection acumen to extract it. Make sure nothing is selected by pressing Ctrl+Shift+A (⌘-Shift-A), switch to the white arrow tool by pressing the A key, and then Alt-click (or Option-click) to select the circle independently of its group.

10. *Cut and paste the circle to the front.* Choose **Edit→Cut**. Now nothing on the layer should be selected, so you're free to choose **Edit→Paste in Front**, assured that the circle will paste to the top of the stack.

11. *Adjust the stroke of the square.* The frame from the Final Lace layer actually uses two stroke attributes to produce the effect you see—a thick black stroke and a thinner white stroke. Here's how to reproduce it:

    • Use the black arrow tool to select the square.

    • Bring up the **Appearance** panel.

    • Clone the existing stroke by selecting it and clicking the ⬚ icon in the lower-right corner of the panel.

    • Change the color of the first-listed stroke to white and the weight to 3 pt, as in Figure 5-83.

12. *Use the eyedropper tool to apply the stroke to the circle.* The circle needs the same stroke, and the eyedropper tool is the easiest way to get it there. Select the circle, press the I key to switch to the eyedropper tool, and click the frame of the square, as in Figure 5-84 on the facing page.

13. ***Join the circle and square.*** If you look closely (as shown in the zoom in Figure 5-85), you'll notice a strange overlap in the frame where the circle sits over the square. To remove this overlap, the two shapes need to be combined into a compound path:

- Press the V key to return to the black arrow tool.

- Shift-click the square to add it to the selection.

- Choose **Object→Compound Path→Make**, or press Ctrl+8 (⌘-8). (We use 8 because the figure 8 is itself a compound path.)

Illustrator is now treating the two paths as one, applying the double stroke seamlessly around the entire element. You're finished with the **One Shy** layer; hide it by clicking its 👁 icon in the **Layers** panel.

Note that compound paths are different from compound shapes; I explain the difference fully in the next lesson.

Figure 5-84.

14. ***Convert the Final Lace layer to a tracing template.*** It's time to move on to creating the lace, but first, you need to turn the final artwork layer into a tracing template. Make the **Final Lace** layer visible, and select everything on the layer by meatballing it. In the control panel, set the **Opacity** to a value of 25. Lastly, lock the layer.

15. ***Make the Just Circles layer active.*** Make the **Just Circles** layer visible and active.

16. ***Select and copy the innermost circle.*** Click to select the innermost circle, and press Ctrl+C (⌘-C) to copy it. We'll bring it back in a later step.

17. ***Select the curved segments of the circle.*** Choose **Select →Object→Direction Handles**. (*Direction handles* is Adobe's term for what I call control handles.) Note that Illustrator doesn't actually select the control handles—it can't—but rather it deselects the anchor points and selects the curved segments of the circle.

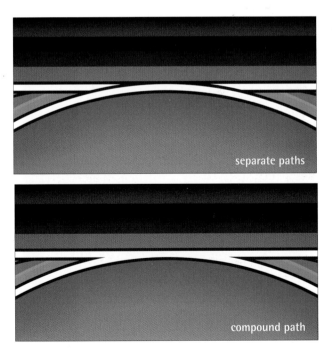

separate paths

compound path

Figure 5-85.

Figure 5-86.

Figure 5-87.

18. *Scale the segments to create a cloverleaf.* Now for the excitement. Switch to the scale tool, and start dragging from the upper-right corner outward, as in Figure 5-86. Hold the Shift key while you drag to constrain the scale. Notice that the anchor points themselves aren't moving, but the curved segments are actually curving in on themselves. Once your shape resembles that in Figure 5-86 (and frankly, the Apple ⌘ key), release the mouse button.

19. *Paste the original circle in front.* Press Ctrl+F (⌘-F) to paste the original circle in front.

20. *Select and copy the middle circle.* Ctrl-click (⌘-click) the middle circle to select it, and press Ctrl+C (⌘-C) to copy it to the clipboard.

21. *Rotate the middle circle.* The next shape to draw is the curlicue diamond—the shape with loops pointing directly up, down, left, and right. And while rotating a circle has no immediate effect, it's a necessary first step to achieving that diamond shape. Double-click the rotate tool, enter an **Angle** value of 45, and click **OK**.

22. *Select and scale the segments.* Switch back to the scale tool by pressing the S key. Again, choose **Select→Object→Direction Handles**, and start dragging as shown in Figure 5-87. Again, press the Shift key to constrain the scale. Release the mouse button when your shape matches the tracing template underneath. Because you rotated the circle 45 degrees, the anchor points (which remained fixed) are now in the diagonal corners, allowing the curves to bend to the desired locations.

23. *Paste the original in front.* Press Ctrl+F (⌘-F) to paste the original circle in front.

24. *Double the anchor points in the circle.* The next shape to draw is the very complex shape just inside the outer circle—which, to me, resembles the retro representations of the atom, electrons zipping around. But this shape is too complex to recreate with just four anchor points. Choose **Object→Path→Add Anchor Points**. Illustrator dutifully

adds anchor points halfway between all the existing anchor points, doubling the number to eight.

25. *Again, select and scale the segments.* Choose **Select→Object→Direction Handles**. Drag as shown in Figure 5-88—this time dragging inward toward the center and across—adding Shift once again.

26. *Quadruple the anchor points in the outermost circle.* Ctrl-click (⌘-click) the outermost circle to select it. Choose **Object→ Path→Add Anchor Points** to double the number of anchor points to eight, and choose the command again to make a total of sixteen.

27. *Scallop the outer circle with the Pucker & Bloat effect.* The Effect menu provides access to Illustrator's effects, which I cover fully in Lesson 10. (Lest you think I'm hyping this lesson with the many references to it thus far, live effects are probably the most powerful and least understood of Illustrator's many wonders. But I digress.) The Pucker & Bloat filter is precisely what you need to finish the lace effect; choose **Effect→Distort & Transform→Pucker & Bloat**. Illustrator presents you with the **Pucker & Bloat** dialog box shown in Figure 5-89. Make sure the **Preview** check box is selected, and move the slider back and forth. Negative (pucker) values create a spiky, star-like effect, while positive (bloat) values create a loopy, pillowy effect. I found that a value of 10 best matches the tracing template; once you've settled on that value, click **OK** to accept your changes.

28. *Expand the appearance of the scalloped circle.* While live effects provide a wealth of flexibility, they don't always behave well when included in a compound path. You'll notice that even though the stroke has changed appearance, the underlying path is still circular, as in Figure 5-89. Before you can move to the next step, you need to make the distortion of the path permanent—that is, a static effect as opposed to a live one. Choose **Object→Expand Appearance**. The path changes to match the shape of the stroke; the effect is no longer live, on the other hand you can now join the path with the others in a compound path.

Figure 5-88.

Figure 5-89.

29. ***Make a compound path of all the distorted circles.*** All your shapes are now in place, but there's the same issue of the strokes overlapping instead of tracing around one contiguous shape. In the **Layers** panel, select everything on the **Just Circles** layer by meatballing it, and then choose **Object→Compound Path→Make**. Your lace is now complete!

30. ***Turn the One Shy layer back on.*** All that's left is to make the **One Shy** layer visible again, so turn it on from the Layers panel. Your final art should look like Figure 5-90.

In just a few exercises, you've seen a wide range of possibilities that the selection and transformation tools provide. (Series duplication alone can be a huge timesaver, as evidenced by the *tonalpohualli*.) And while individual transformations may be small, they can quickly add up to a full metamorphosis of your illustration.

Figure 5-90.

# WHAT DID YOU LEARN?

Match the key concept in the numbered list below with the letter of the phrase that best describes it. Answers appear upside-down at the bottom of the page.

## Key Concepts

1. Transformation
2. Reshaping
3. Outline Stroke
4. Duplication
5. Transform Again
6. Constraining
7. Offset Path
8. Transformation origin
9. Series duplication
10. Object rotation
11. Pattern rotation
12. Transform Each

## Descriptions

A. A technique that forces Illustrator to complete the transformation along a fixed axis or angle, obtained by pressing the Shift key.

B. A command that repeats the transformation operation.

C. A command that converts a stroked path (either open or closed) into a solid filled shape.

D. A technique combining various transformations and the Transform Again command to recreate a repeating pattern of objects.

E. Any number of alterations that can be made to a path, including scaling, rotation, reshaping, or even moving.

F. An operation that creates a new version of the transformed object, while leaving the original unchanged; obtained by pressing the Alt or Option key.

G. A rotation function that allows an object to be rotated independently of its contents.

H. A command that creates a new shape a specified distance out (or in) from an existing path.

I. Adjustments made to the points of a path, either with the pen tool, the white arrow tool, or the tool of the same name.

J. A command that calculates any transformation operation based on independent origin points.

K. A rotation function that allows an object's pattern fill to be rotated independently of its containing shape.

L. The point around which Illustrator calculates all move, rotate, scale, shear, and reflect operations.

## Answers

1E, 2I, 3C, 4F, 5B, 6A, 7H, 8L, 9D, 10G, 11K, 12J

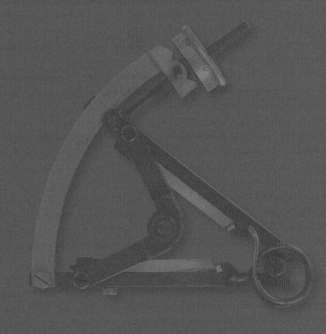
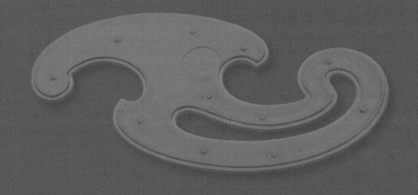

# PATHFINDER OPERATIONS

PRIMITIVES, as you learned in Lesson 2, are the building blocks of all illustrations, but sometimes such simple objects can't accurately represent your work. The alternative—drawing complex shapes by hand with the pen tool—can be tedious and time-consuming. Fortunately, Illustrator provides a shortcut: *pathfinder operations*. Pathfinders allow you to quickly combine simple objects to create more complex ones, as shown in Figure 6-1. A line plus an ellipse is a musical note. Two circles next to each other and a triangle below become a valentine. A circle minus a smaller, offset circle becomes a crescent moon. A door, some drywall, and a couple of windows—not to mention some electrical, plumbing, heating, AC, roofing, and a really big loan—make a house. These are all pathfinder operations (well, except for the house), and they're amazing timesavers, one and all. To get a sense of how they work, keep reading.

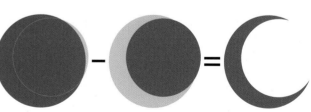

Figure 6-1.

## Compound Paths versus Compound Shapes

The pathfinder joins shapes in a few ways, each with their own level of permanence. By default, the pathfinder will simply perform the operation and permanently alter the target path; this change is irrevocable, short of an undo command. A *compound path* is two or more subpaths that merge to form a single path—hence it appears as a single object in the Layers panel. You can move one subpath independently of another, but intersecting regions are always transparent holes (also called the exclusion mode, which I explain further later in this lesson). Compound shapes are the most flexible. A *compound shape* is composed of two or more paths as well, but you can see individual paths in the Layers panel, and even set each to a differ-

# ABOUT THIS LESSON

## Project Files

Before beginning the exercises, make sure you've downloaded the lesson files from *www.oreilly.com/go/Deke-IllustratorCS5*, as directed in Step 2 on page xiv of the Preface. This should result in a folder called *Lesson Files-Alcs5 1on1* on your desktop. We'll be working with the files inside the *Lesson 06* subfolder.

Pathfinder operations are simple operations, but used wisely, they can produce powerful results. In this lesson, you'll learn how to:

## Video Lesson 6: Shape Builder and Pathfinder

Creating complex paths is often just a matter of combining the right basic shapes. I'll show you how to use the new Shape Builder tool and the classic and more powerful Pathfinder operations to do this, exploiting the fact that the world around us can often be broken down into (and built up with) simple shapes like ellipses and rectangles.

To build shapes and find paths visit *www.oreilly.com/go/ deke-IllustratorCS5*. Click the **Watch** button to view the lesson online or the **Download** button to save it to your computer. During the video, you'll learn these shortcuts:

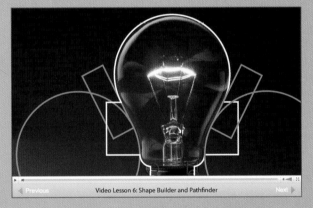

Video Lesson 6: Shape Builder and Pathfinder

| Operation | Windows shortcut | Macintosh shortcut |
|---|---|---|
| Select the Shape Builder tool | Shift+M | Shift-M |
| Subtract shapes from your path | Alt-drag with Shape Builder | Option-drag with Shape Builder |
| Display the Pathfinder panel | Ctrl+Shift+F9 | ⌘-Shift-F9 |
| Apply Shape modes dynamically | Alt-click the panel icon | Option-click the panel icon |
| Display the Attributes panel | Ctrl-F11 | ⌘-F11 |
| Select the reflect tool | Press the O key | Press the O key |
| Select the white arrow tool | Press the A key | Press the A key |
| Repeat the last Pathfinder operation | Ctrl+4 | ⌘-4 |
| Display the Gradients panel | Ctrl+F9 | ⌘-F9 |

ent *shape mode*. Shape modes are identical to pathfinder operations, save for the fact that they can be applied dynamically.

## Meet the Pathfinder Panel

In this first exercise, I'll demonstrate the basics of the Pathfinder panel using a whimsical exercise inspired by the movie *Yellow Submarine* (an animated film that was a vehicle for an obscure band, since forgotten). You'll learn the fundamentals of pathfinder operations, and how different path combinations behave.

1. *Open the submarine artwork.* Navigate to the *Lesson 06* subfolder inside the *Lesson Files-AIcs5 1on1* folder. Locate the file *Violet submarine.ai* and open it. Inside the artwork, you'll find a violet submarine, a red fin shape, and a yellow silhouette of a man. (We'll call him Ringo.)

2. *Bring up the Pathfinder panel.* Open the **Pathfinder** panel, shown in Figure 6-2, by choosing **Window→Pathfinder** or pressing Ctrl+Shift+F9 (⌘-Shift-F9 on the Mac). (Alternately, you can click the ▪ icon in the panel bar.)

3. *Select Ringo and the submarine.* Make sure the black arrow tool is selected. Click the silhouette of Ringo, and Shift-click the submarine to add it to the selection. (Note that to select the paths, you need to click the edge of the paths, not inside the shapes.)

4. *Combine the shapes.* Click the **Unite** icon (▣) to combine the two shapes. Illustrator creates a new path based on the outline of the two shapes, and discards any path information inside the shapes, as in Figure 6-3.

---

Note that Illustrator also assigns the yellow fill and black stroke attributes to the new shape—the program uses the attributes of the topmost object in the stack to determine the new path's attributes.

---

5. *Undo the last step.* That's all well and good, but Illustrator has discarded information in the process of creating the new shape, information you want to keep. It would be better if the combination were dynamic, so press Ctrl+Z (⌘-Z) to undo.

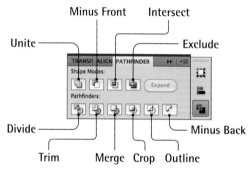

Figure 6-2.

Figure 6-3.

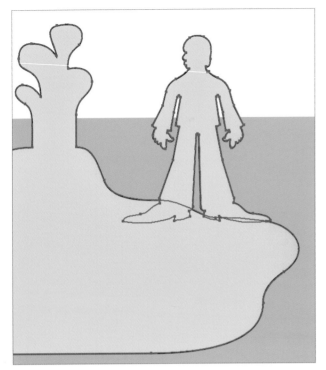

Figure 6-4.

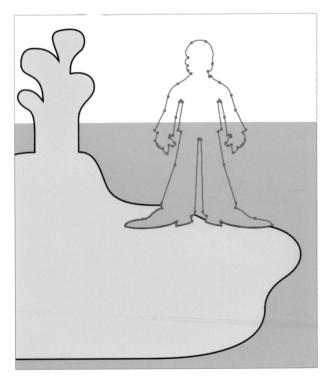

Figure 6-5.

6. **Combine the shapes dynamically.** To force Illustrator to make the joining dynamic, press and hold the Alt (or Option) key while clicking the ⬒ icon in the Pathfinder panel. Illustrator once again combines the shapes, but this time it preserves the path information for each subpath, as in Figure 6-4.

7. **Change the shape mode dynamically.** Since the compound shape allows you to make changes to subpaths on-the-fly, it also affords you the freedom to change the shape mode whenever you'd like. Here's how:

   - Deselect everything by clicking off the artwork (or pressing Ctrl+Shift+A or ⌘-Shift-A).

   - Select Ringo independently by pressing and holding the Ctrl (or ⌘) key and clicking his outline.

   - While pressing and holding the Alt (or Option) key, press the Minus Front (⬔) icon.

   Now Illustrator is treating the Ringo subpath as a "hole" that knocks through the submarine shape, as shown in Figure 6-5.

   It's crucial that you press and hold the Alt (or Option) key when changing pathfinder modes dynamically. Without this modifier key, Illustrator attempts to create a permanent change—but because only one path is selected, it cannot, and instead greets you with a warning message.

8. **Move Ringo independently of the submarine.** Ringo should still be selected independently; click and hold somewhere on the path and drag to center him just below the submarine's spout, his shoes barely overlapping the bottom of the vessel. When you release the mouse button, a hidden figure is revealed, as shown in Figure 6-6 on the next page. Maybe Ringo was the walrus?

9. ***Bring the fin shape to the front.*** When you joined the two paths back in Step 6, the submarine path was moved to just below the Ringo path, placing the path in front of the red fin. To fix this, you could select the fin shape with the black arrow tool and choose Object→Arrange→Bring to Front, or press Ctrl+Shift+⬚ (⌘-Shift-⬚).

But instead, I'd like you to move the fin using the Layers panel, as a preview for the next step. Bring up the **Layers** panel by pressing F7, and make sure the triangles for both the **Up Above** layer and the **Compound Shape** sublayer are twirled open, as in Figure 6-7. Click and hold the **Fin** layer, and drag until a bar appears between Up Above and Compound Shape, as in Figure 6-7, and then release the mouse button.

10. ***Add the fin to the compound shape.*** The next step is to add the Fin layer to the Compound Shape layer, which can be accomplished via the Layers panel. Again, drag the Fin layer, this time until the bar appears between the **Ringo** and **Submarine** path layers. Your results should look like Figure 6-8.

Figure 6-6.

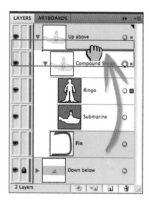

Figure 6-7.

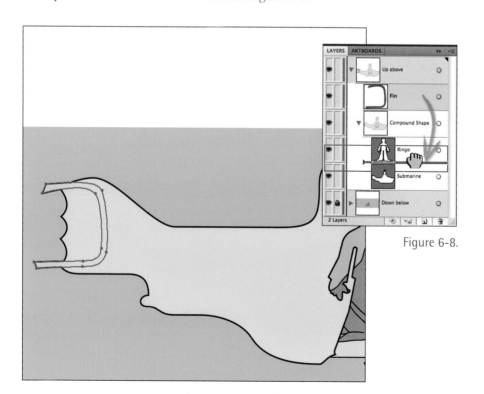

Figure 6-8.

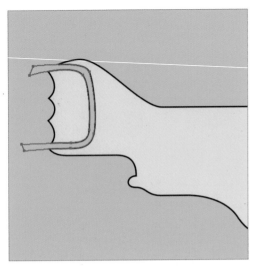

Figure 6-9.

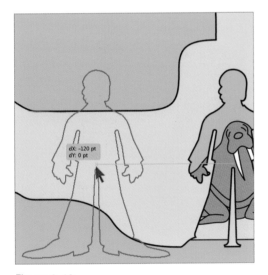

Figure 6-10.

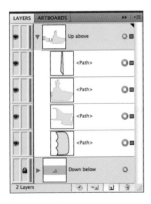

Figure 6-11.

11. *Switch the shape mode to Minus Front.* The Fin path is now part of the compound shape, but it's not the effect I'm looking for—the fin should cut its shape out of the submarine, just as Ringo does. Alt-click (or Option-click) the ○ icon on the right side of the Fin layer to select it independently, and then Alt-click (or Option-click) the Minus Front (▯) icon in the **Pathfinder** panel. The new shape mode should appear like that in Figure 6-9.

12. *Move Ringo independently.* Ctrl+Alt-click (or ⌘-Option-click) on Ringo's outline to select his path separately from the compound shape. Drag Ringo to a spot similar to that shown in Figure 6-10, and release.

13. *Hide the background.* In preparation for the next step, click the 👁 icon next to the Down Below layer in the Layers panel to hide the elements on that layer, leaving just the foreground visible.

14. *Make a compound path from the compound shape.* Still in the Layers panel, meatball the **Compound Shape** layer to select all component subpaths. Switch to the **Pathfinder** panel, and then click the Expand button, paying close attention to what transpires in the Layers panel as you do so. Illustrator converts the compound shape to a compound path, removing any path data from outside the intersection of the original components—but now none of the individual pieces are selectable in the Layers panel. You'll address that in the next step.

15. *Make individual paths from the subpaths.* The only way to have the individual pieces of a compound path appear in the Layers panel is to release the compound path. With the path selected, choose **Object→Compound Path→Release**, or press Ctrl+Alt+Shift+8 (⌘-Option-Shift-8). Now each piece appears in the Layers panel (shown in Figure 6-11) and can be manipulated individually.

PEARL OF WISDOM

Why 8? (You'll notice the other compound path, Make, uses Ctrl+8 or ⌘-8 as its keyboard shortcut.) The reason is this: A figure eight is one of the most common and simple compound paths. If you can remember that tidbit, you can remember these shortcuts.

This was but a brief introduction to the Pathfinder panel. Over the next few exercises, you'll learn the ins and outs of pathfinder operations using a piece of space robot artwork that will carry through to the end of the lesson. Save or discard your submarine artwork as you see fit.

## Adding and Subtracting Shapes

In this, the first of our robot art adventures, we'll be introduced to our protagonist, Ghost Robot, and his sad space opera of unrequited mechanical love. (Hey, it worked for *Battlestar Galactica*.) But more importantly, you'll see how to add and subtract primitive shapes to build more complex ones. You'll start with shapes that I've already created, and—over the next few exercises—assemble them into your own full-fledged masterpiece.

1. *Open the ghost robot artwork.* In the *Lesson 06* subfolder inside the *Lesson Files-AIcs5 1on1* folder, you'll find a piece of art labeled *Ghost Robot.ai*. Open the file, and meet our translucent metal friend—featured as the cover model for a fictitious magazine, shown in Figure 6-12.

2. *Examine the Layers panel.* In the **Layers** panel, you'll notice a total of six layers, as pictured in Figure 6-13. Click the 👁 icon to temporarily turn a layer off and see the layers underneath; click the empty box to turn on the layers. The Type, Frames, and Backdrop layers are window dressing to flesh out the illustration; the Ghost template layer shows my original sketch. These layers can be safely ignored. The two layers of most interest to us are the Pathfinders layer and the Ghost Vectors layer. The Pathfinders layer shows your ultimate goal; you'll be starting with the shapes on the Ghost Vectors layer. To that end, turn off all other layers.

3. *Duplicate the Ghost Vectors layer.* Because many pathfinder operations are destructive—that is to say, they alter paths permanently—it's best to work from a copy and keep your original primitives intact. Duplicate the **Ghost Vectors** layer by dragging it to the 🗐 icon in the Layers panel, as shown in Figure 6-14. Illustrator dutifully copies all the objects on the layer to a brand new layer. To doubly protect your originals, click the 👁 icon to hide the original Ghost Vectors layer.

Figure 6-12.

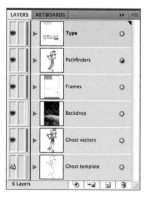

Figure 6-13.

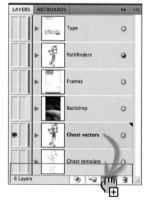

Figure 6-14.

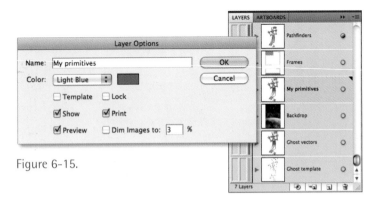

Figure 6-15.

Figure 6-16.

Figure 6-17.

Figure 6-18.

4. *Do some layer cleanup.* It would be nice to have some indication as to what the robot's final appearance might look like, so (still inside the Layers panel) turn the **Backdrop** layer back on. Unfortunately, the ghost robot has now disappeared—it's covered by the Backdrop layer. Drag the Backdrop layer to just under your duplicated vector layer to bring the ghost back; then lock the Backdrop. Finally, to avoid confusion, double-click the duplicated layer, and give it a new name, such as "My Primitives" (as shown in the **Layer Options** dialog in Figure 6-15), and click **OK**.

5. *Select the robot's antennae.* With the black arrow tool, marquee around the right set of antenna rods as shown in Figure 6-16. Click the ⬚ icon to join the two shapes permanently. Repeat the process for the antenna rods on the left side of the robot's head (his right). Note that when you join the shapes, the newly created path jumps to the front of the stack; press Ctrl+Shift+[ (⌘-Shift-[) to send it behind the robot's ear.

---

Should you accidentally Alt-click (or Option-click) the ⬚ icon, not to worry. You can simply click the Expand button in the Pathfinder panel to make the change permanent.

---

6. *Remove the wedge from the left eye.* Marquee the two shapes that make up the left iris (his right), as shown in Figure 6-17. Click the ⬚ (Minus Front) icon to remove the wedge.

7. *Remove the wedge from the right eye.* Select the two shapes for the right iris (his left), as in Figure 6-18. Again, click the ⬚ icon.

This time, the results are unexpected—you are left with a sliver of a shape, not at all what was intended. Instead of the Minus Front shape mode, what is needed here is the Minus Back pathfinder because the wedge is in front of the iris. Press Ctrl+Z (⌘-Z) to undo, and then click the ⬚ icon in the bottom-right corner of the Pathfinder panel; the irises now match.

8. *Subtract one circle from the other.* Marquee the two circles in the left "ear" (his right) as shown in Figure 6-19 on the facing page. Next, click the ⬚ icon in the Pathfinder panel. Illustrator knocks out the inner hole, creating a peach-colored donut. (As always, Illustrator pulls the fill and stroke attributes from the rearmost object.) Repeat for the right ear (his left).

You may be wondering why I had you make compound paths instead of compound shapes, given that I was singing the praises of compound shapes and their flexibility in the introduction to this lesson. While it is true that you have more leeway in terms of later edits with compound shapes, they are not compatible with PostScript output. As PDF becomes more ubiquitous, this is less of a concern—but for legacy projects, compound paths ensure the broadest compatibility.

Figure 6-19.

9. *Make a compound path for both palms.* With the black arrow tool, select the two circles that make up the palm of the hand on the left, as in Figure 6-20, and choose **Object→Compound Path→Make**. (I found it easiest to click the first circle and Shift-click the second; be sure to click the path and not the fill.) The result is the same as clicking the ⊞ icon. Select the two circles for the hand on the right, and repeat the menu command or use the shortcut Ctrl+8 (⌘-8 on the Mac).

You've now learned the fundamentals of compound paths and adding and subtracting shapes. But our robot friend, shown in Figure 6-21, still has a way to go before he's ready for his debut. Save your work, and when you're ready, join me in the next exercise.

Figure 6-20.

Figure 6-21.

Figure 6-22.

Figure 6-23.

Figure 6-24.

## Using the Divide Operation

Now that you've mastered the basic pathfinder operations, we'll continue with one of the more advanced functions, Divide. In this exercise, we'll be focusing on the robot's mouth and fingers, and the cartoon speech bubble.

1. *Open the ghost artwork in progress.* If you still have the artwork open from the last exercise, great. Otherwise, open the file you saved from the previous exercise, or the *Unite and divide.ai* file in the *Lesson 06* subfolder, inside the *Lesson Files-AIcs5 1on1* folder.

2. *Select the paths that make up the mouth.* First, we need to clean up the robot's mouth—the outer shapes are in the way. Using the black arrow tool, click to select one of the paths that makes up the mouth, and then Shift-click to select the other two, as in Figure 6-22.

3. *Divide the paths.* Once you have the paths selected, click the 🔳 icon. Illustrator splits the three paths into all their overlapping components—in this case, a total of six paths. Deselect everything by pressing Ctrl+Shift+A (⌘-Shift-A).

4. *Delete the extraneous paths.* Press the A key to switch to the white arrow tool, and then Alt-click (or Option-click) the top rectangle path, as in Figure 6-23. Press Backspace or Delete to delete it. Repeat the process for the lower rectangular path.

---

It's worth noting that the Divide command creates a group of paths rather than a compound path. Divide suits our purposes in the next step because a group's individual elements can have stroke and path attributes applied independently, but a compound path's cannot.

---

5. *Fill the inner mouth with blue.* Alt-click (or Option-click) the inner mouth segment (the one that resembles a pair of cartoon shorts, shown in Figure 6-24) to select it. Switch to the eyedropper tool by pressing the I key, and then click the outline of the left blue oval to copy its attributes.

6. *Select and divide the two thumb shapes on the left hand.* Now to fix our robot's broken thumbs. Switch back to the white arrow tool by pressing the A key, and while pressing and holding the Alt (or Option) key, marquee the two thumb shapes as shown in Figure 6-25 on the facing page. Click the 🔳 icon to split apart the paths. Press Ctrl+Shift+A (⌘-Shift-A on the Mac) to deselect the new group.

7. *Delete the extraneous pieces.* We don't need the two outer pieces of the thumb. Alt-click (or Option-click) the first, and then Shift+Alt-click (Shift-Option-click) the second, as shown in Figure 6-26. Press Backspace or Delete to remove the pieces.

8. *Unite the remaining pieces.* Switch to the black arrow tool, and select the remaining pieces. Click the ▣ icon in the **Pathfinder** panel to unite them. One thumb repaired!

9. *Repeat for the thumb on the right hand.* Repeat Steps 6 through 8 for the other thumb, taking care to first switch to the white arrow tool before repeating Steps 6 and 7. Your results should look like Figure 6-27.

10. *Move the left endpoint to overlap the right.* Now it's time to turn your attention to the talk balloon—which at the moment looks more like two white flags waving under an oval. But don't surrender yet! You'll whip the talk balloon into shape over the next few steps.

   • Switch to the white arrow tool.

   • Select the endpoint at the bottom of the left squiggle by clicking it, as shown in Figure 6-28, and move it over to overlap the squiggle on the right. If you have Smart Guides turned on, you will see the word *anchor* in green when the points are aligned.

   • Finally, move the control handle to the left to soften the curve, as indicated by the second arrow in the figure.

Figure 6-25.

Figure 6-26.

Figure 6-27.

Figure 6-28.

Figure 6-29.

Figure 6-30.

Figure 6-31.

11. *Join the two points.* Marquee around the two points, as in Figure 6-29, and press Ctrl+J (⌘-J) to join the points.

12. *Change the miter limit.* The point on the talk balloon has been flattened. (You'll need to zoom in to see it, but it's there.) Bring up the **Stroke** panel by pressing Ctrl+F10 (⌘-F10), shown in Figure 6-30. Notice that the join is set to Miter, as indicated by the ⊡ icon, yet Illustrator is rendering a bevel join. What gives?

   The issue is the miter limit. With the Shift key held down, click the up arrow in the ⬍ icon next to **Limit** to increase it. Keep clicking until the join becomes a nice sharp point.

13. *Change the join to rounded.* If your results are like mine, the point is a little *too* sharp. Switch the join to rounded by clicking the ⊡ icon.

14. *Unite the elements of the talk balloon.* Select the white oval and the now-joined squiggly lines just below it, shown in Figure 6-31. Click the ⬚ icon to complete the shape. A finished talk bubble!

15. *Select the OO! in the talk bubble, and unite the shapes.* Using the black arrow tool, marquee around the *OO!* as shown in Figure 6-32. (You'll need to Shift-click the talk balloon to deselect it.) Then click the ⬚ icon to unite the shapes.

   Instead of Illustrator doing what you want, however, it makes a real mess of things. The problem is twofold: Pathfinder operations do not work with open paths that have no fill, and they also ignore stroke attributes on closed paths. We'll need to fix the strokes first, by converting them to closed paths. Undo your changes by pressing Ctrl+Z (⌘-Z).

Figure 6-32.

16. *Fix the strokes of all the text elements.* Marquee around all the text elements. (Again, you'll need to Shift-click the talk balloon to deselect it.) Choose **Object→Path→Outline Stroke** to convert all the strokes to closed paths.

17. *Unite the OO! elements.* As you did in Step 15, select all the elements in the *OO!*, and click the 🗗 icon to unite them.

18. *Apply stroke and fill attributes.* Switch to the eyedropper tool by pressing the I key, and then click the outline of the right blue oval to copy its attributes. Your results should look like mine in Figure 6-33.

For the rest of this exercise, it's important that you set your selection preferences to include the Object Selection by Path Only option, as I instructed in the Preface on page xix. If you haven't yet, take the time to do so now.

EXTRA ★ CREDIT

You've learned quite a few things about the Divide and Unite commands, and if you'd rather skip ahead to the last of the advanced pathfinder operations, turn to "Crop, Exclude, and Intersect" on page 193. However, even though the next few steps may be a bit fussy—and over a single letter no less—it's another way to work with the Divide command, and the only place I show you how to hide the current selection, so stick with me.

19. *Bring the hidden curve in the B to the front.* Somewhere, lost in the stack of yellow and black that make up the *B*, there's a shape hidden behind the other shapes. Hover your mouse cursor over the area shown in Figure 6-34, and when you see the path outlined, click to select it. Press Ctrl+Shift+⬚ (⌘-Shift-⬚) to bring the path to the front of the stack.

20. *Divide the elements that make up the B.* Marquee around all the elements that make up the *B*, as shown in Figure 6-35. Click the 🗗 icon in the **Pathfinder** panel to split apart all the paths.

Figure 6-33.

Figure 6-34.

Figure 6-35.

Figure 6-36.

Figure 6-37.    Figure 6-38.

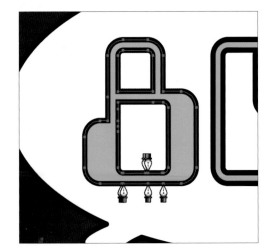

Figure 6-39.

21. *Delete the extraneous paths.* Quite a few paths are unnecessary and, frankly, unwanted. First, switch to the white arrow tool by pressing the A key. Then, holding down the Alt (or Option) key, marquee around the paths as shown in the two frames of Figure 6-36. (The goal is to remove all the shapes inside the lower loop.) After each marquee, press the Backspace or Delete key to get rid of the paths.

22. *Unite all the elements of the B.* Press V to switch back to the black arrow tool, and marquee around all the elements that make up the *B*. Finally, click the 🗗 icon in the Pathfinder panel.

    That's *almost* right. Unfortunately, almost isn't good enough—we have to figure out why the top of the *B* turned solid. Press Ctrl+Z (⌘-Z) to undo your Unite command.

23. *Hide the top of the B.* Now it's time for a nifty trick. I suspect there may be a hidden shape lurking somewhere back there, throwing off the Unite operation, but there's no way to get to it with the top loop of the *B* in the way. Or is there?

    With the white arrow tools, select the top loop, as shown in Figure 6-37. Then, choose **Object→Hide→Hide Selection**. As if by magic, the selection vanishes.

24. *Marquee to see if there are any hidden shapes.* Now that the loop is (literally) out of the way, marquee in roughly the same area as I have in Figure 6-38. Lo and behold, there was a hidden shape! Press Backspace or Delete to ditch it for good.

25. *Show all the elements.* The troublemaking path is now gone, but so is the top of the *B*. Bring it back by choosing **Object→Show All**.

26. *Unite all the remaining B elements.* Once again, marquee all the shapes to select them, and click the 🗗 icon. This time, the results are as expected.

27. *Use the eyedropper to pick up a stroke and fill.* Switch to the eyedropper tool by pressing the I key, and then click the outline of the *OO!* to make the letters match.

28. *Clean up the bottom outside edge.* If you zoom in really close, you may see some little nicks along the bottom edge of the *B*, as in Figure 6-39. To clean up these nicks, switch to the ✎ tool, and when you see the minus sign appear, click to delete the points as shown in the figure. (Your points may vary slightly from mine; if you delete a point that changes the shape, click Ctrl+Z to undo.)

29. *Repeat for the bottom inside edge.* Referring to Figure 6-39, delete the extraneous points to clean up the inside edge as well.

Save your work—you'll be returning to the robot for the final exercise. But as you've learned over the course of this exercise, the Divide command, when put to work with its companion Unite, gives you quite a bit of control of the shapes you can create from a whole host of overlapping primitives. My best pathfinder advice: When in doubt, divide!

## Crop, Exclude, and Intersect

In this, the last of our ghost robot exercises, I'll walk you through the final, most advanced pathfinder operations—crop, exclude, and intersect. In this exercise, we'll focus entirely on the robot's body, and finish with some transparency effects to give our robot friend an appropriate other-worldliness.

1. *Open the last of the ghost artwork.* If you still have the file open from the last exercise, you're ready to go. If not, open the file you saved at the end of the last exercise, or navigate your way to the *Lesson 06* subfolder, inside the *Lesson Files-AIcs5 1on1* folder, and open *Final robot.ai*.

2. *Convert the grill lines to paths.* As with the other pathfinder operations, the Crop operation requires filled closed paths. With the black arrow tool, select a grill line, as shown in Figure 6-40. (They are grouped, so selecting one selects all.) Choose **Object→Path→Outline Stroke** to convert all the strokes to closed paths.

3. *Select and copy the smock path.* Select the robot's smock (the upside-down V shape in the center of the robot's body) and press Ctrl+C (⌘-C) to copy it to the clipboard.

4. *Swap the fill and stroke attributes.* Again, we need a fill for the pathfinder to work properly; press Shift+X to swap the smock's stroke and fill attributes.

5. *Bring the smock to the front.* We want to crop the ribbing lines to the smock shape, so the smock needs to be on top of the other shapes. Bring the smock to the front by pressing Ctrl+Shift+⎀ (⌘-Shift-⎀).

6. *Crop the ribbing lines to the new smock fill.* Shift-click the ribbing lines to add them to the selection, and then press the ⧉ icon in the **Pathfinder** panel to crop the shapes.

Figure 6-40.

Figure 6-41.

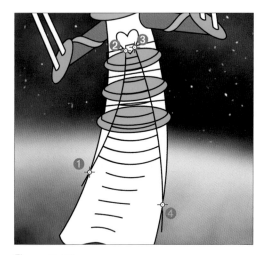

Figure 6-42.

Figure 6-43.

7. *Paste the original smock outline in front.* The smock outline is now missing, but thankfully it's still on the clipboard. Press Ctrl+F (⌘-F) to paste the cape outline at the top of the stack. Your results should look like Figure 6-41.

8. *Use the scissors tool to cut off extra segments of the path.* The smock is looking pretty good, but some bits need to go—namely, the two tails off either side and the segment that pass through the robot's heart. Here's how to separate them:

   - Switch to the scissors tool by pressing the C key.

   - Change to outline mode by pressing Ctrl+Y (⌘-Y). This will allow you to see the precise point of the paths intersecting.

   - Using Figure 6-42 as a guide, click the four points marked. (With smart guides turned on, you'll see a green *intersect* whenever you hover over the path intersection.)

   - Press Ctrl+Y (⌘-Y) again to return to preview mode.

9. *Delete the extra segments.* Switch back to the black arrow tool by pressing the V key, click the first segment, and Shift-click the remaining two to select them all. Press the Backspace or Delete key to get rid of the segments. Afterward, your robot should match that in Figure 6-43.

10. *Select and copy the three discs.* Next we'll focus on the rings around the robot's body. See the three large blue discs that segment the robot's body, shown in Figure 6-44? Select them by clicking the first, and Shift-clicking the next two. Press Ctrl+C (⌘-C) to copy the discs to the clipboard.

Figure 6-44.

11. **Paste the discs to the back.** First, click off the artwork to make sure nothing is selected. Paste the discs to the back of the artwork by pressing Ctrl+B (⌘-B); then press Ctrl+G (⌘-G) to group them. Now, we need to make sure these discs are protected. Bring up the **Layers** panel by pressing F7. Twirl open the **My Primitives** layer, and scroll all the way to the bottom, as in Figure 6-45. You should see the group of three circles. Finally, click the 👁 to hide the group.

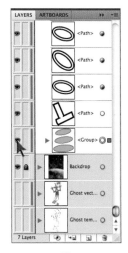

Figure 6-45.

12. **Marquee to select the disc elements.** In the next steps, you'll need to employ the most advanced Divide and Unite operations we've seen thus far. But first, we need to select the required elements. With the black arrow tool, marquee as shown in Figure 6-46, taking care not to select the smock shape.

13. **Divide the selected elements.** Click the 🗐 icon. Illustrator breaks apart the elements; we'll reunite them over the next few steps. Press Ctrl+Shift+A (⌘-Shift-A) to deselect the shapes.

14. **Delete the extraneous shapes.** The transparent shapes outside the robot's body are superfluous and can be removed. Switch to the white arrow tool by pressing the A key, Alt-click (or Option-click) the first shape, and Shift+Alt-click (Shift-Option-click) the rest, as shown in Figure 6-47. Press the Backspace or Delete key to send them into the ether.

Figure 6-46.

15. **Reunite some of the split shapes of the coat.** Alt-click (or Option-click) the topmost disc, and then Shift+Alt-click (Shift-Option-click) the two shapes above to add them to the selection, as in Figure 6-48. Click the 🗐 icon to unite the shapes. Unfortunately, Illustrator fills the resulting shape with blue; press the D key to restore the default fill and stroke.

Figure 6-47.

Figure 6-48.

Figure 6-49.

Figure 6-50.

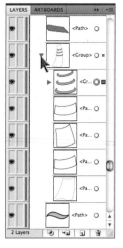

Figure 6-51.

16. *Repeat for the other two disc shapes.* Repeat Step 15 for the other two body segments, as shown in Figure 6-49.

17. *Select the blue-filled objects.* We've repaired the body, but the blue ring shapes are still broken—and into a host of tiny little pieces. Selecting them all by hand would be difficult, and there's no marquee we can draw to select them without selecting other elements. What's a robot to do?

Fortunately, all the elements have the same stroke and fill. Alt-click (or Option-click) any ring shape to select it, and then in the control panel, click the ⬚ icon (equivalent to choosing **Select→Same→Appearance**). This selects all the objects with a matching stroke and fill.

---

If the results aren't as you expect, check to make sure that the pop-up menu next to the ⬚ icon is set to All, and try again.

---

18. *Deselect the unwanted elements with the lasso tool.* The last step selected all the ring elements—and everything else blue in the artwork. A marquee around the elements will reverse the selection, but that would mean while the blue elements will be deselected, the peach, white, violet, and green elements will get selected. This is where the lasso tool comes in handy.

Switch to the lasso tool by pressing the Q key. With the Alt (or Option) key held down, lasso around the highlighted areas shown in Figure 6-50. (You'll need to do it in two steps, as indicated.)

19. *Join the ring shapes.* Now that just the rings are selected, join them by clicking the ⬚ icon.

20. *Cut the shapes from the group and paste them in front.* You're almost finished with the rings, but they're still behind the grill lines from earlier in the exercise. And pressing Ctrl+Shift+⬚ (⌘-Shift-⬚) to bring them to the front appears to do nothing. What's going on?

Bring up the **Layers** panel and scroll down (slowly, so you don't miss it) until you see the highlighted blue square on the right side, shown in Figure 6-51. Twirl open the highlighted group. The Bring to Front command worked, but it brought the shape just to the top of its group. The only way to change the stacking order in this case is to cut the rings. Press Ctrl+X (⌘-X), and then paste them to the front of the entire artwork by pressing Ctrl+F (⌘-F).

The Arrange commands cannot move objects outside any group they are contained in. So if you need to move something out of a group, this cut-and-paste approach is the only surefire method.

21. *Change the opacity of the top of the coat.* At last, you're ready to start giving our ghost his ghostly appearance—that is, make his body translucent. Switch to the white arrow tool, and Alt-click (or Option-click) on the outline of the top of the coat to select it, as in Figure 6-52. Bring up the **Appearance** panel by pressing Shift+F6, and click the fill attribute to make it active. Finally, from the control panel, lower the **Opacity** value to 80.

22. *Repeat for the head and the rest of the coat.* Alt-click (or Option-click) the second body segment, then Shift+Alt-click (Shift-Option-click) the third and fourth segments as well as the head to select them all, as in Figure 6-53. Switch to the eye-dropper tool by pressing the I key, and lift the attributes from the first body segment.

23. *Make the original discs visible.* The discs aren't showing through, but that's because I asked you to hide them in Step 11 on page 195. Again, bring up the **Layers** panel, scroll to the bottom, and click the empty square to the far left of the group to turn on that group. Your results should look like Figure 6-54.

Figure 6-52.

Figure 6-53.

Figure 6-54.

EXTRA ★ CREDIT

You're nearly there, and while there are still a number of steps left in the exercise, they'll conclude your pathfinder work. These steps take the skills you've learned thus far to complete the legs and feet—and then move on to demonstrate Exclude and Intersect, two pathfinder operations you won't see anywhere else in the book. Take a break if need be, but I do hope you'll stick with me.

24. *Select the coat and the legs and divide the shapes.* As is now painfully obvious by the translucent body, I was lazy when drawing the robot—his legs extend only halfway up his shins. And that clearly won't do. Select the legs and the coat shape, and click the ⬚ icon to split them.

25. *Unite the coat and the leg tops.* While it may be tempting to just select the two extraneous bits and delete them, that's not the right approach because that would leave two holes knocked out of the robot's body. Instead, with the white arrow tool, Alt-click (or Option-click) the coat, then Shift-Alt-click (Shift-Option-click) the two leg segments, as in Figure 6-55 on the next page. Unite the shapes by clicking the ⬚ icon.

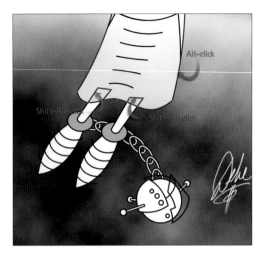

Figure 6-55.

Figure 6-56.

Figure 6-57.

26. ***Convert the shoe lines to paths.*** Select the five grill lines over the left shoe, as in Figure 6-56, and group them. To crop them, we need to convert them to paths as we did all the way back in Step 2 on page 193; choose **Object→Path→Outline Stroke**.

27. ***Copy the shoe outline to the front.*** Select the shoe outline, and copy it by pressing Ctrl+C (⌘-C). Deselect the artwork by clicking off the shoe outline, and then paste the shoe in the front by pressing Ctrl+F (⌘-F).

---

You must deselect the artwork before pasting; otherwise, you will paste directly in front of the selected object, which in this case is still behind the grill lines. When in doubt, select the object you would like to paste in front of before choosing Paste in Front.

---

28. ***Crop the lines to the shoe outline.*** The shoe outline should still be selected; Shift-click the lines to add them to the selection. Click the ⬕ icon to crop the lines to the shoe.

29. ***Repeat for the other shoe.*** Repeat Steps 26 through 28 for the other shoe. Your results should match those in Figure 6-57.

30. ***Create a compound path from the links in the chain.*** Select all the links in the chain by marqueeing as shown in Figure 6-58, Shift-marqueeing to select the last two links. Alt-click (or Option-click) the ⬓ icon in the **Pathfinder** panel to create a compound path from the links. Note that as part of a compound path, each link can still be moved independently, but the Exclude relationship will be maintained.

Figure 6-58.

31. *Copy the bottommost circle of the ball.* Select the bottommost circle of the robot ball, shown in Figure 6-59, and copy it to the clipboard by pressing Ctrl+C (⌘-C).

32. *Set the fill of the two "empty" pieces to white.* Two pieces currently have no fill, and as you've seen in this lesson, the pathfinder doesn't like unfilled shapes. Select the two, and press the D key to give them the default fill and stroke.

33. *Paste the circle to back.* Click the rightmost piece to select it, and then press Ctrl+B (⌘-B) to paste the circle just behind the selection.

34. *Create an intersection with the rightmost piece.* Shift-click the rightmost piece again to add it back to the selection, then Alt-click (or Option-click) the ▣ icon in the **Pathfinder** panel to create a dynamic intersection. Illustrator draws only the section where the two shapes overlap, as shown in Figure 6-60, but each path is still independently movable.

35. *Repeat for the top quadrant.* Repeat Steps 33 and 34 for the top quadrant, which should result in Figure 6-61.

36. *Repeat again for the left quadrant.* Once again, repeat Steps 33 and 34 for the left quadrant. The finished ball should look like Figure 6-62.

37. *Cut and paste the heart.* Lastly, turn your attention to the robot's heart. In the original, the heart knocks out of the body—our poor lonely robot has a hole where his heart should be. Unfortunately, the heart is much further up the stacking order

Figure 6-59.

Figure 6-60.

Figure 6-61.

Figure 6-62.

than the body, and if you used a pathfinder operation now, it would pull the body in front of the collar and the right arm. That would just be adding insult to injury.

The solution, as you may have surmised from my earlier tip, is Paste in Front. Select the heart, and cut it by pressing Ctrl+X (⌘-X). Select the body, and press Ctrl+F (⌘-F) to paste the heart just above the body in the stacking order.

Figure 6-63.

38. *Knock out the heart from the ghost's body.* Shift-click the body to add it back to the selection, and Alt-click (or Option-click) the ⬚ icon in the Pathfinder panel. "*Hole* is where the heart is" may be the new idiom for our robot.

39. *Fix the opacity.* Unfortunately, the Exclude operation picked up the opacity settings from the heart, rendering our ghost body opaque again. Press the I key, and with the eyedropper tool, lift the attributes from the robot's head.

Your robot is now complete, as shown in Figure 6-63. Through creative applications of pathfinder operations—especially the ever-versatile Divide and Unite pairing— you've taken a large group of primitives and built a finished illustration, and started down the road of mastering one of Illustrator's most powerful and practical set of tools.

# WHAT DID YOU LEARN?

Match the key concept in the numbered list below with the letter of the phrase that best describes it. Answers appear upside-down at the bottom of the page.

## Key Concepts

1. Pathfinder operation
2. Compound path
3. Compound shape
4. Shape mode
5. Unite
6. Minus Front
7. Minus Back
8. Divide
9. Crop
10. Lasso tool
11. Exclude
12. Intersect

## Descriptions

A. A selection tool that allows for freeform selection of points or paths.

B. A calculation Illustrator performs to combine two or more paths either permanently or dynamically.

C. A shape mode that subtracts the front shape from the shapes behind it.

D. A shape composed of multiple paths, where each path can have its own shape mode applied.

E. A pathfinder operation that subtracts the rearmost shape from those above it.

F. A pathfinder operation that breaks all overlapping areas of the selected paths into individual pieces that remain grouped.

G. A pathfinder operation that removes all pieces of a path or paths that lie outside of the topmost shape.

H. A single path consisting of multiple subpaths, such as a figure eight.

I. A shape mode that knocks out any areas where the paths overlap.

J. A calculation Illustrator performs to combine two or more paths permanently through a Boolean operation.

K. A shape mode that shows only the areas where the paths overlap.

L. A shape mode that adds two or more paths.

## Answers

1J, 2H, 3D, 4B, 5L, 6C, 7E, 8F, 9G, 10A, 11I, 12K

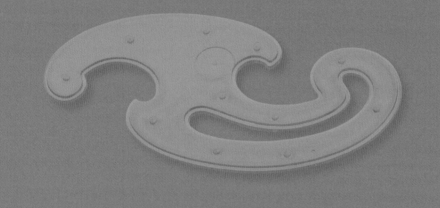

# LESSON

# 7

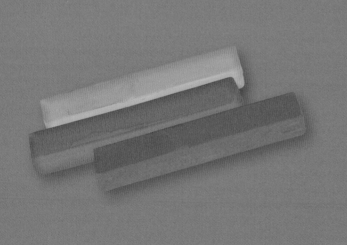

**CONCEPTUALLY, THE** common gradient is a straight-forward creature. Where Illustrator is concerned, a *gradient* is a fill pattern (the program prohibits gradient strokes) in which one color transitions seamlessly into another. You define the location, color, and even opacity of the *stops*—or points of color—in the gradient; Illustrator figures out how the transitional colors should blend in between.

Illustrator provides three kinds of gradients: There's the standard gradient fill that you apply and edit with the gradient tool. You can build a multipath blend, which allows you to design a custom gradient inside a clipping mask. Or you can apply a *gradient mesh*, which lets you add points of color anywhere inside a path outline and blend between those points along a network of subpaths.

I'll explore the distinctions between these three kinds of gradients in a moment. But your larger question might be, why does Illustrator go to such great lengths to support gradients—not to mention, mire you down with so many alternatives—when they are fundamentally so simple? To make sense of that, you need to understand the mechanics of making a standard gradient.

Start by drawing something simple, say, a rectangle. Then select the gradient tool—you can get it by pressing G—and click inside the shape to fill it with a default gradient, most likely white-to-black. (If that doesn't work, just tap the period key.) You'll see a bar inside the shape, known as the *gradient annotator*. Hover your cursor over the annotator and it takes on the appearance pictured in Figure 7-1 (albeit in different colors). A circle marks the beginning, or origin, of the gradient. Drag the circle to move the gradient inside the shape. (And be prepared for the annotator to recenter itself after you release.) A diamond marks the end, or terminus, of the gradient. Drag the diamond to change the length of the gradient; move your cursor slightly beyond the diamond and drag to change the angle.

The gradient annotator (annotated)

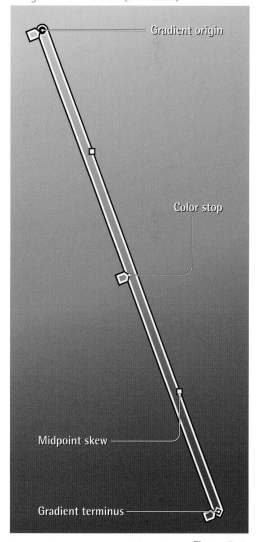

Gradient origin

Color stop

Midpoint skew

Gradient terminus

Figure 7-1.

# ABOUT THIS LESSON

## Project Files

Gradients, blends, masks, and gradient mesh represent perhaps the most surefire ways to take flat path outlines and transform them into volumetric, dimensional objects. The video explains the basics of gradients. In the step-by-step exercises on the following pages, you'll learn how to:

- Blend between two or more colored paths to create a custom gradient . . . . . . . . . . . . . . page 206

- Edit a blend and mask it inside another shape . . . . page 209

- Blend between translucent, distant, and stroked paths to create intermediate steps . . . . . . . . . . page 213

- Use clipping masks to house anything, including other clipping masks . . . . . . . . . . . page 219

- Create a two-dimensional gradient mesh . . . . . . page 226

## Video Lesson 7: Gradients

Creating gradients, blended transitions between colors, allows you to add texture and shading to your artwork without adding a single path. In this video, I'll show you how to create custom gradients and use blends to give your artwork added dimension.

To see gradients in action, visit *www.oreilly.com/go/deke-IllustratorCS5*. Click the **Watch** button to view the lesson online or click the **Download** button to save it to your computer. During the video, you'll learn these shortcuts:

Video Lesson 7: Gradients

| Operation | Windows shortcut | Macintosh shortcut |
|---|---|---|
| Display the Gradient panel | Ctrl+F9 | ⌘-F9 |
| Apply a gradient fill | Press the ⟨.⟩ key (period) | Press the ⟨.⟩ key (period) |
| Apply the last-used solid fill | Press the ⟨,⟩ key (comma) | Press the ⟨,⟩ key (comma) |
| Display the Color Guide panel | Shift+F3 | Shift-F3 |
| Display the Appearance panel | Shift+F6 | Shift-F6 |
| Add a fill to a selected object | Ctrl+⟨/⟩ (forward slash) | ⌘-⟨/⟩ (forward slash) |
| Add a stroke to a selected object | Ctrl+Alt+⟨/⟩ (forward slash) | ⌘-Option-⟨/⟩ (forward slash) |
| Display the Transparency panel | Ctrl+Shift+F10 | ⌘-Shift-F10 |
| Select the gradient tool | Press the G key | Press the G key |
| Blend between two selected paths | Ctrl+Alt+B | ⌘-Option-B |

When you hover over the annotator (the key to getting it to work), you'll also see five-sided color stops and tiny square *midpoint skews*, both labeled in Figure 7-1. Drag a color stop to change its location. Double-click it to display a pop-up Color panel and assign a new color. (You may need to click the ⬇≡ icon and choose CMYK to access anything other than gray values.) Click along the edge of the annotator to add a new color stop. Drag the midpoint skew square to change the speed at which one color stop transitions into the next.

Gradients are all very flexible once you come to terms with them. Problem is, Illustrator offers just two styles of gradient: linear, in which one color transitions directly into another, and radial, which fills the shape with concentric rings of color. (You switch between them from the Gradient panel.) That's fine for design work. The many gradient boxes and backgrounds in this book, for example, are filled with linear gradients. But what if you're trying to approximate real-life or otherwise volumetric shading inside an illustration? That, my friend, is when you resort to blends and meshes.

Figure 7-2.

## Designing Custom Gradients

Despite the fact that it was introduced more than 20 years ago, Illustrator's second gradient solution, *blending*, continues to rank among the program's most powerful capabilities. Blending permits you to design custom gradations and morphs, in which one shape or group of shapes steadily transitions into another, by creating intermediate subpaths, called *steps*, between two selected extremes. You can then mask the blended paths—or any other collection of objects, for that matter—inside a path.

The final solution, gradient mesh, is altogether unique to Illustrator. It allows you to move colors in two-dimensional space—right there in the artboard—and blend between neighboring colors in all directions. You can create bright spots, shaded edges, even rivers of color. Figure 7-2 features an illustration created using just two shapes, each filled with a gradient mesh. Figure 7-3 shows each shape with its mesh exposed as a series of anchor points and segments.

Figure 7-3.

Points in a gradient mesh behave just like anchor points in a path. You can move them, adjust their control handles, and otherwise modify them as selective points in a larger whole.

The beauty of both blends and gradient mesh objects is that they are forever editable. Change the color or shape of a blended path, and all pieces of the blend update immediately. You can even change the path of a blend, so it slows down, speeds up, or curves on its way from one shape to the other. Plus, you can blend between multiple shapes, fill and stroke attributes, and levels of transparency. Meanwhile, each and every point in a gradient mesh lies forever in wait of your next edit, whether it be one of position, curvature, or color.

I demonstrate how to create and modify gradients with the gradient tool in Video Lesson 7, "Gradients." In the exercises that follow, I show you how to exploit the power of blends, masks, and gradient mesh fills.

## Blending Between Paths

The primary purpose of a blend is to create a custom gradient, in which colors flow in controlled patterns. Because a blend transforms one path into another, you need a mechanism for placing those paths inside a larger shape. Hence the *clipping mask*, which is a shape that crops the boundaries of the blended paths below it.

Although blends and masks rank among Illustrator's oldest features, they are some of its most powerful as well. I show you how to create a blend in this exercise. I explain how to mask that blend in the next.

1. *Open an illustration with a gradient background.* Open *Lone ghost.ai*, found in the *Lesson 07* folder inside *Lesson Files-AIcs5 1on1* folder. Pictured in Figure 7-4, this file is the sequel to the ghost robot you built in Lesson 6. He's shrieking the spooky "2oo!"—in case you read it as the large number 200, which would be a curious non sequitur even for a ghost robot. Notice that I've restored some of the original path outlines—including those in the smock, shoes, and ball—so that we can rebuild those details using masks. The file also features a gradient background, which we'll replace with a blend.

Figure 7-4.

2. *Select the large gradient rectangle.* Scroll to the bottom of the **Layers** panel and Alt-click (or on the Mac, Option-click) in the second column to the left of the **Backdrop** layer to lock all the other layers in the illustration. This will make it easier to navigate inside the illustration without selecting the wrong objects. Then, using the black arrow tool, click the outline of the largest rectangle to select it.

3. *Select the gradient tool.* Click the gradient tool in the toolbox, as demonstrated in Figure 7-5, or press the G key. Illustrator shows the gradient annotator (also on display in the figure), with the circular origin point at the top and the square terminus point at the bottom.

Figure 7-5.

---

If the gradient annotator gets in the way of seeing your artwork, you can hide it by choosing View→Hide Gradient Annotator or by pressing Ctrl+Alt+G (⌘-Option-G). To bring it back, choose View→Show Gradient Annotator.

---

4. *Examine the color stops.* Hover your cursor over the gradient annotator to see a total of three color stops, one each at the top, middle, and bottom. Double-click a color stop to bring up a pop-up panel with CMYK values.

The existing fill pattern is a simple linear gradient, progressing from a deep purple to blue and finally ending in peach. The colors are fine, but I'd like to introduce some moderate wave action to the gradient using a blend.

5. *Switch to a solid fill.* The next steps will show up better if you eliminate the existing gradient. Go to the **Color** panel (if you don't see it, press F6) and click a green in the spectrum bar at the bottom of the panel. Although the exact shade of green isn't important, I opted for CMYK values of 100, 0, 100, and 35, respectively.

6. *Turn on the objects.* In the **Layers** panel, twirl open the **Backdrop** layer. Then click the first column in front of the group called **Objects** to display the three paths of color pictured in Figure 7-6.

Figure 7-6.

Figure 7-7.

7. **Blend the three colored paths.** Press V to switch to the black arrow tool and click the outline of any of the newly displayed colored paths. (Note that I drew each path with the rectangle tool, and then modified its anchor points with the white arrow tool.) To blend the paths, choose **Object→Blend→Make**, which has a keyboard shortcut of Ctrl+Alt+B (⌘-Option-B). Illustrator creates a series of gradual shape and color transitions between the paths. That said, they look altogether wrong, as in Figure 7-7.

8. **Change the stacking order.** If a blend misbehaves, your tool for discovering why is the **Layers** panel. Go to the panel and twirl open the **Objects** group. Inside you'll find an item called Blend, which is your new blend object. Click the ▶ in front of **Blend** to twirl it open and therein you'll find three items. The first, <Path>, determines the direction of the blend (and will prove a nuisance in just a moment). The others—Middle, Top, and Base—represent the original path outlines.

The problem is that Middle appears above Top. The Blend command doesn't know top from bottom (or left from right, for that matter). It knows stacking order. So drag **Middle** between Top and Base.

9. **Undo the last two steps.** Boy, did that not work! Thanks to the dictates of the <Path> item, Illustrator has physically moved the Top path to a new location. Our only solution is to undo what we've done and take a new stab at it. So choose **Edit→Undo** or press Ctrl+Z (⌘-Z) twice in a row to return to the original, unblended paths.

10. **Stack the paths first; blend them second.** The trick is to stack the paths properly before blending them, which means reversing the order of Steps 7 and 8. Still in the Layers panel, drag **Middle** between Top and Base. Then with the Objects group still selected, choose **Object→Blend→Make** or press Ctrl+Alt+B (⌘-Option-B). The colors now blend in the proper order.

Unfortunately, now we have a more subtle but equally troubling problem: a diagonal edge between the blue and peach paths, labeled in Figure 7-8. While less disastrous than our previous problem, the edge ruins the effect of a seamless gradient.

Bad edge

Figure 7-8.

11. *Rotate the blue path.* Illustrator tracks blends by connecting an anchor point in one path to what it believes to be an equivalent anchor point in the next. But in connecting the blue and peach paths, the program got it wrong. For example, the bottom-right point in the blue path blends to the bottom-left point in the peach-colored one.

The solution is to reshape, reposition, or transform a path in a way that forces Illustrator to recalculate the blend. In our case, a slight rotation will suffice:

- Again in the Layers panel, twirl open the **Blend** item. Then target the Base path by clicking its circular meatball.

- In the control panel, click the blue **X** (or Y, W, or H) to bring up the Transform panel.

- Click the △ icon on the left side of the panel to highlight the rotate value. Enter 5 degrees, and press the Enter or Return key.

By rotating the blue path a few degrees counter-clockwise—so it's more in keeping with the angle of the purple and peach paths—you make Illustrator reconnect the anchor points, this time with more success, as in Figure 7-9.

Blends create smooth color transitions and update automatically. But the same can be said of gradients (as documented in the video lesson). In fact, the blend in Figure 7-9 isn't all that remarkably different from the one I established back in Figure 7-4 (see page 206), except it required more work and no longer fits tidily inside the original rectangle. But this is just the beginning. You can edit blends with far more control than that afforded by gradients, and you can mask them as well, all of which I explain in the next exercise.

Figure 7-9.

## Editing and Masking a Blend

In this exercise, you'll build on the previous project by modifying the placement of a blended path, adding another color and path outline to the blend, and setting the blend inside a mask.

1. *Open an illustration that contains a blend.* Keep working inside the file you have open from the last exercise. Or if it isn't handy, open *Blended shapes.ai*, found inside the *Lesson 07* folder.

Figure 7-10.

Figure 7-11.

2. *Select the blue path.* Inside the **Layers** panel, Alt-click (or Option-click) the ▶ in front of the **Backdrop** layer to twirl open not only the layer but the **Objects** group and the Blend object inside it. Then meatball the **Middle** item (click the "meatball" circle to the right of Middle) to select the blue path.

3. *Move the blue path down.* Using either of the arrow tools, drag the selected path down so it's more or less centered on the robot's shins. (The exact location isn't important, but be sure to drag the path by its outline.) By now, it hardly comes as a surprise that Illustrator updates the blend automatically, as shown in Figure 7-10.

4. *Clone the blue path.* Illustrator lets you add colors to a blend by duplicating existing paths inside that blend. That is, drag a blended path and then press the Alt key (Option on the Mac) as you release to create another key point of color.

With that in mind, drag the blue path upward so it's even with the hand to the right of the robot's head (his left). Then press and hold Alt (or Option) and release the mouse button to clone the path as opposed to move it. Figure 7-11 illustrates the process.

5. *Change the color of the cloned path.* Figure 7-11 also illustrates a strange behavior inherent in cloning a blended path. Because the clone and its original are precisely the same color, Illustrator perceives no need to create the usual rich array of transitional steps. (The fact that it draws two steps in our case is merely a function of the gaping distance between the paths.) But tweak so much as a single CMYK (or other color) value and the steps fill in. To prove me right, bring up the **Color** panel, change the **M** value to 25, and watch the gaps disappear.

6. *Make the cloned path green.* That's still not quite the color I'm looking for. The C and M values are fine at 100 and 25, respectively, but for purely subjective reasons, the other two need adjusting. Change the **Y** value to 80 and the **K** value to 0 to achieve the vivid green pictured in Figure 7-12.

Figure 7-12.

The final step is to crop the blend inside the confines of the background rectangle. Based on what you learned in Lesson 6, you might naturally assume that this is a job for a Pathfinder operation, specifically Crop. But like most of Illustrator's Pathfinder ops, the static Crop function works exclusively with closed path outlines—no blends or other specialty objects allowed.

The more reliable and flexible solution is a clipping mask, which serves as a container into which you can place closed paths, open paths, groups, text, specialty objects, *anything*. Illustrator CS5 provides two methods for making a clipping mask, both of which I believe you'll find useful.

7. *Paste the blend into the rectangle.* This first method for masking a blend inside a shape is new to CS5 and simulates a behavior pioneered by FreeHand, which some of you may remember nostalgically as Illustrator's primary competition back in the old days:

- In the **Layers** panel, meatball the group labeled **Objects**.

- Choose **Edit→Cut** or press Ctrl+X (⌘-X) to transfer the group to the clipboard.

- Using the black arrow tool, click the bright green rectangle to select it.

- Click the 🔲 icon at the bottom of the toolbox and choose **Draw Inside**, as you see me doing in Figure 7-13. The icon changes to ⊕ and the green rectangle receives dotted corners to show that anything you make will appear clipped inside the selected shape.

- Choose **Edit→Paste in Place** or press the keyboard equivalent Ctrl+Shift+V (or ⌘-Shift-V). The blend fills the rectangle.

Figure 7-13.

Figure 7-14.

The result appears in Figure 7-14. In the everyday average course of things, you would click the ⊕ icon at the bottom of the toolbox and choose **Draw Normal** (or press Shift+D) to return to the standard drawing mode and go about your business.

Which is to say, you're done. But while that approach is straightforward enough, it fails to demonstrate what's going on under the hood. And one of my goals in this book is to help you understand exactly how Illustrator works. So, if you'll forgive me, I'm going to have you recreate the clipping mask using a more traditional technique.

8. *Undo the last two operations.* Press Ctrl+Z (or ⌘-Z) twice in a row to restore the unclipped blend.

9. *Recreate the clipping mask.* Here's how to clip the blend inside the rectangle, whether you use Illustrator CS5 or some older version:

   • First press Shift+D to make sure you're working in the standard drawing mode.

   • Scroll to the bottom of the **Layers** panel and meatball the item called **Rectangle** to select that shape independently of the others.

   • Right-click in the document window, and choose **Arrange→Bring to Front** or press the shortcut Ctrl+Shift+⬚ (that's ⌘-Shift-⬚ on the Mac). The green rectangle now appears in front of the blend. While that might not make a lot of sense, it's important: Illustrator requires a mask to be in front of the paths that it clips.

   • Back in the Layers panel, Shift-click the meatball after **Objects** to select the group and blend.

   • Choose **Object→Clipping Mask→Make** or press its long-time shortcut, Ctrl+7 (⌘-7). The blend once again appears inside the rectangle, only without the blend selection handles as in Figure 7-15.

Figure 7-15.

10. *Inspect the clipping mask.* In addition to providing you with valuable experience, I had you make the mask a second time so you can inspect its structure. Again in the Layers panel, twirl open the one item in the **Backdrop** layer, <Group>. Inside that, you'll see

Rectangle, Objects, Blend, and the others. Note that the thumbnail for Rectangle has changed, with a white rectangle against a gray background, as in Figure 7-16. This is Illustrator's code for a clipping mask. White represents the interior of the mask, the portions of the clipped objects you can see. Gray represents the area outside the mask, the portions that are hidden (or clipped). Click the 👁 icon for **Rectangle** to turn off the mask and you'll see that the blend remains entirely intact and editable. Turn the Rectangle back on, and the blend appears cropped. Now that Rectangle is identified as the mask, you can even change its stacking order. Just so long as it remains inside the item called <Group>, all is well.

11. *Rename the group.* One last bit of housekeeping: Double-click the <Group> item in the Layers panel. Then change the **Name** option to "Mask," and click **OK**.

12. *Save your changes.* Choose **File→Save As** or press Ctrl+Shift+S (⌘-Shift-S on the Mac). Name your revised file "Blend inside clipping mask.ai," and click the **Save** button. You'll use this file as the starting point for the next exercise.

The primary advantage of blends and masks are the same: They afford a high degree of flexibility, editability, and automation in return for a modest amount of work. And once you come to terms with their underlying mechanics and admittedly odd (at times) behavior, they become efficient tools as well.

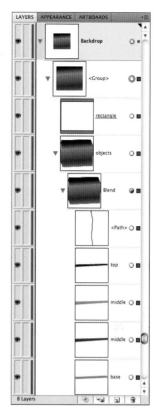

Figure 7-16.

## Creating Specialty Blends

Blends don't have to be gradients. They can represent shading, glows, directional fades, and all varieties of incremental effects. In this exercise, you'll blend between shapes with differing levels of opacity. You'll blend distant shapes to create a trail. And you'll adjust the speed, curvature, and direction of a blend.

1. *Open a file that includes translucent paths.* If you've managed to get through the previous exercises successfully, open the *Blend inside clipping mask.ai* file that you saved in Step 12 above. Or if you prefer, open the file that I've provided for you, *Cropped universe.ai*, found in the *Lesson 07* folder. In addition to the blended background, this file contains a handful of opaque and translucent circles that you'll blend together.

2. *Lock and unlock layers.* In the **Layers** panel, click the second column to the left of the **Backdrop** layer to lock it. (If necessary, twirl it closed as well.) Click the 🔒 icon to the left of the **Shoot Star** layer to unlock it. This is the layer we'll use for this exercise.

Figure 7-17.

Double-click the blend tool to adjust the number of steps

Blend Tool (W)

Figure 7-18.

3. *Expand the Shoot Star layer.* Click the ▶ in front of Shoot Star to reveal six objects, two each named Burst, Star, and Circle.

4. *Blend the Star paths.* Still inside the Layers panel, click the meatball for **Star 1** and then Shift-click that for **Star 2** to select the two star paths to the left of the robot's leg. Then choose **Object→Blend→Make** or press Ctrl+Alt+B (⌘-Option-B) to blend between them. Because both stars are white and 50 percent opaque, Illustrator creates a single step between them, as shown in Figure 7-17.

5. *Add steps between the stars.* One step isn't nearly enough. To add more steps without changing the color of one star or the other, choose **Object→Blend→Blend Options**. In the dialog box, set the **Spacing** option to **Specified Steps** and enter a value of 3 to achieve the effect shown in Figure 7-18. Then click **OK**.

When creating and adjusting blends, you spend a lot of time choosing the Blend Options command. So it may seem curious that it doesn't have a keyboard equivalent—and downright odd that I didn't add one to dekeKeys. That's because Illustrator includes a different kind of shortcut.

---

Illustrator includes a blend tool that lets you create a blend object by clicking the precise anchor point in each path that you want to blend. Although I rarely use the tool—if only because it's less efficient than choosing Object→Blend→Make—it has its purpose: Double-click the blend tool icon (it looks like a square morphing into a circle, 🔲, as labeled in Figure 7-18) to display the Blend Options dialog box. Then change the number of steps for the selected blend. If no blend is selected, your changes determine the future default settings. But be careful when doing this; while requesting a specific number of steps by default may benefit path blends like the ones you'll create in this exercise, it can result in *banding*—that is, obvious steps (or bands) of color—in gradient-style blends.

---

6. *Rename the star blend.* By the end of this exercise, the Shoot Star layer will contain three blends and you'll want to be able to tell them apart. So double-click the **Blend** item in the Layers panel, rename the blend "Star Blend," and click **OK**.

7. *Blend the Burst paths.* In the Layers panel, meatball **Burst 1** and Shift-meatball **Burst 2** to select two circles, one centered within and the other around the stars. (Burst 2 is particularly difficult to select outside the Layers panel because it's invisible.) Press Ctrl+Alt+B (or ⌘-Option-B) to blend the paths. Even though one circle is opaque and the other transparent—that is, their Opacity values in the control panel are 100 and 0 percent, respectively—both paths contain white fills. So once again, Illustrator creates a single step between them.

8. *Rename the burst blend.* Double-click the newest **Blend** item in the Layers panel, call it "Burst Blend," and click **OK**. This kind of layer management can be tedious, but you'll thank yourself later when you're trying to sift your way through a complex illustration.

9. *Increase the number of steps.* Double-click the blend tool in the toolbox (⬚) to display the **Blend Options** dialog box. Set **Spacing** to **Specified Steps**. Increase the value to 30, and click **OK**. The result appears in Figure 7-19.

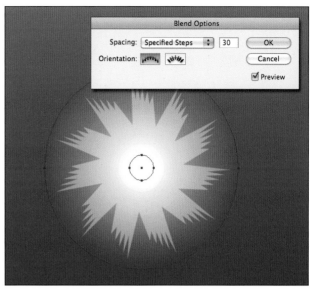

Figure 7-19.

10. *Blend the Circle paths.* Back in the **Layers** panel, meatball **Circle 1** and then Shift-meatball **Circle 2** to select two more circles. The path at the center of the starburst (Circle 1) is set to an Opacity value of 30 percent; the one on the right side of the robot (Circle 2) is set to 0 percent. Press Ctrl+Alt+B (or ⌘-Option-B) to blend the paths. Due to the large distance between the circles, Illustrator automatically adds nineteen steps, as in Figure 7-20.

11. *Rename the circle blend.* You know the routine. Double-click the third **Blend** object in the Layers panel, name it "Comet Trail," and click **OK**.

Figure 7-20.

12. *Increase the number of steps to 100.* Double-click the blend tool in the toolbox to display the **Blend Options** dialog box. Select **Specified Steps** from the **Spacing** pop-up menu. Enter a value of 100, which is the lowest number that results in a moderately smooth transition, with just a few bumps along the way, as evidenced in Figure 7-21. (A low-as-possible Specified Steps value means less work for Illustrator and faster printing.) Then click **OK**.

The path-of-the-blend

Figure 7-21.

Any time two or more blended paths are separated by a distance (rather than being centered on one another, as with the Star and Burst paths), Illustrator adds an invisible path that determines the *path-of-the-blend*, as labeled in the figure above. In the next few steps, you'll add control handles to this path to make the steps in the Comet Trail blend traverse along a curve.

13. *Lock all but the path-of-the-blend.* The endpoints at either side of the path-of-the-blend coincide with center points in the Burst and Circle paths. Therefore, the only way to get to them with any degree of reliability is to lock down the other paths. Here's the easiest way to accomplish that:

   • Alt-click (or Option-click) the **Shoot Star** layer in the **Layers** panel to select all objects on that layer.

- Press the A key to switch to the white arrow tool. Then press the Shift and Alt (or Shift and Option) keys and click the straight path-of-the-blend that cuts through the robot to deselect it.

- Choose **Object→Lock→Selection** or press Ctrl+2 (⌘-2). Now all paths in the Shoot Star layer except the path-of-the-blend are locked.

14. *Change the curvature of the path-of-the-blend.* In this step, you'll add a bit of wave to the currently straight path-of-the-blend. Press Ctrl+A (⌘-A) to select the path. Then do like so:

- Press Shift+C to select the convert point tool (⊦), which is also available from the pen tool flyout menu. Just as this tool allows you to add and subtract anchor points associated with a standard path outline, you can use it to add and subtract control handles inside a blend.

- Drag up and to the right from the left endpoint. The result is the emergence of a control handle that adds curvature to the path. For my part, I dragged to a position just to the left of the robot's near elbow, as demonstrated in Figure 7-22. But there are no hard-and-fast rules here. Feel free to do as you like.

Figure 7-22.

- Still armed with the convert point tool, drag up and to the right from the right-hand endpoint. (As when drawing with the pen tool, the convert point tool requires you to continue the curvature of segments in the direction of your first drag.) Again, a control handle emerges, but this time in the opposite direction of your drag, as illustrated in Figure 7-23.

Figure 7-23.

15. *Further increase the number of steps.* If you zoom in on the blend—try 400 percent or higher—you may notice that it's beginning to break up into a series of lumps. In the process of extracting control handles from the path-of-the-blend, we've stretched the path so that it has to cover a longer distance. Hence, we need more steps. Double-click the blend tool icon (🔳) in the toolbox to display the **Blend Options** dialog box. With the **Spacing** value highlighted, press Shift+↑ to raise the number of steps in increments of 10. When you get to 180— which, to my eye, results in a smooth blend—click **OK**. The final comet trail appears independently of the rest of the illustration in Figure 7-24 on the facing page.

16. *Save your changes.* Press Ctrl+Shift+S (or ⌘-Shift-S), name your file "The blended comet.ai," and click the **Save** button. Then set the file aside for the next exercise.

Step 14 documents just one of many ways to use the path-of-the-blend to adjust the appearance of a trail or other shape-morphing effect. Here are a few other tricks to try out: Using the white arrow tool, drag either endpoint in the path-of-the-blend to change the location of one blended path or the other. If you need more control, use the pen tool to add or subtract anchor points along the path-of-the-blend. With the white arrow tool, you can also drag a control handle to adjust the speed of the blend. Dragging a short control handle results in a fast blend; dragging a long control handle results in a slow one. Stay tuned: I explain how to use control handles for this very purpose in Lesson 8.

Figure 7-24.

## Making the Most of Clipping Masks

In the last exercise, I showed you how to create blends that don't require masks. In this exercise, I demonstrate uses for masks that may or may not involve blends. (And the blends that you will encounter are anything but conventional.) Topics include restoring the fill and stroke of a mask, creating compound masks, and nesting one mask inside another. This is masking at its best.

1. *Open a file with paths to be masked.* If you're happy with the file that you saved in Step 16 of the preceding exercise, open it. If not, open my file, *Shooting star.ai*, found in the *Lesson 07* folder.

2. *Lock and unlock the requisite layers.* Choose **Object→Unlock All** to unlock the blended paths on the Shoot Star layer. In the **Layers** panel, twirl the Shoot Star layer closed (if it's open) and click in the second column to the left of that layer to lock it. Then scroll to the top of the panel, and click the 🔒 icon to the left of the **Ball** layer to unlock it so you can modify the ball attached to the robot's feet without harming the rest of the illustration.

3. *Twirl open the Ball layer.* Click the ▶ in front of the Ball layer to reveal its four groups—Tacks, Front Thing, Edges, and Back Things—along with the ball outline, called Ball. This last layer needs to crop the elements above it. In Lesson 6, we achieved this effect using the Crop Path-finder operation. This time, we'll employ masking, which is slightly more complex but several times more flexible.

4. *Mask the Edges inside the Ball.* Zoom in on the ball below the robot's feet. In the Layers panel, drag the **Ball** path above the **Edges** group. (As you may recall, Illustrator requires that the mask be stacked in front of the objects it will contain.) Meatball both the Ball and Edges objects in the Layers panel. And then choose **Object→Clipping Mask→Make** or press Ctrl+7 (⌘-7). As shown in Figure 7-25, the white fill and the black stroke of the Ball path disappear. It's not that a clipping mask can't have fill and stroke attributes; it can. It's just that Illustrator strangely chooses to dispose of them as a matter of course. Our job now is to reinstate them.

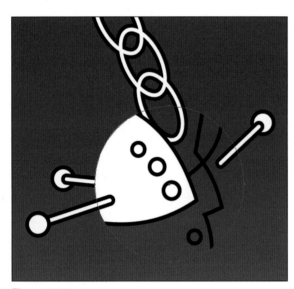

Figure 7-25.

5. *Restore the fill and stroke of the Ball.* With the circular Ball outline selected, press the I key to select the eyedropper tool. Then click the top-left "plate" of the ball—the one that includes a white fill and a black stroke—to copy the fill and stroke to the ball itself, as demonstrated in Figure 7-26.

6. *Move the right plate to the back.* The plate along the right side of the ball should be in back of the others. Unfortunately, now that it's housed inside a clipping mask, it's difficult to select it in the document window. Better to exploit Illustrator's group isolation mode:

   • Press the V key to get the black arrow tool.

   • Double-click along the outline of the outer ball to isolate the clipping mask from the rest of the illustration.

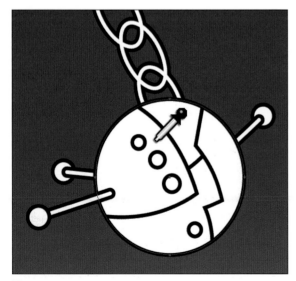

Figure 7-26.

- Double-click the outline of any of the three plates to isolate the Edges group from the clipping mask.

- Select the right plate, and press Ctrl+Shift+[ (or ⌘-Shift-[) to send it to the back of the group, as in Figure 7-27.

- Now press the Esc key to escape the group isolation mode. The plates appear in the proper order, masked inside the ball, as in Figure 7-28.

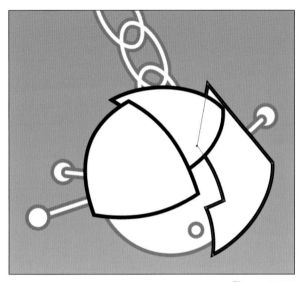

Figure 7-27.

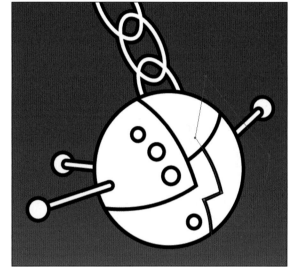

Figure 7-28.

The advantage of working with a clipping mask is that you can move the contents of the mask or even reshape the mask outline, and Illustrator will update the crop automatically. That is to say, the relationship between the mask and its contents is forever dynamic.

7. *Lock the Ball; unlock the feet.* The ball is complete. In the **Layers** panel, twirl the **Ball** layer closed and lock it. Then scroll four layers down and click the 🔒 icon next to the **Feet** layer to unlock it.

8. *Examine the contents of the Feet layer.* Click the Feet layer's ▶ to reveal two blends and two paths. The paths are the shoe outlines; the blends are the laces. I created each set of laces by drawing an arc at the top of the shoe, cloning it to make the bottom lace, and then blending between the two stroked outlines with three steps. If you select either arc with the white arrow tool and drag it to a new location, the blend will update, as in Figure 7-29.

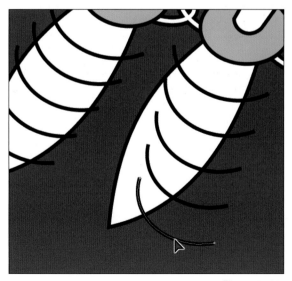

Figure 7-29.

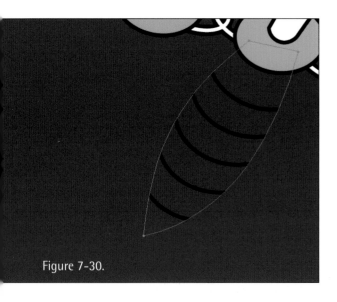

Figure 7-30.

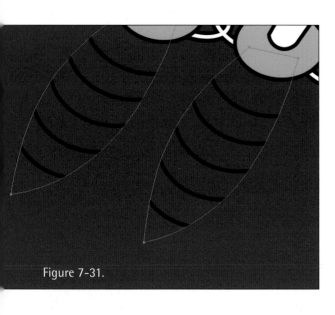

Figure 7-31.

9. *Mask the laces inside the shoes.* If you moved a lace, press Ctrl+Z (or ⌘-Z) to return it to its original position. We want to mask the laces inside the shoes, but as usual the shoes are in back. So select the two items labeled **<Path>** in the Layers panel (click one, Shift-click the other) and drag them above the Blend items. Then Alt-click (or Option-click) the **Feet** layer to select both shoes and laces. Right-click anywhere inside the document window and choose **Make Clipping Mask**—another way to work—or press Ctrl+7 (⌘-7). Unfortunately, instead of masking the two sets of laces inside the two shoes, Illustrator masks everything inside the right shoe, as in Figure 7-30. That's because the program assigns just the front path as a mask, and the right shoe is at the top of the Feet layer.

10. *Combine the shoes into a single compound path.* Press Ctrl+Z (⌘-Z) to undo the previous step. Obviously, you could mask the left laces inside the left shoe and then mask the right laces inside the right one. But is there a way to mask the laces inside both shoe shapes at once?

PEARL OF WISDOM

The answer is, of course. (Why else would I have brought it up?) How? First combine the two shoe paths into a single compound path. In previous lessons, we've seen how compound paths let you use one outline to carve a hole in another. But it doesn't have to work that way. If the paths don't intersect—as is the case with our pointy shoes—they don't interact with each other. Regardless of its form, Illustrator always sees a compound path as a single path outline.

Press Ctrl+Shift+A (⌘-Shift-A) to deselect all. Press the V key to get the black arrow tool. Click one shoe outline and then Shift-click the other. Right-click anywhere in the document window and choose **Make Compound Path** or press Ctrl+8 (⌘-8). The shoes look the same as ever, but Illustrator now regards them as one path.

11. *Reattempt masking the laces inside the shoes.* Press Ctrl+A (⌘-A) to select the shoes and laces. (This assumes all other layers are locked. If not, Alt-click or Option-click the Feet layer in the Layers panel.) Then again right-click in the document window and choose **Make Clipping Mask** or press Ctrl+7 (⌘-7). Illustrator masks the laces inside the shoes, as in Figure 7-31.

12. ***Restore the fill and stroke of the shoes.*** As usual, Illustrator has seen fit to jettison the fill and stroke of the shoes. To reinstate them, press the I key to get the eyedropper tool. Then click anywhere inside the ball at the end of the chain, as in Figure 7-32. Illustrator reapplies the black 1-point stroke and white fill.

Figure 7-32.

13. ***Unlock and expand the Body layer.*** Scroll up to the **Body** layer in the Layers panel—as well as inside the document window for that matter—and both unlock and expand it. (You can lock the Feet layer, too, but we're so far away from the feet that there's no chance that they'll get in the way.) The Body layer contains a total of six objects, but we're concerned with only three of them: Cape, Grill, and Smock. The Grill item is once again a blend between two stroked arcs, this time with eight steps.

14. ***Mask the grill lines in the cape.*** Press the V key to switch back to the black arrow tool. In the document window, click the top or bottom grill line to select the blend, then Shift-click the cape outline to select it. (Or meatball the Cape and Grill items in the Layers panel.) Right-click and choose **Make Clipping Mask** or press Ctrl+7 (on the Mac, ⌘-7). Because the cape outline is in front, it masks the grill lines behind it. Press the I key to get the eyedropper, and click the top or bottom grill line to restore the cape's black stroke. The amazing thing here is that even an open path like the cape can serve as a mask, as witnessed in Figure 7-33.

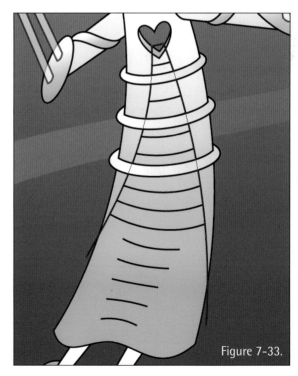

Figure 7-33.

Figure 7-34.

Take a look at the Layers panel, and you'll see that Illustrator has named the combined Cape and Grill items <Group>. Illustrator requires a group to contain a clipping mask, even going so far as prohibiting you from ungrouping them. (Go to the Object menu, and you'll see that Ungroup is dimmed.) Experienced users should note that Illustrator CS5 has made it more difficult to access the contents of a clipped group. Clicking a clipped path in a selected group yields no result. Instead, you have to target (meatball) the contents in the Layers panel, or deselect the group and then use the white arrow to select the contents in the document window.

15. *Rename the new clipping mask.* The group needs a more descriptive name. In the Layers panel, double-click the new **<Group>** item, name it "Reveal" (the idea being that the cape reveals the grill), and click **OK**.

Now to mask the new Reveal object inside the larger Smock. But before we start blindly masking, let's see what we're working with. In the Layers panel, meatball **Smock**. Note that it's a compound path, with a heart clipped out of the larger shape. No concerns there. Here's the issue: Press the G key to select the gradient tool. The gradient annotator shows a two-color linear gradient, with specific origin and terminus points that define an angle. If you were to choose Make Clipping Mask, you'd lose the fill, which means having not only to reassign the gradient but match the origin, terminus, and angle as well. Fortunately, Illustrator CS5 provides a method for creating a clipping mask while preserving the mask's original attributes.

16. *Cut the selection to the clipboard.* Meatball the **Reveal** object in the Layers panel and choose **Edit→Cut** or press Ctrl+X (⌘-X) to send the selection to the clipboard.

17. *Paste the cape and grill lines into the smock.* Press the V key to switch to the black arrow tool, and click the outline of the large gradient smock to select it. Then do the following:

   • Click the 🔲 icon at the bottom of the toolbox and choose **Draw Inside**. Or press Shift+D twice. Illustrator draws dotted lines around the corners of the selection.

   • Choose **Edit→Paste in Place** or press Ctrl+Shift+V (on the Mac, ⌘-Shift-V). The lines appear inside the smock, as in Figure 7-34.

- Click the  icon at the bottom of the toolbox and choose **Draw Normal** (or just press Shift+D).

Happily, Illustrator has maintained the gradient fill assigned to the smock path. (As it invariably should, in my opinion.) Plus, we now have one mask, the cape, nested inside another, the smock. Regardless of your approach, Illustrator permits you to nest as many masks as you like.

18. *Rename the clipping mask.* Again in the Layers panel, double-click the newest <**Group**> item, name it "Torso," and click **OK**. Go ahead and click its meatball as well to select the entire group.

19. *Reduce the Opacity of the torso.* In keeping with the robot's head and arms, his body ought to be translucent. (He is a ghost, after all.) So change the **Opacity** value in the control panel to 70 percent. Problem is, the torso now exposes a series of paths behind it (see Figure 7-35), including the heart-shaped breastplate and a couple of embarrassingly incomplete details. If you're familiar with the concept of a "dickey"—my favorite example being a partial turtleneck sewn into a flannel shirt—you know it's no class act. Tragically, our robot has dickey legs!

20. *Reduce the Opacity of the entire layer.* Press Ctrl+Z (or ⌘-Z) to undo that last mishap. In the **Layers** panel, meatball the entire **Body** layer and again reduce the **Opacity** value to 70 percent. As pictured in Figure 7-36, Illustrator fades all elements of the Body layer as one and maintains the relative levels of opacity between them, so no one will be the wiser to the dickey legs or other disquieting robot failures.

Figure 7-35.

Figure 7-36.

21. *Save your changes.* Choose **File**→**Save As** or press Ctrl+Shift+S (⌘-Shift-S). Name your final file "Final clipped robot.ai," and click the **Save** button. For the sake of comparison, I've included my final file (shown in Figure 7-37) as *Translucent robot.ai*, as ever inside the *Lesson 07* folder.

CS5's Draw Inside mode notwithstanding, blends and clipping masks have changed little since they were introduced back in 1988. And yet they continue to rank among Illustrator's most powerful capabilities. I for one can't imagine drawing without them.

Figure 7-37.

## Creating and Editing a Gradient Mesh

Having spent four exercises on blends and masks and reserving just one for gradient mesh, you might infer some preference on my part for the former. Yes and no. However ancient they may be, blends and masks offer a terrific bang for the buck. You can accomplish an outstanding amount of work in a few minutes. In contrast, Illustrator's gradient mesh function is more powerful—dare I say, more nuanced—but it demands a higher degree of attention in return. This is no in-and-out feature. Fleshing out a single gradient mesh may require a half hour of your time, oftentimes more. Suffice it to say, once you begin, you're in it for the long haul.

Good news: In exchange for your efforts, you can fill a path with a matrix of anchor points, every one of which links to four of its neighbors. And not only does each point represent a potentially unique color, but you can use control handles to define the direction and speed of the transitions. Bad news: Well, same thing. You reign supreme over a dazzling array of point-to-point gradients. If you delighted in my discussion of the pen tool in Lesson 3, you'll love gradient mesh. If not, you may find yourself overwhelmed by it.

Which is why I use the same illustration that I featured in Lesson 3—the Mishipizheu of Ojibwe lore—as a jumping-off point. Those of you who are psyched, get ready to have some fun. Those of you who are psyched out, have no fear. We'll work through it together.

1. *Open an image that contains a gradient.* Open the file called *Mish again.ai* in the *Lesson 07* folder. Notice that I've added a few paths since we last saw this illustration, not to mention a handful of gradients in and around the creature and an enclosing frame, as pictured in Figure 7-38.

Figure 7-38.

2. *Inspect the background gradient.* Exposed in the background, the original painting exhibits a series of green and red rivers running through fields of yellow and orange. In an attempt to mimic the flow (if not the arrangement) of these colors, I've created a base gradient. To check it out, do as follows:

- In the **Layers** panel, click in the first column to the left of the **Gradient** layer (second from bottom) to turn it on. Illustrator displays a rectangle filled with a linear gradient.

- Click the Gradient layer's ▶ to twirl it open. Meatball the path called **Color Rivers** to select it.

- Press the G key to select the gradient tool. Then hover your cursor over the gradient annotator to expose a series of seven color stops. Reading from bottom-left to top-right, these color stops are orange, yellow, green, red, green, orange, and finally red again, as shown in Figure 7-39.

Illustrator offers two ways to create a gradient mesh. The first is to select a shape and choose Object→Create Gradient Mesh. The program assigns a mesh to the shape, but it provides only

Figure 7-39.

the most rudimentary color controls (always fading to a lighter shade of the active color), which means a lot of manual labor for you. The second and more efficient method is to convert an existing gradient—like our seven-color linear gradient—to a mesh. This approach offers the advantage of giving you some starting colors, direction, and placement, as the next step explains.

3. *Convert the gradient to a mesh.* Choose **Object→Expand** or, if you loaded my dekeKeys shortcuts, press Ctrl+M for Mesh (that's ⌘-M on the Mac). Inside the **Expand** dialog box, change the **Expand Gradient To** setting to **Gradient Mesh** (see Figure 7-40), and click **OK**. Illustrator eliminates the annotator and slightly adjusts the position of the colors inside the gradient. Although it may not look like it, you now have a gradient mesh.

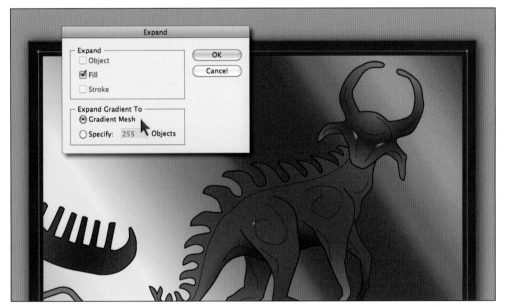

Figure 7-40.

4. *Ungroup and rename.* Illustrator places the new gradient mesh inside a grouped clipping path (perfectly reasonable) that it then nests inside another group (altogether unnecessary). To dispense with the latter, choose **Object→Ungroup** or press Ctrl+Shift+G (⌘-Shift-G). In the **Layers** panel, double-click the remaining object (now called **<Group>**) and name it "Color Rivers," as is was named before. Click **OK**.

5. *Select the mesh.* Twirl open the **Color Rivers** group to see a rectangular clipping path and an item called <Mesh>. Click the meatball to the right of <Mesh> to select it. Illustrator reveals a diagonal washboard of blue lines, one each for the seven key colors in the gradient. This is our base mesh.

PEARL OF WISDOM

When converting a linear gradient to a mesh, the result is a pattern of rows or columns, depending on the angle of the gradient. If you'd prefer to organize your mesh in a pattern of concentric circles, start with a radial gradient. For a mesh that matches the contouring of the shape that it fills, use Object→Create Gradient Mesh.

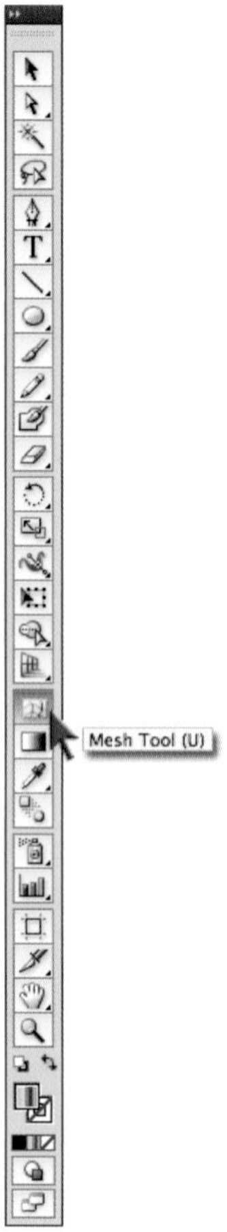

6. *Switch the Gradient layer to the outline mode.* We'll use the bottommost Paint layer as a template for our gradient. And to do that, we need to see that layer through the active one. Ctrl-click (or ⌘-click) on the 👁 icon in front of the **Gradient** layer to switch it to the outline mode while previewing the other layers.

7. *Select the mesh tool in the toolbox.* In Illustrator, a mesh is a matrix of rows and columns that meet at anchor points. So far, all we have is columns; we need to add rows. You add points, which introduce new colors and give rise to new rows and columns, using the mesh tool. Click the mesh tool, which is located immediately above the gradient tool in the toolbox, as highlighted in Figure 7-41. Or press the U key, which is a key Illustrator reserves for units and control.

8. *Click to make new rows and columns.* Given the free-flowing nature of the colors in the painting, it's difficult to know where to position the rows and columns in our linear mesh. Which is why I've provided the elaborate but illustrative Figure 7-42. Start by clicking along the column line that intersects the animal's haunches at each of the points indicated by the blue arrowheads. Then click

Figure 7-41.

Figure 7-42.

at the points along the new row line through the canoe indicated by the orange arrowheads. In all, you'll add six rows (lines such as ╱, going up and to the right) and four columns (like ╲).

---

If you add too many rows or columns, or position one at the wrong location, delete it by Alt-clicking (or Option-clicking) with the mesh tool. But be careful: Alt-clicking an anchor point deletes both its row and its column. If you want to delete a row or column independently of the other, click a line between the anchor points.

---

9. *Switch back to the preview mode.* To witness the effects of the new points on your gradient, press Ctrl+Y (or ⌘-Y), which switches back to the preview mode. If you followed my directions, each of your new points of color will be either transitional (that is, a blend of the colors that already existed) or green. Why green? Because that was the color of the column that you clicked first.

10. *Switch to the lasso tool.* Making a gradient mesh and adding rows and columns is child's play. But as you may recall from having been a child, child's play is the most intricate play there is. Ours has resulted in a grid full of anchor points, each of which conveys color and position information. It is in adjusting these points that the real fun begins.

Recoloring points—as we're about to do—is a matter of selecting those points and setting a color. You can select a point with the mesh tool, but because it also lets you create points, it tends to be a clumsy tool for this purpose. (For a couple of editing tricks that work only when using the mesh tool, see the sidebar, "More Gradient Mesh Tips and Tricks" on page 235.)

Figure 7-43.

My preference: When recoloring a single point, switch to the white arrow. When recoloring multiple points, use the lasso tool, which lets you grab lots of points in a single drag. We'll be coloring entire rows and columns at a time, so select the lasso by clicking the fourth icon in the toolbox (highlighted by way of a reminder in Figure 7-43) or by pressing the Q key.

11. *Select a row of points.* Our goal is to modify the base colors in the gradient so they look like those pictured in Figure 7-44. Note that the gradient sports rows of color on the left and columns of color on the right.

Figure 7-44.

Start by selecting a sample row. Armed with the lasso tool, drag around the five points on the left side of the third row down (the highest of the two running through the canoe), as illustrated in Figure 7-45. Note that these five points include two that are nearly coincident (one on top of the other) on the far left side.

---

Drawing a marquee with the lasso can be tricky if you're unused to it. Should you accidentally deselect the mesh, try this: Press Ctrl+A (⌘-A) to select the entire masked gradient. (The other layers are locked so that's all you'll get.) Then click the second icon on the left side of the control panel, ⊙, just before Opacity. This action takes you back to the mesh, which you can again attempt to select with the lasso tool.

---

12. *Color the selected points green.* Check to make sure the fill icon is active at the bottom of the toolbox, so that the question mark is in front, as in ⬚. (If it isn't, press the X key.) Choose **Window→Swatches** to bring up the **Swatches** panel. Then click the green swatch, which is named, as you might expect, Green. Illustrator adds a row of green cutting away from the green column, as in Figure 7-46.

Figure 7-45.

Figure 7-46.

One of the drawbacks of using the lasso tool to marquee bunches of points at a time is that you end up selecting the rectangular clipping mask as well. Fortunately, that won't affect your results. Changing the clipping mask to green, for example, does not change the color of the gradient because Illustrator gives the gradient mesh priority. If you grow tired of selecting and recoloring the mask, I recommend that you lock it down by clicking the second column to the left of <Clipping path> in the Layers panel.

13. *Select and color the other rows.* In all, you'll need to color six more rows with five points each. Figure 7-47 shows how to color the rows, in each case using the named color found in the Swatches panel. If that's sufficient, excellent. If not, here's an explanation:

    - Lasso the five points on the left side of the row directly above the one you just colored green. Then click the swatch called **Bright Orange** (just left of Green) in the **Swatches** panel.

    - Lasso the corresponding points in the topmost row (along the top of the mesh), and change them to the swatch named **Deep Red**.

    - Lasso those same five points in the row below the green one, and select the swatch called **Pale Yellow**.

    - Color the five points in the next three rows **Bright Orange**, **Deep Red**, and **Pale Yellow**, respectively, as directed by Figure 7-47.

    That leaves one row—the five points along the bottom-left edge of the mesh—unchanged. If you're feeling fastidious, color them **Pale Yellow**. Otherwise, don't worry about them.

14. *Select and color a couple of columns.* Happily, just two columns require your attention. But because of their close proximity to each other, selecting them is a bit challenging.

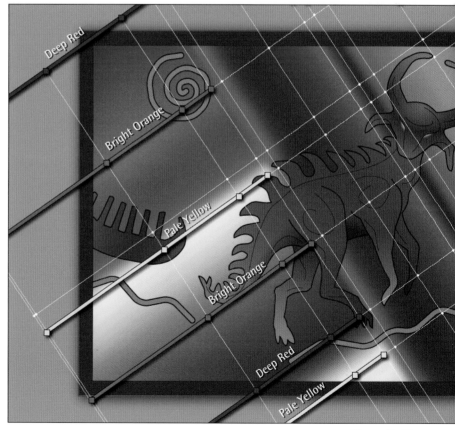

Figure 7-47.

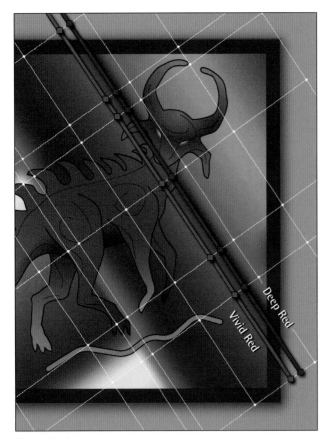

Figure 7-48.

Figure 7-49.

Lasso all eight points in the column that runs through the Mishipizheu's neck—the one labeled Vivid Red in Figure 7-48—and assign the swatch just to the right of Green in the Swatches panel, **Vivid Red**. Then lasso all eight points in the column immediately to the right and change it to **Deep Red** (again, as directed in the figure).

---

If you have trouble maintaining a narrow lasso along the entire length of a column, try multiple passes. Lasso a few points at the top of the column and then Shift-drag around a few points farther down, and so on. You can also Shift-click with the white arrow tool if you find that to be easier.

---

15. *Hide the selection edges.* Press Ctrl+H (or ⌘-H) to hide the rows and column lines and view the new colors. If the colors compare well to those in Figure 7-49, you're ready to move on. If not, you can revisit Steps 11 through 14 to see what went wrong. For the sake of comparison, I'm also including my work as a sample file titled *Mesh colors.ai* found in the *Lesson 07* folder.

Much as I like what we've come up with so far, it's awfully geometric. Which is why your next task, should you choose to accept it, is to turn these various rows and columns into something more closely resembling free-flowing rivers of color. Illustrator offers all kinds of ways to edit a mesh with absolute and sometimes mind-numbing control, the myriad delights of which I document in the facing sidebar. But we're going to get more work done faster by employing a couple of path-editing tools that most illustrators don't even know exist, let alone use: warp and pinch. And did I mention that these tools, and the results they produce, are a lot of fun.

---

16. *Bring back the edges, switch to the outline mode.* To distort the mesh outlines with any degree of accuracy, we need to see the outlines as well as the painting template below. So press Ctrl+H (or ⌘-H) to bring back the selection edges and reveal the mesh lines. Then, in the **Layers** panel, Ctrl-click (or ⌘-click) the **Gradient** layer's 👁 icon to hide the colors inside the mesh and expose the Paint layer and its image file in the background.

In Lesson 3, "Using the Pen Tool," I explained how anchor points, control handles, and intervening segments work together to create a path outline. That kind of path is a one-dimensional object, traveling in a continuous direction, one segment at a time, the trajectory of which is defined by as many as one outgoing and one incoming control handle. The path is like a track that conducts a train in a single direction.

In contrast, a mesh—whether gradient or otherwise—is a network of path outlines projected into two dimensions. For every path outline that might be regarded as a row, another might be called a column. (Or, in the case of a radial mesh, spokes and wheels.) As a result, each anchor point has not two neighbors—one before and another after—but rather four—north, east, south, and west. And where the gradient mesh is concerned, each point conveys a color. This is no longer a track that conducts a train; it's a firework that projects and mingles its light in all directions.

Just about every technique you can use to edit a path outline—from nudging points to dragging control handles—works when editing a mesh as well. But given the more complex nature of a colored, two-dimensional object, you also have a variety of other tricks at your disposal, as follows:

- To select multiple points at a time, draw a marquee around the points with the white arrow or lasso tool. You can then assign a new color (as you saw in the exercise), drag the points to a new location, or nudge the points by pressing the ↑, ↓, ←, or → keys.

- If you turn off the Object Selection by Path Only check box in the second panel of the Preferences dialog box, you can click a "patch"—a colored area between points and segments in a mesh—to select all four points that surround that patch. (Note: If you try this technique, be sure to turn Object Selection by Path Only back on to successfully complete future exercises.)

- Curiously, the mesh tool always works on a single point at a time, even if multiple points were previously selected. But the tool offers a special trick: Press Shift while dragging a point to align it to the existing row or column.

- Using the white arrow or mesh tool, drag a control handle to change the curvature and direction of a segment.

- The control handle also controls the speed of a color transition. Long handles result in slow transitions; short handles make for speedy ones.

- Here's another mesh tool–only trick: Press the Shift key, and drag a control handle to move all four handles that surround an anchor point as a single "jack." For example, Shift-dragging ✗ spins the jack like ✕.

- To break the alignment between two opposing control handles, drag a handle with the convert-point tool (Λ). Drag from the anchor point to redraw all four handles in perpendicular alignment with each other, as in ✗. To break the alignment between one pair of control handles and the other, drag a handle with the white arrow tool.

- Click anywhere along a segment with the add-point tool (⬩⁺) to add an intermediate anchor point. Use such a point to adjust the direction or curvature of the segment; it cannot convey color. To delete an intermediate point (such as one automatically added when painting with the liquify tools), click it with the delete-point tool (⬩⁻).

- To assign a color to one or more selected points, switch focus to the fill (as in ▣) and then select a color from the Color or Swatches panel. You can also drag and drop a swatch onto a deselected point.

- To recolor selected points with a color found elsewhere in the mesh, a different path, or an imported image, click that color with the eyedropper tool. To lift a color from a standard gradient or a stroke, Shift-click with the eyedropper instead.

- You can use the eyedropper also as a color-application tool. Start by pressing Ctrl+Shift+A (or ⌘-Shift-A) to deselect all objects in the illustration. Select the desired color from the Color or Swatches panel. Then Alt-click (Option-click) a point to assign it the active color. You can likewise Alt-click on a segment or inside a patch to recolor multiple points at a time.

- Press Ctrl+H (⌘-H) to hide mesh lines and points, while still being able to modify and color them.

Illustrator's gradient mesh takes time and experience to master. But it's hard to imagine a more powerful or rewarding feature.

Figure 7-50.

17. *Select the warp tool in the toolbox.* Click and hold on the width tool icon, and then select the warp tool from the flyout menu, as demonstrated in Figure 7-50. Or press the keyboard shortcut, Shift+R. The warp tool is the first of Illustrator's seven *liquify tools* (the width tool is not one of them), which allow you to paint distortions into selected paths. While I only rarely use them to adjust path outlines, the liquify tools can be exceedingly useful for modifying a gradient mesh.

18. *Adjust the warp tool settings.* By default, the warp brush is 100 pixels in diameter, too small for our purposes. To enlarge the brush, double-click the warp tool icon in the toolbox. Inside the **Warp Tool Options** dialog box, change both the **Width** and **Height** values to 250 pixels. Then click **OK**.

---

Another way to change the brush size is to press the Alt key (Option on the Mac) and drag in the document window. Drag up or right to enlarge the brush, and down or left to reduce it. I say *or* because you can scale the width and height of the brush independently. To maintain a circular brush, press and hold Shift as you drag.

---

19. *Brush inside the mesh.* If nothing is selected, the warp tool acts on all unlocked objects; otherwise, the warp tool affects just the selection. So check the **Layers** panel to make sure the **<Mesh>** item is selected (with the ◎ meatball). This prevents you from messing up the clipping path, even if it isn't locked.

Then brush inside the gradient mesh to bend and distort it. Your goal is to more or less mold the mesh so it matches the contours of the background painting. Some advice:

- Don't get too hung up on exactly matching the painting. An approximate match with vivid rivers of color will suffice.

- It's going to take several short brushstrokes. I painted perhaps a dozen times to get the results pictured in Figure 7-51 on the facing page. (Note that the figure shows the mesh in the preview mode so you can see the adjusted colors.)

- Brush the central portion of the mesh—around the head, body, and tail of the animal—inward; brush the outer portion of the mesh outward. Look for opportunities to match the general flow and sway of the painting.

- Brush as much as you want. Don't worry about creating crimps and buckles in the mesh. In contrast with path outlines, such crimps and buckles may produce kinetic, gestural, or just plain good-looking results.

Feel free to switch the Gradient layer between the preview and outline modes. You can switch to the preview mode as easily as pressing Ctrl+Y (or ⌘-Y); to switch just the Gradient layer to the outline mode, you'll have to Ctrl-click (⌘-click) its ◉ icon.

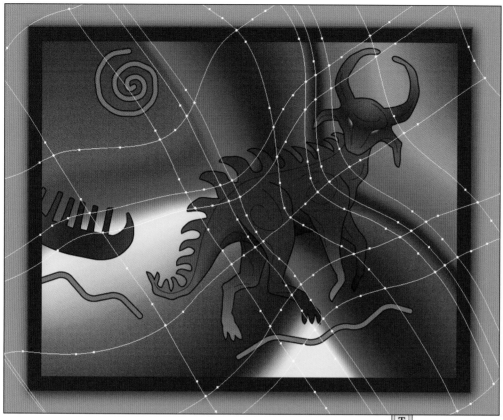

Figure 7-51.

20. *Select the pucker tool from the toolbox.* Click and hold the warp tool and select the pucker tool from the flyout menu, as in Figure 7-52. This tool lets you pinch the mesh. That is to say, it bends the mesh inward, as if in a concave mirror, such as the inside of a spoon.

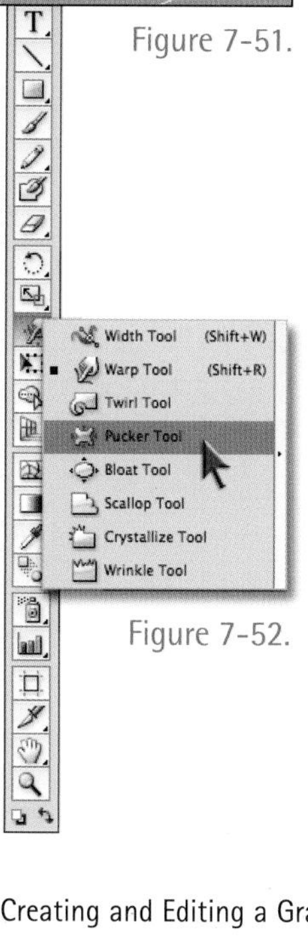

21. *Adjust the pucker tool settings.* If you start right in dragging with the pucker tool, you'll rapidly pinch your flowing mesh into a series of sharply transitioning tornadoes of color. What we need is a larger brush with a more delicate touch. So double-click the pucker tool icon in the toolbox to display the **Pucker Tool Options** dialog box. Increase the **Width** and **Height** values to 400 pixels. Then reduce the **Intensity** value to 5 percent, which causes the tool to behave more subtly. Click the **OK** button to invoke your changes.

Figure 7-52.

22. ***Click and hold in a few spots to pinch the mesh.*** In my experience, painting with the pucker tool rarely yields desirable results. Better to click and hold (for perhaps a second) at a few strategic locations, in our case to tuck the gradient so that the rivers of color appear to emanate from the creature. I clicked in the Mishipizheu's body to tuck the rivers toward the center of the illustration. Then I clicked again at its tail, above the hip and spikes, again in the body, and around the neck to pinch the mesh lines as pictured in Figure 7-53 (again in the preview mode).

Figure 7-53.

23. ***Get the mesh tool, add more columns.*** By now, your results are sure to vary from mine. But if you compare your warped and puckered mesh to the original painting, my guess is you'll see differences, just as I do in mine. For example, the painting features a Y of green to the left of the spiral that's missing from the mesh. The best way to simulate that Y is to add a new column. So press the U key to switch back to the mesh tool. Then click a row line near the right tip of the canoe. I also recommend that you add a column by clicking a row somewhere in the animal's neck. The new columns appear white in Figure 7-54 (facing page), with click points indicated by blue arrowheads.

24. *Assign some new colors.* Fortunately for those of you who had difficulty lassoing the rows and columns in Steps 13 and 14, you don't have to recolor all the new points, just a few of them. Figure 7-55 shows the points in question and the colors from the **Swatches** panel that I suggest you apply. (Note that you have to color only those anchor points that appear at the intersection of rows and columns. The points between intersections—added automatically by the warp and pucker points—convey position and direction in the mesh, not color.) For my money, the easiest way to select the points is to click and Shift-click with the white arrow tool. But you can use the lasso tool if you prefer.

Figure 7-54.

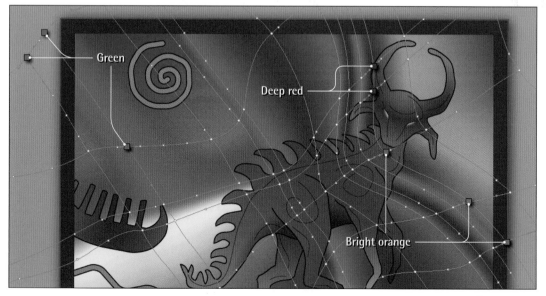

Green

Deep red

Bright orange

Figure 7-55.

25. ***Further warp the gradient mesh as desired.*** If your color rivers don't yet match those in the painting—as mine, alas, do not—you can apply additional modifications with the warp tool:

- Press Shift+R to select the tool.

- Double-click the tool icon in the toolbox, restore the **Intensity** value to 50 percent, and click **OK**.

- In the **Layers** panel, click the meatball (◎) for <**Mesh**>.

Now drag inside the mesh to stretch and bend the lines. I tugged upward on the green and red rows on the left side of the gradient. I also added some sway to the column of green below the Mishipizheu and further tucked the right columns of color in toward the creature's shoulders. Pictured in Figure 7-56, the result is something no other tool in Illustrator can reproduce: a fountain of colors flowing horizontally, vertically, and in every angle in between. This is gradient mesh.

Figure 7-56.

# WHAT DID YOU LEARN?

Match the key concept in the numbered list below with the letter of the phrase that best describes it. Answers appear upside-down at the bottom of the page.

## Key Concepts

1. Stops
2. Gradient annotator
3. Midpoint skew
4. Blending
5. Steps
6. Clipping mask
7. Draw Inside
8. Banding
9. Path-of-the-blend
10. Gradient mesh
11. Expand
12. The liquify tools

## Descriptions

A. This command allows you to convert a standard linear or radial gradient into a more exotic gradient mesh, among other things.

B. The intermediate subpaths that Illustrator draws and updates automatically between two extreme paths in a blend.

C. Obvious steps of color that conflict with the otherwise fluid transitions in a gradient, blend, or mesh.

D. The bar that shows the length and direction of a gradient (as well as the colors and stops when you hover over it) in a selected path when the gradient tool is active.

E. Combined with the Paste in Place command, this new feature lets you place a blend or collection of paths inside a clipping mask.

F. This most complex and powerful of Illustrator's gradient features lets you create and adjust anchor points of color in two-dimensional space, as well as blend between neighboring colors in all directions.

G. Illustrator's oldest gradient option lets you design custom gradations and morphs, in which one path steadily transitions into another.

H. While I use these only rarely to adjust path outlines, the likes of warp and pucker can be exceedingly useful for painting free-form distortions into a gradient mesh.

I. A shape that crops the boundaries of the paths below it, as well as updates dynamically whether you edit the shape or the paths.

J. The locations of the key colors in a gradient.

K. The outline that determines the course and direction of the subpaths inside a blend and is most easily modified when the rest of the blend is locked.

L. Drag this square on the gradient annotator to change the speed at which one color stop transitions into the next.

## Answers

# WORKING WITH TRANSPARENCY

**TRANSPARENCY IS** all about creating interactions between objects. Or put more simply, *blending*. Select a path, group, or even an entire layer and then blend it with the ones behind it. The most basic example of blending is the Opacity value in the Transparency panel. This option lets you mix a selected object with the stuff in the background according to a percentage—from 100, opaque, to 0, transparent. Because I'm a shameless epicure, I draw the analogy of mixing a yummy beverage. Suppose you have a glass of chocolate syrup and a glass of milk behind it. If you select the syrup and set it to an Opacity value of 30 percent, 70 percent of the milk shows through. Alternatively, you could move the milk in front of the syrup and set the former to an Opacity of 70 percent. Either way, you get a glass of chocolate milk. For a more delicious mix, reduce the milk's Opacity to 50 percent.

Not everyone fancies syrupy lactose. And Opacity is just the first of Illustrator's many transparency options. Which is why I offer the cheerful holiday graphic that is Figure 8-1. Here we see examples of differing Opacity values (labeled Normal 100% and Normal 35%) and a few of the most useful *blend modes*. Like the Opacity value, blend modes apply computations. Add *x* of the active layer to *y* of the stuff behind it. But blend modes employ more elaborate arithmetic likely to frighten humanities majors, which is why they have math-free names like Normal (meaning no blend mode at all), Multiply (smooth darkening), Screen (similarly smooth lightening), and Overlay (a bit of both), all documented in the figure.

Figure 8-1.

# ABOUT THIS LESSON

## Project Files

Before beginning the exercises, make sure you've downloaded the lesson files from *www.oreilly.com/go/Deke-IllustratorCS5*, as directed in Step 2 on page xiv of the Preface. This should result in a folder called *Lesson Files-AIcs5 1on1* on your desktop. We'll be working with the files inside the *Lesson 08* subfolder.

Illustrator's Transparency panel lets you create interactions between paths, groups, or whole layers of objects. This panel introduces the topics of opacity, knockout groups, blend modes, and the multifaceted opacity mask. As you follow along with these exercises, you'll learn how to:

## Video Lesson 8: Blend Modes

Blend modes and opacity setting are the mainstays of creating transparency inside your Illustrator artwork. In this video, I'll cover how opacity settings affect the elements in your image. I'll also show you how to use the variety of Illustrator's blend modes, which allow you to determine how layers interact with complex mixing formulas.

To watch blend modes at work, visit *www.oreilly.com/go/deke-IllustratorCS5*. Click the **Watch** button to view the lesson online or the **Download** button to save it to your computer. During the video, you'll learn these shortcuts:

| Operation | Windows shortcut | Macintosh shortcut |
|---|---|---|
| Hide the selection edges | Ctrl+H | ⌘-H |
| Hide all layers but one | Alt-click on 👁 icon | Option-click on 👁 icon |
| Switch between the stroke and fill | Press the X key | Press the X key |
| Display the Gradient panel | Ctrl+F9 | ⌘-F9 |
| Duplicate an entire layer | Drag layer onto 🗔 icon | Drag layer onto 🗔 icon |
| Select the reflect tool | Press the O key | Press the O key |
| Display opacity mask on its own | Alt-click mask's thumbnail | Option-click mask's thumbnail |
| Select the gradient tool | Press the G key | Press the G key |
| Duplicate a gradient color stop | Alt-drag the color stop | Option-drag the color stop |
| Add a fill to a selected object | Ctrl+⃞ (forward slash) | ⌘-⃞ (forward slash) |

But as is so often the case with Illustrator, Opacity and blend modes are just the beginning. There are knockout groups, opacity masks, new uses for gradients and blends, super-rich blacks, and the wonders of rasterization.

If that all sounds a tad overwhelming, don't fret: Believe it or not, you've already worked your way through the toughest Illustrator offerings. This is where the fun begins.

## Yeah, But Will It Print?

When first released, Illustrator was designed to facilitate the power of Adobe's PostScript printing language (and satisfy the design needs of principal John Warnock's wife, if legend is to be believed). The pen tool, for example, exploits the three-point model—anchor point plus two control handles—popularized by PostScript. Type outlines, clipping masks, compound paths, and many of Illustrator's other core objects owe their origins to PostScript.

For years, Illustrator remained in lockstep with PostScript, rendering each and every graphic as a collection of routines that a PostScript imagesetter could render in a matter of seconds. In fact, Illustrator was well known as the program that could do precisely what PostScript could do. If it seemed underpowered compared with its flashier competitors, there was a reason: Illustrator's feature set was aligned with Post-Script; the others' were not.

So it's perhaps only fitting that Illustrator—the program that Adobe once trumpeted for its straight-and-narrow simplicity—is now called into question for veering from the PostScript orthodoxy.

Why do I mention this? Because PostScript has no provision for a translucent object. When you blend a path with the paths behind it, Illustrator has to either rasterize that section of the artwork—that is, convert it to pixels—or break it into subpaths with opaque fills. Illustrator doesn't modify your AI file; the "flattening," as it's called, occurs on-the-fly during the print process. But even so, there's an outside chance that your translucent objects might print opaque or just plain wrong, as in Figure 8-2.

Figure 8-2.

I say "outside chance" because, these days, it's unlikely. Transparency first appeared in Illustrator 9, which was six versions and more than a decade ago. This coincided with the introduction of transparency to version 1.4 of Adobe's Portable Document Format (PDF), which has largely supplanted the limited confines of Post-Script. By default, every AI file includes a PDF description. Which means that, if your translucent objects fail to print properly to a PostScript printer (again, unlikely), you can rasterize the AI file in a PDF-savvy program such as Photoshop, and the work of your printer will be done.

I bring this up because I want you to look upon transparency in Illustrator as your extremely powerful friend. You can use it—you *should* use it—without fear of it interfering with the viability of your artwork. And if printing somehow presents a problem, you can always export your artwork for use in Photoshop, which (based on my experience with thousands of files) *always* produces accurate results, as I'll document in Lesson 12, "Printing and Exporting." In any event, rest assured: Illustrator's brand of transparency is practical, it's adaptable, and it works.

## Opacity and Knockout Group

This lesson features one elaborate project file, in which we'll build on a base image (Figure 8-3 on the facing page) to create a multi-layered photo illustration (Figure 8-4). I've drawn all the paths for you; your job is to apply the transparency effects.

In this first exercise, I'll show you how to change the Opacity value for a single attribute assigned to a path outline. Then you'll set a group of paths so that translucent attributes cancel each other out, resulting in a uniform and highly desirable effect.

1. *Open a piece of layered artwork.* Open the file called *Base image with gloves.ai* in the *Lesson 08* folder inside *Lesson Files-AIcs5 1on1*. Pictured in Figure 8-3, this seven-layer illustration features a low-quality, two-megapixel photograph that I shot years ago of my youngest son, Sam, as a bald, eyebrowless toddler banging on a tragically tuneless piano. Thus far, the illustration sports two vector-based gloves with inset eyes. (Clearly, I was inspired. By what, not so clear.) Many more paths, groups, layers, and sublayers lay in wait.

2. *Inspect the Layers panel.* In the **Layers** panel, you'll see seven layers, four turned on (with 👁s visible) and three off. The **Vectors** layer should appear twirled open; if it isn't, click its ▶ to

Figure 8-3.

Figure 8-4.

make it so. Inside the Vectors layer, you'll find a total of eight objects, two paths and six sublayers. (The paths appear as white, the sublayers—like the layer that contains them—are gray.)

3. *Turn on the Backdrop layer.* Scroll down to the bottom of the Layers panel and click in the first column in front of the **Backdrop** layer to turn it on. As pictured in Figure 8-5, this layer adds a collection of floor and curtain paths that cover up all but Sam's head. (We also see the gloves, but that's because they're on a higher layer.) The head is not a transparency effect, not in the context of this lesson at any rate. Rather, I used a head-shaped path to carve a hole in the beige curtain and floor with the help of the Pathfinder panel, as we explored in Lesson 6, "Pathfinder Operations."

4. *Turn on and expand the Jacket sublayer.* Scroll up to the expanded Vectors layer and turn on the sublayer called **Jacket**, which features various elements of a Liberace-like orange jacket with flouncy cravat and

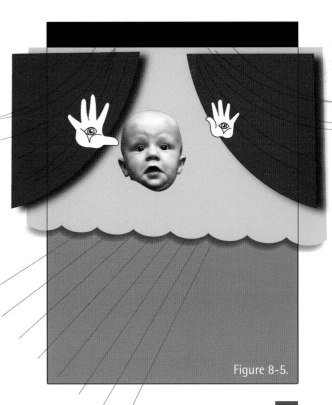

Figure 8-5.

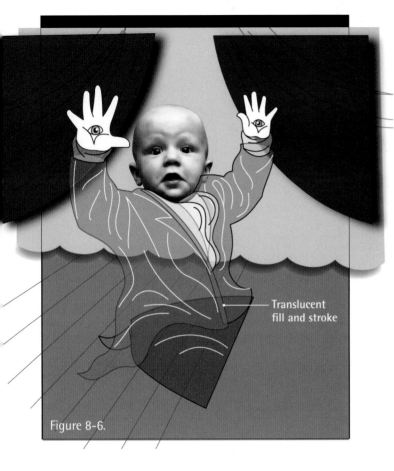

Translucent
fill and stroke

Figure 8-6.

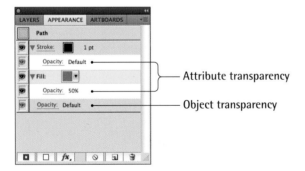

Attribute transparency

Object transparency

Figure 8-7.

sleeves. Click the sublayer's ▶ to twirl it open. Inside Jacket, you'll find a group called **Suit**. Please twirl it open as well.

5. *Make the one opaque object translucent.* Inside the Suit group, meatball the path that I've named **Left Half** (so a ◎ appears to the right of it), which represents the left side of Sam's orange jacket. Then locate the **Opacity** option near the middle of the control panel and change it to 50 percent. The meatball changes to a shaded sphere (◉), indicating that a non-PostScript effect has been applied.

6. *Undo the last step.* Changing the Opacity value fades the left side of the jacket to match the right side, tail, and other elements. But if you press Ctrl+H (or ⌘-H) to hide the selection edges, you'll notice a difference between this path and the others: The stroke for the selected path is translucent; the strokes of the other paths are altogether opaque. Figure 8-6 shows what I mean.

   Obviously, another approach is in order. Press Ctrl+Z (or ⌘-Z) to undo the last step. The Left Half item's meatball changes back to ◎ to show that the non-PostScript effect is gone.

7. *Target Fill in the Appearance panel.* With the Left Half path still selected, press Shift+F6 or choose **Window**→**Appearance** to bring up the **Appearance** panel. Then, click the orange **Fill** item to make the fill attribute active independently of the stroke.

8. *Make the fill translucent.* Again set the control panel's **Opacity** value to 50 percent. In the Appearance panel, click the ▶s in front of **Stroke** and **Fill** to reveal two inset Opacity entries, labeled in Figure 8-7. The one below Stroke reads Opacity: Default; the one below Fill reads Opacity: 50%. Following that is another entry, this time not inset, that says Opacity: Default. The meaning: The overall path is opaque, the stroke is opaque, and the fill is translucent, thus matching the rest of the jacket.

I like the way that you can see through Sam's jacket to the curtain and floor elements on the Backdrop layer. It gives him a phantom quality, as if his Wizard-of-Oz head rises out of a ghostly body. But I hate how the various elements of the jacket, sleeves, and cravat interact with each other, as illustrated in Figure 8-8. You can see the partially drawn tail, for crying out loud. What we want is for each path to clip a hole out of—or "knock out"—the one behind it. Fortunately, the jacket, sleeves, and cravat paths are grouped together. Illustrator lets you clip all paths in a group, regardless of their translucency, by creating a *knockout group.*

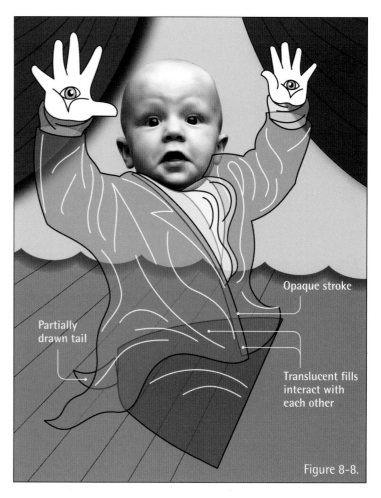

Opaque stroke

Partially drawn tail

Translucent fills interact with each other

Figure 8-8.

9. *Target the Suit group.* Click the meatball to the right of the **Suit** group, two items up from the Left Half path in the **Layers** panel. (Note that the meatball appears as ◎ instead of ◉ because, while it contains translucent paths, the group itself is opaque.) You can tell Suit is a group because the word *Group* appears on the left side of the control panel.

10. *Expand the Transparency panel.* Locate the **Transparency** panel. If you can't find it, choose **Window→Transparency** or press Ctrl+Shift+F10 (on the Mac, ⌘-Shift-F10). Fully unfurled, the Transparency panel appears as shown in Figure 8-9. If you don't see all the options, double-click the **Transparency** tab at the top of the panel until you do.

11. *Turn the selection into a knockout group.* Hover over the **Knockout Group** option to see the tip: "Prevents the elements of a group from showing through each other," pictured in the figure. This sounds perfect, and in fact it is. One small problem: Illustrator requires you to click the check box not once but *twice* to make it active:

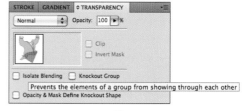

Figure 8-9.

- Click the **Knockout Group** option a first time. For reasons that make no sense to anyone outside Adobe (and few inside the company), this produces no effect except to add a minus sign to the check box, as in ⊟. Your copy of Illustrator is not broken; this is standard behavior.

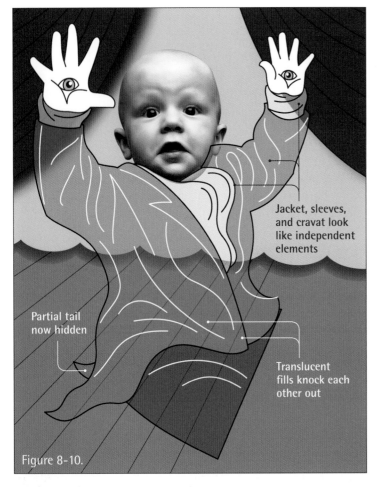

Jacket, sleeves, and cravat look like independent elements

Partial tail now hidden

Translucent fills knock each other out

Figure 8-10.

Figure 8-11.

- Click **Knockout Group** a second time to give it a proper check mark, as in ☑. The jacket, sleeves, and cravat knock each other out, as copiously documented in Figure 8-10.

12. *Save your changes.* Believe it or not, you have completed the first phase of this kooky project. If you hid the selection edges in Step 6, press Ctrl+H (⌘-H) to bring them back. Then choose **File→Save As** or press Ctrl+Shift+S (⌘-Shift-S). Name your revised file "My knockout jacket.ai" and click the **Save** button. Prepare to use this file as the starting point for the next exercise.

With any luck, you now feel familiar with the Opacity option, see the benefits of applying different Opacity settings to the Fill and Stroke attributes, and have a sense for why you might need and how you invoke a knockout group. Even if clicking a check box twice to turn it on doesn't make a lick of sense.

But the jacket paths still encroach on toddler Sam's jowls. (As I mentioned, that snapshot is ages old. Nowadays, Sam's faux musical expressions more closely resemble the one in Figure 8-11. Years from now, Sam will seek revenge for my abusing his likeness in this lesson.) And we have so many more effects to apply. Which means we have much mind-bending, hard-rocking transparency work ahead of us.

# Working with Opacity Masks

If you've ever used Photoshop, you may know that you can erase temporary holes into a layer using a layer mask. Illustrator offers something similar, but because it's not restricted to a layer, it goes by a different name: *opacity mask*. In many ways, an opacity mask is like a path in a compound shape set to Subtract or Intersect, carving a hole or containing other paths. The differences between those modes and an opacity mask are that the latter works with paths that include all varieties of fills and strokes (whereas all paths in a compound shape must subscribe to a single set of attributes); it can convey fades and levels of translucency; and you can apply it to a layer, group, text block, blend, gradient mesh—in short, to anything.

In return for such flexibility, the opacity mask demands that you come to terms with its unusual ways. Which is why I've organized this exercise differently from the others. I'll start things off with a few steps that—while they don't get us any nearer to our ultimate goal—demonstrate how the opacity mask works. Then you'll use this knowledge to clip away the jacket elements along Sam's head, clip away Sam's excess pant legs, and create a fading piano. As a bonus, I'll show you a great use for blending between groups.

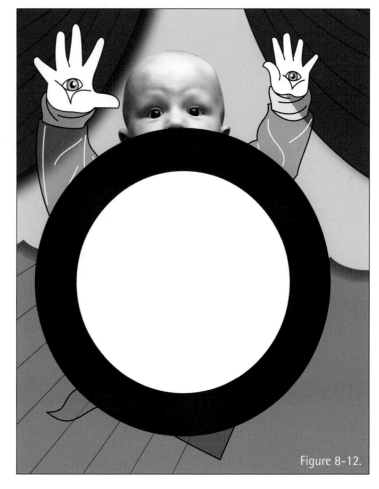

1. *Open your last-saved file.* Continue working with the file that you saved at the end of the preceding exercise. Or open my version of the illustration in progress, *The knockout group.ai*, found in the *Lesson 08* folder.

2. *Turn on the Circle path.* First, a quick tutorial on how opacity paths work. If necessary, in the **Layers** panel, twirl closed the **Jacket** sublayer. Then click in the first column in front of the **Circle** path (just above Jacket) to turn it on. You'll see a white circle with a 40-point black stroke, as in Figure 8-12. What it lacks in beauty, in makes up for in educational value.

3. *Select the Circle and Jacket items.* Again in the Layers panel, click the meatball for the **Jacket** sublayer to select it. And then Shift-click the meatball for the **Circle** path.

Figure 8-12.

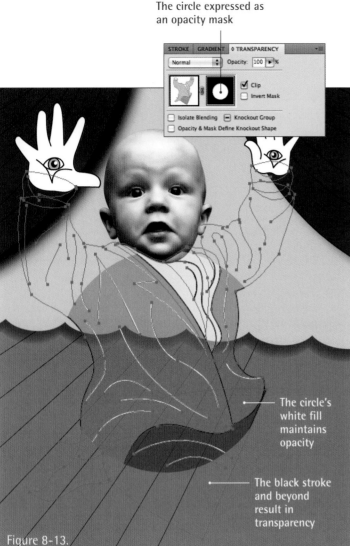

The circle expressed as an opacity mask

The circle's white fill maintains opacity

The black stroke and beyond result in transparency

Figure 8-13.

4. **Combine the selected objects into an opacity mask.** Return to the **Transparency** panel and click the ▾≡ in the panel's top-right corner. Then choose the command **Make Opacity Mask.** Illustrator applies the top path in the selection, Circle, as an opacity mask to the selected object below. These are the repercussions:

- The Circle path disappears from the Layers panel.

- Illustrator gives the Jacket sublayer a <u>dashed underline</u>, showing that it harbors an opacity mask. (Remember this: When reviewing archived art or files from other designers, a dashed underline in the Layers panel means "opacity mask in effect.")

- In the Transparency panel, the white circle appears to the right of the sublayer thumbnail, as shown at the top of Figure 8-13.

- Look closely, and you'll see that the Knockout Group check box in the Transparency panel appears as ⊟. This time, it's accurate: Some items in the selection are knockout groups; others aren't. Leave it as is.

- In the document window, everything outside the white fill of the circle goes transparent, also shown in Figure 8-13.

An opacity mask defines transparency using brightness. White is opaque, black is transparent, and gray is an intermediate level of translucency. Which is why the circle's fill leaves Sam's clothing opaque and anything black—including the stroke and the empty area outside the path—makes the clothing transparent.

5. **Experiment with the check boxes.** When working with an opacity mask, the Transparency panel makes available two mysterious check boxes, Clip and Invert Mask. Perform the following and you'll understand how they work:

- So you can see what you're doing, press Ctrl+H (or ⌘-H) to hide the selection edges.

- Turn off the **Clip** check box. This fills the undefined area of the opacity mask with white, making the area outside the circle opaque, as in Figure 8-14. (In this and the other figures on the right, a black label means the check box is off, and a green label means the option is on.) The result is that only the 40-point black stroke is transparent.

- Turn on the **Invert Mask** check box. The meaning of black and white in the opacity mask path are reversed, so that the circle's fill is transparent and the stroke is opaque. The area outside the circle remains opaque because Clip is turned off, as in Figure 8-15.

- Take a look at Figure 8-16. You've already seen what happens when you turn Clip on and Invert Mask off, but for the sake of comparison, I repeat the effects here. Under these default conditions, the stroke and undefined area are black, so only the circle's white fill is visible.

- Now turn on both the **Clip** and **Invert Mask** check boxes. Clip makes the undefined area black; Invert Mask reverses the meaning of black and white in the path. So only the stroke is opaque, as in Figure 8-17.

**Clip off, Invert Mask off**

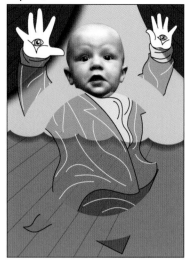

Figure 8-14.

**Clip on, Invert Mask off**

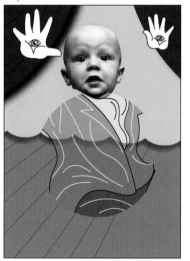

Figure 8-16.

**Clip off, Invert Mask on**

Figure 8-15.

**Clip on, Invert Mask on**

Figure 8-17.

6. *Release and delete the opacity mask.* Having demonstrated the behavior of Clip and Invert Mask, the circle has served its purpose and serves no further use in this project:

- Press Ctrl+H (⌘-H) to bring back the selection edges.

- Click the ▾≡ icon in the top-right corner of the Transparency panel and choose **Release Opacity Mask**.

- The Circle item returns to the **Layers** panel. Click its meatball to select it independently of the Jacket sublayer. Then press Backspace (or Delete) to get rid of the circle.

7. *Unlock and expand the Backdrop layer.* To cut a head-shaped hole in the Jacket sublayer, we need a head-shaped path. Were you to search this book for clues to the location of such a path, you might land on my introduction to the Backdrop layer (Step 3, page 247), which includes the seemingly innocuous passage, "I used a head-shaped path to carve a hole in the beige curtain and floor." To unlock the Backdrop layer and gain access to this path, click the 🔒 icon in front of the **Backdrop** item in the Layers panel. For good measure, also click Backdrop's ▶ to expand the layer and reveal its contents.

8. *Copy the head-shaped path.* Six items down, you'll see a beige thumbnail named Compound Shape. This is the flat-colored curtain behind Sam's chest, arms, and head. Here's what I want you to do with it:

   • Twirl open the **Compound Shape** item.

   • Meatball the first <Path> item, which looks—even in the Layers panel—like the outline of my young son's head.

   • Choose **Edit→Copy** or press Ctrl+C (⌘-C).

   In the name of tidiness and self-protection, I recommend that you now undo the results of the last step. That is: Continuing in the Layers panel, twirl the **Backdrop** layer closed and then click in the second column in front of Backdrop to lock it back down.

9. *Paste the head in front of the Jacket sublayer.* Still inside the Layers panel, meatball the **Jacket** sublayer to select it. Then choose **Edit→Paste in Front** or press Ctrl+F (⌘-F). The head appears as a white silhouette, obliterating Sam's face, as in Figure 8-18.

10. *Rename the path.* In the Layers panel, double-click the newest <Path> item. Type the new name of "Head Outline" and press Enter or Return.

11. *Apply a black fill with no stroke.* In the world of opacity masks, black means hole. So let's prepare for this by filling the head with black and eradicating the stroke. My suggested method:

    • Press Shift+X to reverse the fill and stroke. The head path now has a black fill and a white stroke.

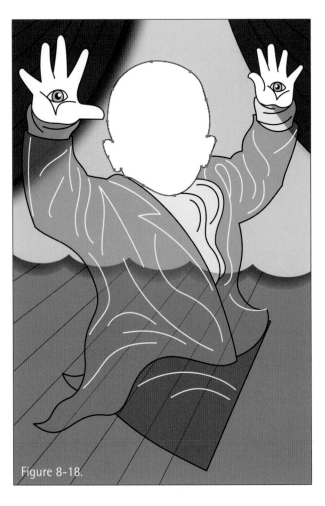

Figure 8-18.

- Select the stroke in the **Color** panel or at the bottom of the toolbox. The icon should look like 🔲.

- Press the slash key, as in ⊘, to make the active attribute (the stroke) transparent.

The Head Outline path is now ready to serve as an opacity mask.

12. *Add the Jacket sublayer to the selection.* Back in the **Layers** panel, Shift-click the meatball for the **Jacket** sublayer to add it to the selection.

13. *Apply the head path as an opacity mask.* First, trust me. Now click the ⬇≡ icon in the top-right corner of the **Transparency** panel, and choose the command **Make Opacity Mask**. Suddenly and somewhat terrifyingly, all of Sam's clothing goes transparent. This is to be expected. Keep reading.

14. *Turn off the Clip check box.* Being black, the head path clips away the tops of the jacket and cravat. But so does the undefined area outside the head, leaving the Jacket layer altogether transparent. The solution? Make the undefined area white (and therefore opaque) by turning off the **Clip** check box in the **Transparency** panel. The result appears in Figure 8-19. Congratulations, my child's head is entirely exposed, as if he grew up in this translucent suit.

Figure 8-19.

15. *Turn on and expand the Piano sublayer.* In the **Layers** panel, click in the first column to the left of the **Piano** sublayer, immediately above Jacket, to display a blue keyboard that I've drawn for you. Then click the ▶ triangle in front of Piano to twirl the sublayer open and reveal three paths and a blend.

16. *Copy the bottom blue path.* Note how Sam's partially rendered pants slide below the piano keyboard. Because the keyboard is translucent, you can see that the pants are incomplete, cut off at the tops of the thighs. My child has dickey legs! Like the orange suit, the pants are part of the Jacket sublayer, which already includes an opacity mask. To clip the legs successfully, we need to add the base of the keyboard to that mask.

    In the Layers panel, meatball the blue path at the bottom of the Piano sublayer. Then choose **Edit**→**Copy** or press Ctrl+C (⌘-C).

17. *Paste the keyboard into the Jacket's opacity mask.* Meatball the **Jacket** sublayer. Then do the following:

    - Go to the **Transparency** panel and click the opacity mask thumbnail, the one that looks like a black head against a white background.

    - Choose **Edit**→**Paste in Place** or press the keyboard shortcut Ctrl+Shift+V (⌘-Shift-V). Illustrator adds the blue path to the opacity mask.

    The blue path diffuses Sam's stumpy legs but does not entirely erase them. When rendered within an opacity mask, a colored path can hide elements of your illustration on an ink-by-ink basis, but that's not what we're looking for. We want to clip the pants entirely under the piano. Which requires black.

18. *Fill the blue path with black.* On the far left side of the control panel, select black for the fill color and none (▢) for the stroke. Illustrator now clips the pants and the bottom of the suit to the left edge of the blue keyboard, as shown in Figure 8-20.

19. *Rename the new masking path.* Note that Illustrator has renamed the Layers panel **Layers (Opacity Mask)** and it contains just one item, **<Opacity Mask>**. Twirl this item open to reveal two paths, one for the piano and the other for Sam's head. Double-click the item called **<Path>** and rename it "piano."

20. *Exit the opacity mask.* Try clicking part of the jacket and note that Illustrator refuses to select it. This is because editing an opacity mask amounts to a kind of isolation mode. You can select the head and the piano—the two paths in the opacity mask—but that's it. It's as if the opacity mask is all that exists.

Figure 8-20.

When otherwise cut off from your illustration—as when editing an artboard—you can escape by pressing the Esc key. But to escape an opacity mask, you have to act more deliberately. As demonstrated in Figure 8-21, click the first thumbnail in the **Transparency** panel, the one that looks like a tiny jacket with its arms up. This is the illustration thumbnail. The Layers panel repopulates and the jacket appears selected in the document window.

Figure 8-21.

---

You can likewise access the illustration and opacity mask thumbnails by clicking the word *Opacity* in the control panel. A few more tips: Shift-click the opacity mask thumbnail to turn off the opacity mask. To turn it back on, Shift-click the thumbnail again. Alt-click (or Option-click) the opacity mask thumbnail to view the opacity mask on its own. Alt-click (or Option-click) the thumbnail again to see the illustration.

---

Now that you're back inside the illustration, take a look at the keyboard. It comprises a mere 47 keys—nearly half of which are black—so it hardly qualifies as realistic. But, happily, nor was it hard to create. In fact, the keys are nothing more than an automated blend between two distant groups. Although this technique has nothing to do with transparency, and we already covered blending in the previous lesson, it is so compelling that I'm setting aside a few steps to share it with you now.

21. *Release the blended keys.* The best way to understand the keyboard blend is to bust it up and recreate it. In the **Layers** panel, meatball the **Blend** item in the **Piano** layer. Then do as follows:

    • Choose **Object→Blend→Release** or press Ctrl+Shift+Alt+B (⌘-Shift-Option-B). The keys disappear, leaving three selected objects: two groups, one each at the top and bottom of the piano, and a path-of-the-blend in between.

    • Still in the Layers panel, click the meatball for the top **<Path>** item in the Piano layer to select the path-of-the-blend independently of the other objects. Then press the Backspace (or Delete) key to get rid of it.

You are now left with the two groups—pictured in close proximity in Figure 8-22 to show their relative sizes—each of which contains three paths. From back to front, they are: a black-stroked line that divides the white keys, a dark gray-filled path that is the black key, and a white-stroked line that serves as a highlight. The size, line weights, and fills vary to impart depth. But the two groups are arranged symmetrically—that is, each path has a corresponding path in the other group, and the stacking order inside the groups is the same.

Figure 8-22.

Figure 8-23.

22. *Blend the two groups.* Select the two key groups, either in the Layers panel or using the black arrow tool in the document window. Then choose **Object→Blend→Make** or press Ctrl+Alt+B (⌘-Option-B) to make a *group blend*. Illustrator automatically assigns nine steps, as in Figure 8-23. That makes for some whopping-big white keys. But it also creates the optical effect of the white keys growing (even though they're all the same size) as the black keys decline into the distance. We'll address these two separate issues in the next steps.

23. *Change the number of steps to 21.* Double-click the blend tool (⬚) in the toolbox to bring up the **Blend Options** dialog box. Change the **Spacing** setting to **Specified Steps**. Then enter a value of 21, and click **OK**. Illustrator packs in way more keys, but because the spacing is identical from one step to the next, the keys don't match the perspective of the scene. Fortunately, you can adjust the blend's pace using the path-of-the-blend.

24. *Adjust the path-of-the-blend using the convert point tool.* When a blend crosses a distance, Illustrator automatically adds a straight path-of-the-blend. Your job now is to bend it.

    • To make the job easier, go to the **Layers** panel, twirl open the **Blend** object, and click in the second column next to each of the two **<Group>** items to lock them down.

    • Select the convert point tool from the pen tool flyout menu. Or just press the shortcut, Shift+C.

    • From the bottom point, drag up—nearly to the bottom of the beige curtain—and a bit to the right to draw forth a control handle and slightly bend the path. Illustrator spaces out the forward keys as well.

    • Drag about a third that distance straight up from the top point to spread the upper keys more naturally as well. Figure 8-24 shows the locations of the control handles. I've also circled the positions of the convert point tool cursor at the ends of each of the drags.

    So ends our brief departure into the rarefied realm of group blending. Whatever your impression, it beats the hell out of duplicating, scaling, filling, and stroking 21 separate object variations.

25. *Collapse and target the Piano sublayer.* The next and final phase of this exercise is to fade the keyboard using a gradient opacity mask. This time, we'll add a blank opacity mask to an

Figure 8-24.

object and draw directly inside it. To prepare, return to the **Layers** panel and twirl closed the **Piano** sublayer. (This isn't strictly necessary, but a little bit of cleanup helps keep the Layers panel from becoming an unmanageable mess.) And then meatball the Piano sublayer to select it in all its fullness.

26. *Add a blank opacity mask.* Click the ▾≡ icon in the top-right corner of the **Transparency** panel and choose **Make Opacity Mask**. Because you selected no path above the Piano sublayer, Illustrator grants you an empty opacity mask. Because the Clip check box is turned on by default, that mask is altogether black, making the blue keyboard and its blended keys invisible (although you can still see their ghostly selection edges). Don't worry, it's all going according to plan.

27. *Switch to the opacity mask.* Despite dutifully creating an opacity mask, Illustrator strangely chooses to leave it inactive. So it's up to you to click the all-black thumbnail in the Transparency panel, which I ask you to do now. You'll know you're in the right place when you see the selection edges disappear and the Layers panel change to Layers (Opacity Mask), which is Illustrator's secret-handshake way of announcing that you have entered the opacity mask mode.

28. *Turn off the Clip option.* The simplest vehicle for a gradient mask is a rectangle. But to draw a rectangular mask boundary, you need to see the thing that you're drawing it around. So deselect the **Clip** check box in the **Transparency** panel. The piano springs back to life in the document window.

29. *Draw a rectangle around the piano.* Press the M key to select the rectangle tool. Then draw a rectangle that completely encircles (or, if you prefer, enrectangles) the blue piano keyboard. Very likely, Illustrator will assign the rectangle neither a fill nor a stroke, as in Figure 8-25. If not, set both the fill and stroke to none (▨).

30. *Assign a gradient to the rectangle.* Make sure that the fill is active at the bottom of the toolbox. (If it isn't, press the X key to make it so.) Then press the period key (⚬) to assign the rectangle the default horizontal black-to-white gradient. The piano will appear to fade in from the right, as in Figure 8-26.

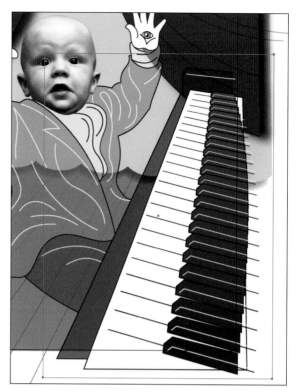

Figure 8-25.

Figure 8-26.

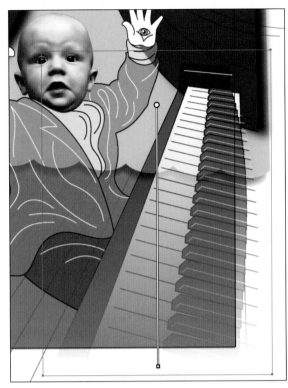

Figure 8-27.

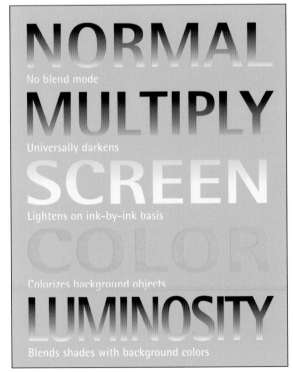

Figure 8-28.

31. *Change the direction of the gradient to vertical.* Press the G key to switch to the gradient tool. Illustrator will display a horizontal gradient annotator in the document window. Now draw a vertical line (press the Shift key as you do) from Sam's elbow down to the bottom of the white edge of the keyboard. The aftermath, complete with annotator and fading piano, appears in Figure 8-27.

32. *Save your changes.* Press the V key to select the black arrow tool. Switch back to the **Transparency** panel and click the first thumbnail, the one that looks like the spine of a piano, to return focus to the illustration. Press Ctrl+Shift+A (⌘-Shift-A) to deselect everything. And then choose **File**→**Save As** or press Ctrl+Shift+S (⌘-Shift-S) to save your most recent changes without overwriting your last ones. Name this file "Opacity masks final.ai," and click the **Save** button.

Opacity masks permit you to employ any of Illustrator's tools in the name of modifying the transparency of a path, group, blend, or layer. Use the blob brush to paint holes. Use gradients and blends to produce soft transitions. You can even use editable text to cut character-shaped holes or house objects inside letters. Opacity masks are beyond PostScript, but they're well within PDF and as flexible as the day is long.

## Applying Blend Modes

Witnessed back in Figure 8-1 (page 243), blend modes are methods for mixing colors with more flexibility than is afforded by a straight Opacity blend. To get a sense of just how much you can do with them, imagine that you're mixing two pigments—traditional paints, for example—to create a new color. And in addition to deciding how much of each pigment to mix, the equivalent of an Opacity adjustment, you can also tweak the chemical reaction so that the mix darkens the pigments, lightens them, increases the color's intensity, or even reverses the pigments entirely.

Illustrator's sixteen blend modes vary wildly in their utility. We'll focus on the most essential. As illustrated in Figure 8-28, such modes as Multiply, Screen, Color, and Luminosity allow you to use a path or other object to darken, lighten, colorize, or shade, respectively, the objects behind it. (The Normal setting is the equivalent of turning off the blend mode.)

If you're new to blend modes, it's easy to write them off as gimmicky, even underwhelming parlor tricks. But in time, you'll recognize them for what they are: highly practical methods for creating color and luminance interactions between the paths, groups, and layers in your illustrations.

1. *Open the file you recently saved.* Assuming you completed the previous exercise, extra credit and all, your file should be called *Opacity masks final.ai.* If you have no such file, open the progress document I created for you, called *My pretentious piano.ai* in the *Lesson 08* folder.

2. *Turn on and select the Bench sublayer.* In the **Layers** panel, click the first column next to the **Bench** sublayer (immediately below Jacket) to turn it on. Then target the sublayer by clicking its meatball. As shown in Figure 8-29, the bench is entirely visible even as it extends under the piano. If that were a problem, you could move the bench into the Jacket sublayer (behind the Lines and Suit items), in which case it would automatically subscribe to the Jacket sublayer's opacity mask. But I like the way the bench, piano, and clothing interact. In fact, my one problem with the bench is that it's opaque, which we'll address with a blend mode in the next step.

3. *Apply the Multiply blend mode.* Although you wouldn't know to look at it, both the bench and the piano are filled with the same shade of blue: 100 percent Cyan plus 60 percent Magenta. The difference is that, whereas the bench is opaque, I imprinted the blue path from the Piano sublayer into the background objects using a blend mode.

To match that same effect, click the top-left option in the **Transparency** panel, the one that reads **Normal**, and select **Multiply** from the ensuing pop-up menu. The bench dims and absorbs some of the color of the tan of the Backdrop layer, as in Figure 8-30. Multiply has many real-world analogies, but for our purposes, the idea of ink blending with colored paper is perhaps the easiest to imagine. For example, if you were to print the blue bench onto a tan sheet of paper, the paper would darken as it received the translucent ink, much like a tattoo applied to flesh. The result is that the vibrant blue ink would appear deeper and somewhat warmer, like the greenish blue blend pictured in Figure 8-30.

Figure 8-29.

Figure 8-30.

Figure 8-31.

Figure 8-32.

4. ***Add a gradient opacity mask.*** As I mentioned, I like the way the bench extends under the piano. But I think the effect would look better if the bench faded in just as the piano fades out. Yet another opacity mask is in order:

- If you haven't copied anything since Step 16 of the previous exercise (see page 256) and you aren't using my sample file, the Clipboard is already filled with the path you need to complete this step. Otherwise, twirl open the **Piano** sublayer in the Layers panel, meatball the blue <**Path**> item at the bottom of that layer, and choose **Edit→Copy** or press Ctrl+C (⌘-C). Then twirl the Piano sublayer closed.

- Now to add the opacity mask: Meatball the **Bench** sublayer. Click the ▾≡ icon in the top-right corner of the **Transparency** panel and choose **Make Opacity Mask**. The bench disappears, leaving nothing but selection edges.

- Turn off the **Clip** check box in the Transparency panel. The bench reappears.

- Click the now-white thumbnail to the right of the bench in the Transparency panel. Then choose **Edit→Paste in Place** or press Ctrl+Shift+V (⌘-Shift-V). The bench dims in response to the blue-piano opacity mask.

- In the control panel, change the stroke to none (⊘). Check that the fill is active at the bottom of the toolbox (if not, press X) and press the period key (⬚) to swap the fill for a default black-to-white gradient.

- Press the G key to switch to the gradient tool. Then press the Shift key and drag from the bottom of the artboard upward to Sam's right-side elbow (that would be his left, were he a real boy instead of a kooky cartoon).

The gradient annotator and fading bench appear in Figure 8-31. Assuming your result more or less matches, press the V key to switch back to the black arrow tool. Then click the bench thumbnail in the Transparency panel to exit the opacity mask edit mode and restore your access to the illustration's layers.

5. ***Turn on the Eyes and Hair sublayers.*** In the **Layers** panel, click in the first column in front of **Eyes** and **Hair**. What results is a collection of additions to Sam's formerly hairless visage (see Figure 8-32). The newest paths may be slightly over the top. But absurdity is a small price to pay for quality education. Besides, if there were formerly any doubt, you now have proof that this is no corporate-seal, by-committee publication.

6. **Set the gray paths to Multiply.** First select the gray clown-makeup paths around Sam's eyes. (Armed with the black arrow tool, click the path outline of one of the paths in the document window, then Shift-click the other.) In the **Transparency** panel, click the top-left option and change the blend mode to **Multiply**. Then reduce the **Opacity** value to 70 percent. As seen in Figure 8-33, the Multiply blend mode lets you transform a couple of plain gray paths into contour-sensitive shadows.

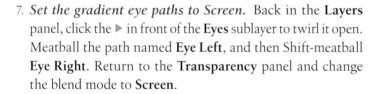

In the random-trivia department: Photoshop, the program that Adobe used to introduce the world to Opacity and Multiply, has historically permitted you to adjust both for no more than a single layer at a time. Photoshop CS5 finally permits you to change the Opacity value for multiple layers at once, but the same cannot be said of blend modes. Illustrator, meanwhile, has permitted you to modify translucency and blend mode for multiple objects since the features were introduced roughly a decade ago. Nothing against Photoshop, but Illustrator rocks.

Figure 8-33.

7. **Set the gradient eye paths to Screen.** Back in the **Layers** panel, click the ▶ in front of the **Eyes** sublayer to twirl it open. Meatball the path named **Eye Left**, and then Shift-meatball **Eye Right**. Return to the **Transparency** panel and change the blend mode to **Screen**.

The Screen mode is Multiply's opposite, so instead of mixing and darkening, it mixes and lightens. Imagine that instead of adding ink (the Multiply analogy), you're shining a colored light. The Eye paths started out as blue-to-black gradients (from left-to-right). If black was a light, it would be invisible, like a light turned off. Any other color brightens. As a result, the Eye paths brighten Sam's eyes on the left and have no effect on the right, as in Figure 8-34.

In other words, Multiply invariably creates shadows; Screen is designed to (but does not always) create highlights. (I'll explain the exceptions, and how to ensure that Screen always works as designed, in the upcoming Step 16 on page 266.)

8. **Select the Hair path in the Hair sublayer.** In the **Layers** panel, twirl closed the **Eyes** sublayer and twirl open the **Hair** sublayer. Then meatball the item also called **Hair**, just below the Lines group. This compound path—so identified on the left side of the control panel (assuming that you selected the correct item)—comprises five subpaths: the great tufts on

Figure 8-34.

Figure 8-35.

Figure 8-36.

the left and right sides of Sam's head, the two eyebrows, and the soul patch below my boy's lower lip. The compound path includes two fills, both of which sport live Scribble effects (hence the back-and-forth patterns of sketchy lines) applied from the Effect menu.

9. *Try out the Color blend mode.* As you work with blending in Illustrator, it's always a good idea to have a specific goal in mind (as opposed to selecting random modes and hoping something will miraculously work). But even with the best plans and intentions, the perfect mode may allude you. In which case, you experiment. In my case, I want to add scribbly fills to both color and shade Sam's bald pate. Just to get a sense of your options, change the blend mode in the top-left corner of the **Transparency** panel to **Color**. As shown in Figure 8-35, the Color mode keeps the blues of the compound path and mixes them with the luminance transitions from the layers below. (By *luminance*, I mean transitions from dark to light.) As a result, the hair replaces the formerly tan flesh tones and background with blue but otherwise leaves the detail intact. (Note that the opaque dark blue hairs are part of the Lines group, which is not affected.)

10. *Try out Luminosity instead.* That leaves us with far too little hair detail, so let's try Color's opposite mode. Click **Color** in the Transparency panel and change the blend mode to **Luminosity**, the last option in the pop-up menu. The Luminosity mode keeps the luminance of the hair elements and mixes then with the color from the rear objects. As a result, we keep the hair texture and merge it with the flesh colors, as evidenced by Figure 8-36.

11. *Undo the last two steps.* Sadly, neither effect is what I'm looking for. So press Ctrl+Z (⌘-Z) twice to undo the results of the last two steps. Or, if you prefer, reset the blend mode in the Transparency panel to **Normal**. It seems we'll need to dig a little deeper.

12. *Set the blue fill to the Color blend mode.* Switch to the **Appearance** panel by clicking its tab or pressing Shift+F6. The panel identifies a compound path with a dark blue stroke, a medium blue fill, and a white-to-black gradient fill. Click the blue fill to make it active. Then return to the **Transparency** panel, and apply the **Color** blend mode. Twirl open the blue fill in the **Appearance** panel to see two items: Scribble (the live effect) and Opacity: 100% Color.

Illustrator is unique in its ability to peel off a single attribute, such as the blue fill, and blend it independently of other attributes associated with that same object. Which is admirable, to be sure. But as Figure 8-37 makes plain, it's still not right.

13. *Set the gradient fill to the Overlay mode.* Once again in the Appearance panel, select the second **Fill** item, which contains the white-to-black gradient. I'm not altogether sure what to do with this fill, so let's try a few blend modes, all available from the **Transparency** panel:

    • Change the blend mode to **Luminosity**. Disappointingly, this does nothing. Because we overrode the colors inside the Hairs path with the blue fill above, the gradient scribbles no longer have an underlying color to interact with. The result appears identical to that in Figure 8-37.

    • Set the blend mode to **Screen**. This keeps the white tip of the gradient in the soul patch but altogether wipes out the dark areas from the sideburns on up.

    • What I need is a blend mode that splits the difference by lightening the hair with the light portion of the gradient and darkening the hair elsewhere. Enter the three contrast modes—Overlay, Soft Light, and Hard Light—which enhance contrast by mapping luminance values like a texture onto the layers in the background. Select the most successful of these, **Overlay**, to turn the gradient into a kind of natural shading attribute.

Having determined that Overlay does the trick, soften the effect by reducing the **Opacity** value to 60 percent. The net result appears in Figure 8-38.

14. *Select the contents of the Gradient layer.* I next want to add a "bounce" of light to the bottom-left corner of the illustration. The simplest solution is to blend a gradient, one that I've created for you. Here's how to get to it:

    • Switch to the **Layers** panel. We're done with the **Hair** sublayer so twirl is closed.

    • Scroll to the top of the Layers list and turn on the **Gradient** layer. A large rectangle filled with a light blue-to-black gradient appears in the document window.

    • Twirl open the Gradient layer and meatball the path inside (also called **Gradient**).

Figure 8-37.

Figure 8-38.

Figure 8-39.

Figure 8-40.

15. ***Apply the Screen blend mode.*** The current gradient doesn't look anything like a bounce of light; it covers the illustration in darkness. But imagine if the blue of the gradient were to brighten the objects behind it and the black were to drop away. As mentioned in Step 7 (page 263), when set to the Screen mode, black becomes invisible and other colors brighten. So go to the **Transparency** panel and change the blend mode to **Screen**. Sure enough, the blue of the gradient brightens. But the black area, rather than dropping out, becomes brighter than the blue, as pictured in Figure 8-39. What gives? Am I a big liar? Is Illustrator broken? Neither, it so happens. All blend modes work on an ink-by-ink basis. And the different inks are telling the Screen mode to do different things.

### PEARL OF WISDOM

Expressed in terms of CMYK ink coverage, white is 0 percent and black is 100 percent. In the case of Screen, 0 percent brightens absolutely, 100 percent brightens not at all. Our gradient contains two colors: a light blue consisting of 75 percent Cyan and 40 percent Magenta, and a weak black of just 100 percent Black. Because Screen (like all blend modes) works on a single ink at a time, the blue lightens absolutely in the Yellow and Black inks (where it's 0 percent), moderately in Magenta, and just slightly in Cyan. Which is why the bottom-left corner of Figure 8-39 appears Cyan + Magenta, or bluish. The weak black brightens the Cyan, Magenta, and Yellow inks absolutely, removing all vestiges of color. But the top-right portion of the gradient turns invisible in the Black ink, which is why all the black lines remain intact.

If that seemed a little dense, take heart. The solution should make things clearer.

16. ***Change the weak black to a super-rich black.*** Press the G key to switch to the gradient tool and display the gradient annotator in the document window. Hover over the annotator to see the color swatches. Then double-click the black stop at the top of the annotator to reveal the color panel. Here are two ways to make the black drop away:

- Change the **Opacity** value to 0 percent, making the black transparent.

- That's the simple solution, but it doesn't help you understand how Screen works. So here's the better way: Change the **C**, **M**, and **Y** values to 100. The black goes invisible in all inks, as in Figure 8-40.

Don't worry that the gradient doesn't quite cover all the illustration. We'll correct that problem with a mask in the next exercise.

17. *Add some black ink to the blue.* The blue of the gradient is washing out too much of the black strokes in the bottom-left corner of the artwork. (The lines on the floor even manage to turn white.) To bring some of that black back, again hover over the annotator. Double-click the bottom blue color stop to bring up the color panel. And change the **K** value from 0 to 35 percent. This ratchets back the Screen mode in the Black ink, as in Figure 8-41.

18. *Save your changes.* Press the V key to reactivate the black arrow tool. Twirl closed the **Gradient** layer in the **Layers** panel and press Ctrl+Shift+A (⌘-Shift-A) to deselect the illustration. Choose **File**→**Save As** or press Ctrl+Shift+S (⌘-Shift-S), name your updated file "Blended objects.ai," and click the **Save** button.

Figure 8-41.

To recap: The Color mode colorizes background objects with the active one, Luminosity colorizes the active object with those behind it, and Overlay heightens contrast. Meanwhile, Multiply darkens the illustration and Screen lightens it. Back off an ink to reduce the effect of the Multiply mode; increase an ink value to back off the effect of the Screen mode.

And that, in a nutshell, is how blend modes work in Illustrator.

## Cropping Entire Layers

Cropping is one of the more difficult issues to come to terms with in Illustrator, in part because it's handled so easily in other print programs. In Photoshop, for example, you select the crop tool and drag around the portion of the image you want to keep. In InDesign, you import a piece of artwork and drag a corner handle. But Illustrator has no canvas (as in Photoshop) or frame (as in InDesign). In other words, Illustrator lacks a natural crop zone.

Some would argue that the crop zone is the artboard. This argument is marginally true for printing and exporting, as you'll learn in Lesson 12, but those tasks are just a fraction of the picture. Which introduces our second problem: Illustrator has so many things to crop that arriving at one solution is impossible.

In Lesson 6, I showed you how to crop from the Pathfinder panel. Then in Lesson 7, we employed a more deft clipping mask. I end this lesson by showing you how to crop the contents of an entire layer in one effortless but arcane operation. In fact, because that operation is so useful and obscure, I'll show you how to apply it twice.

1. **Open your last-saved file.** For those of you scrupulously following along, that's *Blended objects.ai* (see Step 18 on the preceding page). Otherwise, open my progress file, *Blend mode fantasia.ai* in the *Lesson 08* folder.

2. **Select the Vectors layer.** Go to the **Layers** panel. The Vectors layer should still be expanded. Notice the top item in that layer, called Boundary? It is nothing more than a rectangle—with neither fill nor stroke—that matches the size of the gradient rectangle on the Gradient layer. (If that doesn't ring a bell, see Step 14 on page 265.) This path is our crop boundary.

3. **Highlight the Vectors layer.** Still in the Layers panel, click the **Vectors** layer. The layer is now highlighted.

4. **Crop the layer with its top path.** At the bottom of the panel, click the first icon on the left (next to the words 7 *Layers*), the one that looks like ◑. Regardless of which object is selected, Illustrator uses the top path in the layer—in our case, Boundary—to crop the rest of the layer.

5. **Unlock and crop the Backdrop layer.** Twirl closed the **Vectors** layer, if only to get it out of the way. Then click the 🔒 in front of the **Backdrop** layer to unlock it. Click the Backdrop layer to highlight it and click the ◑ icon once again to mask the layer with its top path, another rectangle.

6. **Turn on the Text Items layer.** The artwork needs some text to finish it off. Scroll to the top of the Layers panel list and click in the first column to the left of the **Text Items** layer, which contains a layer of live text set to the Screen mode. The final artwork appears as shown in Figure 8-42.

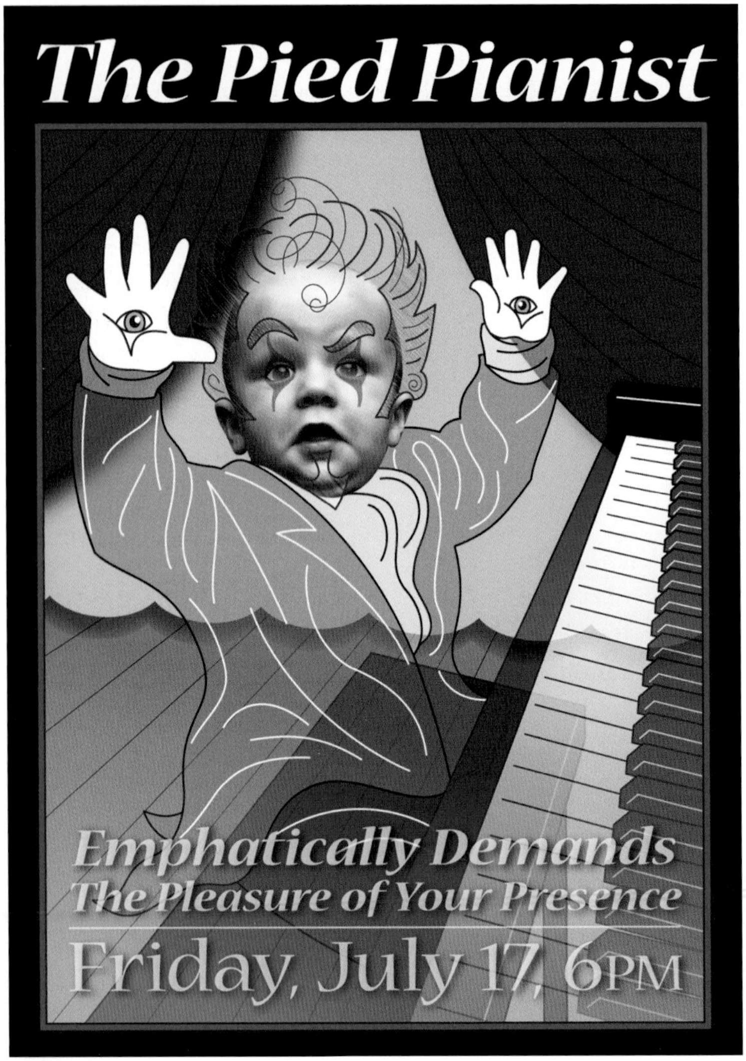

Illustrator's brand of transparency is applicable to any kind of object. You can adjust it from a variety of panels. And it is as core to the creation of vector art as fill and stroke.

Figure 8-42.

# WHAT DID YOU LEARN?

Match the key concept in the numbered list below with the letter of the phrase that best describes it. Answers appear upside-down at the bottom of the page.

## Key Concepts

1. Blending
2. Opacity
3. Flattening
4. Knockout Group
5. Opacity mask
6. Clip
7. Invert Mask
8. Illustration thumbnail
9. Group blend
10. Blend modes
11. Multiply
12. Screen

## Descriptions

A. This numerical option in the control panel and the Transparency panel lets you mix a selected path, a gradient, a group, a layer, or another object with the stuff behind it according to a percentage.

B. This trick blend mode lightens colors on an ink-by-ink basis, with only a super-rich black turning entirely invisible.

C. Analogous to a layer mask in Photoshop, this independent drawing mode allows you to paint in fades and translucency, with black equating to transparent and white meaning opaque.

D. Click this item—located immediately below the blend mode pop-up menu in the Transparency panel—to exit the opacity mask mode.

E. These sixteen named settings permit you to mix colors with more flexibility than that afforded by a straight Opacity blend.

F. The creation of interactions between objects using a combination of Opacity adjustments, knockout groups, opacity masks, and such modes as Multiply, Screen, and Overlay.

G. This blend mode lets you mix and darken colors, much as if you were printing ink onto colored paper.

H. This rarely useful check box reverses the meanings of black and white in an opacity mask, so that white paths cut holes.

I. This process of rasterizing sections of artwork or breaking objects into subpaths to accommodate the discrepancies between transparency and the PostScript printing language occurs on-the-fly during the print process.

J. The best way to create a pattern of step-and-repeat objects between two similarly organized collections of paths.

K. This check box in the Transparency panel—which in its own words "Prevents the elements of a group from showing through each other"—must be clicked twice to work.

L. Unwisely turned on by default, this check box sets everything outside the paths in an opacity mask to transparent.

## Answers

1F, 2A, 3I, 4K, 5C, 6L, 7H, 8D, 9J, 10E, 11G, 12B

# LESSON
# 9

# BRUSHES AND SYMBOLS

**CLIP-ART ASIDE,** there is a real value to prefab repeatable art. Consider for a moment the modern miracle of digital type as made available to and exploited by a run-of-the-mill computer application. When you select a font—TrueType, OpenType, the standard doesn't matter—you're actually selecting a library of hundreds or thousands of character definitions, every one of which is a compound path drawn using a program like Illustrator. By way of an example, Figure 9-1 shows three of the more exotic characters included with Adobe Caslon Pro. Figure 9-2 shows these same characters detailed as compound path outlines, with hole-cutting subpaths in blue crosshatch and tiny square anchor points throughout. Amazingly, all you have to do to call up these simple graphics is bang away at your keyboard. If you later change the font, your application swaps out all the original graphics for new ones. In a very real sense, your operating system draws your words, sentences, and punctuation marks from pieces of prefab art.

Figure 9-1.

Illustrator doesn't yet permit you to draw and export your own fonts. (I wish it did.) But it does let you create, replicate, and update pieces of artwork using a couple of panels and a handful of tools. And instead of entering characters from a keyboard, you paint with them.

This lesson demonstrates two varieties of such repeatable, updatable art: brushes and symbols. Illustrator's Brushes panel lets you save one or more

Figure 9-2.

# ABOUT THIS LESSON

## Project Files

Before beginning the exercises, make sure you've downloaded the lesson files from *www.oreilly.com/go/Deke-IllustratorCS5*, as directed in Step 2 on page xiv of the Preface. This should result in a folder called *Lesson Files-Alcs5 1on1* on your desktop. We'll be working with the files inside the *Lesson 09* subfolder.

Brushes and symbols are bound by their reliance on a piece of base artwork. Meaning that after you draw something, you can convert it into a brush or a symbol and manipulate it six ways to Sunday. This lesson is all about Monday through Saturday, in which you'll learn how to:

## Video Lesson 9: Freehand Painting

Painting inside Illustrator is a diversion from the highly controlled creation of paths. In this video, I'll demonstrate Illustrator's arsenal of freehand painting tools. Of particular interest and usefulness are the paintbrush and the blob brush tools.

To learn how to paint outside the outlines, visit *www.oreilly.com/go/deke-IllustratorCS5*. Click the **Watch** button to view the lesson online or click the **Download** button to save it to your computer. During the video, you'll learn these shortcuts:

Video Lesson 9: Freehand Painting

| Operation | Windows shortcut | Macintosh shortcut |
|---|---|---|
| Select the pencil tool | Press the N key | Press the N key |
| Display the Brushes panel | Press the F5 key | Press the F5 key |
| Create a new brush | Click 🔲 in the Brushes panel | Click 🔲 in the Brushes panel |
| Create a new layer | Ctrl+Alt+L | ⌘-Option-L |
| Select the paintbrush tool | Press the B key | Press the B key |
| Temporarily access the arrow tool | Press the Ctrl key | Press the ⌘ key |
| Deselect your artwork | Ctrl+Shift+A | ⌘-Shift-A |
| Select the blob brush tool | Shift+B | Shift-B |
| Select the eraser brush tool | Shift+E | Shift-E |
| Display the Blob Brush dialog box | Double-click the blob brush tool | Double-click the blob brush tool |

paths as something that you can paint with, the net result being graphics along a path. The Symbols panel lets you create copies of graphics that remain linked to the originals, so that you can edit all copies in a single operation, much like switching fonts. Both brushes and symbols represent powerful means of replication and automation for the intrepid illustrator, which is to say, *you*.

## Dynamic Brushstrokes

Illustrator CS5 offers five varieties of brushes, samples of which appear in Figure 9-3, and all of which I document in Video Lesson 9, "Freehand Painting" (see the facing page). You can either paint a brushstroke using the paintbrush tool, in which case the brush will respond to input from a pressure-sensitive stylus (if you have one). Or you can apply a brush to a path drawn with any other tool, in which case the brush behaves like a specialty stroke.

Two of the brush types, calligraphic and the new bristle brush (first and fourth in the figure), permit you to paint free-form artwork that resembles traditional ink (calligraphic) or paint (bristle). You create brushes by adjusting a dizzying array of numerical options. If you stroke a path with the brush before editing it, you can preview the results of your modifications, which makes the options a lot easier to suss out.

The other brushes paint graphics along the path outline. The scatter brush repeats a graphic, randomly sized, spaced, and scattered (spaced from the path outline), according to your specifications. The pattern brush repeats the graphic with more constraint, stretching and bending the graphic to flow with the path outline. You can also add graphics to accommodate corners and endpoints, all housed inside one brush.

The one that I examine in detail in this lesson is the *art brush*, which stretches a collection of shapes along the length of a path. The result is an entirely new class of graphics that you can bend and distort merely by manipulating a central spine. As a result, an art brush can look like a charcoal stroke, as in Figure 9-3. Or it

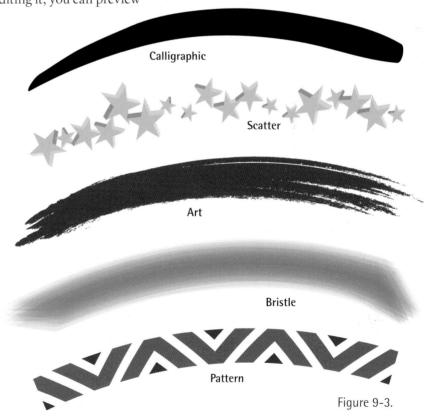

Calligraphic

Scatter

Art

Bristle

Pattern

Figure 9-3.

can appear as a waving design, a distorted graphic, or even a new variety of text along a path. Text expressed as a brush goes well beyond standard path type, with letterforms folding and splaying as they round the curve. Naturally, I'll show you a few examples in the forthcoming exercises.

## Symbols and Instances

The Symbols panel allows you to collect graphics and icons that you use on a regular basis in your artwork. You then drag and drop clones, or *instances*, of those graphics into your illustration and position and scale them to taste. All instances remain linked to the graphic in the Symbols panel. So if you change the graphic, all instances update in kind. For example, if an architect wants to update a Vermont floor plan to suit Hawaii, then it's a simple matter to replace all the pine trees with palms.

Symbols are also well suited to Web graphics, especially Flash-based content. Because instances are just phantoms of a graphic, they save on file size. Repeat a 20K graphic ten times, and it compresses down to just the core 20K.

At this point, you might be thinking that symbols and brushes seem like strange bedfellows. But remember that both art brushes and symbols rely on an original graphic, one that remains linked to either a brushstroke or an instance. Plus, as with brushes, you can paint with symbols using the symbol sprayer tool. That may sound trivial if not downright goofy, but the symbol sprayer can be highly useful for laying down background art.

For the graphically challenged—or those hoping to avoid some up-front work—Illustrator ships with predefined brush and symbol libraries, which include grunge brushes, decorative dividers, highly outfitted border patterns, map icons, flow chart elements, 3D symbols, and more. Figure 9-4 shows the contents of the more interesting symbol libraries, which you can load by clicking the 🖾 icon in the bottom-left corner of the Symbols panel and choosing Grime Vector Pack.

---

All brushes and symbols are raw materials for you to customize. To edit an art, scatter, or pattern brush, drag the brush from the Brushes panel and drop it into your artwork. (You typically need to ungroup a scatter brush once; ungroup an art brush twice.) To customize a symbol, select an instance and click the ⬇ at the bottom of the Symbols panel. That's how I added color to some of the instances in Figure 9-4.

---

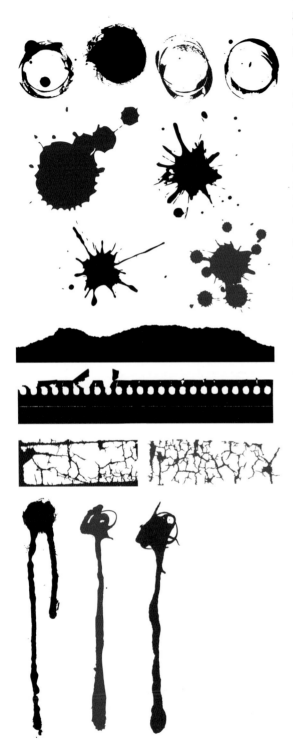

Figure 9-4.

## Enhancing Line Art with Art Brushes

In this first exercise, I'll show you how to apply and customize art brushes in Illustrator. I've created all the paths for you in advance. But remember, if you want to paint your own brushstrokes, you can do so with the paintbrush tool, which you get by pressing the B key. This is particularly useful if you own an art tablet with a pressure-sensitive stylus, such as one of the Intuos line of tablets from Wacom (*www.wacom.com*). That said, standard paths typically offer the most precision, which is why I employ them in the following steps.

1. **Open an illustration with colored lines.** Find the *Lesson 09* folder inside the *Lesson Files-AIcs5 1on1* folder, and open the file called *Eyeliner.ai*. Shown in Figure 9-5, it's the newest version of the Eye of Horus artwork that you first drew in Lesson 2. Only this time Horus is a pop band and Eyeliner is the name of the group's debut single (with the obligatory David Guetta remix and an ill-advised collaboration with Akon).

2. **Open the Brushes panel.** Choose **Window→Brushes** or press the F5 key. Pictured in Figure 9-6, the Brushes panel contains a row of calligraphic brushes, followed by Basic and six art brushes. Like the ✕ icon at the bottom of the panel, Basic removes any brush and restores an unadorned stroke.

**PEARL OF WISDOM**

Like symbols, swatches, and other panel items, Brushes are saved along with an illustration. So the brushes shown in Figure 9-6 are specific to the *Eyeliner.ai* file. The brushes that Illustrator includes with a new document vary from one version of the software to the next. But they always start with a row of calligraphic brushes, followed by Basic and at least a couple of art brushes.

3. **Apply the Rough Charcoal brush to the eyebrow.** Using the black arrow tool, select Horus's dark red eyebrow. Then click the first art brush in the **Brushes** panel, called (if you hover over it) Rough Charcoal. Illustrator stretches the art brush across the length of the eyebrow, as in Figure 9-7.

Figure 9-5.

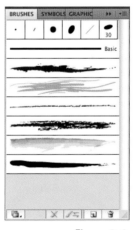

Figure 9-6.

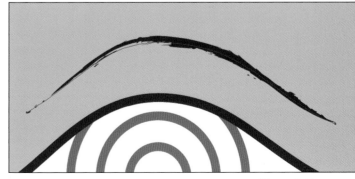

Figure 9-7.

4. *Scale and flip the brushstroke.* Sized by default to fit a 1-point line weight, the brushstroke is too thin, plus it traces the eyebrow in the wrong direction. Fortunately, an art brush is a graphic that flows along a path outline. So it stands to reason that you can transform the brush independently of the path.

There are two ways to edit a brush assigned to a path.

- One is to double-click on the brush in the Brushes panel. But that's a global edit that changes all future applications of the brush, which is rarely what you want.

- The other is to edit the brush as it's applied to the selected path only, which is what we'll do in this step.

With the eyebrow path selected, click the middle icon at the bottom of the Brushes panel (𝒜⸗) to bring up the **Stroke Options (Art Brush)** dialog box. Turn on the **Preview** check box. Then try turning on the **Proportional** check box, which ignores the line weight and scales the brush proportionally to the length of the path. That's too thick for my taste. For something less Neanderthal, turn off Proportional and raise the **Width** value to 400 percent. Select the **Flip Along** check box, which reflects the brush along the length of the path, as in Figure 9-8. Click **OK**.

Figure 9-8.

5. *Scale the path outline.* The now-hairy eyebrow appears too small to fit the eye. Press the S key to select the scale tool. Then click along the top of the purple eye path to set the transformation origin. Position your cursor 45 degrees from the origin point, and drag away from it to scale the path so the top of the eyebrow approaches but doesn't quite touch the *R* in *Horus*, as in Figure 9-9 on the next page. The brush resizes to fit.

6. *Edit the path with the white arrow.* Press the A key to switch to the white arrow tool. Click off the eyebrow path to deselect it. Then click on the leftmost anchor point, the one that would be closest to Horus's beak. Drag the point downward slightly and drag its control handle down as well to produce more of an angry eyebrow. Then adjust the other points and handles to smooth out the effect. Figure 9-10 shows the placement of points and control handles that I arrived at. You may, as always, go your own way. Again, the brush resizes automatically.

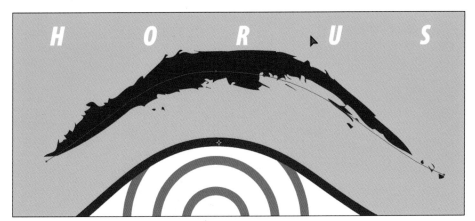

Figure 9-9.

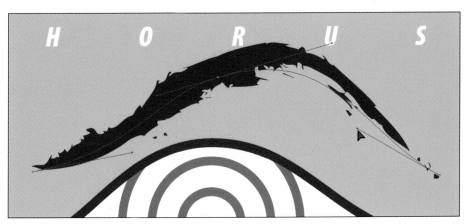

Figure 9-10.

7. *Adjust the thickness of the eyebrow with the width tool.* All of Illustrator's brushes grow thicker and thinner based on pressure-sensitive input from an art tablet. I drew the eyebrow path with the pen tool, so there is no pressure information. Fortunately, you can also add thickness information using CS5's new width tool. Not all brushes respond to width-tool-imposed thickness—conspicuously incompatible is the new bristle brush (shouldn't new features work together?)—but art and pattern brushes do.

In the toolbox, click on the third tool down in the third group, or just press Shift+W to select the width tool. Then drag from the left point to make it thicker, as demonstrated in Figure 9-11. Quite surprisingly—at least, I was surprised—the right side of the eyebrow grows thicker. Because we flipped the eyebrow in Step 4, the brush is responding to opposite width information, which works out fine for the eyebrow.

Add another width point at the top of the eyebrow, about midway into the *R*, so the eyebrow cuts just slightly into the right edge of the letter, as in Figure 9-12.

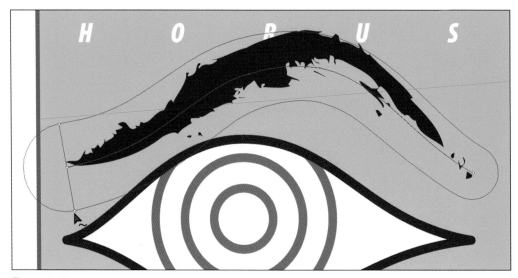

Figure 9-11.

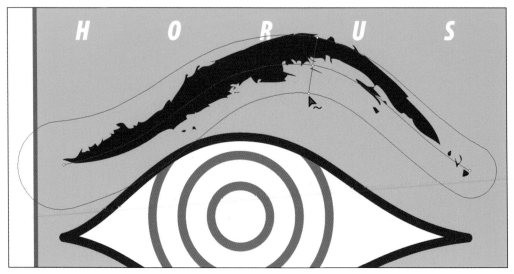

Figure 9-12.

8. **Apply the Fude brush to the purple eyeliner.** Press the V key to switch back to the black arrow tool. (Because the width tool uses an arrowhead cursor, it's easy to forget to switch away from it when you want to select a different path.) Click on the purple path around the eye, then select the last brush in the **Brushes** panel, a tightly woven Japanese brush called Fude.

Pictured in Figure 9-13, the result is a little thin. I'd prefer to see the brush taper away along both the top and bottom edges of the eye. Which means scaling the brush (in a new way) and clipping it in two, as documented in the next steps.

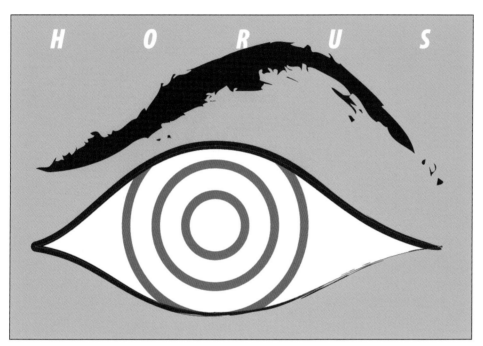

Figure 9-13.

9. **Scale the brush.** You can scale the brush independently of the path (as we saw in Step 4) or by adjusting the line weight. Before applying the art brush, the line weight was 10 points, but upon applying a brush, Illustrator changes it to 1 point. To increase the brush size, go up to the control panel and change the **Stroke** value to 2 points. The brush doubles in thickness.

10. **Clip the path at both ends.** Press the C key to select the scissors tool. Click the far left anchor point to open the path and flip the brush upside-down. Click the right anchor point to sever the path in two, each with its own brushstroke, as in Figure 9-14 on the next page.

11. ***Flip the brush along and across the top path.*** It seems to me that both the top and bottom brushstrokes should emanate from the inside of the eye. So press the V key to switch back to the black arrow tool, and click the top path to select it (just in case it's not already selected). Next, click the ✐⇆ icon at the bottom of the Brushes panel to bring up the **Stroke Options (Art Brush)** dialog box. Turn on the **Flip Along** check box to flip the brush lengthwise. Unfortunately, now the beginning of the brushstrokes (on the left side of the eye) don't align with each other. So also turn on **Flip Across** to flip the brush top-to-bottom and align the strokes, as in Figure 9-15. Click the **OK** button to accept your changes.

Figure 9-14.

Figure 9-15.

280    Lesson 9: Brushes and Symbols

12. ***Remove the white fill inside the eye.*** There's really no way to align the purple brushstrokes with the white inside the eye, so I suggest we just get rid of the latter. In the **Layers** panel, click the ▶ triangle in front of the **Horus** layer to twirl it open. Scroll down to the bottom of that list, and twirl open the Eye group to reveal a group of concentric circles (Hypno) masked by a path called Eye. Click the ◎ to the right the Eye mask (the thumbnail for which shows as white against gray) to select it. Change its fill to none (⬚). The result appears in Figure 9-16.

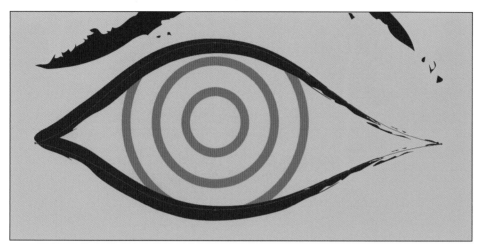

Figure 9-16.

13. ***Apply the Watercolor Stroke brush to the green iris lines.*** Still in the Layers panel, click the ◎ to the right of the Hypno group to select it. Then bring up the **Brushes** panel and select the second-to-last art brush, which is called Watercolor Stroke. As shown in Figure 9-17, the result is hardly inspiring. Don't worry, we'll make it better.

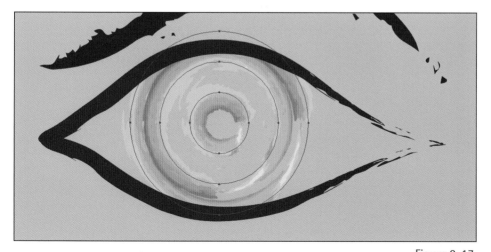

Figure 9-17.

14. *Scale and flip.* My goal is to paint the concentric circles so they eventually look like clouds sitting on top of a globe. For starters, that means that the brushstrokes need to be larger and more spread out. With the circles selected, click the ✐⇥ icon at the bottom of the Brushes panel. Raise the **Width** value to 200 percent. Then turn on the **Flip Across** check box, which moves the strokes outward as in Figure 9-18.

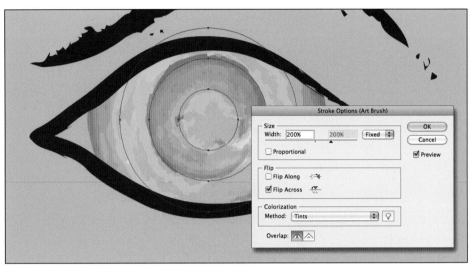

Figure 9-18.

15. *Change the Colorization Method.* Illustrator colorizes the brushstroke with the color assigned to the stroke. You can change how this colorization occurs by selecting one of four options from the Method pop-up menu:

   • The first option, *None*, applies no colorization at all, leaving the brushstroke gray in our case.

   • The default setting, *Tints*, maps the stroke color (in our case, green) to black in the brush. All other brush colors become lighter. This is great for black brushes; otherwise, you end up with wimpy effects like the current one.

   • For a heavier effect, switch to *Tints and Shades*. Black and white in the brush remain unchanged, medium gray changes to the stroke color, and other shades darken and lighten. This is usually the best setting for nonblack brushes.

   • The final option, *Hue Shift*, swaps a key color in the brush for the stroke color and changes all other colors relative to that shift. You can change the key color when creating or editing the brush. Hue Shift is best suited to brushes that include color in them, which none of ours do.

Set the **Method** option to **Tints and Shades** to produce the richer effect pictured in Figure 9-19. Then click the **OK** button.

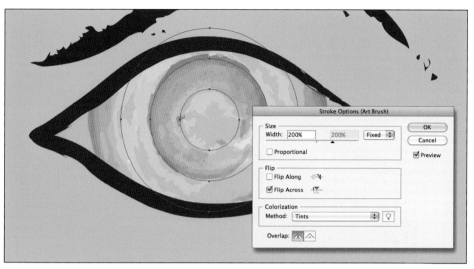

Figure 9-19.

16. *Stroke the individual pattern transitions.* The Watercolor Stroke brush comprises nearly 100 independent paths, filled with varying shades of gray. I imagine if we were to stroke each and every one of these paths, we could create something resembling borders between the clouds and land masses below them.

Bring up the **Appearance** panel. Click the first icon at the bottom of the panel, ◻, or press Ctrl+Alt+⬚ (⌘-Option-⬚ on the Mac), to add a new stroke to the entire group. The stroke should come in as black; if not, make it so. Reduce the **Stroke** weight value at the top of the Appearance panel to 0.5 point. The result, with polar-style cloud and land interactions, appears in Figure 9-20.

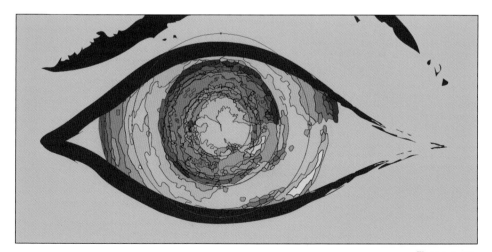

Figure 9-20.

17. ***Establish a series of terraced fills.*** Now to create the bodies of water below the land and cloud forms. Scroll down to the bottom of the **Layers** panel. Alt-click (or Option-click) on the ▶ triangle in front of the Hypno group to expand all groups and paths inside it. Click on the circular meatball for the bottom-most green swirling path to select it, then Shift-click the fill icon in the control panel and dial in 100 for the **C** value followed by 0 for **M**, **Y**, and **K**. The circle of sea blue appears in Figure 9-21.

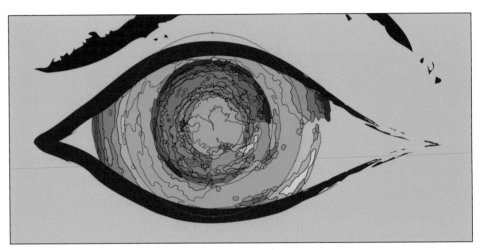

Figure 9-21.

But that's just the starting point. We need to fill the other two circles and add a fourth, as follows:

- Again in the Layers panel, meatball the next path up in the group, and change its fill color to **C**: 100, **M**: 50, **Y**: 0, **K**: 0.

- Meatball the topmost of the three circles (each called <**Path**>) and change its fill to white. Figure 9-22 shows the progress so far.

Figure 9-22.

- Once again, meatball the bottom circle, the one that's now filled with 100 percent Cyan. Press the S key to switch to the scale tool. Begin dragging outward and press and hold Shift and Alt (Shift and Option on the Mac) to create a new circle that's another increment larger than the others, so that the perimeter of the circle touches the far edges of the Watercolor Stroke paths, as demonstrated in Figure 9-23.

- Press Ctrl+Shift+-⬚ (⌘-Shift-⬚) to move the new circle back in the stacking order, so it doesn't cover up it parent.

- The new circle brings with it more watercolor clouds, which do not add to the effect. So in the **Appearance** panel, click the 👁 in front of the green **Stroke** item to turn off the Watercolor Stroke brush.

- Change the fill for the new circle to 50 percent Cyan and nothing else.

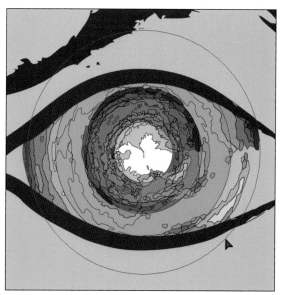

Figure 9-23.

Press Ctrl+Shift+A (⌘-Shift-A) to deselect the circle. If your final eye matches the one in Figure 9-24, you performed the steps flawlessly.

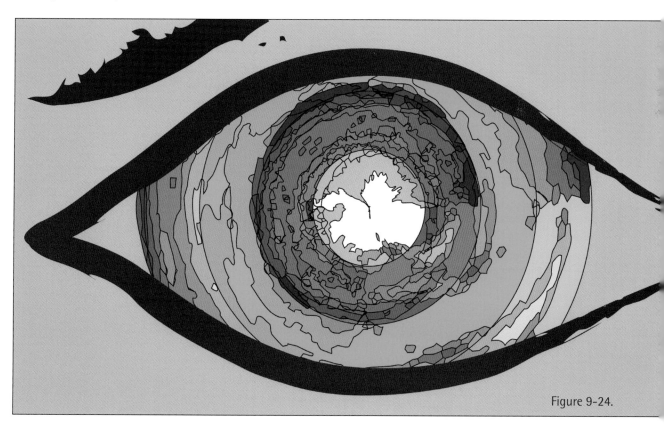

Figure 9-24.

So far, we've managed to transform a few ordinary paths into some extraordinary design elements. And we've done so using predefined brushes that at some point in time shipped with Illustrator. Think of it: A polar grid and a watercolor-type brush are nothing more than found elements, and yet they combine to form an artificial world set inside an eye. Imagine the creative freedom you might gain by designing your own custom brush, just as you will in the next steps.

18. *Select the gray path above the artwork.* Press the V key to return to the black arrow tool. Then scroll to the area of pasteboard above the illustration and click on the gray path. As shown in the enlarged Figure 9-25, the path includes lots of seemingly random details. Although I drew it with the pen tool (along with the pencil and a few Pathfinder operations), the path doesn't subscribe to any of the rules for drawing smooth vector outlines. The path exhibits rough corners, vacillating segments, and even clumsy transitions, all of which work well when applied as an organic brushstroke, which is after all chaotic.

Figure 9-25.

19. *Turn the path into an art brush.* Make sure the **Brushes** panel is open. Drag the selected path and drop it into the Brushes panel. Illustrator displays the **New Brush** dialog box, which asks what kind of brush you want to create. (Notice that the Calligraphic Brush and Bristle Brush choices are dimmed, because those brushes rely on numerical settings as opposed to a base object.) Select **Art Brush**, as in Figure 9-26, and click **OK**.

Figure 9-26.

20. *Name the brush and confirm its settings.* Illustrator next displays the **Art Brush Options** dialog box, which lets you name the brush and establish some basic behavioral settings. Name the brush "Everlasting Brushstroker," in reference to its long trail. (When applied to a path, the brush appears to last a good deal longer than any real brush would.) Here's how the other options work, and how to set them:

- **Width** defines the thickness of the brush relative to the stroke weight. But it's most useful to folks who own an art tablet. If you do, then choose Pressure and adjust the two width values to establish a range. (Setting the first value to 50 percent and the second to 200 percent usually works well.) For purposes of this exercise, skip this option.

- The three **Brush Scale Options** control how the brush sizes to fit the path. There is almost no chance you'll want to select the first option, which makes a brush huge along a long path and tiny along a short one. The final option (new to Illustrator CS5) lets you define an area that will scale independently of one that remains fixed. (Drag the dotted boundaries to adjust.) For most work, and for the purposes of this exercise, leave this option set to **Stretch to Fit Stroke Length**, as by default.

- The **Direction** options let you change the direction in which the brush follows the path. By default, the brush travels against the path, which is typically just what you want. In other words, the point at which the path begins is the point at which the brush begins. Unless you have a reason to change this setting, don't.

- Ignore the **Flip** options. You can always address them after you apply a brush by clicking the ✐ icon at the bottom of the Brushes panel (as we have twice thus far).

- Next comes **Colorization**. Because this is a gray path, select **Tints and Shades** to infuse the gray with color. The Key Color tool works exclusively with Hue Shift, so you can give it the slip. (If you needed to use it—with a colorful brush, for example—you would click on a color in the brush preview inside the dialog box. From then on, the clicked color will "shift" to the stroke color.)

- New to Illustrator CS5, the **Overlap** option reconciles the appearance of the brush at acute corners in a path. Normally, I recommend that you leave this option set to ⌃, as by default. But for the sake of demonstration, I'd like you to select the first icon, ⌃, pictured with its tool tip in Figure 9-27. This will help you to appreciate the difference between the two settings, as I'll demonstrate shortly.

Once the options appear as shown in Figure 9-27, click the **OK** button to create your new brush.

21. *Apply the new brush to the remaining paths.* Below the eye and above the word *Eyeliner* are four paths stroked with blue and brown. Select these using the black arrow tool. (Or, in the **Layers** panel, you can meatball the top four paths in the **Horus** layer.)

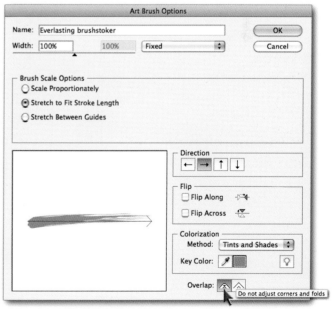

Figure 9-27.

Next, click the new Everlasting Brushstroker brush at the bottom of the **Brushes** panel. The four brushed paths with their long trails of thick paint appear in Figure 9-28.

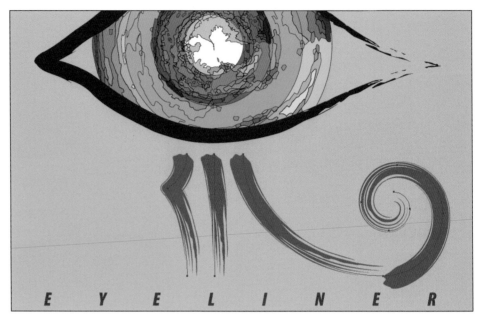

Figure 9-28.

22. *Join the two right-hand paths.* Unlike uniform strokes, an art brush makes plain where one path ends and another begins. So it's obvious that the blue spiral on the right side of the illustration is actually two paths. Let's fix that.

Select just the two right-hand paths under the eye. (Or if you prefer, deselect the leftmost blue path and the brown path.) Then choose **Object**→**Path**→**Join** or press Ctrl+J (⌘-J on the Mac) to fuse the endpoints and join what were formerly two open paths into one. The result is a continuous, spiraling brushstroke, as in Figure 9-29. The upshot is that anything you can do to paths before assigning a brush, you can do afterward, and the brush will update automatically.

Figure 9-29.

23. *Adjust the settings for the custom-brush paths.* The brush-strokes are slightly too thick, and the colors are lighter than the original stroke colors. Select the three paths below the eye by marqueeing partially around them with the black arrow tool. Then click the ✐⇄ icon at the bottom of the **Brushes** panel to adjust the settings, as follows:

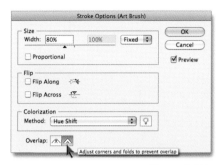

- Reduce the **Width** value to 80 percent to slim the strokes.

- With **Colorization** set to Tints and Shades, Illustrator merges the brightness of the brush with the color of the stroke. If you'd rather merely replace the gray of the brush with the original stroke colors—which I'm now thinking will look better—change this option to **Hue Shift**. Assuming the Preview check box is on, you'll see the colors deepen in the background illustration.

- This next one's subtle: See the corner in the left-hand, elbow-like path? The outside of the elbow is rounded (in keeping with the round join that I originally assigned to the stroke). Inside the elbow you can see tiny gaps, and a bit of brush-stroke overlaps itself. Now switch the **Overlap** option from ⟋⟍ to ⟋⟍, as in Figure 9-30. Illustrator retraces the corner, making the outside of the elbow pointy and eliminating the overlap on the inside. Figure 9-31 highlights the areas of difference in yellow.

Click **OK** to accept your changes.

Figure 9-30.

24. *Expand the brushstrokes.* Like transparency, brushes are one of those items that have been known to cause occasional problems with PostScript printers. If that concerns you at all, here's how to expand the brushstrokes and express them as conventional filled paths:

- In the **Layers** panel, twirl closed the Horus layer. Then drag the layer onto the ⊡ icon at the bottom of the panel. Illustrator duplicates the layer.

- Click the 👁 in front of the original **Horus** layer to turn it off. Now your brushed paths are safe in case you want to edit them in the future.

Figure 9-31.

- Double-click the **Horus Copy** layer. Rename the layer "Expanded Paths," change the **Color** setting to **Green**, and click **OK**.

- To select all the visible brushed paths in the illustration, choose **Select→Object→Brush Strokes**. (The hidden brush-strokes on the Horus layer are protected.)

- Choose **Object→Expand Appearance**. Illustrator converts the selected brushstrokes to path outlines, as well as the stroke colors to fills.

25. *Save your changes.* No sense in going to all that effort without saving your work. Press Ctrl+Shift+A (or ⌘-Shift-A) to deselect the artwork. Then press Ctrl+Shift+S (⌘-Shift-S) to bring up the **Save As** dialog box. Name the new file as desired—I called mine *Horus expanded.ai*, also found in the *Lesson 09* folder—and click the **Save** button.

Figure 9-32 shows the final illustration. Despite its simplicity—just four brushes and nine brushed paths—the effect is bold, verging on overwrought. Who wouldn't want to BitTorrent this single?

Figure 9-32.

# Expressing Text as an Art Brush

Adobe characterizes art brushes and the other brush styles as painting tools. I prefer to think of them as a means of distorting artwork to fit a path. And if that's not enough, you can bring to bear pressure and width information, which are options elsewhere unavailable inside Illustrator (not to mention, ones that I very much envy when working in Photoshop and other graphics programs).

Once you begin thinking of brushes as distortion tools, it frees you from imagining a brush to be simply a brush. Granted, an art brush can resemble a traditional brushstroke. As illustrated in Figure 9-33, however, it may also be a crude scribble, an ornate arrow, a woodcut banner, the silhouette of an aquatic mammal, or a consistently spaced and regularly oriented passage of type.

An art brush is actually a graphic—that is, anything you can draw—traced along a path. The trick is to start with a graphic rendered along a linear horizon. (For example, I drew the original humpback whale from Figure 9-33 with its mouth and tail along a more or less even keel, as in Figure 9-34.) When expressed as an art brush, the graphic blossoms into a living, squirming, breathing element of your design. The path is the vertebra, the brush is the vertebrate. Or put more simply: The brush flexes along the path's infinitely flexible spine.

In this exercise, we'll experiment with one of the most powerful kinds of art brush: a line of type (the final example in Figure 9-33) or what I term the "text brush." We'll see many incarnations of text brushes, learn how to exploit the Hue Shift option's Key Color setting, and even compare the text brush to Illustrator's type-along-a-path feature (see the sidebar "Path Type versus the Text Brush" on page 300).

Figure 9-33.

1. ***Open a document with editable type.*** Open the file *Brush type.ai* found in the *Lesson 09* folder. (If you get a font warning, click whatever button you have to open the file.) The document features three repetitions of the words *Brush Type*, the first of which is a line of live type. The

Figure 9-34.

Figure 9-35.

two lower examples represent steps in the process of creating the text brush. I've left a blank space for you to work, labeled as such in Figure 9-35.

2. *Duplicate the top line of type.* With the black arrow tool, click the first occurrence of the words *Brush Type* to select them. Then press the Enter or Return key to display the **Move** dialog box. Set the **Horizontal** value to 0 point, the **Vertical** value to 111 points, and click the **Copy** button. Illustrator adds a new line of type that exactly fills in the gap.

3. *Convert the type to path outlines.* The Brushes panel can't accommodate editable type. So convert the type to static path outlines by choosing **Type→Create Outlines** or by pressing Ctrl+Shift+O (⌘-Shift-O). Happily, Illustrator retains the black drop shadow effect. Press Ctrl+Shift+A (⌘-Shift-A) to deselect the paths.

4. *Extract an original of the Macworld Brush.* Open the **Brushes** panel by choosing **Window→Brushes** or pressing the F5 key. Then do the following:

   • Hover your cursor over the gray brush above the ones that read *Brush Type* and *Circus Arts*. You should see a hint that reads Macworld Brush, in deference to the fact that I first created this brush a few eons ago for *Macworld* magazine.

   • Drag the Macworld Brush from the panel and drop it between the words *Brush* and *Type* in the new line of outlined type.

Avoid dropping the brush onto a letter, or Illustrator will stroke the letter with the brush. If all goes right, you should see a small brush between the words, as in Figure 9-36.

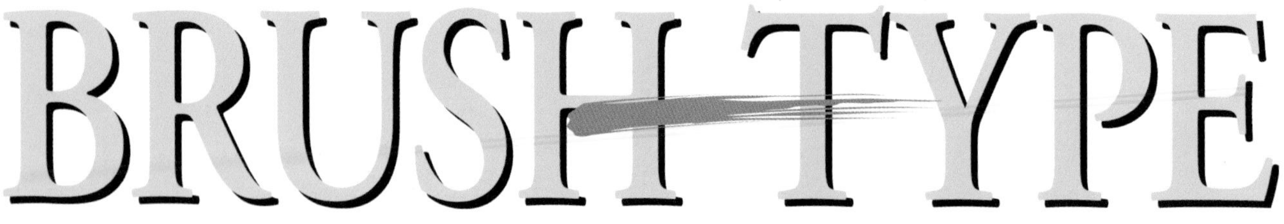

BRUSH TYPE

Figure 9-36.

5. *Remove the brush from its group.* The extracted brush is part of a group that includes a bounding rectangle, one of Illustrator's closely held conventions. We don't

need it. In fact, it's a menace. The following bullets explain how to remove it, all from within the **Layers** panel:

- Click the ▶ triangle in front of the topmost **<Group>** to twirl it open. The group contains two <Path> items, the gray brush and the bounding box.

- Drag the top **<Path>** ( ) up and out of <Group>, so it rests just above the <Group> item.

- Meatball the **<Group>**, and press the Backspace or Delete key to get rid of it, as diagrammed in Figure 9-37.

- Double-click the top **<Path>** item ( ), rename it "Macworld Brush," and click the **OK** button.

The brush is now an independently and unencumbered path outline, with which you can do anything you want.

6. *Scale, rotate, and move the brush to fit the text.* Meatball the Macworld Brush item in the Layers panel. Then choose **Window→Transform** or press Shift+F8 to bring up the **Transform** panel and apply these modifications:

- Confirm that the top-right W and H options are linked, so the chain looks like 🔗. Change either the **W** or **H** value to "400%" (be sure to enter the % character), and press Enter or Return. The brush grows to four times its previous size.

- Click the △ icon in the bottom-left area of the panel and change the value to −2.5 degrees. Press Enter or Return. Illustrator rotates the brush a few seconds clockwise, so that the path is more or less on a horizontal keel.

- Now to move the brush so it aligns to the type. Assuming that the center point is active in the top-left reference point matrix (as in ▦), click the **X** to select its value and change it to 399. Then press the Tab key to advance to the **Y** value and change it to 236.

Assuming all the values worked out according to plan, the brush should align to the letters as shown in Figure 9-38.

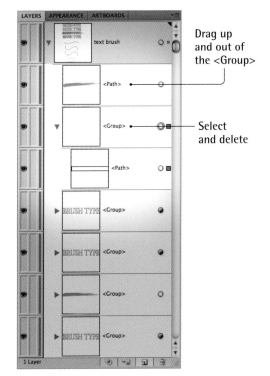

Figure 9-37.

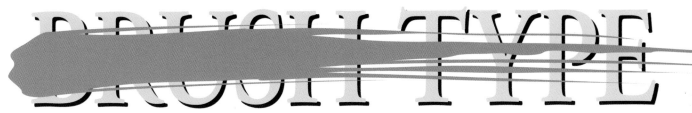

Figure 9-38.

7. *Copy the type to the Clipboard.* Your next task is to mask the brush inside the letters. Because each letter is an independent path, however, any masking technique will result in the letters attempting to clip each other. The solution is to ungroup the letters and combine them into a single compound path. That's easily done, but the black drop shadow is attached, not to the individual letters, but to the group as a whole. Which means the second you ungroup the letters, you'll lose the shadow. To preserve both the letters and their shadows, make sure the type outlines are still selected and choose **Edit**→**Copy** or press Ctrl+C (⌘-C). Now you can retrieve them at a moment's notice.

8. *Ungroup the letters.* In converting the type to path outlines (Step 3), Illustrator thought it was doing you a kindness by grouping the letters together. It was wrong; the group is in your way. So choose **Object**→**Ungroup** or press Ctrl+Shift+G (⌘-Shift-G) to dispense with it. As predicted in the previous step—and pictured in Figure 9-39—the drop shadow disappears. But with the text safe in the Clipboard, you have nothing to worry about. (As long as you don't go copying anything else!)

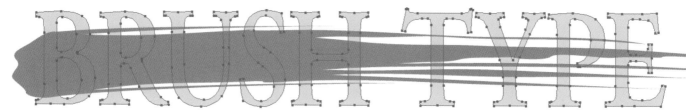

Figure 9-39.

9. *Combine the letters into a compound path.* To convert the letters into one big path, choose **Object**→**Compound Path**→**Make** or press Ctrl+8 (⌘-8). Now Illustrator regards the letters as a single, cohesive path outline, which you can use to clip the gray brush.

---

For those who may find themselves repeating this exercise in the future: You can skip Step 8 with only a slight change in behavior. The act of converting the letters into a compound path (Step 9) automatically ungroups the letters. But in doing so, Illustrator not only deletes the drop shadow, it also deletes the fill. Just FYI.

---

10. *Apply the Intersect operation.* Anyone who read Lesson 7 (as I trust *you* did) might reasonably expect that you should now mask the brush with the letters using a clipping mask. Problem is, brushes don't support clipping masks—such is often the way with Illustrator—so we must instead resort to a static Pathfinder operation.

Here's what I'd like you to do:

- With the black arrow tool, Shift-click on the outline of the gray brush in the document window to select it. (Or Shift-meatball the Macworld Brush item in the Layers panel.)

- Choose **Window**→**Pathfinder** or press Ctrl+Shift+F9 (⌘-Shift-F9) to bring up the **Pathfinder** panel.

- Click the third icon on the top row, 回, to clip the gray brush inside the letters. Illustrator preserves just the intersection of the letters and the brush, as pictured in Figure 9-40.

Figure 9-40.

11. ***Paste the letters in back of the brush fragments.*** It's time to retrieve the Clipboard that you captured in Step 7. Choose **Edit**→**Paste in Back** or press Ctrl+B (⌘-B) to paste the letters in back of the path fragments, as appears in Figure 9-41.

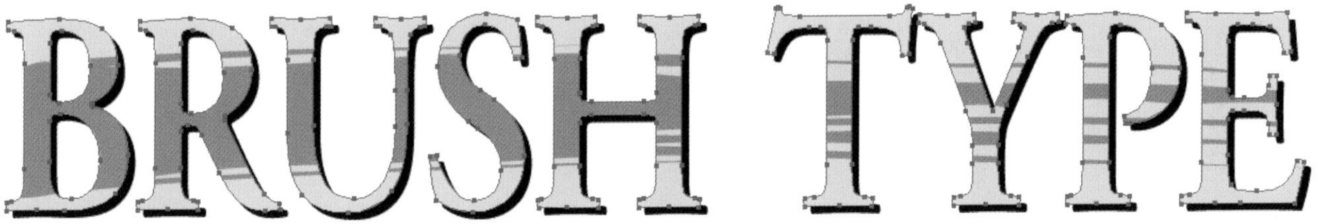

Figure 9-41.

12. ***Turn the letters and fragments into an art brush.*** Select both the fragments and the letters with the black arrow tool. (Alternatively, you can meatball the two <Group> items at the top of the Layers panel.) Then drag the selected objects and drop them into the **Brushes** panel. Then do like so:

- In response to the **New Brush** dialog box, select the **Art Brush** option and click **OK**.

- Next comes the **Art Brush Options** dialog box. This document happens to already contain a text brush called Brush Type. To distinguish yours, name it "Striped Type."

- Most of the other options are fine as is. The one exception: Among the **Colorization** settings in the bottom-right corner of the dialog box, change **Method** to **Tints and Shades**.

- Click the **OK** button. Illustrator adds the new art brush to the Brushes panel.

13. ***Apply the text brush to the first path.*** Scroll down to the red-stroked paths below the type treatments. Select the first path outline and click the new Striped Type brush in the Brushes panel. Illustrator applies the text to the path and distorts its letterforms to fit the contours. (To compare this to the behavior of path type, which does not distort, see the sidebar "Path Type versus the Text Brush" on page 300).

14. ***Reduce the path's line weight.*** The text looks great with one problem: The letters are too tall. Change the **Stroke** value on the left side of the control panel to 0.7 point to size the letters so they appear more proportional, as in Figure 9-42.

Figure 9-42.

15. ***Apply the text brush to the second path.*** Select the next path down with the black arrow tool. As a change of pace, click the item that reads ——— **Basic** in the control panel, then choose the Striped Type brush from the pop-up panel.

16. ***Flip and scale the brushstroke.*** The text comes in upside-down (see Figure 9-43), indicating that I must have drawn the path from right to left. To account for this, click the ✐ icon at the bottom of the **Brushes** panel. In the **Stroke Options (Art Brush)** dialog box, turn on both the **Flip Along** and **Flip Across** check boxes. Reduce the **Width** value to 70 percent. And purely for the sake of variety, change the **Colorization Method** to **Hue**

Figure 9-43.

**Shift**. Then click the **OK** button. The resulting effect appears in the hard-to-miss Figure 9-44. It may not be the world's most elegant type treatment, but it demonstrates the extremes to which you can go without sacrificing spacing or legibility. And in the figure's defense, there's no denying it catches the eye.

Figure 9-44.

17. ***Apply the Circus Arts brush to the third path.*** Select the third and final red path outline. Click —— **Basic** in the control panel, and choose the Circus Arts brush from the ensuing pop-up panel. These letters not only include drop shadows, but they have masked spots as well, as witnessed in Figure 9-45. You may occasionally lament the fact that you can't edit the text, but there are clearly advantages to working with text expressed as a graphic.

Figure 9-45.

18. ***Flip and scale the brushstroke.*** Again, the text is upside-down, so click the ✐⇥ icon at the bottom of the **Brushes** panel. Reduce the **Width** value to 80 percent and turn on both the **Flip Along** and **Flip Across** check boxes. And again change the **Colorization**

**Method** to **Hue Shift**. The Hue Shift method is designed to change the key color to the stroke color. But whereas the stroke is red, Illustrator makes the text a dull blue, as in Figure 9-46. Problem: Hue Shift can be unpredictable when combined with an art brush that was originally designed to work with a different method. Solution: I'll show you in a future step. In the meantime, I was getting tired of the red and the blue comes as a welcome departure. Click **OK** to accept the effect.

Figure 9-46.

19. ***Apply the text brush to the blue paths.*** Select the two blue-stroked paths at the bottom of the artboard, then click on the Striped Type brush in the **Brushes** panel. Illustrator applies the text to both paths at once (see Figure 9-47), which is yet another trick that you can't match using type-along-a-path.

20. ***Flip the brushstrokes.*** I want to adjust the direction of the text brushes so one looks like a crude reflection of the other:

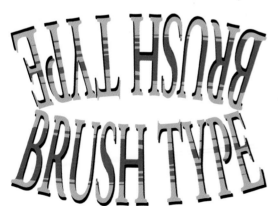

Figure 9-47.

- With both paths still selected, click the ✐⇆ at the bottom of the Brushes panel. Then turn on the **Flip Across** check box, set the **Colorization Method** to **Hue Shift**, and click **OK**.

- Shift-click the bottom path with the black arrow tool to deselect it. Then click the ✐⇆ icon again. Turn on the **Flip Along** check box, and click **OK**.

Now the top line of text reads properly and the bottom line serves as its roughly executed reflection. (Don't worry, we'll make it look better a few steps from now.)

Next, I want to see the middle of the text bend inward, so that it appears to decline slightly into the distance. Naturally, I also want to duplicate this effect in the bottom "reflection" text. Which means adding a width point with the new CS5 width tool and saving a custom width profile that I can apply to other paths.

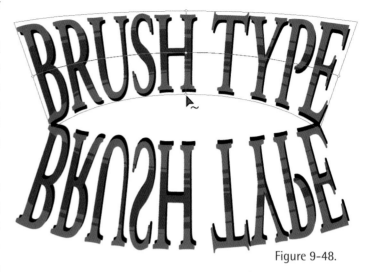

Figure 9-48.

21. ***Bend in the center of the top line of text.*** Press Shift+W to switch to the width tool. Then drag from the center of the top path outline to pinch the text inward, as demonstrated in Figure 9-48.

22. ***Save your changes as a width profile.*** In the control panel, click the blank option between Stroke and BRUSH TYPE. Then click the floppy disk icon (💾) in the bottom-left corner of the pop-up panel. Name the profile "Bowtie," and click **OK**. Now you can apply this same collection of width tool settings to other paths.

23. ***Apply the width profile to the bottom text.*** Press the V key to switch back to the black arrow tool. Select the bottom line of text by marqueeing around where the path outline ought to be. Click in that control panel option between Stroke and BRUSH TYPE, and choose the new Bowtie profile from the bottom of the list.

For a more credible effect, reduce the **Stroke** value for both paths to 0.6 point. Reduce the **Opacity** value for the bottom text to 25 percent, and nudge the text up so that it comes close to but does not touch the top text, as in Figure 9-49.

Figure 9-49.

# Path Type versus the Text Brush

Your first question when expressing text as an art brush—or what I'll call a "text brush"—has to be, why? After all, the very act of making a text brush demands a handful of compromises. You have to convert the text from editable letters to comparably dormant path outlines. You can't change the font or other formatting attributes. And the brush is ultimately a static object, meaning that there's no direct link to a dynamic collection of paths.

---

That said, you can update an existing brush: Drag a collection of selected paths and press the Alt (or Option) key as you drop them onto that brush in the Brushes panel.

---

Meanwhile, there is an alternative: Illustrator's path type feature—which lets you assign type directly to a path outline—offers everything a text brush lacks. You can edit the type, change the formatting, and apply other stylistic modifications at a moment's notice.

But while path type is undeniably more flexible, what ultimately counts is the final product. Getting decent results out of path type takes work; getting great results out of a text brush is easy. Let me explain why:

As throughout the "Expressing Text as an Art Brush" exercise (which began on page 291), I'm working with the original version of *Brush type.ai* found in the *Lesson 09* folder. To create a line of path type, select the *Brush Type* text at the top of the artboard with the black arrow tool and choose **Edit→Copy** Ctrl+C (⌘-C). Then scroll down and select the first red path outline. Press the T key to switch to the type tool. Click on the leftmost point in the selected path to invoke Illustrator's type-on-a-path function. Choose **Edit→Paste** or press Ctrl+V (⌘-V) to paste the copied text onto the path. The word *Brush* appears in the middle of the path, as below.

Already you have a sense for the frustrations associated with this feature. The text is too large to fit the confines of the path, the alignment is off, and we lost the drop shadow.

To address these problems, press the Esc key to return to the black arrow tool with the path type still selected. Reduce the type size value (the third Character option) in the control panel from 120 to 90 points. The text is centered, but because of the shape of the path, Illustrator indents the characters too far to the right. To truly center the text, drag the bracket line to the right of *Type* slightly to the left, as demonstrated below.

To restore the drop shadow, choose **Effect→Stylize→Drop Shadow** or, if you loaded dekeKeys, press the shortcut Ctrl+Alt+E (⌘-Option-E). Change the **Opacity** value to 100 percent, **X Offset** and **Y Offset** to 3 points apiece, and the Blur value to 0. Click **OK** to achieve the effect below.

One problem remains: If you look closely, you'll notice that the word *Brush* appears a bit cramped in the concave portion of the path, while *Type* splays slightly along the convex portion. You can even out the spacing by increasing the tracking of *Brush* and reducing the tracking of *Type*, which may in turn necessitate adjusting the type size.

Spacing becomes a more significant problem when you align text to a more radically curving path. Select the next red path outline. Press the T key to switch to the type tool and click on the first endpoint in the path. Because I drew this path from right to left (recall Step 16 on page 296), the blinking insertion marker appears at the opposite end. Assuming the *Brush Type* text is still in the Clipboard, press Ctrl+V (⌘-V) to paste it along the path, upside-down, as below.

Press the Esc key to escape the text-entry mode and return to the black arrow tool. See that long line that extends between the *B* and the *R*? This *midpoint bracket* lets you move text (when there's room to do so) and flip it to the other side of the path. Drag the bracket up to flip the text so it's right-side-up, as demonstrated below.

Now to adjust the alignment and spacing. Choose **Type→Type on a Path→Type on a Path Options**. In the ensuing dialog box, turn on the **Preview** check box. Then switch the **Align to Path** setting from Baseline to **Center**, which shifts the characters down so that the path runs through their centers. The word *Brush* is bunching up like crazy, and *Type* spreads so much that you could fit another character between the *T* and the *Y*. To compensate for the valleys and swells in the path, change the **Spacing** value to 14 points. As witnessed below, the effect is by no means perfect, and I encourage you to experiment with other adjustments, including changing the Effect setting. But the truth is, this is about as good as we can do with this path and this text. So click the **OK** button.

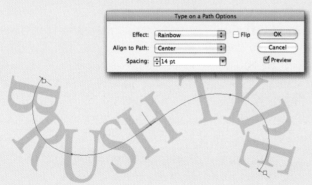

Again, we're missing the drop shadow. Choose **Effect→Stylize→ Drop Shadow** or press the dekeKeys shortcut Ctrl+Alt+E (⌘-Option-E). Illustrator should remember the last settings

you applied (100, 3, 3, and 0). Once you have them in place, click **OK**. The final effect, pictured below, is not only of questionable merit, but it took a lot of effort to create.

Now let's see how much better and easier things would have been if we employed a text brush. Select the third and final red path. Bring up the **Brushes** panel and click on the Brush Type brush that I created for you in advance. Just like that, Illustrator aligns the letters to the path, centers them vertically, sizes them to fit, preserves legible spacing, and keeps the drop shadow, as shown below.

The text is upside-down, so click the ⬿ icon at the bottom of the Brushes panel. In the **Stroke Options (Art Brush)** dialog box, turn on both the **Flip Along** and **Flip Across** check boxes. Reduce the **Width** value to 85 percent. Set the **Colorization Method** to **Tints and Shades**, and click **OK** to accept the adjusted brush settings.

I then chose **Object→Expand Appearance** to bust up the effect into static path outlines. And I stroked and recolored the letters, as below. Granted, I can't edit the text, but it's a better effect in exchange for far less work. You be the judge.

24. *Hide the second line of brushed text.* In the remaining steps, I'll show you how to make predictable use of Hue Shift, which—although mired by a clumsy interface—is a very useful option. (Plus, when used properly, it invokes respect and admiration from fellow designers because no one knows how to use the damn thing.) We'll need room to work, room that's taken up by other effects, so clear some space:

   • Scroll up to the dark red line of *Brush Type*, immediately above the blue *Circus Arts*.

   • Select the path and choose **Object→Hide→Selection** or press Ctrl+3 (⌘-3) to hide it.

   That path was a throwaway effect. But you spent time on it, so you should have the option to bring it back later.

25. *Apply the colorful Art Brush to the first path.* Now select the very first line of red *Brush Type*. In the **Brushes** panel, click the multicolored word *ART*, called Art Brush, to replace it. Then increase the **Stroke** value in the control panel to 3 points to scale the letters to the proportions pictured in Figure 9-50.

Figure 9-50.

Figure 9-51.

26. *Investigate how Hue Shift works.* First, take a look at the brush preview in the Brushes panel. The letters *A*, *R*, and *T* appear purple, orange, and green, respectively, as in Figure 9-51. And yet when applied to a red path, the *A* turns blue, the *R* red, and the *T* olive, as in Figure 9-50. To figure out why this is, make sure the path is still selected and click the ✐⇌ icon at the bottom of the Brushes panel. In the **Stroke Options (Art Brush)** dialog box, notice that the Colorization Method is set to Hue Shift. Which must mean that something in the Art Brush is "shifting" to red. That's got to be the *R*, because it changed from orange to red. So you might extrapolate that the *A* and *T* "shifted" by the same amount. And you'd be exactly right.

Unfortunately, you have no way to modify how this setting is applied. That's because Hue Shift cannot be altered on-the-fly. It's a function of the brush itself.

So much as I hate to tell you to do this, click the **Cancel** button. This dialog box has nothing to offer. We must search elsewhere.

27. *Edit the Art brush.* Still in the Brushes panel, double-click on the multicolored Art Brush item to display the **Art Brush Options** dialog box. Turn your attention to the Colorization box in the bottom-right corner. Notice Key Color followed by an 🖊 icon and an orange swatch. The 🖊 lets you select a new hue-shifting color; the swatch shows you the hue-shifting color that's in force. None of which quite makes sense, I realize. Which is why I want you to do the following:

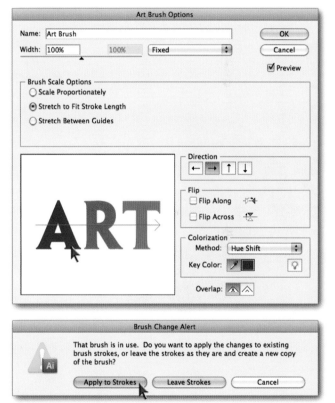

Figure 9-52.

- Click the 🖊 icon to select the tool. The orange swatch, incidentally, is not clickable—stupid, in my humble opinion, but true.

- Move your cursor inside the preview area of the dialog box. (The tool doesn't work outside the dialog box, just inside.) The cursor should be a 🖊 so you know that it's your method for selecting a new key color that will shift to red. But instead, more stupidness, it's a generic ⬉.

- Inside the dialog box preview, click on the purple *A*. As demonstrated in Figure 9-52, the Key Color swatch changes to purple—hooray!

- Unfortunately, even though the Preview check box is on, the illustration in the larger document window remains dormant. Illustrator does not let you preview the effects of two options in the Art Brush Options dialog box: Direction and Hue Shift. You must commit to the change to see it occur. The stupidness rages on unabated, and we are but it's hapless victims. So click **OK**.

- Illustrator displays one of those horrible alert messages that makes you want to close your eyes and click the nearest button. This time it's asking you the equivalent of "Would you like to change the selected art?" Which is reasonable, and to which the obvious answer is Yes. But there is no Yes button. So click the first button, **Apply to Strokes** (again, see Figure 9-52), *which is not highlighted by default.* (Did I mention I have some issues with this feature?)

Okay, so obviously, whoever designed this interface has long since found some other line of employment—but the result is almost worth the effort! The once purple *A* is now red, and the amber *R* and teal *T* have shifted accordingly, as in Figure 9-53.

Key color

Figure 9-53.

---

**PEARL OF WISDOM**

*Hue* is the essential ingredient in color. For example, the hue for brown is orange, because darkening orange and lowering its intensity gives you brown. You can map hues onto a circle, from red through orange, yellow, green, blue, purple, and back to red, as in **Figure 9-54**. The Hue Shift option rotates the colors around that circle. So in rotating the purple *A* to red—a slight shift in the land of hues—Illustrator must also rotate the reddish orange *R* to a yellower color and the green *T* to a bluer color. Figure 9-54 shows the starting hues for our letters as black lines and the ending hues as white lines; the arrows diagram the shifts.

---

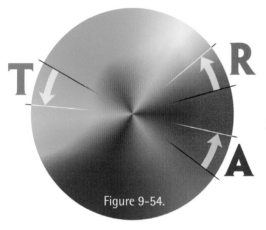

Figure 9-54.

28. ***Do it again.*** Again in the Brushes panel, double-click the many-colored *ART* brush to display the **Art Brush Options** dialog box. Click the ✐ icon next to **Key Color**, then click on the green *T* in the dialog box preview to make the key color green. Next click the **OK** button. When the alert message appears, click **Apply to Strokes**. Illustrator changes the *T* to red and shifts the *A* and *R* to their analogous colors, as in Figure 9-55.

Key color

Figure 9-55.

29. *Fix the Circus Arts brush.* Okay, so let's imagine that by now you understand the basic underpinnings of the Hue Shift option. You might still wonder: Why did the application of Hue Shift to the Circus Arts brush (which happened on page 298) turn a gray brush assigned to a red path blue? That makes no sense, no matter how you split it.

The original sin lies in the fact that the Circus Arts brush was never assigned a key color. When no key color exists, Illustrator ascribes its own bizarre logic.

I can't defend the logic—who knows what's going on in the deeper recesses of this sprawling program's id?—but I can tell you how to fix things:

- Press Ctrl+Shift+A (or ⌘-Shift-A) to deselect the artwork. Otherwise, you'll end up applying Circus Arts to the top path outline.

- In the **Brushes** panel, double-click the Circus Arts brush to display the **Art Brush Options** dialog box.

- Click the ✐ icon next to **Key Color** and then click on a gray portion of the Circus Arts text in the dialog box preview. Illustrator updates the document window, making the brushstroke in question red and upside-down.

- Change the **Colorization Method** to **Hue Shift**. Now the text becomes blue again. Which is wrong, by the way.

- Reduce the **Width** value to 80 percent. Illustrator scales the brush in the document window.

- Click the ⬅ among the **Direction** icons. Illustrator fails to update the preview.

- Click the **OK** button. Then click **Apply to Strokes**. Illustrator finally updates the brushstroke to its proper red and upright appearance, as in Figure 9-56.

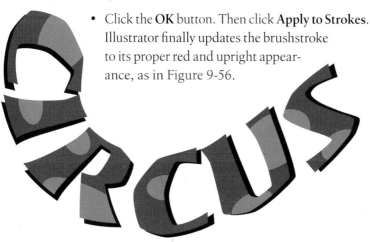

Figure 9-56.

This time, the finished piece isn't really a piece of artwork—more like a rambling collection of disassociated effects. But I guarantee you, you now know more about art brushes and advanced methods for creating type-along-a-path than anyone on your block. My hope is that this knowledge will serve you well when you need to twist and distort all manners of objects in the future.

## Replicating, Updating, and Replacing Symbols

Now we shift from the topic of brushes to that other method for repeating and updating art in Illustrator: symbols. Whereas Illustrator presents brushes as creative features, symbols are a means of efficiency and automation through and through. Take the detail from a map of Yellowstone National Park, featured in Figure 9-57. (This file ships with Illustrator. To find it, search for *Yellowstone Map.ai* on the hard disk that contains the Illustrator CS5 application.) This small detail contains nine repetitions of a picnic table icon, 🛦, with many others strewn elsewhere inside the map, all of which are instances of a central symbol. This means I can change the symbol's fill to green, massage the placement of the table's top and benches, and update all instances in one operation, as indicated by the nine updated (and circled) picnic icons in Figure 9-58.

Figure 9-57.

Figure 9-58.

Details courtesy of U.S. National Park Service staff at the NPS Harper's Ferry Center

The act of creating a symbol is as easy as selecting a piece of artwork and dragging it into the Symbols panel. Which is why I devote this exercise to tasks that are more likely to cause you confusion, that is, replicating, updating, and replacing symbols. Along the way, you'll get a sense of how symbols work and what kinds of benefits they provide.

1. *Open an illustration that contains symbols.* Open the file named *264 symbols.ai* in the *Lesson 09* folder. It features an instance of a single symbol, called Florid Strokes, which appears in Figure 9-59. But if you choose **Window→Symbols** or press Ctrl+Shift+F11 (⌘-Shift-F11),

then you'll see a total of 264 symbols, starting with the six included with a new Print document (both in CS5 and CS4), the eighteen included with a new Web document (again in CS5 and CS4), and moving on to those included with other kinds of documents, and a few excerpts of the most interesting symbol libraries, whether from this or a previous version of Illustrator. It's a kind of one-stop department store for all your symbol needs.

Figure 9-59.

2. *Delete the current occupant of the artboard.* The Florid Strokes instance is attractive to look at, but it's merely a placeholder so that your graphic doesn't look empty if you should preview it from the Bridge. We won't be using it in this project. So press Ctrl+A (or ⌘-A) to select all the artwork, and press the Backspace (or Delete) key to get rid of it.

3. *Place an instance of the Tiki Idol symbol.* Click the Tiki Idol symbol in the Symbols panel. (If you can't find it, see the next page.) Click the ▾≡ icon in the top-right corner of the panel and choose **Place Symbol Instance** to place an instance in the exact center of the artboard. Or drag the symbol from the panel and drop it into the artboard, as in Figure 9-60.

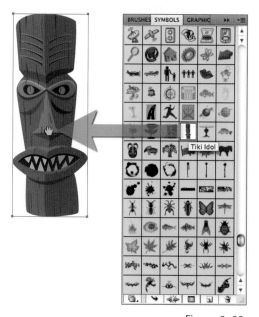

Figure 9-60.

If you're having problems locating the Tiki Idol—does it help that it's the 75th-to-last symbol, located between Fireplace and Table?—here's a strange trick that you may find useful:

---

Drag and drop *any* symbol into the artboard. Then go up to the control panel and click the **Replace** icon (just before Opacity) to bring up a pop-up version of the Symbols panel. Press Ctrl+Alt (or ⌘-Option) and click in the pop-up panel to lock it into focus—a trick that works with Swatches, Brushes, and other library-style panels as well. Type T-I-K to select the first symbol that begins with those letters, which is Tiki Idol. Press Enter or Return to replace the previous symbol with the new one.

---

On the PC, you can Ctrl+Alt-click in the Symbols panel and type T-I-K to find the Tiki Idol. Which saves a step. But the above trick offers the advantage of working on either platform.

4. ***Align the symbol to the center of the artboard.*** If you chose the Place Symbol Instance command in Step 3, you can skip this step. If you dragged and dropped the symbol, then do like so:

- Go to the control panel, and click the ⬚ icon to the right of the Opacity value. Then choose **Align to Artboard**, so the ⬚ icon changes to ▣.

- Click the ≜ and ▯ icons to the right of ▣ to align the selected symbol to the center of the artboard.

5. ***Move the symbol up 200 points.*** Double-click the black arrow icon in the toolbox. Or, assuming the black arrow is active, press Enter or Return. Either way, you get the **Move** dialog box. Make sure that the **Preview** check box is on. Then enter a **Horizontal** value of 0 and a **Vertical** value of –200 points. Watch that the tiki symbol moves up in the artboard and click the **OK** button.

6. ***Add a drop shadow.*** Purely for aesthetic reasons, choose **Effect→Stylize→Drop Shadow**. In the **Drop Shadow** dialog box, change the **Opacity** value to 75 percent. Set **X Offset** and **Y Offset**, and **Blur** to 3 points apiece, and click **OK**.

7. ***Rotate a copy of the tiki symbol.*** Press the R key to select the rotate tool. Then press the Alt (or Option) key and click the center of the artboard, as indicated by the intersection of the two guidelines. (If you can't see the guides, press Ctrl+⬚ or ⌘-⬚ to display them.) In the **Rotate** dialog box, enter an **Angle** value of 45 degrees and click the **Copy** button. Illustrator creates a second, angled tiki a little more than a half inch from the first, as in Figure 9-61.

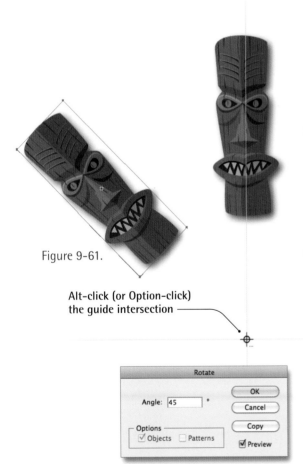

Figure 9-61.

Alt-click (or Option-click)
the guide intersection

8. **Repeat the last transformation six times.** Choose **Object→Transform→Transform Again** or press Ctrl+D (⌘-D) a total of six times in a row to create a circle of tiki masks.

9. **Select the first tiki and scale it by 200 percent.** Press the Ctrl (or ⌘) key and click the top tiki symbol to select it. Then press the S key to switch to the scale tool. Alt-click (or Option-click) at the intersection of the top of the symbol and the vertical guideline. In the **Scale** dialog box, change first **Scale** value (under Uniform) to 200 percent and click **OK**. The central tiki grows into a gigantic alpha-tiki, as depicted in Trader Vic's splendor in Figure 9-62. All that's missing is the Mai Tais.

Figure 9-62.

10. **Break the link with the large tiki symbol.** The actual Tiki is a kind of Adam of Oceanic Maori mythology. (You know the Maori—those warriors who sport facial tattoos and show their tongues.) One time, for example, the lonely Tiki saw his reflection in a pool and became convinced that he had discovered a mate. When the reflection broke, he flew into a rage, covered the pool with mud, and—through sheer force of will—gave birth to the world's first woman. Compare this to the comparatively bland tiki that most of us know. Like the fellow in the symbol, he's slightly dreadful, I suppose, what with his unflinching gaze and razor-sharp teeth. But you might just as easily describe him as glassy-eyed and slack-jawed, the Polynesian equivalent of a drunk uncle at a summertime barbecue. Wouldn't he be so much more authentic if he were plainly aggressive, confidently amorous, and perhaps a little bit red-in-the-face?

Which is why I propose that we edit the symbol. There are two ways to do this: One is to double-click the symbol, either in the Symbols panel or on the artboard. The problem is, this obvious solution requires you to modify your artwork either entirely or largely out of context, in

Figure 9-63.

one of Illustrator's isolation modes. The other is to break the link between the symbol and the art, edit the artwork in context, and update the symbol when you're done.

We'll be taking advantage of the second technique. Press the V key to switch back to the black arrow tool. Click on the large tiki symbol in the artboard to select it. Then at the bottom of the **Symbols** panel, click the icon (the third icon in) to break the link. Illustrator expands the symbol into a sublayer of more than 100 independent paths, as in Figure 9-63. (In the figure, I hid the guides by again pressing Ctrl+⊡ or ⌘-⊡.)

11. ***Apply an envelope-style distortion.*** You could edit this swarm of paths manually, using a combination of the white arrow and pen tools, but that would be insane. Better to manipulate the new sublayer as a group using another of Illustrator's amazing distortion functions, *envelope mesh*, which lets you bend and twist selected objects inside a custom grid.

With the paths still selected, choose **Object→Envelope Distort→Make with Mesh** or press Ctrl+Alt+M (⌘-Option-M). In the **Envelope Mesh** dialog box, set the number of **Rows** to 6 and the **Columns** to 3. Turn on the **Preview** check box so that you can see Illustrator divide the tiki art into a matrix of evenly spaced distortion points, as in Figure 9-64.

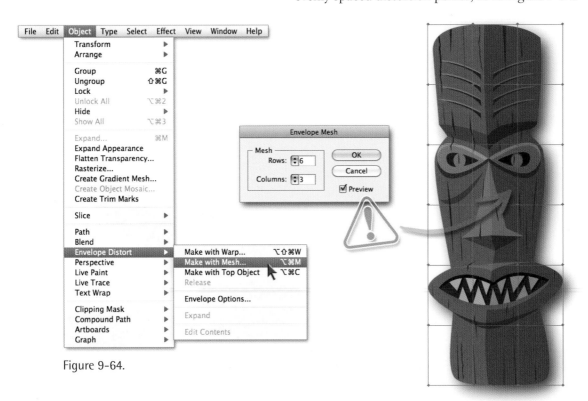

Figure 9-64.

Click the **OK** button to apply the envelope mesh.

12. *Bring the enveloped tiki to the front.* To make the large tiki as easily accessible as possible, choose **Object→Arrange→Bring to Front** or press Ctrl+Shift+⬚ (⌘-Shift-⬚). I also suggest you double-click the top Tiki Idol sublayer in the **Layers** panel and change the **Color** setting from the default Red to something that provides better contrast with the reds and oranges of the wood. (I went with Black because it shows up well in print.)

13. *Slant the eyes and mouth upward.* Switch to the white arrow tool. Then select and reposition the anchor points in Rows 3, 5, and 6 of the envelope mesh, identified by arrows in Figure 9-65. In almost all cases, you'll want to move the points upward, the exception being the two central points at the base of the mouth in Row 6 (those you should nudge down). You'll also need to adjust the control handles to smooth out the transitions. Figure 9-65 shows the final position of my anchor points and control handles, which result is a more animated Tiki.

14. *Expand the contents of the envelope.* True to its name, the envelope mesh acts as a container, anything inside of which is now distorted. To regain access to the path outlines, you have to expand the envelope. To do so, switch to the black arrow tool, click on the object, and choose the command **Object→Expand Appearance**, which renders the distorted tiki to the usual assortment of readily available path outlines.

15. *Make any additional adjustments.* That sliver of a red path under the right eye is still bugging me. The problem is that it comprises two smooth points: the control handles for which overlap each other. Here's how to make things right:

    - Press Shift+C to select the convert point tool.

    - Drag down on the left anchor point and up on the right one to summon the control handles. The path becomes a roundish blob, as in Figure 9-66.

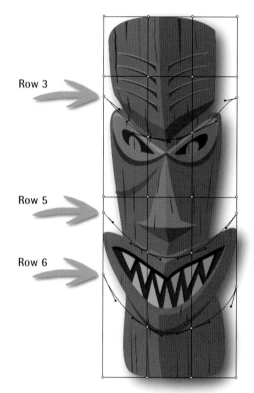

Row 3

Row 5

Row 6

Figure 9-65.

Figure 9-66.

Figure 9-67.

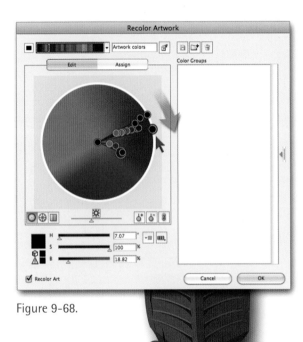

Figure 9-68.

- Drag the top control handles on either side down and inward, to turn the blob into a crescent, as in Figure 9-67.

16. *Select the large, expanded tiki.* Press the V key to get the black arrow tool and click anywhere in the artwork to select it. Notice that the points and handles appear inside a big rectangle. Just so you know, that rectangle represents the drop shadow from Step 6 (page 308), which Illustrator has rendered out as a pixel-based image.

17. *Recolor the artwork.* Now to make Tiki red in the face. Press Ctrl+H (⌘-H) to hide the selection edges. Then choose **Edit→Edit Colors→Recolor Artwork** to display the **Recolor Artwork** dialog box, part of Illustrator's powerful "live color" feature, about which you'll learn more in Lesson 11. Then do the following:

   - Click the **Edit** tab in the top-left corner of the dialog box to modify one or more colors in the tiki mask using a color wheel like the one illustrated back in Figure 9-54 (page 304).

   - To change the colors in the tiki, confirm that the **Recolor Art** check box is turned on in the bottom-left corner of the dialog box.

   - Click the 👁 icon below and to the right of the color wheel to link all the tikis' colors together so you can edit them in one operation.

   - Click the top-right, deep-red color circle in the larger color wheel. To make sure we're on the same page, check that the **H** value (for Hue) at the bottom of the dialog box reads 21.25 degrees.

   - Drag that circle clockwise a few degrees, until the H value shrinks to about 7 degrees. (I got it to 7.07 degrees.) The tiki mask changes to a crimson red, as in Figure 9-68.

   - Click **OK** to recolor the artwork.

18. *Update the Tiki Idol symbol.* Now to update the prefab dead-expression Tiki Idol symbol with the new, more villainous one. Press Ctrl+H (⌘-H) to again see the selection edges. Locate the Tiki Idol item in the **Symbols** panel. Then drag the selection into the panel, press the Alt (or Option) key, and drop it onto the Tiki Idol symbol.

Illustrator turns the upright tiki into an instance—so the symbol definition exists in just one location—and replaces the other instances with the big red one. Because you scaled the central tiki in Step 9 (page 309), the instances grow very large. The result is a kind of Maori sharkfest, as in Figure 9-69.

Figure 9-69.

19. *Reverse the selection.* Assuming that we don't want the other tikis to be this enormous, some scaling is in order. First, select the too-massive symbols by choosing **Select→Inverse**. If you loaded dekeKeys, you also have the keyboard shortcut Ctrl+Shift+I (or ⌘-Shift-I).

20. *Scale the tikis to half their current size.* You need to scale the symbols with respect to independent origin points. So choose **Object→Transform→Transform Each** or press Ctrl+Shift+Alt+D (⌘-Shift-Option-D). In the **Transform Each** dialog box:

- Confirm that the **Preview** check box is on.

- To scale each symbol from its center, click in the middle of the reference point matrix (above Preview), so it looks like ⠿.

- Set both the **Horizontal** and **Vertical** values in the **Scale** area to 50 percent. The other values should be 0.

- The options should look like those in Figure 9-70. If they do, click the **OK** button.

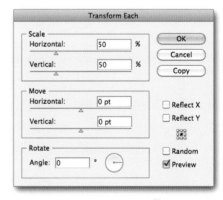

Figure 9-70.

Illustrator scales the lesser tikis to their previous sizes, as pictured in Figure 9-71.

Figure 9-71.

If I were you, I'd be thinking, "Who knew brushes and symbols were such a deep topic that every exercise in the lesson would require an Extra Credit?" Or perhaps I'm just projecting because I'm thinking that very thing myself. But while I think you have a reasonable sense of what you can do with symbols—they're not exactly rocket science, after all—you haven't seen one of the most important functions, how to replace a bunch of instances with a different symbol. Good news for those feeling symbol fatigue: This particular Extra Credit is just nine steps long.

21. *Select a different symbol.* With the outlying instances still selected, scroll to the bottom of the **Symbols** panel and click on the item called Regal Vector Pack 16. This symbol features the silhouette of a bipedal lion, as illustrated by the last of the

Regal Vector Pack symbols in Figure 9-72. By itself, selecting a symbol does not replace the selected instances in the artboard, but it identifies the symbol that you want to work with.

Figure 9-72.

22. *Choose the Replace Symbol command.* Click the ▾▆ icon in the top-right corner of the Symbols panel, and choose the second command in the second set, **Replace Symbol**. (I'm being so specific because I don't want you to select the second command in the *first* set, Redefine Symbol, which does exactly the opposite of what we want.) Illustrator replaces the selected totems with the lion silhouettes. The original lion symbol is quite large—about twice as big as the one featured in Figure 9-72—so the instances appear generously proportioned, despite having been scaled to half size in Step 20.

23. *Remove the drop shadows.* The tikis used to have two drop shadows—one that was part of the updated symbol definition and another attached to the instances—which suited the artificial sculpting of the totems just fine. But even a single drop shadow doesn't suit the lions. So go to the **Appearance** panel and click the 👁 icon in front of **Drop Shadow** to turn off the shadows, thus leaving the lions shadowless as in Figure 9-73.

24. *Copy the instances and paste them in back.* In your Symbols panel wanderings, you may have noticed the eagle silhouette among the Regal Vector Pack artwork (labeled 09 in Figure 9-72). I was sorely tempted to use it, but after some deliberation, I decided to go with the lion adorned in what I considered to be the boldest of the wings (14 in the figure).

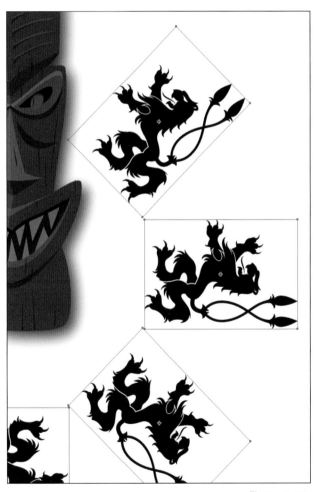

Figure 9-73.

To pull this off, choose **Edit**→**Copy** or press Ctrl+C (⌘-C). Then choose **Paste in Back** or press Ctrl+B (⌘-B). Although your artwork won't look any different, this step results in a collection of selected instances that stand ready to receive another symbol. (Be careful where you click, by the way. You don't want to deselect your artwork at this point!)

25. *Select an alternate symbol from the control panel.* Here's another way to replace one or more selected instances with a different symbol: Go up to the control panel and click the pop-up menu to the right of the word **Replace**. Expand the panel and scroll to the bottom of the symbols list. Then select the wing art called Regal Vector Pack 14. Illustrator replaces the background lions immediately.

26. *Assign a red fill to the wings.* The black lions are altogether unreadable against the black wings. So let's make the wings red. Click the second icon, □, at the bottom of the **Appearance** panel or press Ctrl+⃞ (⌘-⃞) to add a new fill. Then click the **Fill** swatch in the panel to bring up a list of swatches. Select the second red swatch, Ruby, to fill the wings with red.

27. *Scale the wings by 150 percent.* The wings need to be much larger and scooted out a bit. I found a combination of two resizing operations worked best. First, choose **Object**→**Transform**→**Transform Each** or press Ctrl+Shift+Alt+D (⌘-Shift-Option-D). In the **Transform Each** dialog box, change the two **Scale** values to 150 percent. Make sure the matrix is set to ⊞ and click **OK**.

28. *Scale them again by 120 percent.* Now to move the wings outward slightly. Press the S key to switch to the scale tool. Press Ctrl+⃞ (⌘-⃞) to bring back the guidelines. Then press the Alt (or Option) key and click at the intersection of the guides. In the **Scale** dialog box, change the **Uniform Scale** value to 120 percent and click the **OK** button.

29. *Move the central tiki.* Our last step is to center the great and powerful Tiki in his new princely environment. Press the V key to switch to the black arrow tool and click on the tiki to select it. Press the Enter or Return key to display the **Move** dialog box. Change the **Horizontal** value to 4 points and the **Vertical** one to 42, and then click **OK**. The final artwork appears in Figure 9-74.

30. *Save your changes.* Choose **File**→**Save As**. Navigate to the *Lesson 09* folder, name your illustration "Tiki with lions.ai," and click the **Save** button. For reference, I called my file *The regal Tiki.ai*.

If nothing else—and there's more, as you'll see—symbols are great convenience tools. What other feature let's you change your mind and your artwork with such ease? Plus, there's something to be said for throwing together an illustration, however trivial, using someone else's drawings.

Figure 9-74.

## Using the Symbolism Tools

In addition to how they facilitate the replication and transformation of predefined artwork, the tie that binds brushes and symbols is painting. Just as you can paint with brushes (as I demonstrated in Video Lesson 9, "Freehand Painting"), you can likewise paint with symbols. The symbol sprayer tool lets you lay down whole populations of instances. Seven more alliterative tools—each begins with "symbol" and ends with another S word—let you edit these populations. Illustrator calls these tools the *symbolism tools*.

1. ***Open my updated version of the artwork.*** Although it was not my intention, Figure 9-74 suggests that our original man Tiki may have aligned himself with some new breed of dogmatic radicalism, which history has taught us is a Very Bad Thing. Fortunately, Tiki has since grown in his philosophy. To see how, go to the *Lesson 09* folder and open the file called *Green Tiki with fire lions.ai*. As pictured in Figure 9-75, Tiki retains the same alliances. But in deference to his Oceanic roots, he's gone green.

Figure 9-75.

2. ***Inspect the Layers panel.*** The **Layers** panel houses a single layer called Life. Click the ▶ in front of the Life layer to twirl it open. At the very top—above the wings and lions instances and the tiki group—is a <Clipping Path> item. Filled with a light-to-dark radial gradient, this square path masks the contents of the entire layer. It will likewise mask the symbols that you paint in the following steps.

3. *Select the symbol sprayer tool in the toolbox.* Click the symbol sprayer tool (see Figure 9-76) or press Shift+S. Your cursor will change to a big, circular brush with a spray can in the middle.

4. *Select a symbol.* Before you can paint with the symbol sprayer, you have to select a symbol. Scroll to the bottom of the **Symbols** panel and select the second-to-last item, Grass 1, which looks like 〰.

Figure 9-76.

---

PEARL OF WISDOM

---

Grass 1 is another of Adobe's predefined symbols. But it isn't included with Illustrator; it comes to us from Photoshop. Like Illustrator, Photoshop ships with a slew of predefined graphics. But Photoshop calls them *custom shapes*. As an added bonus, I've gone ahead and converted an extensive collection of these shapes to symbols. To load them into any open illustration, click the 🖾 icon in the bottom-left corner of the Symbols panel and choose the Other Library command. Navigate to the *Lesson 09* folder and open the file called *Photoshop shapes.ai*. Then click on the symbols you want to use to add it to your illustration. Alternatively, you can open the *Photoshop shapes.ai* document and use that file as a jumping-off point. As shown in Figure 9-77, the artboard sports sixteen instances. (The leaf above the crown is a Japanese maple, in case you thought otherwise.) But take a look at the Symbols panel and you'll see that the document contains 210 symbols in all.

Figure 9-77.

5. *Paint with the symbol sprayer.* Drag inside the artboard to paint with the Grass 1 symbol. As you drag, Illustrator coats the illustration with a series of gray grass blades. Keep painting until you get an effect similar to the one in Figure 9-78.

Figure 9-78.

As I write this, Illustrator CS5's symbol sprayer suffers from some severe performance problems. After laying down 40 or 50 symbols, the sprayers slows to a crawl. My hope is that Adobe will address the problem in a bug release, which may be available by the time you read this. But if it happens to you, try this: Release the mouse button, and press Ctrl+Z (or ⌘-Z on the Mac) to undo what you've done. Still armed with the symbol sprayer, paint from one corner of the artboard to the other and release. You should see a big bounding box Now paint to fill in the gaps. Whenever the tool slows—which may happen after a second or two—release the mouse button. Then paint another short stroke, and another. Each time, Illustrator will add your newest brushstroke to the existing symbol set. There is no perfect grass pattern, so don't worry if yours ends up looking a bit sparse.

Whether you paint one long brushstroke or 25 short ones, Illustrator pushes the old grass blades out of the way to make room for the new ones. It's as if you're growing a garden of grass symbols as you paint.

---

No matter how you paint, gaps will naturally form between your blades of grass. This is not a golf course! In other words, don't get too obsessed with filling in the gaps. You can always relocate your grass blades later, as I'll explain in a few steps.

---

6. *Send the symbol set to the back.* Take a look at the **Layers** panel and notice that you've created a new item called Symbol Set. A *symbol set* is a collection of instances that you can grow, shrink, and otherwise edit with the symbolism tools. But it shouldn't be in front of the totem head and the other instances. So right-click in the artboard and choose **Arrange**→**Send to Back**. Or press the keyboard shortcut Ctrl+Shift+⬓ (⌘-Shift-⬓).

Figure 9-79.

7. *Select a different symbol.* Illustrator lets you paint as many instances into a symbol set as you like. All you have to do is select a different symbol and paint away. To try it out, again scroll to the bottom of the **Symbols** panel and select the very last item, Grass 2, which is a broad-leaf grass that looks like 🌿.

8. *Paint with the symbol sprayer.* Confirm that the **Symbol Set** remains selected in the **Layers** panel (with its meatball looking like ◎). Then paint in Grass 2 using the symbol sprayer tool. Your brushstrokes mingle the new fat blades of grass with the previous thin blades. Paint one long brushstroke if Illustrator can keep up with you; or paint many short brushstrokes if it can't. On the right, Figure 9-79 shows a detail of what I arrived at.

---

In addition to adding instances by painting inside a symbol set, you can likewise delete instances. Press the Alt (or Option) key and drag to erase instances of the selected symbol. Note that Illustrator erases only those instances of the selected symbol in the Symbols panel; other instances remain intact.

9. ***Drag out the symbolism tools panel.*** Now to modify the active symbol set. Click and hold on the symbol sprayer tool in the toolbox to display a flyout menu of eight tools. Drag to the vertical "tearoff" bar on the right side and release. Illustrator produces a micropanel of eight horizontal tools, as in Figure 9-80. Move the panel to anyplace you like. Here's how this group of eight tools work:

Figure 9-80.

- *Symbol sprayer.* This tool lays down instances as you drag and erases instances as you Alt-drag (or Option-drag). You've already seen it, so I shan't dwell.

- *Symbol shifter.* From here on out, a symbol set or instance must be selected for the tool to work. The symbol shifter tool moves instances of the active symbol in the direction of your drag. You can also move instances forward, in stacking order, by pressing the Shift key as you drag. To move them backward, press Shift+Alt (or on the Mac, Shift-Option).

Note that these various keyboard tricks work on-the-fly. So as you're pressing Shift to bring instances forward, you can add Alt (or Option) to push them back. I'm not sure how useful this trick is for the symbol shifter, but for other tools, it may prove helpful.

- *Symbol scruncher.* Drag with the symbol scruncher tool (hey, I didn't name it!) to move instances together. Press the Alt (or Option) key to move them apart.

- *Symbol sizer.* Paint with this tool to increase the size of the active instances. Press Alt (on the Mac, Option) as you drag to shrink the instances. Perhaps by now, you get the idea that Alt (or Option) reverses a tool's behavior.

- *Symbol spinner.* Except in this case. Drag with the symbol spinner to rotate instances in the direction of your drag. For once, pressing a key does nothing.

- *Symbol stainer.* Although unfortunately named, this is the best instance-alteration tool of the bunch. Drag to imbue the symbols with the active fill color. Alt-drag (or Option-drag) to make the instances more gray. There's also a curious Shift-key trick that I'll explain in a moment.

- *Symbol screener.* Obviously, someone had a field day with these tools. This one reduces the opacity of the active instances as you paint. Press the ever-present Alt (or Option) key to make translucent instances more opaque.

- *Symbol styler.* This final tool applies a style from the Graphic Styles panel to the active instances. You can also press Alt (or Option) to reduce the intensity of an active style. Or Shift to transfer the intensity of a style.

---

As you experiment with these tools, the symbol set may become deselected. If it does, reselect it by scrolling to the bottom of the Layers panel and targeting the Symbol Set item.

---

I'm tempted to lay another tip on you, but if I were you, I'd feel slightly overwhelmed by now. So I'll keep it short: If you're ever curious how one of these kooky symbolism tools works, just double-click on it. The blue info icon near the bottom of the Symbolism Tool Options dialog box, ⓘ, tells you what's going on.

10. **Paint with a random symbolism tool.** For now, grab the second one, the symbol shifter. Then paint inside the active symbol set. You'll set a zillion grass outlines with a zillion radiant lines, showing you the direction in which you're moving the instances. (I think it's those damn center-crosshairs that slow down the program. If you're frustrated by the program's performance, just know, I'm working right along with ya. Yeesh!)

11. **Paint with the symbol stainer.** As I mentioned, although I'm not a fan of its name (stain? *really?*), this is my favorite symbolism tool. Here's how I suggest you use it:

    - Go to the **Swatches** panel and select the medium shade of green, which goes by the name Mint Julep.

    - Select the symbol stainer, which looks like a paint bucket pouring water onto a carbonated doughnut.

    - Paint inside the symbol set. Good news: This tool works at a reasonable pace. Bad news: It doesn't show you what you've done until after you release the mouse button.

After a bit of painting, Illustrator colorizes the grass with Mint Julep green, as in Figure 9-81.

Figure 9-81.

Figure 9-82.

12. *Recolor just the thin grass.* Back to the **Swatches** panel, select the chartreuse swatch—two-left of Mint Julep—known as Little Sprout Green. (Who is the Adobe employee in charge of naming things?) Then switch to the **Symbols** panel, and select the second-to-last symbol, Grass 1. Now paint in the active symbol set. When you release the mouse button, Illustrator imbues the slim grass blades with the yellower hue of green.

13. *Recolor just the thick grass.* Return to the **Swatches** panel, and select the color to the left, Peridot. In the **Symbols** panel, select the final symbol, Grass 2. Paint inside the symbol set. Illustrator recolors the thick grass blades, producing an effect like the one in Figure 9-82. Moral of the story: You can control exactly which instances gets modified and which do not by isolating one or more symbols in the Symbols panel.

Here's a weird one: Press Shift while painting to change the hue of the selected instances without affecting their intensity. I find this trick to be altogether useless. But I invite you to give it a try and see what you think.

14. *Set the blend mode to Overlay.* Goodness knows, I love staining the symbols. But it only gets the job halfway done. To finish off the effect, bring up the **Transparency** panel—if you can't find it, choose **Window**→**Transparency**—click the **Normal** option, and choose the **Overlay** blend mode. The unevenly colored grass blends with the green field behind it, as in the previous page's Figure 9-83.

EXTRA ★ CREDIT

In addition to adjusting a symbol set, the symbolism tools let you modify one or more selected instances. The remaining steps explain how.

15. *Select the lion and wing instances.* We'll be editing two sets of instances, the lions and their wings. Unfortunately, while Illustrator makes it easy to select one collection of instances, it makes it much harder to select two.

Start by pressing the V key to switch to the black arrow tool. Then do the following:

- Click on the outline of one of the lion paths. Then choose **Select→Same→Symbol Instance** to select them all.

- Choose **Select→Save Selection**. Name the collection of selected objects "All Lions," and click the **OK** button.

Figure 9-83.

- Click on the outline of one of the fiery wings. And again choose **Select→Same→Symbol Instance** to select them all.

- You don't need to save this selection, but you might as well. To do so, choose **Select→Save Selection**, name the selection "Wings," and click **OK**.

- Press the Shift key and choose **Select→All Lions**.

Not only does this select all the lion and wing symbols, but it also lets you go back to the selections later just by choosing a command (that you created!) at the bottom of the Select menu.

16. *Scale the selected instances.* Go to the flyout tool panel that you made in Step 9 (page 322) and select the fourth tool, the symbol sizer. Then scale the selected instances like so:

   - In the **Symbols** panel, make sure no symbol is selected. If necessary, click in the empty gray area after the last symbol (Grass 2.)

   - Paint the selected symbols. I recommend that you click and hold (as opposed to dragging) to make the symbols larger. Press the Alt (or Option) key and click and hold to make the symbols smaller.

   For what it's worth, I made all the symbols larger.

17. *Enlarge the green totem.* Press the Ctrl (or ⌘) key to temporarily access the black arrow tool and click on the outline of the large tiki to select him. Then release the key and click and hold briefly on the totem. The main focus of your illustration will grow to a gargantuan size, as in Figure 9-84.

Admittedly, the symbolism tools are more playful than practical. But when they work, they let you lay down and modify big collections of graphics with remarkably little effort.

Figure 9-84.

# WHAT DID YOU LEARN?

Match the key concept in the numbered list below with the letter of the phrase that best describes it. Answers appear upside-down at the bottom of the page.

## Key Concepts

1. Calligraphic, scatter, art, bristle, and pattern
2. Symbols
3. Instances
4. Art brush
5. Stroke Options
6. Flip Along
7. Overlap
8. Text brush
9. Hue Shift
10. Envelope mesh
11. Replace Symbol
12. Symbol sprayer

## Descriptions

A. A means of collecting and replicating graphics—whether simple or complex—that you use on a regular basis in your artwork.

B. Click the middle icon (✎≡) at the bottom of the Brushes panel to bring up this dialog box, which lets you edit the brush settings for one or more selected path outlines.

C. This tool lets you paint an array of instances of the selected symbol in the Symbols panel.

D. Although mired by a clumsy interface, this useful option lets you rotate the colors in a brush to bring them in alignment with the stroke color assigned to a path outline.

E. This extraordinary option lets you bend and twist selected objects inside a custom grid.

F. The styles of brushes that you can create in Illustrator CS5.

G. Select this check box to change the direction of an art brush as it traverses the length of a path outline.

H. Like path type, this option lets you bend a line of type to fit a path outline, but with more predictable and better looking results.

I. Clones of a symbol that remain linked to a graphic that you establish in the Symbols panel.

J. Click the ▾≡ icon in the top-right corner of the Symbols panel and choose this command—the second one in the second set—to replace any and all selected instances with the selected symbol.

K. A way of saving one or more paths as something that you can paint with, the net result being graphics along a path.

L. Pictured as ⟋⟍ and ⟋⟍, these new options in Illustrator CS5 let you reconcile the appearance of an art brush at acute corners in a path.

## Answers

1F, 2A, 3I, 4K, 5B, 6G, 7L, 8H, 9D, 10E, 11J, 12C

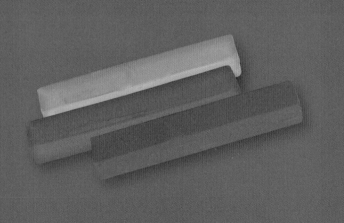
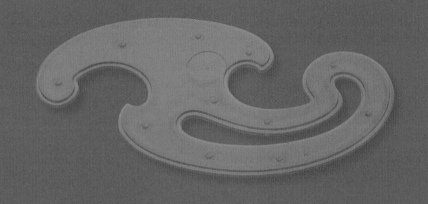
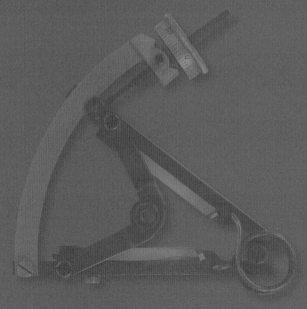

# THE AMAZING WORLD OF DYNAMIC EFFECTS

**WHEN WORKING** with vectors, most folks naturally assume that they have to draw each and every path outline exactly as it appears in the finished illustration. Granted, Pathfinder operations, blends, and other features help to limit your reliance on the pen tool. But if you want, say, flower petals or a starburst, you have to assemble them as one or more path outlines.

In fact, that's not true. Take Figure 10-1, for example. The shapes at the top of the figure are *static* path outlines. That is to say, they exist as they appear. The eight-sided polygon comprises eight anchor points and eight straight segments; the eight-pointed star comprises sixteen anchor points and sixteen straight segments. Press Ctrl+Y (or ⌘-Y) to switch to the outline mode, and you see the very same shapes, albeit without fills and strokes.

The bottom shapes in the figure are *dynamic* path outlines. Meaning that they are not what they appear and can be modified at a moment's notice. In each case, I selected the static path of the same color and chose Effect→Distort & Transform→Pucker & Bloat. The ensuing dialog box supplies a single numerical value that puckers (pinches) when negative and bloats (spreads) when positive. I bent the sides of the polygon outward and gathered in the corners by assigning a value of 100 percent; I pinched the points of the star inward with a value of −50 percent.

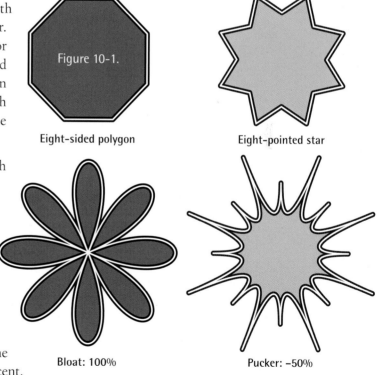

Figure 10-1.

Eight-sided polygon

Eight-pointed star

Bloat: 100%

Pucker: −50%

As with all the commands in the Effect menu, Pucker & Bloat is a *dynamic effect*. Rather than permanently changing the path outline, it leaves the base path unchanged, permitting you to restore the original path or change the settings as the occasion dictates.

# ABOUT THIS LESSON

## Project Files

Before beginning the exercises, make sure you've downloaded the lesson files from *www.oreilly.com/go/Deke-IllustratorCS5*, as directed in Step 2 on page xiv of the Preface. This should result in a folder called *Lesson Files-Alcs5 1on1* on your desktop. We'll be working with the files inside the *Lesson 10* subfolder.

Dynamic effects—whether applied from the Effect menu or the Graphic Styles panel—rank among Illustrator's most powerful and delightfully fun features. In this challenging but exciting lesson, you'll learn how to:

## Video Lesson 10: Introducing Dynamic Effects

If ever a feature needed to be shown in video (as opposed to just described in print) to reveal the true wonder, it's Dynamic Effects. In this video, I show you how to apply these effects, which are amazingly transformable, layerable, and powerful.

To see the amazing dynamic effects in motion, visit *www. oreilly.com/go/deke-IllustratorCS5*. Click the **Watch** button to view the lesson online or click the **Download** button to save it to your computer. During the video, you'll learn these shortcuts:

Video Lesson 10: Introducing Dynamic Effects

| Operation | Windows shortcut | Macintosh shortcut |
|---|---|---|
| Display the Appearance panel | Shift+F6 | Shift-F6 |
| Display the Stroke panel | Ctrl+F10 | ⌘-F10 |
| Apply the Transform effect | Ctrl+E* | ⌘-E* |
| Exactly repeat the last dynamic effect | Ctrl+Shift+E | ⌘-Shift-E |
| Repeat last effect with new settings | Ctrl+Shift+Alt+E | ⌘-Shift-Option-E |
| Send selection to the back of stack | Ctrl+Shift+□ (left bracket) | ⌘-Shift-□ (left bracket) |
| Toggle between the view modes | Ctrl+Y | ⌘-Y |
| Reset the default fill and stroke colors | Press the D key | Press the D key |
| Track selected characters apart | Ctrl+Alt+→ | ⌘-Option-→ |

* Works only if you loaded the dekeKeys keyboard shortcuts (as directed on page xviii of the Preface).

What I love about dynamic effects—also known as "live" effects—is that very few Illustrator users know they exist. And even those that do have only the sketchiest idea of how powerful and flexible they can be. My hope is that once you try them out for yourself, it won't be so much the effects that come alive as your imagination.

## The Best (and Worst) Effects

The Effect menu contains more than 120 commands, all of which produce different results, nearly half of which were designed for Photoshop (and have little practical application in Illustrator), and some of which refuse to work except under very specific conditions. In other words, they're not the friendliest bunch.

Fortunately, Illustrator does a nice job of dividing them into categories. And a few of the effects are exceedingly useful. Here's how the Effect menu (pictured in Figure 10-2, with the best submenus highlighted in red) breaks down, from most useful to least:

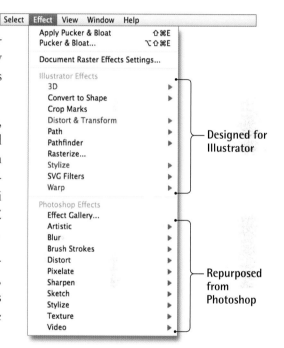

Figure 10-2.

- Effect→Distort & Transform→Transform lets you nudge, scale, rotate, and otherwise transform whole objects (or individual stroke and fill attributes) from a single dialog box. Transform is heads and shoulders the most practical of the dynamic effects, which is why—if you loaded my dekeKeys (see page xviii of the Preface)—I've assigned it a keyboard shortcut of Ctrl+E (on the Mac, ⌘-E) for *Effect*. You'll be seeing a lot of this one.

- Effect→Stylize→Drop Shadow casts a shadow behind a selected path. Many complain that drop shadows get overused, but they're overused for good reason: They help offset objects and create a sense of depth. For dekeKeys loaders, again I have a shortcut: Ctrl+Alt+E (or ⌘-Option-E).

- Most of the other commands in the Effect→Distort & Transform submenu (that is, besides Transform) twist and turn path outlines. I long ago christened these the *path wigglers*. Because that's what they do, and they're very good at it. Pucker & Bloat is just one example.

- Effect→Stylize→Scribble breaks a fill, stroke, or both into a series of back-and-forth crosshatch lines. It offers an intricate dialog box, but it's one of the best commands in all of Illustrator.

- Effect→Stylize→Round Corners smooths away the acute corners along a selected path. And brilliantly, it does so on-the-fly, so that you can make the corner more or less round at a moment's notice.

Select an imported photo,...

Figure 10-3.

add a new stroke from the Appearance panel,...

Add New Stroke

and apply Effect→Convert to Shape→Rectangle with the settings shown below.

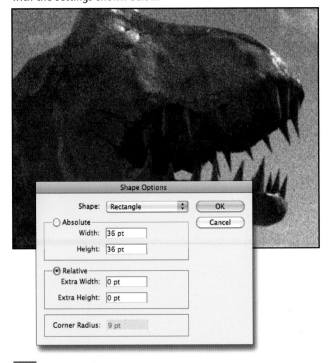

- The remaining Effect→Stylize commands (Feather, Inner Glow, Outer Glow) blur path outlines and add edge effects. If Feather doesn't give you quite the effect you're looking for, try Effect→Blur→Gaussian Blur from the Photoshop effects.

- The three commands in the Effect→3D submenu transform one or more 2D paths into a 3D illustration. Illustrator's 3D opportunities are limited, but with care you can create some eye-popping effects, as you'll learn in "Creating 3D Text and Graphics" on page 372.

- The commands in the Effect→Warp submenu let you distort text blocks and other objects without requiring you to jump through hoops when you later need to apply edits.

- Effect→Crop Marks appends dynamic crop marks to a selected path, group, or layer. It's great for business cards.

Here's an interesting one: Normally, Illustrator doesn't allow you to stroke an imported photograph. But you can force a stroke to frame a photo with the help of an effect. Select the placed image, and click the ■ icon in the bottom-left corner of the Appearance panel. Then, with the Stroke attribute highlighted, choose Effect→Convert to Shape→Rectangle. Select the Relative radio button, set the Extra Width and Extra Height values to 0, and click OK. I've taken the liberty of diagramming the entire process in the gigantic and terrifying **Figure 10-3**.

- The rest.

If that seems glib, permit me to elaborate: Although on occasion powerful, the commands in the Path and Pathfinder submenus are designed less for creative purposes and more for problem solving.

Here's an example. Start with a selected block of point text, with a slim drop shadow, as shown at the top of **Figure 10-4**. Select the text with the black arrow tool and apply a stroke from the Appearance panel. With the Stroke attribute selected, choose Effect→Path→Offset Path. Enter an Offset value and click OK to move the stroke outward. Problem is, the strokes intersect each other. To reconcile the overlaps, choose Effect→Pathfinder→Add. Figure 10-4 tells the story.

My difficulty with this technique is that you can already accomplish a similar and more flexible effect using multiple strokes, as I explain in Video Lesson 10, "Introducing Dynamic Effects" (as outlined on page 330). Only the inclusion of a drop shadow in Figure 10-4 makes this approach unique.

As for the other commands in the Effect menu, the Effect→SVG Filters are dusty relics from the waning days of the twentieth century. And the commands in the second half of the Effect menu—which begin with the dimmed words Photoshop Effects—comprise a bunch of less-than-inspiring filters from Photoshop that few professionals find uses for in *that* program. Which is why I very much doubt you'll have cause to use them in *this* one.

Red text with yellow, 2-point stroke, and black drop shadow

Select Stroke, choose Effect→Path→Offset Path, Offset: 4 point

To get your bearings—and witness the likes of Transform, Outer Glow, Warp, and the path wigglers applied to both path outlines and editable text—watch Video Lesson 10: "Introducing Dynamic Effects." Then jump into the following exercises to gain hands-on experience with the best commands in the Effect menu. Along the way, you'll learn how to manage effects from the Appearance panel, heap multiple dynamic effects on top of each other, and save a set of effects in the Graphic Styles panel. This may be my favorite lesson in the book. I think you'll have a lot of fun with it, too.

Choose Effect→Pathfinder→Add

Figure 10-4.

## Applying and Editing Graphic Styles

If you watched the video (and if you haven't, you should), you know that the standard dynamic effect workflow involves assigning an effect from the Effect menu and editing it from the Appearance panel. But when you're first learning how they work, you can more simply and rapidly apply and adjust effects from the Graphic Styles panel.

Figure 10-5.

A *graphic style* is a collection of effects and other Appearance attributes that you can apply, mix, edit, and ultimately save as a new graphic style. And in the course of editing a graphic style, you can see how the effects are put together as well as gain insights and inspiration for your own techniques. Here's how graphic styles work:

1. *Open a file that contains some graphic styles.* Every new document you make contains a handful of predefined styles,  but I've made one for you that contains a bunch. Go to the *Lesson 10* subfolder in the *Lesson Files-AIcs5 1on1* folder, and open the file called *Napkin art.ai*. The document, which looks nothing like a napkin so far (see Figure 10-5), contains just three objects: a brown circle, a bluish circle cut out of a square, and some green point text. (A fourth object, a jack-o'-lantern face, awaits you on a hidden layer.)

2. *Bring up the Graphics Styles panel.* Choose **Window→Graphic Styles** or press Shift+F5 to bring up the **Graphic Styles** panel, which contains a total of 36 style thumbnails, all of which are saved with this document.

---

Normally, I don't advocate you memorize shortcuts for showing and hiding panels, because they're neither intuitive nor particularly helpful. But this one's different. Shift+F5 brings up Graphic Styles; Shift+F6 brings up Appearance. Fittingly, the two panels work hand-in-hand, as we'll see.

---

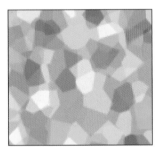
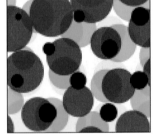

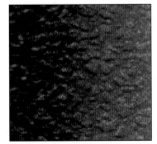
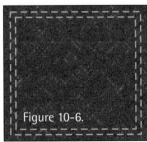
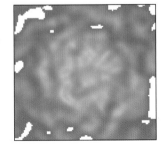

Figure 10-6.

3. *Apply a few styles to the outermost shape.* Use the black arrow tool to select the bluish shape, a compound path in which a circle clips a hole in a square. Then apply a graphic style. Feel free to click on any style thumbnail (except the first three, which I'll explain later); if you don't like it, try another one.

In particular, I'd like you to try out the styles in the third row (assuming that the Graphic Styles panel is scaled to six thumbnails wide). All are the results of multiple fills and strokes combined with pixel-based commands from the Photoshop Effects area. Pictured sequentially in Figure 10-6, these styles look great on screen, but they appear jagged in print.

As I alluded to earlier, you can increase the resolution of these effects. Choose Effect→Document Raster Effects Settings, select High (300 ppi) from the Resolution options, and click OK. But there are three problems with this solution. First, Illustrator is not terribly efficient at handling pixels so you can expect lots of delays and progress bars, commensurate with the quantity and complexity of the effects applied. Second, the fill patterns shrink so that effects such as RGB Brick and RGB Rust become tiny indeed, as in **Figure 10-7**. Some of the effects can be scaled to account for the dramatic increase in resolution, but most cannot. And third, resolution is a document-wide setting. As a result, *all* pixel effects are affected—including effects such as drop shadows and blurs that don't benefit from high resolutions—resulting in teeth-gnashing delays in effects-heavy illustrations.

Which is why my preferred solution—and the solution I'll employ for the rest of this lesson—is to steer clear of the Photoshop Effects.

4. *Apply the Back Rough style.* After experimenting with a few more styles—apply as many as you like, they won't hurt a thing—click the fourth-to-last thumbnail, called Back Rough. Illustrator applies a series of fill, strokes, and dynamic effects that result in three groups of overlapping scribble patterns inside a series of roughly-hewn outlines, a detail of which appears in Figure 10-8.

**Tissue Paper Collage**

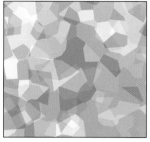

**Color Halftone**

**RGB Brick**

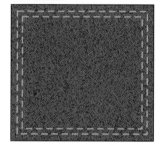

**RGB Rust**

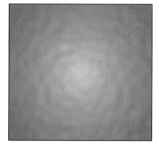

**RGB Denim**

**Ocean Basin**

Figure 10-7.

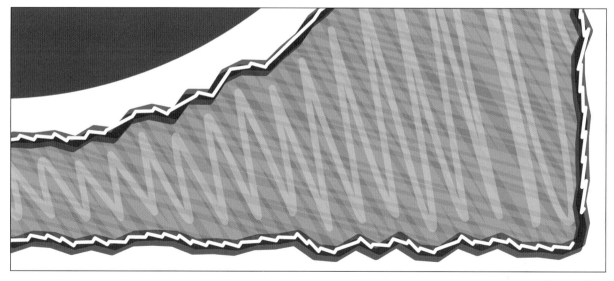

Figure 10-8.

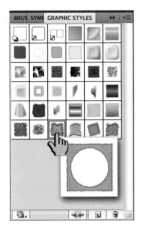

Figure 10-9.

The Graphic Styles panel lets you preview a style on the selected object. Under Windows, right-click on a style thumbnail to see a meaty 100-by-100-pixel preview, as in **Figure 10-9**. (On the Mac, right-clicking doesn't work. You have to press the Control key and click.)

5. *Examine the applied style.* To find out how a style is put together, choose **Window→Appearance** or press Shift+F6 (just one function key up from the Graphic Styles shortcut) to bring up the **Appearance** panel. Initially, you should see a list of three strokes and four fills, sandwiched between two dynamic effects, Roughen at the top and Opacity at the bottom, as in Figure 10-10. This means that Roughen and Opacity affect the entire selected object, as opposed to a single stroke or fill attribute.

The Roughen item is followed by an *fx* icon, which tells you that it's an editable dynamic effect. If you have an interest, click on the underlined Roughen link to bring up its settings, which you can edit by adjusting the dialog box settings (be sure to turn on the Preview check box so you can see what you're doing) and apply by clicking the **OK** button.

Figure 10-10.

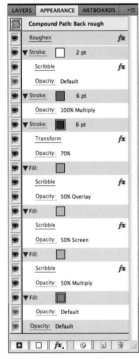

Figure 10-11.

PEARL OF WISDOM

Opacity is not followed by an *fx* icon, but it is ultimately a dynamic effect. (I don't intend to confuse: Opacity is not available from the Effect menu, nor is it a central subject of this lesson, given that I already covered it in Lesson 8, "Working with Transparency." But Opacity is altogether dynamic—you can change your mind any time you like.) Click the Opacity link to bring up a pop-up version of the Transparency panel. Modify the settings as desired. Your changes will affect all fills and strokes associated with the selected object.

The three strokes and four fills are prefaced by ▶ triangles; click a ▶ to reveal any dynamic effect associated with that specific attribute. (I know I'm laying a lot on you; hang in there, it will all make sense in the end.) Figure 10-11 shows how the stroke and fill attributes look when all seven are twirled open. Note that each and every attribute includes an Opacity link. If it reads Opacity: Default, nothing special is going on. Meanwhile, fully five of the attributes harbor an *fx* link—four Scribble and one Transform. Again, these are dynamic effects. Click the link to bring up a dialog box of options.

Much of the magic of this style hinges on the Scribble effect. I don't elaborate on Scribble in this lesson, but here's the skinny: When working in the Scribble dialog box, the first option, Angle, determines the angle of the crosshatched lines. The Path Overlap value permits Illustrator to scribble inside (negative) or outside (positive) the path outline. Within the Line Options, Stroke Width determines the thickness of the scribble lines. Curviness defines how a scribble line bends back on itself; Spacing controls the distance between one scribble line and the next. The three Variation values add random variations to the scribble lines. Turn on the Preview check box and experiment if you have a mind to play.

The upshot is that you can apply dynamic effects to an entire object (as in the case of Roughen) or to specific fill and stroke attributes (as with Scribble). And no matter how nuts you go, you can save the entire collection—fills, strokes, and effects—as a graphic style, as I'll explain shortly.

6. *Apply the Parchment style to the inner circle.* Still armed with the black arrow tool, click the central circle in the document window to select it. Return to the **Graphic Styles** panel and—again assuming six thumbnails per row—click on the fourth style in the second row, which is called Parchment. Illustrator colors the shape yellow and assigns a ragged, dark outline, as pictured in the magnified Figure 10-12.

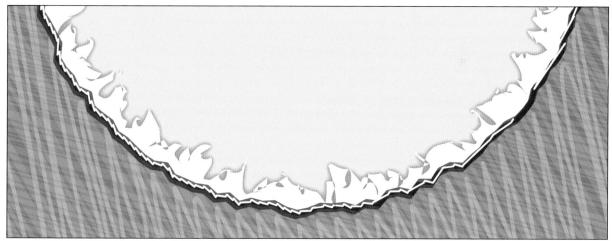

Figure 10-12.

7. *Riff off the Parchment style.* Go to the **Appearance** panel and notice the one and only yellow fill. Click its ▶ triangle to twirl it open and reveal three dynamic effects: Roughen, Tweak, and Inner Glow. (Roughen and Tweak are path wigglers; Inner Glow lets you create bright or, in our case, dark halos around the interior of an object.)

Here's what I want you to do:

- At the bottom of the inset effects list is an item that reads Opacity: 43%. Click the word **Opacity** to bring up a pop-up version of the **Transparency** panel, change the **Opacity** value to 100 percent, and press Enter or Return.

- Click on the **Fill** item to select it. The attribute should appear highlighted.

- Click the ⬓ icon at the bottom of the **Appearance** panel to duplicate the fill. Because Roughen and Tweak introduce random variations, the ragged outline of the new fill is slightly different from that of the original one.

- Shift-click the yellow swatch next to the top Fill attribute, and change the **C** and **M** values to 0 and 40 percent, respectively, to color the new fill orange.

Figure 10-13 shows a detail from the bottom of the circle, which illustrates the customized collection of two-fill effects.

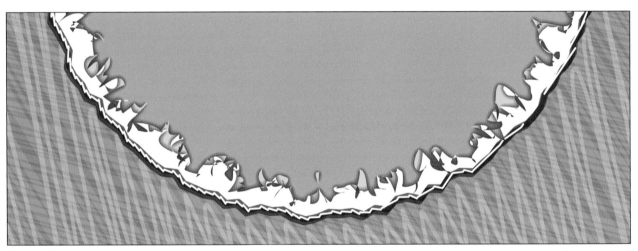

Figure 10-13.

8. *Apply a few styles to the text.* The type (hidden in the figure) looks terrible in its new environment. The solution is to apply a graphic style. Select the point type with the black arrow tool. Then try your hand at applying a few styles. Assuming a **Graphic Styles** panel that's six thumbnails wide, the fourth row and most of the fifth—starting with Ice Type and ending with Metal Silver—comprise styles that Adobe specifically designed to accommodate text; although you can apply any styles you like. Figure 10-14 shows a sample style applied to each line of type. (Illustrator requires you to apply a style to an entire text object, so I had to break the text into three independent lines of point type to pull this off.) The Backdrop layer is hidden.

You can preview a style as it will appear on the selected text by right-clicking (or Control-clicking) its thumbnail. If you're doing a lot of type work, then click the ▾≡ icon in the top-right corner of the Graphic Styles panel and choose Use Text for Preview to change the thumbnails to a bunch of letter *T*'s. To see a *T* larger, deselect your artwork and right-click (Control-click) the thumbnail.

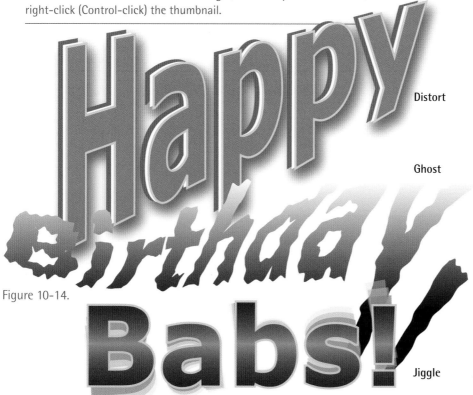

Distort

Ghost

Jiggle

Figure 10-14.

9. *Switch to Beveled & Angled style.* In the end, click on the second-to-last thumbnail in the Graphic Styles panel, Beveled & Angled, which assigns a scribble pattern that matches the background art, as well as rotates the text 15 degrees, as in Figure 10-15.

Most of the styles that I've assembled in this document ship with Illustrator. To load more style libraries, click the 🖿 icon in the bottom-left corner of the panel and choose a library from the list. (The Additive styles are meant to be added to other styles, as I'll explain shortly.) The only non-Adobe styles are the final four, which I created specifically for use in this exercise.

10. *Kern the comma closer to the text.* The comma after *Birthday* is really hanging out there. But finding the character and moving it in is no easy matter, given that the text is not actually where it appears to be.

Figure 10-15.

Figure 10-16.

Choose **View→Outline** or press Ctrl+Y (⌘-Y) to switch to the outline mode. In the outline mode, all dynamic effects disappear. As shown in Figure 10-16, we have precisely what we started with: three path outlines (two of which are part of a single compound path) and three lines of upright type. Illustrator calculates every fill, stroke, and dynamic effect on-the-fly.

In the outline mode, do the following:

- Double-click between the *y* in *Birthday* and its comma to switch to the type tool and set the blinking insertion marker at this location.

- Choose **View→Preview** or press Ctrl+Y (⌘-Y) to switch back to the preview mode. This way, you can see the results of your changes as you work.

- Press Ctrl+Alt+← (⌘-Option-←) five times in a row to kern the comma closer to the *y*.

- Press Esc to escape the text edit mode and return to the black arrow tool. Then press Ctrl+Y (⌘-Y) to restore the preview.

The result is a more tightly spaced comma, consistent with the other letterspacing, as shown in the magnified Figure 10-17.

Figure 10-17.

11. *Combine a few styles.* In addition to applying a style—in which case, all fills, strokes, and effects associated with that style replace those of the previous one—you can combine styles. For example, suppose Style A is a 2-point blue stroke and Style B is a 6-point orange stroke. Apply Style A and you get a 2-point blue stroke. Apply Style B and you get a 6-point orange stroke. But combine Style B with Style A, and you get the best of both worlds: a 6-point orange stroke in back of a 2-point blue stroke.

To combine a style with the attributes already assigned to an object, press the Alt (or Option) key and click on a style thumbnail in the Graphic Styles panel. The new style attributes go back to the bottom of the stack. In other words, the first-applied style is in front; the Alt (or Option)-clicked style is in back.

Figure 10-18 shows a trio of styles added to those that we first saw in Figure 10-14 (page 339). For example, to achieve the first effect, you'd click the Distort thumbnail and then press the Alt (or Option) key and click the Hair Ball thumbnail. (Again, for purposes of this figure, each line of type is its own text block.)

Distort + Hair Ball

Ghost + Metal Silver

Figure 10-18.

Jiggle + Rough

12. *Combine Beveled & Angled with Pink Bevel.* Some styles are invisible or astonishingly unattractive on their own, but lend themselves well to coupling with other styles. To get a sense for what I mean, try this:

- With *Happy Birthday, Babs!* still selected, bring up the **Graphic Styles** panel and click the final thumbnail in the second row, Pink Bevel. The text turns a gooey pink with a slight dark outline. My word, that's ugly.

- Click the third thumbnail in the first row, Live Reflect X. The text disappears entirely. What kind of effect is this?

- Click the second-to-last thumbnail, Beveled & Angled, to restore the text to the way it appeared back in Figure 10-15 (page 339), although with the kerned comma.

- Press the Alt (or Option) key and click the Pink Bevel thumbnail to add that style to Beveled & Angled.

- Alt-click (or Option-click) Live Reflect X. Now Illustrator sports two versions of the text, one reflected horizontally with respect to the original, as in Figure 10-19.

Figure 10-19.

- Press Ctrl+Z (⌘-Z) to undo that last maneuver.

You don't need a dynamic reflection of your type. But you might find uses for such a thing in the future. Dynamic reflection is a function of the powerful Transform effect, as you'll see later.

13. *Apply a drop shadow.* Our next task is to develop the type effects into something that will work for all parts of the artwork, and then save the changes as a new graphic style. Start by assigning a drop shadow. Choose **Effect→Stylize→Drop Shadow** or, if you loaded dekeKeys, press Ctrl+Alt+E (⌘-Option-E). The default settings are fine with one exception: Change the **X Offset** value to −7 points to match the shadow to the angle of the beveled strokes. The final settings appear in Figure 10-20. When your settings match, click the **OK** button.

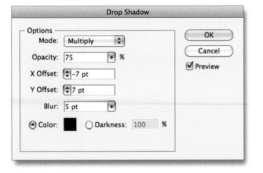

Figure 10-20.

14. *Modify the fill and stroke attributes.* Although you may not know it to look at it, the text comprises three strokes and six fills. In this step, we're going to change all but one of each. While it sounds like a lot of work, it's hardly unusual when customizing complex styles. If along the way, it seems like so much busy work, perish the thought. Each adjustment makes a meaningful (if subtle) contribution to the overall effect. Here are the steps, all of which I document visually in Figure 10-21:

- Shift your attention to the **Appearance** panel. Double-check that the type is selected so you don't waste any time.

- Click to the right of the second Stroke item to select it. (Clicking the word Stroke brings up a pop-up panel of stroke settings, which is not what we want.) Then click its color swatch and select the purple called Plum from the list of swatches. Finally, press Enter or Return.

- In the same manner, change the third stroke to the deep green labeled Forest. (That is, click to the right of the third Stroke, click its color swatch to bring up a list of swatches, select Forest, and press Enter or Return.)

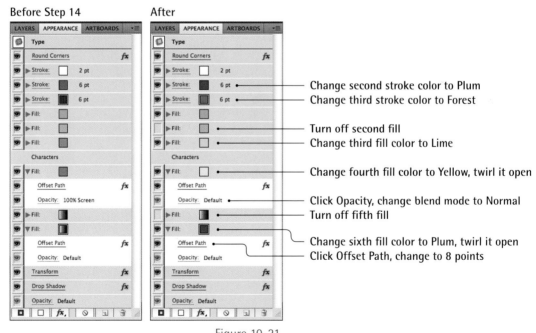

Figure 10-21.

- Click the 👁 icon in front of the second **Fill** item to turn it off.

- Click the third **Fill** item. (When editing a fill, you don't have to click to the right of it.) Click its color swatch, select the light green called Lime, and press Enter or Return.

- Change the fourth fill (the pink one) to the swatch called Yellow. Then click the ▶ in front of that Fill item to twirl it open and reveal the Offset Path and Opacity effects.

- Click the **Opacity** item to display a pop-up version of the Transparency panel. Click the blend mode option (which is set to Screen) and choose **Normal** to make the border around the letters solid yellow. Then press Enter or Return.

- The fifth fill (the first gradient swatch) isn't making a meaningful contribution to the effect. To keep things tidy, click the 👁 icon in front of that Fill item to turn it off.

- Change the final fill (the second gradient) to Plum. Then click its ▶ triangle to twirl it open and reveal its effects.

- Click the **Offset Path** item to display the **Offset Path** dialog box. Change the **Offset** value to 8 points, and click **OK**.

These several adjustments later, the candy-sweet letters are complete, as pictured in Figure 10-22.

Figure 10-22.

15. *Save the effects as a graphic style.* Now I'd like to replicate my fills, strokes, and dynamic effects onto the other paths. The most surefire way to do that is to save a new graphic style. Press Alt (or Option) and click the ⬜ icon at the bottom of the Graphic Styles panel to display the **Graphic Style Options** dialog box, which lets you name your style as you create it. Enter "Candy Coat" into the **Style Name** field, and click **OK**. Illustrator adds a new thumbnail to the end of the style list.

16. *Apply the new style to the circles and square.* Choose **Select→Inverse** or press Ctrl+Shift+I (⌘-Shift-I) to deselect the text and select the paths on the **Backdrop** layer. Then click the new Candy Coat thumbnail at the end of the **Graphic Styles** list to produce the sugary-sweet effect shown in Figure 10-23.

17. *Right the circle-in-square.* The problem with the style is that it rotates the big square shape, which I want to remain upright:

    • Press Ctrl+Shift+A (⌘-Shift-A) to deselect the art. (No need to change the inner circle.)

    • Click the larger circle—the one on the inside of the square shape—to select it.

    • In the **Appearance** panel, click the 👁 in front of the Transform item to turn it off.

Figure 10-23.

Happily, this makes the square upright, but it also changes the angle of the various scribble patterns so they no longer match those of the smaller circle and text, as witnessed by the detail in Figure 10-24. You could adjust the angle of the scribbles by hunting down the problem effect. But searching through three strokes and four active fills is no picnic. The more reliable solution is to update the Candy Coat style so that the scribbles never get rotated in the first place.

18. *Modify the order of the effects assigned to the type.* Select the type with the black arrow tool. Still inside the Appearance panel, note the order of the effects and attributes. The list starts off with the Roughen effect, followed by a series of strokes and fills. Midway into the fills, you'll see the word *Characters*, which represents the letters inside the point type object. The list ends with two effects, Transform and then Drop Shadow. (The final item, Opacity: Default, indicates that the selection is opaque.)

Figure 10-24.

The way in which Illustrator organizes the Appearance panel is a little strange. The fills and strokes make sense, with attributes toward the bottom of the list appearing behind attributes at the top. So in our case, the fills appear behind the strokes. But the effects—Round Corners, Transform, and Drop Shadow—are arranged in the opposite order. Illustrator applies the Roughen effect before any of the fills and strokes, followed by Transform and finally Drop Shadow. (For our purposes, the order of the Characters item is meaningless.) Which means that Round Corners rounds off just the text, while Transform rotates the text as well as all its fill and stroke attributes.

How's that for confusing? But it does afford you control.

To rotate the letters without rotating the scribbles, drag the **Transform** item up to just below Round Corners. Although you have to look carefully to see it happen, the scribbles rotate back into alignment with those in the big square.

19. *Update the Candy Coat style to reflect your change.* The scribbles in the circle remain off-kilter. To rotate them so they match all the others, click the ▾☰ icon in the top-right corner of the Appearance panel and choose **Redefine Graphic Style "Candy Coat"** from the flyout menu. Illustrator updates the circle to match the other objects, as in Figure 10-25.

Here's another way to update a style: Make sure both the Appearance and Graphic Styles panels are open and available. With the text selected, notice the tiny preview thumbnail in the top-left corner of the Appearance panel next to the words *Type: Candy Coat.* Drag this thumbnail into the Graphic Styles panel. While still dragging, press and hold the Alt (or Option) key, and then drop the item onto the Candy Coat thumbnail in the Graphic Styles panel. It's an unusual technique, but it can be more convenient than choosing a command.

You may notice that the big square shape is not affected by this step. The moment you deactivated the Transform effect for that shape (Step 17), Illustrator broke the link between that shape and the Candy Coat style.

Figure 10-25.

That pretty much finishes the napkin project. At least, I think Babs will be pleased. The only reason I include this last section is to demonstrate just how amazingly flexible graphic styles make your artwork. With only a few clicks, we'll altogether transform the appearance of the illustration.

20. *Bring up the jack-o'-lantern face.* Press the F7 key to go to the **Layers** panel, then click the 👁 icon in front of the **Live Text** layer to turn it off. Turn on the **Face** layer to display an orange pumpkin face, which I created in advance as a single compound path.

21. *Apply the Candy Coat style to the face.* Select any of the orange path outlines to select the entire face graphic. Then click the **Candy Coat** thumbnail in the **Graphic Styles** panel to achieve the key-lime-pie effect pictured in Figure 10-26.

22. *Apply the Pumpkin Rough style to the entire graphic.* Properly prepared, key lime pie is yummy, but it doesn't invoke the spirit of a jack-o'-lantern. To alter the mood, press Ctrl+A (⌘-A on the Mac) to select all visible paths. Then click on what is now the fourth-to-last thumbnail in the Graphic Styles panel, Pumpkin Rough. With that single click, Illustrator fills and strokes the shapes with a complex network of overlapping scribble patterns, ultimately reinventing the appearance of the artwork, as in Figure 10-27.

Figure 10-26.

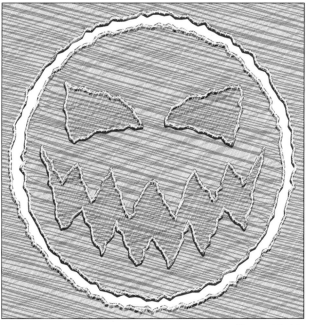

Figure 10-27.

23. *Finish off the artwork.* An orange pumpkin is preferable to a lime green one. But it seems to me it could use some additional flavoring, as follows:

- Using the black arrow tool, Shift-click on the outline of the central circle to deselect it.

- In the Graphic Styles panel, click the second-to-last style, Face Scribbles, to change the angle of the scribble patterns and shift their hues toward a deep olive green.

- In the document window, Shift-click the outline of the square to leave only the eyes and mouth selected.

- Click the **Opacity** link in the control panel to bring up the pop-up version of the **Transparency** panel. Then change the blend mode from Normal to **Multiply** to burn the face into the circle. Figure 10-28 shows the final effect.

Figure 10-28.

The idea behind this exercise is that—thanks to graphic styles, the Appearance panel, and dynamic effects—you can use a single base file to create a series of continuous, fluid variations. If you have any doubt, compare Figures 10-5 (page 334), 10-15 (339), 10-25 (346), and 10-28. What starts as a birthday napkin for Babs becomes a kid's Halloween decoration. And because all effects are scalable, you can make the net result any size you like. Only in Illustrator.

## Exploiting the Transform Effect

As I mentioned at the outset, Effect→Distort & Transform→Transform is my favorite dynamic effect. This one command lets you move, flip, scale, rotate, and clone the appearance of one or more selected objects, all from a central dialog box. The net result is that you can create patterns of paths or text blocks at a moment's notice, and then manipulate the whole pattern in one fell swoop by making adjustments to the original object.

In this exercise, I'll demonstrate how to create a simple rotation pattern, create a beveled stroke effect, and nudge an object using the Transform Effect. You'll also get a chance to try your hand at one of my favorite path wigglers, Pucker & Bloat.

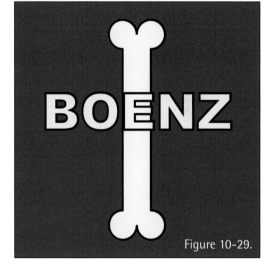

Figure 10-29.

1. *Open a simple line drawing.* Open the file called *Boenz.ai* found inside the *Lesson 10* folder. The file contains three objects: a background square (which will remain unchanged), a compound shape (the cartoon bone) that comprises five subpaths, and an oddly spelled line of point type. Pictured in Figure 10-29, the document can safely be termed unremarkable. But with the help of Transform and Pucker & Bloat, it'll develop into a high-impact graphic design.

2. *Apply a thick stroke to the bones.* Click the outline of any of the four circles or rectangle associated with the vertical bone shape to select it. Open the **Stroke** panel and change the **Weight** value from 20 to 200 points. The result is a chunky outline that nearly obscures the bone-colored fill.

3. *Send the stroke to the back.* By default, Illustrator positions a stroke in front of its fill, in deference to the behavior of the PostScript printing language (which does the same). But you don't have to leave it that way. To restore the fill—so no portion of it is covered—bring up the **Appearance** panel. And drag the Stroke item below Fill (just above the bottom Opacity item). Figure 10-30 shows the result.

Figure 10-30.

4. *Rotate three duplicates of the bones.* Choose **Effect→Distort & Transform→Transform** or, if you loaded dekeKeys back in the Preface, press Ctrl+E (⌘-E on the Mac). In the **Transform Effect** dialog box, turn on the **Preview** check box so you can see the results of your efforts. Change the **Angle** value at the bottom of the dialog box to 45 degrees and press the Tab key to highlight the **Copies** value and invoke the preview. Illustrator rotates the preview of the bone, but its path outlines remain unchanged.

With the **Copies** field active, press the ↑ key to nudge the value up one copy at a time. With Copies set to 1, Illustrator restores a bone at the original position. Once you get to 3, Illustrator completes the pattern, as in Figure 10-31. That's one original plus three copes, for a total of four bones. Then click **OK**.

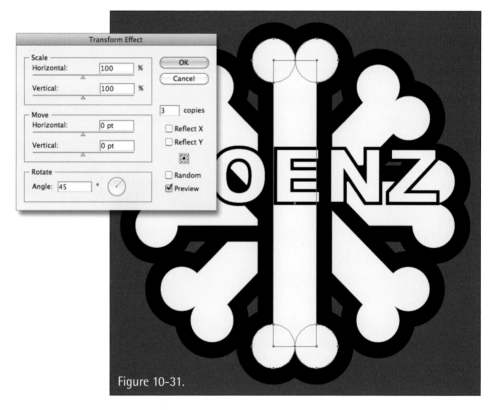

Figure 10-31.

5. *Add the virtual paths together.* Unfortunately, in rotating the paths, we've also managed to rotate the strokes so that they cover each other. To merge the strokes, we need to merge the base bone shape with its virtual copies. To do this, choose **Effect→Pathfinder→Add**.

6. *Move the Transform effect above Add.* Well, that didn't do anything. But that's because the effects are applied in the wrong order. Go to the **Appearance** panel, and notice that Transform

appears below the fill and stroke attributes, while Add appears above. In keeping with Illustrator's strange effect ordering (see the Pearl of Wisdom on page 346), this means Illustrator adds the shape before transforming it. In other words, the Add effect occurs before there's anything to add.

The solution is simple: Grab the **Transform** item, and drag it to the top of the list, before Add. Illustrator immediately merges the rotated bones, granting them a single stroke, as in Figure 10-32.

7. *Offset the stroke around the bones.* To impart a sense of dimension, let's offset the stroke so that it traces the bottom-right edges of the bones more heavily than the top-left edges. Click to the right of the Stroke item in the **Appearance** panel to isolate the stroke. Then once again choose **Effect**→**Distort & Transform**→**Transform** or press Ctrl+E (⌘-E). In the **Move** area (the second box of options), change both the **Horizontal** and **Vertical** values to 30 points. Then click **OK**. Figure 10-33 shows the result.

Figure 10-32.

Figure 10-33.

8. *Prepare the text attributes to receive dynamic effects.* Now it's time to work on the text. Click on the path type with the black arrow tool to select it. See our problem? The Appearance panel shows just three items: Type at the top, followed by Characters, and then Opacity: Default. Where are the fill and stroke? Answer: They're buried inside the letters where they won't do us any good. If you wish, you can double-click on the Characters item to see the fill and stroke, but you can't manipulate them dynamically from that vantage. So if you followed along with the last sentence, press the Esc key to back out.

The trick is to build up new fill and stroke attributes—assigned to the overall text object—and then apply effects to those. Here's how to build up the attributes:

- Click the □ icon at the bottom of the Appearance panel (to the left of *fx*) or press Ctrl+◻ (⌘-◻ on the Mac). This adds new Stroke and Fill items, with Fill active.

- Click the color swatch next to the **Fill** item and select the fifth swatch, Bonewhite. Press the Enter or Return key to accept your change.

- Click the word **Stroke** in the Appearance panel to bring up a pop-up panel. Change the **Weight** value to 120 points, and press the Tab key to accept the change without hiding the panel. Click the center Corner icon, ⊡, to round off the corners. Then press Enter or Return to hide the panel.

    - The stroke will most likely come up automatically as rich black. But in the rare event that it doesn't, click the Stroke item's swatch and select **Rich Black** (fourth in) from the pop-up panel.

    - Drag the **Stroke** item below Fill to position the super-thick stroke behind the fill. Standard character-level attributes do not let you do this; attributes applied to a whole text object from the Appearance panel do.

    - Select the Stroke attribute, and click the ◼ icon in the bottom-left corner of the Appearance panel, or press Ctrl+Alt+◻ (⌘-Option-◻). Illustrator duplicates the active stroke.

    - Click the color swatch next to **Stroke**, select the sixth swatch, Violet, and press Enter or Return to accept your changes and hide the panel. Then change the line weight to 40 points. The final, admittedly arduous result appears in Figure 10-34.

Figure 10-34.

Between you and me, I resent the fact that Illustrator requires you to do this much work to prepare editable text to receive dynamic effects. (I mean, shouldn't live text and line effects go together naturally?) But once the work is done, the rest is smooth sailing.

9. *Pucker the text.* In the Appearance panel, click the top item, **Type**, to make the entire text object active. (This is very important; otherwise, you'll change just the violet stroke.) Choose **Effect→Distort & Transform→Pucker & Bloat** to bring up the **Pucker & Bloat** dialog box. Enter a value of −15 percent (in other words, 15 percent toward Pucker), and click the **OK** button. Figure 10-35 shows the outcome.

Figure 10-35.

Bear in mind that this remains editable text, set, I hasten to add, in Arial Black—the heaviest style of one of the most common and ultimately generic fonts in the world of personal computing. And yet a bit of pucker turns boring old Arial into something quite distinctive. By applying Pucker & Bloat or another path wiggler—namely Roughen, Tweak, or Zig Zag—you can establish the equivalent of customizable type styles that you can assign to any typeface inside Illustrator.

10. *Further pucker the fill.* Nothing says that you can apply an effect just once; in fact, you can do so as many times as you like, oftentimes achieving unique effects (as we'll explore in more detail in the next exercise). First click the **Fill** item to make it active. Then reapply the **Pucker & Bloat** effect with the exact same setting in either (but not both) of the following ways:

- Choose the first command in the **Effect** menu, **Apply Pucker & Bloat**, to reapply the last-used effect. Or press Ctrl+Shift+E (⌘-Shift-E).

- In the **Appearance** panel, press Alt (or Option) and drag the **Pucker & Bloat** item and drop it onto Fill. This duplicates the effect and assigns it to the fill attribute.

Figure 10-36 shows magnified views of the text before and after the second application of Pucker & Bloat. The spikier bone-white fill now extends its way into both the violet and rich-black strokes.

Letters puckered 15 percent

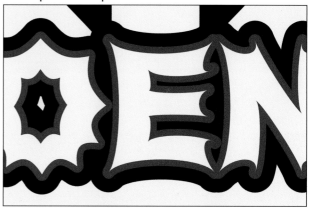

Bone-white fill puckered an additional 15 percent

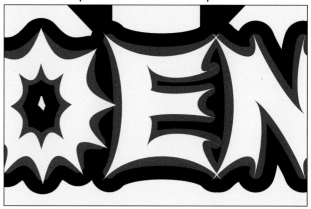

Figure 10-36.

Figure 10-37.

11. *Move the text down.* The point type is currently exactly aligned to the center of artwork, not to mention the artboard. But because the letters rest on the baseline, they're too high with respect to the bone pattern. To center the letters vertically, do the following:

- Click the **Type** item at the top of the Appearance panel.

- Choose **Effect→Distort & Transform→Transform** or press my dekeKeys shortcut, Ctrl+E (⌘-E).

- Turn on the **Preview** check box. (In most of the dynamic effect dialog boxes, Preview does not stay on, so you have to go back and reactivate it on a regular basis.)

- Change the **Vertical** value in the **Move** area to 168 points to move the text down 2 and ⅓ inches.

- Press the Tab key to update the preview. And then click the **OK** button to accept the change, as in Figure 10-37.

Why not *really* move the text instead of temporarily doing so using a dynamic effect? Two reasons: First, this permits you to keep the point type locked into alignment with the violet square that surrounds the artboard. Second, when employing a dynamic effect, you have the option to change your mind in the future.

12. *Rotate the bones another 22.5 degrees.* After taking a moment to gauge the appearance of the artwork, it occurs to me that the bones are off-center, thanks to the fact that I offset their strokes back in Step 7 (page 351). Plus, I think they'd look better if they were grouped into pairs, with two bones on top, two on the left, and so on. This means applying an incremental Transform effect to all the bones. Here's how:

- Use the black arrow tool to select the compound shape that makes up the original bone in the document window.

- Choose the second command from the **Effect** menu, **Transform**, to reapply the last effect with new conditions. This command comes with an intricate shortcut, Ctrl+Shift+Alt+E (or on the Mac, ⌘-Shift-Option-E).

- Illustrator produces an alert message that asks if adding a new effect is really your intention. After all, you might prefer to edit the existing Transform effect by clicking the Transform link in the Appearance panel. But, alas, this won't work. The existing Transform effect includes three copies that are set exactly as they should be. The only solution, then, is to add a new Transform effect. Let Illustrator know your intentions by clicking the **Apply New Effect** button.

- Again, turn on the **Preview** check box.

- In the **Move** area, change both the **Horizontal** and **Vertical** values to –24 pixels. This moves the bones up and to the left.

- You'll need to rotate the bones half their current increment, which is 45 degrees. So in the **Rotate** area, change the **Angle** value to "45/2" and press the Tab key. Illustrator updates the value to 22.5 degrees and rotates the bones accordingly in the background.

- Click **OK** to accept your changes.

Bear in mind that, even though Illustrator updates the preview to show the rotated bones, the original compound shape remains upright, as indicated by the selection edges in Figure 10-38.

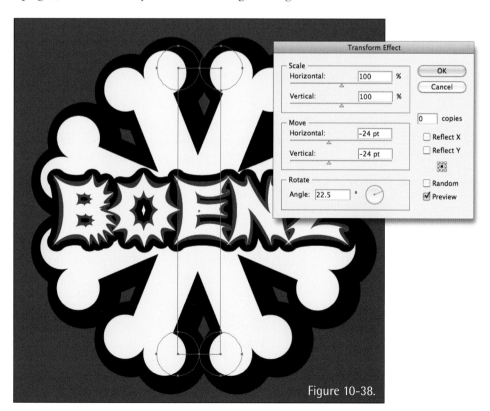

Figure 10-38.

13. *Make a couple of adjustments to the text.* Looking at the logo line, now I think it needs adjustment. (Lest you misinterpret my back-and-forthing as poor organization, I'm actually trying to give you a sense for how dynamic effects keep up with your everyday-average, trial-and-error workflow.) It seems to me that the rich-black stroke should be offset, as with the bones. And thanks to the last step, the centering needs some adjustment. Here's what I came up with:

- Select the point type with the black arrow tool.

- Click to the right of the second **Stroke** item (the black one) in the **Appearance** panel to make it active.

- Choose **Effect→Distort & Transform→Transform** to bring up the **Transform Effect** dialog box with all values reset.

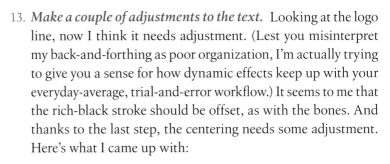
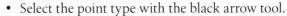

Figure 10-39.

- In the **Move** area, change the **Horizontal** and **Vertical** values to 18 points apiece, as in Figure 10-39. Then click the **OK** button to apply the change.

- Now to adjust the positioning of the point type. Recall that in Step 11 (page 354), you moved the text to its present position by applying a Transform effect. It is precisely this effect that needs adjustment. So rather than choosing a command from the Effect menu, click the final **Transform** item in the **Appearance** panel to edit it.

- In the **Transform Effect** dialog box, turn on the **Preview** check box to verify your movements.

- Tab your way to the **Horizontal** value in the **Move** area. Press Shift+↓ to nudge the text to the left. (Pressing Shift with the ↑ or ↓ key raises or lowers a Move value in six-point increments.) I ultimately arrived at a value of –54 points.

- Press the Tab key again to advance to the **Vertical** value. Press Shift+↓ to reduce the value and nudge the selected text upward. (Because Illustrator measures its movements from the top-left corner of an artboard, positive is down and negative is up.) This time, I arrived at a value of 144 points, as shown in Figure 10-40.

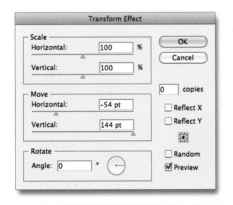

Figure 10-40.

- When you finish, click the **OK** button.

On the facing page, Figure 10-41 shows the final artwork. Recall that the only "real" objects (aside from the violet square) are a vertical bone and some Arial Black type, and I would characterize this as a relatively simple but stunning effect.

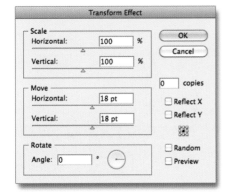

Every once in a while, I get a question from a Macromedia FreeHand user asking how to mimic FreeHand's "power duplication" function in Illustrator. To its credit, the late (and much missed) FreeHand let you apply a series of transformations—scale, rotate, and clone, for example—and then duplicate that entire series to create, say, a declining spiral of objects. In contrast, Illustrator's traditional transformation tools (the topic of Lesson 5) permit you to duplicate a single operation—scale *or* rotate, but not both—at a time. But while the transformation tools may not live up to FreeHand's, the Transform effect does. Select an object, choose Effect→Distort & Transform→Transform, apply all the transformations you like, raise the Copies value to the desired number of duplicates, and click OK. It's a different way of working. But once you come to terms with the Transform effect, it proves itself to be one of the most powerful features in all of Illustrator.

Figure 10-41.

## Building Up a Complex Transformation Series

By now, you have a sense for how transformative the Transform effect can be. But you've seen the merest glimmer of its full potential. You can use Transform not only to change a piece of artwork, but also to *create* one. I first got an inkling of the full power of this command when playing around with one of Adobe's ancient predefined graphic styles. (Other people's styles can be highly illuminating!) Which naturally inspired me to take the Transform effect out for a test drive and see how far I could push it.

The result is this exercise. In the following steps, we'll take a single geometric shape—specifically, the circle pictured in Figure 10-42—and turn it into the costume-jewelry-inspired, Spirographic explosion pictured in Figure 10-43. That lone circle is a kind of foundation that supports one fill, five strokes, three blend modes, a couple of blurring effects, and nineteen applications of Transform—applied as many as seven times to a single attribute—each of which serves a unique and indispensable function. Granted, without the circle, you'd have nothing but the background gradient. But subtract a single fill, stroke, or dynamic effect, and Figure 10-43 would suffer for its absence.

Figure 10-42.

Figure 10-43.

1. *Open a simple path outline.* In the *Lesson 10* subfolder, open the document called *Circle.ai*, which appears in all its glory Figure 10-42.

2. *Stroke the circle with a dashed outline.* Select the circle with the black arrow tool. Then click the second swatch on the left side of the control panel, select the swatch just to the left of bright yellow (called Custard), and press Enter or Return. Next, click the **Stroke** link to bring up a pop-up panel and do the following:

   • Reduce the **Weight** value to 2 points.

   • Turn on the **Dashed Line** check box.

   • Enter a **Dash** value of 6 points and a **Gap** of 2 points.

   Figure 10-44 (facing page) shows the settings. Press Enter or Return to hide the panel and accept your changes.

3. *Scale and rotate the stroke.* As I say, we'll be applying the Transform effect nineteen times. (Although thankfully, in many cases, we'll be replicating it, which will cut down on the grunt work.) This first application is designed to scale and orient the circle in anticipation of repeating it. Here's how:

- Bring up the **Appearance** panel and click on the **Stroke** attribute to select it.

- Choose **Effect→Distort & Transform→Transform** or, if you loaded dekeKeys, press Ctrl+E (⌘-E) to bring up the **Transform Effect** dialog box.

- Turn on the **Preview** check box.

- Change the **Horizontal** value in the **Scale** area to 36 percent.

- Enter a **Rotate Angle** value (at the bottom of the dialog box) of 15 degrees. The settings and effect appear in Figure 10-45.

- Click the **OK** button.

This first transformation may seem arbitrary, but it sets up the stroke for the next transformation. And because this is a dynamic effect, the original circle remains intact.

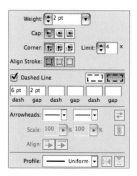

Figure 10-44.

Between the Reflect Y and Random check boxes on the right side of the dialog box is a matrix that permits you to define the transformation origin. Throughout the first portion of this exercise—that is, until I tell you to change it—the matrix should be set to 🔳, as by default.

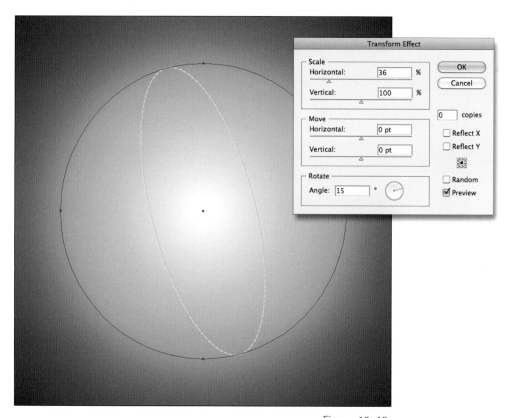

Figure 10-45.

Figure 10-46.

4. *Repeat the Transform effect and bypass the alert.* Choose the second command from the **Effect** menu, **Transform**, or press Ctrl+Shift+Alt+E (⌘-Shift-Option-E). Illustrator warns you that "This will apply another instance of this effect," and then goes on to explain (albeit somewhat inaccurately) how to edit an existing effect, as in Figure 10-46. It's a reasonable warning, but a new instance is precisely what we want. Assuming you understand the implications of what you're doing, turn on the **Don't Show Again** check box and click **Apply New Effect**.

5. *Enter new values, including five copies.* Up comes the **Transform Effect** dialog box with the same settings you applied a moment ago. Reinstate the first **Horizontal** value to 100 percent, and change the **Rotate Angle** value to 30 degrees. Then turn on the **Preview** check box, click the word **Copies** to activate its value, and press the ↑ key to nudge the value upward. A value of 5 (for a total of six ellipses) completes the cycle. When you achieve the effect shown in Figure 10-47, click **OK**.

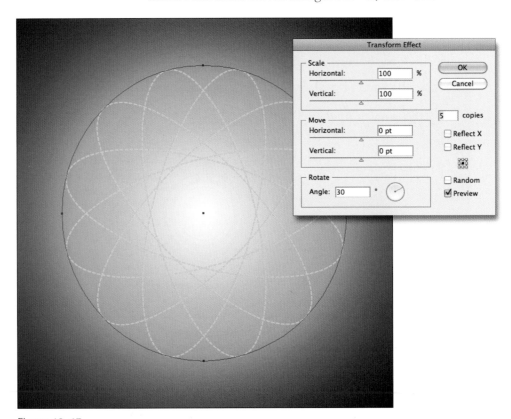

Figure 10-47.

6. *Duplicate the stroke attribute.* Go to the **Appearance** panel and, with the **Stroke** attribute selected, click the ⬓ icon in the bottom-right corner. This duplicates the dashed stroke, complete with its two dynamic Transform effects.

7. *Make the new stroke white with round dots.* Recall that the final artwork (see Figure 10-43 on page 358) features a series of white beads outlined in blue. Here's how to make the white beads:

- Still inside the Appearance panel, change the color of the new stroke to white.

- Click the **Stroke** link, and change the **Weight** to 6 points.

- Tab down to the **Dash** value and make it 0. Then change the **Gap** value to 10. The dashes all but disappear.

- Select the middle ⊖ from the **Cap** icons (directly below Weight) to surround each and every 0-point dash with a white circle.

Figure 10-48 shows the settings and result. Assuming what you see it a match, press the Enter or Return key.

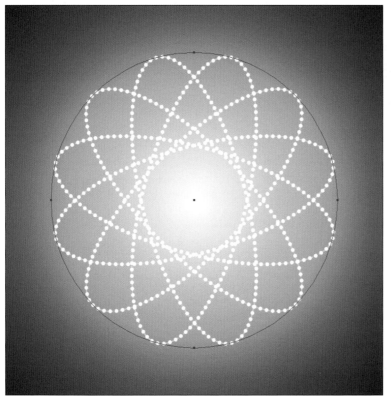

Figure 10-48.

8. *Turn off the first rotation effect.* Now to offset the angle of the white beads with respect to the yellow dashes. In the **Appearance** panel, click the ▶ in front of the new **Stroke** item to reveal its Transform effects. Click the first **Transform** link to edit it. Change the **Rotate Angle** value to 0, and click the **OK** button. Figure 10-49 shows the result.

Figure 10-49.

9. *Add a series of rotated and scaled strokes.* The second Transform effect—which rotates five copies of the white-dot ellipse 30 degrees apiece, as established in Step 5—is fine as is. But I'd like to add yet another effect that scales, rotates, and duplicates the white strokes inward. So choose **Effect→Transform** or press Ctrl+Shift+Alt+E (⌘-Shift-Option-E). Turn on **Preview** and make these changes:

- In the **Scale** area, change both the **Horizontal** and **Vertical** values to 90 percent. (Too bad there's not a link icon!)

- Reduce the **Rotate** value to 15 degrees.

- Change the number of **Copies** to 4 and click **OK**.

The settings and resulting effect appear in Figure 10-50.

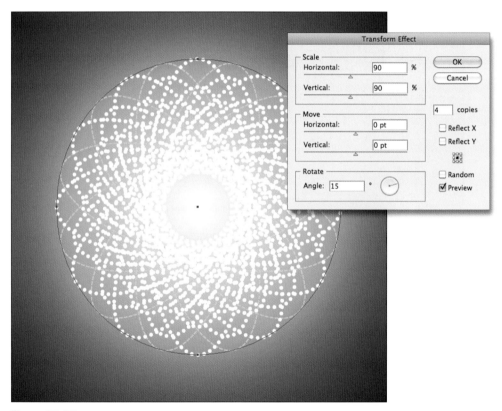

Figure 10-50.

10. *Duplicate and modify the white strokes.* The next trick is to trace the white beads with deep blue, translucent outlines:

- In the **Appearance** panel, click the top **Stroke** item (labeled 6 pt Dashed) to make it active.

- Click the ⬒ icon along the bottom of the panel to copy the stroke and its effects.

- Click on the lower of the two white strokes to select it.

- Click the stroke's color swatch, and select the darkish blue color, called Night Blue, in the pop-up panel. Then press Enter or Return to hide the panel.

- Increase the line weight value to 9 points.

- Click the word **Opacity** in the control panel to bring up a pop-up version of the Transparency panel. Change the blend mode from Normal to **Multiply**, and press Enter or Return.

Illustrator encases the composite of the white beads inside a uniform system of blue borders, as in Figure 10-51. The effect works perfectly without you having to modify a single effect.

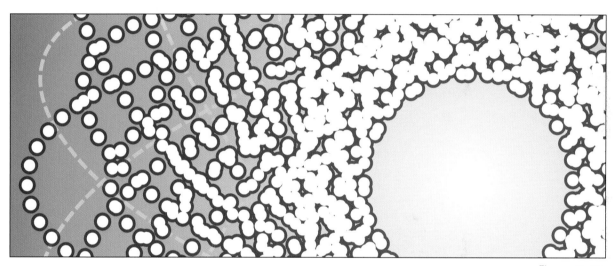

Figure 10-51.

11. *Duplicate the bottom blue stroke.* With the blue stroke still active, click the ▭ icon along the bottom of the **Appearance** panel to duplicate it, along with its dash settings and effects. Then drag the new stroke down the stack and drop it below the yellow stroke, just above the empty fill.

12. *Modify the new stroke.* Click the swatch for the bottom stroke and change it to the purple called Plum. Then click on the **Stroke** link, reduce the **Weight** value to 0.7 point, and turn off the **Dashed Line**. Press Enter or Return to accept your changes.

13. *Change the Transform effect settings.* Make sure the purple stroke is twirled open so you can see all three of its Transform effects. We'll change each one of them:

- Click the first **Transform** link for the purple stroke. Reduce the **Horizontal** value to 8 percent for some skinny ellipses. Then set the **Rotate Angle** to 15 degrees, and click **OK**.

- Click the second **Transform** link for the purple stroke. This time change the **Rotate Angle** to 10 degrees and set **Copies** to 17. Because you have one original, 17 + 1 = 18. Meanwhile, 18 × 10 degrees = 180 degrees, which is all you need to spin a path around in a circle. As always, click **OK**.

- Click the third and final **Transform** link. In the **Scale** area, raise both the **Horizontal** and **Vertical** values to 110 percent. Confirm that the **Rotate Angle** value is 15 degrees, and change the number of **Copies** to 2. These values don't describe a circle; they're just for fun. Click **OK**.

Figure 10-52 shows a detail from the resulting effect. I don't know if it looks more like something drawn with a Spirograph or a work of 1970's string art. But I like it.

Figure 10-52.

14. ***Create a new black stroke*** Our next effects have very little to do with those that we've applied so far. So let's start with a brand new stroke: With the purple stroke active, click the ◻ icon at the bottom of the **Appearance** panel or press Ctrl+Alt+ ⬚ (⌘-Option-⬚). Drag the new stroke all the way to the top of

the stack. Change the line weight from 0.7 to 2 points. Then make the color of the stroke black. In the end, I want the stroke to be white, but starting with black will make it easier to see what we're doing.

15. *Apply a series of offset scale effects.* In all, this stroke will include seven Transform effects. The first three will scale and repeat the stroke, the other four will rotate and repeat the results. Let's start with the scale effects:

    - In the Appearance panel, click to the right of the top **Stroke** item to make it active. Choose **Effect→Distort & Transform→Transform** or press Ctrl+E (⌘-E) to create a fresh effect. In the **Scale** area, change both the **Horizontal** and **Vertical** values to 22.5 percent. Then click the top-right corner in the reference point matrix, so it looks like ⌗, and click **OK**. The result is the offset circle in Figure 10-53.

    - Confirm that the top Stroke is active. (Illustrator sometimes has a habit of turning it off.) Then choose **Effect→Transform** or press Ctrl+Shift+Alt+E (⌘-Shift-Option-E) to repeat the effect with different settings. Change the **Horizontal** and **Vertical** values to 70 percent each. Request 3 **Copies**, click the center point in the matrix (as in ⌗), and click **OK**. You should see three inset circles, as in Figure 10-54.

    - Make sure the Stroke item is selected, and again choose the second **Effect** menu command or press Ctrl+Shift+Alt+E (⌘-Shift-Option-E). Change the **Horizontal** and **Vertical** values to 50 percent apiece. Leave the **Copies** value set to 3 and click the bottom-left corner in the reference point matrix, so it looks like ⌗. Then click **OK**. Illustrator creates a declining series of inset circles, as in Figure 10-55.

16. *Rotate seven copies of the black circles.* Now to rotate and replicate the circles that you've made so far to create a kind of flower effect. Click to the right of the top Stroke item in the **Appearance** panel to make it active. (If you're thinking this constant deactivation of the stroke is a pain in the neck, I hear ya. But you have to do it; otherwise, you'll affect all strokes applied to the path, which would be a mess.) Choose **Effect→Transform** or press the mash-your-fist-E shortcut to bring up the Transform Effect dialog box with the last settings. Restore the **Horizontal** and **Vertical** values to 100 percent each. Change the **Rotate Angle** value to 45 degrees. Request 8 **Copies**, leave the matrix set to ⌗, and click **OK**. Figure 10-56 shows the result.

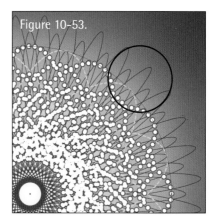
Figure 10-53.

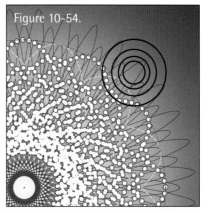
Figure 10-54.

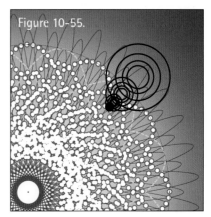
Figure 10-55.

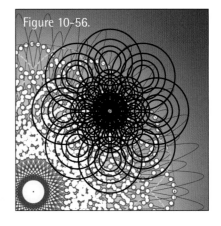
Figure 10-56.

17. *Spin the circle set around the original path outline.* Select the top stroke and choose **Effect→Transform**. Leave the Scale values set to 100 percent each. Change the **Rotate Angle** value to 60 degrees, ask for 5 **Copies**, and leave the reference point set to ⬚. Click **OK** to get the effect pictured in Figure 10-57.

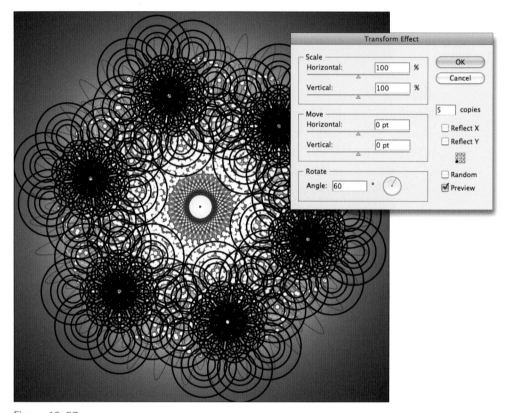

Figure 10-57.

18. *Fix the angle and spacing.* While the various black circle sets are spaced impeccably with respect to each other, the larger shape that they form leans precariously to the right, and it's not centered properly with respect to the other strokes. We'll address these two different problems in two different ways:

- Click the top Stroke item in the **Appearance** panel and choose **Effect→Transform** for the umpteenth time. Reset the **Copies** value to 0, and select the center reference point, ⬚. Turn on the **Preview** check box, and adjust the **Rotate Angle** value until the black strokes appear upright, which happens at 15 degrees. Click the **OK** button to accept the seventeenth Transform effect.

- That first Transform effect—the one you applied at the beginning of Step 15—determined the position of every effect that followed. So to fix the centering of the black circles, click on the topmost **Transform** link in the Appearance panel. Turn on the **Preview** check box, and reduce the two **Scale** values in tenths of a point until the circles shift into place. (Unfortunately, there is no shortcut for this; you'll have to reduce the values manually.) I found that the centering worked out when I set both the **Horizontal** and **Vertical** values to 22.2 percent, as in Figure 10-58. Click **OK** to apply your changes.

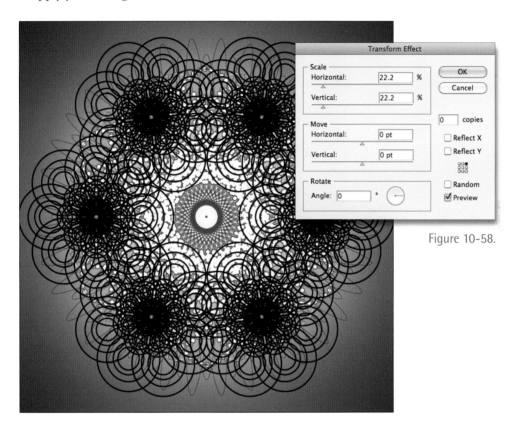

Figure 10-58.

19. *Move the black stroke to the back and make it white.* In the **Appearance** panel, click the color swatch for the black **Stroke** item and switch it to white, making it more in keeping with the rest of the graphic. Then drag the top **Stroke** to the bottom of the stack, between the purple stroke and the empty fill.

20. *Feather the stroke.* Next I want to blur my most recent stroke. Illustrator provides two effects for blurring, Gaussian Blur and Feather. The former has a tendency to blur strokes outward, so they bleed into their background. The latter—known as *feathering* after a traditional technique that employs feathers as brushes—blurs strokes away, making them more fragile. We'll see Gaussian Blur in a moment, but for this particular stroke, I prefer

Feather. Select the rear white Stroke (the one you've been working on) to reactivate it. Then choose **Effect**→**Stylize**→**Feather**. (For once, there is no shortcut.) Change the **Feather Radius** value to 2 points and turn on the **Preview** check box. The circles produce a slight, diaphanous glow, like those in Figure 10-59. Click **OK** to accept your change.

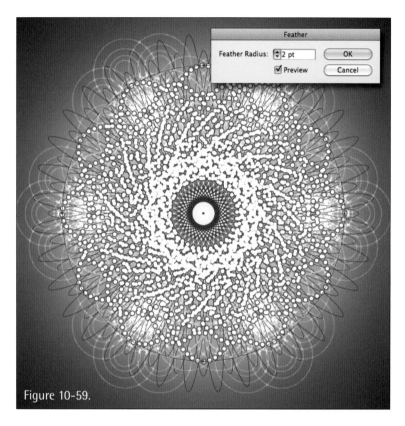

Figure 10-59.

21. *Duplicate the glowing circles.* In this step, I want to increase the density of the feathered white circles and reduce their opacity. Here's how:

- Click the final Stroke item in the Appearance panel to keep it active. Then choose **Effect**→**Distort & Transform**→**Transform** or press my shortcut, Ctrl+E (⌘-E).

- Change the **Rotate Angle** value to 90 degrees.

- Increase the **Copies** value to 1, and turn on the **Preview** check box. Illustrator doubles the number of feathered circles in the artwork.

- Click the **OK** button to close the dialog box and apply your changes.

- Shift your attention to the middle region of the control panel and reduce the **Opacity** value to 70 percent.

The slightly blurred, dare-I-say ghostly strokes appear on the right side of Figure 10-60.

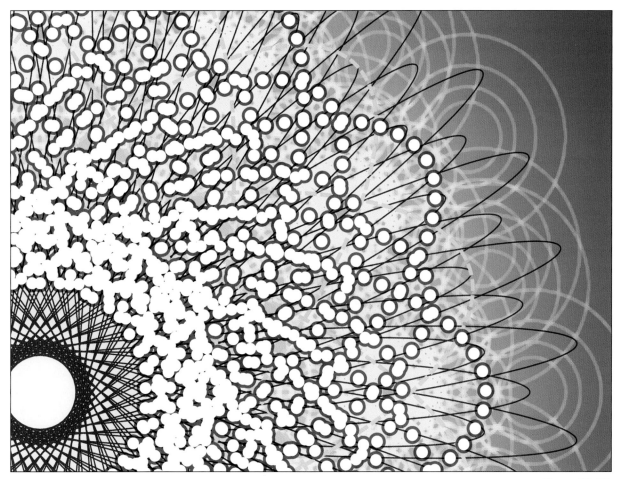

Figure 10-60.

22. *Add a blurry fill.* I really like that intersection of purple lines in the center of the artboard, but I'm finding it distracting in the context of the overall illustration. To cover it with a blurry glow—one that is easier to control than a radial gradient—do the following:

- Click the ⊘ swatch next to the Fill item at the bottom of the **Appearance** panel, and change the fill color to white.

- Drag the **Fill** attribute a couple of items up the list and drop it between the purple and yellow strokes. Then click on Fill to select it.

- Choose **Effect→Distort & Transform→Transform**. (This is it, the nineteenth and final application of the effect!)

- In the **Scale** area, change the **Horizontal** and **Vertical** values to 20 percent apiece, and click the **OK** button.

- Choose **Effect**→**Blur**→**Gaussian Blur** to bring up the **Gaussian Blur** dialog box.

- Good news: Gaussian Blur produces more evenly distributed effects than the Feather effect. Bad news: Its only preview is the tiny one inside the dialog box. So cross your fingers, change the **Radius** value to 8 pixels, and click **OK**.

Figure 10-61 shows how the new fill creates a bright vignette inside the center of the beaded pattern.

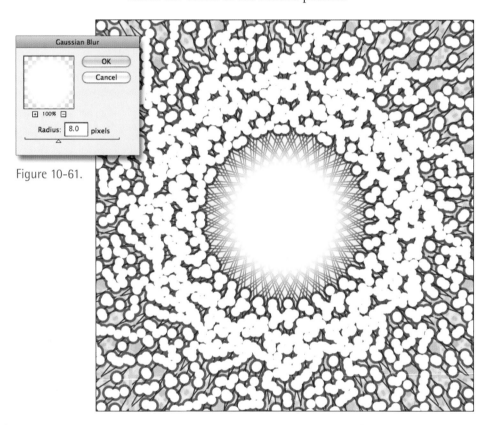

Figure 10-61.

23. *Bolster the details with drop shadows.* Congratulations, the artwork now appears as it did in Figure 10-43 (see page 358). But I'm not entirely happy with it. Specifically, the colors are too light. Throughout this CMYK graphic, black appears only in the background gradient, and even then very lightly. I could add some heft to the stroke colors. But my preferred solution is to add a couple of drop shadows:

- In the **Appearance** panel, click the blue **Stroke** item (labeled 9 pt Dashed) to select it.

- Choose **Effect**→**Stylize**→**Drop Shadow** or press the deke-Keys shortcut Ctrl+Alt+E (⌘-Option-E).

- In the **Drop Shadow** dialog box, leave the Mode option set to Multiply and change the **Opacity** to 100 percent.

- Reduce both the **X Offset** and **Y Offset** values to 1 point, and then change the **Blur** value to 0 point.

- Make sure the **Color** option is selected, then click on its swatch to bring up the **Color Picker** dialog box. Change the **C**, **M**, **Y**, and **K** values to 100, 75, 0, and 50, respectively.

- Click the **OK** button twice to close the dialog boxes and accept your changes.

- Back in the **Appearance** panel, make sure the blue **Stroke** item is twirled open. (If it isn't, click its ▶ triangle.)

- Press the Alt key (Option on the Mac) and drag the **Drop Shadow** item onto the purple stroke to duplicate it.

From a single circle, we now have an symmetrical maelstrom of beads, wires, and gossamer filament, as in Figure 10-62.

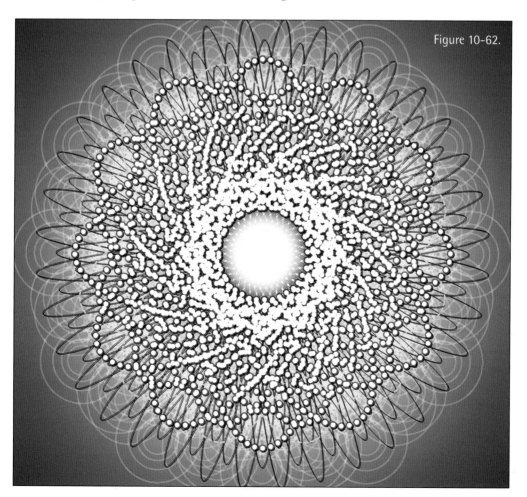

Figure 10-62.

Figure 10-63.

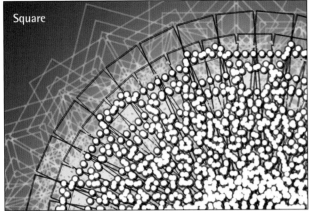

Square

Star

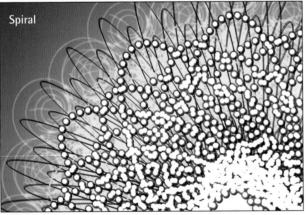

Spiral

Zig

After all that work you might argue that, for all their flexibility, dynamic effects don't necessarily save on brute force or sheer, mind-numbing effort. Which is true. But having done the job once, you can repurpose the fruits of your labors over and over again.

For example, with the big circle still selected, press Shift+F5 to open the Graphic Styles panel. Press the Alt (or Option) key and click the ⊡ icon at the bottom of the panel. Name the new style "Spectral Brooch," and click OK. Now press F7 to switch to the Layers panel. Click the 👁 in front of the Circle layer to turn it off, and then turn on the Other Shapes layer. Now experiment with applying the Spectral Brooch style to each of the four paths on the new layer. Figure 10-63 shows a detail from each and every path, independently of the others.

What I love about this (or any) graphic style is that every path subjected to the style exhibits a unique flaw—which is consistent with the implementation of any piece of artwork, automated or otherwise. And if the symmetry bothers you, then crop it. Change the size of the artboard, move the styled path outline one direction or another, much as I did to create the details in Figure 10-63.

## Creating 3D Text and Graphics

In this last exercise, I'll introduce you to 3D in Illustrator, which is another of the program's dynamic effects. Don't get too excited. Illustrator has always been—and may forever be—a two-dimensional vector drawing program. You can't construct a full 3D scene, establish shared light sources, or set objects so that they cast shadows onto each other. You can't create reflections, refractions, or camera angles. What you *can* do is create single 3D objects at a time, each of which exists altogether independently of each other.

In this project you'll create 3D text and map artwork onto the various surfaces of a 3D jewel case. While Illustrator's brand of 3D is hardly robust, it's a lot of fun.

### FURTHER INVESTIGATION

To learn more about 3D in Illustrator, sign up for your free seven-day trial account at *www.lynda.com/deke*. And then check out my video series *Illustrator CS5 One-on-One: Mastery*. I explore Illustrator's 3D capabilities in Chapter 29, "3D Effects."

1. *Open a basic illustration.* For the final time in this lesson, navigate your way to the *Lesson 10* subfolder in the *Lesson Files-AIcs5 1on1* folder. Then open the file called *Text & symbols.ai*. Pictured in Figure 10-64, this document contains a background grid, a line of point type, a hidden rectangle (which will become the jewel case), and a few symbols to map onto your 3D art.

2. *Apply a few 3D styles to the text.* Click on the type with the black arrow tool to select it. Then press Shift+F5 to open the **Graphic Styles** panel. Assuming that your panel is six thumbnails wide, you'll find 3D styles in the third, fourth, and fifth rows (all of which I culled from the 3D Effects library that ships with Illustrator). To get a feel for how they work, apply a few to the selected type. Figure 10-65 shows three examples. (Sadly, Illustrator sometimes has troubles rendering 3D effects accurately, so some styles may exhibit problems.)

3. *Restore the original type.* When you've had your fill of playing around, choose **File→Revert** or press F12 to reload the saved document.

Figure 10-64.

3D Effect 12

3D Effect 14

3D Effect 18

Figure 10-65.

4. *Add a 3D style to the type.* My goal is to take the text as it originally appears—with three strokes and a yellow fill—and project it into the third dimension. You can do exactly that using Effect→3D→Extrude & Bevel. Or you can add one of the predefined graphic styles that already includes an Extrude & Bevel effect. For the sake of simplicity, we'll do the latter.

Still in the Graphic Styles panel, press the Alt (or Option) key and click on the purple thumbnail in the fourth row, 3D Effect 11. After a few progress bars—Illustrator's 3D is not what you'd call fast—the program leans the letters backward and adds depth to the sides, as in Figure 10-66.

5. *Delete the extra purple fill.* Switch to the **Appearance** panel (by pressing Shift+F6 if need be). With the point type still selected, grab that final purple **Fill** item—which was added by the 3D Effect 11 style—and drag it to the trash at the bottom of the panel. And then wait out the progress bars as Illustrator recalculates the effect. When working with 3D effects, it pays to eliminate any excess attributes.

Figure 10-66.

6. *Adjust the 3D settings.* Click the **3D Extrude & Bevel** link at the bottom of the Appearance panel to edit the effect's settings. The central element of the **3D Extrude & Bevel** dialog box is a blue-faced cube floating inside a concave grid. (Because the 3D Effect 11 style leans the text back, you see the cube straight-on, from below.) You can rotate the cube in 3D space by dragging any of its edges, or by modifying the numerical values to its right.

Here's how the options work, and what I'd like you to do:

- Click the red ⊕ to select the first value, which rotates the selected 3D object around the horizontal X axis. As diagrammed in Figure 10-67, this is also known as *pitch*, after an aviation term for the up-and-down movement of a plane's nose with respect to its wings. Alternatively, you can drag the top and bottom edges of the cube, color-coded red. Lower the value to 20 degrees to pitch the letters forward.

- Press the Tab key to advance to the green ⬩⊅ value, which rotates the 3D object around the vertical Y axis, known as *yaw*. You can likewise drag the left and right sides of the cube, color-coded green. Because I want to view the letters straight on, I'd normally have you set the value to 0 degrees. But if you were to do so, and preview the results, you'd see the render fall apart. To avoid this problem, leave the ⬩⊅ value set to 1 degree.

- Tab to the blue ⊙ value. To understand this new axis, imagine a line extending from your nose straight into the distance. This is the depth, or Z, axis. In aviation and 3D graphics, a Z-axis rotation is called *roll*. Another way to modify this value is to drag the top and bottom sides of the cube, which appear blue when you hover over them (as well as in Figure 10-67). For our purposes, leave ⊙ set to 0.

- Press Tab again to highlight the Perspective value. This one determines the degree to which the extrusion declines into the horizon. For a bold degree of depth that doesn't result in radical render problems, leave it cranked up to 100 degrees.

- Finally, tab to the Extrude Depth value. Calculated in the active unit of measure—in our case, points—this option determines the depth of the extrusion. Raise the **Extrude Depth** value to 40 points.

- Turn on the **Preview** check box to render and confirm your settings. Then click **OK** to close the dialog box.

The settings and the resulting effect—with more deeply extruded letters tipped forward—appear in Figure 10-68.

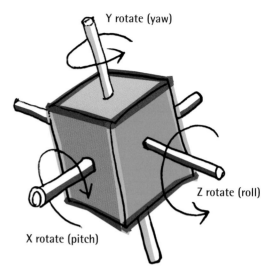

Figure 10-67.

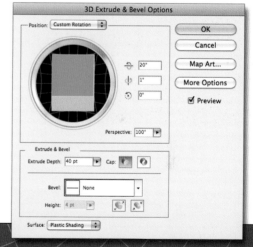

Figure 10-68.

7. *Bend the text upward.* Because 3D is a dynamic effect, you can combine it with other attributes and effects. For example, choose **Effect→Warp→Arch** to display the **Warp Options** dialog box. Reduce the **Bend** value to 10 percent. Turn on

the **Preview** check box and wait patiently (or impatiently, it really doesn't matter) for Illustrator to render the effect, pictured in Figure 10-69. If ever you find yourself frustrated with Illustrator's 3D capabilities—which, based on my experience, you probably will—remember that it can pull off an effect like this in the matter of a few minutes. And then click **OK**.

Figure 10-69.

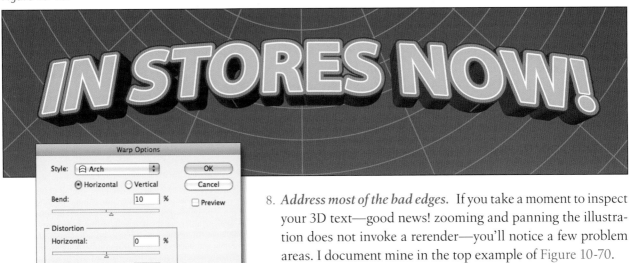

8. *Address most of the bad edges.* If you take a moment to inspect your 3D text—good news! zooming and panning the illustration does not invoke a rerender—you'll notice a few problem areas. I document mine in the top example of Figure 10-70.

---

Two items to bear in mind: First, your problems may differ from those in the figure. Illustrator renders 3D effects based on many shifting variables, including the position of the object, the size and kerning of the text, and your experimentations in the 3D Extrude & Bevel Options dialog box. Second, in my experience, what you see is what you get. In other words, if you see a problem, it's not a screen redraw anomaly, it's part of the illustration that must be remedied or endured.

---

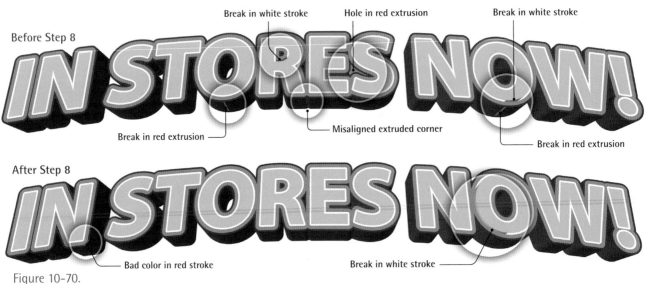

Figure 10-70.

The trick is to simplify the effect. Take a look at the **Appearance** panel and notice that Warp appears at the top of the stack and 3D Extrude & Bevel appears at the bottom. In other words— even though you applied the 3D effect first and the Warp effect second—Illustrator has elected to bend the type before extruding it. Better to reverse the order, so Illustrator does the tough stuff first and the easy stuff second. By which I mean, drag the **Warp: Arch** item down to very bottom of the stack, so Illustrator applies it before 3D Extrude & Bevel.

All the old problems go away. But new problems may arise, as documented at the bottom of Figure 10-70. In my case, the new problems are fewer, just two instead of five. And all but one go away in the next step.

9. *Edit the text.* Let's say I'm advertising a DVD-ROM version of one of the videos that I recorded for my online video publisher, lynda.com. The thing is, unlike this book, my videos are *not* available in stores. So the 3D text, however stunning, is a lie. Fortunately, the text is editable so I can change it at a moment's notice. Unfortunately, because the text has a 3D effect assigned to it, Illustrator will try to update the rendering each and every time I enter a new letter. In other words, were I to start editing the text as is, I'd be in for a world of hurt.

---

The natural trick might be to switch to the outline mode (Ctrl+Y or ⌘-Y) and then edit away. But contrary to everything I've taught you so far, Illustrator is resolute on recalculating 3D effects, even in the outline mode where you can't possibly see them! The solution is to turn off the 3D effect as you edit the text and turn it back on when you're done.

---

Here's the best approach:

- In the **Appearance** panel, click the 👁 in front of the **3D Extrude & Bevel** item to turn it off.

- Double-click in the point type in the document window to switch to the type tool and set the blinking insertion marker in the text.

- Press Ctrl+A (or ⌘-A) to select all the letters.

- Type "Never in stores!" The new text will appear in all caps.

- Press the Esc key to accept your changes and return control to the black arrow tool.

- Back in the Appearance panel, turn the **3D Extrude & Bevel** effect back on.

After a few progress bars, Illustrator rerenders the text, hopefully dispelling most, if not all, of the problems. If an unacceptable slew of problems remain, try nudging the text up or down by pressing the ↑ or ↓ arrow key. But be aware, each nudge requires a new rendering. In the end, you may have to adjust to some degree of imperfection. I was ultimately forced to endure a sliver of brown under the *E* in *STORES*, as in Figure 10-71.

Break in red extrusion

Figure 10-71.

Figure 10-72.

Is such an imperfection okay? I guess it depends on how fussy you are. But let's say the text must be perfect. Then rasterize and correct the effect in Photoshop. Here's how: Save your changes using File→Save. Then switch to the Adobe Bridge, right-click on the illustration file, and choose Open With→Adobe Photoshop CS5. In the following dialog box, specify a very high Resolution value—say, 600 pixels per inch—and click OK. Give Photoshop some time to rasterize the file. Once in Photoshop, you can use your image-editing skills to fill in the problem details. If you don't possess such skills, check out my book on the topic, *Adobe Photoshop CS5 One-on-One*. If you like this book, you'll probably like that one as well.

10. *Display the DVD Case path.* Now that you have some experience with 3D text, let's try out a 3D path outline. Press the F7 key to bring up the **Layers** panel. Click the ▶ triangle in front of the top layer, **3D Object**, to twirl it open. Then click in the first column in front of the **DVD Case** path to turn it on and reveal a beige rectangle in the document window.

11. *Apply the Monolith style to the path.* Select the rectangle in the document window. Then switch to the **Graphic Styles** panel and click the final thumbnail, Monolith. Illustrator fills the rectangle with black, extrudes and rotates it at a slight angle, and adds an Outer Glow effect, as in Figure 10-72. If you like, you may inspect the effect by clicking the 3D Extrude & Bevel link at the bottom of the Appearance panel. Therein, you'll discover that the ⟳, ⟲, and ⟳ values (pitch, yaw, and roll) are –32, –36, and 26 degrees, respectively. Meanwhile, the Perspective value is 62 degrees and Extrude Depth is 50 points.

If you click the More Options button, and you'll learn even more. The Surface option is set to Plastic Shading, which is Illustrator's best (but most time-consuming) rendering setting. The sphere below Surface sports two light sources, the settings for which appear to the sphere's right. The upshot is that the box is lit from the top right and bottom center.

So why does it look like a lifeless, indefinite silhouette of a box, with no shading whatsoever? Because the fill color is a neutral dark gray. Were you to switch the fill to some other color, you would see shading. But rather than changing the fill, we'll add a variety of colors by mapping artwork onto the box.

12. *Check out the symbols.* So far, the 3D box is nothing but a structure that will ultimately hold art. In fact, you might think of it as a plain black box that we'll decorate with stickers. Before adding the stickers, however, you have to save them as symbols, as I've done in advance. Choose **Window→Symbols** to bring up the **Symbols** panel. Figure 10-73 shows the six symbols that I've included with this document, in the order they appear. The final three symbols—Yellow Sun, Sun Logo, and Tiki Idol—are included in the Front and Spine symbols. Illustrator is perfectly fine with you using symbols inside symbols, and integrating the larger symbols into your 3D art.

Figure 10-73.

---

When creating your own symbols, make sure to define one for each and every side of your 3D object. A box, like the one in Figure 10-72, is a six-sided shape. Of those six sides, we can only see three: the front, left side, and top edge. Hence, my Front, Spine, and Top Edge symbols. Also, sides and edges have to be on their sides and sometimes upside-down, as in Figure 10-73.

---

13. *Bring up the Map Art dialog box,* With the rectangle selected, press Shift+F6 to switch to the **Appearance** panel and click the **3D Extrude & Bevel** link. In the top-right corner of the **3D Extrude & Bevel Options** dialog box, click the **Map Art** button. Illustrator displays the **Map Art** dialog box and shows the 3D box as a black-and-red wireframe, as in Figure 10-74.

The wireframe shows the six sides of the box: top and bottom, left and right sides, front, and back. The red outline indicates the active side, which is initially the front.

14. *Assign the Front symbol to the front of the 3D box.* Click the **Symbol** option in the top-left corner of the dialog box and choose the **Front** symbol from the pop-up menu. Then turn on the **Preview** check box to see how the symbol fits the box.

Figure 10-74.

15. *Position and scale the symbol to fit the box.* It's official: The symbol art doesn't fit the front surface of the 3D box worth beans. Illustrator helpfully offers a Scale to Fit button in the bottom-left corner of the Map Art dialog box. But if you were to click it, you'd be in worse shape than ever. The Front symbol includes a clipping mask, so Illustrator thinks the symbol is much larger than it looks.

The only solution is to scale the artwork manually. Drag the symbol in the preview area of the dialog box to position it. And then scale the symbol by dragging the eight bounding box handles as needed. Keep an eye on the document window and be patient. This step requires a lot of back-and-forth work. In the end, you want the symbol to be at least as wide as the front surface of the box, so the artwork fills the entire width of the 3D rendering. But you also want it to be slightly shorter, so a sliver of dark gray shows up at the top and bottom of the red rectangle, as in Figure 10-75. (After all, were this a real jewel case—comprising a black box and a clear plastic sleeve—the paper insert would float inside the larger box's confines. Grab a physical DVD if you need guidance.)

Figure 10-75.

16. *Assign and scale the other symbols.* One symbol down, two to go. Here's how to apply the Spine and Top Edge symbols:

- More or less centered at the top of the Map Art dialog box is a Surface option that lets you select the surface of the 3D object you want to work on. Currently it reads *1 of 6*. Click the ▶ to the right of **Surface** to advance from one surface to the next. In the document window, the red outline shows which surface is active. To select the left side, advance to surface *5 of 6*.

- Choose the **Spine** symbol from the **Symbol** pop-up menu, then position and scale the symbol to fit. Pay careful attention to make sure it matches the seams of the Front symbol, so the artwork looks like one continuous insert.

- Click the ▶ to the right of **Surface** to advance to the final surface, which is the top edge.

- Choose **Top Edge** from the **Symbol** pop-up menu. Click the **Scale to Fit** button to shrink the symbol so it fits entirely inside the top surface. Then scale the symbol by dragging the bounding box handles.

---

Shockingly, Illustrator does not let you nudge a symbol by pressing an arrow key. But you can press the Alt (or Option) key and drag a bounding box handle to scale the symbol with respect to its center.

---

The result of your efforts should look like Figure 10-76.

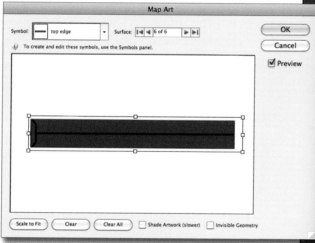

17. *Turn on the shading.* By default, Illustrator doesn't apply any of its lighting or shading variables to mapped artwork. But while it is more computationally intensive to do so, it's hardly worth the effort not to. To shade the artwork, turn on the **Shade Artwork (slower)** check box at the bottom of the dialog box. Then click the **OK** button to accept your changes. Click **OK** in the **3D Extrude & Bevel Options** dialog box exit all the way out and map the symbols to the 3D box art.

18. *Edit the Spine symbol.* In reviewing my artwork, I notice with something resembling horror that, while the front art is up-to-date, the spine reads *Illustrator CS4*, after the previous version of the software.

Figure 10-76.

Fortunately, this is easy to remedy:

- Back in the **Symbols** panel, double-click the Spine thumbnail to edit the symbol in the isolation mode.

- Press T to select the type tool. Drag across the upside-down 4 to highlight the number and replace it with a 5.

- Press the Esc key twice, first to accept your text edits and second to exit the symbol-isolation mode.

- That should be all it takes, but Illustrator misses the edit. So reselect the 3D box art. (If necessary, switch to the outline mode and select the rectangle there.) Switch to the **Appearance** panel, and click on the **3D Extrude & Bevel** link. Turn on the **Preview** check box to inspire Illustrator to pay attention to your symbol adjustment. Click **OK**.

19. *Turn on Cast Shadow path.* To complete the artwork, press F7 to bring up the **Layers** panel. Twirl open the **Background** layer and turn on the item called **Cast Shadow**. The resulting illustration appears in Figure 10-77.

Insofar as Illustrator is concerned, we still have a rectangle and a line of point type. And yet they appear, print, and export as something considerably more, thanks to the power of dynamic effects.

Figure 10-77.

# WHAT DID YOU LEARN?

Match the key concept in the numbered list below with the letter of the phrase that best describes it. Answers appear upside-down at the bottom of the page.

## Key Concepts

1. Static path outlines
2. Dynamic effects
3. The path wigglers
4. Photoshop Effects
5. Document Raster Effects Settings
6. Graphic style
7. Appearance panel
8. Scribble
9. Transform
10. Apply New Effect
11. 3D Bevel & Extrude
12. Pitch, yaw, and roll

## Descriptions

A. This collection of commands in the Distort & Transform submenu—specifically Pucker & Bloat, Roughen, Tweak, and Zig Zag—let you twist and turn path outlines.

B. A saved collection of effects and other Appearance-panel attributes that you can apply, mix, and edit to fit your specific needs.

C. Rather than permanently changing a path outline, these commands apply a series of virtual adjustments, permitting you to change your mind as the occasion dictates.

D. This button accompanies an alert message that implies you shouldn't apply a dynamic effect multiple times in a row—when, in fact, you should!

E. This group of commands in the bottom half of the Effect menu look fine on screen at their default resolution of 72 pixels per inch, but rarely survive in print.

F. One of the best dynamic effects in Illustrator, this command breaks down a fill or stroke attribute into a series of back-and-forth crosshatch lines.

G. The central weigh station for everything you can apply to a path outline, including fills, strokes, and dynamic effects.

H. This command defines the resolution of all pixel-based dynamic effects across an entire illustration.

I. This powerful command lets you add depth to text or path outlines and rotate objects in three-dimensional space.

J. This one command—which lets you nudge, scale, flip, and rotate whole objects or individual stroke and fill attributes—is so outstanding that I've assigned it a keyboard shortcut of Ctrl+E (⌘-E) for *Effect*.

K. These lines and shapes exist as they appear—where you see a corner, there is an anchor point; where you see a curve, there is a segment.

L. When you're in a plane and it buffets like crazy, remember that it's nothing to worry about. It's just the result of riding these three axes of the atmosphere, which are the same as the those of 3D graphics: X, Y, and Z.

## Answers

1K, 2C, 3A, 4E, 5H, 6B, 7G, 8F, 9J, 10D, 11I, 12L

LESSON

# 11

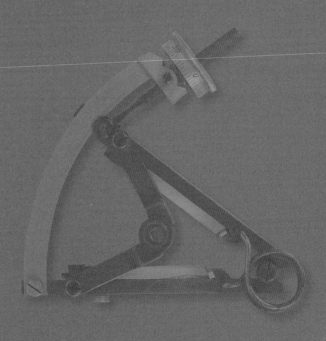

# LIVE TRACE, PAINT, AND COLOR

**THE FEATURES COVERED** in this lesson have one major thing in common: They can make your life easier. Oh yeah, and they each have—or at one point had—the word "live" slapped in front of them, which conveniently allows me to group them all in the same lesson. *Live*, in Adobe-speak, means you can change the parameters of your modifications on the fly, then rethink what you've done and retrace, repaint, or recolor your artwork with no penalties or damage to your illustration. There is no requirement for you to do this in front of an audience or even use a living subject, as is evidenced by the various treatments of our decidedly dead pirate friend in Figure 11-1.

These are all relatively recent features, popping up in Illustrator CS2 or CS3. *Live Trace* is a dialog box-driven function that traces imported raster-based images with vector-defined path outlines. *Live Paint* lets you fill and stroke shapes you *see* (rather than areas specifically defined by paths) using a couple of tools and a few options in the control panel. The *Live Color* group of features (as they were known when they were introduced in CS3) lets you assemble color libraries and recolor selected artwork using an assortment of options divided between two panels and a dialog box. The point is when you use these features, you're sending instructions automatically as opposed to doing meticulous (and tedious) hand-work. All are highly automated and exceedingly powerful. And while the repetition of the term *live* is misleading—the Live Color feature in particular applies static color modifications—one can't help but admire the control and integration that they afford.

Figure 11-1.

# ABOUT THIS LESSON

## Project Files

Before beginning the exercises, make sure you've downloaded the lesson files from *www.oreilly.com/go/Deke-IllustratorCS5*, as directed in Step 2 on page xiv of the Preface. This means you should have a folder called *Lesson Files-Alcs5 1on1* on your desktop (or whatever location you chose). We'll be working with the files inside the *Lesson 11* subfolder.

In this lesson, I'll introduce you to the "live" features in Illustrator, which can seem intimidating at first, but turn out to be some of the easiest, coolest, and most entertaining features in Illustrator.

## Video Lesson 11: The Perspective Grid Tool

Although the new Perspective Grid tool in Illustrator CS5 doesn't go by the name "live" like the other features in this lesson, I've introduced it in this the lesson's video because it too works automatically. With the Perspective Grid tool, you can automate much of the work of putting shapes and even text into alignment with your grid.

To see the new Perspective Grid tool in action, visit *www.oreilly.com/go/deke-IllustratorCS5*. Click the **Watch** button to view the lesson online or click the **Download** button to save it to your computer. During the video, you'll learn these shortcuts:

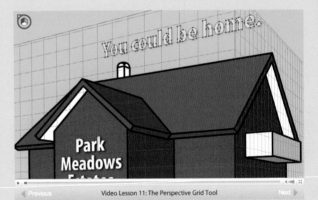

Video Lesson 11: The Perspective Grid Tool

| Operation | Windows shortcut | Macintosh shortcut |
|---|---|---|
| Perspective Grid tool | Shift+P | Shift-P |
| Activate the left plane | Number 1 key | Number 1 key |
| Activate the ground | Number 2 key | Number 2 key |
| Activate the right plane | Number 3 key | Number 3 key |
| Turn off grid | Number 4 key | Number 4 key |
| Toggle in and out of Outline mode | Ctrl+Y | ⌘-Y |
| Add anchor point | Ctrl+Alt+⧵ (backslash key)* | ⌘-Option-⧵ (backslash key)* |
| Increase text size | Ctrl+Shift+Alt+⧠ (period key) | ⌘-Shift-Option-⧠ (period key) |
| Tighten text leading | Ctrl+Shift+↑ | ⌘+Shift+↑ |

* Works only if you loaded the dekeKeys keyboard shortcuts (as directed on page xviii of the Preface).

# Similar Names, Different Features

In general, any one of the features explained in this lesson is less about being "live" than it is "automatic." Consider the following:

- *Live Trace* allows you to convert raster images into vector-based images in an automatic way. You simply place a pixel-based file, like a photograph or piece of scanned art, then give Illustrator a set of objective instructions on how to go about creating paths from it. During the process, you can dynamically effect the outcome with a sophisticated set of controls before turning the resulting outlines into editable paths. Figure 11-2 shows (from top to bottom) my original sketch, the Sharpie-enhanced drawing I scanned, and the resultant trace that I then edited.

- *Live Paint* essentially lets you take a coloring book approach to your work by allowing you to fill or stroke visually discernible areas caused by overlapping shapes (as opposed to having to create or choose discrete paths). As you then move the two paths in relation to each other, the overlapping area in between is recalculated and updated automatically. In the top illustration of Figure 11-3, I filled the overlapping area between two reddish eye shapes with yellow (to give the pirate glowing eyes, naturally). But as I changed the position of the red areas in the bottom illustration, the yellow area automatically updated to fill the new area of overlap (and awesomely gives my pirate flame eyes as it does so). I didn't have to repaint the yellow area at all.

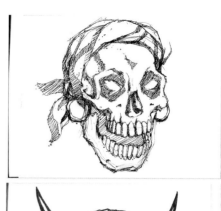

Figure 11-2.

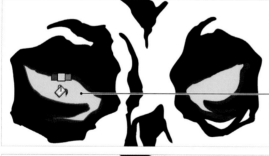

Overlapping area filled with yellow via Live Paint

After moving red shapes, yellow area automatically updates

Figure 11-3.

- *Live Color* is really a feature set as opposed to a specific tool (in fact, Adobe quietly abandoned the phrase "Live Color" in CS4, but I still use it as do many others). With it you can automatically yet systematically replace given colors in your image with completely different ones. For instance, let's say I wanted to change the color motif in the pirate flag in Figure 11-4 to something more tasteful. With a quick trip through a dialog box, I can reassign the colors to go from "1979" to "Cafe Au Lait" color schemes and quickly create a more understated flag, (for your more discerning pirate decorating needs).

Figure 11-4.

The live features explained in this lesson are not only efficient, but fun to use as well. Let's get started with a simple automatic trace.

## Creating a Black-and-White Trace

The Live Trace feature in Illustrator allows you to turn pixels into vectors by tracing over a raster-based image in order to create scalable, editable artwork. Illustrator analyzes the bitmapped image, creates a usable reference, and then traces around that reference file to draw its outlines.

In this exercise, all the vector-based content for this illustration will be created by the Live Trace feature's interaction with an existing Photoshop file. In other words, we'll start with a blank document without a single bit of vector information, and let Illustrator create all the path content on its own. And you'll see how the trace takes shape dynamically as we work our way through Illustrator's controls.

1. ***Create a blank document.*** We'll start with a blank document that will serve as our sheet of virtual tracing paper, so to speak. Choose **File→New**, and name your document "Hand drawn characters." Start with the **New Document Profile** set to **Print**, then change the **Width** value to 1478 points and the **Height** value to 1111 points in order to create a canvas with the same dimensions as the file we're going to trace, as in Figure 11-5. Click **OK**.

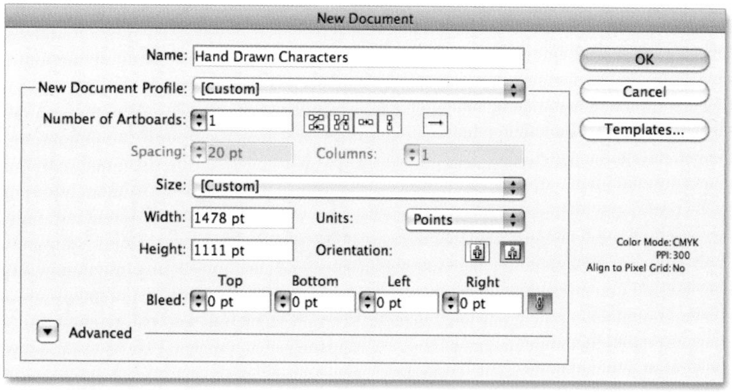


Figure 11-5.

2. ***Rename the default layer.*** To get a really clear vision of how Live Trace works, it's helpful (and good practice in general, of course) to name the layers descriptively. In the Layers panel, double-click on the existing layer with the relatively meaningless name of Layer 1. In the **Layer Options** dialog box rename it "Image," and press the Enter (Return) key.

3. ***Place the file that you want to trace.*** We're going to be tracing a black-and-white image of a handmade alphabet that I drew in Photoshop with a Wacom tablet. To place the source into this document, choose **File→Place** to bring up the **Place** dialog box. Navigate to the *Lesson 11* folder inside *Lesson Files-AIcs5 1on1*. Choose the file called *Alphabet.psd*, make sure the **Link** check box is turned on, and then click the **Place** button. Illustrator will import the file into your document, where its contents appear within a blue bounding box, as you can see in Figure 11-6 on the next page.

PEARL OF WISDOM

Linking to a file—rather than embedding it directly—keeps your file size manageable. The link is also updatable, meaning that if you make changes to the original source, those changes can be updated in your working document. Be warned, Illustrator will need to be able to find that link if you are to work with the linked file's contents. So if you change the name or the location of the original, you'll have to relink by showing Illustrator where the file is. You can use Live Trace with either an embedded or a linked file, but for the purposes of this lesson, we'll stick with the streamlined efficiency of placing linked images.

4. ***Examine the linked file.*** Even though it appears as if we have an image populated with my distinctive characters, what we essentially have is an empty illustration through which we're seeing the contents of the linked file. A linked file exists separately from the illustration to which it is linked, but a preview of its contents are visible from within your working document.

Figure 11-6.

To see what I mean, twirl open the **Image** layer: There is now an *Alphabet.psd* item within. Make sure that item is meatballed, and the control panel will reveal a slew of features for managing the linked file, as documented in Figure 11-7.

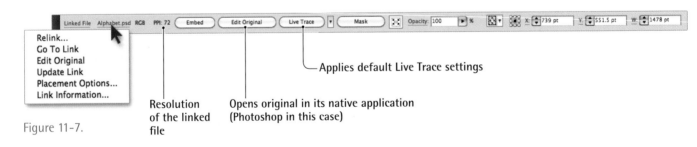

Relink...
Go To Link
Edit Original
Update Link
Placement Options...
Link Information...

Resolution of the linked file

Opens original in its native application (Photoshop in this case)

Applies default Live Trace settings

Figure 11-7.

If you hover over the name of the linked file, in this case *Alphabet.psd*, in the control panel, you can view the path to the file on your hard drive. If you actually click that filename entry, you'll get a pop-up menu (revealed in Figure 11-7) with a variety of options including those for relinking, updating, and examining some basic information about the linked file. You'll also notice that the resolution on the image to be traced is very low, just 72 ppi, which will serve us just fine for tracing.

5. *Apply the Live Trace feature.* Now that you have the trace-able file in place and properly selected, you have four options for tracing:

- You can click the Live Trace button in the control panel to accept Illustrator's default idea of the best tracing options. The results always create a black-and-white image regard-less of the color in your source file.

- You can click the arrow to the right of the Live Trace button and choose Tracing Options from the bottom of the pop-up menu. This brings up an initially daunting dialog box that gives you complete control over the tracing process.

- From that same pop-up menu, you can choose from a variety of preset options that set the tracing parameters based on the type of image you're working with, such as Photo High Fidelity or Inked Drawing. If you use presets, you'll have to investigate which preset gives you the best results for your particular image.

- For immediate access to the path outlines created by the Live Trace process, you can Alt-click (Option-click) the Live Trace button to expand the path outlines that repre-sent Illustrator's best guess at the tracing. You can then dig in and start modifying these paths with the white arrow or pen tools. (Note that this method breaks the link with the traced image, meaning it is no longer a live, dynamic trace.)

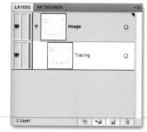

For this particular image, with its black-and-white simplicity yet hand-drawn complexity, we'll start with the simplest approach and work from there. So click the **Live Trace** button and take a look at what Illustrator has created in Figure 11-8. Note that the layer name automatically changes to Tracing (although in my opinion, this is actually the Trac*ee*.) In the image window, you'll see Illustrator's best (default) stab at tracing the Alpha-bet image.

Figure 11-8.

6. *Zoom in to see more detail.* From a distance, the vector-based characters look pretty close to my pixel-based ones. Zoom into the DE section of the image, and you'll notice that Illustrator created smooth vector-based lines from the raster image. However, the traced characters possess some odd bumps and swirly points that weren't there in the original.

7. *Change the preview settings for the vector tracing results.* Illustrator provides a number of preview options that will give you a better idea of how it came up with this default trace. As long as the traced object is meatballed, the control panel will display two pyramid-like icons, circled in Figure 11-9.

Figure 11-9.

The solid, chunky pyramid on the left controls the raster preview settings that are associated with the original placed image; for now, click that icon and set it to **Original Image**. The smooth outlined pyramid on the right controls the preview settings for the tracing results. Click the smooth pyramid to see the following options (all of which are demonstrated in Figure 11-10 using our current illustration):

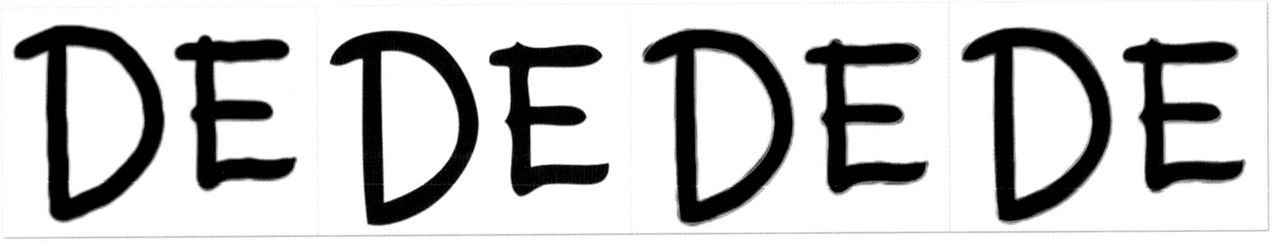

# DE DE DE DE

No Tracing Result          Tracing Result          Outlines          Outlines with Tracing

Figure 11-10.

- *No Tracing Result* turns off the trace to allow you to view the original pixel image. The trace is still there but hidden from view.

- *Tracing Result*, the default setting, shows the current state of the dynamic trace.

- *Outlines* displays a cyan-colored outline of the trace superimposed over the original image.

- *Outlines with Tracing* reveals both the outlines and the fills of the current trace. The fills are displayed with reduced opacity so that you can still see the original below.

In Figure 11-10, transparent display of the fill is particularly visible along the top part of the last D, where you can see that Illustrator filled in the outline to smooth out the antialiased edges of the raster image underneath.

The **Outlines** option is probably best for our purposes. Choose it from the smooth pyramid icon's pop-up menu.

8. *Change the preview settings for the original raster image.* Clicking the chunky pyramid in the control panel will reveal the options for the preview of the raster image. You can choose to view the original, not view it, or set it to Transparent (which is really "translucent" in this case). Each of these options has some obvious uses depending on what you'd like to see behind your trace. The other option, Adjusted Image, will be handy for this exercise, but it requires a little bit of explaining.

When you're creating a black-and-white trace, Illustrator considers every pixel to be either black or white, even when there are shades of gray in the original. (Illustrator is very literal about "black and white.") So the *adjusted image* represents Illustrator's interpretation of our original, with every pixel being assigned to either black or white. The result becomes the sole basis for Illustrator's tracing outline.

Figure 11-11.

To see what I mean, choose **Adjusted Image** from the black pyramid's pop-up menu. See the chunky black-and-white interpreted image and the way the outlines attempt to define it (shown in Figure 11-11)? Illustrator sent all the gray pixels that provided smooth transitions to one or the other extreme, then used that interpretation as a basis for its trace. This intermediary analysis explains some of the otherwise mildly inexplicable choices Illustrator made during the Live Trace process. But fortunately, we can change the settings for that adjusted image to get better results.

9. *Zoom out to another area of the image.* For the next few steps, which center around the settings in the Tracing Options dialog box, we want to focus on a different area of the image, namely the first four rows of alphabet variations. Adjust your view so that you can see each of the first four rows of letters.

10. *Increase the Threshold point.* One of the most useful features for fine-tuning a black-and-white tracing is the Threshold setting. *Threshold* determines the point at which pixels are converted to either black or white in the creation of the adjusted image. This assessment is based on luminance levels: The luminance scale goes from 0 (which is black) to 255 (which is white).

Where all the gray pixels fall in your adjusted image depends on where you set the Threshold. You can see in the control panel, that Threshold is currently set to its default, smack-in-the-middle value of 128, meaning that any pixel with a luminance level of 128 or greater will be converted to white and the rest will become black.

If you click the right-pointing arrow next to the Threshold value, you'll see a slider that indicates where you are on the scale. As you move that slider, you can see changes in the characters in the trace preview.

- For instance, if you moved the Threshold slider all the way to the left to a value of 1, you'd be telling Illustrator that every pixel with a luminance value of 1 or greater should be changed to white. This would have the effect of making our letters very skinny and rough as in the left illustration in Figure 11-12.

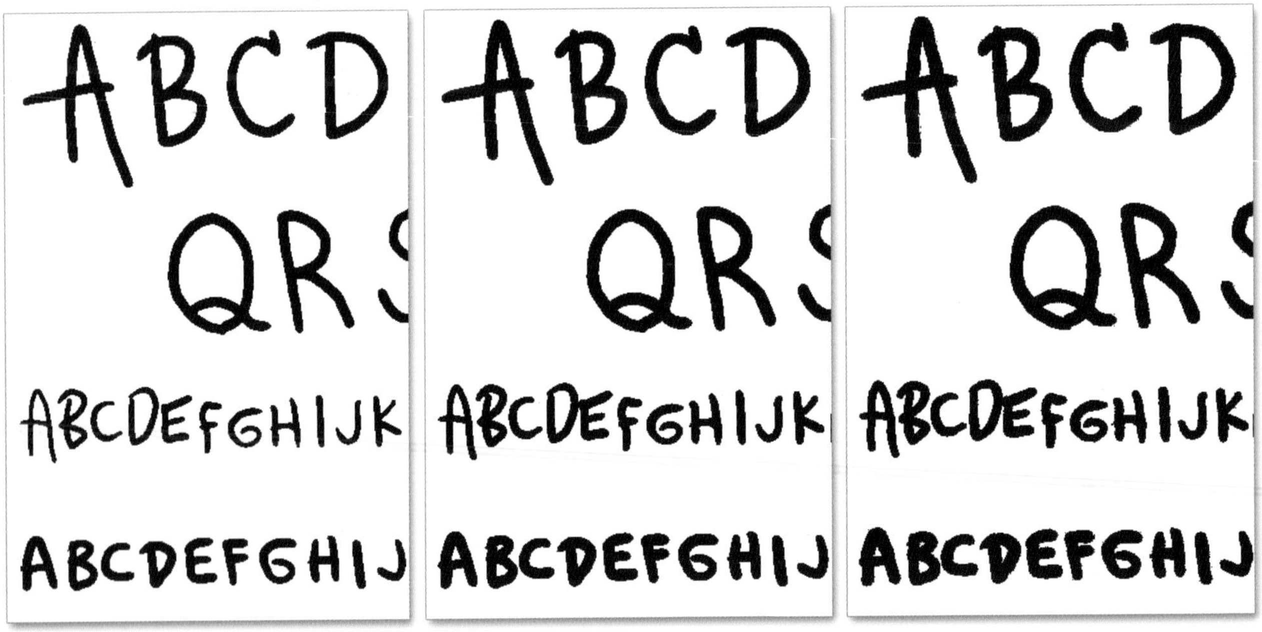

Figure 11-12.

For purposes of clarity, I temporarily turned off the outline preview so you could view the unobscured adjusted image.

- Conversely, if you moved the slider all the way to 255, every pixel that wasn't completely white would turn black, resulting in the illustration on the right side of the figure and turning the bolder characters into sloppy messes.

For this image, set the **Threshold** value to 240 to produce nice plump letters without the gooey effect, as you can see in the center illustration of Figure 11-12.

Note, if you enter a Threshold value manually using the numbers on your keyboard, then you need to press Tab to see the results of any changes.

11. ***Turn the Tracing Result preview back on.*** Remember, the Threshold changes are applied to the adjusted version of the image. To see the current tracing, click the smooth pyramid icon in the control panel. Choose **Tracing Result** to see how the Threshold adjustment will affect the trace. In Figure 11-13, you can see the same three Threshold settings (values of 1, 240, and 255 respectively left to right) with the preview set to show the tracing result.

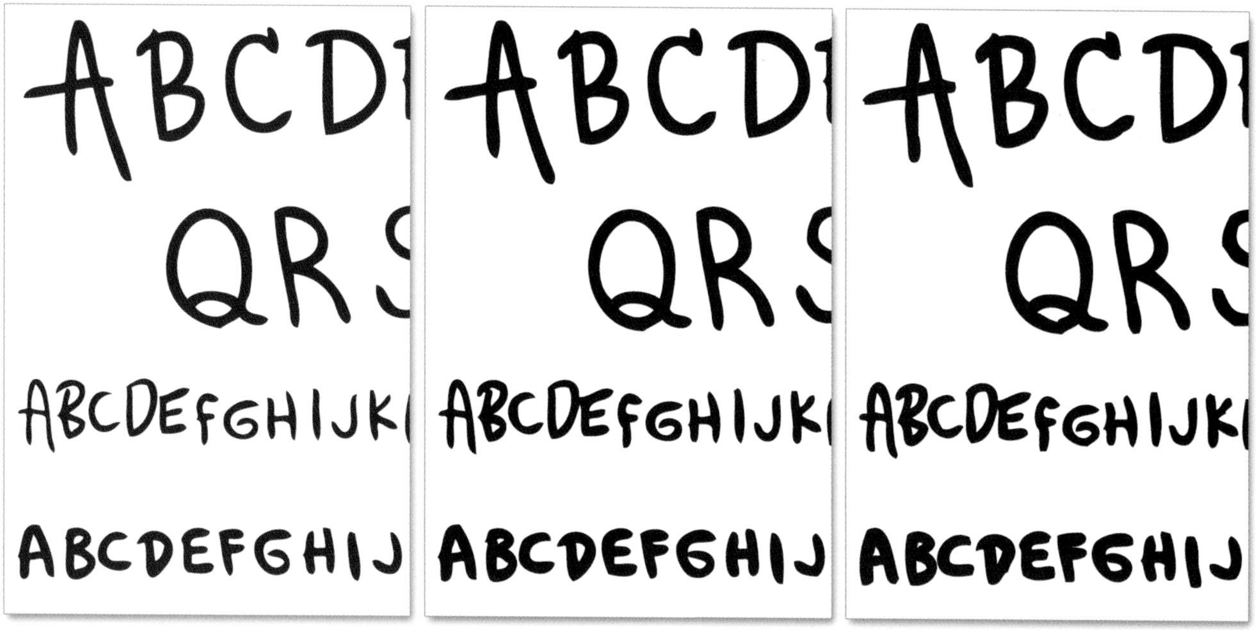


Figure 11-13.

12. *Lower the Min Area value.* The *minimum area*, appropriately shortened in the control panel to Min Area, indicates the smallest particle that will be traced inside a piece of artwork. The Min Area setting allows you to tell Illustrator to ignore groups of pixels that are smaller than the numerical value you've set.

For instance, if you were to take the Min Value in our current project up to 1000 pixels as I've done in Figure 11-14 (don't try this at home kids; I'm just trying to make a point), then any area that is made up of less than that amount will disappear from the trace. Interior cutouts and even entire letters disappear from the illustration, because those lost areas are smaller than 1000 pixels in total area. Obviously not the results we want! For this relatively clean illustration, set the **Min Area** value to 5 pixels.

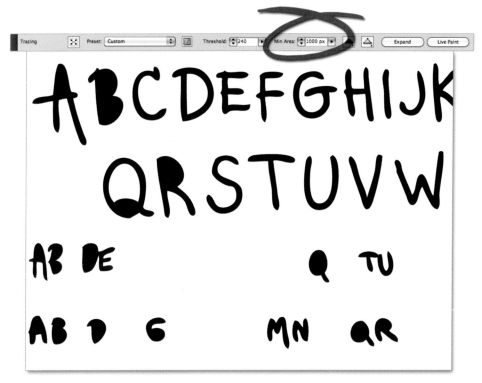

Figure 11-14.

13. *Move to a different area of the image.* For the next few steps, which center around the settings in the Tracing Options dialog box, we want to focus on a different area of the image. So zoom in to the area with that cocky *o* (with the flourish above and within) is visible, as in Figure 11-15.

Figure 11-15.

14. *Open the Tracing Options dialog box.* Having introduced you to all the relevant settings in the control panel, I think you're ready to move on to the real treasure trove of Live Trace settings. Start by clicking the icon indicated in Figure 11-16 to bring up the **Tracing Options** dialog box, an initially daunting but immensely logical and infinitely useful set of controls. Don't worry, we'll take this baby one step at a time.

Figure 11-16.

15. *Turn on the Preview check box.* Every setting you change in the Tracing Options dialog box is a dynamic effect. And those effects will be sooner enjoyed if you turn on the Preview check box so you can watch your trace develop as you work your way through the settings.

16. *Peruse the choices in the left section.* Note that at the bottom of the dialog box there are two sets of View settings. These two pop-up menus are exactly analogous to the chunky and smooth pyramid icons we saw earlier. Their position here also gives you a clue to the other options available. In other words, the Adjustment options on the left side affect the raster image, and the Trace Settings on the right control the vector output. Let's start with the options on the left:

    • The *Mode* setting contains a pop-up menu from which you can choose the type of trace you are performing: Black and White, Grayscale, or Color. For our image, the default Black and White option is appropriate. (We'll take a look at tracing color in the next exercise.)

    • The *Threshold* setting is exactly the same thing we saw earlier in the control panel in Step 8, basically setting the luminance point at which pixels should be considered black or white.

    • The next two options are dimmed because they control color images: The *Palette* setting determines which color palette will be used, and the *Max Colors* value designates how many colors will be traced.

    • The *Output to Swatches* check box allows you to export colors to swatches. Since we're working in black and white, both of which are already represented in the Swatches panel, it's not relevant here.

    • The *Blur* value applies a blur to your raster image based on the radius you set. It's useful for blurring away scratches, dust, or particles from a scanned image, but here it just makes a mess of things so we'll leave it set to 0.

    If you intrepidly want to see the effects of the Blur setting, you can experiment by changing the Mode to Grayscale, and upping the Max Colors setting to 256. I'm not really sure I'd call it a "blur" as much as a "smudge."

- The *Resample* option allows you to reduce or increase the number of pixels in the raster image. This option comes in handy when you're tracing a high resolution color photograph and you want to reduce the number of pixels for more efficient results. (More pixels does not necessarily mean a better trace result, and it can slog the process down considerably.) Nice to know this option exists, but I generally try to reduce the resolution of items I'm going to trace before placing them in Illustrator in the first place.

Admittedly, with this particular image, we didn't find much to adjust in this first half of this dialog box, but that will change in the next steps as we explore the options on the right side.

17. ***Turn on the Ignore White check box.*** Frankly, you don't really want to trace all the white stuff; creating outlines around the black letters will be enough. A quick look at the list of handy information along the right side of the dialog box shows there are 419 paths, 2549 anchors, 2 colors, and 210 areas. At the moment, Illustrator is creating paths (and subpaths) around both the white and black "colors." Turn on the **Ignore White** check box at the bottom of the right column. As you can see in Figure 11-17, the number of paths drops to 209, one less than the number of areas (which also includes the big white area of the background). Also note that the number of colors drops to 1, namely black.

18. ***Change the Raster View.*** Now that we've eliminated the white areas, the letters are looking pretty jagged in the preview window. That's because we're seeing through the trace in some places to the adjusted image behind it, and that adjusted image no longer has any white areas.

Figure 11-17.

Figure 11-18.

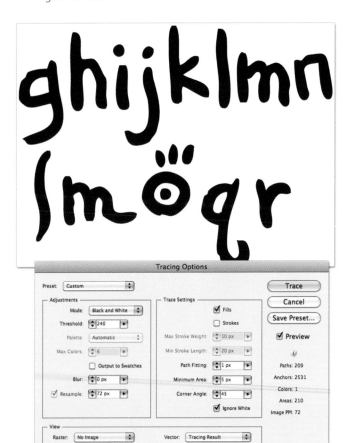

Figure 11-19.

So in the **View** section of the dialog box, choose **No Image** from the **Raster** pop-up menu, as in Figure 11-18. Illustrator now displays just the smooth tracing result.

19. *Adjust the Trace Settings.* With our strictly black letters and nice compound paths, let's take a look at some of the other options available:

- The first two check boxes instruct Illustrator to either create close filled compound paths or attempt to make strokes out of the traced shapes. The default setting of the Fills check box turned on and the Strokes check box turned off is going to be your best bet unless you have very fine, straight lines. In our case, we want to trace around the letters and so leaving just the **Fills** check box turned on is the best option.

- Path Fitting determines how closely Illustrator has to match the pixels in your original art. If you have ratty pixels in clumsy art, you may want to give Illustrator a lot of leeway here. In this case, the artwork is in pretty great shape, so set the **Path Fitting** to 1 pixel.

- The Minimum Area setting is exactly the same as the Min Area value we set in Step 12, so leave it as is.

- The Corner Angle setting indicates how sharp a corner has to be in order to be counted as a corner point. We're a little sharp at the default setting of 20 degrees. So change the **Corner Angle** to 45 degrees and note how the letters smooth out a little.

Figure 11-19 shows the results and all the settings.

20. *Save the settings as a preset.* Before you leave the Tracing Options dialog box, you can save all these settings to use for other compound path tracing. Click the **Save Preset** button and name your preset "Compound Paths," and click **OK**. Next time you check that pop-up menu to the left of the Live Trace button, Compound Paths will be available (and quite useful, actually) from the preset list.

21. *Apply all the changes.* Now that you have optimized all the settings for this image, and you've saved your options as a handy preset for future use, click the **Trace** button to apply all the changes.

22. *Expand the Live Trace.* We've done everything we can with the automated controls, so it's time to expand the trace and get rid of the remaining lumps manually. Start by clicking the **Expand** button in the control panel. All the letters become editable path outlines. To celebrate, choose a nice red from the **Swatches** panel and fill all the newly traced letters with color, as I've done in Figure 11-20.

Figure 11-20.

23. ***Examine the all important letter D.*** The Live Trace settings take us pretty far, but they're obviously not perfect. Examine exhibit D: The first uppercase D in the top row is full of interesting bumps and wobbles. Some of them, like nibble marks I targeted on the left in Figure 11-21 can be easily smoothed by simply selecting the offending anchor points with the white arrow tool and deleting them. You can see the effects of zapping those points on the right.

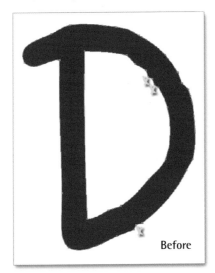
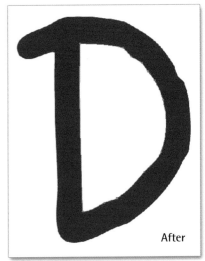

Before      After

Figure 11-21.

---

Yes, in a fit of total metacommentary, I made the happy little Xs of Destruction in the left image out of the same alphabet file. I told you they could be useful. Even for targeting problematic anchor points for annihilation.

---

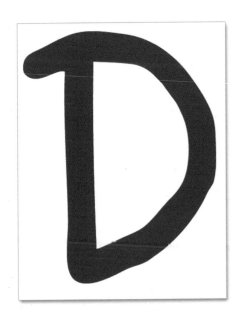

Figure 11-22.

24. ***Smooth the upper edge.*** Although it's satisfying work, removing anchor points for this entire trace could get tedious. If you prefer something a little faster, grab the smooth tool from the toolbox (it lives underneath the pencil tool) and run it multiple times over the wobbly areas. The smoothed top curve of the D in Figure 11-22 is the result of just a few passes with the smooth tool. It's not exacting, but it's effective and it doesn't take pinpoint mouse work.

---

If you use the smooth tool to a subpath (like the interior of the D), you'll deselect the larger path and need to reselect it to work on another area.

---

Make adjustments to each of the letters as you see fit. In the end you have a unique alphabet file that you can edit, scale, mix-and-match, then put to use as you see fit.

# Tracing Full-Color Artwork

Live Tracing in Illustrator is not limited to black-and-white images, either in terms of what you trace or what you create. Starting with a full-color raster image, you can either trace a black-and-white version or create color-filled paths. When I say "full color," I don't mean the 16 some-odd million colors that are digitally possible with an 8-bit per channel image. That would make more paths than you (or even I) could ever want to deal with, and you might as well leave such a file to Photoshop in the first place. But the fact is that in Illustrator, you can distill the colors down to something reasonable while maintaining the relative complexity of the original. And you can save your working color palette for later use, including the ability to adjust, edit, and swap those colors as you see fit.

To trace the scanned full-color drawing in this exercise, we'll be working through virtually the same process we did in the last exercise. But when we get to the Tracing Options dialog box, there are some new considerations to make. And then I'll show you how to save (and alter) colors from the original artwork in order to make color edits to the final results.

1. *Open a file.* Start by opening the file called *B&W Astronaut.ai* from the *Lesson 11* folder inside *Lesson Files-AIcs5 1on1*. This image, shown in Figure 11-23, is based on a scan of an image I drew on cheap paper with a variety of colored Sharpies. You're probably wondering why I named this obviously colorful Mayan Space traveler "B&W." My mysterious ways will become clear in the next step.

2. *Twirl open the Image layer.* I wanted you to get a sense of the original file we were working with at the outset of this exercise, so I started the tracing process for you but saved the file with the preview set to show the original image only. In the **Layers** panel, twirl open the Image layer and notice the Tracing object that's already within. As you learned, in the last exercise, there are controls for setting the preview of both the raster image and the vector output, and I currently have those chunky and smooth pyramids in the control panel to show the Original Image and No Tracing Results, respectively. Thus you get to see our astronaut in full, vibrant color to start.

Figure 11-23.

3. *Change the preview settings.* To see the trace I've already started in this file, meatball the **Tracing** object in the **Layers** panel. Then set the chunky, solid pyramid in the control panel to **No Image** (in order to hide the colored original) and set the smooth, outlined pyramid to **Tracing Result**.

Give Illustrator a moment—this is a high-resolution image and turning off the preview basically turns off the tracing "dynamically" even though the settings are still there—and eventually you'll see the fairly amazing, detailed black-and-white trace shown in Figure 11-24.

Figure 11-24.

4. *Examine the Tracing Options.* As you learned in the preceding exercise, you can revisit the tracing settings at any time by clicking the Trace Options Dialog icon in the control panel. Click it now to open the **Tracing Options** dialog box and reveal the choices I made for the preliminary black and white trace, which you can see in Figure 11-25 on the facing page.

Here's the gist of how I arrived at these results:

- I started with the Compound Paths preset that we created and saved in the previous exercise.

- The preset's Threshold value was 240, which basically made any colored area turn black and made the trace a ghastly mess. I lowered the Threshold value to 50 to open up the white spaces and establish the nice black paths.

- I raised the Minimum Value to 100 pixels to get rid of some schnivelly areas that made my results look like a bad photocopy.

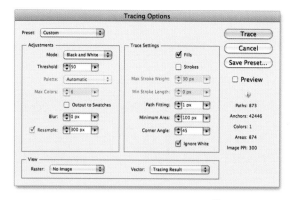

Figure 11-25.

5. *Change the options to make a color trace.* As cool and Machiavellian as our astronaut is as a black-and-white trace, I want to convert it to a color trace. Because Live Trace works dynamically, we can just make changes to the trace we have going. To start, choose **Color** from the **Mode** pop-up menu. You'll note in Figure 11-26 on the next page, that some items that were dimmed when we were working in black and white are now available, and others that were active before have now gone dim. Here's what I want you to change:

---

With this high resolution image, I urge you not to turn on the Preview check box at the moment, because you'll be waiting for Illustrator to update the preview after every step. To avoid frustration, leave it off while you make the changes you can without seeing a preview.

---

- Leave the Palette setting at Automatic so that Illustrator can make its own judgment about which colors to use.

- Set the **Max Colors** value to 24. It can go as high as 256, but 24 is plenty of paths and colors for Illustrator to work with. We don't want to be here all day.

- Turn on the **Output to Swatches** check box. Currently the Swatches panel contains only four swatches (black, white, registration, and none). Illustrator will collect the 24 colors it chooses to trace and plop them in the Swatches panel for our later use.

- Leave Blur set to 0, which is pretty much where I always leave it, everytime.

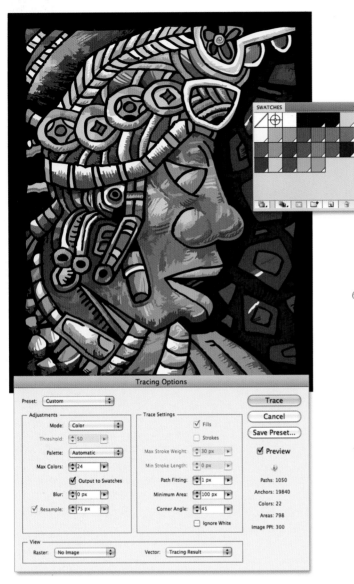

Figure 11-26.

PEARL OF WISDOM

Definitely leave the Ignore White check box turned off for this trace. While it was helpful when we were just trying to capture the all black letters in the previous exercise, in full-color artwork it can make strange things happen.

• Set the **Resample** value to 75 pixels which is exactly 25 percent of our original 300 pixels per inch. When you downsample in this way, it's good to use regular fractions like 25, 50, or 75 percent, rather than some random number. A higher resolution would keep more of the cross hatching, but again, for our purposes simpler and swifter will work fine.

Once you have the left side filled out, turn on the **Preview** check box to see the results so far, as shown in Figure 11-26. Note that the Swatches panel is now filled with colors from the image.

6. *Change the Path Fitting amount.* The Path Fitting setting from our preset was set to a very low number leftover from when we were working on the low-resolution alphabet file. But such a high rate of conformity for tracing the pixels in this high-resolution drawing is giving this trace some wobbly outlines. To plump them up a little change the **Path Fitting** amount to 4 pixels.

7. *Decrease the Minimum Area.* As you recall from the previous exercise, the Minimum Area (or Min Area as it's known in the control panel) determines the number of pixels that must be in a clump for the trace to recognize it. The lower the Minimum Area, the more detail you will have; the higher the Minimum Area, the more you will distill your image into its core components. Of course, lowering the Minimum Area increases the number of paths and the complexity of the artwork (and increases the time it will take for Illustrator to calculate the trace). To keep some cross-hatching detail without completely outlining every single pixel in vector form, set the **Minimum Area** to 50 pixels.

8. *Save a preset.* To keep these settings handy for your next full color art piece, click the **Save Preset** button, name this collection of settings "Full Color Scanned Art," and click **OK**.

9. *Finish the trace.* The final results of the trace area is on display in Figure 11-27. Now that you've saved the settings for future use, click the **Trace** button to close the dialog box.

10. *Sample an unwanted color.* On the whole, the artwork is looking great, and Illustrator has done a particularly nice job on the headdress area of our Mayan's space helmet. But I'm not thrilled with the light blue color in those decorations anymore. Fortunately, because we saved the colors as swatches in the Tracing Options dialog box, all 24 colors are now available as global swatches in the Swatches panel.

---

You can identify a global swatch by its white triangle in the lower-right corner of the swatch.

---

When it comes to swatches, *global* means that any edit you make to the swatch is reflected in the corresponding area of the artwork. To target the unwanted blue I mentioned for alteration, press the I key to grab the eyedropper tool and then click in one of the blue areas of the headdress. The similarly colored swatch will be selected in the Swatches panel. Notice the white border that appears around its edge, as shown in Figure 11-28. Although my case and yours may certainly differ, for me it's the color called Tracing 7. (I've done this exercise a few times, and the numbering of the swatch colors changes each time.)

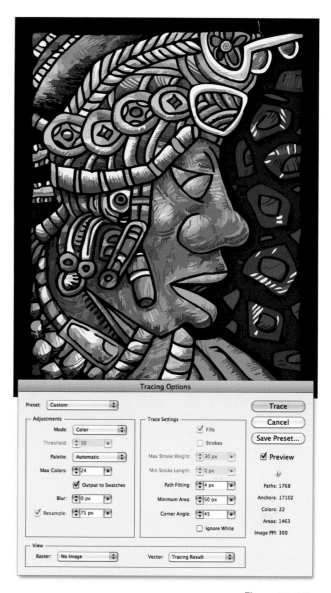

Figure 11-27.

Eyedropping this color...

...selects this swatch.

Figure 11-28.

11. *Swap out the blue for gold.* Double-click the swatch that corresponds to the undesired color to bring up the **Swatch Options** dialog box. Change the color to a nice cosmic gold by setting the CMYK values (shown in Figure 11-29) to **C:** 0, **M:** 35. **Y:** 100. and **K:** 0. Click **OK**, and watch both the swatch and any area that had been filled with that exact blue (formerly known, in my case, as Tracing 7) turn a nice rich gold, as you can see in Figure 11-29.

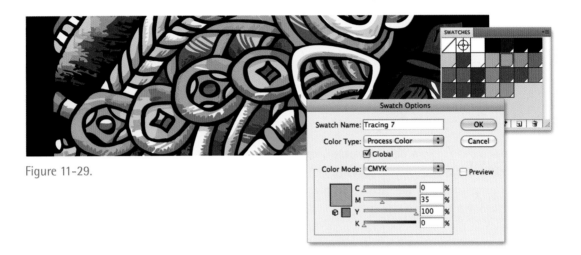

Figure 11-29.

12. *Select another problematic color region.* Modifying global swatches is a great way to get rid of or edit away all occurrences of colors that you don't like, but what if you wanted to change only some instances of a color rather than all of them. Say we wanted to get rid of some of those greenish blotches in our astronaut's face. Eyedropper the greenish brown area shown in Figure 11-30. I can see that, in my case, I've selected Tracing 15, but I can't immediately tell where else in the image Tracing 15 might be.

Figure 11-30.

13. *Change the swatch to something ridiculously noticeable.* To help you see all the areas that are connected to the chosen swatch, double-click it in the **Swatches** panel. When the **Swatch Options** dialog box opens, crank up the color to something immediately noticeable that is far from anything that already exists in the artwork, like **C:** 40, **M:** 100. **Y:** 0, and **K:** 0. Turn on the Preview check box. You can see in Figure 11-31, there are several areas throughout the illustration where Tracing 15 (or whatever number it is in your file) appears, many of them that we don't want affected by a global swatch edit.

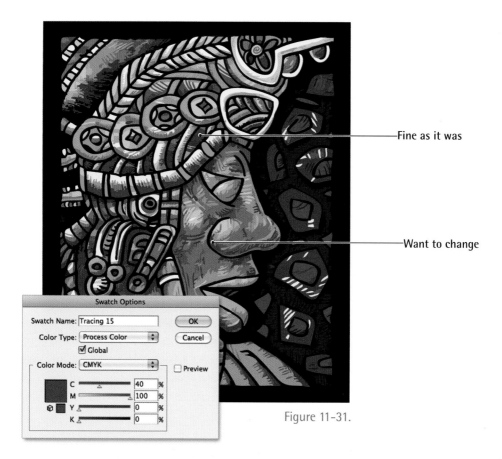

Fine as it was

Want to change

Figure 11-31.

14. *Cancel the swatch change.* We're using the hideous purple for identification purposes only, so click **Cancel** to abandon it. Obviously, the global solution isn't going to work for this edit. Instead I'm going to give you a sneak preview of Live Paint, which we'll see much more of in the next exercise. With it, you can easily repaint selected regions of your image quickly and easily.

PEARL OF WISDOM

You're not limited to scanned art with Live Trace, in fact, it makes interesting work of photographs, especially high contrast portraits, as you can see in the sidebar on page 354, "Live Tracing a Photographic Portrait."

# Live Tracing a Photographic Portrait

One of the most interesting things you can do with Live Trace is to apply it to a full-color photograph, anything from a landscape to a still life can yield interesting results when converted to vector art. But Live Trace is especially effective with portrait shots, particularly high-contrast portraits with lots of detail (and of course, detail is what makes we humans recognize ourselves in portraits, whether they be photographed, drawn, or traced.

By way of example, I applied Live Trace to a lovely photograph from one of my favorite iStockphoto photographers, Alexandra Alexis. The original photograph is shown on the left below.

The initial process is the same one you followed in the first two exercises of this lesson. You place the photograph into an Illustrator document and start tracing. On the right below is a striking black-and-white traced version of the image that I made with one click of the Live Trace button, simply applying the default settings with no alterations whatsoever. Check out the detail in the hair. I want hair like that.

There are a few things to consider when you're working with a color trace of a photograph. For the most part, I started with the preset we created in the Mayan Astronaut exercise with a few small tweaks:

- I did bump up the colors to 27 from our initial preset of 24, just to make sure I gave enough smoothness to the continuous tone spirit of the original.

- I skipped outputting the colors to swatches because I actually wanted to take advantage of using a predetermined color palette during a color trace (I'll demonstrate that shortly).

- I have to say, I'm not still using the Blur setting at all. It may smooth out some of the reticulated areas in her face, but it completely turned her eyes and other facial detail to mush.

- I turned up the Minimum Area to 200 to avoid as much patchy color areas in her skin as possible while still grabbing lots of great detail.

- You have to keep the Path Fitting fairly low, especially for a profile like this, because letting the path get too loose actually changes the shape of her nose.

On the left at the bottom of the facing page is the result of my trace with the Tracing Options I've described. Note that there is still great detail in the hair. On second thought, I think *that's* the hair I want.

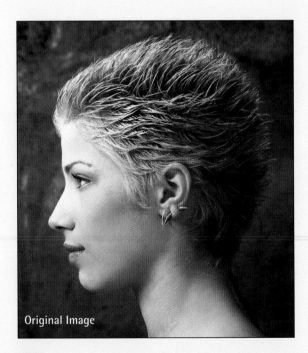

Original Image

Live Trace default

But it did seem as though the model had become a little jaundiced. The colors in the original photograph were much more vibrant. Illustrator has a means for establishing a custom color palette with which to conduct a trace. Here's how it works:

- First set the previews (via the chunky and smoothy pyramids in the control panel) to Original Image and No Tracing Results respectively so that you can lift colors from your original.

- Shift-click a color area that you think reflects the color scheme of the original with the eyedropper tool to set the foreground color. Then Alt-click (Option-click) the New Swatch icon (that looks like a page) at the bottom of the Swatches panel to make a swatch of that color.

(I did this for 27 different colors, because I wanted to stick with the 27 colors I originally requested from Illustrator.)

- Click on the first of your custom colors in the Swatches panel, then Shift-click on the last one to select the entire collection.

- Next, click the first icon on the left of the Swatches panel, known as the Swatch Libraries icon, and choose Save Swatches from the pop-up menu. Let Illustrator save it to wherever it wants (since that's where it will look first). Save the file with some kind of memorable name, I'm using "Alexandra Alexis" for my collection.

- Load the color palette by clicking once again on the Swatch Libraries icon and choosing User Defined→Alexandra Alexis (or whatever you named yours). This loads the palette in a new panel which will pop up on your screen.

- Reopen the Tracing Options dialog box, and now you should be able to choose "Alexandra Alexis" (in my case) from the Palette pop-up menu.

When I redid the trace with my custom colors, I got a much warmer, healthier result, as you can see below.

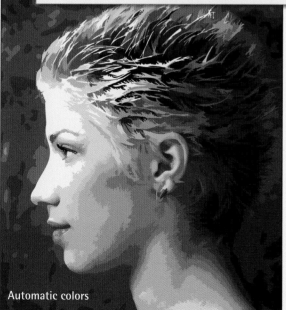

Automatic colors

Custom palette

15. *Evoke Live Paint.* Click the **Live Paint** button in the control panel. When you do, you'll first see the newly expanded paths of your trace appear. Press Ctrl-Shift-A (⌘-Shift-A) to deselect the paths, we aren't going to need them directly.

16. *Choose a color to paint with.* Let's replace the dark greens in the face with a browner shade. For me, the color I want is the swatch called Tracing 12, which has the same general luminance value as the color I'm replacing. Click that swatch, then press the K key to grab the live paint tool.

17. *Fill in the greenish area.* As you'll see in detail in the next exercise, Live Paint recognizes areas where paths or subpaths overlap, without you having to select such a path directly. If you hover over the original greenish area with your live paint cursor, you'll see the border light up with a bright red (I've changed it to neon green in Figure 11-32 for better visibility). You'll also see your chosen replacement color in the center of a triad of color swatches. Click with the cursor in the highlighted area as I'm doing in the figure, and voila, you're painting with the new swatch color.

Figure 11-32.

18. *Continue to click and swap color regions as you see fit.* We'll see much more of Live Paint in a moment, but for now, you can rid yourself of all the greenish tones in the face by clicking on them as they light up. If you'd like to paint with a different color, switch to another color in the Swatches panel using the arrow keys to move through the colors in order. When the color you want is in the center of the triad of swatches, you're set to paint with it.

# Filling and Stroking Path Intersections Dynamically

Live Paint gives Illustrator the ability to detect any color intersecting areas within an illustration. So rather than treating everything in terms of discrete objects that overlap and cover each other, Live Paint sees your illustration as consisting of the lines in a coloring book or the panes of a stained glass window. You don't need to create a specialized object to which you apply your color, you merely select two overlapping shapes and click on the intersection with a paint bucket. No need to draw a new shape or create a subpath. And even better, as you change the intersection, by moving one or both of its components, Illustrator updates the effect to the altered area of overlap.

The convenience of Live Paint has always been pretty obvious to me, but the day I came to appreciate its real power was when I consulted my good friend and former Illustrator product manager Mordy Golding. I wanted to create a set of Olympic-style rings, with all the overlaps and underlaps in the proper places. I was bemoaning Illustrator's inability to create such interlocking objects, when Mordy calmly pointed out that it could in fact be done with Live Paint. And then Mordy proceeded to expand my mind. The following exercise reveals what I learned from that conversation.

1. *Open a file.* Go to the *Lesson 11* folder inside *Lesson Files-AIcs5 1on1* and open *Olympic dreams.ai*. As you can see in Figure 11-33, it's a simple set of decidedly non-interlocking rings created with compound paths. Notice how the blue ring completely covers the yellow one, which completely covers the black one, and so on. This is a by product of standard vector-based stacking order.

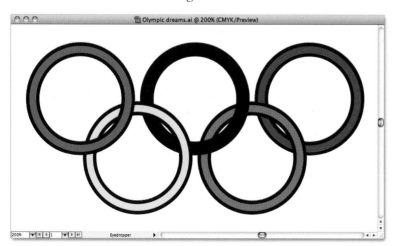

Figure 11-33.

2. *Convert the rings to a Live Paint group* Select all the rings by pressing Ctrl-A (⌘-A on the Mac). Then grab the live paint bucket tool (the one that looks like a bucket of paint) from the toolbox, as in Figure 11-34. If you can't find it, press the K key.

3. *Choose the first paint color.* Live Paint will fill your image with a color from the Swatches panel. Above the paint bucket cursor is a triad of mini-swatches that show you the current selected color in the center, with the previous and proceeding colors on the left and right respectively. Press the right-arrow key until the center color above the bucket is yellow.

4. *Create a live paint group.* Click the lower of the two areas where the yellow ring intersects the blue one (as demonstrated in Figure 11-35). You now have a live paint group.

Figure 11-34.

Figure 11-35.

Move your cursor around the image, and notice how different overlapping areas light up with the thick neon red outline like the one around the small yellow section in Figure 11-24. The outline indicates you could click to paint the areas should you choose to.

Figure 11-36.

5. *Enable Live Paint to work on strokes.* The default setting for Live Paint is to just supply fills, but you can set it to work on strokes as well. Double-click the paint bucket icon in the toolbox to bring up the **Live Paint Bucket Options** dialog box, as shown in Figure 11-36. Turn on the **Paint Strokes** check box, and click **OK**.

6. *Paint the strokes on the yellow ring.* Obviously, the strokes of the blue and yellow rings' intersection are disrupting the interlocking effect. Make sure the **Stroke** is set to 4 points in the control panel. Then, move your cursor over the right side of the yellow-over-blue region so that you get a brush cursor and the small stroke section lights up in the red-orange highlight color, as in Figure 11-37. (Use the arrow keys to advance the color above the cursor to black, if necessary). Click to change the right stroke to black. Do the same for the left stroke.

7. *Set the interrupting strokes to None.* Now we have one too many sets of black strokes. Hover your cursor on the stroke below the boxed-in yellow area. Press the left arrow key a few times to set the swatch above the cursor to None (the red slash) and click to make the bottom stroke invisible. Then click the stroke above to make it disappear as well. As if by magic, the blue ring now passes into, around, and back out of the yellow one, as you can see in Figure 11-38.

8. *Fill more intersections.* Click with black, green, and red, respectively, inside each of the lower areas where the remaining rings intersect. Use the right and left arrow keys to change the center swatch preview above the cursor to the appropriate color for each area. Conveniently, each of the intersections you need to fill in are on the lower set of ring intersections, so they're all on the same horizontal line in the image. (Those Olympic folks, they really know how to plan ahead.) If you want a quick visual guide to confirm which color goes where, check out Figure 11-39 on the next page.

9. *Paint the good strokes.* You now have three new regions of overlapping color, which I'll call (from left to right) black-over-yellow, green-over-black, and red-over-green.

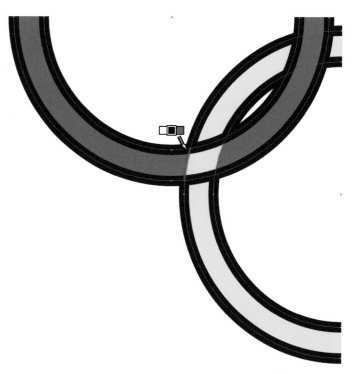

Figure 11-37.

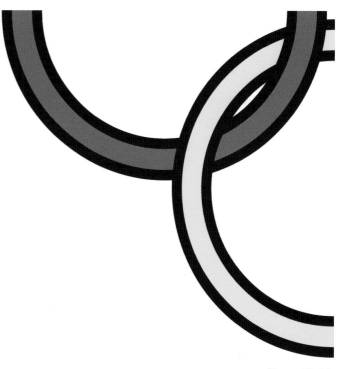

Figure 11-38.

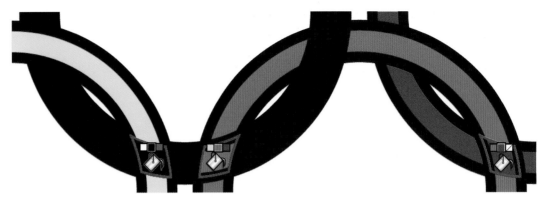

Figure 11-39.

Each intersection has two areas that need stroking with the brush variation of the paint bucket tool (the one we first encountered in Step 6). First the ones you want to be black, as follows:

- Set the **Stroke** attributes to black with a 4-point weight, in the control panel.

- Stroke above and below the black-over-yellow region. (This one's tricky to see because the fill is already black.)

- Stroke to the left and right of the green-over-black region.

- Stroke above and below the red-over-green region.

The results appear in Figure 11-40.

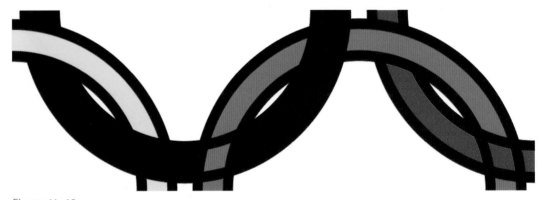

Figure 11-40.

10. *Set the bad strokes to None.* Now to make invisible the strokes that interrupt the overlapping rings. Still armed with the brush variation of the paint bucket, do the following:

- Set the stroke attribute to None in the control panel.

- Click to the left and right of the black-over-yellow region.

- Click above and below the green-over-black region.

- Click to the left and right of the red-over-green region.

Figure 11-41 shows the final results and setting one of the black strokes, which again is tricky because the ring is already black. You still want to remove the interrupting stroke, however. Just remember, if a ring is "on top" it needs black strokes along its edges and invisible strokes (essentially no strokes) across it.

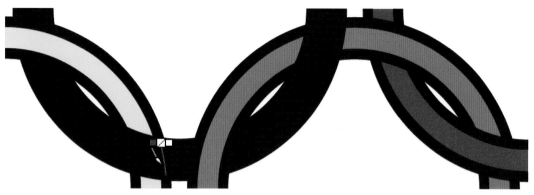

Figure 11-41.

11. *Change all the strokes at once.* Now I know what you're thinking. After all that, the fact is the Olympic rings have *white* strokes, not black ones. To switch all the black strokes to white, start by pressing the V key to get the standard black arrow selection tool. Click on the rings to select them. Then change the **Stroke** color to white and the **Weight** to 2 points in the control panel. The result is the picture-perfect interlocking rings shown in Figure 11-42.

Figure 11-42.

Note that Illustrator, thanks to Live Paint, knows to keep those "invisible" strokes that we established in Step 10 intact. So you can select "all" the strokes in Step 11 and make them white, and not have to reset the strokes that you wanted to be set to None.

12. *Move the black ring.* The great thing about this technique is that it results in a very close approximation of true interlocking objects. To prove my point, grab the white arrow tool by pressing the A key. Alt-marquee (or Option-marquee) the right edges of the black ring, to get the whole thing, then Shift-drag the ring down below the yellow and green rings to make a large medallion-style Olympic necklace. Move it in two or three passes (release and drag a few times), so that the Live Paint strokes that are set to None stay intact. The amazing results are shown in Figure 11-43.

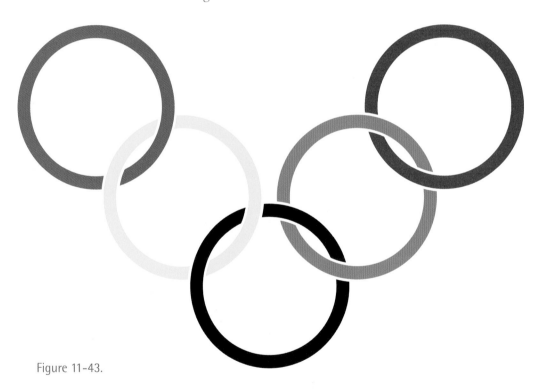

Figure 11-43.

Big modifications may result in stray strokes and gaps, where Illustrator fails to understand what is still considered an overlap. You can always fix them with the Live Paint tool. To effectively move the black ring to the position you see in Figure 11-43 without having to reapply Live Paint, I had to stop and release a few times, then resume dragging the black ring to its final position.

Thanks to good friends showing me the error of my ways and Illustrator's Live Paint feature, the Olympic spirit can continue on—now also available in necklace form.

## Recoloring Artwork with Live Color

Live Color is really an umbrella term for a group of loosely related features that are scattered between a handful of icons, panels, and dialog boxes. With it, you can dynamically alter the colors in your artwork, even going so far as to reassign all the colors across an entire illustration. And you can choose your new color scheme from an existing library, another illustration, or your own custom crafted color group.

After introducing it in CS3, Adobe abandoned the phrase "Live Color" in the actual interface in favor of the prosaic and literal Edit Colors and Recolor Artwork. But I continue to call the over-arching feature set Live Color, because it's alive and it's cool. Changing the entire color theme across an illustration in a matter of seconds? Effortlessly distilling a piece of artwork with 17 colors down to a one-color spot job? If that's not "live," I'm not sure what is. In this exercise, we'll perform such feats with the live color set of tools. It's still invigorating and fun to use, despite the decidedly less vivacious official verbiage.

1. *Open a colored piece of artwork.* We're going to start with the illustration you see in Figure 11-44, entitled *Stock footage.ai,* which you'll find inside the *Lesson 11* folder in *Lesson Files-AIcs5 1on1*. This piece comes from artist Bulent Ince of iStockphoto. As you can see (if not immediately count, just trust me) it contains 13 colors not including black and white, all of which we'll alter during this exercise.

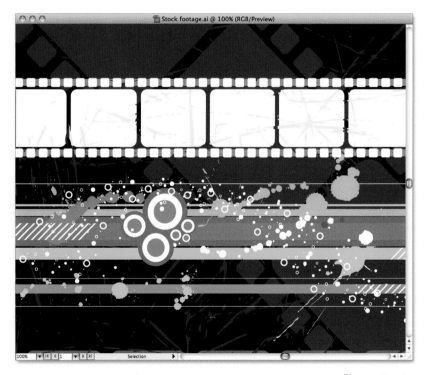

Figure 11-44.

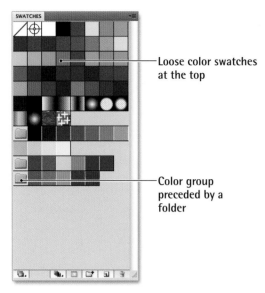

Loose color swatches at the top

Color group preceded by a folder

Figure 11-45.

2. *Examine the Swatch panel organization.* The first thing we'll need is some color options to work with. When it comes to re-coloring artwork, you'll be working with *color groups*—sets of thematically organized colors that live in the Swatches panel. As you can see in Figure 11-45, right now, *Stock footage.ai* houses some loose colors and a few color groups (indicated by the folders that precede them), but we'll soon add more variations to play with.

3. *Open a new file.* One way to add new color groups is to import them from another illustration. So navigate to the *Lesson 11* folder of *Lesson Files-AIcs5 1on1* and open *Electro blisco.ai*. As you can see in Figure 11-46, the file contains some groovy colors that might be fun to experiment with in our destination file. But first we'll have to make a color group within the *Electro blisco.ai* file.

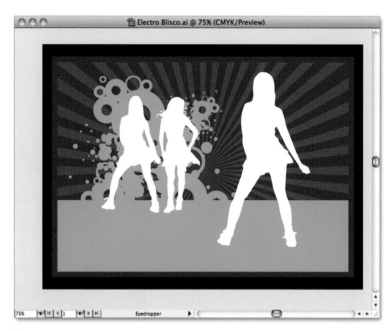

Figure 11-46.

4. *Select all the backdrop colors.* We can skip the white dancers while were collecting colors, since we already have white in our destination artwork. So select the **Backdrop** layer in the **Layers** panel and press Ctrl-Alt-A (⌘-Option-A) to select all the objects in that layer, and more importantly their colors.

5. *Make a new color group.* At the bottom of the **Swatches** panel, click the icon that looks like a folder with a plus sign to make a new color group (as shown in Figure 11-47). In the **New Color Group** dialog box, name the group "Electro Blisco," of course. Instruct Illustrator to create the group from the selected artwork by clicking the **Selected Artwork** option. Turn on both check boxes—although we don't need global swatches or tints per se, we might as well get all the benefits available. Then click **OK**.

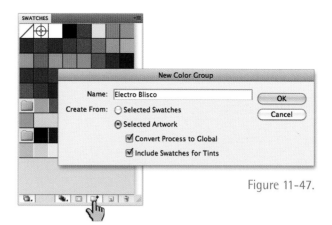

Figure 11-47.

6. *Save the file.* Even though we haven't done anything specific to the actual artwork, color groups are considered a "change," and we're going to steal from it later. So save and close *Electro blisco.ai*.

7. *Import the color group into the original artwork.* Return to *Stock footage.ai*. Now to import that group we just created. Here's how it works:

   • Click the leftmost icon at the bottom of the **Swatches** panel, as shown in Figure 11-48, and choose **Other Library** from the bottom of the pop-up menu.

   • Navigate to the version of *Electro Blisco.ai* that you saved in the last step, and click the **Open** button.

   • A new panel, bearing the name **Electro Blisco** will open inside Illustrator. In that panel, click the folder in front of the final color group (as demonstrated in Figure 11-49), also known as Electro Blisco conveniently enough.

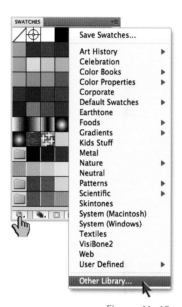

Figure 11-48.

The new color group should now appear in the Swatches panel of *Stock footage.ai*.

8. *Add another color group from an existing swatch library.* Aside from importing from another illustration, there are other ways to add color groups to your artwork. Illustrator ships with a collection of color libraries from which you can add yet another color group. Return to that same icon at the bottom far left of the **Swatches** panel that you used in Step 7, click it once again, and choose the **Textiles** library from the pop-up menu.

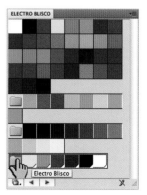

Figure 11-49.

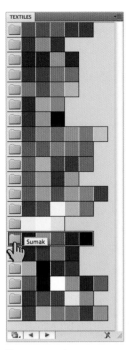

Figure 11-50.

9. *Choose a textile color group.* From the free-floating **Textile** panel that opens in Illustrator, find the color group about two-thirds of the way down, called Sumak, as shown in Figure 11-50. Click on the folder to add it to your working Swatches panel.

---

If you want to read the sometimes prosaic, sometimes inspired, names of the various color groups, simply hover over the folder at the front of the color group until the name appears in a tool tip, as in the figure. If you hover over one of the swatches instead of the folder, you'll get the color breakdown of the swatch in question.

---

10. *Move the Color Guide panel into view.* You needn't strictly rely on importing to create new color groups. As we already saw in Step 5, you can make a color group from all the colors that already exist in the artwork. You can also use the tools within Illustrator to create color groups based on *harmonies*, color patterns that are based on predetermined relationships between colors. The Color Guide panel provides a convenient way to do just that. (Press Shift+F3 if it's not already open.) Because it's convenient to see both the Swatches and the Color Guide panels at the same time, move the **Color Guide** panel from behind the Swatches panel if necessary.

PEARL OF WISDOM

The term "harmony" is sort of misleading in my opinion. A harmony in Illustrator really refers to a pattern of colors that is based on certain spatial or mathematical relationships between the participating colors. Harmony rules are essentially derived from math or geometry. For instance, *triad* just means three colors that divide the color wheel into 3. But just because it's formulaic doesn't guarantee that the color grouping is going to be harmonious, *per se*. So don't take the term too literally.

---

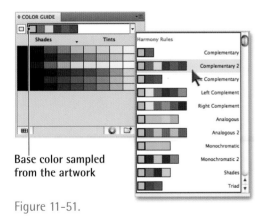

Base color sampled
from the artwork

Figure 11-51.

11. *Choose a color for a custom color group.* To set this process in motion, grab the eyedropper tool and select a color to serve as the base for your new color group. To shake things up, try clicking on the lime green stripe near the bottom of the illustration. Lime green immediately becomes the base color for a collection of swatches, which are displayed in a row across the top of the Color Guide panel, as shown in Figure 11-51.

12. *Choose a harmony rule.* With that lime green as your base, click the downward arrow to the right of the row of colors at the top of the **Color Guide** panel. In the resulting pop-up menu, choose the second harmony down, **Complementary 2** to create a five-color theme based on your base color and the hue directly opposite on the color wheel, in this case purplish magenta.

13. *Save the group to the Swatches panel.* Once you've chosen a harmony, you can save that group to the Swatches panel. Click the now familiar-ish icon (the folder with the plus sign) at the far right of the Color Guide panel to add your new color group.

14. *Add one of the Color Guide suggestions to your new color group.* As you can see, the Color Guide panel does much more than allow you to create groups based on harmony rules. It also supplies you with an array of variations on your current colors. The chosen colors are repeated in the center column, and the grid comprises variations on each color, with shades on the left and tints on the right. You can add any of these colors to the Swatches panel by simply dragging it.

You can also add any of these colors to any of your existing groups. For instance, drag the second from the bottom swatch in the rightmost column into the **Swatches** panel to become part of your new color group, as I've done in Figure 11-52.

15. *Select the entire work.* Now that we have enough colors to experiment with, it's finally time to put them to use. Start by selecting the entire illustration: Press Ctrl-A (⌘-A) to select all, then press Ctrl-H (⌘-H) to hide the edges so you can watch the colors do their magic with an unobstructed view.

16. *Open the Recolor Artwork dialog box.* In the control panel, click the circular icon shown in Figure 11-53 to bring up the **Recolor Artwork** dialog box.

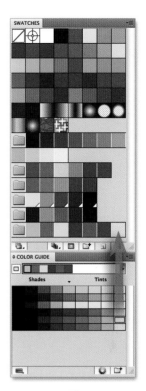

Figure 11-52.

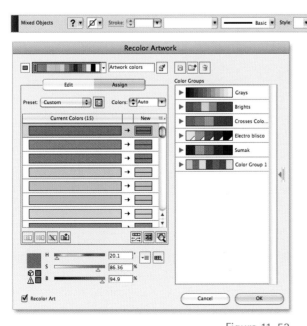

Figure 11-53.

17. *Assign the Electro Blisco colors.* Along the left side of the Recolor Artworks dialog box, all thirteen of the current existing colors are listed, along with black and white. You could reassign any of these colors individually by double-clicking on the box in the New column and changing them to something else in the Color Picker dialog box. But that doesn't leverage the magic of this feature.

Instead, click on the Electro Blisco collection in the Color Groups panel. Illustrator assigns each of the existing colors a new color from Color Group 1. Since there are more existing colors than there are in the chosen color group, Illustrator puts the existing colors together as it sees fit and reassigns them tint variations from the color group swatch, as you can see in Figure 11-54.

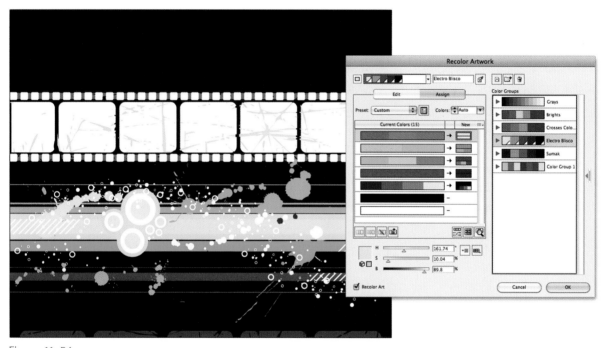

Figure 11-54.

Make sure the Recolor Art check box in the lower left is turned on. It's the equivalent of the Preview check box you've seen elsewhere .

18. *Swap the colors.* Illustrator assigns the color group swatches based on the stacking order of the colors in the original artwork. I don't think assigning the minty green to the oranges does the piece justice. So grab the set of medium pinks in the **New** column that are currently assigned to the blues and move it up to the orange row. Then swap the dark bottom two new colors as well. Illustrator automatically assigns the mint to the blues. Better, as you can see in Figure 11-55.

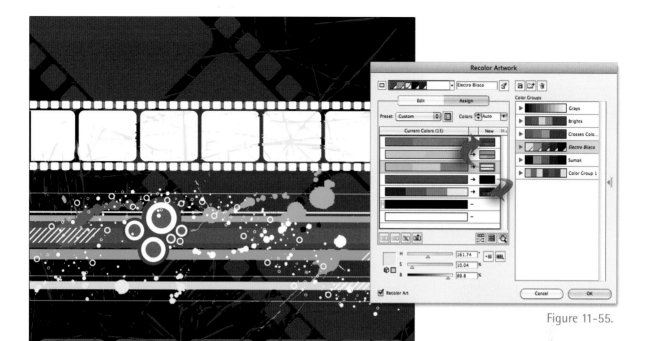

Figure 11-55.

19. *Move a single color to a different assignment.* It makes sense
in a way that Illustrator has mapped all three oranges in the
original to a single color in the new group. I mean, it's trying
to turn thirteen colors into five, after all. But the tint variations
in the pink set aren't quite providing enough contrast for that
big stripe in the middle. You don't have to accept Illustrator's
groupings in the left column, however. Try this instead:

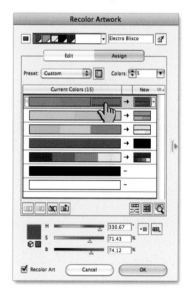

- Click on the darkest orange color in the top bar of the
  Current Colors column, as shown in Figure 11-56. (Your
  position may vary.)

- Drag it to the row below, and release. The darkest orange
  then shares the darker green destination tints with yellow
  and lime.

The result, as you can see in Figure 11-57, is greater contrast in
the thick stripe element.

Figure 11-56.

Figure 11-57.

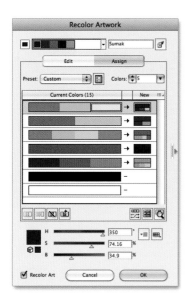

Figure 11-58.

20. *Assign a different color group.* It's been a color whirlwind, but I'm getting dizzy and in the mood for something a little more understated, so let's try another color group instead. Click on the **Sumak** color group on the right. Then adjust:

- Swap the second and fifth new colors, so that we get some tone to the diagonal gray filmstrip element in the background.

- Then swap the second and fourth colors to create a little more contrast in the stripes.

- Move the darkest orange color to the second row, mostly so that the circles now become the darkest of the orange colors and thus get a nice deep reddish color in the destination effect.

- Move the green in the second row up to the top to add a little more variation in the stripes.

- Move the lightest gray color up to the top row so that the splashes across the white filmstrip stand out a little better.

Figure 11-58 shows where each color landed.

21. *Find a specific color to change.* You can see the current effects of the changes thus far in Figure 11-59. Let's say that we want to change the color of the uppermost of the thicker stripes.

Area to change ———

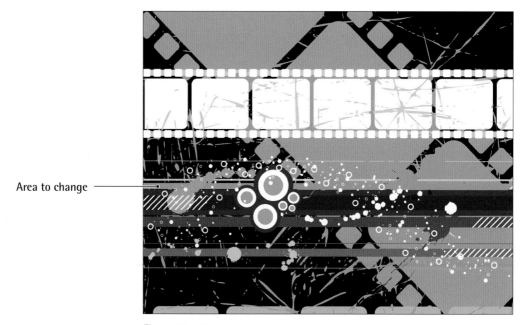

Figure 11-59.

Problem is, at this point, I've lost track of which color that is in the original colors. Illustrator provides an, albeit backward for our current purposes, way to find the target area:

- Click the magnifying glass icon at the lower-right corner, as shown in Figure 11-60.

- Click the color bars in the **Current Colors** rows until you find the one you want. (It would be great if you could actually click the artwork to identify the problem area, but it doesn't work that way.)

- The artwork dims its window. As you click the color bars, the areas of the artwork that are filled with the corresponding color light up against the faded background.

- Turns out the color we're looking for is yellow, as you can see in Figure 11-60. Now that you know, click the magnifying glass again to turn off the feature and restore the artwork to full color.

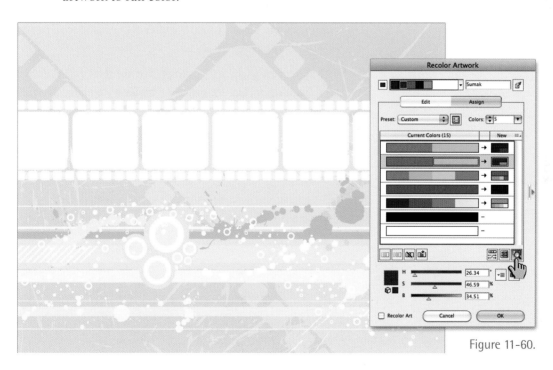

Figure 11-60.

22. *Move the yellow bar to the top row.* Armed with the knowledge we've obtained in the previous step, drag the yellow up to the top row with confidence.

23. **Edit the colors.** Recoloring artwork needn't depend solely on mapping to color groups. To see what I mean, click the **Edit** tab in the left panel. The color wheel that appears will allow you to adjust any of your currently assigned colors. Here's how it works (with the salient features labeled in Figure 11-61).

- By default, the colors are locked into their harmony-based arrangement. If you drag any of the colors around the color wheel, all the colors move together and maintain their relationship.

- The biggest circle represents the base color.

- You can change to a different harmony algorithm by choosing a new one from the pop-up menu to the right of the top row of colors.

- To move colors independently, click the ✪ icon in the lower-right corner to break the link.

- Moving colors around the wheel changes the Hue.

- Dragging the colors toward the center or out toward the edges changes the Saturation.

- The slider below the color wheel controls the Brightness for all the colors at once. You must use the slider at the bottom for establishing Brightness for individual colors.

- Once you've unlinked the colors, you can use the H, S, and B sliders at the bottom to adjust colors individually.

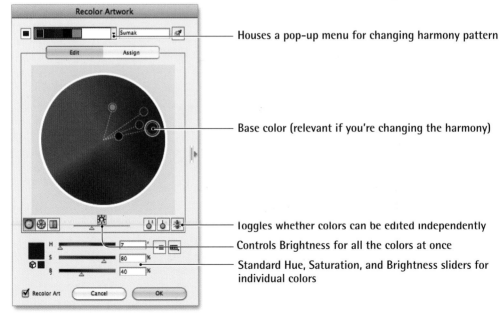

Houses a pop-up menu for changing harmony pattern

Base color (relevant if you're changing the harmony)

Toggles whether colors can be edited independently

Controls Brightness for all the colors at once

Standard Hue, Saturation, and Brightness sliders for individual colors

Figure 11-61.

For my part, I moved the whole group toward a slightly warmer area of the wheel and increased the overall saturation and brightness, then unlocked the colors and adjusted each one slightly to suit my mood. My result are shown in Figure 11-62. Please feel free to have fun and express yourself as you desire. When you have the colors where you want them, click **OK** to save your recoloring work.

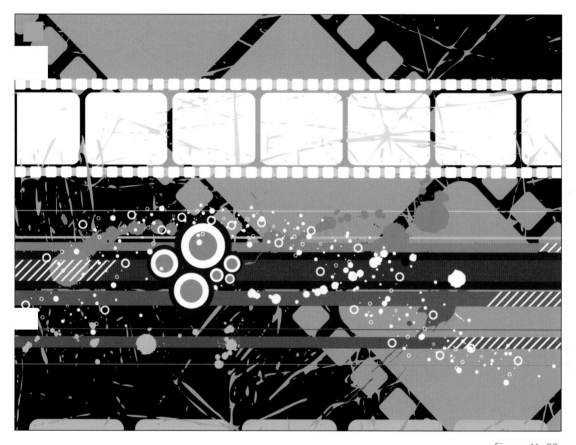

Figure 11-62.

24. *Do* not *save changes to the Sumak color group.* When you click OK, Illustrator is going to ask if you want to save the changes to the Sumak color group. This is one of those dialog boxes where you're going to have to think it through when you're working on your own. In this case, the answer you want to click is **No**. Leave Sumak the way it is for later use, and just preserve the new colors within your document. As you saw way back in Steps 5 and 6, you can always create a new color group from these new colors once they are safely converted in your current artwork.

You've learned quite a bit about the fun you can have with the Recolor Artwork dialog box, and you may feel like you've had enough colorful excitement for the day. But if you stick with me, I'll show you how to have even more fun, and potentially save money as well, as we distill this illustration all the way down to just two colors—black and a spot color.

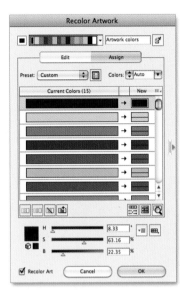

Figure 11-63.

25. *Reopen the Recolor Artwork dialog box.* Once again, click the color wheel icon in the control panel to bring up the **Recolor Artwork** dialog box. At this point, Live Color is not exactly as dynamically live as say, Live Trace. (OK, maybe that's why Adobe changed the official name.) When you reopened the Trace Settings dialog box in the first and second exercises, everything about the original file was still intact.

Here, as you can see in Figure 11-63, that is definitely not the case. Gone are the original bright colors from the image. Every current color is now one of the earthy tones we applied in the last several steps of this exercise.

If you'd like to work with the file that I ended up with in Step 24, I've provided it for you in the *Lesson 11* folder of *Lesson Files-Alcs5 1on1*, called *Recolored artwork.ai.* If you worked through the exercise this far, yours will work just as well for these final steps, but in case you'd like to follow along exactly, you can open mine if you choose.

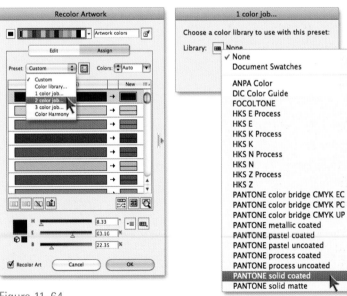

Figure 11-64.

26. *Choose the 2-Color preset.* Let's say the intention of this color reduction is to potentially save some money at the printer by having this document printed with just a couple of spot colors. *Spot colors* are predetermined industry-standard colors that printers can use instead of creating colors by applying combinations of cyan, magenta, yellow, and black inks (known as a *process color*). From the **Preset** pop-up menu, choose **2 Color Job**, as shown in Figure 11-64. In the dialog box that appears, click on the grid-like icon to open the available spot color libraries (color books). Pick **Pantone Solid Coated** from the pop-up menu. Then click **OK**.

The results of our distillation is shown in Figure 11-65. It's cool that Illustrator can take some thirteen colors and turn them into tint variations on one single color, but the one it chose leaves something to be desired.

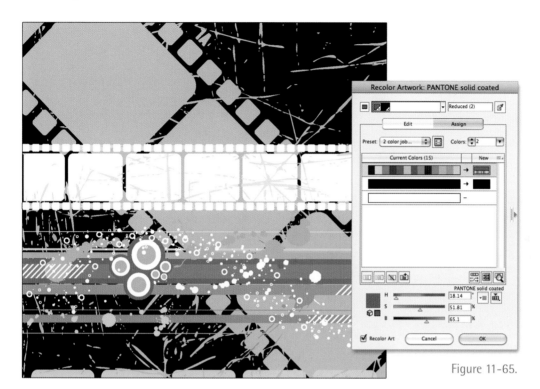

Figure 11-65.

27. *Edit the New color swatch.* In Illustrator's attempt to choose one color to represent all the existing colors in the artwork, it chose an average between the colors we had, which turned out to be an unfortunate rosy brownish color. But it's easy to change while still keeping within the Pantone color library that we have set:

• Start by noting that the words *Pantone Solid Coated* appear wedged between the five icons on the lower right. This means that although it will feel like you're altering the colors freehand, any choice you make will map to a specific color in the Pantone library that we established in Step 26.

• Make sure the swatch in the **New** column that represents all your colors (except black) is selected, as is evidenced by the swatch in the lower left of the dialog box as well. This will be the color from which all tints in the artwork are formulated.

- Adjust the color with the sliders at the bottom of the dialog box. Set the **Hue** to 0 degrees, the **Saturation** to 100 percent, and the **Brightness** to 50 percent, as I've done in Figure 11-65.

- To confirm that you've actually chosen a Pantone color, you can double-click the red swatch and see that Illustrator has assigned your color to Pantone 188 C. (You can also check the Black swatch, which in my case is Pantone Black 6 C.)

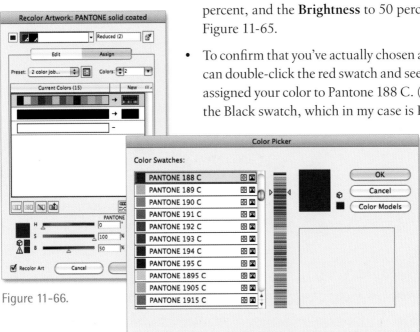

Figure 11-66.

The results are shown in Figure 11-66. Through the magic of Live Color, we've taken a multicolored disco shaded image and turned two colors into a piece of compelling artwork.

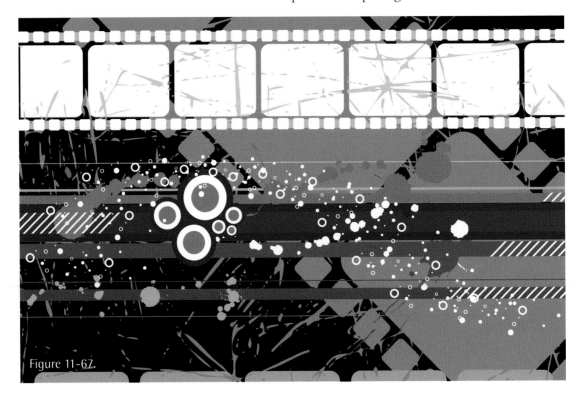

Figure 11-67.

# WHAT DID YOU LEARN?

Match the key concept in the numbered list below with the letter of the phrase that best describes it. Answers appear upside-down at the bottom of the page.

## Key Concepts

1. Live Trace
2. Live Paint
3. Live Color
4. Linked file
5. Threshold
6. Minimum Area
7. Adjusted image
8. Global swatch
9. Color group
10. Harmony
11. Spot color
12. Process color

## Descriptions

A. A Live Trace setting that allows you to instruct Illustrator to ignore smaller areas of pixels during the tracing operation.

B. A feature in Illustrator that allows you to fill visible shapes with color, regardless of whether they are designated paths.

C. An algorithmic pattern of colors that describes the relationship between colors in a group.

D. A file that is placed in Illustrator, but attached as a reference file should any updates be made to the original.

E. A specific color that is predesignated by industry standard.

F. A feature in Illustrator that allows you to dynamically trace a placed file.

G. A color created by the mixing of cyan, magenta, yellow, and black inks at the time of printing.

H. A Live Trace setting that instructs gray pixels in the traced file to be sent to either black or white.

I. A color reference that, if changed, subsequently updates within the artwork.

J. The reference version of an image that Illustrator uses to construct its trace.

K. A partially abandoned umbrella term for the tools that allow you to change colors automatically inside your artwork.

L. A designated collection of swatches that can be stored in a library or passed between Illustrator files.

## Answers

1F, 2B, 3K, 4D, 5H, 6A, 7J, 8I, 9L, 10C, 11E, 12G

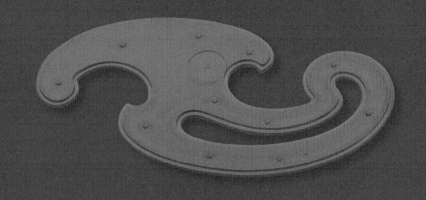

# PRINTING AND EXPORTING

**NO APPLICATION** is an island, and Illustrator users probably understand this better than most. Graphic artists who painstakingly craft artwork inside Illustrator usually have a destination beyond their computers in mind from the outset.

This lesson will help you safely get your artwork where it needs to go—to set it free if you will—like our long-suffering friend in Figure 12-1. Whether you are sending your illustration off to a commercial printer, printing it on your local device, posting it to the Web, or using it in projects involving other applications, Illustrator has the tools and commands you'll need to make sure it arrives at its destination the way you intended it to be seen.

Illustrator has always offered a highly sophisticated set of printing options. Starting with the familiar File→Print command, you enter a world where you can set up virtual bleeds, define crop boundaries, output an array of printer marks, print color separations for commercial reproduction, overprint black, define the flatness of curved paths, tweak color management settings, and adjust how your transparency effects get flattened, all from inside a single Print dialog box.

In addition to Illustrator's printing capabilities, we'll be exploring other means of output, like saving your vector artwork for the Web, exporting it as layered Photoshop images, and creating files for other applications.

This lesson is designed to help you ask the important questions, make the educated decisions, and find the right answers so that your particular document can shine in its life beyond your computer.

Figure 12-1.

# ABOUT THIS LESSON

## Project Files

Before beginning the exercises, make sure you've downloaded the lesson files from www.oreilly.com/go/Deke-IllustratorCS5, as directed in Step 2 on page xiv of the Preface. This means you should have a folder called *Lesson Files-Alcs5 1on1* on your desktop (or whatever location you chose). We'll be working with the files inside the *Lesson 12* subfolder.

In this lesson, I'll show you how to prepare your file for a life outside of Illustrator, whether that be in print or on the web. You'll learn how to:

## Video Lesson 12: Commercial Printing

If you are sending your Illustrator files off to a custom commercial printer, you'll want to ensure you've done everything you can to get the results you desire. In this video lesson, I'll show you how to prepare your artwork for commercial print, including changing your type to outlines, checking your spot colors, and generally making sure there are no surprises.

To review my pre-printer preparations, visit *www.oreilly. com/go/deke-IllustratorCS5*. Click the **Watch** button to view the lesson online or click the **Download** button to save it to your computer. During the video, you'll learn these shortcuts:

Video Lesson 12: Commercial Printing

| Operation | Windows shortcut | Macintosh shortcut |
|---|---|---|
| Create Outlines | Ctrl+Shift+O | ⌘-Option-O |
| Hide selection outlines | Ctrl¡H | ⌘-H |
| Zoom tool | Ctrl-spacebar | ⌘-spacebar |
| Open Preferences | Ctrl+K | ⌘-K |
| Document Setup | Ctrl+Alt+P | ⌘-Option-P |
| Print | Ctrl+P | ⌘-P |

# General Printing Considerations

Illustrator has an incredibly sophisticated print engine built within, which we'll tour in the next exercise. But some Illustrator users may find that they rarely see the inside of the Print dialog box, simply because they're usually handing off their work to the experts at a commercial print house. Your responsibility in such instances is to make sure your artwork is *ready* to relinquish. The video that accompanies this lesson (see Video Lesson 12: "Commercial Printing," on the previous page) walks you through the steps required to make that hand-off go smoothly.

When you watch the video, you'll hear me discuss a variety of concepts and concerns that anyone who's hung around a print shop will find familiar. What follows is a list of things to keep in mind so that you get results worthy of all the hard work you've put into creating your artwork during the first eleven lessons of this book.

- *Converting type to outlines:* Although you may have created your text using standard fonts that come along with Creative Suite 5, there's always a chance that your printer of choice doesn't have your exact fonts, which could lead to disaster. To ensure against this, you can convert your text to paths by choosing Type→Create Outlines. This command converts your font-based text to path outlines, thus guaranteeing it can print on any system without unexpected results.

---

If you choose this route, be sure to choose File→Save As, and save your artwork with outlines in a new file, so that you still have the original file with editable text available should you need it. Once you convert type to outlines, changing the letters of the text dynamically, say to make a spelling correction, is not an option.

---

- *Embed your linked files:* If you have any linked files, like the pixel-based background in my video example, you'll need to decide whether to embed them or send them along separately to the printer. From the Links panel you can embed any selected image by choosing Embed Image from the flyout menu, as shown in Figure 12-2.

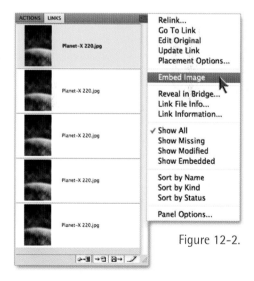

Figure 12-2.

---

Remember that embedding the image can make your artwork disproportionately large (in my case it will embed the cryptically named *Planet-X 220.jpg* five times). So even though embedding seems like the safe bet, it can make for some serious overhead in terms of file size.

---

Custom crop marks around a
single element on the artboard.

Figure 12-3.

- *Trim size* refers to the size of the final trimmed pages after the printer has cut away any extraneous paper. For the purposes of Illustrator, trim size is the same thing as the size of your artboard.

- *Bleed* refers to an area of safety beyond the trim boundary that gives printers a literal margin for error when trimming. If you want to make sure your artwork extends all the way to the edge of the printed document, known as a *full bleed*, then you need to make sure your artwork extends out into this bleed area.

---

Remember, bleed is a protection against unprinted white areas. So any content within the bleed area has to be something that will maintain the general intention of the illustration if it survives the paring process, but can alternately be trimmed off without compromising the piece as well.

---

- *Overprinting* refers to one ink printing over another in the CMYK process, where plates of the four colors each pass over the artwork. Illustrator allows you to preview the overprint to ensure that you mitigate against any white slivers where one color might knock out another, should the print color plates be out of registration.

- *Crop marks* indicate where the artwork should be trimmed, and you can set that for an entire document from the print dialog box, as we'll see. But it's also possible to create custom crop marks around multiple items on a single artboard (business cards come to mind) by simply choosing Effect→Crop Marks. I eschew business cards, so I've placed a custom crop around my much cooler ghost robot surfboard in Figure 12-3.

A couple of other things to remember:

- Although Illustrator gives you many options, simply do not take line weights below a quarter point (hairline width) and expect them to survive the printing process. This is a mistake those new to Illustrator often make.

- Save your file to Illustrator CS5 or CS4 if you have multiple artboards, because Illustrator CS3 (or earlier) will see only your first page. (Multiple artboards hadn't been invented when CS3 came along.) If your printer doesn't use CS4 or later, you'll have to save each artboard as a separate file.

# Printing Artwork to a Local Printer

And by "local printer" I don't mean Joe's Print Shack down the block (though I'm all for supporting neighborhood artisans). Rather, this exercise will take you through the steps of printing on an inkjet or laser printer that's attached directly to your computer or connected via a local network. This makes the most sense if you have a high-quality local printing device and you don't need the volume of copies that would be required to make commercial printing feasible, efficient, or thrifty. In fact, even if your job is destined for a commercial printer eventually, it's sometimes advantageous to create a proof yourself first. Putting your artwork through the print process on your own can help you avoid potential problems down the line, plus you'll sound knowledgeable if you ever need to talk to Joe the Print Guy.

Everything you need to print is housed in one gigantically useful dialog box, evoked with the familiar command File→Print or the keyboard shortcut Ctrl-P (⌘-P). Like many behemoth dialog boxes, the Print dialog box can seem overwhelming at first, with more choices than you'll ever possibly need. But it's truly one of the best in the business in terms of comprehensive print capabilities. So in this exercise, I'll walk you through critical options available to you.

1. ***Open a file to print.*** Start by opening the file called *Murderous assets.ai* from the *Lesson 12* folder inside *Files-AIcs5 1on1*. This image, shown in Figure 12-4, features a poster for an amphibiously disturbing play, as well as some merchandising options: skateboard, surfboard, and t-shirt treatments.

Figure 12-4.

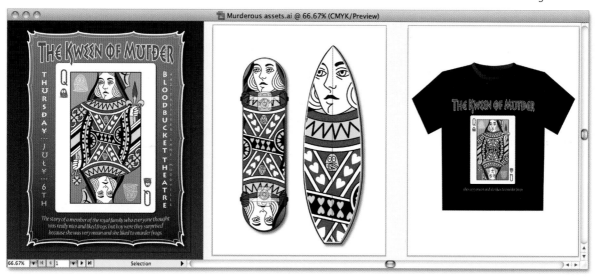

Figure 12-5.

2. *Evoke the Print dialog box.* As I mentioned, Illustrator uses the virtually universal command of **File→Print** or Ctrl-P (⌘-P) to evoke the **Print** command. Whichever method you choose, you'll be presented with the dialog box shown in Figure 12-5.

3. *Choose the appropriate printer.* From the **Printer** pop-up menu, choose one of the printers that's available from your computer or network.

---

The PPD setting just below the Printer selection stands for PostScript Printer Description. PostScript is probably irrelevant for most local printers, but it does represent an industry standard in commercial printing. For more on the decisions you should consider exclusively for PostScript printers, see the sidebar, "PostScript-Only Options in the Print Dialog Box," on page 444.

---

4. *Choose the number of copies.* The **Print** dialog box opens to the **General** panel, as highlighted in the list on the left side of the dialog box. If you've ever printed anything from any application, the first choices in this panel will be quite familiar. A good place to start is by setting the number of copies you would like. For the purposes of this exercise, leave **Copies** set to 1 copy.

5. *Indicate the specific pages you want to print.* By "pages," of course I mean artboards. The default is set to All, but you can also specify a range. Turn on the **Range** option, and the field will immediately register the entire range of artboards, as indicated by the 1–3 setting.

Let's say we want to skip the skateboard/surfboard comp for this presentation. To tell Illustrator to print only the desired artboards, enter "1,3" in the Range field. A comma indicates a list of artboards to be printed, allowing you to skip over pages you don't want to print. Notice that the preview in the lower left of Figure 12-6 updates to show you the requested pages only.

---

You can also include literal ranges separated by commas, in your list. For instance, to print the first and final three out of six artboards, you'd enter "1, 4-6" in the Range field.

---

6. *Make your paper size selection.* The next section of the General panel defines how your artwork will interact with the paper you have available. Leave the Size set to Defined by Driver, so Illustrator will let the printer in question tell us what paper size the printer has queued up and available. (You could also choose specific sizes from the pop-up menu.)

7. *Set the orientation.* Illustrator gives you four page orientation options: the standard vertical and horizontal options you see in most printers and the inverse (upside down and facing left) of each of those. Make sure the **Auto-Rotate** check box is turned on. This gives us the vertical upright setting, which fits the artwork the best in terms of maximizing paper real estate.

8. *Consider the Placement options.* There are three main ways to indicate the placement of your artwork on the page:

    - You can choose to pin your artwork to one of the corners or in the center of the page by choosing the appropriate spot on the nine-point matrix Placement icon.

    - You can set the X and Y coordinates manually. Note that in this dialog box, these measurements indicate the placement of the upper-left corner of your artwork in reference to the upper-left corner of the page.

    - In the preview area, you can grab the artwork thumbnail and move it around the window.

This particular file works well centered on the page, so experiment with any of the options above, then double-click the artwork thumbnail in the preview (labeled in Figure 12-6) area to re-center it.

---

The dotted outline in the preview, as labeled in Figure 12-6, indicates the printable area of the page, i.e., the area that the printer is capable of printing on.

---

Double-click preview thumbnail to center artwork on the page.

Dotted line indicates the printable area of the page.

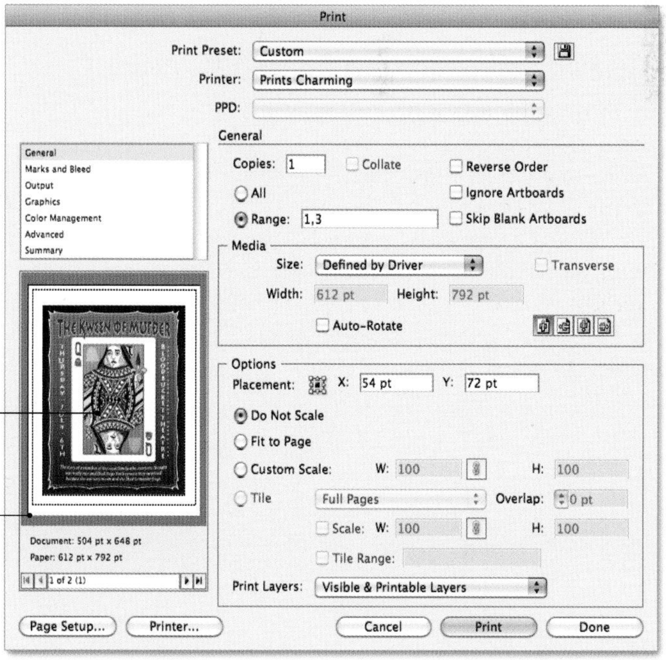

Figure 12-6.

9. *Determine the scale.* In keeping with the spirit of giving you incredible control over your print, Illustrator also gives you several options for scaling your artwork on the page:

- *Do Not Scale* retains your artwork at the exact dimensions you indicated in your file.

- *Fit to Page* sets the largest artboard at its maximum size that still allows it to fit on one page. It then scales the other artboards to that same percentage.

- *Custom Scale* allows you to set a width and height of your own choosing. This scale is applied to every artboard; you can't set a manual custom scale for each page.

- The *Tile* command allows you to breakup the artwork onto multiple pages regardless of how any one element fits on the page. Unless you have a real need to print a large illustration with only small paper sheets available (and copious amounts of tape and patience), you probably want to skip this option.

Since each of the artboards in this artwork fit fairly nicely on the page, leave the setting at Do Not Scale for this document.

---

If you have problems that can't be solved here, at any time, you can click the Page Setup button in the bottom left to switch to the print options offered by your operating system. Illustrator will beg you to change your mind, and, as needy as it's plea is, Illustrator is probably right. Both the current Mac and Windows print options are woefully disappointing compared to the amount of control you have in Illustrator.

---

10. *Turn on all the printer marks.* Having finished with everything relevant in the General category, click **Marks and Bleed** in the list of panels on the left side of the Print dialog box, as I've done in Figure 12-7. For educational purposes, turn on all the **All Printer's Marks** check box to add each of the following:

- *Trim marks* indicate the boundary of the artwork, i.e., where you want to trim away any excess paper.

- *Registration marks* are circular symbols that help printers align the different color plates. *Color Bars* help printers judge the accuracy of the printed colors. Neither one of these options is relevant for printing to a consumer printer, but turning them on here lets you see what they look like

- *Page Information* contains the information about the document like the name, date, etc.

As you turn on each of the check boxes the corresponding mark will appear in the preview window. Each type of mark is labeled in Figure 12-7.

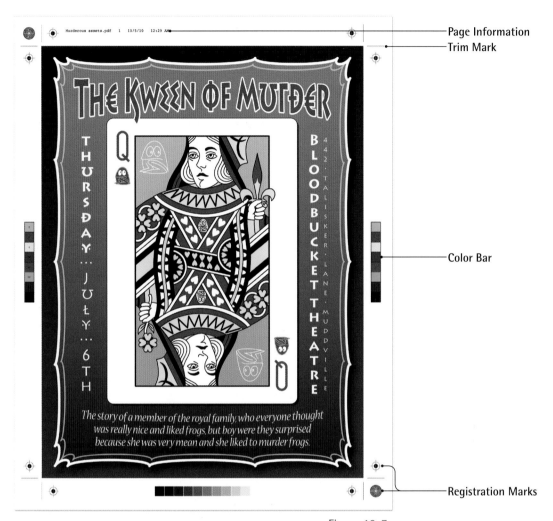

Figure 12-7.

---

The next two panes of the Print dialog box, Output and Graphics, are only relevant if you are working with a PostScript printer, so I discuss them in the sidebar, "PostScript-Only Options in the Print Dialog Box," that starts on page 444.

---

11. *Switch to the Color Management panel.* Click **Color Management** in the list on the left of the dialog box to move to the next set of options. Though the very words "color management" can strike trepidation into the hearts of the less initiated, these options are worth understanding, even when you're printing from your home or office.

# PostScript-Only Options in the Print Dialog Box

PostScript is the industry standard printing language, and virtually every professional level printer and plate-making device uses PostScript. Most home or office printers are not PostScript capable and therefore the Output and Graphics tabs of the Print dialog box are likely to be full of dimmed choices when you have your local printer set as your device of choice. That doesn't mean, however, that you don't want to know about these options in the event you want to have a reasonably informed conversation with your commercial printer.

If you'd like to follow along and see these screens on your computer, open *PostScript ready.ai* from the *Lesson 12* folder of *Lesson Files-AIcs5 1on1*. Press Ctrl-P (⌘-P) to bring up the Print dialog box, click Output in the list on the left, and choose either Adobe PDF or Adobe PostScript File in the Printer setting at the top of the dialog box.

The first thing you'll notice, as you can see in the image below, is the previously dimmed PPD setting actively fills in with the appropriate *PostScript printer description*. The PPD is a file that describes the capabilities, features, and instructions for the PostScript device you (or more likely your commercial printer operator) select. Set it to Adobe PostScript if you'd like to see the options

The first of your now available choices is the Mode setting which gives you three options:

- *Composite* indicates you'll be printing a full-color composite of your artwork, suitable for your desktop device.

- *Separations* (Host-Based) will breakdown your artwork into the appropriate color separations for CMYK printing. The host in question is Illustrator.

- *In-RIP Separations* also creates color separations, but in accordance with the *RIP*, or *raster image processor*, used by your commercial printer to break the work down into printable dots appropriate to the machine in use.

For the purposes of this demonstration, choose Separations (Host-Based) from the Mode pop-up menu.

The next two options, Emulsion and Image, are the domain of your commercial printer, so you can leave those set to their defaults.

Changing the Printer Resolution setting will be useful for examining the screen angles (which I'll explain in a moment), set it to 100 lpi/1200 dpi.

- The *lpi* measurement refers to the lines per inch, which is the measurement for the screen frequency of the half-tone dots. *Half-tone dots* are the dots of ink in varying sizes that simulate continuous tone in a reproduced graphic.

- The *dpi* measurement refers the dots per linear inch that the printer is capable of rendering.

The *Convert All Spot Colors to Process* check box allows you to tell Illustrator to convert any spot colors to their nearest CMYK equivalent. Theoretically, it could save you the cost of adding another ink plate (or plates, depending on how many spot colors you have) to the job. Leave it turned off for now so we can continue to discuss the spot color in this artwork.

The *Overprint Blacks* check box allows you to tell Illustrator to always overprint 100 percent black. In my opinion this should be on by default, because 99 percent of the time it saves you from errors when the print plates are out of alignment. For more on overprinting blacks, review Video Lesson 12, "Commercial Printing," described at the outset of this lesson on page 436.

Finally, there is a table of Document Ink Options which gives you details for how each color separation will be created. Of particular interest here is the Angle column.

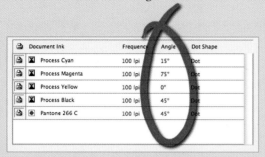

This column indicates the angle at which the half-tone dot pattern will be created on the paper. You generally want each color at a different angle and it's probably a good idea if black, the darkest color, isn't directly vertical or horizontal across the page.

Duplicate angles of interacting colors is probably also best avoided. In the case of this document, it would be wise to see if black and the spot color (which are assigned the same angle) significantly interact in the artwork.

You can check the black and spot interaction in the Separations Preview panel by turning on visibility for only Black and Pantone 266 C. (Note you'll have to leave the Print dialog box, so click Done to save your settings first.) You can see in the image below that the two colors intermingle quite a bit, especially in the ghost robot's body area. So it may be a good idea to change the angle of the spot color so that their respective half-tone patterns don't match.

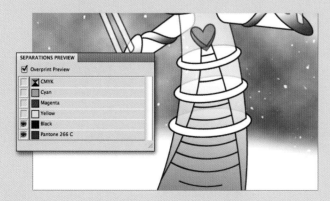

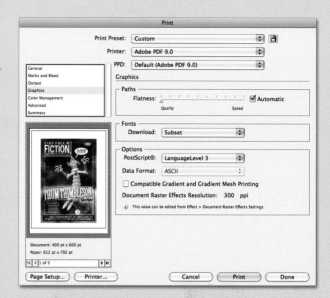

The Graphics panel, shown above, contains settings that you'll probably never encounter in daily life, but are interesting for those of you who like to know how everything works.

The *Flatness* slider is best understood when you accept that PostScript can't really render your smoothly drawn curves. Instead, it breaks down your arcs and circles into multi-sided polygons. The slider tells Illustrator just how small those sides should be; the higher the *Quality* setting the closer you are to the natural infinity of a circle.

The *Fonts Download* setting lets you decide which set of character information you're going to share with the printer. You'd only choose *None* if you'd converted all your text to outlines. *Complete* would share every single character in every font you're using, which is probably overkill. So the *Subset* option in the middle, sanely delivers just those characters used in your artwork.

The *Compatible Gradient and Gradient Mesh Printing* check box will convert your gradients to pixels if you're having problems. Illustrator's obtuse warning when you click this box reminds you to only use it if you're having issues. The most frustrating thing about this check box, aside from Illustrator's odd advice to "check the documentation" (what documentation?), is that the *Document Raster Effects Resolution* is listed but unchangeable from the dialog box. So if you feel like the default of 300 dpi for rasterized gradients is too high (which it may be), you have to close out and reset the value from the Effects menu.

12. *Set the Printer Profile.* This particular piece of artwork began life in the CMYK color mode (which you can confirm by choosing File→Document Color Mode and verifying it reads CMYK Color). And I can be relatively certain that your local printer is not an RGB device. Nonetheless, you'll note that your Printer Profile is set to an RGB space—probably Adobe RGB (1998) if you followed my instructions in the Preface. What gives?

PEARL OF WISDOM

A *profile* is the description of how a given device interprets and produces color. Any color management system is a negotiation between the different profiles employed by the various devices along the workflow chain. The idea is to make color as consistent and predictable as possible.

Your composite color printer is using some variation on the CMYK method of building color with inks, but it's not the standard CMYK system used by commercial printers. Rather, the printer is undoubtedly using a system that employs its own special mixing scheme for its own proprietary inks. So what the various printer manufacturers have decided to do is build printers that accept RGB input and convert it via the printer driver to the appropriate ink colors each respective printer has available.

In practice, virtually all consumer level printers are designed to receive sRGB information specifically, so from the **Printer Profile** pop-up menu, choose **sRGB IEC61966-2.1**.

13. *Designate a Rendering Intent. Rendering intent* specifies how you want Illustrator to deal with *out-of-gamut colors*—that is, those colors in your artwork that aren't reproducible by your printer. If you think it through, we're translating a CMYK image to an RGB color space, then handing it off to a device to retranslate to its own color composition language, so the rendering intent sets a policy for how those translations occur. You have four options:

- *Perceptual* tries to maintain the relationship between colors in a way similar to how the human brain perceives them. This may be a good choice for anything that needs smooth transitions like continuous tone raster images or complex gradients, because the transitions will be preserved perceptually.

- *Saturation* pushes colors to their most vivid. It may be useful if you need strong contrast in presentation graphics, but frankly I never use this one.

- *Relative Colorimetric* assigns the colors to their nearest in-gamut equivalent relative to one another. All the colors may be shifted to some degree, but the overall relationship will reflect the variety of colors in your artwork.

- *Absolute Colorimetric* translates all the colors to their nearest in-gamut equivalent with no attention paid to scaling the overall relationship between colors. The result is that out-of-gamut colors are clipped in the printed document.

---

To see a technical description of each of these options, you can hover over a chosen Rendering Intent option. An explanation of the intent will appear in the Description area at the bottom of the dialog box.

---

Since this particular artwork is highly graphical and we want the widest range of colors available to be printed, set the **Rendering Intent** to **Relative Colorimetric**.

Figure 12-8 shows a summary of the current Color Management settings.

Figure 12-8.

14. *Switch to Advanced panel.* Click **Advanced** in the list on the left side of the dialog box to bring up instructions for how you want Illustrator to deal with overprinting and flattening.

15. *Change the Overprints option.* By default, the Overprints option will be set to Discard. The reason is fairly clear, overprinting is an instruction relevant only to printing with multiple plates; there's no danger on an inkjet printer that your colors are going to knock each other out or you'll have trapping issues. Your local printer is not working with plates, so throwing away that information seems logical. However, anything is worth a try to see if you get better results: Set **Overprints** to Simulate.

16. *Tell Illustrator how you want to handle transparency.* It's hard to tell from the interface, but the item labeled Preset in this panel of the Print dialog box controls the plan for handling areas of transparency in your artwork. Your choices are Low, Medium, and High Resolution, but you can tweak these. Starting with the **Preset** set to Medium Resolution, press the **Custom** button and make the following choices in the **Custom Transparency Flattener Options** dialog box, shown in Figure 12-9 on the facing page:

   • Leave Raster/Vector Balance slider set to 75. This controls how often your paths will be rasterized in order to accommodate producing transparency effects. (Note, this is only a printing option, nothing in your artwork is changed.)

   • The **Line Art and Text Resolution** tells Illustrator your desired resolution for rendering line art or text when necessary (for example when one of these elements crosses paths with something soft that needs to be rasterized). Set it to 600 ppi.

   • Set the **Gradient and Mesh Resolution** to 200 ppi. Gradients are by nature edgeless, so a higher resolution would be overkill.

- Leave the Convert All Text to Outlines check box turned off. If you wanted that to happen, you would have already done it. (See the Video Lesson, "Commercial Printing," described on page 436 for more information on converting text to outlines.)

- Turn on the **Convert All Strokes to Outlines** check box.

- Turn on the **Clip Complex Regions** check box. This allows Illustrator to place a vector-based mask over complex rasterized areas so that the edges smooth out.

- Click **OK** to close the Custom Transparency Flattener Options dialog box..

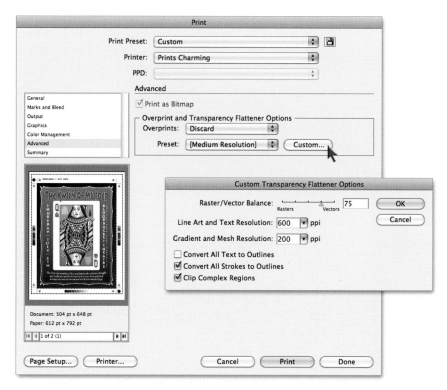

Figure 12-9.

17. *Print or save your settings to print later.* At this point, click the **Print** button to see your artwork in the flesh. If you're not interested in committing to paper at this point, however, click the **Done** button instead. This saves the print settings within the document file for later use. Be sure to save your document as well, since these saved printer settings are an unsaved change until you save the entire artwork file.

## Exporting Artwork for the Web

These days, it's entirely possible your Illustrator artwork will never see the printed page. And even if your work started as a print document, it's important that you know how to prepare your artwork for a digital existence beyond. Adobe realizes this as well, and has created an ever-evolving set of tools designed to optimize your illustrations for inclusion on a Web page, emailing to a colleague, or use in a digital media scenario where quality and file size are competing for primacy. You may still start with print as your primary output expectation, but we'd better have a flight plan in place for exploring the digital universe.

To live in a file format that's Web-compatible, your image will need to be *rasterized*, that is converted to pixels. Pixels are the medium of the digital display, and to exist in the great beyond, your artwork requires conversion to a pixel-friendly format like JPEG, GIF, or PNG. In this particular exercise, we'll be working with a complex graphic with a continuous tone background, so JPEG is going to be our best option. And Adobe's not-so-gracefully but oh-so-descriptively named command, Save for Web and Devices, provides just the right atmosphere for making this transition.

1. *Open a file.* Open the file called *Destination Internet. ai* which you can find by navigating to the *Lesson 12* folder inside *Files-AIcs5 1on1*. As you may recall, this particular graphic (shown in Figure 12-10) contains a backdrop of space that began life as a Photoshop file, and therefore has a continuous tone element you'll want to preserve. It's also chock full of gradients and smooth transition areas.

2. *Add some file information.* Before you go sending your artwork out into the wild, wild Web, you'll want to add information about who created it and how legitimate people might find you to ask permission to use it. (Illegitimate people are going to skip this step.) Start by choosing **File→File Info** or pressing Ctrl+Alt-Shift+I (⌘-Option-Shift-I) to bring up the extensive dialog box for adding metadata to your file. *Metadata* is a general term for information about a file.

The key metadata you enter will be about authorship and ownership, but you can see in **Figure 12-11** on the facing page that there are copious categories of data that you could add to the file. If you click the right pointing arrow at the top right of the dialog box, you'll see the category tabs go past the average attention span.

Figure 12-10.

3. *Enter the Author info.* You an see the title of the document is already filled out for you. In the Author field, add "Deke McClelland" and feel free to go on to add both my title and a description of the illustration.

4. *Append the copyright information.* Click in the copyright notice field and add "©2010 Type & Graphics." Create the © symbol like so:

   • On a PC, hold down the Alt key and type 0169.

   • On a Mac, press Option-G.

   Follow it up by adding my Web site, "deke.com," to the **Copyright Info URL**, and click **OK**. Now anyone who comes across this image in any universe will know who owns this work of genius.

5. *Preview your rasterized image.* To preview how the artwork will look once it's converted to pixels, choose View→Pixel Preview. Then zoom into the area near the robot's head to inspect the potential results. You'll notice that around the letters of the word *BOO* we have extraneous rows of pixels that are degrading the crispness of the letters.

6. *Align the robot element to the pixel grid.* A new feature in Illustrator CS5 allows you to fix this pixel creep, especially for horizontal and vertical lines.

   • With the black arrow tool, click the robot to select both him and his speech bubble.

   • Open the **Transform** panel by pressing Shift-F8.

   • Turn on the **Align to Pixel Grid** check box.

   You can see in Figure 12-12 how the word *BOO* looks before and after aligning to the pixel grid, with the bottom image showing much crisper outlines. I also repeated the steps for the framing elements, and you can see that they too have lost their "ghost pixel" (no pun seriously intended) effect as well.

---

To align everything from this point to the pixel grid, choose Align New Objects to the Pixel Grid from the Transform panel flyout menu.

---

Figure 12-11.

Figure 12-12.

7. *Evoke the Save for Web and Devices command.* With all the preliminary work behind you, choose **File→Save for Web and Devices** or press **Ctrl+Alt+Shift+S** (⌘-Option-Shift-S). Illustrator will open a very large dialog box that contains everything you'll need to create an optimized JPEG from your artwork.

8. *Click the 2-Up Display tab.* Save for Web (for short) allows you four ways of viewing your graphic from within the dialog box. You can choose just the Original or just the Optimized version, or you can choose to see the original compared with one variation or three others. Click the tab that says **2-Up** in the upper-left corner of the dialog box to see your original artwork side-by-side with your working optimized version, as shown in Figure 12-13.

Figure 12-13.

9. *Choose a reasonable download speed.* One of the main purposes of using Save for Web is to make a file small enough, while still maintaining image integrity, that a standard Web surfer won't have to wait an unreasonable amount of time for it to download. To get a sense of how long Illustrator estimates your file will take to display in a Web browser, click the ▾≡ icon on the right above the right preview image and choose **Size/Download Time (256 Kbps Cable/DSL)**. This is a reasonably conservative download estimate for the average Web user.

10. *Zoom in on the upper part of the images.* The default preview size is 100 percent, but we want a closer look. Set the zoom level to 300 percent in the lower left of the dialog box. Then drag one of the preview images around inside the box so the upper part is visible. Both images will move in concert.

11. *Change the quality settings.* You can now make quality/download speed trade off settings for your graphic, keeping an eye on the download speed and estimated time below the preview image as you choose different settings. For this image, here is where I found the best trade off between quality and file size:

- The file format is set to GIF by default, so click to the right of GIF and choose **JPEG** from the pop-up menu.

- The default quality setting of Medium is probably just a bit too compressed, so change the **Quality** setting to 45 to get rid of some of the noisier areas of the background.

- Raising the Blur amount can help get rid of color artifacts but the cost to legibility is too much so leave it set to zero.

- The Matte setting fills in completely transparent areas in your artwork. It's set to white by default which is fine (if irrelevant) for this graphic.

- I've discovered that clicking the **Image Size** tab and choosing **Type Optimization** from the pop-up menu, instead of None or even Art Optimization helps stave off some odd artifacts. You must click **Apply** after changing these settings. Figure 12-14 shows the results.

Figure 12-14.

You can see in the information below the image previews that we've reduced the file size from 938K to 64K (your results may vary slightly). We got a download speed of 3 seconds which seems reasonable for the quality we're getting.

12. *Save your file with a Web-friendly name.* Now that you have a graphic you can feel save sending out to the World Wild Web, click the **Save** button. In the **Save Optimized As** dialog box, name your file something that won't cause confusion on Web servers, namely no spaces. So call it "The-Web-friendly-ghost. jpg" and click the **Save** button.

## Web Optimizing a Low-Color Graphic

If you have a low-color, high-contrast graphic that you'd like to optimize for Web use, you'll want to make different choices during the conversion process than those you used for the previous illustration. While the ghost robot artwork had lots of color transitions and thus indicated the use of JPEG, the three-color, logo-style illustration in Figure 12-15 has different optimization needs.

The Save for Web command that we used to create the JPEG in the last exercise also allows you to export GIF and PNG files, two other Web compatible file formats. If your server supports it, you're probably better off with PNG since you'll get a much wider range of colors available. Most modern browsers support PNG, but your Web server may not, in which case, I'll go over the appropriate GIF settings in this exercise as well. Either way, we'll avoid color artifacts that might occur should we take this low color illustration to JPEG.

Figure 12-15.

1. *Open a file.* Open *Astormann.ai* which you'll find by navigating to the *Lesson 12* folder inside *Files-AIcs5 1on1*. This is a highly articulated graphic with some very complex path outlines, but there are only three colors in all: black, white, and solid blue. The 256 colors available in the GIF format should be more than enough for these three colors and their antialiasing needs.

2. *Change the antialiasing scheme on the white type.* New to CS5 is the ability to change the way Illustrator applies antialiasing to type.

   • Start by choosing **View→Pixel Preview** so you can get a sense of what the rasterized text will look like.

   • Zoom in on the white text, and click to make it active.

   • Open the Character panel by choosing **Window→Type→Character**. Click the ⬍ to the left of the word *Character* to toggle through the panel states until you see all the options.

   • Click the pop-up menu to the right of the ⬛ᵃᵃ icon at the bottom **Character** panel, and choose **Strong**. Figure 12-16 shows Sharp (default), Crisp, and Strong applied to both blocks of text. While I liked Strong for the white type, the smaller black type look best with Sharp antialiasing applied.

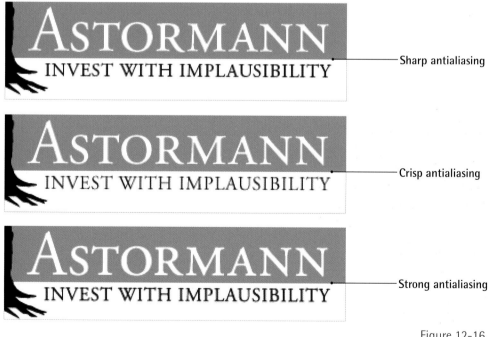

Sharp antialiasing

Crisp antialiasing

Strong antialiasing

Figure 12-16.

3. *Launch Save for Web.* This time I want you take advantage of Save for Web's option to see two possible file formats side by side. Once again, press Ctrl+Alt+Shift+S (⌘-Option-Shift-S) to launch the **Save for Web & Devices** dialog box. Then do the following:

- Click the **2-Up** tab. Then zoom to 200 percent, and position the preview so that you can see the text and the lower branches on the right side of the tree.

- Click the left preview so that it's highlighted (there's a box around it). Then choose **JPEG Medium** from the **Preset** menu to get an idea of what JPEG compression would do to this artwork.

- Click the right preview to select it with the yellow bounding box, and this time set the file type to **GIF**.

You can see the two previews compared in Figure 12-17. Although the file size of the JPEG option on the left is nice and small, the compression that accompanies it wreaks all kinds of havoc around the type and leaf filigree. Meanwhile, even at its default setting, the GIF preview is far smoother and the colors crisper, and yet has a file size that's considerably smaller than the JPEG file.

Figure 12-17.

4. *Customize the GIF settings.* The GIF is already looking vastly improved, but working through the settings will help the output get even better and the file size get even smaller.

- Check out the Color Table and notice of the 256 colors we're allowed in GIF, we're only using a fraction. But we can reduce that list even more and, in turn, get a smaller file size.

- Click the pop-up menu below the file type setting (that currently reads Selective, which is sort of a popularity contest for colors), and change it to **Perceptual**. For this particular image, that color reduction algorithm works well.

- In the next pop-up menu down, choose **No Dither**. Dither is a selective form of noise used to smooth out color transitions. We don't need it for this graphic.

- Turn off the **Transparency** check box, since it's not relevant for this image. You'll notice the Matte setting is set to its default white, so the transparent area fills in just fine.

- Change the number of **Colors** to 16. We still may not need all 16, but this reduces the file size to around 12K.

- To see where the real threshold is, highlight the 16 value and press the ↓ key to move the value down one number at a time until the antialiasing around the letters and the branches becomes too compromised. At about thirteen colors, I felt like I was getting the best compromise between file size and quality.

The results and settings are shown in Figure 12-18. You could save this file now, but I want to keep moving on to the PNG options.

5. *Change the left preview to PNG.* PNG, pronounced "ping," is a versatile, high-quality replacement for GIF. It works well should you need to export your graphic to an application like Microsoft PowerPoint. So click the left preview to make it active, then choose **PNG-8** from the file format pop-up menu that's currently set to JPEG.

Figure 12-18.

You have options for PNG-8 or PNG-24. The numbers refer to bit depth. But since the 256 colors available with PNG-8 are plenty (we already know that from the GIF experiment), you can keep the file size down by choosing PNG-8 for this graphic.

6. *Lower the number of colors back to 13.* The default number of colors for PNG-8 is 256, which we already know we don't need. So lower **Colors** to 13, the same value we had for the GIF output. You'll see in Figure 12-19, with PNG settings for the left preview revealed, that you get pixel-for-pixel results in the PNG file with a slightly smaller file size.

Figure 12-19.

7. *Save your file.* Again, choose a Web-friendly filename for your file.

My advice is to use PNG whenever you can. All the modern browsers currently in use support PNG, and your only real need for GIF is if your Web server doesn't support PNG.

# Exporting a Layered Photoshop Image

Illustrator can be exported to a variety of file formats, way beyond the Web-cooperative JPEG, GIF, and PNG I showed you in the last exercise. The Export command gives you a variety of options including AutoCAD and Flash. But one of the more interesting options is Photoshop.

Exporting to Photoshop gives you the expected raster conversion, but with a few useful nuances. First, you can export with your layers intact, allowing better editing control of the rasterized image. Second, the type in your file can remain editable. And finally, Photoshop even manages to preserve useful vectors (in the form of vector masks) in your images. There are several ways to bring Illustrator content into Photoshop, with varying degrees of ease, speed, and convenience (as I'll show you in the sidebar, "Other Ways to Render Illustrations in Photoshop" on page 461), the particular method I'll show you in this exercise is a way to retain some of the useful features of your existing Illustrator file.

**PEARL OF WISDOM**

You'll need to have Photoshop installed to see the ultimate results of this exercise. You might be able to view the file in another image editor, but only Photoshop will show you the accurate outcome of the Photoshop layers.

1. *Open a file.* If you've just completed the last exercise, then you should still have the original Illustrator file, *Astormann.ai*, open (because Save for Web doesn't close the original file when you're finished with the dialog box.) If not, reopen it; you'll find it in the *Lesson 12* folder of *Lesson Files-AIcs5 1on1*.

2. *Expand the layers panel.* Twirl open the single layer, called **Drawing**, to note the five object components that make up this document. There's a complex shape layer, a compound path, two text layers, and another shape that serves as the primary backdrop for the artwork.

3. *Export the file.* Choose **File→Export** to open the **Export** dialog box. In the **Save As** field, keep the default name, *Astormann.psd*, or change it to something that makes sense to you. Navigate to wherever you'd like to save your work.

4. *Choose the Photoshop format.* From the **Format** pop-up menu, choose P**hotoshop (psd)**, as shown in Figure 12-20. Click the **Export** button.

Figure 12-20.

You can see the wide variety of file types to choose from when you export a file from Illustrator.

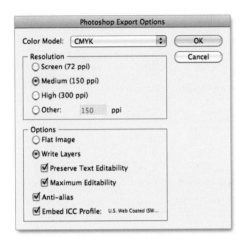

Figure 12-21.

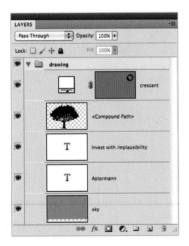

Figure 12-22.

5. **Set the Export options.** In the **Photoshop Export Options** dialog box, make the following choices, as shown in Figure 12-21:

- Leave the Color Mode set to CMYK.

- Set the **Resolution** to **Medium (150 ppi).** I've found with this graphic, in all its complexity, the High setting can choke even the most up-to-date, well outfitted computer.

- In the **Options** area, choose to **Write Layers,** in order to preserve your existing Illustrator layers.

- Turn on the **Preserve Text Editibility** check box so that the text remains editable in Photoshop. (This setting works with a degree of success depending on how elaborate your text is inside the Illustrator file and how much interaction the text has with other complex objects.)

- Turn on the **Maximum Editibility** check box to allow as much post-export editing access to various objects.

- Turn on the **Anti-alias** check box to preserve as much detail as possible.

- Turn on the **Embed ICC Profile.**

Click **OK** to accept your setting and tell Illustrator to get to work.

6. **Switch to the Bridge.** Click the ⧉ icon in the menu bar to open the Bridge, and navigate to the place you saved *Astormann.psd.* From the Bridge, double-click the file to open it in Photoshop.

7. **Examine the Photoshop layers panel.** If the **Layers** panel isn't already open, press F8. You'll see a layer group called **Drawing.** Generally, this is what happens with Illustrator files converted this way: Layers with objects in Illustrator become layer groups in Photoshop. Check out the contents by twirling open the Drawing layer group in Photoshop.

As you can see in Figure 12-22, there are five layers, starting at the bottom:

- The Sky object came in as a pixel-based layer, and interestingly not as a shape.

- The two Text objects are now editable text layers. In fact if you want to check it out, double-click one of the text thumbnails and change the text yourself.

- The layer with the tree element is called <Compound Path> but that's just the name it was given by Illustrator, it's now actually a fully rasterized tree.

# Other Ways to Render Illustrations in Photoshop

Using Illustrator's Export command to create a rasterized, layered PSD file is both easy and useful, but there are other ways to exploit your hard-wrought Illustrator work inside of Photoshop.

One option is to open an AI file directly in Photoshop, which is possible as long as you save your Illustrator file with the Create Compatible PDF File turned on in the Save dialog box (It's the default setting, so not hard to do). Then in the Bridge, right-click your saved Illustrator file, and choose **Open With→Adobe Photoshop CS5**. You'll be presented with the dialog box below:

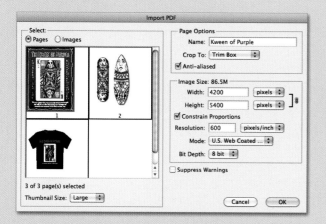

The things to keep in mind during this process:

- You choose your artboard in the Select window. You can Shift-click or Ctrl-click (⌘-click) to choose multiple artboards, but they will each open in a separate Photoshop file (and it could take a while if you have several artboards.)

- To get just the contents of the artboard (no bleed or other extraneous stuff) set the **Crop To** setting to Trim Box.

- I like to bring my illustrations in at a fairly high res (to take advantage of all the detail), and 600 pixels per inch is my go to setting. However, you should consider your scaling needs accordingly.

When you rasterize by opening in Photoshop, you're basically turning Photoshop into your own software-based raster image processor (RIP) and there's no better way to make sure nothing is lost in the process.

Another way to bring your artwork into Photoshop is to use Photoshop's **File→Place** command. You'll be asked to navigate to the image file you want to use.

You can see in the image below that the ensuing dialog box is similar to the Import PDF dialog box, but with far fewer options to choose from, most notably, no way to specify a resolution (though admittedly you get much bigger previews in the Select window). From this dialog box, you can place only one artboard at a time.

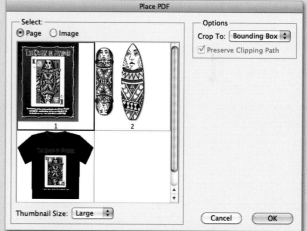

When you place your vector graphic into Photoshop this way, it comes in as a smart object. A *smart object* is a special kind of Photoshop object that holds all the information about the graphic in a protective "container" which allows you to make modifications to the layer non-desructively.

The upshot of your Illustrator graphic being converted to a pixel-based smart object is that you retain all the resolution available in your original artwork. Upon import, you can adjust the scale of the placed file, and at any time you can "reopen" the smart object and readjust the size. Photoshop then re-renders the graphic at the new size. The result is that you can get the resolution you need to complete your work on-the-fly.

Smart objects add a great deal of heft to a file's size, because the entire image is embedded inside the document. However, with the added size, you get to maintain all the flexibility to make ever changeable edits to your graphic.

- The moon, somewhat amazingly, became a fill layer with an editable vector mask. Double-click the vector mask thumbnail in the Crescent layer and you can see that the conversion has actually maintained the compound shape and done a fairly clean job of preserving the original paths. Best part, it's editable.

Figure 12-23 shows the final pixel-based Photoshop file. To demonstrate the edibility of the text and Crescent layers, I changed the message and increased the smile of our man in the moon. Seemed appropriate for him to be smiling watching over two powerful applications play so nicely together.

Figure 12-23.

# WHAT DID YOU LEARN?

Match the key concept in the numbered list below with the letter
of the phrase that best describes it. Answers appear upside-down
at the bottom of the page.

## Key Concepts

1. Create Outlines
2. Trim size
3. Bleed
4. Overprinting
5. Crop marks
6. Registration marks
7. Separations
8. Raster image processor (RIP)
9. Rendering intent
10. Rasterized
11. Metadata
12. Smart object

## Descriptions

A. Marks in a piece of artwork that show where an object should be iso-lated for crop.

B. Specific hardware or software based systems that instruct how a file should be rasterized for print.

C. Converted to pixels.

D. A safety zone area around the artboard that gives the printer a margin for error when trimming.

E. The scheme that indicates how out-of-gamut colors should be handled by the printer.

F. Side information about a file, like author name, description, and copy-right information.

G. The intended size of a printed piece after the unprinted area is pared away.

H. A Photoshop feature that holds all the original data in an object while edits are applied externally and non-destructively.

I. A command that allows you to convert type to vector paths so that you don't have to worry about supplying the correct fonts with the file.

J. Marks in a printed document that assist the printer in putting color plates into alignment.

K. Instructions you can apply that will tell Illustrator to have one color (usually black) print on top of another color rather than knocking it out.

L. Individual renditions of a piece of artwork that break down the file into specific information for each color plate.

## Answers

1I, 2G, 3D, 4K, 5A, 6J, 7L, 8B, 9E, 10C, 11F, 12H

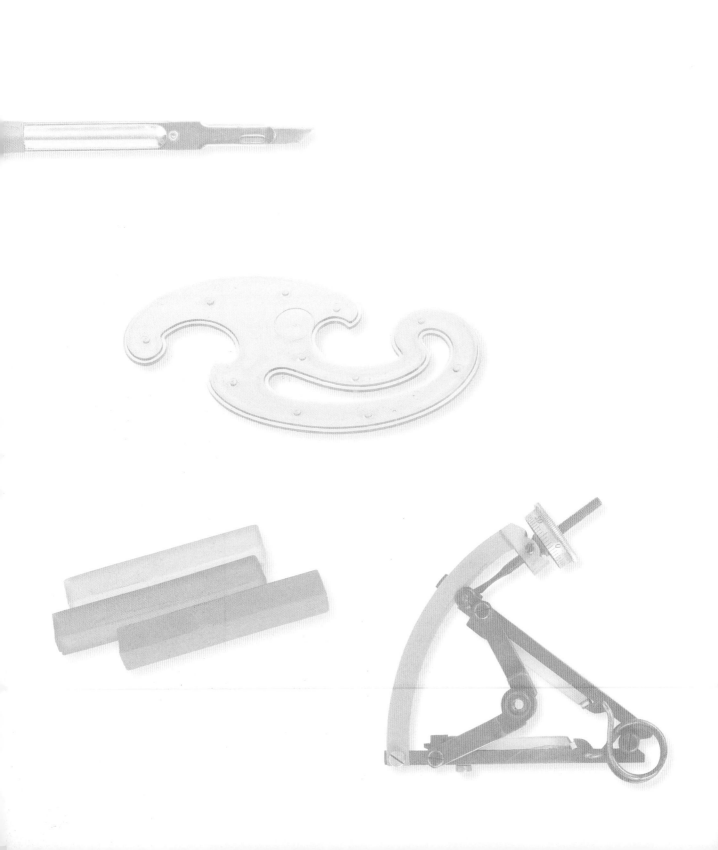

# INDEX

## Symbols

2-Up Display tab, 452
3D
    creating 3D text and graphics,
        372–382
    submenu, 332
    symbols, 274
3D effects
    editing, 374
    Extrude Depth value, 375
    Perspective value, 375
3D Extrude & Bevel, 374–380, 383

## A

accidently deselecting path, 91
Add Anchor Points, 174, 175
Additive styles, 339
add-point tool, 235
Adjusted Image, 393, 433
Adobe Bridge (*see* Bridge)
Adobe Caslon Pro, 271
Adobe Every-line Composer, 131
Adobe PDF (.pdf), 35
Adobe RGB (1998), 446, 448
Advanced settings
    Color Mode, 17
    Preview Mode, 17
        Default setting, 18
    Raster Effects, 17
.ai file format, 35, 37
.ait file format, 34, 35
Alexis, Alexandra, 410
aligning and joining points, 48, 49
Align New Objects to Pixel Grid, 17
Align panel, 31
Align Stroke options, 80
Align to Artboard, 308

align to artboard icon, 90
Align to Pixel Grid check box, 451
alternative measurements, 17
anchor points, 83
    Add Anchor Points, 174, 175
    adding intermediate anchor point,
        235
    Alt (Option) key, 99
    blends, 209
    convert anchor point tool, 98
    converting points from one type to
        another, 98
    corner points (*see* corner points)
    cusp points (*see* cusp points)
    examples of, 98
    filling path with, 227
    lines and shapes, 87
    moving with white arrow tool, 97
    pen tool, 93
    PostScript, 245
    Selection & Anchor Display, 100
    smooth points (*see* smooth points)
    three kinds of, 98
    type, 117
    what makes lines bend, 87
angles, corners of acute angles, 80
antialiasing, 455
Antique Olive typeface, 115
Appearance of Black, xix, 71
Appearance panel, 30, 81, 248, 343, 383
    assigning new attributes, 156
application bar, 8
Apply New Effect, 355, 360, 361
Apply to Strokes, 304
arcs
    drawing lines, arcs, and spirals,
        41–44
    joining bottom points, 64
    joining to spiral, 47

    joining two arc segments, 48
    keyboard shortcuts, 49
    slicing with scissors tool, 46
    splitting, joining, and aligning,
        44–50
    switching to outline mode, 45
arc tool, 43
area type, 110, 111, 118, 129, 135
    editing, 122–126
    versus point type, 118
Area Type Options dialog box, 130
Arial, 114
Arrange, 197
arrowhead options, 80
artboard-editing mode, 19–21
Artboard Options dialog box, 20, 22
    Constrain Proportions box, 20
artboards, 8, 37
    Align to Artboard, 308
    controls, 8
    creating new, 22
    crop zone, 267
    custom sizes, 16, 20–23
    editing size, 22
    modifying, 18–23
    modifying size, 20
    multiple with custom sizes, 20–23
    options, 16
    previewing vector art, 21
    repositioning, 23
    resizing, 21
    saving files, 438
Artboards tool, 21
art brushes, 274–276, 295, 296, 300–
        306, 327
    enhancing line art with, 275–290
Art Brush Options dialog box, 286,
        295, 303, 304, 305

Web gamut warning, 69
Web graphics, 274
Web optimizing low-color graphic,
      454–458
   antialiasing, 455
   customizing GIF settings, 457
   Pixel Preview, 455
   PNG format, 457
   Save for Web and Devices dialog
         box, 456
Web Safe RGB, 69
Welcome Screen, 7
white arrow tool, 47, 48, 107
   adjusting individual points, 92
   moving anchor points, 97
   transformation, 139
   versus black arrow tool, 92
width tool, 277–279, 299
window controls, 9
workspace control, 9
Workspace pop-up menu, 14
workspaces, 37
   custom
      creating, 28–33
      saving, 33
   cycling between different expansion
            settings, 32
   default, 28
      restoring, 33
   deleting, 33
   docking pane
      collapsing, 33
      expanding or reducing width, 32
   Essentials, 29
   Manage Workspaces, 33
   New Workspace command, 33
   One-on-One workspace, 33
   panels
      collapsing, 32
      rearranging, 30–32
      resizing, 32
      toggling visibility, 32
   Part of Workspace check box, 14
   remembering last state, 33
   Save Sort Order as Part of
            Workspace, 14
   saving, 13

## X

x-height, 135

## Z

zooming thumbnails, 12
zoom ratio, 9
zoom tool, 90

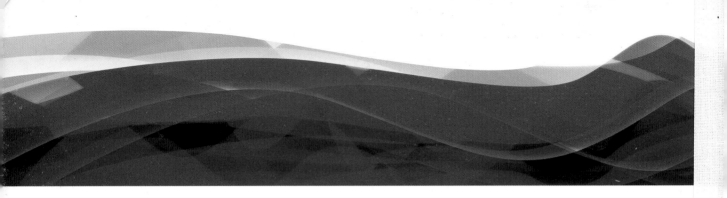